43
58
4
15
80
27
43
70
24
30
29
16
43
61
18
22
39
8
69
43
44
43
35
43
16
17
56
35
85
43
68
43
35
43
35
43
35
43
20
19
35
63
35
43
36
47
43
9
5
43
35
10
11
73
78
21
35
67
43
33
7
13
72
34
3
3
43
65
21
14
52
37
57
87
12
43
92
2
26
35
60
31
86
45

The Wages of War 1816–1965: A Statistical Handbook

The Wages of War 1816-1965 A Statistical Handbook

J. David Singer
Department of Political Science
University of Michigan
and
Melvin Small
Department of History
Wayne State University

JOHN WILEY & SONS, Inc. New York • London • Sydney • Toronto

To those whose research may make a successor volume unnecessary

Library of Congress Cataloging in Publication Data

Singer, Joel David, 1925–
The wages of war, 1816–1965.

Bibliography: p.
1. War—Statistics. I. Small, Melvin, Joint author. II. Title.
U21.2.S57 301.6'334 75-39120
ISBN 0-471-79300-0

Printed in the United States of America
10 9 8 7 6 5 4 3 2 1

Acknowledgments

Since books that are heavy on data and almost barren of theory are seldom written and less often published in the absence of some demand, our first acknowledgment is to the many researchers and practitioners who either urged the publication of this sort of volume or concurred in that judgment when asked for an opinion. To these few who have been working toward a scientific theory of the causes and consequences of war, and to the many more who will soon be doing so, the book is therefore appropriately dedicated.

Then there are the people responsible for getting the Correlates of War project—of which this is an early but essential part—out of the vague idea stage and underway. First, it was our interdisciplinary colleagues at the Center for Research on Conflict Resolution and at the Mental Health Research Institute who encouraged and prodded when the project looked more intractable than attractive. Second, the Carnegie Corporation, then willing to support high-risk research in international politics, financed the first phase of the project as well as a number of related studies at the University of Michigan.

We have benefited greatly from the frequent advice of Karl Deutsch during his monthly visits to Ann Arbor, and that of Bruce Russett who was always available during the critical year 1965–1966. We are equally grateful to that army of historians who alternately delighted us with their painstakingly gathered military statistics, and infuriated us with their Olympian disdain for the comparative and the nomothetic. All are identified, if not classified, in the References section and in the several Appendices.

We thank those who carried out the day-to-day work involved in an enterprise of this nature. In the early data-gathering stage, George Kraft and Bernard Mennis helped us to screen the hundreds of primary and secondary sources that we used. Reponsible for data management and conversion during the long road from raw facts to scientifically useful tables were Marcia Feingold, Vilma Ungerson, Warren Phillips, Michael Wallace, Larry Arnold, Tim Pasich, Urs Luterbacher, John Stuckey, Hugh Wheeler, and Stuart A. Bremer; The latter four were particularly helpful in analyzing the trend and periodicity data. Perhaps more than anyone else, the person who made many of the compilations, prepared most of the draft tables, generally coordinated the entire operation, and repeatedly picked up the loose ends was Susan Jones; along with Ann Clawson and Marsha Stuckey, she also prepared most of the typescript and tabular layouts. Among those who have read parts or all of the manuscript and have given us their suggestions were Bruce Russett, Samuel Huntington, Karl Deutsch, Philip Chase, and Raymond Tanter.

Finally, our gratitude must go to those two pioneers whose intelligence, commitment, and vision are largely responsible for the fact that war is well on the way to becoming an object of scientific inquiry: Lewis Richardson and Quincy Wright.

J. David Singer
Melvin Small

Ann Arbor, 1970

Contents

Part A

Rationale and Procedures

Chapter 1
Introduction

In the opening chapter of Quincy Wright's *Study of War,* completed on the eve of World War II, we are reminded that war has many meanings. "To some it is a plague which ought to be eliminated; to others, a crime which ought to be punished; and to still others, it is an anachronism which no longer serves any purpose. On the other hand, there are some who take a more receptive attitude toward war, and regard it as an adventure which may be interesting, an instrument which may be legitimate and appropriate, or a condition of existence for which one must be prepared." (1942, I, p. 3) Regardless of how we conceive of war, we have made little progress in understanding this most complex and recurring social phenomenon—in terms of either cause or consequence. The speculation has been endless and the verbiage overwhelming, yet anything close to full explanation has eluded us.

Without belittling the efforts of earlier generations, it is only within the past several decades that any intellectual assault of promise has been launched against this organized tribal slaughter. That is, until war has been systematically *described,* it cannot be adequately *understood,* and with such understanding comes the first meaningful possibility of controlling it, eliminating it, or finding less reprehensible substitutes for it. In our judgment, the important turning point is marked by the rise of scientific (and therefore quantitative) analyses of war, manifested primarily in the work of Quincy Wright and Lewis Richardson beginning in the 1930s.

Inspired by the efforts of these scholars, and somewhat encouraged by their successes, we have recently initiated a project that is designed to identify the variables that are most frequently associated with the onset of war during the century and a half since the Congress of Vienna. More specifically, we hope to ascertain which factors characterize those conflicts which terminate in war, and which ones accompany those which find a less violent resolution. One of the first requirements in such a study is to discover the trends and fluctuations in the frequency, magnitude, severity, and intensity of war during that period; once our data are gathered for these variables, a systematic search for the most potent independent and intervening variables may begin. At this writing, then, war data have finally been collected, and a number of correlational analyses are now underway; those already published or in press are listed in the Reference section.

PURPOSES AND EXPECTATIONS

The purpose of this volume is to make our war data available to the scholarly community as early as possible, rather than to wait until the project is completed. Our reasoning is simple. There are altogether too many competing "theories" on the causes of international war for any one group to put to the empirical test in the near future; some of these may well be unknown to us and others may strike us as unpromising. Our hope is that the publication of these data will inspire not only the testing of existing hunches and hypotheses, but the development of newer and perhaps more powerful ones as well.

Two additional motives were also at work. First—as the reader will soon discover—data on wars are not exactly easy to come by and we have therefore had to rely on relatively weak evidence or on pre-operational judgments from time to time. Thus, despite herculean efforts at maximum accuracy and precision, some errors will inevitably have crept in, and we trust that any such errors of fact—as well as objections to our coding rules—will be brought promptly to our attention. A second and more minor consideration is that publication here of our data, and the rather elaborate procedures by which they were generated, will spare us the need for lengthy reiteration in the several papers which will follow in due course, thereby allowing more space for discussion of the other variables and for theoretical analysis.

Thus, our intent here is to supply the sort of evidence which will accelerate and strengthen the trend toward rigorous historical research into the causes of international war. This is not, however, the only use to which this report may be put. After all, war is more than just a dependent variable or an outcome in most formulations of international politics. Its onset and its termination play an important role at many other points in the feedback loops which characterize the processes of international politics. War often brings in its train a dramatic range of phenomena, and the memory or expectation of war is also not without its effects. To illustrate, several of our projected studies will seek to ascertain the extent to which the recency and magnitude of given wars will predict to such subsequent changes in the international system as: the distribution of power and diplomatic status, alliance configurations and polarization, lateral and vertical mobility rates, technological innovation, demographic movement, and trading and investment patterns. Likewise, war experience should be expected to affect a nation's internal politics, social structure, and economy, its alliance and trading propensities, and the way in which it handles subsequent diplomatic and military problems.

Carrying this approach a step further, we are not unaware of the interest that other social scientists might have in data such as these. The sociologist might use them to examine, in addition to the phenomena noted above, the effect of war on crime, health, suicide, divorce, social organization, and the like; the economist might investigate the correlations between our data and such conditions as unemployment, distribution practices, collective bargaining procedures, and economic growth; and the anthropologist or psychologist might well use these data to analyze the impact of war on national character, ethical norms, child-rearing practices, mental illness, or alcoholism. In sum, then, war may be viewed as a dependent, independent, or intervening variable, and we therefore see this volume as contributing not only to peace research but to a great many other theoretical concerns in all the social sciences.

SOME ANTICIPATED CRITICISMS

It is one thing to hope that a compendium such as this will be well received and widely used, and quite another thing to assume that it will not come in for its share of criticism, constructive and otherwise. In order to spare certain of our readers the need to point out those obvious pitfalls of which we are already aware, we thought it might be useful to say a preemptive word or two in anticipation of the inevitable phrases stressing "the authors' hopeless naiveté" and related themes. Four of these criticisms come readily to mind.

First, it will undoubtedly be urged that no two wars are the same and that any such effort at accumulation and comparison will founder on the rocks of apparent, but unreal, similarity. The point is well taken, and as our many alternative categories of war make clear, we are not oblivious to the problem. No two social events ever *are* quite the same, and as a matter of fact, neither are any two physical events; at the very least, they must occur at different points in time or space. But they often are, depending on the scientific interests of the researcher, sufficiently similar to permit meaningful generalization. Clearly, this report, and the project of which it is a part, is not intended to stifle detailed inquiry into each or any of the 93 wars that we describe statistically, but instead, to provide the kind of hard evidence that would make such an inquiry that much more productive. Thus, even as we generalize across all or some of these international wars, we are painfully aware of the inconsistencies and dissimilarities that made the original data-making operations such a source of agony and frustration.

A second and somewhat related criticism is likely to arise over the point that, even if there is sufficient comparability within or between the various classes of wars, the settings in which they occurred and the factors that preceded or caused them will have been appreciably different over the time span covered. This observation is undoubtedly true, but not particularly interesting. The scientifically interesting point concerns the specific dimensions along which the settings and situations *do* differ, and by how much. That, of course, is an empirical question, and one to which we will direct a great deal of attention as the entire project moves ahead.

Another criticism to be anticipated concerns the data themselves. Many will no doubt argue, and not without reason, that it is impossible to find military statistics of sufficient authenticity and accuracy to be worth collecting. They will remind us that not only field commanders and foreign ministries have personal or institutional axes to grind, but that scholars may also have been less than dedicated in their search for *all* of the facts. This is true enough, but largely beside the point. First, if we were to refrain from doing historical analyses because of the relative paucity or unreliability of the available evidence, some of the most important work in archaeology, zoology, and astronomy—not to mention history, philosophy, and political science—would also come to a halt. The job of the scientist is to sift, evaluate, and collate by procedures which are sufficiently rigorous to satisfy his own skepticism, and sufficiently replicable to satisfy the skepticism of his fellow scholars. This we believe we have done, but as we noted earlier, there is no ironclad guarantee that we have utilized only the best sources or drawn our data from them by the best methods.

Finally, as the reader comes to one after another of our combinations, aggregations, and analyses, he may wonder why *other* computations and analyses have not been provided. All we can say is that we have tried to strike the most intelligent balance we could, weighing the possible needs of the research community on the one hand, and the extent to which excessive or redundant tabulations might make the volume less useful, less readable, and less compelling, on the other.

For example, there are a good many frequency distributions for which we do not present any measures of central tendency and dispersion. Where we *have* done so, it seemed essential to any reasonable interpretation of our data, and where we have *not* it might be because the range was so great—and visually apparent—that a mean or mode would have been of no value. Or, in many of the tables in Chapters Six, Seven, Eleven, and Thirteen, where the wars, or years, or nations are shown in rank order, with rank positions indicated, the median score (that of the middle ranked case) is easily discerned by eye. Or, in the Seasonal Concentration chapter, where the most useful measure of central tendency is the mean, that figure is so readily estimated (or computed) as to not justify the addition of yet another set of columns in the several tables. Likewise, many contemporary scientists put a premium on knowing the extent to which any plotted or calculated distribution of scores can be fitted to some well-known equation and its associated curve. By and large, we have resisted that temptation, and have succumbed only in Chapters Six, Eight, and Nine, mostly when dealing with the search for secular trends and periodicities.

Closely related to this is the matter of summarizing a wide variety of indicators in economical form, and this is the subject of considerable controversy in the social sciences today. In these techniques, the objective is to reduce one's data by ascertaining the presence and strength of a few underlying dimensions or factors. One point of view has it that one should gather the maximum amount of data or generate the maximum number of measures, and then go on to combine, compress, or reduce them to their dominant and natural underlying dimensions. Thus, we might take every one of the indicators presented in the chapters which follow, compute the product moment correlations between and among them, and then factor-analyze the resulting matrix. Such an exercise would probably produce a number of factors that might be labeled Amount of War Begun, Amount of War Underway, and Amount of War Terminated. But it could just as likely produce a rather different set of factors, such as Amount of Central System War and Amount of Peripheral System War; this because there is an inevitably high correlation among the amounts of war begun, underway, and terminated for given sub-sets of the world's nations.

The other point of view (or, at least, *one* other point of view) holds that most data reduction or compression procedures tend to blur and conceal many important differences, merging and combining information which is of greater scientific value when left isolated and identifiable. We have not only discussed and debated the merits of these arguments, but have also subjected much of these data to such reduction processes as "construct mapping" (Jones, 1966). The results were essentially as we predicted, and are not sufficiently interesting or useful, in our judgment, to report here.

In brief, each chapter opens with a few of the theoretical questions to which its data might be relevant, and we then apply only such analyses as seem most relevant to those particular concerns. There are many more questions to which our data might suggest or provide answers than we have asked, and there are many more modes of analysis than we have utilized.

In the chapters that follow, we will summarize prior efforts (serious and otherwise) to put together quantitative evidence on the recurrence of war, compare our results with these earlier and incomplete attempts, describe our data-making procedures in detail, present a wide range of figures in a variety of forms, develop a number of frequency distributions, and suggest some of the ways in which these data may be used by others who agree with us that war is important enough to warrant the most thorough and rigorous analysis known to modern social science.

PRIOR QUANTITATIVE COMPILATIONS

There is probably not a single scholar in the field who is not at least partly familiar with Quincy Wright's *A Study of War* (1942, and revised in 1965) and those having more than a passing acquaintance with this monumental study will know that in Appendix XX of Volume I, the author presents a list of 278 "Wars of Modern Civilization," covering the period 1480 to 1940. For each of these wars, he provides (when possible) the opening and closing dates, the name of the peace treaty which terminated it, the nations which participated, their dates of entry, his classification of the initiating and defending sides, the number of participants vis-à-vis the number of states in the system at the time, the number of important battles, and his classification as to whether it was a balance of power, civil, defensive, or imperialistic war. He does not, however, provide casualty figures for the specific nations in the specific wars. He does, on the other hand, move in that direction in Appendix XXI, showing estimates of war casualties and number of combatants for the leading powers over various time periods since the seventeenth century, as well as figures on the proportions of various populations which were killed during those periods and in World War I. Most of these estimates were gathered by James C. King, one of Wright's students and collaborators in the project, and were compared with figures compiled by Pitirim Sorokin for *Social and Cultural Dynamics* (1937).[1] In the revised edition (1965), Wright updated his list to cover the post-World War II period, and included battle-death estimates for each of these more recent wars.

As familiar as Wright's work may be, that of the other researcher whose pioneering efforts we follow was, until quite recently, relatively unknown: Lewis Richardson's *Statistics of Deadly Quarrels* (1960a). As early as 1919, this British physicist-meteorologist had written (and run off 300 copies, since "there was no learned society to which I dared offer so unconventional a work") a paper on the "Mathematical Psychology of War"; and during the 1930s he continued to employ statistical techniques in a variety of papers on war and peace. This serious avocation of Richardson's culminated, due largely to the efforts of Quincy Wright as well as Anatol Rapoport, Nicholas Rashevsky, Ernest Trucco, and Carl Lienau, in the *Statistics of Deadly Quarrels* and *Arms and Insecurity* (1960b), both published seven years after his death. Only a portion of the first of these volumes will concern us here—those chapters in which he sought to uncover and list all wars which terminated between 1820 and 1949 and which resulted in battle-associated deaths of 317 or more.[2] Also included in his tabulation are the protagonists, the initial and terminal dates for each pair of them, the number of deaths, and his evaluations of the protagonists' objectives and the conditions associated with the pre-war conflict.

The chronological interdependence of these two projects is worth noting. *A Study of War* was begun by Wright in 1926, and during the 15 years preceding publication, several of his colleagues and many of his students participated in the enterprise. About two years before Wright's opus went to press, Richardson published his "Generalized Foreign Politics" (1939), a monograph which Wright evaluated highly enough to cite 15 times and to summarize in a special Appendix. But since it included almost none of the later war figures, it had no effect on Wright's listing; furthermore, when Richardson's first publication of deadly quarrel statistics finally appeared in November 1941 (four days after the date in Wright's Foreword) it was too late to have any impact on the latter's tabulations. The first interaction between the two projects occurred shortly after the appearance of *A Study of War;* Richardson noted it as "a stimulus to further inquiry, which involved the consultation of some seventy history books," and on the basis of these further investigations, he published a revised listing in 1945, and then went on to incorporate it with further minor changes in 1948 and again in the 1950 manuscript of the 1960 volume under discussion here. In his Introduction to Richardson's *Statistics of Deadly Quarrels,* Wright appraises the final results as "the most complete list of wars which exists for the period" (1960a, p. vi). Although we agree with this characterization, *completeness* is not quite sufficient. As the balance of this volume should indicate, neither Wright's nor Richardson's listings are adequately refined or classified for the purposes of the study which engages us here, nor

[1] In comparing these two sets of estimates for British and French casualties between 1626 and 1925, Sorokin's tend to run about two or three times higher than King's. To some extent, this is due to King's inclusion of "principal battles" only, but even then, Sorokin's procedures seem to overestimate by an appreciable amount; see Wright (1942, Vol. I), Table 52, p. 657. The reader should be advised that the decimal point was omitted from the ratio columns, so that when Sorokin's estimate exceeded King's by a factor of 2.63 for a given period and nation, the figure shown is 263.

[2] For a coherent overview and analysis of Richardson's work, see Rapoport (1957); while preceding the publication of the final two-volume series, that monograph is based on, and reflects close familiarity with, its eventual contents.

are Richardson's casualty estimates. Our responsibility, therefore, is to build on the impressive foundations laid for us by these forerunners.

While these two scholars have done the most valuable work to date, there are several others whose work should be mentioned, however briefly. Thus, a third important figure is the sociologist, Pitirim A. Sorokin, whose *Social and Cultural Dynamics* (1937) also presents a wide range of figures on the frequency and severity of war. But while his time span began with antiquity, he was concerned with only the most diplomatically active nations and their wars. Moreover, his theoretical purposes required much less precision than do ours; instead of conducting one more exhaustive search in a project which had already led to many such empirical expeditions, he devised an ingenious, but highly approximate, set of estimation procedures. Taking rough account of the military tactics and technology of the time, and introducing a range of intuitively reasonable weighting factors, he produced a number of war lists which were quite satisfactory for the "order of magnitude" requirements demanded by his *Fluctutations of Social Relationships, War, and Revolution* (1937, Vol. III) study. A valuable by-product of that investigation is his most penetrating discussion (in Chapter Nine) on the uses and limits of precision in longitudinal social science research.

A fourth researcher who attempted a fairly exhaustive compendium is the Russian scholar Boris T. Urlanis, and if a personal note may be permitted, the discovery of his study was quite fortuitous. As of the completion of our first set of tabulations, his work had not been cited in a single one of the hundred-odd sources and bibliographies (in English, French, German, and a number of other languages) we had used. While the senior author was on a visit to Prague in 1964, discussing this project with a group of Czechoslovakian disarmament specialists, Urlanis' work came up, but no one knew his exact name, or the specific title, year, or publisher of his study. Two days of inquiring in almost every bookstore in downtown Prague and describing its putative contents (in a variety of inadequate phrases) produced nothing. Several months later, however, a Czechoslovakian colleague finally located and forwarded the Czech translation of the elusive tome; with the information found therein, it was a simple matter to track down and confirm the existence in Russian of *Wars and the Population of Europe* (1960). The effort, however, was only partially rewarding. In addition to an ideological preoccupation with the differential class suffering imposed by "imperialist wars," the volume also suffers from certain methodological difficulties. Its casualty categories were not always comparable from war to war and analysis to analysis; many estimates for a given war did not include some of the most active combatant nations, and compilations were often for time periods embracing a number of wars which were not specified. In addition, since Urlanis and we relied on many of the same original sources, it was more feasible to apply our own explicit criteria to those sources than to rely on his less visible coding rules.

A fifth and extremely valuable series of studies which should be mentioned is that inaugurated in 1911 by the Division of Economics and History of the Carnegie Endowment for International Peace. Two of the volumes in the series, which was established "to promote a thorough and scientific investigation of the causes and results of war," were especially useful: Gaston Bodart's *Losses of Life in Modern Wars* (1916), and Samuel Dumas and Knud Otto Vedel-Peterson's *Losses of Life Caused by War* (1923).[3] Bodart examined the wars of France and Austria-Hungary from the seven-

[3] A comprehensive outline for investigating the causes and effects of war was presented in an Appendix to the Bodart study, but the scheme was never carried out in its entirety. A brief history of the Carnegie and related projects—including a bibliography of completed reports—can be found in Appendix II of Wright (1942, Vol. I, pp. 414–422).

teenth to the twentieth centuries, and since these two nations participated in most of the major wars in that period, his results are quite valuable. For their part, Dumas and Vedel-Peterson examined most of the "important" wars from the Seven Years War through the First World War. Both studies were concerned with civilian deaths, ratios between officer and enlisted battle deaths, disease and prisoner of war figures, and treatments of separate battles and separate campaigns. In many ways, these two volumes served as our most valuable point of departure, and without them the enterprise would have been more costly and our results less reliable.

A sixth effort along these lines was that undertaken by Frank Klingberg (1945 and 1966), an associate of Wright's in the Study of War project. Toward the closing days of World War II, with Allied speculation running high as to when, and under what conditions, the Japanese might surrender, a consultant to Secretary of War Henry L. Stimson (William Shockley, later the joint winner of a Nobel Prize for the development of transistors) suggested that an historical survey of casualties might help ascertain under what conditions Japan might capitulate. At Wright's urging, the study was soon begun, but it was not completed in time to exercise any impact on strategic planning. Klingberg did, however, gather a large number of casualty estimates, and while they were subjected to a most insightful analysis, they were seldom in a form which we could use directly. Most often, the estimates (largely based on Bodart, 1916) were for given battles rather than total wars, and when a war's figures were given, they generally included civilian casualties as well. This suggestive study, which had remained virtually unknown for 20 years, was finally resurrected at our urging, and subsequently published by Klingberg in abbreviated form in the *Journal of Conflict Resolution* (1966). We will allude to it further in Chapter Fourteen where we analyze the ratios between victor and vanquished, in terms of the magnitude of their war experiences and the severity of their losses.

Then there were a number of statistical studies which dealt with either a single war or at most a few, and usually for only a handful of nations or battles. Among the most useful to us were: Perce (1858), Berndt (1897), Harbottle (1904), Bodart (1908), Beebe and deBakey (1952), and Eggenberger (1967). These and the others that served to provide, corroborate, or correct our battle death and duration estimates for each specific war are listed in Appendix B, and are fully cited in the References.

Another investigation, motivated by many of the considerations that entered into our own study, was Woods and Baltzly's *Is War Diminishing?* (1915). They tell us that it was their "wholesome disgust at the unscientific nature" of existing work that led them to "collect these humble facts" on trends in the incidence of war. Covering the war experiences of about a dozen nations for the period 1450–1900, the study was nevertheless of marginal value. Even though they turned up a number of general patterns, their coding rules and measuring procedures were much too vague and imprecise to permit our use of their figures. Equally ambitious and somewhat more rigorous is the series of studies conducted by the Paris-based Institut de Polémologie under the direction of Gaston Bouthoul. Most fully reported in *Guerre et Paix* in 1968 (No. 2), the figures are too gross, and the coding procedures too invisible, for us to have much confidence in them.

Insensitivity to scientific method is, however, only one of the reasons for the poor state of war research. In the course of our investigation we also turned up a series of reports whose appearance can only be explained by a complete disregard for the most elementary rules of traditional scholarship. Reference is to what another curious and skeptical investigator called *The Great Statistics of Wars Hoax* (Haydon, 1962). In a number of relatively authoritative sources, including The United States Naval Institute *Proceedings* ("The Art of War," 1960), the *New York Times Magazine*

(1963), *Military Review* ("The Art of War," 1960, 1962), and *Time Magazine* (1965), we discovered almost identical articles on the frequency and magnitude of war.[4] They reported that there had been only 292 years of peace since 3600 B.C., and that 3,640,000,000 people had been killed in a total of 14,531 wars during that period. They also reported that since 650 B.C. there had been 1656 arms races, of which only 16 did not end in war. Each of these articles referred to research conducted, "with the aid of an electronic computer, by a team of international historians headed by a former president of the Norwegian Academy of Sciences." Having encountered these "data" shortly before his departure for a year's stay in Oslo, the senior author inquired of many Norwegian scholars and officials as to the nature of the research project, but without result. Finally, an operations analyst was encountered who knew that "someone" at the Rand Corporation had tried to trace the source, and a letter of inquiry to Santa Monica quickly produced the memorandum by Brownlee Haydon mentioned above.

His reasons for so labeling the memorandum soon became clear. After considerable library work and correspondence, he discovered that Norman Cousins had written for the *St. Louis Post-Dispatch* of 13 December 1953 an article entitled "Electronic Brain on War and Peace: A Report of an Imaginary Experiment." The next year, Cousins wrote an editorial in the *Saturday Review* (1954), beginning with the sentence: "The following editorial is of course fanciful." In both articles, there were casual speculations about the sorts of figures that could be *expected* to turn up in a systematic inquiry, but for reasons and by routes undiscoverable for the moment, these guesses soon began to appear as *facts* in the serious media of several nations, including those cited above. We, and all of those who labor in this particular vineyard, can be extremely grateful to Haydon for his patient sleuthing and understated exposé, and trust that those who were unable to distinguish between authoritative imprimatur and reproducible evidence will be a shade more skeptical in the future.

SUMMARY

A glance at the Contents will reveal the basic arrangement of the volume. After outlining our rationale and general procedure and comparing our compilation to those of our predecessors, we divide the book into three major parts, depending on the unit of analysis. In Part B, the individual wars represent our unit of analysis, and there we describe each of them in terms of their magnitude, severity and intensity and then go on to rank them according to each of these measures. In Part C, we aggregate the separate wars in order to generalize about the incidence of war in the international system. In that Part, the system is our unit of analysis, and our concern is to identify the amount of war which began, was underway, or which terminated each year in the total system and in its several regional and functional sub-systems. Finally, in Part D, we shift to the individual nation as our unit of analysis, indicating the total amount of war experienced by each during its tenure in the system, and comparing and ranking the nations (and regions) according to a variety of raw and normalized measures of war experience. This

[4] The second article in *Military Review* was written by Lt. Col. Fielding L. Greaves, as was that in the *New York Times Magazine*. Since Haydon's exposé, only one appearance of the story has been found, and that (not surprisingly) was in *Time* (24 September 1965, pp. 30–31).

final part also presents the data by which certain systematic comparisons might be made between the battle losses of the victors and the vanquished, and by which one might discover whether the termination of wars can be predicted on the basis of such fatality figures.

In sum, we believe that these results represent a significant advance in accuracy and comparability over any prior compilation, and hope that they will not only be useful to those scholars who are already engaged in research on the causes, characteristics, and consequences of war, but will by their mere availability encourage a rapid acceleration in such research in the months and years ahead.[5]

[5] Most of the basic data sets presented here, as well as a few of the derived and generated sets, are available from the International Relations archive of the Inter-University Consortium for Political Research at the University of Michigan, Ann Arbor.

Chapter 2
Identifying International Wars: The Inclusion and Exclusion Problem

We now turn to the task at hand, and try to explain the procedures we used in arriving at the results that are reported in Chapter Four and those following. Here, of course, is where we part company with many of our colleagues in political science and history. If we look at the international scene over the 1816–1965 period, we find at first glance a bewildering array of events. And for our concerns, there seem to be many periods and places characterized by war, others characterized by peace, and others which appear to represent neither war nor peace. But can we generalize on the basis of these impressions? Can we honestly do any more than say that there has indeed been a "great deal" of war among nations over these 150 years? Given the haziness of the line between war and peace, and the elusiveness of these boundaries in time and in space, some will contend that any sharp delineations are either impossible, or so arbitrary as to be politically meaningless. Others will urge that the exercise is hardly necessary in the first place. So be it. All we can do is advise readers who are so persuaded to skip Chapters Two and Three, and turn immediately to the results which emerge.

But for those who recognize that the quality of a product is often determined by the procedures by which it is created, and that creativity devoid of rigor may be aesthetically pleasing but scientifically dubious, our preoccupation with method will be seen as essential. Here, and at appropriate places later on, we will therefore spell out our data-making steps in considerable detail. What we intend to do is to articulate the procedures and criteria employed in our conversion of the vast, buzzing confusion of military history so that any user of the results can do two things. First, this description will permit him to apply the same coding and classifying criteria to the same period, and come up with almost exactly the same results. Few, if any, will actually do this, but it is a cardinal rule in scientific investigations that such replication be possible; if it is not, there is no way of knowing whether the resulting figures are indeed reliable enough for the theorizer to use with any confidence. The second, and equally important, consequence of this self-conscious delineation of procedures is that others will easily be able to discover not only *how* we arrived at our descriptions, but *why* their intuitive expectations differ from our results, if any surprises do indeed turn up.

Given this set of considerations, and seeking to discover the frequency, magnitude, severity, and intensity of war in the international system since the end of the Napoleonic Wars, it behooves us to begin with a delineation and justification of the spatial-temporal domain to which the study is confined.

THE SPATIAL-TEMPORAL DOMAIN

In order to generalize, it is imperative to first specify the spatial-temporal domain to which one's generalizations apply. As obvious as this dictum may be, it is violated all too frequently in the study of international politics. It is an easy matter to find contemporary as well as relatively ancient writings in which the author either fails to specify the boundaries in time and space to which his generalizations should be confined or, worse yet, generalizes to a broad domain on the basis of evidence drawn from a very limited number of years or a very few political entities. Only by a very explicit specification of one's domain can this type of sin be avoided, and it is to that specification which we now turn.

The Temporal Boundaries

As the movement toward greater quantification in international politics research has accelerated, there seems to have been a decreasing emphasis on the long, historical view. While this apparent correlation is all too understandable, it is in our judgment most unfortunate. It is understandable because there clearly are less and less hard data available on many variables as we go back in time. That is, the post-World War II period is characterized by a rapid increase in the availability and reliability of comparative and cumulative cross-national data, thanks largely to the United Nations, OECD, and many other international governmental organizations. Likewise, while both the quantity and quality of such data for the inter-War period are lower than for the post-1945 era, the statistical compilations of the League of Nations and the International Labor Organization, for example, represent an impressive advance over what was available prior to World War I.

But it can be argued that such compilations, despite their great value for social science (and social policy) may well be ignoring the variables that are most critical for an understanding of international politics. One might even agree with the charge that, to some extent, the social sciences have tended to lose in relevance what they have gained in precision. Or, to use a familiar metaphor, we may—like the drunk on a dark street—be looking under the lamp post for things that were lost further down the block. Moreover, if the socioeconomic variables that are most widely measured and reported are not the ones which will best explain the phenomena that concern us (and this remains an empirical question), and if we must eventually get back to the traditional variables of diplomacy, strategy, decision making, and the like, then there is an additional argument in favor of taking the longer view. That is, if most of the information from which such diplomatic data might be generated is found in the collections of documents and communications of the relevant foreign and defense ministries, and these archives are withheld from public scrutiny for periods of from two to five decades, there is no way to acquire a full and accurate picture of the immediate past.

In addition to these two considerations, there is a third and perhaps more important reason for not restricting one's research to a brief (and usually quite contemporary) time span. This is our conviction that no social phenomena are comprehensible except in the context of the historical flow in which they are embedded. Prior events and conditions, along with the direction and rate of change in them, must be taken into account if we hope to explain the present or predict the future.

As to how far back in time one might go, the considerations are myriad, and we have no intention of going into all of them here. But it does seem to us that the burden of proof should rest on those who argue for the briefer time span (usually on the grounds that "things" are radically different now than they were then), rather than on those who urge the longer span. By and large, there is insufficient evidence behind most assertions of radical change, and often there is not even a specification of which variables have so changed as to make earlier and later periods incomparable. We certainly recognize the problem, and one of the by-products of the Correlates of War project will be a set of longitudinal observations for a wide variety of phenomena, on the basis of which one might be able to ascertain precisely which attributes of the global system—or behavioral regularities of its constituent parts—did indeed change, and to what degree, at any particular point in time.

With these often incompatible considerations in mind, we finally decided to look for the correlates (and causes) of war within a time span which runs from the close of the Napoleonic Wars and the Congress of Vienna up until the very recent past. Partly for the sake of arithmetical symmetry, but primarily because of the incompleteness and unreliability of information on those wars that are still underway at this writing or have ended in the past few years, we set 31 December 1965 as our terminal date. To make exactly 150 years, we set 1 January 1816 as our beginning date, even though the Napoleonic era ended several months earlier. That is, the Congress of Vienna opened in September of 1814, was dramatically interrupted by Napoleon's landing at Cannes the following March and his restoration of 100 days, and closed on 8 June 1815. But it was late June before the Battle of Waterloo and Napoleon's second abdication, and 20 November 1815 when the second Peace of Paris agreements were finally signed, the Quadruple Alliance renewed, and the so-called "Concert system" launched.

Social System Levels

While the selection of chronological cutting points is essentially a matter of data availability and research strategy, the delineation of one's spatial domain raises a host of awkward and controversial definitional issues. If we hope to describe and analyze the amount of international war which began, was underway, and terminated every year, it is essential to identify either the locale within which such war occurred, or the specific political entities which participated in these recurrent exercises in legitimized homicide. The *geographical* loci are, from our point of view, of limited interest, and we therefore devote only one chapter to a discussion of the regions in which these wars have occurred. Our major concern is with the *political* systems within which, and among which, international war occurs, and it is to their specification that we now turn.

To begin, we consider the concept of system a useful (as well as currently popular) one, and take the view that a system exists largely in the eye of the beholder. However, we believe that the construct should be applied only to social entities and aggregations, and not to the behavior, interaction, or relationships in which such entities become involved. Thus, we define a social system as any aggregation of individuals or groups who manifest a modest (and for the moment, undefined) degree of interdependence, similarity, or common destiny, and whose treatment as a single unit is scientifically useful to the researcher. Combined with this relatively loose set of requirements, however, is our conviction that it is not scientifically useful to treat as *separate* and successive systems those interdependent aggregates made up of a given class of component units (individuals or groups) merely because some or many of that system's attributes change in magnitude over time. Thus, we reject the notion that there have been many different and successive international systems in the world since 1648 or 1713 or 1815, if the same general territorial area and the same class of social entities (that is, nations) are embraced during the period under examination.

On the other hand, we fully agree that, at any given moment, there exist several different systems (or more precisely, systems and sub-systems), embracing ever smaller aggregations of units, at lower and lower levels of analysis. Thus, at the highest level of analysis for our purposes we postulate the existence of a *global* system, comprising all of mankind and any of the worldwide groupings which men have formed and are of interest to the scientific enterprise at hand. At the next lower, and more restricted level, is the *international* system, comprised of all the national political units in existence at a given time, all of the people who live in these nations, and any of the many existing sub-national and extra-national groupings which are of interest to the researcher. Somewhat more restricted is the *interstate* system, embracing all those national entities that satisfy certain criteria of statehood (discussed below) along with the individuals, the sub-national, and the extra-national groupings which are found within or among these national states. Our primary focus in this enterprise is on this interstate system, and whenever the word "system" is used without a modifier, we refer to the interstate system. We also focus, but to a lesser extent, on those nations which, while not meeting our criteria for inclusion in the interstate system, combine with those which do to form the larger international system. In principle, depending on the era under investigation and the criteria employed, all national entities may qualify as states, making the interstate and the international systems identical and coterminous.

Within the interstate system are two sub-systems of a more restricted nature. One is called the *central* system, and it embraces all those states which are particularly interdependent and which play especially vigorous parts in interstate politics. Essentially identical to what was known as the European state system plus a handful of other states, the specific criteria for inclusion in it are described below. Finally, at the lowest of our five main levels of analysis (global, international, interstate, and central are the first four) is the *major power* system, or once again and more precisely, the major power sub-system. Let us turn in a moment to the criteria by which we define these five nested system levels, but a preliminary step is to discuss the general benchmarks which permit us to identify the several types of war that concern us here.

CRITERIA FOR INCLUSION

Having specified our temporal boundaries fully and our spatial ones less completely, we can now discuss the criteria by which one might differentiate between and among those numerous instances of armed violence which qualify as wars of one type or another, and those which do not. We begin with a description and critique of the criteria used by the two pioneers in the field and then revert to those system levels outlined above, as the major basis for selection—and subsequent classification of—those wars which are included in the present enterprise.

At the outset, we find in Wright's *Study of War* an effort to distinguish among four different types of war: "(a) balance of power war, in the sense of a war *among* state members of the modern family of nations; (b) civil war, in the sense of war *within* a state member of the modern family of nations; (c) defensive war, in the sense of a war to *defend* modern civilization against an alien culture; and (d) imperial war, in the sense of a war to *expand* modern civilization at the expense of an alien culture" (1942, p. 641, italics added). In the *Statistics of Deadly Quarrels,* however, Richardson eschews any effort to establish such a typology. As his editors (one of whom was Wright) remind us, he sought to avoid "conventional and legal distinctions difficult to quantify." Rather, he chose to classify strictly on the basis of casualties, in order to put them into a single series, "whether they occurred in Europe, America, Asia, or Africa, whether between recognized states, between revolutionary groups within a state, between primitive tribes, or between a government and rebels, insurgents, or colonials" (1960a, p. vii).

Since our concern here is to describe, and later to account for, various attributes of *international* wars only, and since we are ignoring civil wars for the time being, it might make perfect sense to proceed to a delineation of our population by (a) ignoring Richardson's undifferentiated list, and (b) merely including Wright's balance of power, defensive, and imperial wars, excluding those wars he classifies as civil. However reasonable such a procedure would be in the abstract, it turns out in practice to be insufficient. As the following paragraphs indicate, Wright goes on to introduce certain additional criteria which lead to the omission of certain wars which *do* seem relevant, and to include several which appear to be irrelevant in establishing a consistent and complete population of such events. Thus it might be useful to examine both his and Richardson's criteria in more detail, and the classificatory effects of each, before articulating the ones employed here.

Among the criteria that might reasonably be used in determining whether or not a given sequence of military combat should be classified as an international war at all are the following: (a) the objectives of the participants, (b) the political consequences, (c) the legal status of the hostilities, (d) the political attributes or status of the participants, (e) the duration of hostilities, (f) the number of troops involved, and (g) the casualties arising from the hostilities. Although Richardson rejects all but the last of these criteria, Wright uses four of them in determining whether the event qualified for his list of 278 wars between 1480 and 1940. Thus, he ignores the participants' objectives but goes on to indicate that "the legal recognition of the warlike action, the scale of such action, and the importance of its legal and political consequences have . . . all have been taken into consideration in deciding whether a given incident was sufficiently important to include in a list of wars." More specifically, Wright includes "all hostilities involving members of the family of nations, whether international, civil, colonial, or imperial, which were recognized as states of war in the legal sense or which involved over 50,000 troops." Also included are "some other incidents . . . in which hostilities of considerable but lesser magnitude, not recognized as legal states of war, led to important legal results such as the creation or extinction of states, territorial transfers, or changes of government" (1942, p. 636).

Richardson, though recognizing that Wright's criteria are "probably more objective" than those he found employed by earlier experts, concludes that they are "hardly satisfactory for statistical purposes: because the *importance* of results is surely a matter of opinion; because opposing belligerents have often differed about what was *legal;* and because important legal and political effects, such as the separation of Norway from Sweden, have been arranged *without* war" (1960a, p. 5). Although these criticisms may not be fully justified, one may nevertheless be slightly uncomfortable with Wright's mixture of coding rules. First, he does not specify the criteria used for determining whether a participant is in fact a "member of the family of nations," and second, he apparently discards all his other criteria if over 50,000 troops were involved. This observation brings us, then, to Richardson's almost sole emphasis on the casualties—what he calls the magnitude—of the belligerent action. He insists often that no other criteria are worth considering, but this is so only because of his prime interest in all deadly quarrels in which casualties reached what he terms a magnitude of 2.5 (317) or greater.[1]

Given these valuable but inconsistent precedents, we decided to employ somewhat more discriminating—as well as more complex—coding procedures in preparing our combined tabulation of international wars. The opening step was to identify and list,

[1] The problem of computing casualties will be discussed below, but it is worth mentioning here that Richardson, justifiably suspicious of many of his figures, decided that the "meaningful part of the record can be separated from its uncertainty by taking the logarithm to the base ten, and rounding the logarithm off to a whole number, or to the first decimal, according to the quality of the information" (1960a, p. 6). A logarithmic scale assumes that errors are likely to be greater and more frequent as magnitude increases, but that accuracy is also less important at the high end of the scale. In Richardson's scale, 2 = 100; 3 = 1000; 4 = 10,000; 5 = 100,000; 6 = 1,000,000; and 7 = 10,000,000; thus, 2.5 = 317 and 6.5 = 3,170,000, for example.

in chronological order, all deadly quarrels between 1816 and 1965 that had been identified as wars by Wright or Richardson, by the standard diplomatic and military histories, or by the many other sources noted in the References and the Appendix. Once this hopefully exhaustive tabulation was completed (and the three most thorough tabulations are combined and compared with our own in Chapter Five), the elimination process began, during which we screened out those quarrels which failed of inclusion because of: (a) the inadequate political status of their participants; or (b) their failure to meet a minimum threshold of battle-connected casualties or troops in combat. Let us describe these exclusion criteria in some detail.

POLITICAL STATUS OF WAR PARTICIPANTS

For a war to be classified as international, it is quite reasonable to require that it occur within the international system of the moment and that it involve at least one national entity on each side. Of course, neither the practitioners of global politics nor the scholars who study their behavior have ever agreed on a set of hard and fast rules by which membership in the system could be unambiguously ascertained, and it was therefore incumbent on us to offer such a set of criteria. In two prior papers, we have moved partially toward that goal, and it would not be amiss to summarize and then expand on those criteria here.

In the more recent and more inclusive of these papers (Russett, Singer, and Small, 1968), we attempt to list all national or quasi-national political entities which have existed since 1900, and which have a population of at least 10,000. We further categorize the degree of each entity's independence, that is, the extent to which it has effective control over its foreign policy, as (a) an independent nation, (b) a colony or dependency, (c) a mandate or trust territory, as established by the League or the United Nations, and (d) militarily occupied; we go on to specify the periods during which each such status was in effect for each entity. Each of these entities is also assigned a geographically determined three-digit code number, to maximize the efficient exchange of machine-readable cross-national data among researchers in comparative and international politics. The earlier and more restricted listing (Singer and Small, 1966a) goes further back in time (to 1815), but only includes the entities that met our criteria for inclusion in the inter*state* system. Unfortunately, we did not at that time make the interstate-international distinction which is followed here, and we thus applied the label of international system to what is really the more restricted interstate system; one effect of that label was to treat as outside the international system the many national entities (colonies, mandates, annexed or occupied regions, etc.) that, while clearly not in the sovereign state category, definitely are constituent units of that larger inter*national* system. The distinction will become clear in the following paragraphs, as we summarize the classification procedures we used for inter*state* system membership in the 1816–1919 and 1920–1965 periods. The criteria established by the later article thus constitute an operational definition of the inter*national system.*

Interstate System Membership Criteria, 1816–1919

Whether or not a national political entity qualifies as a member of the interstate system should be a function of two factors. First, was it large enough in population or other resources to play a moderately active role in world politics, to be a player more than a pawn, and to generate more signal than noise in the system? Several criteria other than population come to mind (territory, unity, self-sufficiency, armed might, etc.) but it would be premature to screen out nations which were deficient on such grounds, even assuming the availability of reasonably accurate evidence. Some minimum population, on the other hand, is always a basic requirement of national survival; moreover, it frequently correlates highly with a number of other criteria of national power. Finally, it is one of the variables for which adequate data have existed over a long period of time.

Thus, our first criterion for treating a nation—no matter what its legal status—as an active member of the interstate system was gross population; and the threshold decided on here was a minimum of 500,000 as opposed to a mere 10,000 for inclusion in our "national entity" list. This figure precluded the need to deal with such minor entities as the smaller of the pre-unification Italian or German states, and more recently, Monaco, Andorra, Liechtenstein, San Marino, or the like. An indication of the sensitivity of that particular threshold may be seen in the fact that, if it had been raised to one million, the following would have been excluded during the specified period: Baden, 1816–1820; Greece, 1830–1845; Argentina, 1841–1850; Chile, 1839–1950; Ecuador, 1854–1860; Salvador, 1875–1900; Guatemala, 1849–1862; and Haiti, 1859–1897. Excluded during the entire 1816–1919 (when we shifted to alternate criteria described below) period would be Albania, Hanover, Hesse Electoral, Hesse Grand Ducal, Mecklenburg-Schwerin, Modena, Parma, Dominican Republic, Honduras, Nicaragua, Paraguay, and Uruguay.

Second, was the entity sufficiently unencumbered by legal, military, economic, or political constraints to exercise a fair degree of sovereignty and independence? The apparent pre-operational nature of this criterion is largely compensated for by the great consistency of diplomatic practice, such that almost all national governments tended to agree on the status of another national entity, at least prior to World War I. That agreement was manifested in a most operational fashion via the granting or withholding of diplomatic recognition, and it will be remembered that this was rarely used as a political weapon until after World War I. Such decisions were not based on one government's approval or disapproval of another, but strictly on the judgment as to whether it could and would effectively assume its international obligations.

At first, our criterion was to ask whether the nation in question was extended such recognition by the majority of the international community, but it soon became evident that so thorough an investigation was not necessary. For the period up to World War I, dominated as the system was by the major European powers, we found that, as Britain and France went, so went the majority. Thus, we designated them as our "legitimizers," and once both of these major powers had established diplomatic missions at or above the rank of chargé d'affaires in the capital of any nation with the requisite half-million population, that nation was classed as a member of the interstate system. We used the establishment of the mission rather than the granting of recognition, since there were occasions on which one government might "recognize" another, but delay sending its representative for long periods. For example, during the 1820s most of the newly independent Latin American states were recognized by European powers, but few permanent missions were dispatched for several decades. This, then, provided us with a highly operational pair of criteria by which we could identify the composition of the interstate system from the Congress of Vienna to the Versailles Conference after World War I.

Interstate System Membership Criteria, 1920–1965

For the post-Versailles era, however, the problem was not solved quite so easily. The "big two" may have emerged victorious from the War, but they found their supremacy somewhat less secure, with power in the system somewhat more diffused. Their capacity to extend or withhold legitimacy became increasingly a perquisite to be shared with other nations, directly, as well as through international organizations. In this later period, then, a nation was classified as a system member if it either: (a) was a member of the League or the United Nations at any time during its existence, or (b) met the half-million population minimum and received diplomatic missions from *any two* (rather than the *specific* two) *major* powers; membership in the latter oligarchy is defined below. We could no longer find two specific legitimizers to replace France and Britain, and even if we could, the norms of recognition had so changed that too many obviously qualified states would have been excluded; hence the reliance on *any* two major powers. Moreover, with the appearance of the League and then the United Nations, we were provided with an institutionalized legitimation procedure by which the comity of nations told us, in effect, which national entities satisfied the requirements for inclusion in the interstate system and which did not. (While the principle of universality of membership is not explicitly stated in the League Covenant nor practiced in effect, the United Nations Charter not only asserts the fundamental aim, but has moved increasingly toward its realization.) Thus, the post-World War I period is one in which we utilize either of two rather different sets of criteria. Even though the results of either set would be quite similar, it is worth noting that if we had not used international organization membership as an alternative route to inclusion in our interstate system, such low population nations as Panama, Costa Rica, Iceland, Malta, Kuwait, Gambia, and the Maldives would have been excluded. In our judgment, it would be wrong to exclude from the interstate system any nation which belonged to the League or its successor.

Despite their apparent reasonableness, however, these rules nevertheless required us to make several intuitive exceptions. First, among those entities which qualified by one or both of the above criteria, but which we excluded, were India, Slovakia, and Manchukuo. India did not qualify for system membership during the 1920s and 1930s because she did not control her own foreign policy. Her membership in the League, as well as her representation at Versailles, was a concession to the British, in much the same way that the inclusion of the Ukraine and Byelorussia (two exceptions for the post-1945 period) in the United Nations was a concession to the Russians.

Both Manchukuo and Slovakia were puppet states which also did not control their own foreign policies in any meaningful sense. Established by Japan, and ruled by Emperor Henry Pu Yi from 1932 to 1945, Manchukuo never achieved League membership (not surprising, considering the ramifications of the Lytton Report), although it did receive its requisite second major power mission in 1937. Slovakia, on the other hand, posed a more difficult problem. More than 25 states recognized her, including three major powers before the start of World War II. Yet a careful analysis of the sources suggests that when Monseigneur Tiso placed his country under the protection of Germany some days after Germany took over Bohemia and Moravia, Slovakia signed over her freedom of action in foreign policy (Mikus, 1963; Lettrich, 1955). In other words, Slovakia resembled occupied Poland more than Rumania or Bulgaria, two of Germany's "independent" allies.

As for the states which we *in*cluded even though they did not meet our admission rules, Outer Mongolia, Nepal, Saudi Arabia, and Yemen are the obvious outliers. We have treated Outer Mongolia as an independent system member from 1921 to the present, despite the fact that she was not a League member and enjoyed recognition from only one major power, the Soviet Union. Our inquiries have led us to conclude that the remote republic was at least as independent as Panama and Nicaragua during the interwar period, for example; for conflicting interpretations, see Friters (1949), Tang (1959), and Rupen (1964). Nepal, even more remote than Outer Mongolia in terms of relationship to the system, and thus without major power recognition, was nevertheless considered independent by almost all observers. Both Saudi Arabia and Yemen existed as independent entities prior to Versailles, but were not treated as system members until recognized by Italy and Britain in the "legitimizing" treaties of the mid-1920s.

In the post-1945 period, aside from the aforementioned cases of the Ukraine and Byelorussia, China caused us some difficulty. While not represented in the United Nations, the mainland regime was recognized promptly by both the U.S.S.R. and England; Taiwan, conversely, qualified via United Nations membership. Thus, we classify China as a continuing system member and successor state to the Nationalist regime after 1949, at which time Taiwan is added to the list as a new member.

An additional consideration in determining whether or not a political entity qualified as a system member in either of the periods—and, therefore, as a war participant—was that of governments that may have been forced by war into exile or into a small salient of their own national territory. The rule we adopted here was that as long as a government could field, and maintain in active combat, an independent fighting force of 100,000 or more, it continued to exist as a system member and war participant, and therefore to contribute to our computations of the war's magnitude, severity, and intensity. For example, Belgium and Serbia were almost completely overrun and occupied in 1914 and 1915 respectively, but each managed to keep relatively large and effective forces fighting against the Central Powers. On the other hand, in World War II, even though contingents identified with their home countries were maintained by the Dutch, the Poles, and the French, neither the Dutch nor the Polish air, ground, and naval forces met the 100,000 threshold, and the Free French did not meet it until De Gaulle and his troops helped to liberate Paris in 1944.

Central System Membership Criteria, 1816–1919

Once the basic list of the nations that qualified for membership in the interstate system was compiled, a further coding procedure seemed necessary. For a number of purposes, mere identification of the members of the system as of any given year may not be adequate. Much of our theorizing in international politics focuses on the most active or influential nations, and quite legitimately ignores or depreciates the others. Recognizing this need, we have gone a step further and differentiated between national states which played a fairly vigorous part in global diplomacy, and those whose role was much more peripheral. The former constitute a sub-system which we have labeled the *central* system, and it will be seen that it is almost identical to that more intuitive grouping known to diplomatic history as the European state system. We are persuaded, however, that our dichotomy makes sense only up through the First World War, after which the total system seems to have become sufficiently interdependent to no longer justify this sharp distinction. Thus, from 1920 on, the central and peripheral systems are treated as a single, interdependent one. How do we differentiate between central and peripheral system membership, then, during the 1816–1919 period?

Here is the point at which our criteria become somewhat softer, and more intuitive than operational. Basically, our classification required that a central system member be active and influential in European-centered diplomacy. Thus, we follow the scholarly consensus, and exclude and include as follows. First, there were several European nations which did not qualify for central system membership during part or all of the 1816–1919 period. Although several of the German states met both the population and recognition criteria, all of them other than Austria and Prussia are relegated to the peripheral system. The major reason is that their 1815 treaty of confederation prohibited entrance into any alliance directed against other members of the confederation, and thus markedly restricted their freedom of activity. Likewise, the Italian states other than Sardinia enjoyed a very limited independence prior to their unification in the 1860s. Linked in a very intimate fashion to Austria by dynastic ties, Modena, Parma, Tuscany, and the Two Sicilies became little more than satellites of Vienna. In the same vein, the Papal States were effectively precluded from any significant diplomatic activity by the French and Austrian guarantees.

On the other hand, certain non-European nations moved into positions of influence and activity during the period under consideration. Following the Sino-Japanese War and the Treaty of Shimonoseki in 1895, both the victor and the vanquished became increasingly involved in European affairs, and are therefore included in the central system. The other extra-continental nation to be included in the central system was the United States, which qualified following its easy victory over Spain in 1898.

Major Power System Membership Criteria, 1816–1965

One last point must be considered in completing our hierarchical scheme. On the one hand, a political entity may have most of the earmarks of statehood but not qualify for system membership, or it may merit inclusion in the system but remain peripheral enough in activity, power, or importance to fail of inclusion in the central system prior to 1920. At the other end of the status or power spectrum, all students of world politics use, or appreciate the relevance of, the concept of "major power." Sharing that appreciation, and recognizing its relevance for establishing a wide range of war data categories, we add this smallest sub-system to our classification scheme.

Although the criteria for differentiation between major powers and others are not as operational as we might wish, we do achieve a fair degree of reliability on the basis of "intercoder agreement." That is, for the period up to World War II, there is high scholarly consensus on the composition of this oligarchy. As we interpret this consensus, the major powers and the period during which that august status was maintained, seem to be as follows: Austria-Hungary, from 1816 to defeat and dismemberment in 1918; Prussia, from 1816 to 1870, and its successor state of Germany, from 1871 to 1918 and 1925 to 1945; Russia, from 1816 to 1917 and the U.S.S.R. from 1922 on; France, from 1816 to its defeat and occupation in 1940; England, from 1816 on; Italy, from its unification in 1860 to its defeat in 1943; Japan, from its victory over China in 1895 to its surrender in 1945; and the United States, from its victories over Spain in 1898 to the final defeat of the Axis.

For the post-World War II period, there is somewhat less consensus, but it would seem difficult to disagree with the continuation of major power status for the U.S.S.R. and the United States, as well as for England, despite the dramatic gap between her and the two super-powers. And, bearing in mind their ultimate possession of limited nuclear capabilities and permanent seats on the U. N. Security Council, it seems reasonable to include France as of the Allied victory in 1945 and China as of the Communist victory in 1949.

The Composition of the Several Systems

Given this range of considerations, and the decisions we adopted, the hope is that we have defined a number of populations and sub-populations by criteria that satisfy not only the requirements of reliability and reproducibility, but those of validity and reasonableness as well. Throughout this volume, the reader will note the often conflicting pulls of these two sets of requirements, and our conviction is that scientific work on theoretically and socially significant problems just cannot go forward unless we are willing to engage in these trade-offs and try to come up with the best (or least bad) of both worlds.

The ultimate results of these necessarily complex coding and classifying procedures are shown in the two tables which follow. First (Table 2.1), we provide a list of all those entities which met our criteria for inclusion in the interstate system at any point during the century and a half under study, along with the year in which it first qualified for, and (occasionally) later lost, membership. This list also shows which states qualified for inclusion in the 1816–1919 central system and when; no state in the central system lost membership in it unless it also lost membership in the overall system. It further identifies the major powers by the years during which that status was enjoyed, according to our criteria. In addition, note that the states are arranged in order of approximate geographical propinquity within each of the major continental regions, and are identified by the standardized (Russett et al., 1968) code numbers that we discussed above. Finally, it should be reiterated here that the entities that are in the larger international system, but not in the more restricted interstate system, are not listed here.

2.1 NATION MEMBERS OF THE INTERSTATE SYSTEM, 1816-1965

NAT#	ABB.	NATION	INCLUSIVE YEARS IN INTERSTATE SYSTEM	INCLUSIVE YEARS IN CENTRAL SYSTEM	INCLUSIVE YEARS A MAJOR POWER
WESTERN HEMISPHERE (002-199)					
2	USA	UNITED STATES	1816-1965	1899-1919	1899-1965
20	CAN	CANADA	1920-1965		
40	CUB	CUBA	1902-1965		
41	HAI	HAITI	1859-1965		
42	DOM	DOMINICAN REPUBLIC	1887-1965		
51	JAM	JAMAICA	1962-1965		
52	TRI	TRINIDAD-TOBAGO	1962-1965		
70	MEX	MEXICO	1831-1965		
90	GUA	GUATEMALA	1849-1965		
91	HON	HONDURAS	1899-1965		
92	SAL	SALVADOR	1875-1965		
93	NIC	NICARAGUA	1900-1965		
94	COS	COSTA RICA	1920-1965		
95	PAN	PANAMA	1920-1965		
100	COL	COLOMBIA	1831-1965		
101	VEN	VENEZUELA	1841-1965		
130	ECU	ECUADOR	1854-1965		
135	PER	PERU	1838-1965		
140	BRA	BRAZIL	1826-1965		
145	BOL	BOLIVIA	1848-1965		
150	PAR	PARAGUAY	1896-1965		
155	CHI	CHILE	1839-1965		
160	ARG	ARGENTINA	1841-1965		
165	URU	URUGUAY	1882-1965		
EUROPE (200-399)					
200	ENG	ENGLAND	1816-1965	1816-1919	1816-1965
205	IRE	IRELAND	1922-1965		
210	HOL	HOLLAND	1816-1940 1945-1965	1816-1919	
211	BEL	BELGIUM	1830-1940 1945-1965	1830-1919	
212	LUX	LUXEMBURG	1920-1940 1944-1965		
220	FRN	FRANCE	1816-1942 1944-1965	1816-1919	1816-1940 1945-1965

NAT#	ABB.	NATION	INCLUSIVE YEARS IN INTERSTATE SYSTEM	INCLUSIVE YEARS IN CENTRAL SYSTEM	INCLUSIVE YEARS A MAJOR POWER
225	SWZ	SWITZERLAND	1816-1965	1816-1919	
230	SPN	SPAIN	1816-1965	1816-1919	
235	POR	PORTUGAL	1816-1965	1816-1919	
240	HAN	HANOVER	1838-1866		
245	BAV	BAVARIA	1816-1870		
255	GMY	GERMANY/PRUSSIA	1816-1945	1816-1919	1816-1918 1925-1945
260	GMW	GERMANY WEST	1955-1965		
265	GME	GERMANY EAST	1954-1965		
267	BAD	BADEN	1816-1870		
269	SAX	SAXONY	1816-1867		
271	WRT	WUERTTEMBERG	1816-1870		
273	HSE	HESSE ELECTORAL	1816-1866		
275	HSG	HESSE GRAND DUCAL	1816-1867		
280	MEC	MECKLENBURG-SCHWERIN	1843-1867		
290	POL	POLAND	1919-1939 1945-1965	1919-1919	
300	AUH	AUSTRIA-HUNGARY	1816-1918	1816-1919	1816-1918
305	AUS	AUSTRIA	1919-1938 1955-1965	1919-1919	
310	HUN	HUNGARY	1919-1965	1919-1919	
315	CZE	CZECHOSLOVAKIA	1918-1939 1945-1965	1918-1919	
325	ITA	ITALY/SARDINIA	1816-1965	1816-1919	1860-1943
327	PAP	PAPAL STATES	1816-1860		
329	SIC	TWO SICILIES	1816-1861		
332	MOD	MODENA	1842-1860		
335	PMA	PARMA	1851-1860		
337	TUS	TUSCANY	1816-1860		
338	MLT	MALTA	1964-1965		
339	ALB	ALBANIA	1914-1939 1944-1965	1914-1919	
345	YUG	YUGOSLAVIA/SERBIA	1878-1941 1944-1965	1878-1919	
350	GRC	GREECE	1828-1941 1945-1965	1828-1919	
352	CYP	CYPRUS	1960-1965		
355	BUL	BULGARIA	1908-1965	1908-1919	
360	RUM	RUMANIA	1878-1965	1878-1919	
365	RUS	RUSSIA	1816-1965	1816-1919	1816-1917 1922-1965
366	EST	ESTONIA	1918-1940	1918-1919	
367	LAT	LATVIA	1918-1940	1918-1919	
368	LIT	LITHUANIA	1918-1940	1918-1919	
375	FIN	FINLAND	1919-1965	1919-1919	
380	SWD	SWEDEN	1816-1965	1816-1919	
385	NOR	NORWAY	1905-1940 1945-1965	1905-1919	
390	DEN	DENMARK	1816-1940 1945-1965	1816-1919	
395	ICE	ICELAND	1944-1965		
AFRICA (400-599)					
420	GAM	GAMBIA	1965-1965		
432	MLI	MALI	1960-1965		
433	SEN	SENEGAL	1960-1965		
434	DAH	DAHOMEY	1960-1965		
435	MAU	MAURITANIA	1960-1965		
436	NIR	NIGER	1960-1965		
437	IVO	IVORY COAST	1960-1965		
438	GUI	GUINEA	1958-1965		
439	UPP	UPPER VOLTA	1960-1965		
450	LBR	LIBERIA	1920-1965		
451	SIE	SIERRA LEONE	1961-1965		
452	GHA	GHANA	1957-1965		
461	TOG	TOGO	1960-1965		
471	CAO	CAMEROUN	1960-1965		
475	NIG	NIGERIA	1960-1965		
481	GAB	GABON	1960-1965		
482	CEN	CENTRAL AFRICAN REPB	1960-1965		
483	CHA	CHAD	1960-1965		
484	CON	CONGO (BRAZZAVILLE)	1960-1965		
490	COP	CONGO (KINSHASA)	1960-1965		
500	UGA	UGANDA	1962-1965		
501	KEN	KENYA	1963-1965		
510	TAZ	TANZANIA	1961-1965		
511	ZAN	ZANZIBAR	1963-1964		
516	BUI	BURUNDI	1962-1965		

2.1 NATION MEMBERS OF THE INTERSTATE SYSTEM, 1816-1965

NAT#	ABB.	NATION	INCLUSIVE YEARS IN INTERSTATE SYSTEM	INCLUSIVE YEARS IN CENTRAL SYSTEM	INCLUSIVE YEARS A MAJOR POWER
517	RWA	RWANDA	1962-1965		
520	SOM	SOMALIA	1960-1965		
530	ETH	ETHIOPIA	1898-1936		
			1941-1965		
551	ZAM	ZAMBIA	1964-1965		
553	MAW	MALAWI	1964-1965		
560	SAF	SOUTH AFRICA	1920-1965		
580	MAG	MALAGASY	1960-1965		
MIDDLE EAST (600-699)					
600	MOR	MOROCCO	1847-1911		
			1956-1965		
615	ALG	ALGERIA	1962-1965		
616	TUN	TUNISIA	1956-1965		
620	LBY	LIBYA	1952-1965		
625	SUD	SUDAN	1956-1965		
630	IRN	IRAN	1855-1965		
640	TUR	TURKEY	1816-1965	1816-1919	
645	IRQ	IRAQ	1932-1965		
651	UAR	U.A.R.	1937-1965		
652	SYR	SYRIA	1946-1958		
			1961-1965		
660	LEB	LEBANON	1946-1965		
663	JOR	JORDAN	1946-1965		
666	ISR	ISRAEL	1948-1965		
670	SAU	SAUDI ARABIA	1927-1965		
678	YEM	YEMEN	1926-1965		
690	KUW	KUWAIT	1961-1965		
ASIA (700-999)					
700	AFG	AFGHANISTAN	1920-1965		
710	CHN	CHINA	1860-1965	1895-1919	1950-1965
712	MON	MONGOLIA	1921-1965		
713	TAW	TAIWAN	1949-1965		
730	KOR	KOREA	1888-1905		
731	KON	KOREA NORTH	1948-1965		
732	KOS	KOREA SOUTH	1949-1965		
740	JAP	JAPAN	1860-1945	1895-1919	1895-1945
			1952-1965		
750	IND	INDIA	1947-1965		
770	PAK	PAKISTAN	1947-1965		
775	BUR	BURMA	1948-1965		
780	CEY	CEYLON	1948-1965		
781	MAD	MALDIVE ISLANDS	1965-1965		
790	NEP	NEPAL	1920-1965		
800	THI	THAILAND	1887-1965		
811	CAM	CAMBODIA	1953-1965		
812	LAO	LAOS	1954-1965		
816	VTN	VIETNAM NORTH	1954-1965		
817	VTS	VIETNAM SOUTH	1954-1965		
820	MAL	MALAYSIA (MALAYA)	1957-1965		
830	SIN	SINGAPORE	1965-1965		
840	PHI	PHILIPPINES	1946-1965		
850	INS	INDONESIA	1949-1965		
900	AUL	AUSTRALIA	1920-1965		
920	NEW	NEW ZEALAND	1920-1965		

Having specified which national entities met our criteria for membership in the interstate system at one point or another in their histories, the next step is to convert those facts into more useful form. This we do in Table 2.2, which presents a cumulative picture of the system, indicating its size and composition after each fluctuation because of departure from, or entry into, the interstate system or its central subsystem.

2.2 - FLUCTUATING COMPOSITION OF THE INTERSTATE SYSTEM, 1816-1965

YEAR	NO. IN SYSTEM	QUALIFIES AS MEMBER OF SYSTEM	LOSES MEMBERSHIP IN INTERSTATE SYSTEM	NO. IN CENTRAL SYSTEM	QUALIFIES AS MEMBER OF CENTRAL SYSTEM
1816	23	UNITED STATES ENGLAND HOLLAND FRANCE SWITZERLAND SPAIN PORTUGAL BAVARIA GERMANY/PRUSSIA BADEN SAXONY WUERTTEMBERG HESSE ELECTORAL HESSE GRAND DUCAL AUSTRIA-HUNGARY ITALY/SARDINIA PAPAL STATES TWO SICILIES TUSCANY RUSSIA SWEDEN DENMARK TURKEY		13	ENGLAND HOLLAND FRANCE SWITZERLAND SPAIN PORTUGAL GERMANY/PRUSSIA AUSTRIA-HUNGARY ITALY/SARDINIA RUSSIA SWEDEN DENMARK TURKEY
1826	24	BRAZIL		13	
1828	25	GREECE		14	GREECE
1830	26	BELGIUM		15	BELGIUM
1831	28	MEXICO COLOMBIA		15	
1838	30	PERU HANOVER		15	
1839	31	CHILE		15	
1841	33	VENEZUELA ARGENTINA		15	
1842	34	MODENA		15	
1843	35	MECKLENBURG-SCHWERIN		15	
1847	36	MOROCCO		15	
1848	37	BOLIVIA		15	
1849	38	GUATEMALA		15	
1851	39	PARMA		15	
1854	40	ECUADOR		15	
1855	41	IRAN		15	
1859	42	HAITI		15	
1860	44	CHINA JAPAN	PAPAL STATES MODENA PARMA TUSCANY	15	
1861	40		TWO SICILIES	15	
1862	39			15	
1866	39		HANOVER HESSE ELECTORAL	15	
1867	37		SAXONY HESSE GRAND DUCAL MECKLENBURG-SCHWERIN	15	
1868	34			15	

2.2 - FLUCTUATING COMPOSITION OF THE INTERSTATE SYSTEM, 1816-1965

YEAR	NO. IN SYSTEM	QUALIFIES AS MEMBER OF SYSTEM	LOSES MEMBERSHIP IN INTERSTATE SYSTEM	NO. IN CENTRAL SYSTEM	QUALIFIES AS MEMBER OF CENTRAL SYSTEM
1870	34		BAVARIA BADEN WUERTTEMBERG	15	
1871	31			15	
1875	32	SALVADOR		15	
1878	34	YUGOSLAVIA/SERBIA RUMANIA		17	YUGOSLAVIA/SERBIA RUMANIA
1882	35	URUGUAY		17	
1887	37	DOMINICAN REPUBLIC THAILAND		17	
1888	38	KOREA		17	
1895	38			19	CHINA JAPAN
1896	39	PARAGUAY		19	
1898	40	ETHIOPIA		19	
1899	41	HONDURAS		20	UNITED STATES
1900	42	NICARAGUA		20	
1902	43	CUBA		20	
1905	44	NORWAY	KOREA	21	NORWAY
1906	43			21	
1908	44	BULGARIA		22	BULGARIA
1911	44		MOROCCO	22	
1912	43			22	
1914	44	ALBANIA		23	ALBANIA
1918	48	CZECHOSLOVAKIA ESTONIA LATVIA LITHUANIA	AUSTRIA-HUNGARY	27	CZECHOSLOVAKIA ESTONIA LATVIA LITHUANIA
1919	51	POLAND AUSTRIA HUNGARY FINLAND		31	POLAND AUSTRIA HUNGARY FINLAND
				************************************ CENTRAL AND PERIPHERAL SYSTEMS COMBINED AS OF 1920	
1920	61	CANADA COSTA RICA PANAMA LUXEMBURG LIBERIA SOUTH AFRICA AFGHANISTAN NEPAL AUSTRALIA NEW ZEALAND			
1921	62	MONGOLIA			
1922	63	IRELAND			
1926	64	YEMEN			
1927	65	SAUDI ARABIA			
1932	66	IRAQ			
1936	66		ETHIOPIA		
1937	66	U.A.R.			
1938	66		AUSTRIA		

2.2 - FLUCTUATING COMPOSITION OF THE INTERSTATE SYSTEM, 1816-1965

YEAR	NO. IN SYSTEM	QUALIFIES AS MEMBER OF SYSTEM	LOSES MEMBERSHIP IN INTERSTATE SYSTEM
1939	65		POLAND CZECHOSLOVAKIA ALBANIA
1940	62		HOLLAND BELGIUM LUXEMBURG ESTONIA LATVIA LITHUANIA NORWAY DENMARK
1941	55	ETHIOPIA	YUGOSLAVIA/SERBIA GREECE
1942	53		FRANCE
1943	52		
1944	57	LUXEMBURG FRANCE ALBANIA YUGOSLAVIA/SERBIA ICELAND	
1945	64	HOLLAND BELGIUM POLAND CZECHOSLOVAKIA GREECE NORWAY DENMARK	GERMANY/PRUSSIA JAPAN
1946	66	SYRIA LEBANON JORDAN PHILIPPINES	
1947	68	INDIA PAKISTAN	
1948	72	ISRAEL KOREA NORTH BURMA CEYLON	
1949	75	TAIWAN KOREA SOUTH INDONESIA	
1952	77	LIBYA JAPAN	
1953	78	CAMBODIA	
1954	82	GERMANY EAST LAOS VIETNAM NORTH VIETNAM SOUTH	
1955	84	GERMANY WEST AUSTRIA	
1956	87	MOROCCO TUNISIA SUDAN	
1957	89	GHANA MALAYSIA (MALAYA)	
1958	90	GUINEA	SYRIA
1959	89		
1960	107	CYPRUS MALI SENEGAL DAHOMEY MAURITANIA NIGER IVORY COAST	

2.2 - FLUCTUATING COMPCSITION OF THE INTERSTATE SYSTEM, 1816-1965

YEAR	NO. IN SYSTEM	QUALIFIES AS MEMBER OF SYSTEM	LOSES MEMBERSHIP IN INTERSTATE SYSTEM
		UPPER VOLTA	
		TOGO	
		CAMEROUN	
		NIGERIA	
		GABCN	
		CENTRAL AFRICAN REPB	
		CHAI	
		CONGO (ERAZZAVILLE)	
		CONGO (KINSHASA)	
		SOMALIA	
		MALAGASY	
1961	111	SIERRA LEONE	
		TANZANIA	
		SYRIA	
		KUWAIT	
1962	117	JAMAICA	
		TRINIDAD-TCEAGO	
		UGANDA	
		BURUNDI	
		RWANDA	
		ALGERIA	
1963	119	KENYA	
		ZANZIBAR	
1964	122	MALTA	ZANZIBAR
		ZAMEIA	
		MALAWI	
1965	124	GAMEIA	
		MALCIVE ISLANDS	
		SINGAPORE	

TYPES OF WAR

We have now, admittedly at some length, defined the criteria by which national entities are assigned to the international, interstate, central, and major power systems, and presented the populations that emerge from these classification procedures. And since, as mentioned earlier in the chapter, the political status (that is, system or subsystem membership) of the combatant nations serves as our major basis for categorizing each war, we can now move on to a summary of the war types that emerge therefrom. We should note in passing, however, that an additional set of criteria—the level of military participation at which a nation may be said to have been sufficiently involved in a given war—needs to be considered, and we will return to that matter in the next section. For the moment, however, we can say that our general rule was to exclude any war which did not lead to at least 1000 battle fatalities among all the participating system members.

It will be recalled that Wright differentiated among balance of power, defensive, imperial, and civil wars, and we expressed certain reservations then in regard to his coding procedures. We would also question the basic conceptualization. In our judgment, his definition of defensive and imperial wars in terms of whether "modern civilization" was defending against, or expanding at the expense of, "an alien culture" is not only risky in that it requires us to ascertain the motives of decision makers and to distinguish between initiator and defender, but in that it also calls for indefensible and invidious distinctions between civilized and alien cultures. As a matter of fact, our non-Western colleagues may detect the degree of embarrassment we feel because of the relatively ethnocentric criteria which we already have—in our judgment, unavoidably—been obliged to employ. Thus, even while adhering to Wright's general categories, we propose and utilize here a typology which is not only more operational, but more neutral in the normative sense. Using the political status and system memberships of the participants as our dominant classificatory benchmark, we began by differentiating between two basic types of international war: *intra*-systemic, or interstate, war, and *extra*-systemic, or imperial and colonial war. A third basic type—civil war—is of concern to us here only if it becomes "internationalized," and will be discussed in a later section. Let us now examine each of these types and their subtypes in turn.

Intra-systemic (Interstate) Wars

Our primary focus in this project is, as was already noted, on fluctuations in the frequency, magnitude, severity, and intensity of interstate war between 1816 and 1965, and the bulk of this handbook will be devoted to the measurement and reportage of these phenomena. We will, therefore, be returning to these intra-systemic or interstate wars in considerable detail, and need only give the summary definition here. An interstate war is defined as one in which at least one sufficiently active participant on each side is a qualified nation member of the interstate system; hence the interchangeable use of the "intra-systemic" and "interstate" labels. Since the criteria for "sufficiently active" participation are discussed in the next section, it will suffice to say here that the number of battle fatalities and the size of the combatant forces constitute the key dimensions.

Central System and Major Power Wars

Even though our dominant preoccupation is with the interstate system as a whole, there will certainly be occasions on which we (or other users of this volume) may want to limit our attention to somewhat more restricted empirical domains. In order to do this, it would be useful to have tabulations which separate out from the larger setting the wars that occur entirely or primarily within the central or major power sub-systems. Moreover, some types of analysis may best be restricted to the war experience of nations within these two smaller domains even though the wars themselves may have involved nations which fall outside of them. Thus, we will in several places compute and present data which are restricted to these two sub-systems of the interstate system.

Let us shift our attention for the moment, then, to the international wars that involve not only national entities which are members of the interstate system, but also those which fall outside of that fairly restricted system. These we call extra-systemic wars, and they are of two basic types: imperial and colonial. In using these two labels, it should be emphasized that we do so in the most neutral fashion, and mean to convey a minimum of ideological and normative baggage.

Extra-systemic (Imperial and Colonial) Wars

Although our chief theoretical interest is in wars between and among state members of the international system, it is evident that any understanding of international war in general cannot rest on interstate wars alone; we must also consider other international wars in which one or more system members have been engaged. Reference is, of course, to wars in which the system member's forces fought against those (however irregular and disorganized) of a political entity which was *not* a qualified system member, but in which the member nevertheless sustained a minimum of 1000 battle-connected fatalities. Within this category, there are three subtypes, depending once more on the political status of the adversary. The adversary might be an independent political entity which did not qualify for membership because of serious limitations on its independence, a population insufficiency, or a failure of other states to recognize it as a legitimate member. These are classed as *imperial* wars (indicated by I after the dates in Table 2.3) and would include the British-Zulu War of 1879 and the Franco-Madagascan War of 1896, for example.

If, on the other hand, the adversary were a colony, dependency, or protectorate composed of ethnically different people and located at some geographical distance from the given system member, or at least peripheral to its center of government, the war was classed as colonial (indicated by a *C* in Table 2.3). Among these were the Greek War for Independence of 1821–1828, the Texan War of 1835–1836, the Polish rebellions of 1831 and 1863, and the French-Indochinese War of 1945–1954.

The third type of extra-systemic war is one in which the adversary was an insurgent or rebellious group located within the territory of *another* system member, and in which the first system member intervened on the side of the regime against its insurgents. This is, of course, an *internationalized civil war* which has become internationalized by virtue of the military intervention of the outside state's forces. The entire question of civil wars is dealt with in the next section, but in closing it should be noted that what gives these three types of war their identity and similarity is that they involve a system member's active participation in a war beyond its own metropolitan territory, against the forces of a political entity which is not a legitimate and recognized member of the system.

Ambiguities and Exclusions

Most of the wars that fall into one of the above categories cause us some, but relatively little, difficulty in coding. The political status criterion plus the military participation threshold (described in the next section) seem to solve most of our selection and classification problems. There are, however, certain kinds of wars which might pose some awkward problems, and even though these are all excluded from the study, it seems worthwhile to say a few words about them. In the process, the boundaries between the wars that are *included* and those which are *excluded* should be sharpened, thus further clarifying our coding rules and reassuring the reader that our criteria are neither capricious nor inconsistent.

The major source of ambiguity arises out of those cases in which the political status of a participant undergoes change either during, or just before, the war in question. This problem falls, in turn, into two classes. First, there is the possible conversion of a sufficiently severe imperial or colonial war into an interstate war and, second, there is the possible internationalization of a civil war, either through outside intervention or the changing status of the insurgent or rebel forces. Since the latter are more complicated, and account for most of the exclusions from our compilation, we might deal first with the former and simpler set of cases.

Our rules for dealing with imperial and colonial wars are quite straightforward. It will be recalled that these are wars (of sufficient severity) in which a nation member of the interstate system is engaged against either a national entity which fails of system inclusion on grounds of population or recognition, or against an entity which is a colony, dependency, or mandate, and therefore fails of system inclusion on grounds of non-independence. Taking the latter class first, the mere proclamation of independence by a colonial entity which was fighting against its former mother country would not be sufficient to convert the colonial war into an interstate war. The rebellious faction or self-proclaimed independent entity must have satisfied our criteria of system membership six months *prior to the onset* of hostilities to merit participation in an interstate war. Thus, the battles of the Poles and Baltic groups against Soviet Russia from 1918 to 1921 were not classified as interstate wars despite their 1918 declarations of independence; these remained in the colonial war category. By way of a contrary example, Finland's "second war for independence" in 1939–1940, fought some 20 years after the initial and successful colonial war, *is* treated as an interstate one because the ex-dependency's independent political status had by then been established.

As to the imperial wars, it might appear at first glance that a similar sort of rule should apply to these as well. There is, however, an important difference. In the case of colonies, as distinct from independent but non-member entities, system membership depends not only on diplomatic recognition and population but, most important, on the establishment of de facto independence. For the entity which engages a system member in an imperial war, this is no problem at all, since it is by definition already an independent entity.

Turning now to civil wars, there are in principle the two aforementioned ways by which they may become internationalized, and thereby qualify for inclusion in this particular investigation. As should be evident by now, even though a standard civil war between a member government and its domestic insurgents might be classified technically as an international war (since it involves at least one system member), it differs substantially in its nature, and usually in its political implications, from those which we call internationalized. Among the civil wars that become internationalized, however, an important distinction must be made. When the intervening system member comes into a civil war *alongside another member* government and against the insurgents, the war clearly falls into the extra-systemic category since it is international and it is against a non-member entity. Even though we make no distinction as to whether the rebellious forces are granted insurgency status under international law or not, if they are sufficiently successful militarily to eventually gain control of all, or a large part of, the national territory and population (thus replacing the original government), and subsequently satisfy the other requirements for system membership, this extra-systemic war is said to have terminated and to have become intra-systemic or interstate, as of the date of such qualification. For the period under review, this is a purely hypothetical problem since there has only been one such case which comes close to qualifying. This is the Spanish Civil War, and in that case the evidence seems to be that the Franco regime had not successfully replaced the regime until after the hostilities had terminated. We will return to this case in a moment.

Civil wars can and do, however, become internationalized interstate wars through an alternative process. We refer, of course, to those which involve the armed forces and the insurgents of a single nation at the outset, but in which there is subsequent intervention by an outside system member's forces on the side of the insurgents and *against* the existing regime. There have been only two cases of sufficient severity in which the intervening forces did indeed come in against the system member's regime and sustained the necessary fatalities: during the Russian Civil War of 1917–1921, and the aforementioned Spanish one of 1936–1939; in the latter, system members intervened on both sides. We have identified (and listed in Appendix B) 34 cases of such intervention, but in which the level of military participation was below the requisite threshold, as outlined in the next section.

A word or two regarding our exclusion of the Russian and Spanish Civil Wars (as well as such contemporary conflicts as that now underway in Vietnam) is in order here. We have, after considerable discussion, reluctantly decided to omit these wars from our data presentation and statistical summaries, while recognizing that other scholars with other theoretical concerns might well have decided otherwise. Let us, however, explain our decision, and include here whatever figures we have been able to gather. As we have reiterated more than once already, we see our mission here as one of shedding light on the military aspects of international politics, concentrating primarily on events which flow from, and exercise an impact on, certain properties of the international system and its interstate sub-system. Admittedly, very few domestic political events (especially in the twentieth century) are fully isolated from international politics, but some division is necessary, even if for purposes of manageability alone. Further, it is incumbent on those of us who advocate a quantitative approach to political science to avoid doing violence to what is intuitively reasonable in the name of operational measurement.

On the one hand, the Russian and Spanish Civil Wars both became internationalized via sufficiently active intervention of outside system members on the side of the insurgents and against the regime; in principle, then, they should be treated—at some point in their unfolding—as interstate wars. There are, on the other hand, a number of specific reasons—in addition to the general considerations just mentioned—for excluding them here.

In the Russian case, we were persuaded that we had in front of us something very different, militarily and politically, from any of the standard interstate wars. Beyond the fact that it began as a civil war, there is the fact that all of the intervening powers were hardly fighting alongside one another against a common enemy; it would be more accurate to describe them as each engaged in a different region for its own peculiar (and often obscure) reasons, seldom engaging Red forces in more than a brief skirmish. The French contingent, which apparently came closest to qualifying as engaged in a military counter-revolution, sustained an unrecorded number of battle deaths, and the British and American forces each lost perhaps 500 men, more by disease and freezing than by combat. The Japanese, Italians, Serbs, and others lost men fighting both in Siberia and South Russia, while Germans lost their lives aiding the Whites in Finland.

The Spanish Civil War was perhaps an even more difficult case to justify including, and to have shown a war in which Spain and Russia were arrayed against Germany, Italy, and Portugal would have overlooked such facts as these: the German contribution was largely the aerial squadron known as the Condor Legion; the Italians were "volunteers" (with their government's approval); the Russian and Portuguese contingents were small; and there were several international brigades, totaling about 30,000, coming from all corners of the globe. Since most of these brigades were financed, organized, and commanded by Communists, even though many of those who fought were not, should these 30,000 men have been classified as Russian troops? In addition to the military and political discontinuities between these two cases and the other interstate wars, the coding and measuring problems also seemed insurmountable. Who fought against whom, and alongside of whom? When did the insurgents become members of the system? What would constitute valid dates of onset and termination? When did the civil war become an interstate war?

We might have dismissed these two civil wars more readily were it not for the fact that a highly parallel case confronts us now in Vietnam. At the moment, however, we cannot disentangle matters sufficiently or predict the future confidently enough either to include this category of international war in our tabulations or to propose the establishment of an additional category. Moreover, since this struggle is not yet over, it is not possible to provide a complete (and therefore comparable) set of measures.

On the other hand, we are all too aware of the possibility that the clear division between civil and international wars is disappearing, and that wars of the Vietnamese type may become more frequent in the future. Thus, even though we feel that it is necessary to set some well-defined limits to our study, others may criticize it for being of little relevance to the conflicts of the future. If this type of war does, unfortunately, erupt more and more often, then it behooves us at least to suggest some likely coding rules. A war could be considered *internationalized* from the point when the nation that intervened on the side of the regime in power suffered 100 battle deaths during one year or was represented by 1000 or more soldiers engaged in active, sustained combat. A civil war could be considered an *interstate* war when an outside system member, in support of the non-member insurgents, intervened and suffered 100 battle deaths in one year or fielded an army of more than 1000 in the nation experiencing civil war. If we accept these general procedures, then the coding and measuring problems raised by the Russian and Spanish cases might well be manageable. A full discussion of the very complex wars in Indochina appears in the Epilogue (Appendix D).

LEVEL OF MILITARY PARTICIPATION

As we suggested above, the political status and system or sub-system membership of the participants do not of themselves suffice for the inclusion of a deadly quarrel in a rigorously defined population of international or interstate wars. Nor does a simple declaration of war, or the dispatch of personnel, supplies, or equipment necessarily mean that the concerned system member has participated in the war in a meaningful way. We have, therefore, imposed the additional requirement of active participation, measured in terms of battle-connected fatalities and/or size of armed forces engaged in active combat. In Chapter Three, we spell out in considerable detail the measurement procedures we used, but let us summarize the general criteria here.

Interstate Wars

Very simply, no hostilities involving one or more system members qualified as an interstate war unless it led to a minimum of 1000 battle fatalities among all of the system members involved.[2] Any *individual* member nation could qualify as a participant through either of two alternative criteria. The most frequently used threshold was a minimum of 100 fatalities, and this sufficed to take care of almost all ambiguous cases. There were, however, a few cases in which a member not only declared war, but sent combat units into the war theater, without sustaining even this low

[2] Interestingly, Bodart (1916, p. 79) defines an "important engagement" as one in which the antagonists suffered *combined* losses in killed, wounded, missing, and prisoners of 2000 or more. Using this rule, he reported that there were 1700 such military engagements since 1614, including 1044 land battles, 122 naval battles, 490 sieges, and 44 capitulations on open fields.

number of casualties. The problem was to differentiate between a nation which committed many troops but fortunately sustained few casualties, and one which sent only limited numbers of troops, many of whom were killed. That is, if only battle deaths are used as the basis for a system member's inclusion, one which dispatches 2000 troops but uses them so skillfully or cautiously as to lose only 50 would not qualify, whereas one which sent 200 and lost half of them would be included. In such cases, an alternative route to qualified participation was necessary: a minimum of 1000 armed personnel engaged in active combat within the war theater.

We found only three cases in which it was necessary to invoke this consideration as a basis for *including* certain nations: France, England, and Russia at Navarino Bay in 1827; England in the Second Syrian War of 1839–1840; and France and England in the Sinai War of 1956. On the other hand, there were eight cases in which marginal participants were ultimately *excluded* on the grounds that they neither sustained the necessary 100 battle deaths nor committed 1000 troops to *active* combat: England and France in the La Plata wars of the 1830s and 1840s; Austria in the Second Syrian War of 1839–1840; Mexico and Thailand in World War II; and South Africa and New Zealand in the Korean War.

A third criterion was considered, but as our data began to come in, it was apparent that the battle death threshold itself would cover most cases, and the 1000 combat troops would cover the remaining few. Thus, we might have required that the system member's forces be involved in active combat for some minimum period of time in order to exclude brief skirmishes and isolated engagements. But very rarely in the past has an extremely brief conflict had a sufficiently large number of combat units and battle fatalities. (Of course, any nuclear war of the future could easily produce a fantastic number of fatalities in a mere matter of hours.) In the one case which defies this proposition, exclusion would have been clearly unreasonable. Reference is to the battle of Navarino Bay, on 20 October 1827, which was not only quite short but which would have failed of inclusion as an interstate war because none of the British, French, or Russian navies appears to have sustained 100 battle deaths. The opposing Turkish fleet, however, was destroyed with a loss of about 3000 men; and since the allied fleets all included at least 1000 men, they qualified as war participants.

Imperial and Colonial Wars

Turning to wars involving a system member against extra-systemic polities or dependencies, we found it necessary to use slightly different threshold criteria. Whereas an interstate war which qualified on the basis of battle deaths would be included if the total fatality figure for the protagonists on each side reached the 1000 mark, the member *itself* (including system member allies, if any) had to sustain 1000 battle fatalities in order for the extra-systemic war to be included.

That is, we do not consider the fatalities sustained by non-member forces in ascertaining whether an extra-systemic war is to be included in our tabulations. Thus, even though the net battle death requirement for inclusion is the same for the intra- and extra-systemic wars (at least 1000 for all participating system members), it is incumbent on us to justify our failure to account for non-member fatalities in the imperial and colonial wars. While such deaths did not go unmourned, they often went uncounted or unrecorded. And given the dubious authenticity of the figures they produce, it is doubtful whether the earlier institution of the contemporary "body count" would have made the task any easier.

On the other hand, we did impose an additional requirement on the system member's fatalities in order to have the war included; if the war lasted more than a year, its battle deaths had to reach an *annual* average of 1000.[3] This coding rule also requires some justification. One of our measures of international war is its frequency, meaning that we must be able to count the *number* of wars, extra-systemic as well as interstate, and here we were faced with what would otherwise have been a serious coding problem. A great many colonial and imperial struggles tended to drag on for quite a few years, with a decade's duration by no means infrequent, but they seldom generated the same amount of combat year after year. Generally, the European governments (who account for most of these wars) were quite content to permit these conflicts to continue at length, providing the casualty levels were not too high; several hundred fatalities a year were often accepted as the price of empire. But if the tempo of the struggle quickened, the still familiar cry of "win or get out!" was often raised—and heeded. Usually, when more than a thousand of their soldiers were killed in a given year, the system member either escalated to a degree sufficient for victory, or withdrew.

Thus, even though our coding rules could have, in principle, led to the exclusion of an extra-systemic war which killed several thousand system member troops over a number of years, it in fact did not. A representative case is that of the Spanish struggle for control of parts of Morocco from 1909 into the mid-1930s. In 1909 and 1910, they fought a full-scale war against the independent state of Morocco, but from 1910 to 1921, they engaged in mopping-up campaigns against paramilitary, semiorganized bands which resisted their rule. These engagements were limited both in terms of the amount of troops committed and the casualty rate. Then, in 1921, Abd-el-Krim rallied many of the rebels around him and raised an organized insurrection against the Spanish, and later against the French. After his capture, in 1926, the rebels continued desultory warfare similar to that waged from 1910 through 1921. We have treated this sequence as follows: (a) the Spanish-Moroccan War of 1909–1910 was included as an interstate war, with Morocco losing its independence in 1910; (b) the Spanish pacification campaign of 1910–1921 was excluded because the Spanish did not suffer anything near the requisite average annual 1000 battle deaths over the 11-year period; (c) the rebellion of Abd-el-Krim of 1921–1926 was included as a colonial war; and (d) the pacification effort from 1926 on to the mid-1930s was excluded because the annual death rate was again not satisfied. While it is too early to tell, every indication is that the present Portuguese effort to maintain control of Angola will follow a rather similar pattern.

THE POPULATION IDENTIFIED

We have now specified, in as clear and operational terms as we can, the criteria that must be satisfied in order for a sequence of military hostilities to be classified as an international war. To summarize, we first had to decide whether a political entity was a member nation of the interstate system; then we had to decide whether it had been sufficiently involved in the war to count as a participant; third, on the basis of which entities participated in the hostilities, and whether a minimum of 1000 fatalities were

[3] We deviated from this rule on one occasion. In 20.2 months of fighting in Madagascar in 1895–1896, the French lost about 1500 men. Theoretically, they should have lost around 1670 in order to qualify the war for our extra-systemic listing. Given the relatively small numbers involved in this case and the roughness of our original estimate, we decided to include the Franco-Madagascan conflict in the study.

2.3 SIMPLE LIST OF INTERSTATE AND EXTRA-SYSTEMIC WARS, 1816–1965

Interstate Wars ($N = 50$)

Franco-Spanish (1823)
Navarino Bay (1827)
Russo-Turkish (1828–1829)
Mexican-American (1846–1848)
Austro-Sardinian (1848–1849)
First Schleswig-Holstein (1848–1849)
Roman Republic (1849)
La Plata (1851–1852)
Crimean (1853–1856)
Anglo-Persian (1856–1857)
Italian Unification (1859)
Spanish-Moroccan (1859–1860)
Italo-Roman (1860)
Italo-Sicilian (1860–1861)
Franco-Mexican (1862–1867)
Ecuadorian-Colombian (1863)
Second Schleswig-Holstein (1864)
Spanish-Chilean (1865–1866)
Seven Weeks (1866)
Franco-Prussian (1870–1871)
Russo-Turkish (1877–1878)
Pacific (1879–1883)
Sino-French (1884–1885)
Central American (1885)
Sino-Japanese (1894–1895)
Greco-Turkish (1897)
Spanish-American (1898)
Russo-Japanese (1904–1905)
Central American (1906)
Central American (1907)
Spanish-Moroccan (1909–1910)
Italo-Turkish (1911–1912)
First Balkan (1912–1913)
Second Balkan (1913)
World War One (1914–1918)
Hungarian-Allies (1919)
Greco-Turkish (1919–1922)
Manchurian (1931–1933)
Chaco (1932–1935)
Italo-Ethiopian (1935–1936)
Sino-Japanese (1937–1941)
Russo-Japanese (1939)
World War Two (1939–1945)
Russo-Finnish (1939–1940)
Palestine (1948–1949)
Korean (1950–1953)
Russo-Hungarian (1956)
Sinai (1956)
Sino-Indian (1962)
Second Kashmir (1965)

Extra-systemic Wars ($N = 43$)

British-Maharattan (1817–1818) I
Greek (1821–1828) C
First Anglo-Burmese (1823–1826) I
Javanese (1825–1830) C
Russo-Persian (1826–1828) I
First Polish (1831) C
First Syrian (1831–1832) C
Texan (1835–1836) C
First British-Afghan (1838–1842) I
Second Syrian (1839–1840) C
Peruvian-Bolivian (1841) I
First British-Sikh (1845–1846) I
Hungarian (1848–1849) C
Second British-Sikh (1848–1849) I
First Turco-Montenegran (1852–1853) I
Sepoy (1857–1859) C
Second Turco-Montenegran (1858–1859) I
Second Polish (1863–1864) C
La Plata (1864–1870) I
Ten Years (1868–1878) C
Dutch-Achinese (1873–1878) I
Balkan (1875–1877) C
Bosnian (1878) C
Second British-Afghan (1878–1880) I
British-Zulu (1879) I
Franco-Indochinese (1882–1884) I
Mahdist (1882–1885) C
Serbo-Bulgarian (1885) I
Franco-Madagascan (1894–1895) I
Cuban (1895–1898) C
Italo-Ethiopian (1895–1896) I
First Philippine (1896–1898) C
Second Philippine (1899–1902) C
Boer (1899–1902) C
Russian Nationalities (1917–1921) C
Riffian (1921–1926) C
Druze (1925–1926) C
Indonesian (1945–1946) C
Indochinese (1945–1954) C
Madagascan (1947–1948) C
First Kashmir (1947–1949) I
Algerian (1954–1962) C
Tibetan (1956–1959) C

sustained by these participants, we decided on whether the event was an interstate war or not; finally, if it did not qualify for the category of interstate war, we classified it as imperial or colonial, depending on the status of the entities which participated. The results of this series of screening procedures appear in Table 2.3.

The coding rules, of course, not only produced the table of wars for inclusion in the book, but also served to exclude a good many that might, intuitively, be expected to appear in such a compilation. In Table 5.2, where our list is compared to those of our more systematic predecessors, those which we excluded will be apparent; for the more ambiguous and debatable exclusions, we have provided a brief explanation in Appendix B, accompanied by the sources from which our information was derived.

The detailed discussion above was necessary on two grounds. First, there is the complex question of whether each of a multitude of military conflicts does or does not qualify for inclusion in a list of wars whose compilation is theoretically defensible and methodologically operational. Needless to say, few of our coding criteria were completely *a priori,* and most were determined after we had proceeded well into the examination of a good many cases. Once these rules had been applied, and our population had been defined and then subdivided into the interstate and extra-systemic categories, our second set of problems came to the fore. Reference is to the matter of scaling these wars and their various attributes.

International wars may be classified and differentiated along any number of dimensions, depending on one's theoretical needs. Among the possible criteria might be: location, time, the issues, the types or number of nations involved, the size, strength, military organization, technologies, strategies or ideologies of the participants, number of major battles, duration, casualties, political results, etc. The concern may be with the war's effect on the demography, industrial base, transport net, internal stability, or power of each participant, on the strength and direction of a given relationship between any two protagonists and/or non-belligerents, or on the structure, status ordering, centralization, or rate of change in the international system, for example. We will be looking primarily for more general indicators of the war's impact on both the belligerents and on the system; that is, we are looking for measures which not only reflect the destructive and disruptive effects of the war, but for those which could also be used as predictor variables in the examination of the political, social, or economic *consequences* of any given wars. Given these requirements, and persuaded of the need to establish such measures, we proceeded to develop three sets of indicators, which we define in detail in Chapter Three.

Chapter 3

Quantifying International War: Three Sets of Indicators

In the previous chapter we dealt with the first of the steps necessary in the conversion of qualitative phenomena into quantitative, scientifically useful data. That is the step which differentiates between the cases which we want to examine later on, and those in which we are *not* interested; with the application of those inclusion-exclusion criteria, we are able to *enumerate.* And while the criteria which lead to enumeration need not be quantitative in nature—or, as in the case here, may be a mixture of the logical and the quantitative—the *results* are definitely quantitative. Once we have identified and counted the cases that interest us, we are free to go on to the second step, and to differentiate among those which remain in the population of cases that satisfied our screening criteria. Measurement, then, must be preceded by identification and enumeration.

With that step out of the way, our next assignment is to make explicit the dimensions along which such differentiation should be made, in light of the theoretical purposes to which the data will later be put. Our major concern is a simple one: to ascertain the "amount" of war which began, or was underway, or ended, in any given time-place domain. Measures or indicators which reflect the amount of war that *began* in each such domain would normally serve as the outcome (or dependent) variable in most studies, and those which reflect the amount that *ended* would usually serve as the predictor (independent or intervening) variable. The amount of war underway, in turn, might be used either as the predictor or the outcome variable, depending on one's theoretical focus and the resulting research design. To put it another way, when war is the "effect," we may want to use a different measure of its amount than is the case when war is the putative "cause" of some subsequent set of events or conditions. Since the major concern of the Correlates of War project is with the amount of war as the *effect* or *consequence* of certain prior phenomena, we will be more interested in measuring the amount that began within certain specified spatial-temporal domains. But since we are also using feedback models, we also require measures of the amount of war that *ended* within such domains. Moreover, others who will be using our data may be more interested in treating war as a predictor than as an outcome variable, and it thus behooves us to generate indicators reflecting the amount of war underway and ending, as well as beginning. We call these onset, underway, and termination measures, and will return to them in Chapter Seven.

Turning, then, to the construction of these measures, we note immediately that nothing can be said about the amount of war that occurred within a given spatial-temporal domain until we have measured each separate war that falls into our population of cases. Only then can we aggregate the separate and single war amounts into a combined onset (or underway or termination) amount for a given region and time period. How, then, do we differentiate among the 93 wars that met our criteria for inclusion, and how do we compare them to one another in a quantitative fashion?

Given the above considerations, we settled on three sets of indicators, one reflecting the *magnitude* of a given war, another its *severity,* and a third its *intensity.* The *magnitude* indicator is intended to get at the spatial and temporal extent of the war—how many nations participated in it and how long it lasted; we measure this in "nation months." *Severity* is intended to get at the human destructiveness of the war, and is measured in battle-connected deaths. And *intensity* is supposed to reflect the ratio between these battle deaths and several base line measures.

A word or two in defense of our verbal labels is in order. On the one hand, we were most reluctant to part company with Richardson, who labels his battle fatalities as "magnitude." On the other hand, magnitude connotes *size,* and the reader is more likely to associate size and magnitude with the spatial—and, to a lesser extent, temporal—attributes of the event or condition being measured than with its destructiveness. Second, since our coding rules differ from Richardson's, the use of identical labels might obscure that difference in our measures. Third, when one thinks of the wounds and bloody deaths of battle, the word "severity" comes to mind well before magnitude. Fourth, since we develop these two rather different measures of the "amount" of war, it would be confusing to assign the same label—such as magnitude—to both. To do so would require constant use of the distinguishing phrase: magnitude in battle deaths or magnitude in nation months.

Finally, since intensity almost invariably connotes some sort of ratio, the use of this label to identify battle deaths per nation month or per capita seemed quite obvious. However, because the three intensity ratios are rather artificial and will probably be used less frequently than magnitude and severity in studies based on our data, we decided to put all three of these "derived" measures under the same rubric. Considering the trade-off between having to specify which intensity measure is being used at a given time, and the need for memorizing three different—and perhaps artificial—labels, the former seemed less costly. The *intensity* measures, which are discussed later in this chapter, reflect a number of ratios between battle-connected deaths and such base lines as population, armed forces size, and the war's magnitude.

MAGNITUDE: NATION MONTHS

Addressing ourselves first to the measurement of a war's magnitude, it seemed reasonable to develop one index which reflected space and time in the broadest sense. The "spatial" dimension could be represented by square mileage (or, more recently, even cubic mileage) of the combat zone, the number or territorial area of the participants, their population size, industrial acreage, and so forth; the "temporal" dimension, or duration, could be in any "real time" measure (days, weeks, months) or in some such artificial measure as diplomatic, communication, or military "time," so as to permit meaningful comparisons between wars fought in differing technological settings. In addition, the sheer number of battles might offer a sensitive measure of magnitude.

The magnitude of war indicator which we decided to use for getting at the time-space dimension is an extremely simple one, characterized by high reliability and face validity. Labeled "nation months," this measure is nothing more than the sum of all the participating nations' separate months of active involvement in each war.

This measure has, of course, certain liabilities. For example, it does not differentiate between a British war month and a Peruvian war month, nor does it differentiate between an early nineteenth century war month and a mid-twentieth century one. These factors could, without too much difficulty, be taken into account, were certain types of data available. One could, for example, weight each nation's war month by: its diplomatic importance score, various indicators of its industrial or military capability, domestic cohesion or stability scores, and so forth.[1] Likewise, one might weight months as a function of the technological period in which the war was fought, on the assumption that such technology might well compress the amount and scale of combat and perhaps the fatality rates accompanying wars of different epochs. However, as the calculations in Chapter Eight show, there seems to be almost no secular

[1] For some of these, data are, or soon will be available. Diplomatic importance scores are reported in Singer and Small (1966a), and the data on which a military-industrial capability index might be constructed are now being assembled and codified.

trend toward a greater number of battle dead per month over the century and a half covered here, despite the radical developments in weapon technology.

In partial response to the need for differentiation among various classes of nation month, however, we have gone on to distinguish between those experienced by peripheral system nations, those of the central system members, and those experienced by major powers, thus providing a first approximation to some more sophisticated weighting scheme. In addition, so that the user of our data will be able to distinguish between the nation months of those who are engaged in savage fighting and those nations whose participation is less bloody, we present in Chapter Eleven a possible criterion by which certain nations might reasonably be omitted, even though they satisfied our criteria. There we compute one index of the intensity of each nation's participation by dividing its fatalities in all of its wars by the length of its participation in all wars. Other researchers will thus have an operational threshold by which to eliminate certain low-level participants from their own computations, as they see fit.

Measuring Duration

How do we convert the nation month concept into hard numbers by which one aspect of a war's magnitude may be measured? Once the participants in any given war have been identified (see p. 45), the next step is to ascertain, as precisely as possible, the dates on which each qualified participant entered and left the war. This, in turn, raises the problem of measuring the duration of the war itself.

Both of our predecessors recognized the pitfalls involved in adhering strictly to legal documents as one's time boundaries. Among the possible sources of confusion, Richardson suggested the following: (a) provocative incidents prior to the formal declaration; (b) prolonged hostilities without a declaration of war; (c) pauses between battles which are not armistices, and are therefore included in the total duration; (d) irregular warfare which continued after the main defeat or after the declaration of peace; and (e) the cessation of hostilities without a declaration of peace. As a consequence, he accepted the conventional dates if the historical authorities agreed, but where they differed, he preferred "common sense to legalism; that is to say, I have been guided by actual warlike alertness rather than by formal declarations of war or peace" (1960a, pp. 15–16).

Likewise, Wright encountered "no small difficulty . . . in determining when a given war began and ended." Thus, "the date of beginning is generally taken as the first important hostilities," since "formal declarations of war have been rare [we tend to disagree] and, when they have occurred, have often *followed* active hostilities." But when it comes to terminal dates, Wright reverted to legal criteria again and used "the date of signature of a treaty of peace, or the date of its going into effect if that is different." In a good many cases, however, he recognized that there was no formal treaty; then, "the date of armistice, capitulation, or actual ending of active hostilities is given" (1965, p. 638).

Given the ambiguities and inconsistencies of these and other previously used rules, plus the fact that precise duration figures are more important to us than to our predecessors, we developed the following procedures. Each war's opening date is that of the formal declaration, but only if it is followed immediately by sustained military combat. If hostilities precede the formal declaration, and continue in a sustained fashion up to and beyond that latter date, the first day of combat is used. Even in the absence of a declaration, the sustained continuation of military incidents or battle, producing the requisite number of battle deaths, is treated as a war, with the first day of combat again used for computing duration.[2]

Turning to *termination,* we again rely on a combination of legal and military events, with the latter more dominant. That is, the war's duration continues as long as there is sustained military action. If such combat comes to an end on the same day as an armistice is signed, and does not resume after the armistice, there is no problem. But if there is a delay between the cessation of military action and the armistice (which is very rare) or if the armistice fails to bring combat to an end, we then ascertain and use the day which most clearly demarcates the close of sustained military conflict. Similarly, the date of the peace treaty would not be used unless it coincided with the end of combat.

Temporary Interruptions

In addition to the identification of a war's onset and termination dates, there is the complication arising out of truces, temporary cease-fires, and armistice agreements. In general, a cessation of hostilities which endured for less than 30 days is not treated as an interruption of the war, whereas a longer break *is* so treated, and would lead to a reduction in the war's overall duration measure equal to the exact length of the interruption. To illustrate,the three-week truce (19 December 1933 to 8 January 1934) arranged by the League of Nations during the Chaco War is not counted as a break, and the war is treated as if it had run continuously for the three years from 15 June 1932 through 12 June 1935, for a duration of 35.9 months. On the other hand, because a formal truce lasted for two of the total six months between the onset and termination of the Second Schleswig-Holstein War (1 February through 20 August. 1864), that war is treated as having a duration of only 3.6 months.[3]

Measuring Each Nation's Participation

Once the problem of defining a given war's duration is resolved, we can go on to the measurement of its magnitude, counted in nation months. To do so, we must face two separate questions: a) what constitutes "participation" in a war by a given nation, and b) what are the opening and closing dates of such participation? As to participation, the criteria outlined in Chapter Two may be summarized as follows. First, the nation must be a qualified member of the interstate system. Second, it must have had regular, uniformed, national military personnel in sustained combat. Third, no matter how brief or lengthy that combat, those forces must have either numbered at least 1000 or have sustained at least 100 battle-connected deaths. Fourth, a nation need not have been, either formally or physically, at war with *all* of the nations on the opposing side in order to be classed as an active participant. Its forces need only have been in sustained combat with those of any *one* adversary in order to qualify, providing that the first three requirements were satisfied.

As to the total duration of each single nation's participation in a given war—and

[2] A useful summary of the problem, from the legal viewpoint, is available in another of Wright's studies (1932).

[3] In the case of the Roman Republic War (1849), we do include a break in hostilities of less than 30 days. In that war, France engaged the Papal States in a one-day battle on 30 April. Fighting resumed on 8 May between the Papal States, and Austria-Hungary and Two Sicilies; France did not reenter the war until 3 June. Therefore it would have been misleading to have included the seven days between 30 April and 8 May as part of the total duration of the war.

hence its contribution to that war's magnitude—there are 14 interstate and four extra-systemic wars in which some participants either did not become involved on the opening day of hostilities or did not continue fighting until the end of the war. In those cases, as we noted in Chapter Two, the active participation period is that marked by the beginning and end of their forces' involvement in sustained military combat. In addition, there is the logical extension of our rule that only qualified members of the interstate system are included as participants. From that, it follows that, even if a nation participated in a given war for its total duration, only that period during which it was a system member is counted when we compute the war's magnitude or that nation's war months. An example is the Franco-Prussian War of 1870–1871; even though Baden, Bavaria, and Wuerttemberg had troops in active combat during the entire war, they were not qualified system members after November 1870, when they became integrated into the new German empire. Thus their participation after that date did not contribute to the magnitude of the war as a systemic event. Similarly, in the Russo-Turkish War of 1877–1878, the military participation of Serbia, Rumania, and Montenegro did not contribute to the nation months of that war, because they were not qualified system members during any part of the war.

Computation and Levels of Confidence

Before closing our description of the ways in which we measured nation months of war, a word regarding the precision and accuracy of our data is in order. First, and despite our rather thorough investigations, we were unable to pin down the *exact* dates for the termination of the Second Turco-Montenegran War of 1858–1859, the Dutch-Achinese War of 1873–1878, the Bosnian revolt of 1878, and the Druze rebellion of 1925–1927. While the exact durations of these imperial and colonial wars are of less importance to our central concern, they may be quite important to others, and we therefore call attention to such lacunae by placing a 00 in the place where an exact date should go. For computation purposes in such cases, however, we have treated the ending date as the 15th of the month.

One scholar (Weiss, 1963, pp. 103–104) found a certain pattern in the relative accuracy of Richardson's data. When he dichotomized those duration figures (on the basis of Richardson's judgments, discussed in the next section) into either the "accurate" or the "approximate" category, he found that the fewer the fatalities produced by the war, the less likely were the precise dates to be known. In tabular form, the estimates were distributed as follows:

Fatality Range	Number of Accurate Figures	Number of Approximate Figures	Total in Range	Percent Accurate
2.5–3.5	65	144	209	31
3.5–4.5	53	18	71	75
4.5–5.5	19	7	26	73

In other words, when the fatalities from a war are fewer, there appears to be less detailed reporting and less thorough research on that war.

Our experience was not quite the same, in that we generally found as high a percentage of uncertain dates for high fatality wars as for those which produced relatively few battle deaths. This discrepancy is, however, not surprising, since we had the advantage of looking at fewer deadly quarrels, especially at the lower end of the fatality range. Another point to keep in mind is that whether we speak of dates or of fatalities, the accuracy—or even the availability—of data is largely a function of the industrial and educational level of the nation involved, with the nation months and battle deaths of many of the non-Western nations much more a matter of intelligent estimate than retrieval of authentic information.

Second, there is the question of how precise we want our duration and magnitude measures to be, given some of the problems we encountered. In order to avoid conveying greater precision than was possible, we considered rounding only to the nearest half-month for both duration and magnitude. However, that rounding procedure not only led to inconsistencies between our war duration score and the separate national war month figures, but would seem to discard too much accurate information unnecessarily. Thus, we ended up by computing simple duration, the combat time of the individual national participants, and the nation month war magnitudes in months and tenths of months. One year was standardized as 365.25 days (taking into account the extra day in leap years), and one month was set equal to one twelfth of one year, or 30.44 days. Then we counted the total number of days of each combat experience, including the first and last days, and divided by 30.44, with the resulting figures given to one decimal place; that is, to the nearest tenth of a month.[4]

To summarize this section, then, our ultimate objective is to measure the magnitude of war which began, was underway, or terminated in a given time-space domain. But in order to do this, we must first ascertain the magnitude of *each war* that began, was underway, or ended in that domain. And in order to measure each war's magnitude, we must, in turn, begin by measuring the war's duration and then the number of months that each qualified nation spent as a participant in that war. Let us now shift from the measurement of magnitude to that of severity.

SEVERITY: BATTLE-CONNECTED DEATHS

The second of our basic measures is that of severity, operationalized in terms of battle-connected deaths. Let us begin by recapitulating Richardson's procedures, since his is the only study comparable in this regard to the one reported here.

In computing his figures, he first listed *all possible* war-connected death categories, which we rearrange and paraphrase as follows: (a) belligerent military personnel killed in fighting or drowned in action at sea, or who died from wounds, or from poison, or from starvation in a siege, or from other malicious acts of their enemies; (b) belligerent military personnel who died from disease or exposure; (c) civilians belonging to the belligerent nations, who died from malicious acts of their enemies; (d) members of neutral populations (civilian or military) accidentally killed in the war; (e) neutral or belligerent civilians who died from exposure and

[4] In the case of the Navarino Bay War, which lasted only one day, the duration figure was rounded up from .03 to .1 months, and each nation's war participation was also put at .1 instead of at .03. But the magnitude of the war (the total of the national war months) was .1 also, reflecting the *actual* total of 4 (nations) times .03 (national war months), rather than 4 times .1, the individual war month figure given.

disease; and (f) the additional number of babies that would presumably have been born if war had not occurred. In Richardson's estimates, the military and civilian deaths resulting from enemy action were included "because they were intentionally inflicted," and military deaths due to disease and exposure were included "because they were accepted as a risk contingent to planned operations" (1960a, p. 9). In sum, he included military *and* civilian deaths which could be attributed to the hostile actions of the participants (a, b, and c), but excluded those which could not reasonably be so explained (d, e, and f).

Inclusion Criteria

Although we found ourselves in general agreement with Richardson's line of reasoning in trying to develop a valid and reliable indicator of a war's severity, we finally decided to restrict our figures to combat-connected deaths of military personnel only. Our reasons for excluding civilian casualties are twofold. First, there is the concern for validity. In seeking a measure of the severity of wars which occur as much as a century and a half apart, it was essential to minimize the effects of the tremendous technological changes which have taken place during this period. In the early nineteenth century, there was not only little military incentive for inflicting civilian casualties, but little technological capacity for doing so. Wars were won by the destruction and disorganization of enemy armies (and navies) and by the successful occupation of territory. But as industrial production and civilian support became more critical to military success, the incentive to destroy them increased markedly, as did, of course, the capability. At the same time, despite great advances in weaponry, there was little increase in the efficiency with which combat personnel could be killed; even the availability of tactical nuclear weapons, given the political as well as military costs associated with their use, has had little impact so far on battle-connected deaths. Thus, by restricting ourselves to military casualties only, we maximize the comparability of our indices over the entire period. To support this contention, we can note (Table 8.8) the absence of any strong upward secular trend in the various war *intensity* measures.

It might also be added that, as a quantitative matter, the inclusion of civilian deaths in our severity measure would not have done much for validity via a somewhat broader index. That is, we soon discovered that civilian deaths were quantitatively negligible in most of the international (as distinguished from civil) wars during our time span, except for the World Wars; and given the fact that the approximately 9 and 15 million battle-connected *military* deaths in those wars so overshadowed all other wars, there seemed no good analytical and comparative reason to include civilian casualties. On the other hand, no study of civil or guerrilla war could afford to exclude non-military deaths.

This brings us to considerations of reliability. First, as difficult as it might be to gather and evaluate military fatality estimates over so wide a domain in space and time, the problem of doing this for civilian fatalities is more difficult still. Even for World War II, civilian death estimates range from 20 to 35 million. The second consideration was the fact that civilians could have died in so wide a variety of situations and at so many different sets of hands that no reasonable and operational criteria could be developed. Third, our researches revealed that few of the investigators or reporters on whom we would be relying to develop our refined estimates had included civilian fatalities in their analyses.

Given this range of considerations, then, we settled on *battle-connected fatalities among military personnel only* as our measure of war's severity. This was defined to include not only those personnel who were killed in combat, but those who subsequently died from combat wounds or from diseases contracted in the war theater.[5] It should also be noted that these figures include not only personnel of the system member, but native troops from their colonies, protectorates, and dominions, who were fighting alongside them.

Estimating Procedures

Shifting from classificatory schemes to the straightforward matter of ascertaining the casualty figures within each category, Richardson again provides us with a valuable point of departure. In addition to perusing Harbottle (1904), Bodart (1916), Dumas and Vedel-Peterson (1923), and Sorokin (1937), he conducted "long searches in the pages of literary history." That the search was frustrating as well as long is reflected in his comment that such histories were "deplorably vague on the subject of casualties. We look for numbers but find instead phrases such as 'many fell in the battle' or 'routed their enemies' or 'suffered heavy loss'. . . . The number killed in one or two outstanding battles may be mentioned, but these melancholy statistics are seldom totaled for the whole war. Military historians . . . sometimes give precise casualties for their own forces, but only very vague statements about their enemies." Thus his pique at "those historians who prefer rhetoric to numbers" (1960a, pp. 9-10).

Given the absence or unreliability of many wartime casualty figures, Richardson introduced a procedure designed both to indicate the level of reliability and to reduce the effects of low reliability when it is present. This is the logarithmic (to the base 10) scale mentioned earlier, and he illustrates its applicability by reference to three different sources of Union death statistics in the American Civil War. The estimates are 359,528; 279,376; and 166,623, and "each, if seen alone [is] apparently accurate to a man." Although the first is over twice the size of the third estimate, the assumption is that on a casualty scale that ranges from 317 to 20,000,000 (World War II), all three estimates cluster very closely together. This clustering is seen when the three absolute figures are converted to their logarithmic scale equivalents: 5.6, 5.4, and 5.2.

In order to indicate the degree of confidence in the final digits of his figures, Richardson utilized a standard notational form. The ladder of diminishing confidence in a battle death estimate of magnitude 4 (that is 10,000) is reflected in the following forms: 4.00, 4,0, $4._{0}$, 4, and 4?. When he was willing to include a final digit, but not with complete confidence, he printed it below the line, or dropped it entirely, depending on his confidence level; and if he was even uncertain as to the reliability of the gross magnitude class, he followed it with a question mark.

It should be evident now that, despite the solid foundation laid by Richardson's explorations, his estimates were unsatisfactory for our purposes. Interested as he was in almost all of the casualty statistics of almost all deadly quarrels, his sample is much larger and less discriminating than ours: too many wars and too many categories of casualty. We did, however, often begin with his estimates, and then go on to revise them for differences in duration, participants, and casualty types.

Our procedure was first to prepare our list of wars, participants, and their dates of involvement in the hostilities as described in the previous sections. Next, we entered all available estimates from earlier general studies under separate columns (somewhat as in Chapter Five), indicating whether they were for the entire war or

[5] For a fuller discussion of the impact of disease, wounds, and medical care, see Prinzing (1916), and Beebe and de Bakey (1952).

some geographical or chronological part, and which nation months and casualty classes were included. Whether a ready concurrence among them could be established, or not, we next turned to the specialized treatises and monographs which so frustrated Richardson; the assumption here was that such high agreement could often be traced to the fact that some or all of the general studies had found their original figures in the same sources or in ones based on the same source. What this return to the monographs often involved was a wading through such literary accounts as Hozier's massive two volumes on the Russo-Turkish War of 1877–1878, recording his estimates of battle deaths for every engagement, and finally adding up the hundreds of figures.[6] While it would have been simpler to accept Richardson's estimates, in retracing his steps we discovered not only a failure to explore all available sources, but a distressing propensity to base his final count on mere guesswork or intuition.[7]

Once all the available estimates were in for a given war, and adjustments were made of the varying classificatory criteria, the semi-operational estimating began. Among the considerations affecting our final figure were: army size, weapons and medical technology available, number of major battles, others' estimates of the wounded-to-killed ratio (Bodart seems to have discovered a constant of about 3.5 to 1), and the historians' appraisal of the war's intensity. A final "reality test" required us to compare victorious and defeated, major and minor, central and peripheral, and active and passive nations across a number of wars. As Klingberg (1966) discovered, in wars of a given duration among nations of given strength there tend to be some rough but fairly constant ratios among population size and casualties, for both victor and vanquished.[8]

Confidence Levels

Despite these multiple cross-checks and a large dose of skepticism at every turn, we must reemphasize the fact that our battle death figures are only estimates. To reiterate, it is worth bearing in mind the possible sources of erroneous data. First, not all armed forces have been consistent in differentiating among dead, captured, missing, wounded, and deserting; as Dumas in *Losses of Life Caused by War* (1923, p. 21) reminds us, the field commander "attaches no importance to the cause of the absences . . . for him it is all the same." Second, there is the simple matter of accurate estimates, compounded by the fact that the size of a force may not even be known

[6] In another illustrative case, that of the Franco-Spanish War of 1823, our estimating procedure can be traced by examining pages 132, 133, 159, 171, and 177 of Geoffrey de Grandmaison (1928).

[7] Richardson implies that he sometimes used a 3 or 3.5 to 1 wounded-to-killed ratio when he knew either sum but not both; unfortunately, those cases are not identified. An alternate estimating procedure is possible since most nations have distinguished between officers and enlisted men in their official casualty reports. In many cases, as would be expected, the figures on officers are more complete and reliable than those on the enlisted men. Consequently, scholars like Bodart (1916, p. 18) have used officer death ratios ("ever-recurring normal proportional loss of officers") to fill in the occasional empty cells for enlisted men. Traditionally, officers have suffered a higher proportion of casualties than the men, a result noted by Bodart of "the effort of the officer to set before his men a good example in cool and courageous combat." At the same time, officers enjoy a lower death ratio when it comes to disease, a phenomenon most likely reflecting their better care, clothing, food, and lodging (Dumas and Vedel-Peterson, 1923, p. 66).

[8] For a fuller discussion of the reliability problem, see Dumas and Vedel-Peterson (1923, Ch. 1); Bodart (1916, Ch. 2); and Richardson (1960a, Ch. 1).

with any accuracy by its commanders. Third, there are the tactical reasons for exaggerating the enemy's losses and minimizing one's own. Finally, the archivists and historians who eventually sift through the reports and provide our basic sources of data may well suffer not only from a lack of statistical sophistication, but even occasionally from personal and national biases of their own.

To make more explicit our own relative sense of confidence in the battle fatality figures, let us classify them as follows, but without using the conventional percentage error ranges, which would themselves be little more than educated guesses. Among the interstate wars, we have high confidence in the estimates for the following 22 cases:

Franco-Spanish, 1823
Navarino Bay, 1827
Mexican-American, 1846–1848
Austro-Sardinian, 1848–1849
First Schleswig-Holstein, 1848–1849
Roman Republic, 1849
Crimean, 1853–1856
Italian Unification, 1859
Italo-Roman, 1860
Italo-Sicilian, 1860–1861
Ecuadorian-Colombian, 1863
Second Schleswig-Holstein, 1864
Spanish-Chilean, 1865–1866
Seven Weeks, 1866
Franco-Prussian, 1870–1871
Central American, 1885
Greco-Turkish, 1897
Spanish-American, 1898
Central American, 1906
Central American, 1907
Chaco, 1932–1935
Italo-Ethiopian, 1935–1936

The 28 interstate wars for which our confidence level is somewhat lower are (if only certain participants' figures proved elusive, they are italicized):

Russo-*Turkish,* 1828–1829
La Plata, 1851–1852
Anglo-*Persian,* 1856–1857
Spanish-*Moroccan,* 1859–1860
Franco-*Mexican,* 1862–1867
Russo-*Turkish,* 1877–1878
Pacific, 1879–1883
Sino-French, 1884–1885
Sino-Japanese, 1894–1895
Russo-*Japanese,* 1904–1905
Spanish-*Moroccan,* 1909–1910
Italo-*Turkish,* 1911–1912
First Balkan, 1912–1913
Second Balkan, 1913
World War I, 1914–1918
Hungarian-Allies, 1919
Greco-Turkish, 1919–1922
Manchurian, 1931–1933
Sino-Japanese, 1937–1941
Russo-Japanese, 1939
World War II, 1939–1945
Russo-Finnish, 1939
Palestine [Isr.-*Arabs*], 1948–1949
Korean [U.N.-*China, N. Korea*], 1950–1953
Russo-Hungarian, 1956
Sinai [Isr., Eng., France-*U.A.R.*], 1956
Sino-Indian, 1962
Second Kashmir, 1965

Ironically enough, as the above lists indicate, the post-1945 period gave us more difficulty than earlier periods.

As for extra-systemic wars we are confident in our estimates of system member battle deaths for the following wars:

British-Maharattan 1817
First Anglo-Burmese, 1823–1826
Javanese, 1825–1830
Texan, 1835–1836
First British-Afghan, 1838–1842
Peruvian-Bolivian, 1841
First British-Sikh, 1845–1846
Hungarian, 1848–1849
Second British-Sikh, 1848–1849
Sepoy, 1857–1859
La Plata, 1864–1870
Dutch-Achinese, 1873–1878
Second British-Afghan, 1878–1880
British-Zulu, 1879

Franco-Indochinese, 1882–1884
Serbo-Bulgarian, 1885
Franco-Madagascan, 1894–1895
Italo-Ethiopian, 1895–1896
Second Philippine, 1899–1902
Boer, 1899–1902
Riffian, 1921–1926
Druze, 1925–1926
Indonesian, 1945–1947
Indochinese, 1945–1954
Madagascan, 1947–1948
Algerian, 1954–1962

We are somewhat less confident in the system member fatality estimates for the following extra-systemic wars:

Greek, 1821–1828
Russo-Persian, 1826–1828
First Polish, 1831
First Syrian, 1831–1832
Second Syrian, 1839–1840
First Turco-Montenegran, 1852–1853
Second Turco-Montenegran, 1858–1859
Second Polish, 1863–1864
Ten Years, 1868–1878
Balkan, 1875–1877
Bosnian, 1878
Mahdist, 1882–1884
Cuban, 1895–1896
First Philippine, 1896–1898
Russian Nationalities, 1917–1921
First Kashmir, 1947–1949
Tibetan, 1956–1959

Thus, in the case of extra-systemic wars, we were quite confident of our estimates for four of the six post-1945 wars, and also for four of the five other extra-systemic wars that were waged in this century. Interestingly, our confidence was quite high for 14 of the 18 "imperial" wars, but for only 12 of the 25 "colonial" wars.

It should also be noted here—in accordance with our discussion of the accuracy of our battle death estimates—that we have rounded off the *total* battle death figures for the three bloodiest wars (World War I, World War II, and Korean) to the nearest million. While the figure given for *each nation* in each war is the most accurate possible estimate, the range of precision varies considerably; sometimes this accuracy is expressed only to the nearest 100,000 (as is the case of such major protagonists as Russia and Germany in World War II and China in the Korean conflict), but in the case of several of the less active participants (such as Belgium and South Africa in World War II), our estimates are expressed to the nearest 100 deaths, or even to the nearest 10 (for some U.N. nations fighting in Korea). Given this range of precision, it would be misleading to assume that the exact sum of each nation's fatalities in those three wars is indeed a precise reflection of their severity. Thus, in Table 4.2 we have rounded off these severity figures as follows: World War I, from 8,555,800 to 9,000,000; World War II, from 15,164,300 to 15,000,000; and the Korean War, from 1,892,100 to 2,000,000. These changes were made by hand to emphasize the fact that they were rounded off *after* summing the nations' battle deaths. In subsequent chapters, however, all war totals will be based on the summation of the national totals, and so reflected in the computerized data decks. Our purpose here, then, is merely to alert the reader and user to the dangers of misplaced precision.

INTENSITY: FATALITY RATIOS

Whereas the magnitude and severity measures outlined above may be quite useful in describing the *extensiveness* of the wars included here, they tell us nothing about their *intensiveness.* One might want to know, for example, whether a particular war was brief but bloody, whether it exacted a higher relative toll in bloodshed than another, whether it was receiving a high concentration of attention or resources, or whether the rate at which deaths were being sustained might predict to its termination. Several such indicators are readily calculated, once the data have been gathered for a number of base lines.

We use three indicators of intensity, and all of them proceed from the estimate of battle-connected deaths, with base lines reflecting: (a) nation months; (b) the total size of the pre-war armed forces of all member nations which participated; and (c) the total pre-war population of all of the member nations that participated. In each case, the war's intensity index is computed by dividing the base line figure into the total number of fatalities that the war produced.[9] The nation month base line is calculated as in the previous section, but the other two sets of figures come from another source. Armed forces size and gross population are two of the six tentative dimensions we are using to estimate a nation's military-industrial capability for rather different analytical purposes. The sources and data-making procedures for these two variables are therefore outlined in a separate study (Singer and Small, forthcoming), but suffice it to say here that a nation's gross population is fairly self-explanatory, being the most accurate possible estimate of a nation's total population on the eve of that nation's entry into a given war; armed forces size includes only those national and colonial military personnel who were on active duty, excluding reserves, militia, and such paramilitary personnel as police and border guards.

We might note in passing, however, that this latter (BD/AF) ratio still poses some problems of reliability and might be used more safely as an ordinal than as an interval measure, since there remain the uncertainties arising, for example, from the recruitment of foreign mercenaries, or the reinforcement of European armies by native conscripts and volunteers. Moreover, the resulting figures for any given war may often be a very inaccurate reflection of the number of military personnel who eventually served in the war. First, the growth rates of armies differ radically during the months prior to the onset of war, and the figure may therefore be an artifact of the precise week or month on which the estimate or report is based. And once a nation gets into war, there may be a dramatic increase in its armed forces size; this will vary, of course, with the nation's basic manpower reserve and with the amount of time it had to mobilize before hostilities actually began. For these reasons, then, we only report the intensity ratio based on battle deaths per capita of pre-war military personnel in Tables 4.2 and 4.4 for those who might find it a useful measure, but exclude it subsequently because of our reservations about its validity.

SUMMARY

In this chapter, then, we have gone beyond the steps of merely identifying and classifying the international wars of the past century and a half. That is, as useful as frequency counts may be, they permit only the most primitive sort of theorizing and hypothesis testing; to

[9] In this volume, we will present straight ratio figures for these three measures, but for certain data-analysis reasons, two of them (BD/Pop. and BD/AF) were also punched in a natural logarithmic transformation. We have not, of course, included all conceivable ratio, or derived, measures; many other permutations are indeed possible, depending on one's theoretical needs. They may be generated by the user himself, or may be requested on special order from the International Relations Archive, University of Michigan. Our ratios in $\log_e$ transformation are also available through the Archive.

the extent that we can go beyond such enumeration and develop measures of an ordinal, interval, or ratio scale nature, more subtle sorts of inquiry become possible. Moreover, we must not only be able to describe any particular war, but also to compare many wars, many nations or regions, and many time periods as well. In the chapters that follow, we present the various measures and transformations by which such comparisons might be made, along with detailed descriptions of the procedures by which such indices have been generated.

Part B
The Wars

Chapter 4

The Qualifying Wars and Their Quantitative Attributes

In the preceding two chapters, we described in some detail the way in which we—as well as our predecessors—defined our population of wars and estimated the duration, participation, and human destructiveness of each. This chapter presents the quantitative results arising out of those data-making and scaling procedures.

Table 4.1 is merely a chronological listing of all 93 international wars which met our inclusion criteria, along with the dates and the war's code number. Because many analyses will deal with interstate and extra-systemic wars separately, they are numbered in two different series; interstate wars run from 1 through 50, and colonial and imperial wars are combined in the 51 through 93 series.

INTERSTATE WARS

In Table 4.2, we single out the 50 interstate wars, list them chronologically, and then present the following basic information for each. On the left is the war number and name, and the number and name of the participants, followed by the opening and closing dates of the war; and for those nations which only participated in part of the war, the dates of such participation are indented below. Then come the three basic indicators for each war: duration in months, magnitude in nation months, and severity in battle-connected deaths among military personnel. Under the gross magnitude and severity figures, we show the nation months and battle deaths for each qualifying participant.

These data are followed by the two variables which are needed to compute the intensity ratios: the total combined prewar populations of all the system members which actively participated, and their total prewar armed force sizes. Next are shown the three intensity ratios for the wars and for each qualifying participant: battle deaths per nation month; battle deaths per capita based on total population; and battle deaths per capita based on armed forces size.

Table 4.2 offers additional information which is relevant for analyses done in later chapters. Since all but one of the interstate wars included in our list resulted in clear-cut victory for one side (with the criteria spelled out in Chapter Fourteen), we have shown this by placing the victor or victors first in the list of participants. For the 20 of these 50 wars which had more than one participant on a side, a space has been left between the victorious side and the vanquished, with the participating nations listed in the order of their three-digit nation code number. As a final refinement of this table, we have asterisked those participating nations which, from 1816 through 1919, were members of the peripheral subset only, and did not qualify for the more restricted central system membership.

Later on in the volume a number of calculations will be made for the central and major power sub-systems, as distinct from the entire interstate system. Therefore, we list in Table 4.3 the interstate wars that were fought by nations belonging to these more restricted groupings. In these wars, at least one of the participants—on *either* side—belonged to the central or to the major power sub-system. In this list, we give the war number and name only, and also indicate, for those who might want an even more restricted list, which wars included at least one participant on *each* side from the central or major power sub-systems respectively. Such wars are marked with an asterisk.

4.1 ALL INTERNATIONAL WARS LISTED CHRONOLOGICALLY, WITH WAR NUMBER, NAME, AND YEARS

51. British-Maharattan (1817–1818)
52. Greek (1821–1828)
1. Franco-Spanish (1823)
53. First Anglo-Burmese (1823–1826)
54. Javanese (1825–1830)
55. Russo-Persian (1826–1828)
2. Navarino Bay (1827)
3. Russo-Turkish (1828–1829)
56. First Polish (1831)
57. First Syrian (1831–1832)
58. Texan (1835–1836)
59. First British-Afghan (1838–1842)
60. Second Syrian (1839–1840)
61. Peruvian-Bolivian (1841)
62. First British-Sikh (1845–1846)
4. Mexican-American (1846–1848)
5. Austro-Sardinian (1848–1849)
6. First Schleswig-Holstein (1848–1849)
63. Hungarian (1848–1849)
64. Second British-Sikh (1848–1849)
7. Roman Republic (1849)
8. La Plata (1851–1852)
65. First Turco-Montenegran (1852–1853)
9. Crimean (1853–1856)
10. Anglo-Persian (1856–1857)
66. Sepoy (1857–1859)
67. Second Turco-Montenegran (1858–1859)
11. Italian Unification (1859)
12. Spanish-Moroccan (1859–1860)
13. Italo-Roman (1860)
14. Italo-Sicilian (1860–1861)
15. Franco-Mexican (1862–1867)
68. Second Polish (1863–1864)
16. Ecuadorian-Colombian (1863)
17. Second Schleswig-Holstein (1864)
69. La Plata (1864–1870)
18. Spanish-Chilean (1865–1866)
19. Seven Weeks (1866)
70. Ten Years (1868–1878)
20. Franco-Prussian (1870–1871)
71. Dutch-Achinese (1873–1878)
72. Balkan (1875–1877)
21. Russo-Turkish (1877–1878)
73. Bosnian (1878)
74. Second British-Afghan (1878–1880)
75. British-Zulu (1879)
22. Pacific (1879–1883)
76. Franco-Indochinese (1882–1884)
77. Mahdist (1882–1885)
23. Sino-French (1884–1885)
24. Central American (1885)
78. Serbo-Bulgarian (1885)
25. Sino-Japanese (1894–1895)
79. Franco-Madagascan (1894–1895)
80. Cuban (1895–1898)
81. Italo-Ethiopian (1895–1896)
82. First Philippine (1896–1898)
26. Greco-Turkish (1897)
27. Spanish-American (1898)
83. Second Philippine (1899–1902)
84. Boer (1899–1902)
28. Russo-Japanese (1904–1905)
29. Central American (1906)
30. Central American (1907)
31. Spanish-Moroccan (1909–1910)
32. Italo-Turkish (1911–1912)
33. First Balkan (1912–1913)
34. Second Balkan (1913)
35. World War One (1914–1918)
85. Russian Nationalities (1917–1921)
36. Hungarian-Allies (1919)
37. Greco-Turkish (1919–1922)
86. Riffian (1921–1926)
87. Druze (1925–1926)
38. Manchurian (1931–1933)
39. Chaco (1932–1935)
40. Italo-Ethiopian (1935–1936)
41. Sino-Japanese (1937–1941)
42. Russo-Japanese (1939)
43. World War Two (1939–1945)
44. Russo-Finnish (1939–1940)
88. Indonesian (1945–1946)
89. Indochinese (1945–1954)
90. Madagascan (1947–1948)
91. First Kashmir (1947–1949)
45. Palestine (1948–1949)
46. Korean (1950–1953)
92. Algerian (1954–1962)
93. Tibetan (1956–1959)
47. Russo-Hungarian (1956)
48. Sinai (1956)
49. Sino-Indian (1962)
50. Second Kashmir (1965)

4.2 - LIST OF INTERSTATE WARS, WITH PARTICIPANTS, DURATION, MAGNITUDE, SEVERITY, AND INTENSITY

NUMBER AND NAME OF WAR / PARTICIPANTS AND CODE NUMBER	DATES OF WAR / NATIONAL DATES WHEN DIFFERENT	DURATION IN MONTHS	MAGNITUDE IN NATION MONTHS	SEVERITY IN BATTLE DEATHS	POPULATION (MILLIONS PRE-WAR)	ARMED FORCES SIZE (000'S PRE-WAR)	BATTLE DEATHS PER NATION MONTH	BATTLE DEATHS PER MILLION POPULATION	BATTLE DEATHS PER 1000 ARMED FORCES
1 FRANCO-SPANISH	4/07/1823-11/13/1823	7.3	14.6	1000	42.9	370	68.5	23	2.7
220 FRANCE			7.3	400	31.6	250	54.8	13	1.6
230 SPAIN			7.3	600	11.3	120	82.2	53	5.0
2 NAVARINO BAY	10/20/1827-10/20/1827	0.1	0.1	3180	132.6	1185	31800.0	24	2.7
200 ENGLAND			0.1	80	23.1	120	800.0	3	0.7
220 FRANCE			0.1	40	32.1	235	400.0	1	0.2
365 RUSSIA			0.1	60	53.6	610	600.0	1	0.1
640 TURKEY			0.1	3000	23.8	220	30000.0	126	13.6
3 RUSSO-TURKISH	4/26/1828- 9/14/1829	16.7	33.4	130000	78.3	830	3892.2	1660	156.6
365 RUSSIA			16.7	50000	54.4	610	2994.0	919	82.0
640 TURKEY			16.7	80000	23.9	220	4790.4	3347	363.6
4 MEXICAN-AMERICAN	5/12/1846- 2/12/1848	21.1	42.2	17000	30.6	29	402.8	556	586.2
* 2 UNITED STATES			21.1	11000	23.1	11	521.3	476	1000.0
* 70 MEXICO			21.1	6000	7.5	18	284.4	800	333.3
5 AUSTRO-SARDINIAN	3/24/1848- 8/09/1848; 3/20/1849- 3/23/1849	4.7	9.4	9000	39.2	350	957.4	230	25.7
300 AUSTRIA-HUNGARY			4.7	5600	34.3	320	1191.5	163	17.5
325 ITALY/SARDINIA			4.7	3400	4.9	30	723.4	694	113.3
6 FIRST SCHLESWIG-HOLSTEIN	4/10/1848- 8/26/1848; 3/25/1849- 7/10/1849	8.1	16.2	6000	18.3	150	370.4	328	40.0
255 GERMANY/PRUSSIA			8.1	2500	16.0	120	308.6	156	20.8
390 DENMARK			8.1	3500	2.3	30	432.1	1522	116.7

NOTES: * - NATION NOT IN CENTRAL SUBSYSTEM (1816-1919)
- FOR EACH WAR, VICTOR NATIONS APPEAR FIRST, FOLLOWED BY A BLANK LINE, THEN THE DEFEATED NATIONS

NUMBER AND NAME OF WAR PARTICIPANTS AND CODE NUMBER	DATES OF WAR NATIONAL DATES WHEN DIFFERENT	DURATION IN MONTHS	MAGNITUDE IN NATION MONTHS	SEVERITY IN BATTLE DEATHS	POPULATION (MILLIONS PRE-WAR)	ARMED FORCES SIZE (000'S PRE-WAR)	BATTLE DEATHS PER NATION MONTH	BATTLE DEATHS PER MILLION POPULATION	BATTLE DEATHS PER 1000 ARMED FORCES
7 ROMAN REPUBLIC	4/30/1849- 4/30/1849; 5/08/1849- 7/01/1849	1.8	6.4	2200	76.0	810	343.8	29	2.7
220 FRANCE	4/30/1849- 4/30/1849; 6/03/1849- 7/01/1849		1.0	500	35.6	370	500.0	14	1.4
300 AUSTRIA-HUNGARY	5/08/1849- 7/01/1849		1.8	100	34.4	320	55.6	3	0.3
*329 TWO SICILIES	5/08/1849- 7/01/1849		1.8	100	3.1	101	55.6	32	1.0
*327 PAPAL STATES			1.8	1500	2.9	19	833.3	517	78.9
8 LA PLATA	7/19/1851- 2/03/1852	6.6	13.2	1300	8.4	27	98.5	155	48.1
*140 BRAZIL			6.6	500	7.3	16	75.8	68	31.3
*160 ARGENTINA			6.6	800	1.1	11	121.2	727	72.7
9 CRIMEAN	10/23/1853- 3/01/1856	28.3	116.5	264200	166.6	1380	2267.8	1586	191.4
200 ENGLAND	3/31/1854- 3/01/1856		23.1	22000	28.7	180	952.4	767	122.2
220 FRANCE	3/31/1854- 3/01/1856		23.1	95000	36.0	430	4112.6	2639	220.9
325 ITALY/SARDINIA	1/10/1855- 3/01/1856		13.7	2200	5.2	80	160.6	423	27.5
640 TURKEY			28.3	45000	25.5	140	1590.1	1765	321.4
365 RUSSIA			28.3	100000	71.2	550	3533.6	1404	181.8
10 ANGLO-PERSIAN	10/25/1856- 3/14/1857	4.6	9.2	2000	33.6	200	217.4	60	10.0
200 ENGLAND			4.6	500	29.2	170	108.7	17	2.9
*630 IRAN			4.6	1500	4.4	30	326.1	341	50.0
11 ITALIAN UNIFICATION	4/29/1859- 7/12/1859	2.5	7.3	22500	77.0	820	3082.2	292	27.4
220 FRANCE	5/03/1859- 7/12/1859		2.3	7500	37.2	390	3260.9	202	19.2
325 ITALY/SARDINIA			2.5	2500	5.2	80	1000.0	481	31.3
300 AUSTRIA-HUNGARY			2.5	12500	34.6	350	5000.0	361	35.7

NOTES: * - NATION NOT IN CENTRAL SUBSYSTEM (1816-1919)
- FOR EACH WAR, VICTOR NATIONS APPEAR FIRST, FOLLOWED BY A BLANK LINE, THEN THE DEFEATED NATIONS

4.2 - LIST CF INTERSTATE WARS, WITH PARTICIPANTS, DURATION, MAGNITUDE, SEVERITY, AND INTENSITY

NUMBER AND NAME OF WAR PARTICIPANTS AND CODE NUMBER	DATES OF WAR NATIONAL DATES WHEN DIFFERENT	DURATION IN MONTHS	MAGNITUDE IN NATION MONTHS	SEVERITY IN BATTLE DEATHS	POPULATION (MILLIONS PRE-WAR)	ARMED FORCES SIZE (000'S PRE-WAR)	BATTLE DEATHS PER NATION MONTH	BATTLE DEATHS PER MILLION POPULATION	BATTLE DEATHS PER 1000 ARMED FORCES
12 SPANISH-MOROCCAN	10/22/1859- 3/26/1860	5.2	10.4	10000	18.7	140	961.5	535	71.4
230 SPAIN			5.2	4000	16.1	100	769.2	248	40.0
*600 MCROCCC			5.2	6000	2.6	40	1153.8	2308	150.0
13 ITALO-ROMAN	9/11/1860- 9/29/1860	0.6	1.2	1000	25.0	274	833.3	40	3.6
325 ITALY/SARDINIA			0.6	300	21.9	250	500.0	14	1.2
*327 PAPAL STATES			0.6	700	3.1	24	1166.7	226	29.2
14 ITALO-SICILIAN	10/15/1860- 1/19/1861	3.2	6.4	1000	31.6	393	156.2	32	2.5
325 ITALY/SARDINIA			3.2	600	21.9	250	187.5	27	2.4
*329 TWO SICILIES			3.2	400	9.7	143	125.0	41	2.8
15 FRANCC-MEXICAN	4/16/1862- 2/05/1867	57.7	115.4	20000	46.1	541	173.3	434	37.0
* 70 MEXICC			57.7	12000	8.4	91	208.0	1429	131.9
220 FRANCE			57.7	8000	37.7	450	138.6	212	17.8
16 ECUADORIAN-COLOMBIAN	11/22/1863-12/06/1863	0.5	1.0	1000	4.4	6	1000.0	227	166.7
*100 CCICMBIA			0.5	300	3.0	2	600.0	100	150.0
*130 ECUADCR			0.5	700	1.4	4	1400.0	500	175.0
17 SECOND SCHLESWIG-HOLSTEIN	2/01/1864- 4/25/1864; 6/25/1864- 7/20/1864	3.6	10.8	4500	56.5	510	416.7	80	8.8
255 GERMANY/PRUSSIA			3.6	1000	19.3	220	277.8	52	4.5
300 AUSTRIA-HUNGARY			3.6	500	35.3	260	138.9	14	1.9
390 DENMARK			3.6	3000	1.9	30	833.3	1579	100.0

NOTES: * - NATICN NOT IN CENTRAL SUBSYSTEM (1816-1919)
- FOR EACH WAR, VICTOR NATIONS APPEAR FIRST, FOLLOWED BY A BLANK LINE, THEN THE DEFEATED NATIONS

NUMBER AND NAME OF WAR / PARTICIPANTS AND CODE NUMBER	DATES OF WAR / NATIONAL DATES WHEN DIFFERENT	DURATION IN MONTHS	MAGNITUDE IN NATION MONTHS	SEVERITY IN BATTLE DEATHS	POPULATION (MILLIONS PRE-WAR)	ARMED FORCES SIZE (000'S PRE-WAR)	BATTLE DEATHS PER NATION MONTH	BATTLE DEATHS PER MILLION POPULATION	BATTLE DEATHS PER 1000 ARMED FORCES
18 SPANISH-CHILEAN	10/25/1865- 5/09/1866	6.5	16.8	1000	21.4	278	59.5	47	3.6
*135 PERU	1/14/1866- 5/09/1866		3.8	600	3.2	13	157.9	188	46.2
*155 CHILE			6.5	100	1.8	5	15.4	56	20.0
230 SPAIN			6.5	300	16.4	260	46.2	18	1.2
19 SEVEN WEEKS	6/15/1866- 7/26/1866	1.4	14.5	36100	94.1	1032	2489.7	384	35.0
255 GERMANY/PRUSSIA			1.4	10000	23.6	350	7142.9	424	28.6
325 ITALY/SARDINIA			1.4	4000	22.3	240	2857.1	179	16.7
*240 HANOVER	6/15/1866- 6/29/1866		0.5	500	0.1	20	1000.0	5000	25.0
*245 BAVARIA			1.4	500	4.8	53	357.1	104	9.4
*267 BADEN			1.4	100	1.4	5	71.4	71	20.0
*269 SAXONY			1.4	600	2.4	32	428.6	250	18.8
*271 WUERTTEMBERG			1.4	100	1.8	7	71.4	56	14.3
*273 HESSE ELECTORAL			1.4	100	0.7	13	71.4	143	7.7
*275 HESSE GRAND DUCAL			1.4	100	0.8	7	71.4	125	14.3
*280 MECKLENBURG-SCHWERIN			1.4	100	0.6	5	71.4	167	20.0
300 AUSTRIA-HUNGARY			1.4	20000	35.6	300	14285.7	562	66.7
20 FRANCO-PRUSSIAN	7/19/1870- 2/26/1871	7.3	27.0	187500	85.5	990	6944.4	2193	189.4
*245 BAVARIA	7/19/1870-11/15/1870		3.9	5500	4.9	92	1410.3	1122	59.8
255 GERMANY/PRUSSIA			7.3	40000	38.3	410	5479.4	1044	97.6
*267 BADEN	7/19/1870-11/22/1870		4.2	1000	1.5	22	238.1	667	45.5
*271 WUERTTEMBERG	7/19/1870-11/25/1870		4.3	1000	1.8	26	232.6	556	38.5
220 FRANCE			7.3	140000	39.0	440	19178.1	3590	318.2
21 RUSSO-TURKISH	4/12/1877- 1/03/1878	8.8	17.6	285000	122.0	930	16193.2	2336	306.5
365 RUSSIA			8.8	120000	93.8	780	13636.4	1279	153.8
640 TURKEY			8.8	165000	28.2	150	18750.0	5851	1100.0
22 PACIFIC	2/14/1879-12/11/1883	57.9	170.3	14000	7.0	15	82.2	2000	933.3
*155 CHILE			57.9	3000	2.0	7	51.8	1500	428.6
*135 PERU	4/05/1879-10/20/1883		54.5	10000	2.7	5	183.5	3704	2000.0
*145 BOLIVIA			57.9	1000	2.3	3	17.3	435	333.3

NOTES: * - NATION NOT IN CENTRAL SUBSYSTEM (1816-1919)
- FOR EACH WAR, VICTOR NATIONS APPEAR FIRST, FOLLOWED BY A BLANK LINE, THEN THE DEFEATED NATIONS

4.2 - LIST OF INTERSTATE WARS, WITH PARTICIPANTS, DURATION, MAGNITUDE, SEVERITY, AND INTENSITY

NUMBER AND NAME OF WAR / PARTICIPANTS AND CODE NUMBER	DATES OF WAR / NATIONAL DATES WHEN DIFFERENT	DURATION IN MONTHS	MAGNITUDE IN NATION MONTHS	SEVERITY IN BATTLE DEATHS	POPULATION (MILLIONS PRE-WAR)	ARMED FORCES SIZE (000'S PRE-WAR)	BATTLE DEATHS PER NATION MONTH	BATTLE DEATHS PER MILLION POPULATION	BATTLE DEATHS PER 1000 ARMED FORCES
23 SINO-FRENCH	6/15/1884- 6/09/1885	11.8	23.6	12100	468.1	1484	512.7	26	8.2
220 FRANCE			11.8	2100	38.1	500	178.0	55	4.2
*710 CHINA			11.8	10000	430.0	984	847.5	23	10.2
24 CENTRAL AMERICAN	3/28/1885- 4/15/1885	0.6	1.2	1000	2.0	61	833.3	500	16.4
* 92 SALVADOR			0.6	200	0.7	26	333.3	286	7.7
* 90 GUATEMALA			0.6	800	1.3	35	1333.3	615	22.9
25 SINO-JAPANESE	8/01/1894- 3/30/1895	8.0	16.0	15000	480.0	200	937.5	31	75.0
*740 JAPAN			8.0	5000	40.0	100	625.0	125	50.0
*710 CHINA			8.0	10000	440.0	100	1250.0	23	100.0
26 GRECO-TURKISH	2/15/1897- 5/19/1897	3.1	6.2	2000	26.7	400	322.6	75	5.0
640 TURKEY			3.1	1400	24.3	370	451.6	58	3.8
350 GREECE			3.1	600	2.4	30	193.5	250	20.0
27 SPANISH-AMERICAN	4/21/1898- 8/12/1898	3.7	7.4	10000	94.4	330	1351.4	106	30.3
* 2 UNITED STATES			3.7	5000	76.0	130	1351.4	66	38.5
230 SPAIN			3.7	5000	18.4	200	1351.4	272	25.0
28 RUSSO-JAPANESE	2/08/1904- 9/15/1905	19.3	38.6	130000	187.9	1400	3367.9	692	92.9
740 JAPAN			19.3	85000	47.1	200	4404.1	1805	425.0
365 RUSSIA			19.3	45000	140.8	1200	2331.6	320	37.5
29 CENTRAL AMERICAN	5/27/1906- 7/20/1906	1.8	5.4	1000	3.7	105	185.2	270	9.5
* 90 GUATEMALA			1.8	400	1.9	63	222.2	211	6.3
* 91 HONDURAS			1.8	300	0.7	21	166.7	429	14.3
* 92 SALVADOR			1.8	300	1.1	21	166.7	273	14.3

NOTES: * - NATION NOT IN CENTRAL SUBSYSTEM (1816-1919)
- FOR EACH WAR, VICTOR NATIONS APPEAR FIRST, FOLLOWED BY A BLANK LINE, THEN THE DEFEATED NATIONS

NUMBER AND NAME OF WAR PARTICIPANTS AND CODE NUMBER	DATES OF WAR NATIONAL DATES WHEN DIFFERENT	DURATION IN MONTHS	MAGNITUDE IN NATION MONTHS	SEVERITY IN BATTLE DEATHS	POPULATION (MILLIONS PRE-WAR)	ARMED FORCES SIZE (000'S PRE-WAR)	BATTLE DEATHS PER NATION MONTH	BATTLE DEATHS PER MILLION POPULATION	BATTLE DEATHS PER 1000 ARMED FORCES
30 CENTRAL AMERICAN	2/19/1907- 4/23/1907	2.1	6.3	1000	2.4	46	158.7	417	21.7
* 93 NICARAGUA			2.1	400	0.6	4	190.5	667	100.0
* 91 HCNDURAS			2.1	300	0.7	21	142.9	429	14.3
* 92 SALVADOR			2.1	300	1.1	21	142.9	273	14.3
31 SPANISH-MOROCCAN	7/07/1909- 3/23/1910	8.5	17.0	10000	24.5	130	588.2	408	76.9
230 SPAIN			8.5	2000	19.5	90	235.3	103	22.2
*600 MCROCCC			8.5	8000	5.0	40	941.2	1600	200.0
32 ITALO-TURKISH	9/29/1911-10/18/1912	12.7	25.4	20000	59.7	700	787.4	335	28.6
325 ITALY/SARDINIA			12.7	6000	34.9	280	472.4	172	21.4
640 TURKEY			12.7	14000	24.8	420	1102.4	565	33.3
33 FIRST BALKAN	10/17/1912- 4/19/1913	6.1	20.4	82000	31.9	550	4019.6	2571	149.1
345 YUGOSLAVIA/SERBIA	10/17/1912-12/03/1912; 2/03/1913- 4/19/1913		4.1	15000	2.9	40	3658.5	5172	375.0
350 GREECE			6.1	5000	2.7	30	819.7	1852	166.7
355 BULGARIA	10/17/1912-12/03/1912; 2/03/1913- 4/19/1913		4.1	32000	4.3	60	7804.9	7442	533.3
640 TURKEY			6.1	30000	22.0	420	4918.0	1364	71.4
34 SECOND BALKAN	6/30/1913- 7/30/1913	1.0	4.2	60500	37.6	820	14404.8	1609	73.8
345 YUGOSLAVIA/SERBIA			1.0	18500	4.5	360	18500.0	4111	51.4
350 GREECE			1.0	2500	2.7	60	2500.0	926	41.7
360 RUMANIA	7/11/1913- 7/30/1913		0.7	1500	7.1	130	2142.9	211	11.5
640 TURKEY	7/15/1913- 7/30/1913		0.5	20000	18.5	210	40000.0	1081	95.2
355 BULGARIA			1.0	18000	4.8	60	18000.0	3750	300.0

NOTES: * - NATION NOT IN CENTRAL SUBSYSTEM (1816-1919)
- FOR EACH WAR, VICTOR NATIONS APPEAR FIRST, FOLLOWED BY A BLANK LINE, THEN THE DEFEATED NATIONS

4.2 - LIST OF INTERSTATE WARS, WITH PARTICIPANTS, DURATION, MAGNITUDE, SEVERITY, AND INTENSITY

NUMBER AND NAME OF WAR / PARTICIPANTS AND CODE NUMBER	DATES OF WAR / NATIONAL DATES WHEN DIFFERENT	DURATION IN MONTHS	MAGNITUDE IN NATION MONTHS	SEVERITY IN BATTLE DEATHS	POPULATION (MILLIONS PRE-WAR)	ARMED FORCES SIZE (000'S PRE-WAR)	BATTLE DEATHS PER NATION MONTH	BATTLE DEATHS PER MILLION POPULATION	BATTLE DEATHS PER 1000 ARMED FORCES
35 WORLD WAR I	7/29/1914-11/11/1918	51.5	607.8	9,000,000	605.2	5630	14076.7	14137	1519.7
2 UNITED STATES	4/17/1917-11/11/1918		18.9	126000	96.0	150	6666.7	1313	840.0
200 ENGLAND	8/05/1914-11/11/1918		51.2	908000	46.2	410	17734.4	19654	2214.6
211 BELGIUM	8/04/1914-11/11/1918		51.3	87500	7.6	50	1705.7	11513	1750.0
220 FRANCE	8/03/1914-11/11/1918		51.3	1350000	41.0	870	26315.8	32927	1551.7
235 PORTUGAL	3/01/1916-11/11/1918		32.4	7000	6.2	40	216.0	1129	175.0
325 ITALY/SARDINIA	5/23/1915-11/11/1918		41.7	650000	35.2	360	15587.5	18466	1805.6
345 YUGOSLAVIA/SERBIA			51.5	48000	4.5	360	932.0	10667	133.3
350 GREECE	6/29/1917-11/11/1918		16.5	5000	2.7	60	303.0	1852	83.3
360 RUMANIA	8/27/1916-12/09/1917		15.4	335000	7.1	130	21753.2	47183	2576.9
365 RUSSIA	8/01/1914-12/05/1917		40.2	1700000	162.0	1400	42288.6	10494	1214.3
740 JAPAN	8/23/1914-11/11/1918		50.7	300	53.4	300	5.9	6	1.0
255 GERMANY/PRUSSIA	8/01/1914-11/11/1918		51.4	1800000	67.0	870	35019.5	26866	2069.0
300 AUSTRIA-HUNGARY	7/29/1914-11/03/1918		51.2	1200000	53.0	360	23437.5	22642	3333.3
355 BULGARIA	10/12/1915- 9/29/1918		35.6	14000	4.8	60	393.3	2917	233.3
640 TURKEY	10/28/1914-11/11/1918		48.5	325000	18.5	210	6701.0	17568	1547.6
36 HUNGARIAN-ALLIES	4/16/1919- 8/04/1919	3.6	10.8	11000	37.0	310	1018.5	297	35.5
315 CZECHOSLOVAKIA			3.6	2000	13.0	150	555.6	154	13.3
360 RUMANIA			3.6	3000	16.0	130	833.3	188	23.1
310 HUNGARY			3.6	6000	8.0	30	1666.7	750	200.0
37 GRECO-TURKISH	5/05/1919-10/11/1922	41.3	82.6	50000	13.7	160	605.3	3650	312.5
640 TURKEY			41.3	20000	11.0	100	484.3	1818	200.0
350 GREECE			41.3	30000	2.7	60	726.4	11111	500.0
38 MANCHURIAN	12/19/1931- 5/06/1933	16.6	33.2	60000	591.0	590	1807.2	102	101.7
740 JAPAN			16.6	10000	64.8	290	602.4	154	34.5
710 CHINA			16.6	50000	526.2	300	3012.0	95	166.7

NOTES: * - NATION NOT IN CENTRAL SUBSYSTEM (1816-1919)
- FOR EACH WAR, VICTOR NATIONS APPEAR FIRST, FOLLOWED BY A BLANK LINE, THEN THE DEFEATED NATIONS

NUMBER AND NAME OF WAR PARTICIPANTS AND CODE NUMBER	DATES OF WAR NATIONAL DATES WHEN DIFFERENT	DURATION IN MONTHS	MAGNITUDE IN NATION MONTHS	SEVERITY IN BATTLE DEATHS	POPULATION (MILLIONS PRE-WAR)	ARMED FORCES SIZE (000'S PRE-WAR)	BATTLE DEATHS PER NATION MONTH	BATTLE DEATHS PER MILLION POPULATION	BATTLE DEATHS PER 1000 ARMED FORCES
39 CHACO	6/15/1932- 6/12/1935	35.9	71.8	130000	3.4	7	1810.6	38235	18571.4
150 PARAGUAY			35.9	50000	0.9	3	1392.8	55556	16666.7
145 BOLIVIA			35.9	80000	2.5	4	2228.4	32000	20000.0
40 ITALO-ETHIOPIAN	10/03/1935- 5/09/1936	7.2	14.4	20000	52.6	430	1388.9	380	46.5
325 ITALY/SARDINIA			7.2	4000	42.6	330	555.6	94	12.1
530 ETHIOPIA			7.2	16000	10.0	100	2222.2	1600	160.0
41 SINO-JAPANESE	7/07/1937-12/07/1941	53.1	106.2	1000000	606.8	700	9416.2	1648	1428.6
740 JAPAN			53.1	250000	69.4	400	4708.1	3602	625.0
710 CHINA			53.1	750000	537.4	300	14124.3	1396	2500.0
42 RUSSO-JAPANESE	5/11/1939- 9/16/1939	4.2	12.6	19000	241.7	2940	1507.9	79	6.5
365 RUSSIA			4.2	1000	170.5	1900	238.1	6	0.5
712 MONGOLIA			4.2	3000	0.6	40	714.3	5000	75.0
740 JAPAN			4.2	15000	70.6	1000	3571.4	212	15.0
43 WORLD WAR II	9/01/1939- 8/14/1945	71.5	875.6	15,000,000	1389.7	7761	17318.8	10912	1953.9
2 UNITED STATES	12/07/1941- 8/14/1945		44.3	408300	130.0	300	9216.7	3141	1361.0
20 CANADA	9/10/1939- 8/14/1945		71.2	39300	11.4	13	552.0	3447	3023.1
140 BRAZIL	7/06/1944- 5/07/1945		10.1	1000	39.5	83	99.0	25	12.0
200 ENGLAND	9/03/1939- 8/14/1945		71.4	270000	47.5	400	3781.5	5684	675.0
210 HOLLAND	5/10/1940- 5/14/1940		0.2	6200	8.7	60	31000.0	713	103.3
211 BELGIUM	5/10/1940- 5/28/1940		0.6	9600	8.4	30	16000.0	1143	320.0
220 FRANCE	9/03/1939- 6/22/1940; 10/23/1944- 8/14/1945		19.4	210000	41.1	800	10824.7	5109	262.5
290 POLAND	9/01/1939- 9/27/1939		0.9	320000	34.9	300	355555.6	9169	1066.7
325 ITALY/SARDINIA	10/18/1943- 5/07/1945		18.7	17500	43.6	380	935.8	401	46.1
345 YUGOSLAVIA/SERBIA	4/06/1941- 4/17/1941		0.4	5000	15.4	130	12500.0	325	38.5
350 GREECE	10/25/1940- 4/23/1941		5.9	10000	7.1	70	1694.9	1408	142.9
355 BULGARIA	9/09/1944- 5/07/1945		7.9	1000	6.3	20	126.6	159	50.0
360 RUMANIA	9/09/1944- 5/07/1945		7.9	10000	20.0	160	1265.8	500	62.5
365 RUSSIA	6/22/1941- 5/07/1945; 8/08/1945- 8/14/1945		46.7	7500000	170.5	1900	160599.6	43988	3947.4
385 NORWAY	4/09/1940- 6/09/1940		2.0	2000	2.9	14	1000.0	690	142.9
530 ETHIOPIA	1/24/1941- 7/03/1941		5.3	5000	10.0	100	943.4	500	50.0
560 SOUTH AFRICA	9/06/1939- 8/14/1945		71.3	8700	10.0	4	122.0	870	2175.0

NOTES: * - NATION NOT IN CENTRAL SUBSYSTEM (1816-1919)
- FOR EACH WAR, VICTOR NATIONS APPEAR FIRST, FOLLOWED BY A BLANK LINE, THEN THE DEFEATED NATIONS

4.2 - LIST OF INTERSTATE WARS, WITH PARTICIPANTS, DURATION, MAGNITUDE, SEVERITY, AND INTENSITY

NUMBER AND NAME OF WAR / PARTICIPANTS AND CODE NUMBER	DATES OF WAR / NATIONAL DATES WHEN DIFFERENT	DURATION IN MONTHS	MAGNITUDE IN NATION MONTHS	SEVERITY IN BATTLE DEATHS	POPULATION (MILLIONS PRE-WAR)	ARMED FORCES SIZE (000'S PRE-WAR)	BATTLE DEATHS PER NATION MONTH	BATTLE DEATHS PER MILLION POPULATION	BATTLE DEATHS PER 1000 ARMED FORCES
710 CHINA	12/07/1941- 8/14/1945		44.3	1350000	541.0	300	30474.0	2495	4500.0
712 MONGOLIA	8/10/1945- 8/14/1945		0.2	3000	0.6	40	15000.0	5000	75.0
900 AUSTRALIA	9/03/1939- 8/14/1945		71.4	29400	6.8	12	411.8	4324	2450.0
920 NEW ZEALAND	9/03/1939- 8/14/1945		71.4	17300	1.6	12	242.3	10813	1441.7
255 GERMANY/PRUSSIA	9/01/1939- 5/07/1945		68.2	3500000	78.8	1000	51319.6	44416	3500.0
310 HUNGARY	6/27/1941- 1/20/1945		42.8	40000	9.2	40	934.6	4348	1000.0
325 ITALY/SARDINIA	6/10/1940- 9/02/1943		38.8	60000	43.6	380	1546.4	1376	157.9
355 BULGARIA	12/08/1941- 9/08/1944		33.0	9000	6.3	20	272.7	1429	450.0
360 RUMANIA	6/22/1941- 8/23/1944		38.1	290000	20.0	160	7611.5	14500	1812.5
375 FINLAND	6/25/1941- 9/19/1944		38.9	42000	3.9	33	1079.7	10769	1272.7
740 JAPAN	12/07/1941- 8/14/1945		44.3	1000000	70.6	1000	22573.4	14164	1000.0
44 RUSSO-FINNISH	11/30/1939- 3/12/1940	3.4	6.8	90000	174.4	1933	13235.3	516	46.6
365 RUSSIA			3.4	50000	170.5	1900	14705.9	293	26.3
375 FINLAND			3.4	40000	3.9	33	11764.7	10256	1212.1
45 PALESTINE	5/15/1948- 7/18/1948; 10/22/1948- 1/07/1949	4.7	19.4	8000	30.8	272	412.4	260	29.4
666 ISRAEL			4.7	3000	1.4	7	638.3	2143	428.6
645 IRAQ	5/15/1948- 7/18/1948; 10/22/1948-10/31/1948		2.5	500	4.6	45	200.0	109	11.1
651 U.A.R.			4.7	2000	19.2	160	425.5	104	12.5
652 SYRIA	5/15/1948- 7/18/1948; 10/22/1948-10/31/1948		2.5	1000	3.1	40	400.0	323	25.0
660 LEBANON	5/15/1948- 7/18/1948; 10/22/1948-10/31/1948		2.5	500	1.2	6	200.0	417	83.3
663 JORDAN	5/15/1948- 7/18/1948; 10/22/1948-10/31/1948		2.5	1000	1.3	14	400.0	769	71.4
46 KOREAN	6/24/1950- 7/27/1953	37.1	514.0	2,000,000	977.2	9387	3681.1	1936	201.6
2 UNITED STATES	6/27/1950- 7/27/1953		37.0	54000	155.3	1610	1459.5	348	33.5
20 CANADA	12/19/1950- 7/27/1953		31.3	310	13.7	80	9.9	23	3.9
100 COLOMBIA	6/06/1951- 7/27/1953		25.7	140	13.6	25	5.4	10	5.6
200 ENGLAND	8/29/1950- 7/27/1953		35.0	670	50.1	830	19.1	13	0.8
210 HOLLAND	1/20/1951- 7/27/1953		30.2	110	10.2	180	3.6	11	0.6
211 BELGIUM	1/20/1951- 7/27/1953		30.2	100	8.7	70	3.3	11	1.4
220 FRANCE	1/01/1951- 7/27/1953		30.8	290	42.0	1113	9.4	7	0.3
350 GREECE	1/20/1951- 7/27/1953		30.2	170	7.6	130	5.6	22	1.3
530 ETHIOPIA	5/01/1951- 7/27/1953		26.9	120	15.8	20	4.5	8	6.0
640 TURKEY	10/18/1950- 7/27/1953		33.3	720	21.0	370	21.6	34	1.9

NOTES: * - NATION NOT IN CENTRAL SUBSYSTEM (1816-1919)
- FOR EACH WAR, VICTOR NATIONS APPEAR FIRST, FOLLOWED BY A BLANK LINE, THEN THE DEFEATED NATIONS

NUMBER ANC NAME OF WAR PARTICIPANTS AND CODE NUMBER	DATES OF WAR NATIONAL DATES WHEN DIFFERENT	DURATION IN MONTHS	MAGNITUDE IN NATION MONTHS	SEVERITY IN BATTLE DEATHS	POPULATION (MILLIONS PRE-WAR)	ARMED FORCES SIZE (000'S PRE-WAR)	BATTLE DEATHS PER NATION MONTH	BATTLE DEATHS PER MILLION POPULATION	BATTLE DEATHS PER 1000 ARMED FORCES
732 KCREA SOUTH			37.1	415000	20.8	154	11186.0	19952	2694.8
800 THAILAND	1/20/1951- 7/27/1953		30.2	110	20.2	30	3.6	5	3.7
840 PHILIPPINES	9/16/1950- 7/27/1953		34.4	90	20.3	40	2.6	4	2.2
900 AUSTRALIA	12/10/1950- 7/27/1953		31.6	270	8.2	60	8.5	33	4.5
710 CHINA	10/27/1950- 7/27/1953		33.0	900000	560.0	4500	27272.7	1607	200.0
731 KCREA NORTH			37.1	520000	9.7	175	14016.2	53608	2971.4
47 RUSSO-HUNGARIAN	10/23/1956-11/14/1956	0.8	1.6	32000	209.6	4520	20000.0	153	7.1
365 RUSSIA			0.8	7000	199.8	4350	8750.0	35	1.6
310 HUNGARY			0.8	25000	9.8	170	31250.0	2551	147.1
48 SINAI	10/31/1956-11/07/1956	0.3	1.0	3230	120.6	2550	3230.0	27	1.3
200 ENGLAND	11/02/1956-11/07/1956		0.2	20	51.6	920	100.0	0	0.0
220 FRANCE	11/02/1956-11/07/1956		0.2	10	43.8	1280	50.0	0	0.0
666 ISRAEL			0.3	200	1.9	250	666.7	105	0.8
651 U.A.R.			0.3	3000	23.3	100	10000.0	129	30.0
49 SINO-INDIAN	10/20/1962-11/22/1962	1.1	2.2	1000	1112.1	3550	454.5	1	0.3
710 CHINA			1.1	500	660.0	3000	454.5	1	0.2
750 INDIA			1.1	500	452.1	550	454.5	1	0.9
50 SECOND KASHMIR	8/05/1965- 9/23/1965	1.6	3.2	6800	600.6	1260	2125.0	11	5.4
770 PAKISTAN			1.6	3800	113.9	260	2375.0	33	14.6
750 INDIA			1.6	3000	486.7	1000	1875.0	6	3.0

NOTES: * - NATICN NCT IN CENTRAL SUBSYSTEM (1816-1919)
- FOR EACH WAR, VICTOR NATIONS APPEAR FIRST, FOLLOWED BY A BLANK LINE, THEN THE DEFEATED NATIONS

4.3 CENTRAL SYSTEM AND MAJOR POWER INTERSTATE WARS

Central System Wars (N = 29)	Major Power Wars (N = 30)
* 1. Franco-Spanish	1. Franco-Spanish
* 2. Navarino Bay	2. Navarino Bay
* 3. Russo-Turkish	3. Russo-Turkish
* 5. Austro-Sardinian	5. Austro-Sardinian
* 6. First Schleswig-Holstein	6. First Schleswig-Holstein
7. Roman Republic	7. Roman Republic
* 9. Crimean	* 9. Crimean
10. Anglo-Persian	10. Anglo-Persian
*11. Italian Unification	*11. Italian Unification
12. Spanish-Moroccan	
13. Italo-Roman	13. Italo-Roman
14. Italo-Sicilian	14. Italo-Sicilian
15. Franco-Mexican	15. Franco-Mexican
*17. Second Schleswig-Holstein	17. Second Schleswig-Holstein
18. Spanish-Chilean	
*19. Seven Weeks	*19. Seven Weeks
*20. Franco-Prussian	*20. Franco-Prussian
*21. Russo-Turkish	21. Russo-Turkish
23. Sino-French	23. Sino-French
*26. Greco-Turkish	
27. Spanish-American	
*28. Russo-Japanese	*28. Russo-Japanese
31. Spanish-Moroccan	
*32. Italo-Turkish	32. Italo-Turkish
*33. First Balkan	
*34. Second Balkan	
*35. World War One	*35. World War One
*36. Hungarian-Allies	
*37. Greco-Turkish	
	38. Manchurian
	40. Italo-Ethiopian
	41. Sino-Japanese
	*42. Russo-Japanese
	*43. World War Two
	44. Russo-Finnish
	*46. Korean
	47. Russo-Hungarian
	48. Sinai
	49. Sino-Indian

* = Central System Member or Major Power on *both* sides, N = 19 for Central, N = 9 for Major Powers

EXTRA-SYSTEMIC WARS

Turning to the extra-systemic wars—those in which the adversary is not a member of the interstate system but is an independent nonmember or a nonindependent national entity—we present Table 4.4 similar in format to Table 4.2. But this table presents data only for the system members involved and not for their extra-systemic adversaries. Furthermore, since only 5 of the 43 extra-systemic wars actively involved more than a single member, the *war* totals are usually the same as the individual *national* totals.

As before, we have identified the peripheral system participants by an asterisk, revealing that all but three of these imperial and colonial wars were fought by members of the central sub-system. Since the extra-systemic war experience of the interstate system members *is* largely accounted for by those nations comprising its central sub-system, we have not replicated the sort of list found in Table 4.3. It is also noteworthy that most of this limited group's experience in extra-systemic wars is accounted for by an even more limited group: the major powers. That is, 32 of these 43 wars were fought by major powers. The 11 exceptions were: Greek (1821–1828), Javanese (1825–1830), First Turco-Montenegran (1852–1853), Second Turco-Montenegran (1858–1859), Ten Years (1868–1878), Dutch-Achinese (1873–1878), Balkan (1875–1877), Serbo-Bulgarian (1885), Cuban (1895–1898), First Philippine (1896–1898), and First Kashmir (1947–1949).

Finally, since the extra-systemic listing presents only the system members' experiences, we could not indicate the victorious side as we did in Table 4.2. Instead, we refer the reader to Table 14.5, in which we list the system members who won and those who lost in extra-systemic combat, along with certain pertinent data from those engagements.

These, then, constitute our two basic bodies of data, and all of the subsequent compilations will represent little more than a wide variety of rearrangements and new combinations of the data shown in this chapter. Before turning to those extensions of the basic data, however, an intermediate question is in order: to what extent do our coding criteria and scaling procedures produce results similar to those of our predecessors? That will be our concern in the chapter that follows.

4.4 - EXTRA-SYSTEMIC WARS WITH SYSTEM MEMBER PARTICIPANTS, DURATION, MAGNITUDE, SEVERITY, AND INTENSITY

NUMBER AND NAME OF WAR SYSTEM MEMBER PARTICIPANTS AND CODE NUMBER	DATES OF WAR NATIONAL DATES WHEN DIFFERENT	DURA-TION IN MONTHS	MAGNI-TUDE IN NATION MONTHS	SEVERITY IN BATTLE DEATHS	POPULA-TION (MIL-LIONS PRE-WAR)	ARMED FORCES SIZE (000'S PRE-WAR)	BATTLE DEATHS PER NATION MONTH	BATTLE DEATHS PER MILLION POPULA-TION	BATTLE DEATHS PER 1000 ARMED FORCES
51 BRITISH-MAHAFATTAN	11/06/1817- 6/03/1818	6.9	6.9	2000	20.4	350	289.9	98	5.7
200 ENGLANC			6.9	2000	20.4	350	289.9	98	5.7
52 GREEK	3/25/1821- 4/25/1828	85.1	85.1	15000	24.7	130	176.3	607	115.4
640 TURKEY			85.1	15000	24.7	130	176.3	607	115.4
53 FIRST ANGLC-EURMESE	9/24/1823- 2/24/1826	29.1	29.1	15000	21.9	120	515.5	685	125.0
200 ENGLANC			29.1	15000	21.9	120	515.5	685	125.0
54 JAVANESE	7/23/1825- 3/28/1830	56.2	56.2	15000	5.9	40	266.9	2542	375.0
210 HCLLAND			56.2	15000	5.9	40	266.9	2542	375.0
55 RUSSO-PERSIAN	9/28/1826- 2/28/1828	17.0	17.0	5000	52.8	610	294.1	95	8.2
365 RUSSIA			17.0	5000	52.8	610	294.1	95	8.2
56 FIRST POLISH	2/07/1831-10/18/1831	8.3	8.3	15000	56.6	600	1807.2	265	25.0
365 RUSSIA			8.3	15000	56.6	600	1807.2	265	25.0
57 FIRST SYRIAN	11/01/1831-12/21/1832	13.7	13.7	10000	23.1	280	729.9	433	35.7
640 TURKEY			13.7	10000	23.1	280	729.9	433	35.7
58 TEXAN	10/01/1835- 4/22/1836	6.7	6.7	1000	7.7	6	149.3	130	166.7
* 70 MEXICC			6.7	1000	7.7	6	149.3	130	166.7
59 FIRST BRITISH-AFGHAN	10/01/1838-10/12/1842	48.4	48.4	20000	25.8	110	413.2	775	181.8
200 ENGLANC			48.4	20000	25.8	110	413.2	775	181.8
60 SECOND SYRIAN	6/10/1839- 6/24/1839; 9/09/1840-11/27/1840	3.1	5.7	10010	50.3	430	1756.1	199	23.3
200 ENGLAND	9/09/1840-11/27/1840		2.6	10	26.3	150	3.8	0	0.1
640 TURKEY			3.1	10000	24.0	280	3225.8	417	35.7

NOTE: * - NATICN NOT IN CENTRAL SUESYSTEM (1816-1919)

NUMBER AND NAME OF WAR SYSTEM MEMBER PARTICIPANTS AND CODE NUMBER	DATES OF WAR NATIONAL DATES WHEN DIFFERENT	DURATION IN MONTHS	MAGNITUDE IN NATION MONTHS	SEVERITY IN BATTLE DEATHS	POPULATION (MILLIONS PRE-WAR)	ARMED FORCES SIZE (000'S PRE-WAR)	BATTLE DEATHS PER NATION MONTH	BATTLE DEATHS PER MILLION POPULATION	BATTLE DEATHS PER 1000 ARMED FORCES
61 PERUVIAN-BOLIVIAN	10/19/1841-11/18/1841	1.0	1.0	1000	1.3	6	1000.0	769	166.7
*135 PERU			1.0	1000	1.3	6	1000.0	769	166.7
62 FIRST BRITISH-SIKH	12/13/1845- 3/09/1846	2.9	2.9	1500	27.0	190	517.2	56	7.9
200 ENGLAND			2.9	1500	27.0	190	517.2	56	7.9
63 HUNGARIAN	9/09/1848- 8/13/1849	11.1	12.1	59500	102.7	710	4917.4	579	83.8
300 AUSTRIA-HUNGARY			11.1	45000	34.3	320	4054.1	1312	140.6
365 RUSSIA	7/16/1849- 8/13/1849		1.0	14500	68.4	390	14500.0	212	37.2
64 SECOND BRITISH-SIKH	10/10/1848- 3/12/1849	5.1	5.1	1500	27.3	190	294.1	55	7.9
200 ENGLAND			5.1	1500	27.3	190	294.1	55	7.9
65 FIRST TURCO-MONTENEGRAN	12/02/1852- 3/13/1853	3.4	3.4	5000	25.2	140	1470.6	198	35.7
640 TURKEY			3.4	5000	25.2	140	1470.6	198	35.7
66 SEPOY	5/10/1857- 4/07/1859	22.9	22.9	3500	29.4	170	152.8	119	20.6
200 ENGLAND			22.9	3500	29.4	170	152.8	119	20.6
67 SECOND TURCO-MONTENEGRAN	5/04/1858- 6/00/1859	12.9	12.9	3000	26.1	140	232.6	115	21.4
640 TURKEY			12.9	3000	26.1	140	232.6	115	21.4
68 SECOND POLISH	1/22/1863- 4/19/1864	14.9	14.9	5000	77.1	640	335.6	65	7.8
365 RUSSIA			14.9	5000	77.1	640	335.6	65	7.8
69 LA PLATA	11/12/1864- 3/01/1870	63.6	123.5	110000	13.7	35	890.7	8029	3142.9
*140 BRAZIL			63.6	100000	11.8	29	1572.3	8475	3448.3
*160 ARGENTINA	3/05/1865- 3/01/1870		59.9	10000	1.9	6	166.9	5263	1666.7
70 TEN YEARS	10/10/1868- 2/10/1878	112.1	112.1	100000	16.6	260	892.1	6024	384.6
230 SPAIN			112.1	100000	16.6	260	892.1	6024	384.6
71 DUTCH-ACHINESE	3/26/1873- 9/00/1878	65.2	65.2	6000	3.7	100	92.0	1622	60.0
210 HOLLAND			65.2	6000	3.7	100	92.0	1622	60.0

NOTE: * - NATION NOT IN CENTRAL SUBSYSTEM (1816-1919)

4.4 - EXTRA-SYSTEMIC WARS WITH SYSTEM MEMBER PARTICIPANTS, DURATION, MAGNITUDE, SEVERITY, AND INTENSITY

NUMBER AND NAME OF WAR / SYSTEM MEMBER PARTICIPANTS AND CODE NUMBER	DATES OF WAR / NATIONAL DATES WHEN DIFFERENT	DURATION IN MONTHS	MAGNITUDE IN NATION MONTHS	SEVERITY IN BATTLE DEATHS	POPULATION (MILLIONS PRE-WAR)	ARMED FORCES SIZE (000'S PRE-WAR)	BATTLE DEATHS PER NATION MONTH	BATTLE DEATHS PER MILLION POPULATION	BATTLE DEATHS PER 1000 ARMED FORCES
72 BALKAN	7/03/1875- 4/12/1877	21.4	21.4	10000	28.2	150	467.3	355	66.7
640 TURKEY			21.4	10000	28.2	150	467.3	355	66.7
73 BOSNIAN	7/29/1878-10/00/1878	2.1	2.1	3500	38.5	290	1666.7	91	12.1
300 AUSTRIA-HUNGARY			2.1	3500	38.5	290	1666.7	91	12.1
74 SECOND BRITISH-AFGHAN	11/20/1878- 5/26/1879; 9/03/1879- 9/02/1880	18.2	18.2	4000	33.9	250	219.8	118	16.0
200 ENGLAND			18.2	4000	33.9	250	219.8	118	16.0
75 BRITISH-ZULU	1/11/1879- 7/04/1879	5.7	5.7	3500	34.2	250	614.0	102	14.0
200 ENGLAND			5.7	3500	34.2	250	614.0	102	14.0
76 FRANCO-INDOCHINESE	4/25/1882- 6/14/1884	25.7	25.7	4500	37.9	500	175.1	119	9.0
220 FRANCE			25.7	4500	37.9	500	175.1	119	9.0
77 MAHDIST	9/13/1882-12/30/1885	39.6	39.6	20000	35.2	250	505.1	568	80.0
200 ENGLAND			39.6	20000	35.2	250	505.1	568	80.0
78 SERBO-BULGARIAN	11/02/1885-12/07/1885	1.2	1.2	2000	1.9	10	1666.7	1053	200.0
345 YUGOSLAVIA/SERBIA			1.2	2000	1.9	10	1666.7	1053	200.0
79 FRANCO-MADAGASCAN	12/12/1894-10/01/1895	9.7	9.7	6000	38.4	590	618.6	156	10.2
220 FRANCE			9.7	6000	38.4	590	618.6	156	10.2
80 CUBAN	2/24/1895- 4/02/1898	37.3	37.3	50000	18.1	130	1340.5	2762	384.6
230 SPAIN			37.3	50000	18.1	130	1340.5	2762	384.6
81 ITALO-ETHIOPIAN	12/07/1895-10/21/1896	10.5	10.5	9000	31.3	290	857.1	288	31.0
325 ITALY/SARDINIA			10.5	9000	31.3	290	857.1	288	31.0
82 FIRST PHILIPPINE	5/30/1896- 5/01/1898	23.1	23.1	2000	18.2	130	86.6	110	15.4
230 SPAIN			23.1	2000	18.2	130	86.6	110	15.4

NOTE: * - NATION NOT IN CENTRAL SUBSYSTEM (1816-1919)

NUMBER AND NAME OF WAR / SYSTEM MEMBER PARTICIPANTS AND CODE NUMBER	DATES OF WAR / NATIONAL DATES WHEN DIFFERENT	DURATION IN MONTHS	MAGNITUDE IN NATION MONTHS	SEVERITY IN BATTLE DEATHS	POPULATION (MILLIONS PRE-WAR)	ARMED FORCES SIZE (000'S PRE-WAR)	BATTLE DEATHS PER NATION MONTH	BATTLE DEATHS PER MILLION POPULATION	BATTLE DEATHS PER 1000 ARMED FORCES
83 SECOND PHILIPPINE	2/04/1899- 7/04/1902	40.9	40.9	4500	76.0	130	110.0	59	34.6
2 UNITED STATES			40.9	4500	76.0	130	110.0	59	34.6
84 BOER	10/11/1899- 5/31/1902	31.6	31.6	22000	41.4	290	696.2	531	75.9
200 ENGLAND			31.6	22000	41.4	290	696.2	531	75.9
85 RUSSIAN NATIONALITIES	12/09/1917- 3/18/1921	39.3	39.3	50000	162.0	1400	1272.3	309	35.7
365 RUSSIA			39.3	50000	162.0	1400	1272.3	309	35.7
86 RIFFIAN	7/18/1921- 5/27/1926	58.3	71.8	29000	62.7	976	403.9	463	29.7
220 FRANCE	4/12/1925- 5/27/1926		13.5	4000	40.7	746	296.3	98	5.4
230 SPAIN			58.3	25000	22.0	230	428.8	1136	108.7
87 DRUZE	7/18/1925- 6/00/1927	22.4	22.4	4000	40.7	746	178.6	98	5.4
220 FRANCE			22.4	4000	40.7	746	178.6	98	5.4
88 INDONESIAN	11/10/1945-10/15/1946	11.2	22.4	1400	58.7	1759	62.5	24	0.8
200 ENGLAND			11.2	1000	49.4	1709	89.3	20	0.6
210 HOLLAND			11.2	400	9.3	50	35.7	43	8.0
89 INDOCHINESE	12/01/1945- 6/01/1954	102.0	102.0	95000	39.0	880	931.4	2436	108.0
220 FRANCE			102.0	95000	39.0	880	931.4	2436	108.0
90 MADAGASCAN	3/29/1947-12/01/1948	20.2	20.2	1500	40.0	1000	74.3	38	1.5
220 FRANCE			20.2	1500	40.0	1000	74.3	38	1.5
91 FIRST KASHMIR	10/26/1947- 1/01/1949	14.3	14.3	1500	389.0	2000	104.9	4	0.8
750 INDIA			14.3	1500	389.0	2000	104.9	4	0.8
92 ALGERIAN	11/01/1954- 3/17/1962	88.5	88.5	15000	43.0	1280	169.5	349	11.7
220 FRANCE			88.5	15000	43.0	1280	169.5	349	11.7
93 TIBETAN	3/01/1956- 3/22/1959	36.7	36.7	40000	610.0	3000	1089.9	66	13.3
710 CHINA			36.7	40000	610.0	3000	1089.9	66	13.3

NOTE: * - NATION NOT IN CENTRAL SUBSYSTEM (1816-1919)

Chapter 5

Comparisons with Prior Compilations

In Chapters Two and Three, we indicated the sense of incompleteness with which we view the work of our predecessors in identifying and measuring the incidence of war. It was, of course, this very dissatisfaction that led to our decision to start afresh in the acquisition of such data, and now that our own basic results are in, it is possible to compare the several compilations. If the Sorokin, Richardson, and Wright studies had: (a) all been largely independent of one another, and (b) had produced essentially the same results, we might have been justified in using *their* data, singly or in some combination. While the first condition appears to be satisfied, it was clear, even by visual inspection, that there were not only sharp differences in the magnitude and severity figures arrived at by our predecessors, but in the very populations of wars which each defined.

In addition to the obvious reasons for deciding to more or less begin afresh in the acquisition of war data, there is another reason of some consequence. Reference is to the recurrent issue in scientific research as to whether—and to what extent—a new or improved data base leads to findings different from those emerging out of the original data. As will soon be quite evident, our inclusion criteria have produced a markedly smaller universe than those used by Richardson and the others; to some extent it is also qualitatively different. Exactly how different these empirical domains are remains a matter of detailed inquiry, but one indication will be the extent to which they reveal similar patterns and regularities. Thus, we will want to ask whether—as far as our questions parallel those of our predecessors—our frequency distributions, trend lines, periodicities, and so forth differ appreciably from those of Richardson, Sorokin, and to a lesser extent, Wright. That is, the first two of these did indeed search for many of the statistical patterns that concern us, and in Part C we will explicitly compare our descriptive findings with those uncovered by these and other pioneers, despite the obvious differences in the respective data bases.

With these considerations in mind, let us now examine all four sets of estimates in order to see how dissimilar those basic lists are, and how ours compares with the other three in terms of the various measures.

STATISTICAL AGREEMENT

If we add up all of the wars that are included in at least one of the four compilations, we get a total of 367 for the period 1816–1965. Needless to say, if other lists or studies (including those mentioned in Chapter Two) had been included in this merged compilation, the number might well be half again as large; indeed, our Appendix B includes 40 wars which were excluded not only by ourselves but by the other three studies as well.

Of these 367 wars, Richardson (even though his compilation does not begin until 1819 and ends in 1949) includes the largest number: 289. Wright's population (for the period 1815–1964) is next, with 133; Sorokin's figure (for 1819–1925) is 97; and ours for 1816–1965 is smallest with 93. What is the degree of commonality and overlap in these four potentially similar populations?

We compute this commonality in percentage terms by a simple procedure: for each of the six pairs of studies, we divide the number of wars which *both* included by the number which *either* of them included, for the period covered by both studies. The percentage agreement in each pair of studies is as follows:

Richardson-Wright: 28.6
Richardson-Sorokin: 22.9
Richardson-Singer & Small: 22.6
Wright-Sorokin: 40.0
Wright-Singer & Small: 45.8
Sorokin-Singer & Small: 31.5

As low as these paired scores are, the commonality declines even further if we compute the score for all of the four studies. That is, if we take the number of wars found in *every* one of the four lists ($N = 36$), and divide by the total found in *any* one of them (but only for the period of total time overlap, 1819–1925, with $N = 305$), we get an overall interstudy agreement of only 12 percent.

On the other hand, these figures do tend to exaggerate the discrepancies between and among the studies, and suggest that there is almost *no* agreement in several of the cases. That is, they are overly sensitive to the fact that Richardson's list, for example, is more than three times the size of ours. An alternative and more conservative index might be constructed by asking a simpler question: for each pair of studies, what percentage of the first's wars are also in the second's list, and what percentage of the second's wars are found in the first's list? These figures are shown in Table 5.1, and reveal that the discrepancies are not nearly so great as they first appeared. The top row of the matrix shows that, indeed, the other three studies only include 30.4, 25.8, and 23.5 percent, respectively, of the wars which Richardson included for those periods embraced by both projects. But the left-most column shows that Richardson's list includes the rather high 75.9, 63.9, and 80 percent of those also found in each of the others. The point, of course, is that when we more or less control for the fact that each study had somewhat different theoretical foci, and therefore used criteria of varying exclusiveness, we find that all four projects were not really that far apart after all.

5.1 PAIRWISE AGREEMENT ON WAR INCLUSIONS: PERCENT OF ALL WARS IN ROW'S LIST WHICH ARE ALSO FOUND IN COLUMN'S LIST

	Richardson	Wright	Sorokin	Singer & Small
Richardson ($N = 289$)	—	30.4	25.8	23.5
Wright ($N = 133$)	75.9	—	52.4	53.4
Sorokin ($N = 97$)	63.9	54.5	—	41.4
Singer & Small ($N = 93$)	80.0	77.2	56.9	—

DETAILED COMPARISONS

The precise extent of agreement, however, is best revealed in Table 5.2, where a case-by-case comparison is available. In this matrix, taking up the balance of this chapter, one finds enough information to make a more detailed comparison among and between the four basic compilations, both in terms of a defined population of international wars and in terms of the quantitative attributes of these wars.

In the left-hand column (Entities at War) are listed all of the political entities—national states or not, system members or not—that are considered to have participated, by any one of the authors, in each of the wars included in any of the four studies. Thus, even when two of the studies agree that a given sequence of military combat meets the criteria for inclusion in the list of wars, they may readily disagree as to which political entities merit listing as participants.

Because there is such a variety of names assigned to many of the wars by ourselves, our three predecessors, and countless other scholars of diverse nationalities, disciplines, generations, and viewpoints, we make no effort to label the wars in this composite list; furthermore, there is a wide divergence as to whether a given sequence of hostilities is best treated as a single war or as a number of separate ones. Hence, we list only the putative participants, assuming that this information, plus the more or less converging dates, will permit ready identification of the war. If there were more than two participants, one side is indented and italicized in order to distinguish the allegiance of the warring parties. And if only one participant is listed, it is because the event in question is a civil war. If the locale of the war is not readily indicated by the identity of the participants, the list is followed by a region name in parentheses.

Moving from sheer inclusion or exclusion to the more detailed descriptions which each of the four studies produced, a few words of clarification are in order. First, we reiterate that none of the four embraces exactly the same time span, with Richardson beginning later than we do (1819) and all three ending earlier: Richardson (1949); Wright (1964); and Sorokin (1925). To indicate when disagreement is merely a function of the time spans covered, a double horizontal line is drawn across each of the other three scholars' columns just above the first war and just after the last war contained in his time frame. As to the sequence in which the wars are listed, it is chronological and generally based on Richardson's month and year since his is the largest population. When two or more begin in the same month and year, that which terminated first is listed first. In a few places, one study will list as two or more separate wars a conflict which another study identifies as one long war. The several wars in the former case are listed with the single war and all are set off by heavy lines; for example, Richardson treats as a continuing conflict the hostilities between Russia and Turkey in the late 1820s, while we treat the Russo-Turkish War of 1828–1829, Navarino Bay, 1827, and the Greek Independence War of 1821–1828 as three separate wars. Even though this necessitates a temporary departure from strict chronological order, the reader can readily compare how the different studies treated the interrelated set of conflicts.

The next four columns show the opening and closing dates as ascertained by those of the studies which include the war. While we established a specific date for the onset and termination of every war that we included, the others, particularly Sorokin, did not always do so; thus, when the month and/or day is not indicated, only the year is shown. And in those cases in which the participating dates of the separate entities differ from that of the entire war, such dates are shown alongside the entity name. When one of the four studies excluded a war, a dash (–) is shown in the corresponding cell, and when one of them included the war but not a participant which one of the others *did* include, that exclusion is indicated by an X. Finally, whenever *we* exclude a war, we indicate the reason, as follows:

bd —the war did not meet our minimum battle death requirements
mem—the participants were not qualified system members according to our criteria
civ —the war was civil rather than international in nature
con —the war continued beyond 31 December 1965[1]

In this particular presentation, no specific effort was made to indicate why any of the *other* studies decided to exclude a given war.

Shifting over to the last three columns (Casualty Estimates), we show the losses resulting from hostilities as estimated by the separate authorities. Since Sorokin's study extends only to 1925, and since Wright includes casualty figures only for World War II and after (in his second edition), we use the same column for both studies, with

[1] We cited battle deaths as a reason for exclusion 185 times, civil war as a reason 75 times, membership in the system 20 times, and continuing after 1965 5 times. Some wars were excluded for multiple reasons.

the break clearly labeled.[2] It will be recalled that none of the four projects utilized precisely the same criteria and procedures for estimating casualties; thus the figures will often differ even when there is agreement on the duration and participants.

To recapitulate, Richardson did not ascertain battle deaths for the participants individually, but for the war as a whole; furthermore, he included civilian deaths. We show his estimates exactly as he did. First there is the $\log_{10}$ figure, with the digits to the right of the decimal reflecting his confidence in the estimate; one or two digits on the same line as the base figure indicate medium confidence, and a question mark indicates low confidence in any precision beyond the figure shown. Below each of his $\log_{10}$ figures we show in parentheses the whole number equivalent. As for Sorokin, his estimates are restricted to those sustained by major powers, and often include the missing, wounded, prisoners, and desertions along with battle fatalities. In presenting his casualty figures for the period between 1945 and 1964, Wright follows Richardson in using the $\log_{10}$ notation for all participants in the war as a whole, but does not specify which classes of casualty are included beyond indicating that it is "the number killed." And, as was discussed in earlier chapters, we computed figures for battle-associated deaths for each system member participating. Under all columns but Richardson's, an X is used to signify that a given participant was not included in the war and that casualty estimates were therefore not made. And as before, a dash signifies that the entire war was excluded from the study in question.

[2] Wright does, however, present casualties per decade for England and France (1630–1919) and the United States (1770–1929), as well as for some of the participants in World War I; see Tables 53–56 in his Appendix 22 (1965). We should also note that he treats the Russo-Finnish War of 1939 separately in his first edition but includes it under World War II in the 1965 version.

5.2 THE FOUR STUDIES COMPARED

Entities at War	Inclusion and Date				Casualty Estimates		
	Richardson	Wright	Sorokin	Singer and Small	Richardson	Sorokin	Singer and Small
Russia Georgians (Caucausus)		—	16–25	bd		5,000 X	—
England Maharattas (India)		11/6/17–8/4/18	17–18	11/6/17–6/3/18		1,500 X	2,000 X
Argentina	10/19–10/20	—	—	civ	3? (1,000)	—	—
Holland Sumatrans	19–6/21	—	—	bd	3 (1,000)	—	—
Turkey Arabs (Syria)	20	—	—	bd	3? (1,000)	—	—
Austria-Hungary Neopolitan Republics	20–3/21	—	—	bd	<3? (<1,000)	—	—
Turkey Janina (Epirus)	20–22	—	—	bd	3? (1,000)	—	—
Turkey Nubians	20–22	—	—	bd	3? (1,000)	—	—

Austria-Hungary Sardinia *Carbonarists*	21	–	–	bd	<3? (<1,000)	–	–
Siam Kedah (Malay Peninsula)	21	–	–	mem	3? (1,000)	–	–
Turkey Persia	8/21–22	–	–	bd	3? (>1,000)	–	–
England Ashanti (Gold Coast)	4/21–9/26	–	24–25	bd	3.4 (2,500)	50 X	–
England France Russia Greeks *Turkey* [Greek Independence]	7–10/27 7–10/27 7–10/27 4/21–9/28 4/21–9/28	27 27 27 3/21–2/3/30 3/21–2/3/30	–	X X X 3/25/21–4/25/28 3/25/21–4/25/28	4 (10,000)	–	X X X X 15,000
England France Russia *Turkey* (Navarino Bay)	–	–	27 27 X 27	10/20/27	–	270 229 X X	80 40 60 3,000
Russia Bulgarians *Turkey*	5/28–9/29	4/26/28–9/14/29	28–29 X 28–29	4/26/28–9/24/29	5 (100,000)	36,000 X	50,000 X 80,000
Khokand Khojas *China* (Kashgaria)	6/26 22–2/28 22–2/28	–	–	mem	4.3 (20,000)	–	–

5.2 THE FOUR STUDIES COMPARED – continued

Entities at War	Inclusion and Date				Casualty Estimates		
	Richardson	Wright	Sorokin	Singer and Small	Richardson	Sorokin	Singer and Small
France Spain	23	12/12/21–10/1/23	23	4/7/23–11/13/23	3? (1,000)	3,000 3,500	400 600
Haiti Santo Domingo	–	23	–	mem/civ	–	–	–
Costa Rica Guatemala Honduras Nicaragua Salvador	–	23	–	mem/civ	–	–	–
England Burma	9/23–2/26	3/5/24–2/20/26	24–26	9/24/23–2/24/26	4.3 (20,000)	2,250 X	15,000 X
Holland Bonians	25	–	–	bd	3 (1,000)	–	–
England Bharatpur (India)	12/25–1/26	–	–	bd	3.7 (5,000)	–	–
Argentina Uruguayans *Brazil*	4/25–8/28	3/27/25–9/15/28	–	bd	3.3 (2,000)	–	–
Russia Persia	25–28	9/28/26–2/28/28	26–28	9/28/26–2/28/28	3.4 (2,500)	7,200 X	5,000 X

England Tasmania	25–30	—	—	bd	3.3 (2,000)	—	—
Holland Javanese	7/25–2/30	—	—	7/23/25–3/28/30	4 (10,000)	—	15,000 X
Turkey Janissaries (Egypt)	6/26–10/26	—	—	bd	4.6 (40,000)	—	—
England Portugal *Spain*	 —	11/22/26–27	26 X 26	 bd	 —	200 X X	 —
Costa Rica Guatemala Honduras Nicaragua Salvador	27–29	—	—	bd/civ	3? (1,000)	—	—
France Algerians	4/27–5/30	—	—	bd	3? (1,000)	—	—
Morocco Algerians *France*	1/44–10/44, 10/47 11/39–10/47 11/39–10/47	X 6/14/30–12/23/47 6/14/30–12/23/47	X 30–47 30–47	bd	3.6 (4,000)	X X 10,200	—
Argentina	28–31	—	—	civ	2.6? (400)	—	—
England France Spain *Portugal*	1/29, 4/34– 5/34 7/31, 4/34– 5/34 4/34–5/34 7/28–5/34	31–5/24/34	26 34 34 26, 34	bd/civ	4?	200 200 500 X	—

5.2 THE FOUR STUDIES COMPARED—continued

Entities at War	Inclusion and Date				Casualty Estimates		
	Richardson	Wright	Sorokin	Singer and Small	Richardson	Sorokin	Singer and Small
Mexico Spain	29	—	—	bd	3 (1,000)	—	—
Chile	29–4/30	—	—	civ	2.6 (400)	—	—
Muscat Zanzibar	29–37	—	—	mem	3? (1,000)	—	—
Russia Circassians	29–40	—	26–50	bd	4 (10,000)	71,750 X	—
France Madagascar	—	—	29	bd	—	100 X	—
China Khokand	9/30–11/30	—	—	mem	3? (1,000)	—	—
France	7/30	—	—	civ	3.3 (2,000)	—	—
Russia Poles	11/30–9/31	7/29/30–9/7/31	30–31	2/7/31–10/18/31	4.2 (16,000)	20,800 X	15,000 X
Turkey Herzogovinans *Bosnians* *Albanians*	30–11/31	—	—	bd	3? or 4? (1,000 or 10,000)	—	—

England France Belgians *Holland*	X X 30–33 30–33	31 31 8/25/30–33 8/25/30–33	30–33 32 30–33 30–33	bd	$3._{3}$ (2,000)	200 500 X 10,000	–
Austria-Hungary *Modena* *Parma*	–	–	31	bd	–	100 X X	–
Turkey Syrians *Egyptians*	11/31–5/32 3/32–3/33 3/32–3/33	11/31–4/15/33 X 11/31–4/15/33	–	11/1/31–12/21/32	4 (10,000)	–	10,000 X X
Costa Rica Guatemala Honduras Nicaragua Salvador	–	31–45	–	mem/civ	–	–	–
Argentina	4/33–4/34	–	–	civ	3? (1,000)	–	–
Portugal Matahanganans (Mozambique)	33–36	–	–	bd	3 (1,000)	–	–
France Annamese	33–39	–	–	bd	$3._{4}$ (2,500)	–	–
England Portugal *Spain*	10/33–6/40 4/34–8/39 10/33–6/40	10/14/33–9/12/47 44 10/14/33–9/12/47	X X 33–40	bd/civ	4 (10,000)	X X 16,000	–
Turkey (Egyptians) Palestinians	34	–	–	bd	3? (1,000)	–	–

5.2 THE FOUR STUDIES COMPARED—continued

Entities at War	Inclusion and Date				Casualty Estimates		
	Richardson	Wright	Sorokin	Singer and Small	Richardson	Sorokin	Singer and Small
England Hottentots Boers *Kaffirs* (South Africa)	12/34–5/35	–	–	bd	$2._7$ (500)	–	–
Austria-Hungary *Bosnians* *Herzogovinans*	–	–	35–46	bd	–	1,100 X X	–
Brazil	9/35–3/45	–	–	civ	3? (1,000)	–	–
Argentina Boliva Peru *Chile*	X 7/36–1/39 7/36–1/39 7/16–1/39	38 34 34 38	–	bd	3 (1,000)	–	–
Turkey Bosnians	36–37	–	–	bd	3 (1,000)	–	–
Mexico Texans	36	35–36	–	10/1/35–4/22/36	$3._0$ (1,000)	–	1,000 X
Argentina Chile	–	36	–	mem	–	–	–
Boers Matabele	36–37	–	–	mem	3 (1,000)	–	–

		9/2/39–2/3/52					
Argentina	36–2/52	38	X	7/19/51–2/3/52	4.4	X	800
Brazil	5/51–2/52	52	X	7/19/51–2/3/52	(25,000)	X	500
England	7/45– 47	X	45	X		600	X
France	3/38–10/40	X	30–40, 45–48	X		200	X
	7/45–8/50						
Uruguay	8/36–2/52	38	X	X		X	X
Ma-Kalanga	37	–	–	mem	3?	–	–
Matabele					(1,000)		
(South Africa)							
Afghanistan	37–38	–	–	mem	3?	–	–
Persia					(1,000)		
Austria-Hungary	–	–	38	bd	–	100	–
Montenegro						X	
France	–	–	38–39	bd	–	200	–
Mexico						X	
England	2/38–2/40	–	–	bd	4.2	–	–
Zulus					(16,000)		
(Natal)							
England	10/38–10/42	10/11/38–9/42	38–42	10/1/38–10/12/42	4.3	1,000	20,000
Afghanistan					(20,000)	X	X
England	11/13/39	–	–	bd	2.6	–	–
Khelat					(400)		
(India)							
Austria-Hungary	9/40–11/40	6/8/39–11/27/41	40	X	4	100	X
		40					
England	8/40–11/40	40	40–41	9/9/40–11/27/40	(10,000)	400	10
Egyptians	5/39–1/41	39	X	X		X	X
France	X	39	X	X		X	X
Turkey	5/39–1/41	39	40–41	6/10/39–6/24/39, 9/9/40–11/27/40		X	10,000

5.2 THE FOUR STUDIES COMPARED—continued

Entities at War	Inclusion and Date				Casualty Estimates		
	Richardson	Wright	Sorokin	Singer and Small	Richardson	Sorokin	Singer and Small
Russia Khiva (Central Asia)	39	39–42	39–40	bd	3? (1,000)	80 X	—
Columbia	39	—	—	civ	3? (1,000)	—	—
England France *China*	9/39–8/42 X 9/39–8/42	6/22/40–8/29/42	40–42 X 40–42	bd	4? (10,000)	2,250 X X	—
Matabele Mashonas (South Africa)	40	—	—	mem	3? (1,000)	—	—
Tibet Dogras	41	—	—	bd	3.6 (4,000)	—	—
Peru Bolivia	—	—	—	10/19/41–11/18/41	—	—	1,000 X
Turkey Bosnia	41	—	—	bd	3? (1,000)	—	—
England Sind (India)	1/43–6/43	—	—	bd	3.6 (4,000)	—	—

England Gwalior (India)	12/43	–	–	bd	3.2 (1,600)	–	–
France Morocco	–	7/6/44–9/10/44	43–44	bd	–	200 X	–
England Borneo Pirates	45	–	–	bd	3? (1,000)	–	–
France Madagascar	–	–	45	bd	–	100 X	–
Turkey Maronites *Druzes* (Syria)	45	–	–	bd	3? (1,000)	–	–
England Sikhs	12/45–3/46	–	43–49	12/13/45–3/9/46	3.6 (4,000)	1,050 X	1,500 X
Austria-Hungary Poles (Galicia)	46	–	–	bd	3 (1,000)	–	–
Mexico United States	4/46–2/48	5/13/46–2/2/48	–	5/12/46–2/12/48	4.2 (16,000)	–	6,000 11,000
Holland Balinese	46–6/49	–	–	bd	3.3 (2,000)	–	–
France Cochin China	–	–	47	bd	–	100 X	–
China Kashgaria	47–1/48	–	–	mem	3? (1,000)	–	–

5.2 THE FOUR STUDIES COMPARED—continued

Entities at War	Inclusion and Date				Casualty Estimates		
	Richardson	Wright	Sorokin	Singer and Small	Richardson	Sorokin	Singer and Small
Spain	—	—	47–49	civ	—	6,000	—
Austria-Hungary	—	3/19/48–3/23/49	48–49	3/24/48–8/9/48, 3/20/49–3/23/49	—	3,200	5,600
France			X	X		X	X
Sardinia			48–49	3/24/48–8/9/48, 3/20/49–3/23/49		7,000	3,400
Austria-Hungary	48–49	—	—	civ	4.9	—	—
France							
Germany					(80,000)		
Italy							
Russia							
Turkey							
Wallachia							
Revolutionaries							
England	—	—	—	10/10/48–3/12/49	—	—	1,500
Sikhs							X
Austria-Hungary	X	3/24/48–1/11/51	X	X		X	X
Prussia	48–50		48–49	4/10/48–8/26/48, 3/25/49–7/10/49	3?	2,800	3,500
Denmark	48–50		48–49	4/10/48–8/26/48, 3/25/49–7/10/49	(1,000)	X	2,500
Austria-Hungary	—	10/3/48–9/13/49	48–49	9/9/48–8/13/49	—	3,200	45,000
Russia			49	7/16/49–8/13/49		600	14,500
Hungarians			48–49	9/9/48–8/13/49		X	X

Austria-Hungary	–	–	X	5/8/49–7/1/49	–	X	100
France			49	4/30/49		100	500
				6/3/49–7/1/49			
Two Sicilies			X	5/8/49–7/1/49			100
				4/30/49			
Rome (Papal States)			49	5/8/49–7/1/49			1,500
		49–58					
Costa Rica	–	54	–	bd	–	–	–
Honduras		49					
Salvador		49					
Guatemala		49					
Nicaragua		49					
England	12/50–12/52	–	51–52	bd	$3._{2}$	400	–
Basutos	1/52–12/52					X	
Hottentots	3/51–12/52				(1,600)	X	
Kaffirs	12/50–12/52					X	
Chile	9/51–12/51	–	–	civ	$3._{3}$	–	–
					(2,000)		
France	12/51	–	–	civ	$2._{7}$	–	–
					(500)		
China	51–64	8/50–7/19/64	–	civ	6.3	–	–
					(2,000,000)		
Dards	52	–	–	mem	$3._{3}$	–	–
Dogras					(2,000)		
(India)							
Russia	–	7/52–1/31/64	51–75	bd	–	1,750	–
Turkestan						X	
England	4/52–1/53	–	52–53	bd	3	1,500	–
Burma					(1,000)	X	

5.2 THE FOUR STUDIES COMPARED—continued

Entities at War	Inclusion and Date				Casualty Estimates		
	Richardson	Wright	Sorokin	Singer and Small	Richardson	Sorokin	Singer and Small
Turkey Montenegro	12/52–3/53	2/12/53–3/13/53	—	12/2/52–3/13/53	$3._8$ (6,500)	—	5,000 X
France England Sardinia Turkey *Russia*	4/54–2/56 4/54–2/56 1/55–2/56 10/53–2/56 10/53–2/56	10/23/53–3/30/56 54 54 54 53 53	54–56 54–56 55–56 53–56 53–56	3/31/54–3/1/56 1/10/55–3/1/56 3/31/54–3/1/56 10/23/53–3/1/56 10/23/53–3/1/56	5.4 (250,000)	27,450 52,200 3,360 X 144,000	22,000 95,000 2,200 45,000 100,000
Colombia	4/54–11/54	—	—	civ	3? (1,000)	—	—
England (Boers) Bantu	54	—	—	bd	3.4_5 (2,800)	—	—
British Santals (Bengal)	55	—	—	bd	3? (1,000)	—	—
Haiti Santo Domingo	—	55–56	—	mem	—	—	—
Nicaragua	5/55–5/57	—	—	civ	$3._3$ (2,000)	—	—
England Persia	11/56–4/57	—	56–57	10/25/56–3/14/57	3 (1,000)	400 X	500 1,500

England France *China*	10/56–6/58, 4/59–10/60 11/57–6/58, 6/59–10/60 10/56–6/58, 6/59–10/60	10/22/56–10/24/60	56–60 X 56–60	bd	4? (10,000)	3,750 X X	—
China Khokand (Kashgaria)	57	—	—	mem	3.$_4$ (2,500)	—	—
France Fulas (Senegal)	57	—	—	bd	3? (1,000)	—	—
England Indians	5/57–4/59	5/10/57–7/8/59	57–58	5/10/57–4/7/59	4? (10,000)	1,500 X	3,500 X
France Annam	—	—	57–62	bd	—	1,200 X	—
Turkey Montenegro	58	—	—	5/4/58–6/5/59	3.$_4$ (2,500)	—	3,000 X
Mexico	58–1/61	—	—	civ	3 or 4? (1,000 or 10,000?)	—	—
Peru Ecuador	—	59	—	bd	—	—	—
Austria-Hungary *France* *Sardinia* *Italians*	4/59–7/8/59	4/23/59–11/10/59 4/23/59–11/10/59 4/23/59–11/10/59 X	59	4/29/59–7/12/59 5/3/59–7/12/59 4/29/59–7/12/59 X	4.3$_4$ (22,000)	13,000 6,800 6,000 X	12,500 7,500 2,500 X

5.2 THE FOUR STUDIES COMPARED—continued

Entities at War	Inclusion and Date				Casualty Estimates		
	Richardson	Wright	Sorokin	Singer and Small	Richardson	Sorokin	Singer and Small
Morocco Spain	10/59–4/60	10/22/59–4/27/60	59–60	10/22/59–3/26/60	3.9 (8,000)	X 2,100	6,000 4,000
Holland Boninese (Celebes)	2/59–1/60	–	–	bd	3 (1,000)	–	–
Argentina	10/59–9/61	–	–	civ	3? (1,000)	–	–
Colombia	59–62	–	–	civ	3? (1,000)	–	–
Holland Banjermasinese (South Borneo)	4/59–63	–	–	bd	3? (1,000)	–	–
Russia Circassians	59–64	–	–	bd	3 (1,000)	–	–
France Arabs (Syria)	–	–	60	bd	–	100 X	–
Druses Moslems *Christians* (Lebanon)	60	–	–	bd	3.4 (2,500)	–	–

Italy	5/60–3/61	5/11/60–2/13/61	60–61	9/11/60–9/29/60	3.3 (2,000)	1,100	300
Papal States	5/60–3/61	X	X	9/11/60–9/29/60		X	700
France	X	5/11/60–2/13/61	60–61	X		600	X
Italy			–	10/15/60–1/19/61		–	600
Two Sicilies	5/60–3/61	5/11/60–2/13/61					400
Arabs Africans (Tanganyika)	60–69	–	–	mem	3? (1,000)	–	–
Ethiopia	61	–	–	civ	3.3 (2,000)	–	–
France Cochinchinese	–	–	61–62	bd	–	200 X	–
United States	4/61–4/65	4/19/61–4/2/66	–	civ	5.8 (630,000)	–	–
England	12/61–4/62	4/4/62–6/27/67	X	X	4 (10,000)	X	X
France	12/61–3/67		61–67	4/16/62–2/5/67		140,000	8,000
Spain	12/61–4/62		X	X		X	X
Mexico	12/61–3/67		61–67	4/16/62–2/5/67		X	12,000
China	61–10/73, 76–1/78	–	–	civ	5.4 (250,000)	–	–
Turkey Montenegro	62	–	–	bd	3? (1,000)	–	–
Turkey Serbs	62	–	–	bd	3? (1,000)	–	–
Italy Garibaldians	–	–	62	bd	–	X 400	–

5.2 THE FOUR STUDIES COMPARED—continued

Entities at War	Inclusion and Date				Casualty Estimates		
	Richardson	Wright	Sorokin	Singer and Small	Richardson	Sorokin	Singer and Small
England France Holland *Japan*	62–64	8/13/63–4/17/69 64 X 63	—	bd	3.? (1,000)	—	—
France China	—	—	62–64	bd	—	600 X	—
United States Sioux (Minnesota)	62–67	—	—	bd	3 (1,000)	—	—
Guatemala *Honduras* *Nicaragua* *Salvador*	—	1/23/63–11/15/63	—	bd/civ	—	—	—
England Wahabis (N. W. India)	10/18/63– 12/22/63	—	—	bd	2.95 (900)	—	—
Colombia Ecuador	63	10/63–12/30/63	—	11/22/63–12/6/63	3 (1,000)	—	300 700
Russia Poles	1/63–65	1/22/63–8/1/64	63–64	4/19/64–1/22/65	3? (1,000)	2,070 X	5,000 X
Argentina	63–64	—	—	civ	3? (1,000)	—	—

Spain	–	–	63–65	bd	–	2,000	–
Santo Domingo						X	
England	4/63–2/66	–	63–69	bd	2.6	1,400	–
Maoris					(400)	X	
(New Zealand)							
Austria-Hungary	2/64–4/64,	2/1/64–10/30/64	64	2/1/64–4/25/64,	3.6	1,000	500
Prussia	6/64–8/64				(4,000)	1,110	1,000
Denmark				6/25/64–7/20/64		X	3,000
Bolivia	X	9/25/65–5/9/66	–	X	3	–	X
		64					
Chile	9/65	64		10/25/65–5/9/66	(1,000)		100
Peru	64–65	63		1/14/66–5/9/66			600
Ecuador	X	64		X			X
Spain	64	63		10/25/65–5/9/66			300
England	65	–	–	bd	3?	–	–
Bhutan					(1,000)		
England	10/11/65–	–	–	bd	2.67	–	–
Jamaicans	11/65				(470)		
Boers	65–67	–	–	bd	2.6	–	–
Basutos					(400)		
Russia	12/65–6/68	–	–	bd	3	–	–
Bokhara					(1,000)		
Argentina	3/65–3/70	4/14/65–3/1/70	–	3/5/65–3/1/70	6	–	10,000
Brazil	10/64–3/70	63		11/12/64–3/1/70	(1,000,000)		100,000
Uruguay	4/64–3/70	64		X			X
Paraguay	11/64–3/70	63		11/12/64–3/1/70			X

5.2 THE FOUR STUDIES COMPARED—continued

Entities at War	Inclusion and Date				Casualty Estimates		
	Richardson	Wright	Sorokin	Singer and Small	Richardson	Sorokin	Singer and Small
Austria-Hungary	6/16/66–8/22/66	6/15/66–8/23/66	66	6/15/66–7/26/66	4.6	42,000	20,000
Baden	X		X	6/15/66–7/26/66		X	100
Bavaria	7/66–8/66		X	6/15/66–7/26/66	(40,000)	X	500
France	X		X	X		X	X
Hanover	6/14/66–6/29/66		X	6/15/66–6/29/66		X	500
Hesse	X		X	6/15/66–7/26/66		X	200
North German States	X		X	X		X	X
Saxony	6/15/66–7/66		X	6/15/66–7/26/66		X	600
Wuerttemberg	X		X	6/15/66–7/26/66		X	100
Prussia	6/14/66–8/22/66		66	6/15/66–7/26/66		25,978*	10,000
Sardinia	6/20/66–8/12/66		66	6/15/66–7/26/66		11,000 *Includes lesser German states	4,000
Japan	66–68	–	–	civ	3 (1,000)	–	–
Spain	–	1/3/66–9/28/68	–	civ	–	–	–
England France Greece *Turkey* (Crete)	–	9/2/66–69	–	bd	–	–	–

France Papal States *Garibaldians*	67	–	67	bd	2.6 (400)	100 X 300	–
Ethiopia	67	–	–	civ	3.5 (3,100)	–	–
England Ethiopia	10/67–5/68	–	67–68	bd	3.0 (1,000)	400 X	–
Spain	–	–	68–74	civ	–	14,000	–
Spain Cuba	10/68–1/78	10/10/68–2/10/78	–	10/10/68–2/10/78	5.3 (200,000)	–	100,000 X
Egypt Zobeir's Army (Bahr-el-Ghazel)	69	–	–	mem	3? (1,000)	–	–
Italy Papal States	–	–	70	bd	–	600 X	–
Baden Bavaria Prussia (N. German Confederation) Wuerttemberg *France*	7/70–1/71	7/19/70–5/10/71	X X 70–71 X 70–71	7/19/70–11/22/70 7/19/70–11/15/70 7/19/70–2/26/71 7/19/70–11/25/70 7/19/70–2/26/71	5.4 (250,000)	X X 267,874 X 396,000	1,000 5,500 40,000 1,000 140,000
France (Paris)	3/18/71– 5/29/71	–	–	civ	4.3 (20,000)	–	–
France Algerians	3/71–1/72	–	–	bd	3 or less (–1,000)	–	–
Spain	5/72–2/76	4/8/72–2/28/76	76–85	civ	4 (10,000)	20,000	–

5.2 THE FOUR STUDIES COMPARED—continued

Entities at War	Inclusion and Date				Casualty Estimates		
	Richardson	Wright	Sorokin	Singer and Small	Richardson	Sorokin	Singer and Small
England Ashanti (Gold Coast)	1/73–2/74	10/14/73–2/13/74	74	bd	3 (1,000)	48 X	—
France Tonkin	73–74	—	73–74	bd	3? (1,000)	4 X	—
Egypt Dafurians	73–75	—	—	mem	3? (1,000)	—	—
Holland Achin (East Indies)	4/73–9/79, 9/80–1908	—	—	3/26/73–9/–/78	5.4 (250,000)	—	6,000 X
Argentina	10/74–5/75	—	—	civ	3? (1,000)	—	—
Egypt Ethiopia	9/75–3/76	—	—	mem	3.8 (6,400)	—	—
Turkey Balkan Peoples	—	—	—	7/3/75–4/12/77	—	—	10,000 X
United States Sioux	76–77	—	—	bd	3 (1,000)	—	—
Colombia	76–77	—	—	civ	3? (1,000)	—	—

Japan	1/77–9/77	–	–	civ	4.0 (10,000)	–	–
Russia	4/77–2/78	5/13/77–7/13/78 77	77–78	4/12/77–1/3/78	5.4	66,000	120,000
Bulgarians	5/76–2/78	X	X	X		X	X
Montenegrins	8/76–11/76, 5/77–2/78	76	X	X	(250,000)	X	X
Serbians	7/76–11/76, 12/77–2/78	76	X	X		X	X
Rumanians	8/75–2/78	X	X	X		X	X
Bosnians	8/75–2/78	X	X	X		X	X
Herzogovinans	8/75–2/78	X	X	X		X	X
Turkey	8/75–2/78	77	77–78	4/12/77–1/3/78		X	165,000
England Kaffirs (South Africa)	77–78	–	–	bd	3? (1,000)	–	–
Austria-Hungary Bosnia-Herzogovina	7/78–10/78	–	–	7/29/78–10/–/78	3.8 (6,400)	–	3,500 X
England Afghanistan	11/78–5/79, 9/79–9/80	1/1/79–10/3/81	78–80	11/20/78–5/26/79, 9/13/79–9/2/80	3.6 (4,000)	2,250 X	4,000 X
Russia Turkomans	78–81	–	–	bd	4.3 (20,000)	–	–
Egypt Slavers (Bahr-el-Ghazel)	78–79	–	–	mem	3.4 (2,500)	–	–
Argentina Patagonians	78–83	–	–	bd	3? (1,000)	–	–
England Zulus	1/79–8/79	1/23/79–9/1/79	79	1/11/79–7/4/79	3.6 (4,000)	260 X	3,500 X

5.2 THE FOUR STUDIES COMPARED—continued

Entities at War	Inclusion and Date				Casualty Estimates		
	Richardson	Wright	Sorokin	Singer and Small	Richardson	Sorokin	Singer and Small
England Basutos	79–81	—	—	bd	3? (1,000)	—	—
Bolivia Peru *Chile*	2/79–12/83 4/79–10/83 2/79–12/83	4/5/79–3/28/84	—	2/14/79–12/11/83	$4._{1}$ (12,000)	—	1,000 3,000 10,000
Argentina	80	—	—	civ	3 (1,000)	—	—
Uganda	80	—	—	civ	$3._{3}$ (2,000)	—	—
England Transvaal	—	12/20/80–8/8/81	80–81	bd	—	1,700 X	—
Austria-Hungary Dalmatians	82	—	—	bd	3 (1,000)	—	—
France Tunisia	4/81–12/81	3/31/81–4/4/82	81–82	bd	3 (1,000)	800 X,	—
England Egypt *Sudanese*	3/83–5/85 8/81–5/85 8/81–5/85	—	81–85	9/13/82–12/30/85	4.44 (28,000)	1,500 X X	20,000* X *Eng. and Egypt
England Italy	6/85–95 12/93–7/94	—	—	bd	4	—	—

Ethiopia Egyptians Suakin Tribes Sudanese Darfurians Shilluks	85–3/89 6/85–95 10/86–1/91 6/85–95 88–2/89 90–92				(10,000)		
England Egypt *Sudan*	3/96–1/00	–	96–99	bd	4.2 (16,000)	3,000 X X	–
England Egypt	4/82–9/82	7/11/82–9/7/82	82–84	bd	3.2 (1,600)	2,250 X	–
China Annam *France* (Franco-Tonkinese)	83–6/85 3/82–6/85 3/82–6/85	12/82–8/9/85 X 12/82–8/9/85	X 83–85 83–85	X 4/25/82–6/14/84 4/25/82–6/14/84	4 (10,000)	X X 4,200	X X 4,500
China France (Sino-French)	–	–	84–84	6/15/84–6/9/85		X 800	10,000 2,100
Oman *Indabayin* *Rehbayin*	83–85	–	–	mem	3? (1,000)	–	–
France Hovas (Madagascar)	83–85	–	–	bd	3? (1,000)	–	–
Costa Rica Guatemala *Honduras* *Nicaragua* *Salvador*	–	3/18/84–4/14/85	–	X 3/28/85–4/14/85 X X 3/28/85–4/14/85	–	–	X 800 X X 200

5.2 THE FOUR STUDIES COMPARED—continued

Entities at War	Inclusion and Date				Casualty Estimates		
	Richardson	Wright	Sorokin	Singer and Small	Richardson	Sorokin	Singer and Small
Colombia	11/84–8/85	–	–	civ	3? (1,000)	–	–
Russia Afghanistan	3/30/85	–	–	bd	$2._8$ (640)	–	–
Serbia Bulgaria	85	11/13/85–3/3/86	–	11/2/85–12/7/85	$3._4$ (2,500)	–	2,000 X
England Burma	11/85–86	–	85–89	bd	$3._8$ (6,400)	3,750 X	–
Uganda	85–90	–	–	civ	3? (1,000)	–	–
England *Arabs* *Yaos* (Nyasaland)	85–96	–	–	bd	3? (1,000)	–	–
Italy Ethiopia	1/87	–	–	bd	$2._4$ (200)	–	–
Germany *Arabs* *Swahili* (Tanganyika)	8/88–90	–	–	bd	3? (1,000)	–	–

Guatemala Salvador	—	7/23/89–11/15/89	—	bd	—	—	—
United States Sioux	11/90–1/91	—	—	bd	2.6 (400)	—	—
France Senegalese	90–91	—	90–92	bd	3? (1,000)	700 X	—
Chile	1/91	—	—	civ	4.0 (10,000)	—	—
Holland Sasaks *Balinese*	7/94–11/94 91–11/94 91–11/94	—	—	bd	3 (1,000)	—	—
Uganda	92	—	—	civ	3? or less? (<1,000)	—	—
France Senegalese (Dahomey)	92–94	—	—	bd	3? (1,000)	—	—
Belgium Congolese *Arabs*	10/92–2/94	—	—	bd	4.3 (20,000)	—	—
Brazil	6/92–6/94	—	—	civ	3? (1,000)	—	—
France Sudanese	—	—	93	bd	—	100 X	—
France Siam	—	—	93	bd	—	100 X	—

5.2 THE FOUR STUDIES COMPARED—continued

Entities at War	Inclusion and Date				Casualty Estimates		
	Richardson	Wright	Sorokin	Singer and Small	Richardson	Sorokin	Singer and Small
Bornu Raheb's Army (Chad)	93	—	—	mem	3.6 (4,000)	—	—
Uganda	93	—	—	civ	3? (1,000)	—	—
Morocco Spain	—	—	93–94	bd	—	X 2,500	—
France Morocco	—	—	93–94	bd	—	800 X	—
France Tuaregs (Timbuctou)	93–04	—	—	bd	3? (1,000)	—	—
France Tonkinese	—	—	94	bd	—	400 X	—
China Japan	7/94–3/95	8/1/94–4/17/95	—	8/1/94–3/30/95	4 (10,000)	—	10,000 5,000
Peru	94–95	—	—	civ	3 (1,000)	—	—
Italy Ethiopia	4/94–10/96	96–10/26/96	95–96	12/7/95–11/21/96	4.2 (16,000)	2,100 X	9,000 X

Turkey Armenians	94–97	—	—	bd	4.6 (40,000)	—	—
Germans Wahemes (East Africa)	10/94–7/98	—	—	bd	3? (1,000)	—	—
France Madagascar	11/94–1/01	3/1/95–8/8/96	83–97	12/12/94–10/1/95	3.8 (6,400)	6,350 X	6,000 X
England Ashanti (Gold Coast)	3/00–*9/03*	1/96–1/19/96	95–96	bd	3? (1,000)	400 X	—
England Masrui (Kenya)	95–96	—	—	bd	3 or less? (1,000)	—	—
Turkey Druzes (Syria)	96	—	—	bd	3 or less? (1,000)	—	—
Spain Filipinos	—	—	—	5/30/96–5/1/98	—	—	5,000 X
Brazil	96–97	—	—	civ	3.2 (1,600)	—	—
England Mashonas Matabele (Rhodesia)	96–99	—	—	bd	3? (1,000)	—	—
England *Cretans* *Greece*	—	5/24/96–11/26/98 96 X 97	97–98	bd	—	400 X X	—

5.2 THE FOUR STUDIES COMPARED—continued

Entities at War	Inclusion and Date				Casualty Estimates		
	Richardson	Wright	Sorokin	Singer and Small	Richardson	Sorokin	Singer and Small
Greece Turkey	2/97–5/97	4/17/97–12/4/97	–	2/15/97–5/19/97	$3._{3}$ (2,000)	–	600 1,400
Costa Rica Nicaragua	–	3/20/97–4/29/97	–	mem	–	–	–
England Beni (Nigeria)	1/97	–	–	bd	3? (1,000)	–	–
England *Bunyoro* *Buganda*	6/97	–	–	bd	3 (1,000)	–	–
England Moslems (N. W. India)	97–98	–	–	bd	3? (1,000)	–	–
England Sierra Leone	98	–	–	bd	$3._{4}$? (2,500)	–	–
Spain Cuba	–	–	–	2/24/95–4/2/98		–	50,000 X
Spain *United States* *Cubans* *Filipinos*	2/95–8/98 4/98–8/98 2/95–8/98 X	4/21/98–12/10/98	98 98 X X	4/21/98–8/12/98 X X	5.3 (200,000)	25,000 X X X	5,000 5,000 X X

France Bornu (Chad)	99–01	–	–	bd	3? (1,000)	–	–
United States Filipinos	2/99–4/02	–	–	2/4/99–7/04/02	4? (10,000)	–	4,500
Colombia	7/99–11/02	–	–	civ	5.$_{2}$ (160,000)	–	–
England *Orange Free State* *Transvaal*	10/99–5/02	12/12/99–5/31/02	99–00	10/11/99–5/31/02	4.4 (25,000)	2,200 X X	20,000 X X
England Italy Ethiopia *Somalians*	99–04	–	01–02 X X 01–02	bd	3.$_{2}$ (1,600)	600 X X X	–
Austria-Hungary Belgium England France Germany Holland Italy Japan Russia Spain United States *China (Boxers)*	6/00–9/00 X 6/00–9/00 6/00–9/00 6/00–9/00 X 6/00–9/00 6/00–9/00 6/00–9/00 X 6/00–9/00 6/00–9/00	6/17/00–9/7/01	X X 00 00 00 X X X 00 X X 00	bd/civ	4.$_{2}$ (16,000)	X X 80 100 200 X X X 1,000 X X X	–
England Germany Italy *Venezuela*	–	12/11/02–2/13/03	–	bd	–	–	–

5.2 THE FOUR STUDIES COMPARED—continued

Entities at War	Inclusion and Date				Casualty Estimates		
	Richardson	Wright	Sorokin	Singer and Small	Richardson	Sorokin	Singer and Small
England Moslems (Nigeria)	1/03–5/03	–	–	bd	3? or 2? (1,000 or 100)	–	–
England Tibet	04	00	03–04	bd	3? (1,000)	200 X	–
Germany *Herreros* *Hottentots* (S. W. Africa)	03–08 04–08 03–08	–	04	bd	$4._9$ (80,000)	100 X X	–
Japan Russia	2/04–8/05	2/6/04–9/15/05	04–05	2/8/04–9/15/05	5.1 (127,000)	X 170,000	85,000 45,000
France Senussi (Central Africa)	04–11	–	–	bd	3? (1,000)	–	–
England Nandi (Victoria Nyanza)	05	–	–	bd	3? or 2? (1,000 or 100)	–	–
Russia	1/22/05	–	–	civ	$3._0$ (1,000)	–	–
Russia Jews	10/05	–	–	bd	3.4_8 (3,040)	–	–

China Tibet	4/05–9/06	—	—	bd	3? (1,000)	—	—
Germany Wangoni (Tanzania)	7/05–1/07	—	—	bd	5.4 (250,000)	—	—
England Zulus	3/06–7/06	—	—	bd	3.7 (5,000)	—	—
Honduras Salvador *Guatemala*	—	7/06–12/20/07	—	5/27/06–7/20/06	—	—	300 300 400
Honduras Salvador *Nicaragua*	—	07	—	2/19/07–4/23/07	—	—	300 300 400
Rumanians Jews	3/07	—	—	bd	3? (1,000)	—	—
France Moroccans	3/07, 10/10–11, 12	—	07–12	bd	3? (1,000) 3.2 (1,600)	6,000 X	—
Holland Venezuela	08	—	—	bd	3? (1,000)	—	—
England Indians	—	—	08	bd	—	750 X	—
Turkey Armenians	4/09	—	—	bd	3.8 (6,400)	—	—
Morocco Spain	7/09–10	—	09	7/7/09–3/23/10	4? (10,000)	42,000 X	12,000 8,000

5.2 THE FOUR STUDIES COMPARED—continued

Entities at War	Inclusion and Date				Casualty Estimates		
	Richardson	Wright	Sorokin	Singer and Small	Richardson	Sorokin	Singer and Small
Mexico United States	10–20 13–7/14, 1/16–2/17	11/20/10–	–	civ/bd	5.4 (250,000)	–	–
England Italy	11/15–2/17 9/29/11– 10/12/17	9/29/11–10/18/12	X 11–12	9/29/11–10/18/12	4.2	X 3,000	X 6,000
Turkey	9/29/11– 10/12/17		11–12		(16,000)	X	14,000
Sanusi	9/29/11–4/17		X	X		X	X
China	10/10/11–2/12 13 13–14 4/18/17–4/25/18 7/6/17–3/18 5/19/20–20 12/27–12/36 28 3/29–5/29 10/29–12/29 4/30–10/30	–	–	civ	3? (1,000) 4 (10,000) 4 (10,000) 2.6 (400) 3.4 (2,500) 3.6 (4,000) 6.1 (1,275,000) 5.3 (200,000) 3? (1,000) 3? (1,000) 4.8 (64,000)	–	–

Bulgaria Greece Montenegro Serbia *Turkey*	10/12–5/13	10/1/12–5/30/13	–	10/17/12–12/3/12 2/3/13–4/19/13 X 10/17/12–12/3/12 2/3/13–4/19/13	4_8 (64,000)	–	32,000 5,000 X 15,000 30,000
China Tibet	12–13	–	–	bd	3? (1,000)	–	–
France *El Hiba* *Caids* S. Morocco	12–5/13	–	–	bd	2_7 (500)	–	–
Bulgaria *Greece* *Rumania* *Serbia* *Turkey*	6/30/13– 8/10/13 6/30/13– 8/10/13 7/13–8/10/13 6/30/13– 8/10/13 7/13–8/10/13	6/30/13–8/10/13	–	6/30/13–7/30/13 6/30/13–7/30/13 7/11/13–7/30/13 6/30/13–7/30/13 7/15/13–7/30/13	4? (10,000)	–	18,000 2,500 1,500 18,500 20,000
China Banditry	13–14	–	–	civ	4 (10,000)	–	–
British Dervishas (Somaliland)	13–20	–	–	bd	3? (1,000)	–	–
France Moroccans *Zaians*	14–17	–	–	bd	3 (1,000)	–	–

5.2 THE FOUR STUDIES COMPARED—continued

Entities at War	Inclusion and Date				Casualty Estimates		
	Richardson	Wright	Sorokin	Singer and Small	Richardson	Sorokin	Singer and Small
Armenians	2/15–8/18	X	X	X	7.2	X	X
Australia	8/14–11/18	X	X	X		X	X
Belgium	8/3/14–11/18	8/28/14–11/11/18	X	8/4/14–11/11/18	16,000,000	X	87,500
Brazil	X	10/26/17–11/11/18	X	X		X	X
Canada	8/14–11/18	X	X	X		X	X
China	X	8/14/17–11/11/18	X	X		X	X
Costa Rica	X	5/24/18–11/11/18	X	X		X	X
Czechoslovakia	7/17–11/18	6/30/18–11/11/18	X	X		X	X
Cuba	X	4/7/17–11/11/18	X	X		X	X
England	8/14–11/18	8/4/14–11/11/18	14–18	8/5/14–11/11/18		3,070,000	908,000
France	8/14–11/18	8/3/14–11/11/18	14–18	8/3/14–11/11/18		3,660,000	1,350,000
Greece	6/17–11/18	11/24/16–11/11/18	X	6/29/17–11/11/18		X	5,000
Guatemala	X	4/22/18–11/11/18	X	X		X	X
Hungary	X	7/28/14–11/3/18	X	X		X	X
Hejaz	5/16–1/19	3/19/17–10/30/18	X	X		X	X
Haiti	X	7/15/18–11/11/18	X	X		X	X
Honduras	X	7/19/18–11/11/18	X	X		X	X
India	8/14–11/18	X	X	X		X	X
Italy	5/15–11/18	5/24/15–11/11/18	14–18	5/23/15–11/11/18		1,780,000	650,000
Japan	8/23/14–11/18	8/23/14–11/11/18	X	8/23/14–11/11/18		X	330
Liberia	X	8/14/17–11/11/18	X	X		X	X
Luxembourg	X	8/2/14–11/11/18	X	X		X	X
Montenegro	X	8/7/14–11/11/18	X	X		X	X
Panama	X	11/10/17–11/11/18	X	X		X	X
Poland	X	11/2/18–11/11/18	X	X		X	X
Portugal	3/16–11/18	3/9/16–11/11/18	X	3/1/16–11/11/18		X	7,000
Nicaragua	X	5/6/18–11/11/18	X	X		X	X
New Zealand	8/14–11/18	X	X	X		X	X
Rumania	8/16–12/17	8/28/16–11/11/18	X	8/27/16–12/9/17		X	335,000
Russia	8/14–3/18	8/1/14–12/16/17	14–18	8/1/14–12/5/17		5,500,000	1,700,000
San Marino	X	6/1/15–11/3/18	X	X		X	X
Serbia	7/28/14–11/18	7/28/14–11/11/18	X	7/29/14–11/11/18		X	48,000
Siam	X	7/22/17–11/11/18	X	X		X	X

South Africa	8/14–11/18	X	X	X		X	X
United States	4/17–11/18	4/6/17–11/11/18	X	4/17/17–11/11/18		X	126,000
Austria-Hungary	7/28/14–11/18	7/28/14–11/3/18	14–18	7/29/14–11/3/18		3,000,000	1,200,000
Bulgaria	10/15–9/18	10/15/15–2/29/18	X	10/12/15–9/29/18		X	14,000
Germany	8/14–11/18	8/1/14–11/11/18	14–18	8/1/14–11/11/18		6,060,000	1,800,000
Turkey	11/14–10/18	11/5/14–10/30/18	X	10/28/14–11/11/18		X	325,000
Haiti United States	15–20	–	–	bd	3.3_5 (2,250)	–	–
Russia Turkestan	16	–	–	bd	3.9_5 (9,000)	–	–
France Chief Kaossen (Niger)	16–17	–	–	bd	3? or 2? (1,000 or 100)	–	–
France Caids *El Hiba* (Morocco)	11/16–17	–	–	bd	$3._2$ (1,600)	–	–
		11/15/17–2/20	18–20	bd/civ			
Czechoslovakia	5/18–2/20	X			*2.6	X	–
England	4/18–11/20	18			(400)	X	
France	8/18–11/20	18				X	
Japan	4/18–22	18			3	X	
Russia	7/16/17–7/18/17 11/6/17–3/18 6/18–12/20	17			(1,000) 5.7	5,000,000	
United States	8/18–11/20	18			(500,000)	X	
Ukraine	11/18–12/20	X				X	
[International and Civil Wars Relating to the Russian Revolutions]					*Kornilov Coup, Bolshevik Revolution, and Civil War, in that order		
[continued]							

5.2 THE FOUR STUDIES COMPARED—continued

Entities at War	Inclusion and Date				Casualty Estimates		
	Richardson	Wright	Sorokin	Singer and Small	Richardson	Sorokin	Singer and Small
Russia Subject Peoples	—	—	—	12/9/17–3/18/21	—	—	50,000 X
Finland Germany *Russia*	1/18–6/18	—	—		4.3 (20,000)	—	
France Poland *Russia*	7/20–10/20 11/18–10/20	4/16/19–4/17/21	—		4? (10,000)	—	
China Tibet	1/18–7/18	—	—	bd	3 (1,000)	—	—
Poland Ukraine	1/19–6/19	—	—	bd	3?	—	—
Czechoslovakia Rumania *Hungary*	X 2/19 2/19	—	—	4/16/19–8/4/19	3 (1,000)	—	2,000 3,000 6,000
British Punjab	6/19	—	—	bd	2.6 (400)	—	—
Greece France Armenians *Turkey*	5/19–10/22 1/20–10/21 2/20–1/21 5/19–10/22	4/21–8/6/24 X X 4/21–8/6/24	—	5/5/19–10/11/22	4.6 (40,000)	—	30,000 X X 20,000

England Afghanistan	5/19–8/19	5/6/19–8/18/19	19	bd	3? (1,000)	1,000 X	–
England Irish	1/19–22	4/24/16–7/20/22	–	bd	3? (1,000)	–	–
France Syrians	18–20	–	–	bd	3.7 (5,000)	–	–
England Iraquis	6/20–21	–	–	bd	3.3 (2,000)	–	–
France Spain *Riffs*	4/25–12/26 4/20–24, 8/25–27 4/20–24, 4/25–27	7/21–5/30/25 25 21 21	25–26 19–25 X	7/18/21–5/27/26	4.4 (25,000)	16,000 42,000	4,000 25,000 X
Lithuania Poland	10/9/20	4/8/20–12/10/27	End of Sorokin's estimates	bd	3? (1,000)	End of Sorokin's estimates	–
Italians Sanusi (Libya)	20–1/32	–		bd	4.6 (40,000)		–
England Moplahs (N. W. India)	8/21–22	–		bd	4 (10,000)		–
France Tache de Taza (Morocco)	23	–		bd	3? (1,000)		–

5.2 THE FOUR STUDIES COMPARED—continued

Entities at War	Inclusion and Date			Casualty Estimates	
	Richardson	Wright	Singer and Small	Richardson	Singer and Small
Japan Koreans	10/23	–	bd	4 (10,000)	–
Afghanistan	24–25	–	civ	3? (1,000)	–
Hejaz Wahabi	24–25	–	mem	3? (1,000)	–
France *Arabs* *Druzes* (Syria)	7/25–12/26 8/25–7/26 7/25–12/26	–	7/18/25–6/27	$3._4$ (2,500)	4,000 X X
Holland Javanese	12/11/26–27	–	bd	3? (1,000)	–
Afghanistan	29	–	civ	3 (1,000)	–
France Moroccans	29–9/33	–	bd	$3._4$ (2,500)	–
Bolivia Paraguay	1/30–6/35	12/15/28–6/2/35	6/15/32–6/12/35	$5._3$ (200,000)	80,000 50,000
France Vietnamese	30–31	–	bd	3? (1,000)	–

China Japan	9/31–5/33	9/18/31–5/31/33	12/19/31–5/6/33	$4._8$ (64,000)	50,000 10,000
Ecuador	32	–	civ	2.9 (800)	–
Brazil Sao Paulo	6/9/32– 8/31/32	–	civ	3? (1,000)	–
Iraq Kurds	33	–	bd	3? (1,000)	–
Austria	2/12/34– 2/15/34	–	civ	3.2 (1,600)	–
Germany	6/30/34–7/34	–	civ	3 (1,000)	–
Spain	34	–	civ	2.7 (500)	–
Ethiopia Italy	11/35–9/37	10/3/35–7/4/36	10/3/35–5/9/36	4 (10,000)	16,000 4,000
China Mongols	11/36–37	–	bd	3? (1,000)	–
England Hindus	36–38	–	bd	3? (1,000)	–
Spain Italy Germany Russia Volunteers	7/36–4/39 10/36–4/39 7/36–4/39 36–39 36–39	7/17/36–4/1/39 7/17/36–4/1/39 7/17/36–4/1/39 X X	civ	$6._3$ (2,000,000)	–

5.2 THE FOUR STUDIES COMPARED—continued

Entities at War	Inclusion and Date			Casualty Estimates		
	Richardson	Wright	Singer and Small	Richardson	Wright	Singer and Small
China	part of World War II	7/7/37–40	7/7/37–12/1/41	–		750,000
France						
Japan						250,000
Thailand						
Mongolia	–	–	5/11/39–9/16/39	–		3,000
Russia						1,000
Japan						15,000
					Wright's estimates begin	
Australia	9/39–8/45	9/3/39–9/1/45	9/3/39–8/14/45	7.3	27,000	29,400
Belgium	4/40–5/45	5/10/40–	5/10/40–5/28/40		8,000	9,600
Brazil	8/42–5/45	8/22/42–	7/6/44–5/7/45		1,000	1,000
Canada	9/39–8/45	9/10/39–9/1/45	9/10/39–8/14/45		32,000	39,300
China	7/37–8/45	7/7/37–9/1/45	12/7/41–8/14/45	20,000,000	2,200,000	1,350,000
Costa Rica	X	1/1/42–	X		X	X
Cuba	X	1/1/42–	X		X	X
Denmark	8/43–5/45	4/9/40–	X		4,000	X
Egypt	X	2/26/45–	X		X	X
England	9/3/39–8/45	9/3/39–9/1/45	9/3/39–8/14/45		557,000	270,000
Ethiopia	7/13/40–11/41	10/10/42–	1/24/41–7/3/41		X	5,000
France	9/3/39–8/45	9/3/39–9/1/45	9/3/39–6/22/40, 10/23/44–8/14/45*		202,000	210,000
Greece	4/6/41–5/45	4/9/41–	10/25/40–4/23/41		73,000	10,000
Guatemala	X	1/1/42–	X		X	X
Haiti	X	1/1/42–	X		X	X

Holland	5/40–5/45	5/10/40–9/1/45	5/10/40–5/14/40		7,000	6,200
Honduras	X	1/1/42–	X		X	X
India	9/39–6/45	9/3/39–	X		36,000	X
Luxembourg	X	5/10/40–	X		X	X
New Zealand	9/39–8/45	9/3/39–9/1/45	9/3/39–8/14/45		12,000	17,300
Nicaragua	X	1/1/42–	X		X	X
Norway	X	4/9/40–	4/9/40–6/9/40		2,000	2,000
Panama	X	1/1/42–	X		X	X
Poland	9/1/39–5/45	9/1/39–	9/1/39–9/27/39		64,000	320,000
Russia	6/22/41–5/8/45, 8/45	6/22/41–9/1/45	6/22/41–5/7/45, 8/8/45–8/14/45		7,500,000	7,500,000
Salvador	X	1/1/42–	X		X	X
South Africa	9/39–5/8/45	9/6/39–	9/6/39–8/14/45		7,000	8,700
United States	12/41–8/45	12/7/41–9/1/45	12/7/41–8/14/45		292,000	408,300
Jews	33–5/45	X	X		X	X
Mongolia	X	X	8/10/45–8/14/45		X	3,000
Bulgaria†	4/7/41–5/45	6/22/41–10/28/44	12/8/41–9/8/44, 9/9/44–5/7/45		10,000	10,000
Czechoslovakia	40–5/45	1/1/42–	X		10,000	X
Finland	6/22/41–9/44	11/30/39–9/19/44	6/25/41–9/19/44		79,000	42,000
Germany	33–5/45	9/1/39–5/7/45	9/1/39–5/7/45		3,250,000	3,500,000
Hungary	3/39–5/45	6/26/41–1/20/45	6/27/41–1/20/45		147,000	40,000
Italy†	6/40–9/43, 10/43–5/45	6/10/40–9/3/43	6/10/40–9/2/43, 10/18/43–5/7/45		149,000	77,000
Japan	7/37–8/45	7/7/37–9/1/45	12/7/41–8/14/45		1,507,000	1,000,000
Rumania†	10/40–5/45	6/22/41–8/23/44	6/22/41–5/7/45, 8/8/45–8/14/45		520,000	300,000
Thailand	1/25/42–8/19/45	X	X		X	X
Yugoslavia	4/6/41–5/45	4/6/41–	4/6/41–4/17/41		410,000	5,000

* Vichy—11/30/40–1/31/41, 11/8/42–11/11/42
† Fought on both sides

Russia Finland	11/39–3/40	11/30/39–3/12/40 (1942 ed.)	11/30/39–3/12/40	4.83 (68,000)	incl. WW II (1965)	50,000 40,000

5.2 THE FOUR STUDIES COMPARED–continued

Entities at War	Inclusion and Date			Casualty Estimates		
	Richardson	Wright	Singer and Small	Richardson	Wright	Singer and Small
England Greece	12/5/44– 1/11/45	–	bd/civ	4 (10,000)	–	–
France Algerians	5/45	–	bd	3 (1,000)	–	–
France *Lebanon* *Syria*	5/17/45– 6/5/45	45	bd	2.8 (640)	3 (1,000)	–
England	10/45– 11/29/46	X	11/10/45–10/15/46	3.2	3	1,000
Holland	10/45–11/46, 7/20/47– 8/1/47, 12/19/48–1/49	47–48	11/10/45–10/15/46	(1,600)	(1,000)	400
Chinese *Indonesians*	6/46 10/45–11/46, 7/20/47– 8/1/47, 12/19/48–1/49	X	X 11/10/45–10/15/46			X X
France Indochinese	–	47–54	12/10/45–6/1/54	–	4 (10,000)	95,000 X

England	2/46–8/14/47	X	civ	5.9	6	–
India	8/15/47–1/18/48	47–48			(1,000,000)	
Pakistan	8/15/47–1/18/48	47–48		(794,300)		
Moslems	2/46–1/18/48	X				
Hindus	2/46–1/18/48	X				
Bolivia	7/18/46–7/22/46, 4/9/52–4/12/52	46–52	civ	3 (1,000) 2.65 (450)	3 (1,000)	–
Bulgaria	X	46–48	civ/bd	4.65	4	–
Rumania	X					
Yugoslavia	X			(44,670)	(10,000)	
Communists	46–49					
Greece	46–49					
China	2/28/47–	47	bd	3.2	3	–
Formosans	3/21/47			(1,600)	(1,000)	
Paraguay	3/7/47–8/2/47	47	civ	2.7 (500)	3 (1,000)	
France	3/29/47–7/47	47	3/29/47–12/1/48	3?	3	1,500
Madagascans				(1,000)	(1,000)	X
India	10/47–3/49	48–49	10/26/47–1/1/49	3	3	1,500
Kashmir	10/47–3/49	X	10/26/47–1/1/49	(1,000)	(1,000)	X
Pakistan	5/48–3/49	48–49	X			X
Moslems	10/47–3/49	X	X			X
England	–	47–52	bd	–	3	–
Malayans					(1,000)	

5.2 THE FOUR STUDIES COMPARED – continued

Entities at War	Inclusion and Date			Casualty Estimates		
	Richardson	Wright	Singer and Small	Richardson	Wright	Singer and Small
Egypt	5/14/48–6/1/48*	48–49	5/15/48–7/18/48, 10/22/48–1/7/49	3.5_5	3	2,000
England	11/30/47–5/14/48	X	X	(3,600)	(1,000)	X
Iraq	5/14/48–6/1/48	X	5/15/48–7/18/48, 10/22/48–10/31/48			500
Lebanon	5/14/48–6/1/48	48–49	5/15/48–7/18/48, 10/22/48–10/31/48			500
Syria	5/14/48–6/1/48	48–49	5/15/48–7/18/48, 10/22/48–10/31/48			1,000
Transjordan	5/14/48–6/1/48	48–49	5/15/48–7/18/48, 10/22/48–10/31/48			1,000
Palestinians	11/47–7/49	X	X			X
Jews (Israel)	11/47–7/49	48–49	5/15/48–7/18/48, 10/22/48–1/7/49			3,000
India Hyderabad	9/13/48–9/17/48	48	bd	3.3 (2,000)	3 (1,000)	–
South Korea	10/20/48	–	civ	3 (1,000)	–	–
Colombia	4/9/48–4/12/48, 9/49–11/49	48–64	civ	2.7 (500) 3.3 (2,000)	5 (100,000)	–
China	End of Richardson's estimates	49	civ	End of Richardson's estimates	5 (100,000)	–

Australia		X	12/10/50–7/27/53		6	270
Belgium		X	1/20/51–7/27/53		(1,000,000)	100
Canada		X	12/19/50–7/27/53			310
Colombia		X	6/24/50–7/27/53			140
Ethiopia		X	5/1/51–7/27/53			120
France		X	1/1/51–7/27/53			290
Great Britain		X	8/29/50–7/27/53			670
Greece		X	1/20/51–7/27/53			170
Holland		X	1/20/51–7/27/53			110
Philippines		X	9/16/50–7/27/53			90
South Korea		50–53	6/24/50–7/27/53			415,000
Thailand		X	1/20/51–7/27/53			110
Turkey		X	10/18/50–7/27/53			720
United Nations		50–53	X			X
United States		50–53	6/27/50–7/27/53			54,000
China		50–53	10/27/50–7/27/53			900,000
North Korea		50–53	6/24/50–7/27/53			520,000
China		54–56	bd		3	–
Taiwan					(1,000)	
France		54–62	11/1/54–3/17/62		5	15,000
Algeria					(100,000)	X
Hungary		56	10/23/56–11/14/56		3	25,000
Russia					(1,000)	7,000
Egypt		56–57	10/31/56–11/7/56		3	3,000
England					(1,000)	20
France						10
Israel						200
China		59	3/1/56–3/22/59		4	4,000
Tibet					(10,000)	X
Laos		59–64	civ		4	–
					(10,000)	

5.2 THE FOUR STUDIES COMPARED—continued

Entities at War	Inclusion and Date		Casualty Estimates	
	Wright	Singer and Small	Wright	Singer and Small
Egypt England Saudi Arabia *Yemen*	59–64	con	3 (1,000)	–
Belgium Congo U.N.	60–64	bd/civ	5 (100,000)	–
Cuba United States	61–63	bd/civ	3 (1,000)	–
South Vietnam United States *North Vietnam*	61–64	con	5 (100,000)	–
China India	62	10/20/62–11/22/62	4 (10,000)	500 500
Portugal Angolans	62–63	con	4 (10,000)	–
Burundi Rwanda	62–63	bd	3 (1,000)	–
Cyprus	63–64	civ	3 (1,000)	–
India Pakistan	End of Wright's estimates	8/5/65–9/23/65	End of Wright's estimates	3,800 3,000

Chapter 6

Ranking the Wars by Severity, Magnitude and Intensity

In Chapter Four, we identified all of the wars that satisfied our criteria for inclusion, and then went on to present our estimates of their duration, magnitude, and severity, as well as the pre-war population and armed forces figures on which their intensity scores are calculated. With these basic data, we also gave the three intensity ratios: battle deaths/nation months, battle deaths/population, and battle deaths/armed forces size. In both our basic listing and in the comparison of our results with the Richardson, Wright, and Sorokin compilations (Chapter Five), we followed a chronological order. For certain purposes such a format is quite useful, but it does not readily lend itself to the needs of those with more restricted interests. Some scholars for example, may want only to analyze wars of a particular type (interstate or extra-systemic, central interstate, major power, etc.). Others may be primarily interested in those which fall above or below a certain threshold on one or more of our measures. Therefore, we devote the present chapter to a computation and presentation of the wars' rankings on five different dimensions: battle-connected deaths, nation months, the total population of the system members involved, battle deaths per nation month, and battle deaths per capita.

RANKING ALL INTERNATIONAL WARS

Although there might be some limited usefulness in presenting a separate rank order tabulation for each of the five dimensions and for both interstate and extra-systemic wars, it does not seem to merit the space required. Thus, we present only four such tabulations, but include additional rank position data in each. Table 6.1, to illustrate, lists all of the 93 international wars, ranked according to battle deaths, but following the column showing the war's rank position on that dimension, there are separate columns indicating each war's rank on the four other dimensions.

One new measure appears here for the first time: a ranking based on the total population of all of the system members that participated in each of the wars. It is probably best thought of as an additional measure of magnitude, since it reflects both the number and the size (and, therefore, indirectly, the "power") of the states involved in the war. The population rankings are also introduced because the figures on which they are based serve as the denominator in computing one of the intensity measures: battle deaths per capita.

A word of justification is in order as to why we select severity rather than one of the other indicators as the primary basis for ranking the wars. As was suggested earlier, we strongly share Richardson's implied view that the single most valid and sensitive indicator of the "amount of war" experienced by the system is that of battle deaths, or severity. To illustrate its advantage over the nation month (magnitude) measure, compare the rank position of the Russo-Turkish War of 1877–1878 as shown in Table 6.1. This is considered by most historians as one of the most important and "great" conflicts of the epoch under study. Because it involved only two powers and lasted less than 9 months, its magnitude is a relatively low 17.8 nation months, for a rank position of 43. But the ferocity with which it was fought and the human resources allocated to it are dramatically revealed in its 285,000 battle deaths, giving it the more representative fifth position in the severity rankings.

It should be noted, of course, that interstate wars dominate these rankings, and not only because they tended to be of higher severity, magnitude, and intensity

6.1 - RANK ORDER OF ALL INTERNATIONAL WARS BY SEVERITY

WAR NO.	NAME OF WAR	BATTLE DEATHS 1	NATION MONTHS 2	POPULATION 3	BATTLE DEATHS PER NATION MONTH 4	BATTLE DEATHS PER CAPITA 5
43	WORLD WAR II	1.0	1.0	1.0	3.0	3.0
35	WORLD WAR I	2.0	2.0	6.0	6.0	2.0
46	KOREAN	3.0	3.0	3.0	13.0	14.0
41	SINO-JAPANESE	4.0	9.0	5.0	8.0	16.0
21	RUSSO-TURKISH	5.0	43.0	19.0	4.0	11.0
9	CRIMEAN	6.0	6.0	16.0	18.0	19.0
20	FRANCO-PRUSSIAN	7.0	30.0	24.0	9.0	12.0
3	RUSSO-TURKISH	9.0	26.0	25.0	12.0	15.0
28	RUSSO-JAPANESE	9.0	23.0	14.0	14.0	23.0
39	CHACO	9.0	14.5	89.0	20.0	1.0
69	LA PLATA	11.0	5.0	80.5	41.0	4.0
70	TEN YEARS	12.0	8.0	79.0	40.0	5.0
89	INDOCHINESE	13.0	10.0	45.0	39.0	10.0
44	RUSSO-FINNISH	14.0	70.0	15.0	7.0	31.0
33	FIRST BALKAN	15.0	39.0	55.0	11.0	8.0
34	SECOND BALKAN	16.0	80.0	49.0	5.0	18.0
38	MANCHURIAN	17.0	27.0	8.0	21.5	66.0
63	HUNGARIAN	18.0	58.0	21.0	10.0	26.0
37	GRECO-TURKISH	20.0	13.0	80.5	50.0	6.0
80	CUBAN	20.0	24.0	78.0	30.0	7.0
85	RUSSIAN NATIONALITIES	20.0	22.0	17.0	31.0	44.0
93	TIBETAN	22.0	25.0	4.0	32.0	74.0
19	SEVEN WEEKS	23.0	51.0	23.0	17.0	38.0
47	RUSSO-HUNGARIAN	24.0	86.0	13.0	2.0	57.0
86	RIFFIAN	25.0	14.5	30.0	61.0	33.0
11	ITALIAN UNIFICATION	26.0	68.0	27.0	16.0	46.0
84	BOER	27.0	28.0	41.0	47.0	30.0
15	FRANCO-MEXICAN	30.0	7.0	38.0	78.0	34.0
32	ITALO-TURKISH	30.0	32.0	31.0	45.0	42.0
40	ITALO-ETHIOPIAN	30.0	52.0	36.0	28.0	39.0
59	FIRST BRITISH-AFGHAN	30.0	18.0	66.0	59.0	21.0
77	MAHDIST	30.0	21.0	51.0	55.0	27.0
42	RUSSO-JAPANESE	33.0	57.0	12.0	26.0	72.0
4	MEXICAN-AMERICAN	34.0	19.0	59.0	62.0	28.0
25	SINO-JAPANESE	37.5	48.0	9.0	38.0	84.0
52	GREEK	37.5	12.0	69.0	76.0	25.0
53	FIRST ANGLO-BURMESE	37.5	29.0	72.0	53.0	24.0
54	JAVANESE	37.5	17.0	85.0	70.0	9.0
56	FIRST POLISH	37.5	66.0	33.0	21.5	49.0
92	ALGERIAN	37.5	11.0	39.0	79.0	41.0
22	PACIFIC	41.0	4.0	84.0	89.0	13.0
23	SINO-FRENCH	42.0	33.0	10.0	54.0	87.0
36	HUNGARIAN-ALLIES	43.0	59.5	50.0	33.0	45.0
60	SECOND SYRIAN	44.0	76.5	37.0	23.0	53.0
12	SPANISH-MOROCCAN	47.0	62.0	75.0	36.0	29.0
27	SPANISH-AMERICAN	47.0	67.0	22.0	29.0	64.0
31	SPANISH-MOROCCAN	47.0	44.5	70.0	51.0	37.0
57	FIRST SYRIAN	47.0	54.0	71.0	46.0	35.0
72	BALKAN	47.0	38.0	61.0	56.0	40.0
5	AUSTRO-SARDINIAN	50.5	64.0	44.0	37.0	51.0
81	ITALO-ETHIOPIAN	50.5	61.0	57.0	42.0	47.0
45	PALESTINE	52.0	41.0	58.0	60.0	50.0
50	SECOND KASHMIR	53.0	82.0	7.0	19.0	91.0
6	FIRST SCHLESWIG-HOLSTEIN	55.0	47.0	76.0	63.0	43.0
71	DUTCH-ACHINESE	55.0	16.0	87.5	87.0	17.0
79	FRANCO-MADAGASCAN	55.0	63.0	47.0	48.0	55.0
55	RUSSO-PERSIAN	58.0	44.5	35.0	68.0	69.0
65	FIRST TURCO-MONTENEGRAN	58.0	81.0	67.0	27.0	54.0
68	SECOND POLISH	58.0	49.0	26.0	65.0	75.0
17	SECOND SCHLESWIG-HOLSTEIN	61.0	59.5	34.0	58.0	71.0
76	FRANCO-INDOCHINESE	61.0	31.0	48.0	77.0	60.0
83	SECOND PHILIPPINE	61.0	20.0	28.5	84.0	77.0
74	SECOND BRITISH-AFGHAN	63.5	42.0	53.0	72.0	61.0
87	DRUZE	63.5	36.5	42.0	75.0	67.0
66	SEPOY	66.0	35.0	60.0	82.0	59.0
73	BOSNIAN	66.0	85.0	46.0	24.0	70.0
75	BRITISH-ZULU	66.0	76.5	52.0	49.0	65.0
48	SINAI	68.0	91.0	20.0	15.0	86.0
2	NAVARINO BAY	69.0	93.0	18.0	1.0	88.0
67	SECOND TURCO-MONTENEGRAN	70.0	56.0	65.0	71.0	62.0
7	ROMAN REPUBLIC	71.0	72.5	28.5	64.0	85.0
10	ANGLO-PERSIAN	74.0	65.0	54.0	73.0	76.0
26	GRECO-TURKISH	74.0	75.0	64.0	66.0	73.0
51	BRITISH-MAHARATTAN	74.0	69.0	74.0	69.0	68.0
78	SERBO-BULGARIAN	74.0	88.0	92.0	25.0	20.0

6.1 - RANK ORDER OF ALL INTERNATIONAL WARS BY SEVERITY

WAR NO.	NAME OF WAR	BATTLE DEATHS 1	NATION MONTHS 2	POPULA-TION 3	BATTLE DEATHS PER NATION MONTH 4	BATTLE DEATHS PER CAPITA 5
82	FIRST PHILIPPINE	74.0	34.0	77.0	88.0	63.0
62	FIRST BRITISH-SIKH	78.5	83.0	63.0	52.0	78.0
64	SECOND BRITISH-SIKH	78.5	79.0	62.0	67.0	79.0
90	MADAGASCAN	78.5	40.0	43.0	90.0	82.0
91	FIRST KASHMIR	78.5	53.0	11.0	85.0	92.0
88	INDONESIAN	81.0	36.5	32.0	92.0	89.0
8	LA PLATA	82.0	55.0	82.0	86.0	56.0
1	FRANCO-SPANISH	88.0	50.0	40.0	91.0	90.0
13	ITALO-ROMAN	88.0	88.0	68.0	43.5	81.0
14	ITALO-SICILIAN	88.0	72.5	56.0	81.0	83.0
16	ECUADORIAN-COLOMBIAN	88.0	91.0	86.0	34.5	52.0
18	SPANISH-CHILEAN	88.0	46.0	73.0	93.0	80.0
24	CENTRAL AMERICAN	88.0	88.0	91.0	43.5	32.0
29	CENTRAL AMERICAN	88.0	78.0	87.5	74.0	48.0
30	CENTRAL AMERICAN	88.0	74.0	90.0	80.0	36.0
49	SINO-INDIAN	88.0	84.0	2.0	57.0	93.0
58	TEXAN	88.0	71.0	83.0	83.0	58.0
61	PERUVIAN-BOLIVIAN	88.0	91.0	93.0	34.5	22.0

than the extra-systemic wars, but also because of the limits of our data. That is, since our major theoretical concern is with the interstate system, we have (as we acknowledged in Chapter Three) gathered severity and magnitude data only for the entities that were qualified system members. Moreover, even if we *were* interested in the additional data, the problems of availability and reliability would have been even more formidable than for the interstate wars. Thus, the extra-systemic wars reflect only the severity, magnitude, and intensity figures for the national members of the system, and therefore understate the *total* range and destructiveness of the hostilities. To illustrate, the Ten Years War of 1868–1878 between Spain and Cuba appears in twelfth place in the severity column, even though the battle deaths sustained by the Cuban forces (as a non-member of the system) are not included in the total; our estimate is that this war might have been in fifth position on that dimension if the Cuban military fatalities had been included.

In addition to the listing of these international wars according to their severity, it seemed to us that a ranking based on at least one other measure could be quite useful: intensity, measured in terms of battle deaths per nation month. As Table 6.2 makes clear, there is an appreciable difference between the rankings produced by

6.2 - RANK ORDER OF ALL INTERNATIONAL WARS BY INTENSITY

WAR NO.	NAME OF WAR	BATTLE DEATHS PER NATION MONTHS 1	BATTLE DEATHS PER CAPITA 2	POPULA-TION 3	BATTLE DEATHS 4	NATION MONTHS 5
2	NAVARINO BAY	1.0	88.0	18.0	69.0	93.0
47	RUSSO-HUNGARIAN	2.0	57.0	13.0	24.0	86.0
43	WORLD WAR II	3.0	3.0	1.0	1.0	1.0
21	RUSSO-TURKISH	4.0	11.0	19.0	5.0	43.0
34	SECOND BALKAN	5.0	18.0	49.0	16.0	80.0
35	WORLD WAR I	6.0	2.0	6.0	2.0	2.0
44	RUSSO-FINNISH	7.0	31.0	15.0	14.0	70.0
41	SINO-JAPANESE	8.0	16.0	5.0	4.0	9.0
20	FRANCO-PRUSSIAN	9.0	12.0	24.0	7.0	30.0
63	HUNGARIAN	10.0	26.0	21.0	18.0	58.0
33	FIRST BALKAN	11.0	8.0	55.0	15.0	39.0
3	RUSSO-TURKISH	12.0	15.0	25.0	9.0	26.0
46	KOREAN	13.0	14.0	3.0	3.0	3.0
28	RUSSO-JAPANESE	14.0	23.0	14.0	9.0	23.0
48	SINAI	15.0	86.0	20.0	68.0	91.0

6.2 - RANK ORDER OF ALL INTERNATIONAL WARS BY INTENSITY

WAR NO.	NAME OF WAR	BATTLE DEATHS PER NATION MONTHS 1	BATTLE DEATHS PER CAPITA 2	POPULATION 3	BATTLE DEATHS 4	NATION MONTHS 5
11	ITALIAN UNIFICATION	16.0	46.0	27.0	26.0	68.0
19	SEVEN WEEKS	17.0	38.0	23.0	23.0	51.0
9	CRIMEAN	18.0	19.0	16.0	6.0	6.0
50	SECOND KASHMIR	19.0	91.0	7.0	53.0	82.0
39	CHACO	20.0	1.0	89.0	9.0	14.5
38	MANCHURIAN	21.5	66.0	8.0	17.0	27.0
56	FIRST POLISH	21.5	49.0	33.0	37.5	66.0
60	SECOND SYRIAN	23.0	53.0	37.0	44.0	76.5
73	BOSNIAN	24.0	70.0	46.0	66.0	85.0
78	SERBO-BULGARIAN	25.0	20.0	92.0	74.0	88.0
42	RUSSO-JAPANESE	26.0	72.0	12.0	33.0	57.0
65	FIRST TURCO-MONTENEGRAN	27.0	54.0	67.0	58.0	81.0
40	ITALO-ETHIOPIAN	28.0	39.0	36.0	30.0	52.0
27	SPANISH-AMERICAN	29.0	64.0	22.0	47.0	67.0
80	CUBAN	30.0	7.0	78.0	20.0	24.0
85	RUSSIAN NATIONALITIES	31.0	44.0	17.0	20.0	22.0
93	TIBETAN	32.0	74.0	4.0	22.0	25.0
36	HUNGARIAN-ALLIES	33.0	45.0	50.0	43.0	59.5
16	ECUADORIAN-COLOMBIAN	34.5	52.0	86.0	88.0	91.0
61	PERUVIAN-BOLIVIAN	34.5	22.0	93.0	88.0	91.0
12	SPANISH-MOROCCAN	36.0	29.0	75.0	47.0	62.0
5	AUSTRO-SARDINIAN	37.0	51.0	44.0	50.5	64.0
25	SINO-JAPANESE	38.0	84.0	9.0	37.5	48.0
89	INDOCHINESE	39.0	10.0	45.0	13.0	10.0
70	TEN YEARS	40.0	5.0	79.0	12.0	8.0
69	LA PLATA	41.0	4.0	80.5	11.0	5.0
81	ITALO-ETHIOPIAN	42.0	47.0	57.0	50.5	61.0
13	ITALO-ROMAN	43.5	81.0	68.0	88.0	88.0
24	CENTRAL AMERICAN	43.5	32.0	91.0	88.0	88.0
32	ITALO-TURKISH	45.0	42.0	31.0	30.0	32.0
57	FIRST SYRIAN	46.0	35.0	71.0	47.0	54.0
84	BOER	47.0	30.0	41.0	27.0	28.0
79	FRANCO-MADAGASCAN	48.0	55.0	47.0	55.0	63.0
75	BRITISH-ZULU	49.0	65.0	52.0	66.0	76.5
37	GRECO-TURKISH	50.0	6.0	80.5	20.0	13.0
31	SPANISH-MOROCCAN	51.0	37.0	70.0	47.0	44.5
62	FIRST BRITISH-SIKH	52.0	78.0	63.0	78.5	83.0
53	FIRST ANGLO-BURMESE	53.0	24.0	72.0	37.5	29.0
23	SINO-FRENCH	54.0	87.0	10.0	42.0	33.0
77	MAHDIST	55.0	27.0	51.0	30.0	21.0
72	BALKAN	56.0	40.0	61.0	47.0	38.0
49	SINO-INDIAN	57.0	93.0	2.0	88.0	84.0
17	SECOND SCHLESWIG-HOLSTEIN	58.0	71.0	34.0	61.0	59.5
59	FIRST BRITISH-AFGHAN	59.0	21.0	66.0	30.0	18.0
45	PALESTINE	60.0	50.0	58.0	52.0	41.0
86	RIFFIAN	61.0	33.0	30.0	25.0	14.5
4	MEXICAN-AMERICAN	62.0	28.0	59.0	34.0	19.0
6	FIRST SCHLESWIG-HOLSTEIN	63.0	43.0	76.0	55.0	47.0
7	ROMAN REPUBLIC	64.0	85.0	28.5	71.0	72.5
68	SECOND POLISH	65.0	75.0	26.0	58.0	49.0
26	GRECO-TURKISH	66.0	73.0	64.0	74.0	75.0
64	SECOND BRITISH-SIKH	67.0	79.0	62.0	78.5	79.0
55	RUSSO-PERSIAN	68.0	69.0	35.0	58.0	44.5
51	BRITISH-MAHARATTAN	69.0	68.0	74.0	74.0	69.0
54	JAVANESE	70.0	9.0	85.0	37.5	17.0
67	SECOND TURCO-MONTENEGRAN	71.0	62.0	65.0	70.0	56.0
74	SECOND BRITISH-AFGHAN	72.0	61.0	53.0	63.5	42.0
10	ANGLO-PERSIAN	73.0	76.0	54.0	74.0	65.0
29	CENTRAL AMERICAN	74.0	48.0	87.5	88.0	78.0
87	DRUZE	75.0	67.0	42.0	63.5	36.5
52	GREEK	76.0	25.0	69.0	37.5	12.0
76	FRANCO-INDOCHINESE	77.0	60.0	48.0	61.0	31.0
15	FRANCO-MEXICAN	78.0	34.0	38.0	30.0	7.0
92	ALGERIAN	79.0	41.0	39.0	37.5	11.0
30	CENTRAL AMERICAN	80.0	36.0	90.0	88.0	74.0
14	ITALO-SICILIAN	81.0	83.0	56.0	88.0	72.5
66	SEPOY	82.0	59.0	60.0	66.0	35.0
58	TEXAN	83.0	58.0	83.0	88.0	71.0
83	SECOND PHILIPPINE	84.0	77.0	28.5	61.0	20.0
91	FIRST KASHMIR	85.0	92.0	11.0	78.5	53.0
8	LA PLATA	86.0	56.0	82.0	82.0	55.0
71	DUTCH-ACHINESE	87.0	17.0	87.5	55.0	16.0
82	FIRST PHILIPPINE	88.0	63.0	77.0	74.0	34.0
22	PACIFIC	89.0	13.0	84.0	41.0	4.0
90	MADAGASCAN	90.0	82.0	43.0	78.5	40.0
1	FRANCO-SPANISH	91.0	90.0	40.0	88.0	50.0
88	INDONESIAN	92.0	89.0	32.0	81.0	36.5
18	SPANISH-CHILEAN	93.0	80.0	73.0	88.0	46.0

battle death figures alone and those which result when we control for the war's nation months.

RANKING THE INTERSTATE WARS

As we pointed out in our discussion of Table 6.1, any listing which combines war indicators based on two rather different measuring criteria can be quite misleading. That is, even though it seemed important to combine interstate and extra-systemic wars in the above tables, there is some lack of comparability because the non-members' populations, battle deaths, and nation months are not included in computing the severity and magnitude of the extra-systemic wars. We avoid that distortion now by treating and ranking the two types of wars separately.

Hence, in Table 6.3 we list the 50 interstate wars only, ranked according to their severity in battle deaths, but also showing their rank position on the magnitude, population, and intensity dimensions.

6.3 - RANK ORDER OF INTERSTATE WARS BY SEVERITY

WAR NO.	NAME OF WAR	BATTLE DEATHS 1	NATION MONTHS 2	POPULATION 3	BATTLE DEATHS PER NATION MONTH 4	BATTLE DEATHS PER CAPITA 5
43	WORLD WAR II	1.0	1.0	1.0	3.0	3.0
35	WORLD WAR I	2.0	2.0	5.0	6.0	2.0
46	KOREAN	3.0	3.0	3.0	12.0	9.0
41	SINO-JAPANESE	4.0	7.0	4.0	8.0	11.0
21	RUSSO-TURKISH	5.0	19.0	16.0	4.0	6.0
9	CRIMEAN	6.0	5.0	14.0	17.0	13.0
20	FRANCO-PRUSSIAN	7.0	14.0	20.0	9.0	7.0
3	RUSSO-TURKISH	9.0	12.0	21.0	11.0	10.0
28	RUSSO-JAPANESE	9.0	11.0	12.0	13.0	14.0
39	CHACO	9.0	9.0	48.0	19.0	1.0
44	RUSSO-FINNISH	11.0	36.0	13.0	7.0	17.0
33	FIRST BALKAN	12.0	17.0	33.0	10.0	5.0
34	SECOND BALKAN	13.0	42.0	30.0	5.0	12.0
38	MANCHURIAN	14.0	13.0	7.0	20.0	35.0
37	GRECO-TURKISH	15.0	8.0	43.0	32.0	4.0
19	SEVEN WEEKS	16.0	25.0	19.0	16.0	22.0
47	RUSSO-HUNGARIAN	17.0	45.0	11.0	2.0	33.0
11	ITALIAN UNIFICATION	18.0	35.0	22.0	15.0	27.0
15	FRANCO-MEXICAN	20.0	6.0	27.0	44.0	19.0
32	ITALO-TURKISH	20.0	15.0	24.0	31.0	24.0
40	ITALO-ETHIOPIAN	20.0	26.0	26.0	22.0	23.0
42	RUSSO-JAPANESE	22.0	28.0	10.0	21.0	37.0
4	MEXICAN-AMERICAN	23.0	10.0	36.0	38.0	15.0
25	SINO-JAPANESE	24.0	23.0	8.0	28.0	43.0
22	PACIFIC	25.0	4.0	45.0	48.0	8.0
23	SINO-FRENCH	26.0	16.0	9.0	34.0	46.0
36	HUNGARIAN-ALLIES	27.0	29.5	31.0	24.0	26.0
12	SPANISH-MOROCCAN	29.0	31.0	41.0	26.0	16.0
27	SPANISH-AMERICAN	29.0	34.0	18.0	23.0	34.0
31	SPANISH-MOROCCAN	29.0	20.0	39.0	33.0	21.0
5	AUSTRO-SARDINIAN	31.0	32.0	29.0	27.0	30.0
45	PALESTINE	32.0	18.0	35.0	37.0	29.0
50	SECOND KASHMIR	33.0	43.0	6.0	18.0	49.0
6	FIRST SCHLESWIG-HOLSTEIN	34.0	22.0	42.0	39.0	25.0
17	SECOND SCHLESWIG-HOLSTEIN	35.0	29.5	25.0	36.0	36.0
48	SINAI	36.0	48.5	17.0	14.0	45.0
2	NAVARINO BAY	37.0	50.0	15.0	1.0	47.0
7	ROMAN REPUBLIC	38.0	37.5	23.0	40.0	44.0
10	ANGLO-PERSIAN	39.5	33.0	32.0	42.0	39.0
26	GRECO-TURKISH	39.5	40.0	37.0	41.0	38.0
8	LA PLATA	41.0	27.0	44.0	47.0	32.0
1	FRANCO-SPANISH	46.0	24.0	28.0	49.0	48.0
13	ITALO-ROMAN	46.0	46.5	38.0	29.5	41.0
14	ITALO-SICILIAN	46.0	37.5	34.0	46.0	42.0
16	ECUADORIAN-COLOMBIAN	46.0	48.5	46.0	25.0	31.0
18	SPANISH-CHILEAN	46.0	21.0	40.0	50.0	40.0
24	CENTRAL AMERICAN	46.0	46.5	50.0	29.5	18.0
29	CENTRAL AMERICAN	46.0	41.0	47.0	43.0	28.0
30	CENTRAL AMERICAN	46.0	39.0	49.0	45.0	20.0
49	SINO-INDIAN	46.0	44.0	2.0	35.0	50.0

RANKING THE EXTRA-SYSTEMIC WARS

In Table 6.4, we do the same thing as in 6.3, but for the extra-systemic wars only. That is, we rank them according to the number of battle deaths sustained in each by the system members, and also show their rank position on the other four dimensions.

6.4 - RANK ORDER OF EXTRA-SYSTEMIC WARS BY SEVERITY

WAR NO.	NAME OF WAR	BATTLE DEATHS 1	NATION MONTHS 2	POPULATION 3	BATTLE DEATHS PER NATION MONTH 4	BATTLE DEATHS PER CAPITA 5
69	LA PLATA	1.0	1.0	38.0	13.0	1.0
70	TEN YEARS	2.0	2.0	37.0	12.0	2.0
89	INDOCHINESE	3.0	3.0	16.0	11.0	5.0
63	HUNGARIAN	4.0	30.0	4.0	1.0	12.0
80	CUBAN	5.5	13.0	36.0	7.0	3.0
85	RUSSIAN NATIONALITIES	5.5	12.0	3.0	8.0	19.0
93	TIBETAN	7.0	14.0	1.0	9.0	36.0
86	RIFFIAN	8.0	6.0	7.0	24.0	15.0
84	BOER	9.0	15.0	13.0	16.0	14.0
59	FIRST BRITISH-AFGHAN	10.5	9.0	29.0	23.0	8.0
77	MAHDIST	10.5	11.0	20.0	21.0	13.0
52	GREEK	14.0	5.0	31.0	33.0	11.0
53	FIRST ANGLO-BURMESE	14.0	16.0	33.0	20.0	10.0
54	JAVANESE	14.0	8.0	40.0	29.0	4.0
56	FIRST POLISH	14.0	33.0	9.0	2.0	21.0
92	ALGERIAN	14.0	4.0	12.0	35.0	18.0
60	SECOND SYRIAN	17.0	36.5	11.0	3.0	22.0
57	FIRST SYRIAN	18.5	28.0	32.0	15.0	16.0
72	BALKAN	18.5	22.0	25.0	22.0	17.0
81	ITALO-ETHIOPIAN	20.0	31.0	23.0	14.0	20.0
71	DUTCH-ACHINESE	21.5	7.0	41.0	40.0	6.0
79	FRANCO-MADAGASCAN	21.5	32.0	18.0	17.0	24.0
55	RUSSO-PERSIAN	24.0	25.0	10.0	27.0	34.0
65	FIRST TURCO-MONTENEGRAN	24.0	39.0	30.0	6.0	23.0
68	SECOND POLISH	24.0	26.0	5.0	25.0	37.0
76	FRANCO-INDOCHINESE	26.5	17.0	19.0	34.0	27.0
83	SECOND PHILIPPINE	26.5	10.0	6.0	38.0	38.0
74	SECOND BRITISH-AFGHAN	28.5	24.0	22.0	31.0	28.0
87	DRUZE	28.5	20.5	14.0	32.0	32.0
66	SEPOY	31.0	19.0	24.0	36.0	26.0
73	BOSNIAN	31.0	41.0	17.0	4.0	35.0
75	BRITISH-ZULU	31.0	36.5	21.0	18.0	31.0
67	SECOND TURCO-MONTENEGRAN	33.0	29.0	28.0	30.0	29.0
51	BRITISH-MAHARATTAN	35.0	34.0	34.0	28.0	33.0
78	SERBO-BULGARIAN	35.0	42.0	42.0	5.0	7.0
82	FIRST PHILIPPINE	35.0	18.0	35.0	41.0	30.0
62	FIRST BRITISH-SIKH	38.5	40.0	27.0	19.0	39.0
64	SECOND BRITISH-SIKH	38.5	38.0	26.0	26.0	40.0
90	MADAGASCAN	38.5	23.0	15.0	42.0	41.0
91	FIRST KASHMIR	38.5	27.0	2.0	39.0	43.0
88	INDONESIAN	41.0	20.5	8.0	43.0	42.0
58	TEXAN	42.5	35.0	39.0	37.0	25.0
61	PERUVIAN-BOLIVIAN	42.5	43.0	43.0	10.0	9.0

RANK ORDER CORRELATIONS

As will be evident from visual inspection of Tables 6.1 to 6.4, there tends to be a fairly strong and positive correlation between the rank orderings of all types of war based on severity and those based on magnitude, but when we look at the two intensity indicators and the population base line, the picture is much less clear. As a matter of fact, this should not be surprising, since any war which is low on battle deaths and relatively high on nation months (such as the War of the Pacific of 1879–1883) will inevitably have a low battle deaths per nation month intensity rank, and one which ranks high on battle deaths and low on total population (such as the Chaco War of 1932–1935) will inevitably have a high battle deaths per capita intensity rank, and so on.

If we think of the five indicators used for ranking these international wars as falling into two rather distinct groupings, we can then examine a rank order correlation matrix and make some sense of it. That is, if we had no information at all, it would be reasonable to expect that: (a) wars that lead to a great many battle deaths are those which involve quite a few nations and/or endure for many months; and (b) wars that were very intense in terms of battle deaths per nation month would also rank high on battle deaths per capita. In Table 6.5, we can see the extent to which such expectations are borne out; given the number of tied scores, we used the Kendall's tau (B statistic), from the Constat Analysis Package, written by the Statistical Research Laboratory at the University of Michigan.

6.5 RANK ORDER CORRELATIONS AMONG SEVERAL WAR INDICATORS, BY TYPE OF WAR

	Pop	Nat-Mos	Bat-Dths	B-Dths/Nm	B-Dths/Cap
Population (All Wars)	1.00				
Interstate wars	1.00				
Extra-systemic wars	1.00				
Nation-Months (All Wars)	.08	1.00			
Interstate wars	.15	1.00			
Extra-systemic wars	.02	1.00			
Battle-Deaths (All Wars)	.31	.47	1.00		
Interstate wars	.39	.53	1.00		
Extra-systemic wars	.12	.48	1.00		
B-Dths per Nat-Mnth (All Wars)	.30	−.08	.47	1.00	
Interstate wars	.41	.05	.55	1.00	
Extra-systemic wars	.01	−.18	.36	1.00	
B-Dths per capita (All Wars)	−.18	.39	.53	.26	1.00
Interstate wars	−.09	.46	.55	.29	1.00
Extra-systemic wars	−.36	.32	.54	.28	1.00

As we suggested earlier, there are just enough cases that deviate from the naively expected to make some of the correlations fairly low. That is, the battle death rank positions tend to correlate strongly and positively with those of the other four ranking criteria, but we find that population rankings are less closely associated with battle deaths than are the others. This stems from the very low (.01) correlation between these two variables in the extra-systemic wars; and even in the interstate wars, the relationship is not as strong as the others. Additional correlations of a fairly strong and positive character are those between rankings on nation months and battle deaths per capita, and (at least for interstate wars) between population and battle deaths per nation month. The only notable correlation in the *negative* direction is that between population and battle deaths per capita, and this is, of course, fully expected. We can conclude, therefore, that the statistical relationships predicted in the above paragraph are generally what we do indeed find.

FREQUENCY DISTRIBUTIONS

Having now identified the various types of war, described them in terms of several quantitative indicators, and ranked them according to those indicators, we are in a position to attempt a summary of the results. What sorts of patterns emerge? How many large wars are there, are many of them particularly bloody, what fraction of them are quite short in duration, etc.? Through the computation of frequency distributions, we can efficiently answer these and other questions. Such distribution matrices not only make these simple descriptive statements possible, but answer that question so dear to the heart of statistically oriented scholars: are these events randomly distributed or is there some underlying pattern and regularity? The corollary question, of course, is whether these distributions fit one or more well-known equations: Poisson, polynomial, binomial, log normal, etc.

Our general view is that this latter "curve fitting" operation is better conducted in the context of a theoretical inquiry, where one is explicitly trying to discover relationships among variables, and testing alternative hypotheses which might account for the observed distributions. And, since this volume is expressly limited to the presentation and systematic arrangement of our war data only, with no attention to the factors that account for them, there are some good reasons for not going beyond the descriptive statements mentioned above. But in order to emphasize the regularity of some of our distributions, and to compare them with the work of others, we have computed the goodness of fit in a few places here.

First we looked at all 93 international wars and determined the number that fell into each of five different groupings along the *severity* (battle death) dimension. As

6.6 - FREQUENCIES OF INTERNATIONAL WAR BY SEVERITY

LOG_{10} RANGE	2.5-3.5	3.5-4.5	4.5-5.5	5.5-6.5	6.5-7.5
ABSOLUTE BATTLE DEATH RANGE	310- 3,100	3,100- 31,000	31,000- 310,000	310,000- 3,100,000	3,100,000 31,000,000
ALL INTERNATIONAL WARS	24	45	20	2	2
INTERSTATE WARS	13	20	13	2	2
CENTRAL SYSTEM WARS	13	34	13	0	1
MAJOR POWER WARS	11	30	12	2	2
EXTRA-SYSTEMIC WARS	11	25	7	0	0

Table 6.6 makes clear, if we use Richardson's $\log_{10}$ breakdown (and the numerical equivalents in battle deaths), there are a good many wars of low severity, somewhat more of moderate severity, and very few in the upper ranges. The same pattern seems, moreover, to hold for all classes of war. And, even though Richardson (1960a, p. 147) uses different criteria and includes more wars, it turns out that his observed frequencies would not be sharply different from ours if they did not embrace so many of those wars in which only a few hundred were killed. But it should also be noted that, in regard to any variable, appreciably different distributions can be obtained with different scale intervals.

Shifting now to the *magnitude* measure, we may again summarize the distributions in the same fashion. By treating all wars of 12 nation months or less as the smallest range and those of 192–960 nation months (16–80 nation years) as the largest, we find a pattern rather similar to that of the severity distributions (Table 6.7).

6.7 - FREQUENCIES OF INTERNATIONAL WAR BY MAGNITUDE

NATION MONTHS NATION YEARS	12 OR LESS 1 OR LESS	13-48 1-4	49-96 4-8	97-192 8-16	193-960 16-80
ALL INTERNATIONAL WARS	36	40	7	7	3
INTERSTATE WARS	22	19	2	4	3
CENTRAL SYSTEM WARS	25	28	4	3	1
MAJOR POWER WARS	22	26	2	4	3
EXTRA-SYSTEMIC WARS	14	21	5	3	0

Here, perhaps, we might profitably succumb to the temptation of curve fitting, since the range in magnitude of wars is fairly manageable. We hypothesize that our distribution is very close to a natural logarithmic curve (skewed to the right), and one way of testing this is to transform the actual values to more nearly approximate normal curve (bell-shaped) values, and then test the transformed values for normality via the Chi-square.

First, we transformed our raw magnitude scores to natural log ($\log_e$) values in order to collapse the extreme high scores; we had to add .9 nation months to the actual magnitude of each war so that no $\log_e$ scores were negative. (The total magnitude of the Navarino Bay war, being only .1 nation months, produced a negative log value of -2.34). Then we calculated the mean and standard deviation of the transformed scores, from which point we could determine what percent of our observed cases could be expected to fall within a given distance from the mean. With a normal curve distribution, 50 percent of the cases occur on each side of the mean, and approximately two thirds of all events fall within one standard deviation from the mean on both sides. We chose to divide the area under the normal curve into 10 interval ranges, each of which was expected to contain 10 percent of the total (transformed) cases; we used a Normal Curve Areas table, employing the standard score (z) formula: $z = x - \bar{x}/\text{s.d.}$, and solving for x at the 10, 20, 30, etc., percent intercepts of the area under a normal curve.

Table 6.8 presents the $\log_e$ intervals for all 93 international wars, the 50 interstate and 43 extra-systemic wars, along with the actual, untransformed, values for each interval division. The "expected" values—10 percent of the total number of wars of each type in each interval—and the "observed" number of wars whose transformed magnitudes fell into each interval are reported, along with the means and standard deviations used to compute the interval ranges.

6.8 OBSERVED AND EXPECTED FREQUENCIES OF INTERNATIONAL WAR BY MAGNITUDE, NATURAL LOGARITHMIC TRANSFORMATION

International Wars $N = 93$										
Interval range—$\log_e$	0–1.24	1.25–1.81	1.82–2.22	2.23–2.58	2.59–2.90	2.91–3.23	3.24–3.58	3.59–3.99	4.00–4.56	4.57+
Interval range—nation months	0–3.4	3.5–6.1	6.2–9.2	9.3–13.2	13.3–18.2	18.3–25.3	25.4 35.9	36.0–54.1	54.2–95.6	95.7+
Expected frequencies	9.3	9.3	9.3	9.3	9.3	9.3	9.3	9.3	9.3	9.3
Observed frequencies	9	6	13	8	14	10	8	8	7	10

mean = 2.90; standard deviation = 1.3

Interstate Wars $N = 50$										
Interval range—Log$_e$	0–.94	.95–1.59	1.60–2.07	2.08–2.46	2.47–2.83	2.84–3.20	3.21–3.60	3.61–4.07	4.08–4.72	4.73+
Interval range—nation months	0–2.5	2.6–4.9	5.0–7.9	8.0–11.7	11.8–16.9	17.0–24.5	24.6–36.6	36.7–58.6	58.7–112.2	112.3+
Expected frequencies	5	5	5	5	5	5	5	5	5	5
Observed frequencies	6	2	7	7	6	7	4	2	3	6
mean = 2.83; standard deviation = 1.48										

Extra-systemic Wars $N = 43$										
Interval range—Log$_e$	0–1.36	1.37–1.88	1.89–2.26	2.27–2.58	2.59–2.88	2.89–3.18	3.19–3.50	3.51–3.88	3.89–4.40	4.41+
Interval range—nation months	0–3.9	4.0–6.6	6.7–9.6	9.7–13.2	13.3–17.8	17.9–24.0	24.1–33.1	33.2–48.4	48.5–81.5	81.6+
Expected frequencies	4.3	4.3	4.3	4.3	4.3	4.3	4.3	4.3	4.3	4.3
Observed frequencies	4	2	5	3	5	7	3	5	4	5
mean = 2.88; standard deviation = 1.19										

With the values in Table 6.8, we could compute the similarity between the expected and observed frequencies for each type of war. We used the Chi-square ($\Sigma\,(f_{\text{observed}} - f_{\text{expected}})^2/f_{\text{expected}}$), which would be equal to zero if all expected and observed values were identical, and increasingly higher as the differences between the values were greater.

We present in fig. 6.9 not only the Chi-square values themselves, but also a visual representation of the observed and expected frequencies in the form of cumulative

6.9a Cumulative probability, expected and observed, of international war magnitudes, and chi-square measures of similarity.

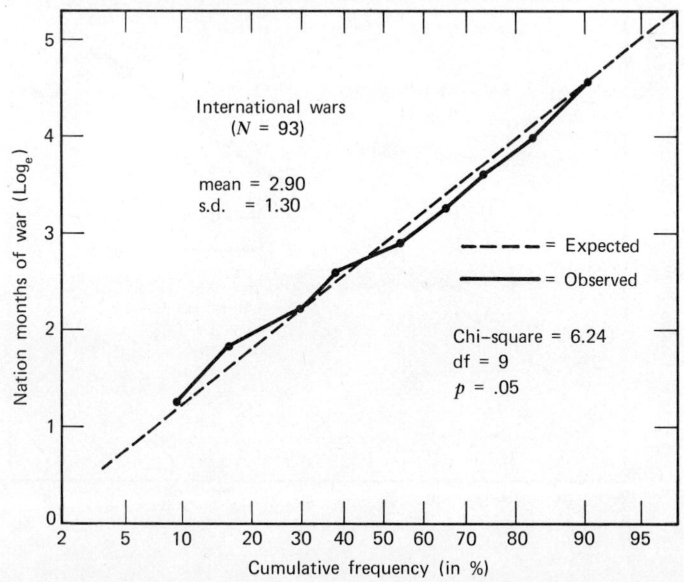

6.9b Cumulative probability, expected and observed, of interstate war magnitudes, and chi-square measures of similarity.

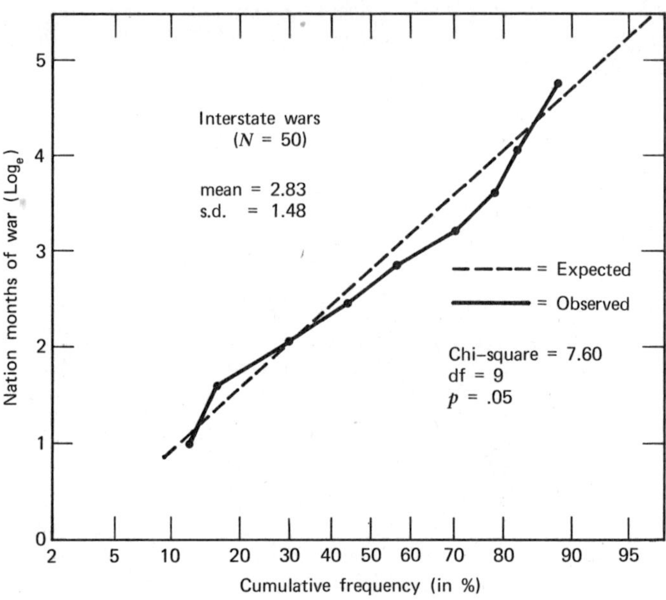

6.9c Cumulative probability, expected and observed, of extra-systemic war magnitudes, and chi-square measures of similarity.

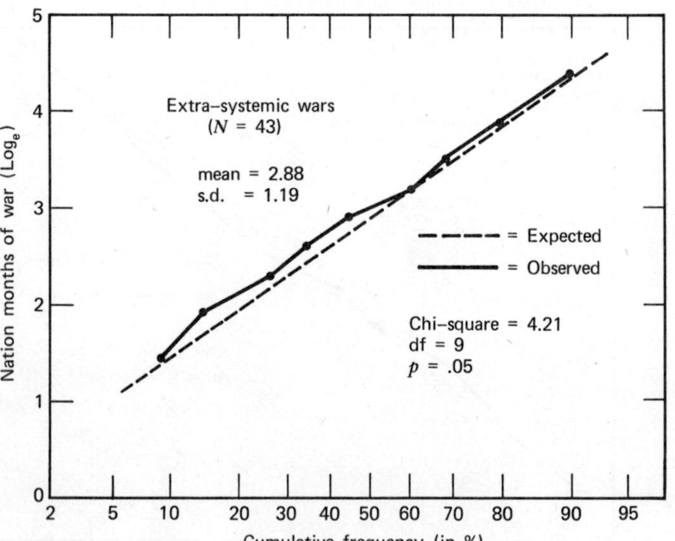

probability graphs. The broken line represents the expected frequency at each percentage level given on the horizontal axis; the $\log_e$ scale is given as the vertical axis. The line connecting the heavy dots represents the observed number of wars, each dot showing the actual percent of the wars included in each successive $\log_e$ range. All three distributions thus tested "fit" the expected distribution at a .05 level of significance, which permits us to say that the distributions of war magnitude scores in our populations of international, interstate, and extra-systemic wars can be described as natural logarithmic curves.

Finally, the 93 wars embraced in this study may be grouped according to their *intensity* ranges, as measured by battle deaths per nation month. Here we note, not too surprisingly, that the distribution frequencies of the extra-systemic wars differ somewhat from those of the other classes of war. To some extent, this is probably a statistical artifact arising from the fact that the non-members' battle deaths are not included. But it also may be accounted for by the fact that the colonial powers seldom allocated as much in material and manpower per year to these wars as to those fought against other system members.

6.10 - FREQUENCIES OF INTERNATIONAL WARS BY INTENSITY (BD/NM)

INTENSITY RATIO	0-66	66-286	286-1000	1000-3000	3000-8000	>8000
ALL INTERNATIONAL WARS	2	23	36	16	9	7
INTERSTATE WARS	1	8	18	8	8	7
CENTRAL SYSTEM WARS	1	14	26	10	7	3
MAJOR POWER WARS	1	12	21	9	8	6
EXTRA-SYSTEMIC WARS	1	15	18	8	1	0

SUMMARY

Having already summarized the way in which these wars rank on a variety of dimensions, there is little to add here. Not surprisingly, the World Wars rank at the very top on severity and magnitude, and within the first five on intensity, with the Korean War third on severity and magnitude, but in positions 12 and 13 on the two intensity dimensions. Further, the wars that rank high on severity tend also to rank high on magnitude and intensity, and those which are low on one tend to be low on the others. We also found that the interstate wars which engaged more nations (and/or the more populous ones) were also those which saw more battle deaths per nation month, but fewer battle deaths per capita. Finally, there seems to be a rather close fit between the frequencies that were observed and those that were predicted by the log normal distribution.

This chapter marks the end of our concern with the wars themselves. In the next chapter, we shift our object of analysis to the system, and to the way in which the wars are distributed throughout the system across time.

Part C
The System

Chapter 7

Annual Amounts of War Begun, Underway and Terminated

Up to this juncture, we have focused exclusively on wars as separate, discrete events occurring at different points in time and space within our empirical domain. For those who want to examine a given war in isolation, or do a comparative analysis of several (or many) such cases, this type of presentation is perfectly satisfactory. That is, one may generalize about all of the wars included in our compilation, or a specified subset of them, on the basis of these original presentations.

One cannot, however, discover very much about the international system (or its interstate, central, and major power sub-systems) on the basis of such raw data. In order to generalize about the role of war in these settings, it is necessary to rearrange and recombine our figures and convert them from a war-by-war basis to a period-by-period (year, decade, etc.) basis. Furthermore, to the extent that we care to ascertain the strength of the correlation between war and a variety of other conditions or events in the international system, some such recombination is absolutely essential. The literature abounds with hypotheses (and, all too often, assertions) about the way in which certain discrete or cyclical phenomena constitute the necessary and/or the sufficient preconditions of war. Some scholars argue, for example, that wars are unlikely until a sufficient interval has elapsed such that the relevant nations can recover from (or forget) the previous carnage, or until a new generation has come to power. Others suggest that the onset of war is intimately related to cyclical processes of an economic, demographic, or even a meteorological nature. Then there are the frequent but undocumented allusions to increases and decreases in the frequency, severity, or magnitude of war over the past century or two. But outside of the partial figures assembled by our predecessors, no sufficient data base exists by which these and other propositions of a bivariate or multivariate nature might be put to the test. Hence the need for a reordering of our compilations along some sort of time scale.

As to the particular unit of time which best serves this need for a chronological breakdown of our war data, one might select the microsecond, hour, day, week, month, quarter, year, half-decade, decade, generation, or century, depending on the independent or intervening variables to be used and the types of analyses contemplated. We have selected the year as our unit here; it is not only the most widely used unit in longitudinal societal science research, but appears to be most practical as well. All sorts of political, economic, and social data are traditionally presented on a year-by-year basis, and annual figures may readily be combined to make for longer periods. And if units of less than a year are needed—as when we shift from structural and cultural phenomena to behavioral ones, or when we do case studies—we can always go back to the raw data and compute our onset, underway, and termination figures for a shorter period.

Nor can we leave this subject without a brief allusion to the distinction between "real" (that is, chronological) time and diplomatic, military, technological, or political "time." Depending on the variables under consideration, there is always the possibility that certain relevant environmental factors may change sufficiently over the years and centuries to make one's measurements not quite comparable from one epoch to another. This is particularly true when factors which show definite secular trends (such as technology, demography, or system size) are at work. One may partially solve the comparability problem by controlling for these environmental factors via the use of an artificial and shifting unit of time. As a matter of fact, as our data on many of the variables considered in the project become available, we will attempt to construct such measures as diplomatic time, reflecting the extent to which it has become compressed or (perhaps as likely) elongated over the past century and a half.

THREE TYPES OF ANNUAL INDICATOR

With the above considerations in mind, we can now turn to the types of annual indicator that are used in this book. At first glance, the most obvious description of annual systemic war experience would appear to be the amount of war going on, or *underway,* during that year. Here, we would report the number of nations engaged in given types of wars during the year, the number of wars underway, and the number of nation months and battle deaths experienced during that year. But it should be clear that this particular form, while meriting attention, is not entirely useful for our purposes. For certain descriptive or comparative purposes, or for use as an *independent* or predictor variable, measures of the amount of war underway during a given year may be quite appropriate, but as a *dependent* or outcome variable, a different form of aggregation is mandatory. Given our theoretical predilections (as spelled out in Chapters One and Two), we are most interested in the period immediately *preceding the outbreak* of war, and the circumstances that resulted in some conflicts being settled peacefully while others terminated in war. In other words, if the causes of war are best understood by studying the configurations of variables on the eve of that war, we might well prefer to know how much war *began* in a given year rather than how much war was *underway.* Although 20 of our interstate wars begin and end in the same year, and would therefore show the same figures whether we look at onset or underway data, the remaining 30 begin in one year and end in another, and thus produce appreciable differences between the onset and underway figures for a given year.

To take one example—the central system's experiences in interstate war in 1897 and in 1911—the number of nation months *underway* is exactly the same (6.2), but, whereas the 1897 figure for nation months *begun* was 6.2, it was 25.4 for 1911. All things being equal, the latter year would appear to be much bloodier than the former, despite the fact that the system experienced the same amount of war *during* those two 12-month periods. Consequently, although we are also concerned with how much war is going on each year, we emphasize the amount of war begun in each year—the total nation months and battle deaths resulting from wars begun in that year, whether those wars terminated during that year or a subsequent one. By adopting this approach, we may ascertain the extent to which the frequency, magnitude, and severity of war might be associated with the state of the system or the properties of the actors during any defined preceding period.

A third type of annual indicator relates to the amount and kind of war experience *terminated* during each year. While not as interesting to us as the onset and underway data, termination figures will be important when we consider intervals between wars and search for indications of periodicity. Moreover, for those who seek to discover the systematic *consequences* of war, these termination figures represent the most useful type of independent (or intervening) variable.

FORMAT AND EXPLANATION

The tables in this chapter, then, will include the three different types of measure outlined above. And, in addition to the distinctions among onset, underway, and terminated figures, we must also specify the particular domain which is embraced by each set of figures: the international, the interstate, the central, or the major power system. Thus, we begin with a table showing the annual amounts of war which began, were underway, and terminated for the entire international system (Table 7.1), then go on to show the same figures for the interstate system wars only (Table 7.2), after which we take a brief look at the *nation* entries into and departures from interstate war (Table 7.3). We follow with tables showing the war experiences of the central system members in all their wars (Table 7.4) and in interstate wars only (Table 7.5), and the annual figures for the major powers in all wars (Table 7.6) and interstate wars only (Table 7.7). Finally, we present data for the extra-systemic wars (Table 7.8). Since the format for these tables will be essentially the same regardless of which system is covered, we may deal with all of them together, beginning with our data for the onset of war.

Amount of War Begun

For each year, from 1816 through 1965 (or from 1816 to 1919 for central system tables), we will first show (column 1) the number of nations in the system or sub-system at hand as of the close of that year; even if a nation did not qualify for membership until December (and the exact day or month is often difficult to ascertain), it is treated as if it were a member during the entire year.

Then (column 2) we show the number of wars of the given type which *began* during that year; this is the factor from which all other indicators in the tables will flow. Next (column 3), we indicate the number of nations that participated in all qualifying wars within that system, regardless of when they *entered* those wars.

From there, we move on to the more refined indicators of magnitude and severity; the first (column 4) is the number of battle deaths (in thousands) of war resulting from those wars which began each year in the particular system or sub-system at hand. Again, let us emphasize that we are not interested here in the years in which these wars ended, but only in the total battle deaths arising out of war begun during any given year. Next (column 5) is the number of nation months resulting from all qualifying wars which began in that system during that year. Then, with that figure, we can proceed to the compilation of the two intensity measures that were described in Chapter Three: battle deaths per nation month of war begun (column 6) and battle deaths per capita based on the total prewar population of all the nations participating in wars begun that year (columns 7 and 8). (Battle deaths per prewar armed personnel will not, as was indicated earlier, be used.) The last ratio is presented in natural logarithmic form, as well as in raw figures, since the raw, nontransformed figure offers only a moderately useful index. Because the denominator is so large and the numerator so small, it is sometimes difficult to make an intelligent interpretation of the ratio. And while the raw ratio is based on 100 for total population and therefore results in a percentage figure, the transformed $\log_e$ figure for battle deaths is based on 1,000,000 population in order to avoid negative $\log_e$ values.

Amount of War Underway

Shifting now from the annual onset data to data on the amount of war *underway* and *terminated,* we find somewhat less detailed presentations. We list (column 9) the number of qualifying wars that were underway at any time during the year, regardless of when they began or ended. Following this is the number of nations that were at war at any time during the year (column 10). This figure is then normalized by computing (column 11) the *percentage* of nations in the system that were at war during each year. Then in column 12 is the more sensitive underway magnitude, measured in nation months. Finally (column 13), there is perhaps the most sensitive and generally useful of the underway indicators: the percentage of *possible* nation months of war which were exhausted during the year. This is computed by multiplying the number of nations in the system by 12 (months in a year), and dividing that figure into the total number of nation months underway during the year. The virtue of this measure is that we are able to make meaningful comparisons between years in which the system size differed drastically; but the drawback of this indicator is that it does not take into account the fact that a nation *can* have more than 12 nation months of war per year via participation in more than one war simultaneously. Therefore, our posited "maximum" number of nation months per year is incorrect in theory, but in fact reflects the situation accurately most of the time.

As to battle deaths sustained by system members during each year, we recognize that such information might be quite useful for some researchers, but we finally decided against any effort to gather these estimates. To do so would require us to ascertain the approximate date on which these fatalities occurred, and like those "body counts" prepared by others, would necessarily be extremely rough; for most theoretical purposes the figures just are not sufficiently useful to merit the research time that would be required.

Amount of War Terminated

As we noted earlier, one can seldom use onset or underway figures if the inquiry at hand treats war as the *independent* variable, or when one hopes to find the extent to which war predicts to certain future consequences over some sustained period. For that purpose, some measure of the amount of war which *ended* in a given period is almost always essential. In this section of the tables, therefore, we offer a number of indicators of the amount of war that terminated each year, beginning (column 14) with the number of wars that ended that year. Next, we show the number of nations in each particular system or sub-system that had at any time fought in the qualifying wars which ended that year, regardless of when those nations left those wars. Finally, we show the number of nation months of war that constitute the magnitude of all wars which ended in a given year (column 16), and the number of battle deaths that were sustained by members of the system as a consequence of those wars (column 17).

As to normalization of these last two figures, we chose not to compute such refinements both because our own interest in termination data is quite low and because they raise certain difficulties. That is, even though we might normalize the nation month figure by merely controlling for system size, we cannot compute the more sensitive figure of percentage of *possible* nation months of war which could have ended; as opposed to nation months which could have been *underway* in any year, there is no logical upper limit. Nor could we produce a particularly useful normalization of the severity measure, based on armed forces size for example, since such data are now only available for the years preceding each nation's entry into war.

THE SYSTEMIC AND SUB-SYSTEMIC COMPILATIONS

In opening this chapter, we noted the distinction between a compilation in which each war is measured separately and one in which all relevant wars are combined to show fluctuations over time within the interstate system or its sub-systems. Here, then, we shift our unit of analysis from the war to the year, and treat each of the systemic and sub-systemic contexts separately, showing for each the amount of war that began, was underway, or terminated each year, with a brief recapitulation of the considerations that were discussed at length in Chapter Two.

International War

The first of our tables here (7.1) presents these annual data for all 93 wars fought by members of the interstate system, either against one another or against a non-member entity. In it, we show the 7 measures of the amount of war that *began* in each year, the 5 measures of the amount *underway,* and the 4 measures of the amount *terminated.* That is, we provide here the figures that reflect the annual amount of war arising out of sustained military combat in which at least one participant is a member of the interstate system. As was pointed out in Chapter Three, only the entities that were members of the system and that qualified as active participants can contribute to the nation months and battle deaths by which a war is measured. On the other hand, no discrimination is made between central or peripheral, or major and minor, sub-system members for the moment; these more limited contexts are treated in the sub-sections that follow.

Interstate War

Our second table (7.2) follows the same format but covers only the 50 wars that had at least one system member on *each* side. In a later table we will return to the extra-systemic conflicts that were excluded here.

Nation Entries and Departures

There are, however, certain limitations inherent in these "annual amounts of war" measures. One problem with the onset figures is that they tend to exaggerate that figure for the *first* year of a relatively long or large war, and understate the figures for the remaining year(s) of such a war. Thus, in order to provide an alternative measure —and one less vulnerable to that criticism—we compute a set of "nation entry" and "nation departure" measures. These show the amount of war *resulting from the nation entries and departures that occurred in each particular year,* instead of assigning all such nation months and battle deaths to the single year in which the *war* began or ended. But we only do this for interstate wars, since so few nations entered into and departed from extra-systemic wars in different years. There are 5 interstate wars which saw a total of 34 nations *entering* the conflicts in a year following the formal initiation of war, and 2 interstate wars which saw a total of 16 nations departing the conflict in a year preceding the formal termination of the war. In 4 extra-systemic wars one nation entered each in a different year, and there were no extra-systemic wars from which nations departed in a different year. The most noticeable differences in the onset and termination figures for interstate wars are to be seen in the data on the two World Wars.

Specifically, Table 7.3 differs from Table 7.2 in the following ways: After the system size for each year is given in column 1, we show (column 2) the number of nation entries into wars each year, rather than the number of nations which *ever* participated in a war that began in a given year. In the rare instances when a nation entered more than one interstate war in a given year (for example, Russia in 1939), we count it as two nation entries into interstate war. We follow (column 3) with number of wars begun (which is column 2 in the other tables). Columns 4 and 5 show the battle deaths and war months, respectively, of *those nations entering* interstate wars that year. Likewise, the intensity measures in columns 6 to 8 reflect the individual nations' entries rather than the totals for the entire war. Shifting to the "underway" measures, we return to the same format as used in the prior tables, with the number of nations engaged in interstate war (column 9), the number of interstate wars underway (column 10), and the fraction of interstate system members actually at war (column 11). Column 12 shows the number of nation months of interstate war underway, and column 13 converts that figure to a percentage of possible nation months exhausted.

Finally, in column 14 we give the number of nations leaving interstate wars each year, whether or not the wars themselves terminated, and in column 15 we show the number of wars ending. The war months (column 16) and battle deaths (column 17) of those departing nations complete the table.

Table 7.3 provides an alternative method of measuring the amount of interstate war begun and ended each year. We now return to an examination of the annual amounts of central system, major power, and extra-systemic war in the form established in Tables 7.1 and 7.2. We have, however, computed the nation entries and departures for all seven data sets presented in this chapter; they are available from the International Relations Archive, University of Michigan. Let us turn now to the annual amounts of war experienced by central system members during the 1816–1919 period.

Central System War

There will be many scholars who, for a variety of reasons, prefer to focus their attention on a somewhat smaller domain than that embraced by the entire interstate system. Recognizing the arguments for limiting one's examination of war and its associated conditions to a more restricted set of nations—especially during the century preceding World War I—we have recomputed our data to partially exclude the role of the peripheral nations from 1816 through 1919. Thus, in Table 7.4 we show the same set of figures as in tables 7.1 and 7.2, but only for those *active participants who were central system members,* regardless of how many peripheral nations were involved or how costly or sustained their combat was. Before examining these figures it should be noted that there is an alternative, and more restricted, way in which central system war might be defined. That is, we might require that a central system member be involved on *each* side before including a given war in this category. But given the fact that 19 of the 29 central system wars from 1816 through 1919—when the central-peripheral distinction is dropped—did indeed find at least one such nation on each side, there seemed little use in calculating and presenting two separate and largely redundant sets of annual data for this particular sub-system. We have, however, presented the annual war experience of the central system participants in *interstate* wars only, and excluded the data from those conflicts in which central system members fought against non-member entities (Table 7.5).

Major Power War

For those who require, or prefer, an even more restricted empirical domain on which to focus, we have gone a step further and tabulated the annual indicators on the basis of major power wars only. As in the case of the central system, we have used the less restrictive of the two possible definitions, and treated as major power wars those which involved at least one nation from this particular oligarchy; here, of the 30 major power wars, only 9 involved a major power participant on each side. We follow the same measurement procedures as in the central system wars and include only the nation months and battle deaths that are accounted for by nations which fall into this select sub-system (Tables 7.6 and 7.7).

7.1 - ANNUAL AMOUNTS OF INTERNATIONAL WAR

	ONSET--BY WAR							UNDERWAY					TERMINATION--BY WAR			
YEAR	NO. IN SYSTEM 1	NO. OF WARS BEGUN 2	NO. OF PARTIC-IPANTS 3	BATTLE DEATHS 000'S 4	NATION MONTHS 5	BATTLE DEATHS 000'S PER NATION MONTH 6	BATTLE DEATHS PER HUNDRED POPULA-TION 7	LOG OF BATTLE DEATHS PER MILLION POPULA-TION 8	NO. OF WARS UNDER-WAY 9	NO. OF NATIONS IN WAR 10	% OF NATIONS IN WAR 11	NATION MONTHS UNDER-WAY 12	% OF NATION MONTHS EX-HAUST-ED 13	NO. OF WARS ENDING 14	NO. OF PARTIC-IPANTS 15	NATION MONTHS 16	BATTLE DEATHS 000'S 17
1816	23	0	0	0.0	0.0	0.0	0.0	0.0	0	0	0.0	0.0	0.0	0	0	0.0	0.0
1817	23	1	1	2.0	6.9	0.29	0.0098	4.59	1	1	4.3	1.8	0.7	0	0	0.0	0.0
1818	23	0	0	0.0	0.0	0.0	0.0	0.0	1	1	4.3	5.1	1.8	1	1	6.9	2.0
1819	23	0	0	0.0	0.0	0.0	0.0	0.0	0	0	0.0	0.0	0.0	0	0	0.0	0.0
1820	23	0	0	0.0	0.0	0.0	0.0	0.0	0	0	0.0	0.0	0.0	0	0	0.0	0.0
1821	23	1	1	15.0	85.1	0.18	0.0607	6.41	1	1	4.3	9.3	3.4	0	0	0.0	0.0
1822	23	0	0	0.0	0.0	0.0	0.0	0.0	1	1	4.3	12.0	4.3	0	0	0.0	0.0
1823	23	2	3	16.0	43.7	0.37	0.0247	5.51	3	4	17.4	29.9	10.8	1	2	14.6	1.0
1824	23	0	0	0.0	0.0	0.0	0.0	0.0	2	2	8.7	24.0	8.7	0	0	0.0	0.0
1825	23	1	1	15.0	56.2	0.27	0.2542	7.84	3	3	13.0	29.3	10.6	0	0	0.0	0.0
1826	24	1	1	5.0	17.0	0.29	0.0095	4.55	4	4	16.7	28.9	10.0	1	1	29.1	15.0
1827	24	1	4	3.2	0.4	7.95	0.0024	3.18	4	5	20.8	36.0	12.5	1	4	0.4	3.2
1828	25	1	2	130.0	33.4	3.89	0.1660	7.41	4	3	12.0	34.1	11.4	2	2	102.1	20.0
1829	25	0	0	0.0	0.0	0.0	0.0	0.0	2	3	12.0	28.8	9.6	1	2	33.4	130.0
1830	26	0	0	0.0	0.0	0.0	0.0	0.0	1	1	3.8	2.9	0.9	1	1	56.2	15.0
1831	28	2	2	25.0	22.0	1.14	0.0314	5.75	2	2	7.1	10.3	3.1	1	1	8.3	15.0
1832	28	0	0	0.0	0.0	0.0	0.0	0.0	1	1	3.6	11.7	3.5	1	1	13.7	10.0
1833	28	0	0	0.0	0.0	0.0	0.0	0.0	0	0	0.0	0.0	0.0	0	0	0.0	0.0
1834	28	0	0	0.0	0.0	0.0	0.0	0.0	0	0	0.0	0.0	0.0	0	0	0.0	0.0
1835	28	1	1	1.0	6.7	0.15	0.0130	4.87	1	1	3.6	3.0	0.9	0	0	0.0	0.0
1836	28	0	0	0.0	0.0	0.0	0.0	0.0	1	1	3.6	3.7	1.1	1	1	6.7	1.0
1837	28	0	0	0.0	0.0	0.0	0.0	0.0	0	0	0.0	0.0	0.0	0	0	0.0	0.0
1838	30	1	1	20.0	48.4	0.41	0.0775	6.65	1	1	3.3	3.0	0.8	0	0	0.0	0.0
1839	31	1	2	10.0	5.7	1.76	0.0199	5.29	2	2	6.5	12.5	3.4	0	0	0.0	0.0
1840	31	0	0	0.0	0.0	0.0	0.0	0.0	2	2	6.5	17.2	4.6	1	2	5.7	10.0
1841	33	1	1	1.0	1.0	1.00	0.0769	6.65	2	2	6.1	13.0	3.3	1	1	1.0	1.0
1842	34	0	0	0.0	0.0	0.0	0.0	0.0	1	1	2.9	9.4	2.3	1	1	48.4	20.0
1843	35	0	0	0.0	0.0	0.0	0.0	0.0	0	0	0.0	0.0	0.0	0	0	0.0	0.0
1844	35	0	0	0.0	0.0	0.0	0.0	0.0	0	0	0.0	0.0	0.0	0	0	0.0	0.0
1845	35	1	1	1.5	2.9	0.52	0.0056	4.02	1	1	2.9	0.6	0.1	0	0	0.0	0.0
1846	35	1	2	17.0	42.2	0.40	0.0556	6.32	2	3	8.6	17.6	4.2	1	1	2.9	1.5
1847	36	0	0	0.0	0.0	0.0	0.0	0.0	1	2	5.6	24.0	5.6	0	0	0.0	0.0
1848	37	4	6	76.0	42.8	1.78	0.0405	6.00	5	7	18.9	27.6	6.2	1	2	42.2	17.0
1849	38	1	4	2.2	6.4	0.34	0.0029	3.37	5	9	23.7	24.3	5.3	5	9	49.2	78.2
1850	38	0	0	0.0	0.0	0.0	0.0	0.0	0	0	0.0	0.0	0.0	0	0	0.0	0.0
1851	39	1	2	1.3	13.2	0.10	0.0155	5.04	1	2	5.1	11.0	2.4	0	0	0.0	0.0
1852	39	1	1	5.0	3.4	1.47	0.0198	5.29	2	3	7.7	3.2	0.7	1	2	13.2	1.3

YEAR	NO. IN SYSTEM 1	NO. OF WARS BEGUN 2	NO. OF PARTIC-IPANTS 3	BATTLE DEATHS 000'S 4	NATION MONTHS 5	BATTLE DEATHS 000'S PER NATION MONTH 6	BATTLE DEATHS PER HUNDRED POPULA-TION 7	LOG OF BATTLE DEATHS PER MILLION POPULA-TION 8	NO. OF WARS UNDER-WAY 9	NO. OF NATIONS IN WAR 10	% OF NATIONS IN WAR 11	NATION MONTHS UNDER-WAY 12	% OF NATION MONTHS EX-HAUST-ED 13	NO. OF WARS ENDING 14	NO. OF PARTIC-IPANTS 15	NATION MONTHS 16	BATTLE DEATHS 000'S 17
	ONSET--BY WAR								UNDERWAY					TERMINATION--BY WAR			
1853	39	1	5	264.2	116.5	2.27	0.1586	7.37	2	2	5.1	7.0	1.5	1	1	3.4	5.0
1854	40	0	0	0.0	0.0	0.0	0.0	0.0	1	4	10.0	42.2	8.8	0	0	0.0	0.0
1855	41	0	0	0.0	0.0	0.0	0.0	0.0	1	5	12.2	59.7	12.1	0	0	0.0	0.0
1856	41	1	2	2.0	9.2	0.22	0.0060	4.09	2	6	14.6	14.4	2.9	1	5	116.5	264.2
1857	41	1	1	3.5	22.9	0.15	0.0119	4.78	2	2	4.9	12.6	2.6	1	2	9.2	2.0
1858	41	1	1	3.0	12.9	0.23	0.0115	4.74	2	2	4.9	20.0	4.1	0	0	0.0	0.0
1859	42	2	5	32.5	17.7	1.84	0.0340	5.83	4	7	16.7	20.1	4.0	3	5	43.1	29.0
1860	44	2	3	2.0	7.6	0.26	0.0035	3.56	3	5	11.4	12.0	2.3	2	4	11.6	11.0
1861	40	0	0	0.0	0.0	0.0	0.0	0.0	1	2	5.0	1.2	0.2	1	2	6.4	1.0
1862	39	1	2	20.0	115.4	0.17	0.0434	6.07	1	2	5.1	17.0	3.6	0	0	0.0	0.0
1863	39	2	3	6.0	15.9	0.38	0.0074	4.30	3	5	12.8	36.3	7.8	1	2	1.0	1.0
1864	39	2	5	114.5	134.3	0.85	0.1631	7.40	4	7	17.9	40.3	8.6	2	4	25.7	9.5
1865	39	1	3	1.0	16.8	0.06	0.0047	3.84	3	6	15.4	50.3	10.7	0	0	0.0	0.0
1866	39	1	11	36.1	14.5	2.49	0.0384	5.95	4	18	46.2	74.7	16.0	2	14	31.3	37.1
1867	37	0	0	0.0	0.0	0.0	0.0	0.0	2	4	10.8	26.4	5.9	1	2	115.4	20.0
1868	34	1	1	100.0	112.1	0.89	0.6024	8.70	2	3	8.8	26.7	6.5	0	0	0.0	0.0
1869	34	0	0	0.0	0.0	0.0	0.0	0.0	2	3	8.8	36.0	8.8	0	0	0.0	0.0
1870	34	1	5	187.5	27.0	6.94	0.2193	7.69	3	8	23.5	39.4	9.7	1	2	123.5	110.0
1871	31	0	0	0.0	0.0	0.0	0.0	0.0	2	3	9.7	15.8	4.2	1	5	27.0	187.5
1872	31	0	0	0.0	0.0	0.0	0.0	0.0	1	1	3.2	12.0	3.2	0	0	0.0	0.0
1873	31	1	1	6.0	65.2	0.09	0.1622	7.39	2	2	6.5	21.2	5.7	0	0	0.0	0.0
1874	31	0	0	0.0	0.0	0.0	0.0	0.0	2	2	6.5	24.0	6.5	0	0	0.0	0.0
1875	32	1	1	10.0	21.4	0.47	0.0355	5.87	3	3	9.4	30.0	7.8	0	0	0.0	0.0
1876	32	0	0	0.0	0.0	0.0	0.0	0.0	3	3	9.4	36.0	9.4	0	0	0.0	0.0
1877	32	1	2	285.0	17.6	16.19	0.2336	7.76	4	4	12.5	44.8	11.7	1	1	21.4	10.0
1878	34	2	2	7.5	20.3	0.37	0.0104	4.64	5	6	17.6	13.0	3.2	4	5	197.0	394.5
1879	34	2	4	17.5	176.0	0.10	0.0425	6.05	3	4	11.8	44.3	10.9	1	1	5.7	3.5
1880	34	0	0	0.0	0.0	0.0	0.0	0.0	2	4	11.8	44.1	10.8	1	1	18.2	4.0
1881	34	0	0	0.0	0.0	0.0	0.0	0.0	1	3	8.8	36.0	8.8	0	0	0.0	0.0
1882	35	2	2	24.5	65.3	0.38	0.0335	5.81	3	5	14.3	47.8	11.4	0	0	0.0	0.0
1883	35	0	0	0.0	0.0	0.0	0.0	0.0	3	5	14.3	56.2	13.4	1	3	170.3	14.0
1884	35	1	2	12.1	23.6	0.51	0.0026	3.25	3	3	8.6	30.7	7.3	1	1	25.7	4.5
1885	35	2	3	3.0	2.4	1.25	0.0769	6.65	4	6	17.1	25.0	6.0	4	6	65.6	35.1
1886	35	0	0	0.0	0.0	0.0	0.0	0.0	0	0	0.0	0.0	0.0	0	0	0.0	0.0
1887	37	0	0	0.0	0.0	0.0	0.0	0.0	0	0	0.0	0.0	0.0	0	0	0.0	0.0
1888	38	0	0	0.0	0.0	0.0	0.0	0.0	0	0	0.0	0.0	0.0	0	0	0.0	0.0
1889	38	0	0	0.0	0.0	0.0	0.0	0.0	0	0	0.0	0.0	0.0	0	0	0.0	0.0
1890	38	0	0	0.0	0.0	0.0	0.0	0.0	0	0	0.0	0.0	0.0	0	0	0.0	0.0
1891	38	0	0	0.0	0.0	0.0	0.0	0.0	0	0	0.0	0.0	0.0	0	0	0.0	0.0
1892	38	0	0	0.0	0.0	0.0	0.0	0.0	0	0	0.0	0.0	0.0	0	0	0.0	0.0

7.1 - ANNUAL AMOUNTS OF INTERNATIONAL WAR

	ONSET--BY WAR								UNDERWAY					TERMINATION--BY WAR			
YEAR	NO. IN SYSTEM 1	NO. OF WARS BEGUN 2	NO. OF PARTIC-IPANTS 3	BATTLE DEATHS 000'S 4	NATION MONTHS 5	BATTLE DEATHS 000'S PER NATION MONTH 6	BATTLE DEATHS PER HUNDRED POPULA-TION 7	LOG OF BATTLE DEATHS PER MILLION POPULA-TION 8	NO. OF WARS UNDER-WAY 9	NO. OF NATIONS IN WAR 10	% OF NATIONS IN WAR 11	NATION MONTHS UNDER-WAY 12	% OF NATION MONTHS EX-HAUST-ED 13	NO. OF WARS ENDING 14	NO. OF PARTIC-IPANTS 15	NATION MONTHS 16	BATTLE DEATHS 000'S 17
1893	38	0	0	0.0	0.0	0.0	0.0	0.0	0	0	0.0	0.0	0.0	0	0	0.0	0.0
1894	38	2	3	21.0	25.7	C.82	0.0041	3.70	2	3	7.9	10.7	2.3	0	0	0.0	0.0
1895	38	2	2	59.0	47.8	1.23	0.1194	7.09	4	5	13.2	25.8	5.7	2	3	25.7	21.0
1896	39	1	1	2.C	23.1	0.09	0.0110	4.70	3	2	5.1	28.8	6.2	1	1	10.5	9.0
1897	39	1	2	2.0	6.2	0.32	0.0075	4.32	3	3	7.7	30.2	6.5	1	2	6.2	2.0
1898	40	1	2	10.C	7.4	1.35	0.0106	4.66	3	2	5.0	14.4	3.0	3	2	67.8	62.0
1899	41	2	2	26.5	72.5	0.37	0.0226	5.42	2	2	4.9	13.6	2.8	0	0	0.0	0.0
1900	42	0	0	0.0	0.0	0.0	0.0	0.0	2	2	4.8	24.0	4.8	0	0	0.0	0.0
1901	42	0	C	0.0	0.0	0.0	0.0	0.0	2	2	4.8	24.0	4.8	0	0	0.0	0.0
1902	43	0	0	0.0	0.0	0.0	0.0	0.0	2	2	4.7	11.1	2.2	2	2	72.5	26.5
1903	43	0	0	C.0	0.0	0.0	0.0	0.0	0	0	0.0	0.0	0.0	0	0	0.0	0.0
1904	43	1	2	130.0	38.6	3.37	0.0692	6.54	1	2	4.7	21.6	4.2	0	0	0.0	0.0
1905	44	0	0	0.0	0.0	0.0	0.0	0.0	1	2	4.5	17.0	3.2	1	2	38.6	130.0
1906	43	1	3	1.0	5.4	0.19	0.0270	5.60	1	3	7.0	5.4	1.0	1	3	5.4	1.0
1907	43	1	3	1.0	6.3	0.16	0.0417	6.03	1	3	7.0	6.3	1.2	1	3	6.3	1.0
1908	44	0	0	0.0	0.0	0.0	0.0	0.0	0	0	0.0	0.0	0.0	0	0	0.0	0.0
1909	44	1	2	10.0	17.0	0.59	0.0408	6.01	1	2	4.5	11.6	2.2	0	0	0.0	0.0
1910	44	0	0	0.0	0.0	0.0	0.0	0.0	1	2	4.5	5.4	1.0	1	2	17.0	10.0
1911	44	1	2	20.0	25.4	0.79	0.0335	5.81	1	2	4.5	6.2	1.2	0	0	0.0	0.0
1912	43	1	4	82.0	20.4	4.02	0.2571	7.85	2	5	11.6	27.4	5.3	1	2	25.4	20.0
1913	43	1	5	60.5	4.2	14.40	0.1609	7.38	2	5	11.6	16.4	3.2	2	5	24.6	142.5
1914	44	1	15	8555.8	607.8	14.08	1.4137	9.56	1	9	20.5	41.4	7.8	0	0	0.0	0.0
1915	44	0	0	0.0	0.0	0.0	0.0	0.0	1	11	25.0	118.0	22.3	0	0	0.0	0.0
1916	44	0	0	0.0	0.0	0.0	0.0	0.0	1	13	29.5	146.3	27.7	0	0	0.0	0.0
1917	44	1	1	50.0	39.3	1.27	0.0309	5.73	2	15	34.1	169.8	32.2	0	0	0.0	0.0
1918	48	0	0	0.0	0.0	0.0	0.0	0.0	2	14	29.2	144.3	25.1	1	15	607.8	8555.8
1919	51	2	5	61.0	93.4	0.65	0.1203	7.09	3	6	11.8	38.6	6.3	1	3	10.8	11.0
1920	61	0	0	0.0	0.0	0.0	0.0	0.0	2	3	4.9	36.0	4.9	0	0	0.0	0.0
1921	62	1	2	29.0	71.8	0.40	0.0463	6.14	3	4	6.5	32.0	4.3	1	1	39.3	50.0
1922	63	0	0	0.0	0.0	0.0	0.0	0.0	2	3	4.8	30.6	4.0	1	2	82.6	50.0
1923	63	0	0	0.0	0.0	0.0	0.0	0.0	1	1	1.6	12.0	1.6	0	0	0.0	0.0
1924	63	0	0	0.0	0.0	0.0	0.0	0.0	1	1	1.6	12.0	1.6	0	0	0.0	0.0
1925	63	1	1	4.0	22.4	0.18	0.0098	4.59	2	2	3.2	26.2	3.5	0	0	0.0	0.0
1926	64	0	0	0.0	0.0	0.0	0.0	0.0	2	2	3.1	21.6	2.8	1	2	71.8	29.0
1927	65	0	0	0.0	0.0	0.0	0.0	0.0	1	1	1.5	5.0	0.6	1	1	22.4	4.0

	ONSET--BY WAR								UNDERWAY					TERMINATION--BY WAR			
YEAR	NO. IN SYSTEM 1	NO. OF WARS BEGUN 2	NO. OF PARTIC-IPANTS 3	BATTLE DEATHS 000'S 4	NATION MONTHS 5	BATTLE DEATHS 000'S PER NATION MONTH 6	BATTLE DEATHS PER HUNDRED POPULA-TION 7	LOG OF BATTLE DEATHS PER MILLION POPULA-TION 8	NO. OF WARS UNDER-WAY 9	NO. OF NATIONS IN WAR 10	% OF NATIONS IN WAR 11	NATION MONTHS UNDER-WAY 12	% OF NATION MONTHS EX-HAUST-ED 13	NO. OF WARS ENDING 14	NO. OF PARTIC-IPANTS 15	NATION MONTHS 16	BATTLE DEATHS 000'S 17
1928	65	0	0	0.0	0.0	0.0	0.0	0.0	0	0	0.0	0.0	0.0	0	0	0.0	0.0
1929	65	0	0	0.0	0.0	0.0	0.0	0.0	0	0	0.0	0.0	0.0	0	0	0.0	0.0
1930	65	0	0	0.0	0.0	0.0	0.0	0.0	0	0	0.0	0.0	0.0	0	0	0.0	0.0
1931	65	1	2	60.0	33.2	1.81	0.0102	4.62	1	2	3.1	0.8	0.1	0	0	0.0	0.0
1932	66	1	2	130.0	71.8	1.81	3.8235	10.55	2	4	6.1	37.2	4.7	0	0	0.0	0.0
1933	66	0	0	0.0	0.0	0.0	0.0	0.0	2	4	6.1	32.2	4.1	1	2	33.2	60.0
1934	66	0	0	0.0	0.0	0.0	0.0	0.0	1	2	3.0	24.0	3.0	0	0	0.0	0.0
1935	66	1	2	20.0	14.4	1.39	0.0380	5.94	2	4	6.1	16.8	2.1	1	2	71.8	130.0
1936	66	0	0	0.0	0.0	0.0	0.0	0.0	1	2	3.0	8.6	1.1	1	2	14.4	20.0
1937	66	1	2	1000.0	106.2	9.42	0.1648	7.41	1	2	3.0	11.6	1.5	0	0	0.0	0.0
1938	66	0	0	0.0	0.0	0.0	0.0	0.0	1	2	3.0	24.0	3.0	0	0	0.0	0.0
1939	65	3	28	15273.3	895.0	17.07	0.8458	9.04	4	13	20.0	66.8	8.6	1	3	12.6	19.0
1940	62	0	0	0.0	0.0	0.0	0.0	0.0	3	16	25.8	118.2	15.9	1	2	6.8	90.0
1941	55	0	0	0.0	0.0	0.0	0.0	0.0	2	18	32.7	144.0	21.8	1	2	106.2	1000.0
1942	53	0	0	0.0	0.0	0.0	0.0	0.0	1	15	28.3	180.0	28.3	0	0	0.0	0.0
1943	52	0	0	0.0	0.0	0.0	0.0	0.0	1	16	30.8	178.5	28.6	0	0	0.0	0.0
1944	57	0	0	0.0	0.0	0.0	0.0	0.0	1	19	33.3	184.3	26.9	0	0	0.0	0.0
1945	64	2	3	96.4	124.4	0.77	0.0987	6.89	3	18	28.1	97.3	12.7	1	28	875.6	15164.3
1946	66	0	0	0.0	0.0	0.0	0.0	0.0	2	3	4.5	31.0	3.9	1	2	22.4	1.4
1947	68	2	2	3.0	34.5	0.09	0.0007	1.94	3	2	2.9	23.3	2.9	0	0	0.0	0.0
1948	72	1	6	8.0	19.4	0.41	0.0260	5.56	4	8	11.1	53.4	6.2	1	1	20.2	1.5
1949	75	0	0	0.0	0.0	0.0	0.0	0.0	3	4	5.3	12.4	1.4	2	7	33.7	9.5
1950	75	1	16	1892.1	514.0	3.68	0.1936	7.57	2	10	13.3	44.2	4.9	0	0	0.0	0.0
1951	75	0	0	0.0	0.0	0.0	0.0	0.0	2	16	21.3	192.5	21.4	0	0	0.0	0.0
1952	77	0	0	0.0	0.0	0.0	0.0	0.0	2	16	20.8	204.0	22.1	0	0	0.0	0.0
1953	78	0	0	0.0	0.0	0.0	0.0	0.0	2	16	20.5	120.8	12.9	1	16	514.0	1892.1
1954	82	1	1	15.0	88.5	0.17	0.0349	5.85	2	1	1.2	7.0	0.7	1	1	102.0	95.0
1955	84	0	0	0.0	0.0	0.0	0.0	0.0	1	1	1.2	12.0	1.2	0	0	0.0	0.0
1956	87	3	7	75.2	39.3	1.91	0.0080	4.38	4	7	8.0	24.7	2.4	2	6	2.6	35.2
1957	89	0	0	0.0	0.0	0.0	0.0	0.0	2	2	2.2	24.0	2.2	0	0	0.0	0.0
1958	90	0	0	0.0	0.0	0.0	0.0	0.0	2	2	2.2	24.0	2.2	0	0	0.0	0.0
1959	89	0	0	0.0	0.0	0.0	0.0	0.0	2	2	2.2	14.7	1.4	1	1	36.7	40.0
1960	107	0	0	0.0	0.0	0.0	0.0	0.0	1	1	0.9	12.0	0.9	0	0	0.0	0.0
1961	111	0	0	0.0	0.0	0.0	0.0	0.0	1	1	0.9	12.0	0.9	0	0	0.0	0.0
1962	117	1	2	1.0	2.2	0.45	0.0001	-0.11	2	3	2.6	4.7	0.3	2	3	90.7	16.0
1963	119	0	0	0.0	0.0	0.0	0.0	0.0	0	0	0.0	0.0	0.0	0	0	0.0	0.0
1964	122	0	0	0.0	0.0	0.0	0.0	0.0	0	0	0.0	0.0	0.0	0	0	0.0	0.0
1965	124	1	2	6.8	3.2	2.12	0.0011	2.43	1	2	1.6	3.2	0.2	1	2	3.2	6.8

7.2 - ANNUAL AMOUNTS OF INTERSTATE WAR

	ONSET--BY WAR							UNDERWAY					TERMINATION--BY WAR			
YEAR	NO. IN SYSTEM 1	NO. OF WARS BEGUN 2	NO. OF PARTIC-IPANTS 3	BATTLE DEATHS 000'S 4	NATION MONTHS 5	BATTLE DEATHS 000'S PER NATION MONTH 6	BATTLE DEATHS PER HUNDRED POPULA-TION 7	LOG OF BATTLE DEATHS PER MILLION POPULA-TION 8	NO. OF WARS UNDER-WAY 9	NO. OF NATIONS IN WAR 10	% OF NATIONS IN WAR 11	NATION MONTHS UNDER-WAY 12	% OF NATION MONTHS EX-HAUST-ED 13	NO. OF WARS ENDING 14	NO. OF PARTIC-IPANTS 15	NATION MONTHS 16	BATTLE DEATHS 000'S 17
1816	23	0	0	0.0	0.0	0.0	0.0	0.0	0	0	0.0	0.0	0.0	0	0	0.0	0.0
1817	23	0	0	0.0	0.0	0.0	0.0	0.0	0	0	0.0	0.0	0.0	0	0	0.0	0.0
1818	23	0	0	0.0	0.0	0.0	0.0	0.0	0	0	0.0	0.0	0.0	0	0	0.0	0.0
1819	23	0	0	0.0	0.0	0.0	0.0	0.0	0	0	0.0	0.0	0.0	0	0	0.0	0.0
1820	23	0	0	0.0	0.0	0.0	0.0	0.0	0	0	0.0	0.0	0.0	0	0	0.0	0.0
1821	23	0	0	0.0	0.0	0.0	0.0	0.0	0	0	0.0	0.0	0.0	0	0	0.0	0.0
1822	23	0	0	0.0	0.0	0.0	0.0	0.0	0	0	0.0	0.0	0.0	0	0	0.0	0.0
1823	23	1	2	1.0	14.6	0.07	0.0023	3.15	1	2	8.7	14.6	5.3	1	2	14.6	1.0
1824	23	0	0	0.0	0.0	0.0	0.0	0.0	0	0	0.0	0.0	0.0	0	0	0.0	0.0
1825	23	0	0	0.0	0.0	0.0	0.0	0.0	0	0	0.0	0.0	0.0	0	0	0.0	0.0
1826	24	0	0	0.0	0.0	0.0	0.0	0.0	0	0	0.0	0.0	0.0	0	0	0.0	0.0
1827	24	1	4	3.2	0.4	7.95	0.0024	3.18	1	4	16.7	0.0	0.0	1	4	0.4	3.2
1828	25	1	2	130.0	33.4	3.89	0.1660	7.41	1	2	8.0	16.4	5.5	0	0	0.0	0.0
1829	25	0	0	0.0	0.0	0.0	0.0	0.0	1	2	8.0	16.8	5.6	1	2	33.4	130.0
1830	26	0	0	0.0	0.0	0.0	0.0	0.0	0	0	0.0	0.0	0.0	0	0	0.0	0.0
1831	28	0	0	0.0	0.0	0.0	0.0	0.0	0	0	0.0	0.0	0.0	0	0	0.0	0.0
1832	28	0	0	0.0	0.0	0.0	0.0	0.0	0	0	0.0	0.0	0.0	0	0	0.0	0.0
1833	28	0	0	0.0	0.0	0.0	0.0	0.0	0	0	0.0	0.0	0.0	0	0	0.0	0.0
1834	28	0	0	0.0	0.0	0.0	0.0	0.0	0	0	0.0	0.0	0.0	0	0	0.0	0.0
1835	28	0	0	0.0	0.0	0.0	0.0	0.0	0	0	0.0	0.0	0.0	0	0	0.0	0.0
1836	28	0	0	0.0	0.0	0.0	0.0	0.0	0	0	0.0	0.0	0.0	0	0	0.0	0.0
1837	28	0	0	0.0	0.0	0.0	0.0	0.0	0	0	0.0	0.0	0.0	0	0	0.0	0.0
1838	30	0	0	0.0	0.0	0.0	0.0	0.0	0	0	0.0	0.0	0.0	0	0	0.0	0.0
1839	31	0	0	0.0	0.0	0.0	0.0	0.0	0	0	0.0	0.0	0.0	0	0	0.0	0.0
1840	31	0	0	0.0	0.0	0.0	0.0	0.0	0	0	0.0	0.0	0.0	0	0	0.0	0.0
1841	33	0	0	0.0	0.0	0.0	0.0	0.0	0	0	0.0	0.0	0.0	0	0	0.0	0.0
1842	34	0	0	0.0	0.0	0.0	0.0	0.0	0	0	0.0	0.0	0.0	0	0	0.0	0.0
1843	35	0	0	0.0	0.0	0.0	0.0	0.0	0	0	0.0	0.0	0.0	0	0	0.0	0.0
1844	35	0	0	0.0	0.0	0.0	0.0	0.0	0	0	0.0	0.0	0.0	0	0	0.0	0.0
1845	35	0	0	0.0	0.0	0.0	0.0	0.0	0	0	0.0	0.0	0.0	0	0	0.0	0.0
1846	35	1	2	17.0	42.2	0.40	0.0556	6.32	1	2	5.7	15.4	3.7	0	0	0.0	0.0
1847	36	0	0	0.0	0.0	0.0	0.0	0.0	1	2	5.6	24.0	5.6	0	0	0.0	0.0
1848	37	2	4	15.0	25.6	0.59	0.0261	5.56	3	6	16.2	21.2	4.8	1	2	42.2	17.0
1849	38	1	4	2.2	6.4	0.34	0.0029	3.37	3	7	18.4	13.6	3.0	3	7	32.0	17.2
1850	38	0	0	0.0	0.0	0.0	0.0	0.0	0	0	0.0	0.0	0.0	0	0	0.0	0.0
1851	39	1	2	1.3	13.2	0.10	0.0155	5.04	1	2	5.1	11.0	2.4	0	0	0.0	0.0
1852	39	0	0	0.0	0.0	0.0	0.0	0.0	1	2	5.1	2.2	0.5	1	2	13.2	1.3

	ONSET--BY WAR								UNDERWAY					TERMINATION--BY WAR			
YEAR	NO. IN SYSTEM 1	NO. OF WARS BEGUN 2	NO. OF PARTIC- IPANTS 3	BATTLE DEATHS 000'S 4	NATION MONTHS 5	BATTLE DEATHS 000'S PER NATION MONTH 6	BATTLE DEATHS PER HUNDRED POPULA- TION 7	LOG OF BATTLE DEATHS PER MILLION POPULA- TION 8	NO. OF WARS UNDER- WAY 9	NO. OF NATIONS IN WAR 10	% OF NATIONS IN WAR 11	NATION MONTHS UNDER- WAY 12	% OF NATION MONTHS EX- HAUST- ED 13	NO. OF WARS ENDING 14	NO. OF PARTIC- IPANTS 15	NATION MONTHS 16	BATTLE DEATHS 000'S 17
1853	39	1	5	264.2	116.5	2.27	0.1586	7.37	1	2	5.1	4.6	1.0	0	0	0.0	0.0
1854	40	0	0	0.0	0.0	0.0	0.0	0.0	1	4	10.0	42.2	8.8	0	0	0.0	0.0
1855	41	0	0	0.0	0.0	0.0	0.0	0.0	1	5	12.2	59.7	12.1	0	0	0.0	0.0
1856	41	1	2	2.0	9.2	0.22	0.0060	4.09	2	6	14.6	14.4	2.9	1	5	116.5	264.2
1857	41	0	0	0.0	0.0	0.0	0.0	0.0	1	2	4.9	4.8	1.0	1	2	9.2	2.0
1858	41	0	0	0.0	0.0	0.0	0.0	0.0	0	0	0.0	0.0	0.0	0	0	0.0	0.0
1859	42	2	5	32.5	17.7	1.84	0.0340	5.83	2	5	11.9	11.9	2.4	1	3	7.3	22.5
1860	44	2	3	2.0	7.6	0.26	0.0035	3.56	3	5	11.4	12.0	2.3	2	4	11.6	11.0
1861	40	0	0	0.0	0.0	0.0	0.0	0.0	1	2	5.0	1.2	0.2	1	2	6.4	1.0
1862	39	1	2	20.0	115.4	0.17	0.0434	6.07	1	2	5.1	17.0	3.6	0	0	0.0	0.0
1863	39	1	2	1.0	1.0	1.00	0.0227	5.43	2	4	10.3	25.0	5.3	1	2	1.0	1.0
1864	39	1	3	4.5	10.8	0.42	0.0080	4.38	2	5	12.8	35.1	7.5	1	3	10.8	4.5
1865	39	1	3	1.0	16.8	0.06	0.0047	3.84	2	4	10.3	28.4	6.1	0	0	0.0	0.0
1866	39	1	11	36.1	14.5	2.49	0.0384	5.95	3	16	41.0	50.7	10.8	2	14	31.3	37.1
1867	37	0	0	0.0	0.0	0.0	0.0	0.0	1	2	5.4	2.4	0.5	1	2	115.4	20.0
1868	34	0	0	0.0	0.0	0.0	0.0	0.0	0	0	0.0	0.0	0.0	0	0	0.0	0.0
1869	34	0	0	0.0	0.0	0.0	0.0	0.0	0	0	0.0	0.0	0.0	0	0	0.0	0.0
1870	34	1	5	187.5	27.0	6.94	0.2193	7.69	1	5	14.7	23.4	5.7	0	0	0.0	0.0
1871	31	0	0	0.0	0.0	0.0	0.0	0.0	1	2	6.5	3.8	1.0	1	5	27.0	187.5
1872	31	0	0	0.0	0.0	0.0	0.0	0.0	0	0	0.0	0.0	0.0	0	0	0.0	0.0
1873	31	0	0	0.0	0.0	0.0	0.0	0.0	0	0	0.0	0.0	0.0	0	0	0.0	0.0
1874	31	0	0	0.0	0.0	0.0	0.0	0.0	0	0	0.0	0.0	0.0	0	0	0.0	0.0
1875	32	0	0	0.0	0.0	0.0	0.0	0.0	0	0	0.0	0.0	0.0	0	0	0.0	0.0
1876	32	0	0	0.0	0.0	0.0	0.0	0.0	0	0	0.0	0.0	0.0	0	0	0.0	0.0
1877	32	1	2	285.0	17.6	16.19	0.2336	7.76	1	2	6.2	17.4	4.5	0	0	0.0	0.0
1878	34	0	0	0.0	0.0	0.0	0.0	0.0	1	2	5.9	0.2	0.0	1	2	17.6	285.0
1879	34	1	3	14.0	170.3	0.08	0.2000	7.60	1	3	8.8	29.9	7.3	0	0	0.0	0.0
1880	34	0	0	0.0	0.0	0.0	0.0	0.0	1	3	8.8	36.0	8.8	0	0	0.0	0.0
1881	34	0	0	0.0	0.0	0.0	0.0	0.0	1	3	8.8	36.0	8.8	0	0	0.0	0.0
1882	35	0	0	0.0	0.0	0.0	0.0	0.0	1	3	8.6	36.0	8.6	0	0	0.0	0.0
1883	35	0	0	0.0	0.0	0.0	0.0	0.0	1	3	8.6	32.2	7.7	1	3	170.3	14.0
1884	35	1	2	12.1	23.6	0.51	0.0026	3.25	1	2	5.7	13.2	3.1	0	0	0.0	0.0
1885	35	1	2	1.0	1.2	0.83	0.0500	6.21	2	4	11.4	11.8	2.8	2	4	24.8	13.1
1886	35	0	0	0.0	0.0	0.0	0.0	0.0	0	0	0.0	0.0	0.0	0	0	0.0	0.0
1887	37	0	0	0.0	0.0	0.0	0.0	0.0	0	0	0.0	0.0	0.0	0	0	0.0	0.0
1888	38	0	0	0.0	0.0	0.0	0.0	0.0	0	0	0.0	0.0	0.0	0	0	0.0	0.0
1889	38	0	0	0.0	0.0	0.0	0.0	0.0	0	0	0.0	0.0	0.0	0	0	0.0	0.0
1890	38	0	0	0.0	0.0	0.0	0.0	0.0	0	0	0.0	0.0	0.0	0	0	0.0	0.0
1891	38	0	0	0.0	0.0	0.0	0.0	0.0	0	0	0.0	0.0	0.0	0	0	0.0	0.0
1892	38	0	0	0.0	0.0	0.0	0.0	0.0	0	0	0.0	0.0	0.0	0	0	0.0	0.0

7.2 - ANNUAL AMOUNTS OF INTERSTATE WAR

	ONSET--BY WAR							UNDERWAY					TERMINATION--BY WAR			
YEAR	NO. IN SYSTEM 1	NO. OF WARS BEGUN 2	NO. OF PARTIC-IPANTS 3	BATTLE DEATHS 000'S 4	NATION MONTHS 5	BATTLE DEATHS 000'S PER NATION MONTH 6	BATTLE DEATHS PER HUNDRED POPULA-TION 7	LOG OF BATTLE DEATHS PER MILLION POPULA-TION 8	NO. OF WARS UNDER-WAY 9	NO. OF NATIONS IN WAR 10	% OF NATIONS IN WAR 11	NATION MONTHS UNDER-WAY 12	% OF NATION MONTHS EX-HAUST-ED 13	NO. OF WARS ENDING 14	NO. OF PARTIC-IPANTS 15	NATION MONTHS 16	BATTLE DEATHS 000'S 17
1893	38	0	0	0.0	0.0	0.0	0.0	0.0	0	0	0.0	0.0	0.0	0	0	0.0	0.0
1894	38	1	2	15.0	16.0	0.94	0.0031	3.44	1	2	5.3	10.0	2.2	0	0	0.0	0.0
1895	38	0	0	0.0	0.0	0.0	0.0	0.0	1	2	5.3	5.8	1.3	1	2	16.0	15.0
1896	39	0	0	0.0	0.0	0.0	0.0	0.0	0	0	0.0	0.0	0.0	0	0	0.0	0.0
1897	39	1	2	2.0	6.2	0.32	0.0075	4.32	1	2	5.1	6.2	1.3	1	2	6.2	2.0
1898	40	1	2	10.0	7.4	1.35	0.0106	4.66	1	2	5.0	7.4	1.5	1	2	7.4	10.0
1899	41	0	0	0.0	0.0	0.0	0.0	0.0	0	0	0.0	0.0	0.0	0	0	0.0	0.0
1900	42	0	0	0.0	0.0	0.0	0.0	0.0	0	0	0.0	0.0	0.0	0	0	0.0	0.0
1901	42	0	0	0.0	0.0	0.0	0.0	0.0	0	0	0.0	0.0	0.0	0	0	0.0	0.0
1902	43	0	0	0.0	0.0	0.0	0.0	0.0	0	0	0.0	0.0	0.0	0	0	0.0	0.0
1903	43	0	0	0.0	0.0	0.0	0.0	0.0	0	0	0.0	0.0	0.0	0	0	0.0	0.0
1904	43	1	2	130.0	38.6	3.37	0.0692	6.54	1	2	4.7	21.6	4.2	0	0	0.0	0.0
1905	44	0	0	0.0	0.0	0.0	0.0	0.0	1	2	4.5	17.0	3.2	1	2	38.6	130.0
1906	43	1	3	1.0	5.4	0.19	0.0270	5.60	1	3	7.0	5.4	1.0	1	3	5.4	1.0
1907	43	1	3	1.0	6.3	0.16	0.0417	6.03	1	3	7.0	6.3	1.2	1	3	6.3	1.0
1908	44	0	0	0.0	0.0	0.0	0.0	0.0	0	0	0.0	0.0	0.0	0	0	0.0	0.0
1909	44	1	2	10.0	17.0	0.59	0.0408	6.01	1	2	4.5	11.6	2.2	0	0	0.0	0.0
1910	44	0	0	0.0	0.0	0.0	0.0	0.0	1	2	4.5	5.4	1.0	1	2	17.0	10.0
1911	44	1	2	20.0	25.4	0.79	0.0335	5.81	1	2	4.5	6.2	1.2	0	0	0.0	0.0
1912	43	1	4	82.0	20.4	4.02	0.2571	7.85	2	5	11.6	27.4	5.3	1	2	25.4	20.0
1913	43	1	5	60.5	4.2	14.40	0.1609	7.38	2	5	11.6	16.4	3.2	2	5	24.6	142.5
1914	44	1	15	8555.8	607.8	14.08	1.4137	9.56	1	9	20.5	41.4	7.8	0	0	0.0	0.0
1915	44	0	0	0.0	0.0	0.0	0.0	0.0	1	11	25.0	118.0	22.3	0	0	0.0	0.0
1916	44	0	0	0.0	0.0	0.0	0.0	0.0	1	13	29.5	146.3	27.7	0	0	0.0	0.0
1917	44	0	0	0.0	0.0	0.0	0.0	0.0	1	15	34.1	169.0	32.0	0	0	0.0	0.0
1918	48	0	0	0.0	0.0	0.0	0.0	0.0	1	13	27.1	132.3	23.0	1	15	607.8	8555.8
1919	51	2	5	61.0	93.4	0.65	0.1203	7.09	2	5	9.8	26.6	4.3	1	3	10.8	11.0
1920	61	0	0	0.0	0.0	0.0	0.0	0.0	1	2	3.3	24.0	3.3	0	0	0.0	0.0
1921	62	0	0	0.0	0.0	0.0	0.0	0.0	1	2	3.2	24.0	3.2	0	0	0.0	0.0
1922	63	0	0	0.0	0.0	0.0	0.0	0.0	1	2	3.2	18.6	2.5	1	2	82.6	50.0
1923	63	0	0	0.0	0.0	0.0	0.0	0.0	0	0	0.0	0.0	0.0	0	0	0.0	0.0
1924	63	0	0	0.0	0.0	0.0	0.0	0.0	0	0	0.0	0.0	0.0	0	0	0.0	0.0
1925	63	0	0	0.0	0.0	0.0	0.0	0.0	0	0	0.0	0.0	0.0	0	0	0.0	0.0
1926	64	0	0	0.0	0.0	0.0	0.0	0.0	0	0	0.0	0.0	0.0	0	0	0.0	0.0
1927	65	0	0	0.0	0.0	0.0	0.0	0.0	0	0	0.0	0.0	0.0	0	0	0.0	0.0

	ONSET--BY WAR								UNDERWAY					TERMINATION--BY WAR			
YEAR	NO. IN SYSTEM 1	NO. OF WARS BEGUN 2	NO. OF PARTIC-IPANTS 3	BATTLE DEATHS 000'S 4	NATION MONTHS 5	BATTLE DEATHS 000'S PER NATION MONTH 6	BATTLE DEATHS PER HUNDRED POPULA-TION 7	LOG OF BATTLE DEATHS PER MILLION POPULA-TION 8	NO. OF WARS UNDER-WAY 9	NO. OF NATIONS IN WAR 10	% OF NATIONS IN WAR 11	NATION MONTHS UNDER-WAY 12	% OF NATION MONTHS EX-HAUST-ED 13	NO. OF WARS ENDING 14	NO. OF PARTIC-IPANTS 15	NATION MONTHS 16	BATTLE DEATHS 000'S 17
1928	65	0	0	0.0	0.0	0.0	0.0	0.0	0	0	0.0	0.0	0.0	0	0	0.0	0.0
1929	65	0	0	0.0	0.0	0.0	0.0	0.0	0	0	0.0	0.0	0.0	0	0	0.0	0.0
1930	65	0	0	0.0	0.0	0.0	0.0	0.0	0	0	0.0	0.0	0.0	0	0	0.0	0.0
1931	65	1	2	60.0	33.2	1.81	0.0102	4.62	1	2	3.1	0.8	0.1	0	0	0.0	0.0
1932	66	1	2	130.0	71.8	1.81	3.8235	10.55	2	4	6.1	37.2	4.7	0	0	0.0	0.0
1933	66	0	0	0.0	0.0	0.0	0.0	0.0	2	4	6.1	32.2	4.1	1	2	33.2	60.0
1934	66	0	0	0.0	0.0	0.0	0.0	0.0	1	2	3.0	24.0	3.0	0	0	0.0	0.0
1935	66	1	2	20.0	14.4	1.39	0.0380	5.94	2	4	6.1	16.8	2.1	1	2	71.8	130.0
1936	66	0	0	0.0	0.0	0.0	0.0	0.0	1	2	3.0	8.6	1.1	1	2	14.4	20.0
1937	66	1	2	1000.0	106.2	9.42	0.1648	7.41	1	2	3.0	11.6	1.5	0	0	0.0	0.0
1938	66	0	0	0.0	0.0	0.0	0.0	0.0	1	2	3.0	24.0	3.0	0	0	0.0	0.0
1939	65	3	28	15273.3	895.0	17.07	0.8458	9.04	4	13	20.0	66.8	8.6	1	3	12.6	19.0
1940	62	0	0	0.0	0.0	0.0	0.0	0.0	3	16	25.8	118.2	15.9	1	2	6.8	90.0
1941	55	0	0	0.0	0.0	0.0	0.0	0.0	2	18	32.7	144.0	21.8	1	2	106.2	1000.0
1942	53	0	0	0.0	0.0	0.0	0.0	0.0	1	15	28.3	180.0	28.3	0	0	0.0	0.0
1943	52	0	0	0.0	0.0	0.0	0.0	0.0	1	16	30.8	178.5	28.6	0	0	0.0	0.0
1944	57	0	0	0.0	0.0	0.0	0.0	0.0	1	19	33.3	184.3	26.9	0	0	0.0	0.0
1945	64	0	0	0.0	0.0	0.0	0.0	0.0	1	17	26.6	92.9	12.1	1	28	875.6	15164.3
1946	66	0	0	0.0	0.0	0.0	0.0	0.0	0	0	0.0	0.0	0.0	0	0	0.0	0.0
1947	68	0	0	0.0	0.0	0.0	0.0	0.0	0	0	0.0	0.0	0.0	0	0	0.0	0.0
1948	72	1	6	8.0	19.4	0.41	0.0260	5.56	1	6	8.3	18.4	2.1	0	0	0.0	0.0
1949	75	0	0	0.0	0.0	0.0	0.0	0.0	1	2	2.7	0.4	0.0	1	6	19.4	8.0
1950	75	1	16	1892.1	514.0	3.68	0.1936	7.57	1	9	12.0	32.2	3.6	0	0	0.0	0.0
1951	75	0	0	0.0	0.0	0.0	0.0	0.0	1	16	21.3	180.5	20.1	0	0	0.0	0.0
1952	77	0	0	0.0	0.0	0.0	0.0	0.0	1	16	20.8	192.0	20.8	0	0	0.0	0.0
1953	78	0	0	0.0	0.0	0.0	0.0	0.0	1	16	20.5	108.8	11.6	1	16	514.0	1892.1
1954	82	0	0	0.0	0.0	0.0	0.0	0.0	0	0	0.0	0.0	0.0	0	0	0.0	0.0
1955	84	0	0	0.0	0.0	0.0	0.0	0.0	0	0	0.0	0.0	0.0	0	0	0.0	0.0
1956	87	2	6	35.2	2.6	13.55	0.0107	4.67	2	6	6.9	2.6	0.2	2	6	2.6	35.2
1957	89	0	0	0.0	0.0	0.0	0.0	0.0	0	0	0.0	0.0	0.0	0	0	0.0	0.0
1958	90	0	0	0.0	0.0	0.0	0.0	0.0	0	0	0.0	0.0	0.0	0	0	0.0	0.0
1959	89	0	0	0.0	0.0	0.0	0.0	0.0	0	0	0.0	0.0	0.0	0	0	0.0	0.0
1960	107	0	0	0.0	0.0	0.0	0.0	0.0	0	0	0.0	0.0	0.0	0	0	0.0	0.0
1961	111	0	0	0.0	0.0	0.0	0.0	0.0	0	0	0.0	0.0	0.0	0	0	0.0	0.0
1962	117	1	2	1.0	2.2	0.45	0.0001	-0.11	1	2	1.7	2.2	0.2	1	2	2.2	1.0
1963	119	0	0	0.0	0.0	0.0	0.0	0.0	0	0	0.0	0.0	0.0	0	0	0.0	0.0
1964	122	0	0	0.0	0.0	0.0	0.0	0.0	0	0	0.0	0.0	0.0	0	0	0.0	0.0
1965	124	1	2	6.8	3.2	2.12	0.0011	2.43	1	2	1.6	3.2	0.2	1	2	3.2	6.8

7.3 - ANNUAL NATIONAL ENTRIES INTO AND DEPARTURES FROM INTERSTATE WAR

	ONSET--BY NATION								UNDERWAY				TERMINATION--BY NATION			
YEAR	NO. IN SYSTEM 1	NO. OF NATIONS ENTER-ING WAR 2	NO. OF WARS BEGUN 3	BATTLE DEATHS 000'S 4	NATION MONTHS 5	BATTLE DEATHS 000'S PER NATION MONTH 6	BATTLE DEATHS PER HUNDRED POPULA-TION 7	LOG OF BATTLE DEATHS PER MILLION POPULA-TION 8	NO. OF NATIONS IN WAR 9	NO. OF WARS UNDER-WAY 10	% OF NATIONS IN WAR 11	NATION MONTHS UNDER-WAY 12	% OF NATION MONTHS EX-HAUST-ED 13	NO. OF NATIONS LEAVING WAR 14	NO. OF WARS ENDING 15	NATION MONTHS 16	BATTLE DEATHS 000'S 17
1816	23	0	0	0.0	0.0	0.0	0.0	0.0	0	0	0.0	0.0	0.0	0	0	0.0	0.0
1817	23	0	0	0.0	0.0	0.0	0.0	0.0	0	0	0.0	0.0	0.0	0	0	0.0	0.0
1818	23	0	0	0.0	0.0	0.0	0.0	0.0	0	0	0.0	0.0	0.0	0	0	0.0	0.0
1819	23	0	0	0.0	0.0	0.0	0.0	0.0	0	0	0.0	0.0	0.0	0	0	0.0	0.0
1820	23	0	0	0.0	0.0	0.0	0.0	0.0	0	0	0.0	0.0	0.0	0	0	0.0	0.0
1821	23	0	0	0.0	0.0	0.0	0.0	0.0	0	0	0.0	0.0	0.0	0	0	0.0	0.0
1822	23	0	0	0.0	0.0	0.0	0.0	0.0	0	0	0.0	0.0	0.0	0	0	0.0	0.0
1823	23	2	1	1.0	14.6	0.07	0.0023	3.15	2	1	8.7	14.6	5.3	2	1	14.6	1.0
1824	23	0	0	0.0	0.0	0.0	0.0	0.0	0	0	0.0	0.0	0.0	0	0	0.0	0.0
1825	23	0	0	0.0	0.0	0.0	0.0	0.0	0	0	0.0	0.0	0.0	0	0	0.0	0.0
1826	24	0	0	0.0	0.0	0.0	0.0	0.0	0	0	0.0	0.0	0.0	0	0	0.0	0.0
1827	24	4	1	3.2	0.4	7.95	0.0024	3.18	4	1	16.7	0.0	0.0	4	1	0.4	3.2
1828	25	2	1	130.0	33.4	3.89	0.1660	7.41	2	1	8.0	16.4	5.5	0	0	0.0	0.0
1829	25	0	0	0.0	0.0	0.0	0.0	0.0	2	1	8.0	17.0	5.7	2	1	33.4	130.0
1830	26	0	0	0.0	0.0	0.0	0.0	0.0	0	0	0.0	0.0	0.0	0	0	0.0	0.0
1831	28	0	0	0.0	0.0	0.0	0.0	0.0	0	0	0.0	0.0	0.0	0	0	0.0	0.0
1832	28	0	0	0.0	0.0	0.0	0.0	0.0	0	0	0.0	0.0	0.0	0	0	0.0	0.0
1833	28	0	0	0.0	0.0	0.0	0.0	0.0	0	0	0.0	0.0	0.0	0	0	0.0	0.0
1834	28	0	0	0.0	0.0	0.0	0.0	0.0	0	0	0.0	0.0	0.0	0	0	0.0	0.0
1835	28	0	0	0.0	0.0	0.0	0.0	0.0	0	0	0.0	0.0	0.0	0	0	0.0	0.0
1836	28	0	0	0.0	0.0	0.0	0.0	0.0	0	0	0.0	0.0	0.0	0	0	0.0	0.0
1837	28	0	0	0.0	0.0	0.0	0.0	0.0	0	0	0.0	0.0	0.0	0	0	0.0	0.0
1838	30	0	0	0.0	0.0	0.0	0.0	0.0	0	0	0.0	0.0	0.0	0	0	0.0	0.0
1839	31	0	0	0.0	0.0	0.0	0.0	0.0	0	0	0.0	0.0	0.0	0	0	0.0	0.0
1840	31	0	0	0.0	0.0	0.0	0.0	0.0	0	0	0.0	0.0	0.0	0	0	0.0	0.0
1841	33	0	0	0.0	0.0	0.0	0.0	0.0	0	0	0.0	0.0	0.0	0	0	0.0	0.0
1842	34	0	0	0.0	0.0	0.0	0.0	0.0	0	0	0.0	0.0	0.0	0	0	0.0	0.0
1843	35	0	0	0.0	0.0	0.0	0.0	0.0	0	0	0.0	0.0	0.0	0	0	0.0	0.0
1844	35	0	0	0.0	0.0	0.0	0.0	0.0	0	0	0.0	0.0	0.0	0	0	0.0	0.0
1845	35	0	0	0.0	0.0	0.0	0.0	0.0	0	0	0.0	0.0	0.0	0	0	0.0	0.0
1846	35	2	1	17.0	42.2	0.40	0.0556	6.32	2	1	5.7	15.4	3.7	0	0	0.0	0.0
1847	36	0	0	0.0	0.0	0.0	0.0	0.0	2	1	5.6	24.0	5.6	0	0	0.0	0.0
1848	37	4	2	15.0	25.6	0.59	0.0261	5.56	6	3	16.2	21.2	4.8	2	1	42.2	17.0
1849	38	4	1	2.2	6.4	0.34	0.0029	3.37	7	3	18.4	13.6	3.0	7	3	32.0	17.2
1850	38	0	0	0.0	0.0	0.0	0.0	0.0	0	0	0.0	0.0	0.0	0	0	0.0	0.0
1851	39	2	1	1.3	13.2	0.10	0.0155	5.04	2	1	5.1	11.0	2.4	0	0	0.0	0.0
1852	39	0	0	0.0	0.0	0.0	0.0	0.0	2	1	5.1	2.2	0.5	2	1	13.2	1.3
1853	39	2	1	145.0	56.6	2.56	0.1499	7.31	2	1	5.1	4.6	1.0	0	0	0.0	0.0

	ONSET--BY NATION								UNDERWAY					TERMINATION--BY NATION			
YEAR	NO. IN SYSTEM 1	NO. OF NATIONS ENTER-ING WAR 2	NO. OF WARS BEGUN 3	BATTLE DEATHS 000'S 4	NATION MONTHS 5	BATTLE DEATHS 000'S PER NATION MONTH 6	BATTLE DEATHS PER HUNDRED POPULA-TICN 7	LOG OF BATTLE DEATHS PER MILLION POPULA-TION 8	NO. OF NATIONS IN WAR 9	NO. OF WARS UNDER-WAY 10	% OF NATIONS IN WAR 11	NATION MONTHS UNDER-WAY 12	% OF NATION MONTHS EX-HAUST-ED 13	NO. OF NATIONS LEAVING WAR 14	NO. OF WARS ENDING 15	NATION MONTHS 16	BATTLE DEATHS 000'S 17
1854	40	2	0	117.0	46.2	2.53	0.1808	7.50	4	1	10.0	42.2	8.8	0	0	0.0	0.0
1855	41	1	0	2.2	13.7	0.16	0.0423	6.05	5	1	12.2	59.7	12.1	0	0	0.0	0.0
1856	41	2	1	2.0	9.2	0.22	0.0060	4.09	6	2	14.6	14.4	2.9	5	1	116.5	264.2
1857	41	0	0	0.0	0.0	0.0	0.0	0.0	2	1	4.9	4.8	1.0	2	1	9.2	2.0
1858	41	0	0	0.0	0.0	0.0	0.0	0.0	0	0	0.0	0.0	0.0	0	0	0.0	0.0
1859	42	5	2	32.5	17.7	1.84	0.0340	5.83	5	2	11.9	11.9	2.4	3	1	7.3	22.5
1860	44	3	2	2.0	7.6	0.26	0.0035	3.56	5	3	11.4	12.2	2.3	4	2	11.6	11.0
1861	40	0	0	0.0	0.0	0.0	0.0	0.0	2	1	5.0	1.4	0.3	2	1	6.4	1.0
1862	39	2	1	20.0	115.4	0.17	0.0434	6.07	2	1	5.1	17.0	3.6	0	0	0.0	0.0
1863	39	2	1	1.0	1.0	1.00	0.0227	5.43	4	2	10.3	25.0	5.3	2	1	1.0	1.0
1864	39	3	1	4.5	10.8	0.42	0.0080	4.38	5	2	12.8	35.3	7.5	3	1	10.8	4.5
1865	39	2	1	0.4	13.0	0.03	0.0022	3.09	4	2	10.3	28.4	6.1	0	0	0.0	0.0
1866	39	12	1	36.7	18.3	2.01	0.0377	5.93	16	3	41.0	50.9	10.9	14	2	31.3	37.1
1867	37	0	0	0.0	0.0	0.0	0.0	0.0	2	1	5.4	2.4	0.5	2	1	115.4	20.0
1868	34	0	0	0.0	0.0	0.0	0.0	0.0	0	0	0.0	0.0	0.0	0	0	0.0	0.0
1869	34	0	0	0.0	0.0	0.0	0.0	0.0	0	0	0.0	0.0	0.0	0	0	0.0	0.0
1870	34	5	1	187.5	27.0	6.94	0.2193	7.69	5	1	14.7	23.4	5.7	3	0	12.4	7.5
1871	31	0	0	0.0	0.0	0.0	0.0	0.0	2	1	6.5	3.8	1.0	2	1	14.6	180.0
1872	31	0	0	0.0	0.0	0.0	0.0	0.0	0	0	0.0	0.0	0.0	0	0	0.0	0.0
1873	31	0	0	0.0	0.0	0.0	0.0	0.0	0	0	0.0	0.0	0.0	0	0	0.0	0.0
1874	31	0	0	0.0	0.0	0.0	0.0	0.0	0	0	0.0	0.0	0.0	0	0	0.0	0.0
1875	32	0	0	0.0	0.0	0.0	0.0	0.0	0	0	0.0	0.0	0.0	0	0	0.0	0.0
1876	32	0	0	0.0	0.0	0.0	0.0	0.0	0	0	0.0	0.0	0.0	0	0	0.0	0.0
1877	32	2	1	285.0	17.6	16.19	0.2336	7.76	2	1	6.2	17.4	4.5	0	0	0.0	0.0
1878	34	0	0	0.0	0.0	0.0	0.0	0.0	2	1	5.9	0.2	0.0	2	1	17.6	285.0
1879	34	3	1	14.0	170.3	0.08	0.2000	7.60	3	1	8.8	29.9	7.3	0	0	0.0	0.0
1880	34	0	0	0.0	0.0	0.0	0.0	0.0	3	1	8.8	36.3	8.9	0	0	0.0	0.0
1881	34	0	0	0.0	0.0	0.0	0.0	0.0	3	1	8.8	36.0	8.8	0	0	0.0	0.0
1882	35	0	0	0.0	0.0	0.0	0.0	0.0	3	1	8.6	36.0	8.6	0	0	0.0	0.0
1883	35	0	0	0.0	0.0	0.0	0.0	0.0	3	1	8.6	32.5	7.7	3	1	170.3	14.0
1884	35	2	1	12.1	23.6	0.51	0.0026	3.25	2	1	5.7	13.2	3.1	0	0	0.0	0.0
1885	35	2	1	1.0	1.2	0.83	0.0500	6.21	4	2	11.4	11.8	2.8	4	2	24.8	13.1
1886	35	0	0	0.0	0.0	0.0	0.0	0.0	0	0	0.0	0.0	0.0	0	0	0.0	0.0
1887	37	0	0	0.0	0.0	0.0	0.0	0.0	0	0	0.0	0.0	0.0	0	0	0.0	0.0
1888	38	0	0	0.0	0.0	0.0	0.0	0.0	0	0	0.0	0.0	0.0	0	0	0.0	0.0
1889	38	0	0	0.0	0.0	0.0	0.0	0.0	0	0	0.0	0.0	0.0	0	0	0.0	0.0
1890	38	0	0	0.0	0.0	0.0	0.0	0.0	0	0	0.0	0.0	0.0	0	0	0.0	0.0
1891	38	0	0	0.0	0.0	0.0	0.0	0.0	0	0	0.0	0.0	0.0	0	0	0.0	0.0
1892	38	0	0	0.0	0.0	0.0	0.0	0.0	0	0	0.0	0.0	0.0	0	0	0.0	0.0
1893	38	0	0	0.0	0.0	0.0	0.0	0.0	0	0	0.0	0.0	0.0	0	0	0.0	0.0

7.3 - ANNUAL NATIONAL ENTRIES INTO AND DEPARTURES FROM INTERSTATE WAR

	ONSET--BY NATION								UNDERWAY					TERMINATION--BY NATION			
YEAR	NO. IN SYSTEM 1	NO. OF NATIONS ENTERING WAR 2	NO. OF WARS BEGUN 3	BATTLE DEATHS 000'S 4	NATION MONTHS 5	BATTLE DEATHS 000'S PER NATION MONTH 6	BATTLE DEATHS PER HUNDRED POPULATION 7	LOG OF BATTLE DEATHS PER MILLION POPULATION 8	NO. OF NATIONS IN WAR 9	NO. OF WARS UNDERWAY 10	% OF NATIONS IN WAR 11	NATION MONTHS UNDERWAY 12	% OF NATION MONTHS EXHAUSTED 13	NO. OF NATIONS LEAVING WAR 14	NO. OF WARS ENDING 15	NATION MONTHS 16	BATTLE DEATHS 000'S 17
1894	38	2	1	15.0	16.0	0.94	0.0031	3.44	2	1	5.3	10.0	2.2	0	0	0.0	0.0
1895	38	0	0	0.0	0.0	0.0	0.0	0.0	2	1	5.3	6.0	1.3	2	1	16.0	15.0
1896	39	0	0	0.0	0.0	0.0	0.0	0.0	0	0	0.0	0.0	0.0	0	0	0.0	0.0
1897	39	2	1	2.0	6.2	0.32	0.0075	4.32	2	1	5.1	6.2	1.3	2	1	6.2	2.0
1898	40	2	1	10.0	7.4	1.35	0.0106	4.66	2	1	5.0	7.4	1.5	2	1	7.4	10.0
1899	41	0	0	0.0	0.0	0.0	0.0	0.0	0	0	0.0	0.0	0.0	0	0	0.0	0.0
1900	42	0	0	0.0	0.0	0.0	0.0	0.0	0	0	0.0	0.0	0.0	0	0	0.0	0.0
1901	42	0	0	0.0	0.0	0.0	0.0	0.0	0	0	0.0	0.0	0.0	0	0	0.0	0.0
1902	43	0	0	0.0	0.0	0.0	0.0	0.0	0	0	0.0	0.0	0.0	0	0	0.0	0.0
1903	43	0	0	0.0	0.0	0.0	0.0	0.0	0	0	0.0	0.0	0.0	0	0	0.0	0.0
1904	43	2	1	130.0	38.6	3.37	0.0692	6.54	2	1	4.7	21.6	4.2	0	0	0.0	0.0
1905	44	0	0	0.0	0.0	0.0	0.0	0.0	2	1	4.5	17.0	3.2	2	1	38.6	130.0
1906	43	3	1	1.0	5.4	0.19	0.0270	5.60	3	1	7.0	5.4	1.0	3	1	5.4	1.0
1907	43	3	1	1.0	6.3	0.16	0.0417	6.03	3	1	7.0	6.3	1.2	3	1	6.3	1.0
1908	44	0	0	0.0	0.0	0.0	0.0	0.0	0	0	0.0	0.0	0.0	0	0	0.0	0.0
1909	44	2	1	10.0	17.0	0.59	0.0408	6.01	2	1	4.5	11.6	2.2	0	0	0.0	0.0
1910	44	0	0	0.0	0.0	0.0	0.0	0.0	2	1	4.5	5.4	1.0	2	1	17.0	10.0
1911	44	2	1	20.0	25.4	0.79	0.0335	5.81	2	1	4.5	6.2	1.2	0	0	0.0	0.0
1912	43	4	1	82.0	20.4	4.02	0.2571	7.85	5	2	11.6	27.4	5.3	2	1	25.4	20.0
1913	43	5	1	60.5	4.2	14.40	0.1609	7.38	5	2	11.6	16.4	3.2	5	2	24.6	142.5
1914	44	9	1	7418.8	447.3	16.59	1.6370	9.70	9	1	20.5	41.4	7.8	0	0	0.0	0.0
1915	44	2	0	664.0	77.3	8.59	1.6600	9.72	11	1	25.0	118.0	22.3	0	0	0.0	0.0
1916	44	2	0	342.0	47.8	7.15	2.5714	10.15	13	1	29.5	147.4	27.9	0	0	0.0	0.0
1917	44	2	0	131.0	35.4	3.70	0.1327	7.19	15	1	34.1	169.1	32.0	2	0	55.6	2035.0
1918	48	0	0	0.0	0.0	0.0	0.0	0.0	13	1	27.1	133.5	23.2	13	1	552.2	6520.8
1919	51	5	2	61.0	93.4	0.65	0.1203	7.09	5	2	9.8	26.6	4.3	3	1	10.8	11.0
1920	61	0	0	0.0	0.0	0.0	0.0	0.0	2	1	3.3	24.2	3.3	0	0	0.0	0.0
1921	62	0	0	0.0	0.0	0.0	0.0	0.0	2	1	3.2	24.0	3.2	0	0	0.0	0.0
1922	63	0	0	0.0	0.0	0.0	0.0	0.0	2	1	3.2	18.8	2.5	2	1	82.6	50.0
1923	63	0	0	0.0	0.0	0.0	0.0	0.0	0	0	0.0	0.0	0.0	0	0	0.0	0.0
1924	63	0	0	0.0	0.0	0.0	0.0	0.0	0	0	0.0	0.0	0.0	0	0	0.0	0.0
1925	63	0	0	0.0	0.0	0.0	0.0	0.0	0	0	0.0	0.0	0.0	0	0	0.0	0.0
1926	64	0	0	0.0	0.0	0.0	0.0	0.0	0	0	0.0	0.0	0.0	0	0	0.0	0.0
1927	65	0	0	0.0	0.0	0.0	0.0	0.0	0	0	0.0	0.0	0.0	0	0	0.0	0.0
1928	65	0	0	0.0	0.0	0.0	0.0	0.0	0	0	0.0	0.0	0.0	0	0	0.0	0.0
1929	65	0	0	0.0	0.0	0.0	0.0	0.0	0	0	0.0	0.0	0.0	0	0	0.0	0.0
1930	65	0	0	0.0	0.0	0.0	0.0	0.0	0	0	0.0	0.0	0.0	0	0	0.0	0.0
1931	65	2	1	60.0	33.2	1.81	0.0102	4.62	2	1	3.1	0.8	0.1	0	0	0.0	0.0

YEAR	NO. IN SYSTEM 1	NO. OF NATIONS ENTER-ING WAR 2	NO. OF WARS BEGUN 3	BATTLE DEATHS 000'S 4	NATION MONTHS 5	BATTLE DEATHS 000'S PER NATION MONTH 6	BATTLE DEATHS PER HUNDRED POPULA-TICN 7	LOG OF BATTLE DEATHS PER MILLION POPULA-TION 8	NO. OF NATIONS IN WAR 9	NO. OF WARS UNDER-WAY 10	% OF NATIONS IN WAR 11	NATION MONTHS UNDER-WAY 12	% OF NATION MONTHS EX-HAUST-ED 13	NO. OF NATIONS LEAVING WAR 14	NO. OF WARS ENDING 15	NATION MONTHS 16	BATTLE DEATHS 000'S 17
	ONSET--BY NATION								UNDERWAY					TERMINATION--BY NATION			
1932	66	2	1	130.0	71.8	1.81	3.8235	10.55	4	2	6.1	37.4	4.7	0	0	0.0	0.0
1933	66	0	0	0.0	0.0	C.0	0.0	0.0	4	2	6.1	32.4	4.1	2	1	33.2	60.0
1934	66	0	0	0.0	0.0	0.0	0.0	0.0	2	1	3.0	24.0	3.0	0	0	0.0	0.0
1935	66	2	1	20.0	14.4	1.39	0.0380	5.94	4	2	6.1	16.8	2.1	2	1	71.8	130.0
1936	66	0	0	C.0	0.0	0.0	0.0	0.0	2	1	3.0	8.6	1.1	2	1	14.4	20.0
1937	66	2	1	1000.0	106.2	9.42	0.1648	7.41	2	1	3.0	11.6	1.5	0	0	0.0	0.0
1938	66	0	0	0.0	0.0	0.0	0.0	0.0	2	1	3.0	24.0	3.0	0	0	0.0	0.0
1939	65	12	3	4503.7	464.6	9.69	0.6948	8.85	13	4	20.0	66.8	8.6	4	1	13.5	339.0
1940	62	5	0	87.8	47.5	1.85	0.1242	7.12	16	3	25.8	119.0	16.0	5	1	9.6	107.8
1941	55	10	0	10649.3	338.1	31.50	1.0901	9.30	18	2	32.7	144.0	21.8	5	1	117.8	1020.0
1942	53	0	0	0.0	0.0	0.0	0.0	0.0	15	1	28.3	180.0	28.3	0	0	0.0	0.0
1943	52	1	0	17.5	18.7	0.94	0.0401	5.99	16	1	30.8	178.6	28.6	1	0	38.8	60.0
1944	57	3	0	12.0	25.9	0.46	0.0182	5.21	19	1	33.3	185.6	27.1	3	0	110.0	341.0
1945	64	1	0	3.0	0.2	15.00	0.5000	8.52	17	1	26.6	93.8	12.2	17	1	711.5	14405.5
1946	66	0	0	0.0	0.0	0.0	0.0	0.0	0	0	0.0	0.0	0.0	0	0	0.0	0.0
1947	68	0	0	0.0	0.0	C.0	0.0	0.0	0	0	0.0	0.0	0.0	0	0	0.0	0.0
1948	72	6	1	8.0	19.4	0.41	0.0260	5.56	6	1	8.3	18.4	2.1	4	0	10.0	3.0
1949	75	0	0	0.0	0.0	0.0	0.0	0.0	2	1	2.7	0.6	0.1	2	1	9.4	5.0
1950	75	9	1	1891.1	309.8	6.10	0.2201	7.70	9	1	12.0	32.2	3.6	0	0	0.0	0.0
1951	75	7	0	1.0	204.2	0.01	0.0009	2.18	16	1	21.3	180.5	20.1	0	0	0.0	0.0
1952	77	0	0	0.0	0.0	0.0	0.0	0.0	16	1	20.8	193.6	21.0	0	0	0.0	0.0
1953	78	0	0	0.0	0.0	0.0	0.0	0.0	16	1	20.5	110.4	11.8	16	1	514.0	1892.1
1954	82	0	0	0.0	0.0	0.0	0.0	0.0	0	0	0.0	0.0	0.0	0	0	0.0	0.0
1955	84	0	0	0.0	0.0	0.0	0.0	0.0	0	0	0.0	0.0	0.0	0	0	0.0	0.0
1956	87	6	2	35.2	2.6	13.55	0.0107	4.67	6	2	6.9	2.6	0.2	6	2	2.6	35.2
1957	89	0	0	0.0	0.0	0.0	0.0	0.0	0	0	0.0	0.0	0.0	0	0	0.0	0.0
1958	90	0	0	0.0	0.0	0.0	0.0	0.0	0	0	0.0	0.0	0.0	0	0	0.0	0.0
1959	89	0	0	0.0	0.0	0.0	0.0	0.0	0	0	0.0	0.0	0.0	0	0	0.0	0.0
1960	107	0	0	0.0	0.0	0.0	0.0	0.0	0	0	0.0	0.0	0.0	0	0	0.0	0.0
1961	111	0	0	0.0	0.0	0.0	0.0	0.0	0	0	0.0	0.0	0.0	0	0	0.0	0.0
1962	117	2	1	1.0	2.2	0.45	0.0001	-0.11	2	1	1.7	2.2	0.2	2	1	2.2	1.0
1963	119	0	0	0.0	0.0	0.0	0.0	0.0	0	0	0.0	0.0	0.0	0	0	0.0	0.0
1964	122	0	0	0.0	0.0	0.0	0.0	0.0	0	0	0.0	0.0	0.0	0	0	0.C	0.0
1965	124	2	1	6.8	3.2	2.12	0.0011	2.43	2	1	1.6	3.2	0.2	2	1	3.2	6.8

7.4 - ANNUAL AMOUNTS OF WAR FOR CENTRAL SYSTEM MEMBERS

	ONSET--BY WAR							UNDERWAY					TERMINATION--BY WAR			
YEAR	NO. IN SYSTEM 1	NO. OF WARS BEGUN 2	NO. OF PARTIC-IPANTS 3	BATTLE DEATHS 000'S 4	NATION MONTHS 5	BATTLE DEATHS 000'S PER NATION MONTH 6	BATTLE DEATHS PER HUNDRED POPULA-TION 7	LOG OF BATTLE DEATHS PER MILLION POPULA-TION 8	NO. OF WARS UNDER-WAY 9	NO. OF NATIONS IN WAR 10	% OF NATIONS IN WAR 11	NATION MONTHS UNDER-WAY 12	% OF NATION MONTHS EX-HAUST-ED 13	NO. OF WARS ENDING 14	NO. OF PARTIC-IPANTS 15	NATION MONTHS 16	BATTLE DEATHS 000'S 17
1816	13	0	0	0.0	0.0	0.0	0.0	0.0	0	0	0.0	0.0	0.0	0	0	0.0	0.0
1817	13	1	1	2.0	6.9	0.29	0.0098	4.59	1	1	7.7	1.8	1.2	0	0	0.0	0.0
1818	13	0	0	0.0	0.0	0.0	0.0	0.0	1	1	7.7	5.1	3.3	1	1	6.9	2.0
1819	13	0	0	0.0	0.0	0.0	0.0	0.0	0	0	0.0	0.0	0.0	0	0	0.0	0.0
1820	13	0	0	0.0	0.0	0.0	0.0	0.0	0	0	0.0	0.0	0.0	0	0	0.0	0.0
1821	13	1	1	15.0	85.1	0.18	0.0607	6.41	1	1	7.7	9.3	6.0	0	0	0.0	0.0
1822	13	0	0	0.0	0.0	0.0	0.0	0.0	1	1	7.7	12.0	7.7	0	0	0.0	0.0
1823	13	2	3	16.0	43.7	0.37	0.0247	5.51	3	4	30.8	29.9	19.2	1	2	14.6	1.0
1824	13	0	0	0.0	0.0	0.0	0.0	0.0	2	2	15.4	24.0	15.4	0	0	0.0	0.0
1825	13	1	1	15.0	56.2	0.27	0.2542	7.84	3	3	23.1	29.3	18.8	0	0	0.0	0.0
1826	13	1	1	5.0	17.0	0.29	0.0095	4.55	4	4	30.8	28.9	18.5	1	1	29.1	15.0
1827	13	1	4	3.2	0.4	7.95	0.0024	3.18	4	5	38.5	36.0	23.1	1	4	0.4	3.2
1828	14	1	2	130.0	33.4	3.89	0.1660	7.41	4	3	21.4	34.1	20.3	2	2	102.1	20.0
1829	14	0	0	0.0	0.0	0.0	0.0	0.0	2	3	21.4	28.8	17.1	1	2	33.4	130.0
1830	15	0	0	0.0	0.0	0.0	0.0	0.0	1	1	6.7	2.9	1.6	1	1	56.2	15.0
1831	15	2	2	25.0	22.0	1.14	0.0314	5.75	2	2	13.3	10.3	5.7	1	1	8.3	15.0
1832	15	0	0	0.0	0.0	0.0	0.0	0.0	1	1	6.7	11.7	6.5	1	1	13.7	10.0
1833	15	0	0	0.0	0.0	0.0	0.0	0.0	0	0	0.0	0.0	0.0	0	0	0.0	0.0
1834	15	0	0	0.0	0.0	0.0	0.0	0.0	0	0	0.0	0.0	0.0	0	0	0.0	0.0
1835	15	0	0	0.0	0.0	0.0	0.0	0.0	0	0	0.0	0.0	0.0	0	0	0.0	0.0
1836	15	0	0	0.0	0.0	0.0	0.0	0.0	0	0	0.0	0.0	0.0	0	0	0.0	0.0
1837	15	0	0	0.0	0.0	0.0	0.0	0.0	0	0	0.0	0.0	0.0	0	0	0.0	0.0
1838	15	1	1	20.0	48.4	0.41	0.0775	6.65	1	1	6.7	3.0	1.7	0	0	0.0	0.0
1839	15	1	2	10.0	5.7	1.76	0.0199	5.29	2	2	13.3	12.5	6.9	0	0	0.0	0.0
1840	15	0	0	0.0	0.0	0.0	0.0	0.0	2	2	13.3	17.2	9.6	1	2	5.7	10.0
1841	15	0	0	0.0	0.0	0.0	0.0	0.0	1	1	6.7	12.0	6.7	0	0	0.0	0.0
1842	15	0	0	0.0	0.0	0.0	0.0	0.0	1	1	6.7	9.4	5.2	1	1	48.4	20.0
1843	15	0	0	0.0	0.0	0.0	0.0	0.0	0	0	0.0	0.0	0.0	0	0	0.0	0.0
1844	15	0	0	0.0	0.0	0.0	0.0	0.0	0	0	0.0	0.0	0.0	0	0	0.0	0.0
1845	15	1	1	1.5	2.9	0.52	0.0056	4.02	1	1	6.7	0.6	0.3	0	0	0.0	0.0
1846	15	0	0	0.0	0.0	0.0	0.0	0.0	1	1	6.7	2.2	1.2	1	1	2.9	1.5
1847	15	0	0	0.0	0.0	0.0	0.0	0.0	0	0	0.0	0.0	0.0	0	0	0.0	0.0
1848	15	4	6	76.0	42.8	1.78	0.0405	6.00	4	5	33.3	24.8	13.8	0	0	0.0	0.0
1849	15	1	2	0.6	2.8	0.21	0.0009	2.15	5	7	46.7	20.7	11.5	5	7	45.6	76.6
1850	15	0	0	0.0	0.0	0.0	0.0	0.0	0	0	0.0	0.0	0.0	0	0	0.0	0.0
1851	15	0	0	0.0	0.0	0.0	0.0	0.0	0	0	0.0	0.0	0.0	0	0	0.0	0.0
1852	15	1	1	5.0	3.4	1.47	0.0198	5.29	1	1	6.7	1.0	0.6	0	0	0.0	0.0

	ONSET--BY WAR								UNDERWAY					TERMINATION--BY WAR			
YEAR	NO. IN SYSTEM 1	NO. OF WARS BEGUN 2	NO. OF PARTIC-IPANTS 3	BATTLE DEATHS 000'S 4	NATION MONTHS 5	BATTLE DEATHS 000'S PER NATION MONTH 6	BATTLE DEATHS PER HUNDRED POPULA-TION 7	LOG OF BATTLE DEATHS PER MILLION POPULA-TION 8	NO. OF WARS UNDER-WAY 9	NO. OF NATIONS IN WAR 10	% OF NATIONS IN WAR 11	NATION MONTHS UNDER-WAY 12	% OF NATION MONTHS EX-HAUST-ED 13	NO. OF WARS ENDING 14	NO. OF PARTIC-IPANTS 15	NATION MONTHS 16	BATTLE DEATHS 000'S 17
1853	15	1	5	264.2	116.5	2.27	0.1586	7.37	2	2	13.3	7.0	3.9	1	1	3.4	5.0
1854	15	0	0	0.0	0.0	0.0	0.0	0.0	1	4	26.7	42.2	23.4	0	0	0.0	0.0
1855	15	0	0	0.0	0.0	0.0	0.0	0.0	1	5	33.3	59.7	33.2	0	0	0.0	0.0
1856	15	1	1	0.5	4.6	0.11	0.0017	2.84	2	5	33.3	12.2	6.8	1	5	116.5	264.2
1857	15	1	1	3.5	22.9	0.15	0.0119	4.78	2	1	6.7	10.2	5.7	1	1	4.6	0.5
1858	15	1	1	3.0	12.9	0.23	0.0115	4.74	2	2	13.3	20.0	11.1	0	0	0.0	0.0
1859	15	2	4	26.5	12.5	2.12	0.0285	5.65	4	6	40.0	17.8	9.9	3	5	43.1	29.0
1860	15	2	1	0.9	3.8	0.24	0.0021	3.02	3	2	13.3	6.0	3.3	2	2	5.8	4.3
1861	15	0	0	0.0	0.0	0.0	0.0	0.0	1	1	6.7	0.6	0.3	1	1	3.2	0.6
1862	15	1	1	8.0	57.7	0.14	0.0212	5.36	1	1	6.7	8.5	4.7	0	0	0.0	0.0
1863	15	1	1	5.0	14.9	0.34	0.0065	4.17	2	2	13.3	23.3	12.9	0	0	0.0	0.0
1864	15	1	3	4.5	10.8	0.42	0.0080	4.38	3	5	33.3	26.7	14.8	2	4	25.7	9.5
1865	15	1	1	0.3	6.5	0.05	0.0018	2.91	2	2	13.3	14.2	7.9	0	0	0.0	0.0
1866	15	1	3	34.0	4.2	8.10	0.0417	6.03	3	5	33.3	20.4	11.3	2	4	10.7	34.3
1867	15	0	0	0.0	0.0	0.0	0.0	0.0	1	1	6.7	1.2	0.7	1	1	57.7	8.0
1868	15	1	1	100.0	112.1	0.89	0.6024	8.70	1	1	6.7	2.7	1.5	0	0	0.0	0.0
1869	15	0	0	0.0	0.0	0.0	0.0	0.0	1	1	6.7	12.0	6.7	0	0	0.0	0.0
1870	15	1	2	180.0	14.6	12.33	0.2329	7.75	2	3	20.0	23.0	12.8	0	0	0.0	0.0
1871	15	0	0	0.0	0.0	0.0	0.0	0.0	2	3	20.0	15.8	8.8	1	2	14.6	180.0
1872	15	0	0	0.0	0.0	0.0	0.0	0.0	1	1	6.7	12.0	6.7	0	0	0.0	0.0
1873	15	1	1	6.0	65.2	0.09	0.1622	7.39	2	2	13.3	21.2	11.8	0	0	0.0	0.0
1874	15	0	0	0.0	0.0	0.0	0.0	0.0	2	2	13.3	24.0	13.3	0	0	0.0	0.0
1875	15	1	1	10.0	21.4	0.47	0.0355	5.87	3	3	20.0	30.0	16.7	0	0	0.0	0.0
1876	15	0	0	0.0	0.0	0.0	0.0	0.0	3	3	20.0	36.0	20.0	0	0	0.0	0.0
1877	15	1	2	285.0	17.6	16.19	0.2336	7.76	4	4	26.7	44.8	24.9	1	1	21.4	10.0
1878	17	2	2	7.5	20.3	0.37	0.0104	4.64	5	6	35.3	13.0	6.4	4	5	197.0	394.5
1879	17	1	1	3.5	5.7	0.61	0.0102	4.63	2	1	5.9	14.4	7.1	1	1	5.7	3.5
1880	17	0	0	0.0	0.0	0.0	0.0	0.0	1	1	5.9	8.1	4.0	1	1	18.2	4.0
1881	17	0	0	0.0	0.0	0.0	0.0	0.0	0	0	0.0	0.0	0.0	0	0	0.0	0.0
1882	17	2	2	24.5	65.3	0.38	0.0335	5.81	2	2	11.8	11.8	5.8	0	0	0.0	0.0
1883	17	0	0	0.0	0.0	0.0	0.0	0.0	2	2	11.8	24.0	11.8	0	0	0.0	0.0
1884	17	1	1	2.1	11.8	0.18	0.0055	4.01	3	2	11.8	24.1	11.8	1	1	25.7	4.5
1885	17	1	1	2.0	1.2	1.67	0.1053	6.96	3	3	17.6	18.5	9.1	3	3	52.6	24.1
1886	17	0	0	0.0	0.0	0.0	0.0	0.0	0	0	0.0	0.0	0.0	0	0	0.0	0.0
1887	17	0	0	0.0	0.0	0.0	0.0	0.0	0	0	0.0	0.0	0.0	0	0	0.0	0.0
1888	17	0	0	0.0	0.0	0.0	0.0	0.0	0	0	0.0	0.0	0.0	0	0	0.0	0.0
1889	17	0	0	0.0	0.0	0.0	0.0	0.0	0	0	0.0	0.0	0.0	0	0	0.0	0.0
1890	17	0	0	0.0	0.0	0.0	0.0	0.0	0	0	0.0	0.0	0.0	0	0	0.0	0.0
1891	17	0	0	0.0	0.0	0.0	0.0	0.0	0	0	0.0	0.0	0.0	0	0	0.0	0.0
1892	17	0	0	0.0	0.0	0.0	0.0	0.0	0	0	0.0	0.0	0.0	0	0	0.0	0.0

7.4 - ANNUAL AMOUNTS OF WAR FOR CENTRAL SYSTEM MEMBERS

	ONSET--BY WAR								UNDERWAY					TERMINATION--BY WAR			
YEAR	NO. IN SYSTEM 1	NO. OF WARS BEGUN 2	NO. OF PARTIC-IPANTS 3	BATTLE DEATHS 000'S 4	NATION MONTHS 5	BATTLE DEATHS 000'S PER NATION MONTH 6	BATTLE DEATHS PER HUNDRED POPULA-TION 7	LOG OF BATTLE DEATHS PER MILLION POPULA-TION 8	NO. OF WARS UNDER-WAY 9	NO. OF NATIONS IN WAR 10	% OF NATIONS IN WAR 11	NATION MONTHS UNDER-WAY 12	% OF NATION MONTHS EX-HAUST-ED 13	NO. OF WARS ENDING 14	NO. OF PARTIC-IPANTS 15	NATION MONTHS 16	BATTLE DEATHS 000'S 17
1893	17	0	0	0.0	0.0	0.0	0.0	0.0	0	0	0.0	0.0	0.0	0	0	0.0	0.0
1894	17	1	1	6.0	9.7	0.62	0.0156	5.05	1	1	5.9	0.7	0.3	0	0	0.0	0.0
1895	19	2	2	59.0	47.8	1.23	0.1194	7.09	3	3	15.8	20.0	8.8	1	1	9.7	6.0
1896	19	1	1	2.0	23.1	0.09	0.0110	4.70	3	2	10.5	28.8	12.6	1	1	10.5	9.0
1897	19	1	2	2.0	6.2	0.32	0.0075	4.32	3	3	15.8	30.2	13.2	1	2	6.2	2.0
1898	19	1	1	5.0	3.7	1.35	0.0272	5.60	3	1	5.3	10.7	4.7	3	1	64.1	57.0
1899	20	2	2	26.5	72.5	0.37	0.0226	5.42	2	2	10.0	13.6	5.7	0	0	0.0	0.0
1900	20	0	0	0.0	0.0	0.0	0.0	0.0	2	2	10.0	24.0	10.0	0	0	0.0	0.0
1901	20	0	0	0.0	0.0	0.0	0.0	0.0	2	2	10.0	24.0	10.0	0	0	0.0	0.0
1902	20	0	0	0.0	0.0	0.0	0.0	0.0	2	2	10.0	11.1	4.6	2	2	72.5	26.5
1903	20	0	0	0.0	0.0	0.0	0.0	0.0	0	0	0.0	0.0	0.0	0	0	0.0	0.0
1904	20	1	2	130.0	38.6	3.37	0.0692	6.54	1	2	10.0	21.6	9.0	0	0	0.0	0.0
1905	21	0	0	0.0	0.0	0.0	0.0	0.0	1	2	9.5	17.0	6.7	1	2	38.6	130.0
1906	21	0	0	0.0	0.0	0.0	0.0	0.0	0	0	0.0	0.0	0.0	0	0	0.0	0.0
1907	21	0	0	0.0	0.0	0.0	0.0	0.0	0	0	0.0	0.0	0.0	0	0	0.0	0.0
1908	22	0	0	0.0	0.0	0.0	0.0	0.0	0	0	0.0	0.0	0.0	0	0	0.0	0.0
1909	22	1	1	2.0	8.5	0.24	0.0103	4.63	1	1	4.5	5.8	2.2	0	0	0.0	0.0
1910	22	0	0	0.0	0.0	0.0	0.0	0.0	1	1	4.5	2.7	1.0	1	1	8.5	2.0
1911	22	1	2	20.0	25.4	0.79	0.0335	5.81	1	2	9.1	6.2	2.3	0	0	0.0	0.0
1912	22	1	4	82.0	20.4	4.02	0.2571	7.85	2	5	22.7	27.4	10.4	1	2	25.4	20.0
1913	22	1	5	60.5	4.2	14.40	0.1609	7.38	2	5	22.7	16.4	6.2	2	5	24.6	142.5
1914	23	1	15	8555.8	607.8	14.08	1.4137	9.56	1	9	39.1	41.4	15.0	0	0	0.0	0.0
1915	23	0	0	0.0	0.0	0.0	0.0	0.0	1	11	47.8	118.0	42.8	0	0	0.0	0.0
1916	23	0	0	0.0	0.0	0.0	0.0	0.0	1	13	56.5	146.3	53.0	0	0	0.0	0.0
1917	23	1	1	50.0	39.3	1.27	0.0309	5.73	2	15	65.2	169.8	61.5	0	0	0.0	0.0
1918	27	0	0	0.0	0.0	0.0	0.0	0.0	2	14	51.9	144.3	44.5	1	15	607.8	8555.8
1919	31	2	5	61.0	93.4	0.65	0.1203	7.09	3	6	19.4	38.6	10.4	1	3	10.8	11.0

7.5 - ANNUAL AMOUNTS OF INTERSTATE WAR FOR CENTRAL SYSTEM MEMBERS

		ONSET--BY WAR							+++ UNDERWAY +++					--- TERMINATION--BY WAR ---			
YEAR	NO. IN SYSTEM 1	NO. OF WARS BEGUN 2	NO. OF PARTIC-IPANTS 3	BATTLE DEATHS 000'S 4	NATION MONTHS 5	BATTLE DEATHS 000'S PER NATION MONTH 6	BATTLE DEATHS PER HUNDRED POPULA-TION 7	LOG OF BATTLE DEATHS PER MILLION POPULA-TION 8	NO. OF WARS UNDER-WAY 9	NO. OF NATIONS IN WAR 10	% OF NATIONS IN WAR 11	NATION MONTHS UNDER-WAY 12	% OF NATION MONTHS EX-HAUST-ED 13	NO. OF WARS ENDING 14	NO. OF PARTIC-IPANTS 15	NATION MONTHS 16	BATTLE DEATHS 000'S 17
1816	13	0	0	0.0	0.0	0.0	0.0	0.0	0	0	0.0	0.0	0.0	0	0	0.0	0.0
1817	13	0	0	0.0	0.0	0.0	0.0	0.0	0	0	0.0	0.0	0.0	0	0	0.0	0.0
1818	13	0	0	0.0	0.0	0.0	0.0	0.0	0	0	0.0	0.0	0.0	0	0	0.0	0.0
1819	13	0	0	0.0	0.0	0.0	0.0	0.0	0	0	0.0	0.0	0.0	0	0	0.0	0.0
1820	13	0	0	0.0	0.0	0.0	0.0	0.0	0	0	0.0	0.0	0.0	0	0	0.0	0.0
1821	13	0	0	0.0	0.0	0.0	0.0	0.0	0	0	0.0	0.0	0.0	0	0	0.0	0.0
1822	13	0	0	0.0	0.0	0.0	0.0	0.0	0	0	0.0	0.0	0.0	0	0	0.0	0.0
1823	13	1	2	1.0	14.6	0.07	0.0023	3.15	1	2	15.4	14.6	9.4	1	2	14.6	1.0
1824	13	0	0	0.0	0.0	0.0	0.0	0.0	0	0	0.0	0.0	0.0	0	0	0.0	0.0
1825	13	0	0	0.0	0.0	0.0	0.0	0.0	0	0	0.0	0.0	0.0	0	0	0.0	0.0
1826	13	0	0	0.0	0.0	0.0	0.0	0.0	0	0	0.0	0.0	0.0	0	0	0.0	0.0
1827	13	1	4	3.2	0.4	7.95	0.0024	3.18	1	4	30.8	0.0	0.0	1	4	0.4	3.2
1828	14	1	2	130.0	33.4	3.89	0.1660	7.41	1	2	14.3	16.4	9.8	0	0	0.0	0.0
1829	14	0	0	0.0	0.0	0.0	0.0	0.0	1	2	14.3	16.8	10.0	1	2	33.4	130.0
1830	15	0	0	0.0	0.0	0.0	0.0	0.0	0	0	0.0	0.0	0.0	0	0	0.0	0.0
1831	15	0	0	0.0	0.0	0.0	0.0	0.0	0	0	0.0	0.0	0.0	0	0	0.0	0.0
1832	15	0	0	0.0	0.0	0.0	0.0	0.0	0	0	0.0	0.0	0.0	0	0	0.0	0.0
1833	15	0	0	0.0	0.0	0.0	0.0	0.0	0	0	0.0	0.0	0.0	0	0	0.0	0.0
1834	15	0	0	0.0	0.0	0.0	0.0	0.0	0	0	0.0	0.0	0.0	0	0	0.0	0.0
1835	15	0	0	0.0	0.0	0.0	0.0	0.0	0	0	0.0	0.0	0.0	0	0	0.0	0.0
1836	15	0	0	0.0	0.0	0.0	0.0	0.0	0	0	0.0	0.0	0.0	0	0	0.0	0.0
1837	15	0	0	0.0	0.0	0.0	0.0	0.0	0	0	0.0	0.0	0.0	0	0	0.0	0.0
1838	15	0	0	0.0	0.0	0.0	0.0	0.0	0	0	0.0	0.0	0.0	0	0	0.0	0.0
1839	15	0	0	0.0	0.0	0.0	0.0	0.0	0	0	0.0	0.0	0.0	0	0	0.0	0.0
1840	15	0	0	0.0	0.0	0.0	0.0	0.0	0	0	0.0	0.0	0.0	0	0	0.0	0.0
1841	15	0	0	0.0	0.0	0.0	0.0	0.0	0	0	0.0	0.0	0.0	0	0	0.0	0.0
1842	15	0	0	0.0	0.0	0.0	0.0	0.0	0	0	0.0	0.0	0.0	0	0	0.0	0.0
1843	15	0	0	0.0	0.0	0.0	0.0	0.0	0	0	0.0	0.0	0.0	0	0	0.0	0.0
1844	15	0	0	0.0	0.0	0.0	0.0	0.0	0	0	0.0	0.0	0.0	0	0	0.0	0.0
1845	15	0	0	0.0	0.0	0.0	0.0	0.0	0	0	0.0	0.0	0.0	0	0	0.0	0.0
1846	15	0	0	0.0	0.0	0.0	0.0	0.0	0	0	0.0	0.0	0.0	0	0	0.0	0.0
1847	15	0	0	0.0	0.0	0.0	0.0	0.0	0	0	0.0	0.0	0.0	0	0	0.0	0.0
1848	15	2	4	15.0	25.6	0.59	0.0261	5.56	2	4	26.7	18.4	10.2	0	0	0.0	0.0
1849	15	1	2	0.6	2.8	0.21	0.0009	2.15	3	5	33.3	10.0	5.6	3	5	28.4	15.6
1850	15	0	0	0.0	0.0	0.0	0.0	0.0	0	0	0.0	0.0	0.0	0	0	0.0	0.0
1851	15	0	0	0.0	0.0	0.0	0.0	0.0	0	0	0.0	0.0	0.0	0	0	0.0	0.0
1852	15	0	0	0.0	0.0	0.0	0.0	0.0	0	0	0.0	0.0	0.0	0	0	0.0	0.0

7.5 - ANNUAL AMOUNTS OF INTERSTATE WAR FOR CENTRAL SYSTEM MEMBERS

	ONSET--BY WAR							UNDERWAY					TERMINATION--BY WAR			
YEAR	NO. IN SYSTEM 1	NO. OF WARS BEGUN 2	NO. OF PARTIC-IPANTS 3	BATTLE DEATHS 000'S 4	NATION MONTHS 5	BATTLE DEATHS 000'S PER NATION MONTH 6	BATTLE DEATHS PER HUNDRED POPULA-TION 7	LOG OF BATTLE DEATHS PER MILLION POPULA-TION 8	NO. OF WARS UNDER-WAY 9	NO. OF NATIONS IN WAR 10	% OF NATIONS IN WAR 11	NATION MONTHS UNDER-WAY 12	% OF NATION MONTHS EX-HAUST-ED 13	NO. OF WARS ENDING 14	NO. OF PARTIC-IPANTS 15	NATION MONTHS 16	BATTLE DEATHS 000'S 17
1853	15	1	5	264.2	116.5	2.27	0.1586	7.37	1	2	13.3	4.6	2.6	0	0	0.0	0.0
1854	15	0	0	0.0	0.0	0.0	0.0	0.0	1	4	26.7	42.2	23.4	0	0	0.0	0.0
1855	15	0	0	0.0	0.0	0.0	0.0	0.0	1	5	33.3	59.7	33.2	0	0	0.0	0.0
1856	15	1	1	0.5	4.6	0.11	0.0017	2.84	2	5	33.3	12.2	6.8	1	5	116.5	264.2
1857	15	0	0	0.0	0.0	0.0	0.0	0.0	1	1	6.7	2.4	1.3	1	1	4.6	0.5
1858	15	0	0	0.0	0.0	0.0	0.0	0.0	0	0	0.0	0.0	0.0	0	0	0.0	0.0
1859	15	2	4	26.5	12.5	2.12	0.0285	5.65	2	4	26.7	9.6	5.3	1	3	7.3	22.5
1860	15	2	1	0.9	3.8	0.24	0.0021	3.02	3	2	13.3	6.0	3.3	2	2	5.8	4.3
1861	15	0	0	0.0	0.0	0.0	0.0	0.0	1	1	6.7	0.6	0.3	1	1	3.2	0.6
1862	15	1	1	8.0	57.7	0.14	0.0212	5.36	1	1	6.7	8.5	4.7	0	0	0.0	0.0
1863	15	0	0	0.0	0.0	0.0	0.0	0.0	1	1	6.7	12.0	6.7	0	0	0.0	0.0
1864	15	1	3	4.5	10.8	0.42	0.0080	4.38	2	4	26.7	23.1	12.8	1	3	10.8	4.5
1865	15	1	1	0.3	6.5	0.05	0.0018	2.91	2	2	13.3	14.2	7.9	0	0	0.0	0.0
1866	15	1	3	34.0	4.2	8.10	0.0417	6.03	3	5	33.3	20.4	11.3	2	4	10.7	34.3
1867	15	0	0	0.0	0.0	0.0	0.0	0.0	1	1	6.7	1.2	0.7	1	1	57.7	8.0
1868	15	0	0	0.0	0.0	0.0	0.0	0.0	0	0	0.0	0.0	0.0	0	0	0.0	0.0
1869	15	0	0	0.0	0.0	0.0	0.0	0.0	0	0	0.0	0.0	0.0	0	0	0.0	0.0
1870	15	1	2	180.0	14.6	12.33	0.2329	7.75	1	2	13.3	11.0	6.1	0	0	0.0	0.0
1871	15	0	0	0.0	0.0	0.0	0.0	0.0	1	2	13.3	3.8	2.1	1	2	14.6	180.0
1872	15	0	0	0.0	0.0	0.0	0.0	0.0	0	0	0.0	0.0	0.0	0	0	0.0	0.0
1873	15	0	0	0.0	0.0	0.0	0.0	0.0	0	0	0.0	0.0	0.0	0	0	0.0	0.0
1874	15	0	0	0.0	0.0	0.0	0.0	0.0	0	0	0.0	0.0	0.0	0	0	0.0	0.0
1875	15	0	0	0.0	0.0	0.0	0.0	0.0	0	0	0.0	0.0	0.0	0	0	0.0	0.0
1876	15	0	0	0.0	0.0	0.0	0.0	0.0	0	0	0.0	0.0	0.0	0	0	0.0	0.0
1877	15	1	2	285.0	17.6	16.19	0.2336	7.76	1	2	13.3	17.4	9.7	0	0	0.0	0.0
1878	17	0	0	0.0	0.0	0.0	0.0	0.0	1	2	11.8	0.2	0.1	1	2	17.6	285.0
1879	17	0	0	0.0	0.0	0.0	0.0	0.0	0	0	0.0	0.0	0.0	0	0	0.0	0.0
1880	17	0	0	0.0	0.0	0.0	0.0	0.0	0	0	0.0	0.0	0.0	0	0	0.0	0.0
1881	17	0	0	0.0	0.0	0.0	0.0	0.0	0	0	0.0	0.0	0.0	0	0	0.0	0.0
1882	17	0	0	0.0	0.0	0.0	0.0	0.0	0	0	0.0	0.0	0.0	0	0	0.0	0.0
1883	17	0	0	0.0	0.0	0.0	0.0	0.0	0	0	0.0	0.0	0.0	0	0	0.0	0.0
1884	17	1	1	2.1	11.8	0.18	0.0055	4.01	1	1	5.9	6.6	3.2	0	0	0.0	0.0
1885	17	0	0	0.0	0.0	0.0	0.0	0.0	1	1	5.9	5.3	2.6	1	1	11.8	2.1
1886	17	0	0	0.0	0.0	0.0	0.0	0.0	0	0	0.0	0.0	0.0	0	0	0.0	0.0
1887	17	0	0	0.0	0.0	0.0	0.0	0.0	0	0	0.0	0.0	0.0	0	0	0.0	0.0
1888	17	0	0	0.0	0.0	0.0	0.0	0.0	0	0	0.0	0.0	0.0	0	0	0.0	0.0
1889	17	0	0	0.0	0.0	0.0	0.0	0.0	0	0	0.0	0.0	0.0	0	0	0.0	0.0

	ONSET--BY WAR								UNDERWAY					TERMINATION--BY WAR			
YEAR	NO. IN SYSTEM	NO. OF WARS BEGUN	NO. OF PARTIC-IPANTS	BATTLE DEATHS 000'S	NATION MONTHS	BATTLE DEATHS 000'S PER NATION MONTH	BATTLE DEATHS PER HUNDRED POPULA-TION	LOG OF BATTLE DEATHS PER MILLION POPULA-TION	NO. OF WARS UNDER-WAY	NO. OF NATIONS IN WAR	% OF NATIONS IN WAR	NATION MONTHS UNDER-WAY	% OF NATION MONTHS EX-HAUST-ED	NO. OF WARS ENDING	NO. OF PARTIC-IPANTS	NATION MONTHS	BATTLE DEATHS 000'S
	1	2	3	4	5	6	7	8	9	10	11	12	13	14	15	16	17
1890	17	0	0	0.0	0.0	0.0	0.0	0.0	0	0	0.0	0.0	0.0.	0	0	0.0	0.0
1891	17	0	0	0.0	0.0	0.0	0.0	0.0	0	0	0.0	0.0	0.0	0	0	0.0	0.0
1892	17	0	0	0.0	0.0	0.0	0.0	0.0	0	0	0.0	0.0	0.0	0	0	0.0	0.0
1893	17	0	0	0.0	0.0	0.0	0.0	0.0	0	0	0.0	0.0	0.0	0	0	0.0	0.0
1894	17	0	0	0.0	0.0	0.0	0.0	0.0	0	0	0.0	0.0	0.0	0	0	0.0	0.0
1895	19	0	0	0.0	0.0	0.0	0.0	0.0	0	0	0.0	0.0	0.0	0	0	0.0	0.0
1896	19	0	0	0.0	0.0	0.0	0.0	0.0	0	0	0.0	0.0	0.0	0	0	0.0	0.0
1897	19	1	2	2.0	6.2	0.32	0.0075	4.32	1	2	10.5	6.2	2.7	1	2	6.2	2.0
1898	19	1	1	5.0	3.7	1.35	0.0272	5.60	1	1	5.3	3.7	1.6	1	1	3.7	5.0
1899	20	0	0	0.0	0.0	0.0	0.0	0.0	0	0	0.0	0.0	0.0	0	0	0.0	0.0
1900	20	0	0	0.0	0.0	0.0	0.0	0.0	0	0	0.0	0.0	0.0	0	0	0.0	0.0
1901	20	0	0	0.0	0.0	0.0	0.0	0.0	0	0	0.0	0.0	0.0	0	0	0.0	0.0
1902	20	0	0	0.0	0.0	0.0	0.0	0.0	0	0	0.0	0.0	0.0	0	0	0.0	0.0
1903	20	0	0	0.0	0.0	0.0	0.0	0.0	0	0	0.0	0.0	0.0	0	0	0.0	0.0
1904	20	1	2	130.0	38.6	3.37	0.0692	6.54	1	2	10.0	21.6	9.0	0	0	0.0	0.0
1905	21	0	0	0.0	0.0	0.0	0.0	0.0	1	2	9.5	17.0	6.7	1	2	38.6	130.0
1906	21	0	0	0.0	0.0	0.0	0.0	0.0	0	0	0.0	0.0	0.0	0	0	0.0	0.0
1907	21	0	0	0.0	0.0	0.0	0.0	0.0	0	0	0.0	0.0	0.0	0	0	0.0	0.0
1908	22	0	0	0.0	0.0	0.0	0.0	0.0	0	0	0.0	0.0	0.0	0	0	0.0	0.0
1909	22	1	1	2.0	8.5	0.24	0.0103	4.63	1	1	4.5	5.8	2.2	0	0	0.0	0.0
1910	22	0	0	0.0	0.0	0.0	0.0	0.0	1	1	4.5	2.7	1.0	1	1	8.5	2.0
1911	22	1	2	20.0	25.4	0.79	0.0335	5.81	1	2	9.1	6.2	2.3	0	0	0.0	0.0
1912	22	1	4	82.0	20.4	4.02	0.2571	7.85	2	5	22.7	27.4	10.4	1	2	25.4	20.0
1913	22	1	5	60.5	4.2	14.40	0.1609	7.38	2	5	22.7	16.4	6.2	2	5	24.6	142.5
1914	23	1	15	8555.8	607.8	14.08	1.4137	9.56	1	9	39.1	41.4	15.0	0	0	0.0	0.0
1915	23	0	0	0.0	0.0	0.0	0.0	0.0	1	11	47.8	118.0	42.8	0	0	0.0	0.0
1916	23	0	0	0.0	0.0	0.0	0.0	0.0	1	13	56.5	146.3	53.0	0	0	0.0	0.0
1917	23	0	0	0.0	0.0	0.0	0.0	0.0	1	15	65.2	169.0	61.2	0	0	0.0	0.0
1918	27	0	0	0.0	0.0	0.0	0.0	0.0	1	13	48.1	132.3	40.8	1	15	607.8	8555.8
1919	31	2	5	61.0	93.4	0.65	0.1203	7.09	2	5	16.1	26.6	7.2	1	3	10.8	11.0

7.6 - ANNUAL AMOUNTS OF MAJOR POWER WAR

	ONSET--BY WAR							UNDERWAY					TERMINATION--BY WAR			
YEAR	NO. IN SYSTEM 1	NO. OF WARS BEGUN 2	NO. OF PARTIC-IPANTS 3	BATTLE DEATHS 000'S 4	NATION MONTHS 5	BATTLE DEATHS 000'S PER NATION MONTH 6	BATTLE DEATHS PER HUNDRED POPULA-TICN 7	LOG OF BATTLE DEATHS PER MILLION POPULA-TION 8	NO. OF WARS UNDER-WAY 9	NO. OF NATIONS IN WAR 10	% OF NATIONS IN WAR 11	NATION MONTHS UNDER-WAY 12	% OF NATION MONTHS EX-HAUST-ED 13	NO. OF WARS ENDING 14	NO. OF PARTIC-IPANTS 15	NATION MONTHS 16	BATTLE DEATHS 000'S 17
1816	5	0	0	0.0	0.0	0.0	0.0	0.0	0	0	0.0	0.0	0.0	0	0	0.0	0.0
1817	5	1	1	2.0	6.9	0.29	0.0098	4.59	1	1	20.0	1.8	3.0	0	0	0.0	0.0
1818	5	0	0	0.0	0.0	0.0	0.0	0.0	1	1	20.0	5.1	8.5	1	1	6.9	2.0
1819	5	0	0	0.0	0.0	0.0	0.0	0.0	0	0	0.0	0.0	0.0	0	0	0.0	0.0
1820	5	0	0	0.0	0.0	0.0	0.0	0.0	0	0	0.0	0.0	0.0	0	0	0.0	0.0
1821	5	0	0	0.0	0.0	0.0	0.0	0.0	0	0	0.0	0.0	0.0	0	0	0.0	0.0
1822	5	0	0	0.0	0.0	0.0	0.0	0.0	0	0	0.0	0.0	0.0	0	0	0.0	0.0
1823	5	2	2	15.4	36.4	0.42	0.0288	5.66	2	2	40.0	10.6	17.7	1	1	7.3	0.4
1824	5	0	0	0.0	0.0	0.0	0.0	0.0	1	1	20.0	12.0	20.0	0	0	0.0	0.0
1825	5	0	0	0.0	0.0	0.0	0.0	0.0	1	1	20.0	12.0	20.0	0	0	0.0	0.0
1826	5	1	1	5.0	17.0	0.29	0.0095	4.55	2	2	40.0	4.9	8.2	1	1	29.1	15.0
1827	5	1	3	0.2	0.3	0.60	0.0002	0.50	2	3	60.0	12.0	20.0	1	3	0.3	0.2
1828	5	1	1	50.0	16.7	2.99	0.0919	6.82	2	1	20.0	10.1	16.8	1	1	17.0	5.0
1829	5	0	0	0.0	0.0	0.0	0.0	0.0	1	1	20.0	8.4	14.0	1	1	16.7	50.0
1830	5	0	0	0.0	0.0	0.0	0.0	0.0	0	0	0.0	0.0	0.0	0	0	0.0	0.0
1831	5	1	1	15.0	8.3	1.81	0.0265	5.58	1	1	20.0	8.3	13.8	1	1	8.3	15.0
1832	5	0	0	0.0	0.0	0.0	0.0	0.0	0	0	0.0	0.0	0.0	0	0	0.0	0.0
1833	5	0	0	0.0	0.0	0.0	0.0	0.0	0	0	0.0	0.0	0.0	0	0	0.0	0.0
1834	5	0	0	0.0	0.0	0.0	0.0	0.0	0	0	0.0	0.0	0.0	0	0	0.0	0.0
1835	5	0	0	0.0	0.0	0.0	0.0	0.0	0	0	0.0	0.0	0.0	0	0	0.0	0.0
1836	5	0	0	0.0	0.0	0.0	0.0	0.0	0	0	0.0	0.0	0.0	0	0	0.0	0.0
1837	5	0	0	0.0	0.0	0.0	0.0	0.0	0	0	0.0	0.0	0.0	0	0	0.0	0.0
1838	5	1	1	20.0	48.4	0.41	0.0775	6.65	1	1	20.0	3.0	5.0	0	0	0.0	0.0
1839	5	0	0	0.0	0.0	0.0	0.0	0.0	1	1	20.0	12.0	20.0	0	0	0.0	0.0
1840	5	1	1	0.0	2.6	0.00	0.0000	-0.97	2	1	20.0	14.6	24.3	1	1	2.6	0.0
1841	5	0	0	0.0	0.0	0.0	0.0	0.0	1	1	20.0	12.0	20.0	0	0	0.0	0.0
1842	5	0	0	0.0	0.0	0.0	0.0	0.0	1	1	20.0	9.4	15.7	1	1	48.4	20.0
1843	5	0	0	0.0	0.0	0.0	0.0	0.0	0	0	0.0	0.0	0.0	0	0	0.0	0.0
1844	5	0	0	0.0	0.0	0.0	0.0	0.0	0	0	0.0	0.0	0.0	0	0	0.0	0.0
1845	5	1	1	1.5	2.9	0.52	0.0056	4.02	1	1	20.0	0.6	1.0	0	0	0.0	0.0
1846	5	0	0	0.0	0.0	0.0	0.0	0.0	1	1	20.0	2.2	3.7	1	1	2.9	1.5
1847	5	0	0	0.0	0.0	0.0	0.0	0.0	0	0	0.0	0.0	0.0	0	0	0.0	0.0
1848	5	4	4	69.1	30.0	2.30	0.0383	5.95	4	3	60.0	15.6	26.0	0	0	0.0	0.0
1849	5	1	2	0.6	2.8	0.21	0.0009	2.15	5	5	100.0	17.1	28.5	5	5	32.8	69.7
1850	5	0	0	0.0	0.0	0.0	0.0	0.0	0	0	0.0	0.0	0.0	0	0	0.0	0.0
1851	5	0	0	0.0	0.0	0.0	0.0	0.0	0	0	0.0	0.0	0.0	0	0	0.0	0.0
1852	5	0	0	0.0	0.0	0.0	0.0	0.0	0	0	0.0	0.0	0.0	0	0	0.0	0.0

	ONSET--BY WAR								UNDERWAY					TERMINATION--BY WAR			
YEAR	NO. IN SYSTEM 1	NO. OF WARS BEGUN 2	NO. OF PARTIC-IPANTS 3	BATTLE DEATHS 000'S 4	NATION MONTHS 5	BATTLE DEATHS 000'S PER NATICN MONTH 6	BATTLE DEATHS PER HUNDRED POPULA-TICN 7	LOG OF BATTLE DEATHS PER MILLION POPULA-TION 8	NO. OF WARS UNDER-WAY 9	NO. OF NATIONS IN WAR 10	% OF NATIONS IN WAR 11	NATION MONTHS UNDER-WAY 12	% OF NATION MONTHS EX-HAUST-ED 13	NO. OF WARS ENDING 14	NO. OF PARTIC-IPANTS 15	NATION MONTHS 16	BATTLE DEATHS 000'S 17
1853	5	1	3	217.0	74.5	2.91	0.1597	7.38	1	1	20.0	2.3	3.8	0	0	0.0	0.0
1854	5	0	0	0.0	0.0	0.0	0.0	0.0	1	3	60.0	30.2	50.3	0	0	0.0	0.0
1855	5	0	0	0.0	0.0	0.0	0.0	0.0	1	3	60.0	36.0	60.0	0	0	0.0	0.0
1856	5	1	1	0.5	4.6	0.11	0.0017	2.84	2	3	60.0	8.2	13.7	1	3	74.5	217.0
1857	5	1	1	3.5	22.9	0.15	0.0119	4.78	2	1	20.0	10.2	17.0	1	1	4.6	0.5
1858	5	0	0	0.0	0.0	0.0	0.0	0.0	1	1	20.0	12.0	20.0	0	0	0.0	0.0
1859	5	1	2	20.0	4.8	4.17	0.0279	5.63	2	3	60.0	8.0	13.3	2	3	27.7	23.5
1860	6	2	1	0.9	3.8	0.24	0.0021	3.02	2	1	16.7	3.2	4.4	1	1	0.6	0.3
1861	6	0	0	0.0	0.0	0.0	0.0	0.0	1	1	16.7	0.6	0.8	1	1	3.2	0.6
1862	6	1	1	8.0	57.7	0.14	0.0212	5.36	1	1	16.7	8.5	11.8	0	0	0.0	0.0
1863	6	1	1	5.0	14.9	0.34	0.0065	4.17	2	2	33.3	23.3	32.4	0	0	0.0	0.0
1864	6	1	2	1.5	7.2	0.21	0.0027	3.31	3	4	66.7	23.0	31.9	2	3	22.1	6.5
1865	6	0	0	0.0	0.0	0.0	0.0	0.0	1	1	16.7	12.0	16.7	0	0	0.0	0.0
1866	6	1	3	34.0	4.2	8.10	0.0417	6.03	2	4	66.7	16.2	22.5	1	3	4.2	34.0
1867	6	0	0	0.0	0.0	0.0	0.0	0.0	1	1	16.7	1.2	1.7	1	1	57.7	8.0
1868	6	0	0	0.0	0.0	0.0	0.0	0.0	0	0	0.0	0.0	0.0	0	0	0.0	0.0
1869	6	0	0	0.0	0.0	0.0	0.0	0.0	0	0	0.0	0.0	0.0	0	0	0.0	0.0
1870	6	1	2	180.0	14.6	12.33	0.2329	7.75	1	2	33.3	11.0	15.3	0	0	0.0	0.0
1871	6	0	0	0.0	0.0	0.0	0.0	0.0	1	2	33.3	3.8	5.3	1	2	14.6	180.0
1872	6	0	0	0.0	0.0	0.0	0.0	0.0	0	0	0.0	0.0	0.0	0	0	0.0	0.0
1873	6	0	0	0.0	0.0	0.0	0.0	0.0	0	0	0.0	0.0	0.0	0	0	0.0	0.0
1874	6	0	0	0.0	0.0	0.0	0.0	0.0	0	0	0.0	0.0	0.0	0	0	0.0	0.0
1875	6	0	0	0.0	0.0	0.0	0.0	0.0	0	0	0.0	0.0	0.0	0	0	0.0	0.0
1876	6	0	0	0.0	0.0	0.0	0.0	0.0	0	0	0.0	0.0	0.0	0	0	0.0	0.0
1877	6	1	1	120.0	8.8	13.64	0.1279	7.15	1	1	16.7	8.7	12.1	0	0	0.0	0.0
1878	6	2	2	7.5	20.3	0.37	0.0104	4.64	3	3	50.0	3.6	5.0	2	2	10.9	123.5
1879	6	1	1	3.5	5.7	0.61	0.0102	4.63	2	1	16.7	14.4	20.0	1	1	5.7	3.5
1880	6	0	0	0.0	0.0	0.0	0.0	0.0	1	1	16.7	8.1	11.2	1	1	18.2	4.0
1881	6	0	0	0.0	0.0	0.0	0.0	0.0	0	0	0.0	0.0	0.0	0	0	0.0	0.0
1882	6	2	2	24.5	65.3	0.38	0.0335	5.81	2	2	33.3	11.8	16.4	0	0	0.0	0.0
1883	6	0	0	0.0	0.0	0.0	0.0	0.0	2	2	33.3	24.0	33.3	0	0	0.0	0.0
1884	6	1	1	2.1	11.8	0.18	0.0055	4.01	3	2	33.3	24.1	33.5	1	1	25.7	4.5
1885	6	0	0	0.0	0.0	0.0	0.0	0.0	2	2	33.3	17.3	24.0	2	2	51.4	22.1
1886	6	0	0	0.0	0.0	0.0	0.0	0.0	0	0	0.0	0.0	0.0	0	0	0.0	0.0
1887	6	0	0	0.0	0.0	0.0	0.0	0.0	0	0	0.0	0.0	0.0	0	0	0.0	0.0
1888	6	0	0	0.0	0.0	0.0	0.0	0.0	0	0	0.0	0.0	0.0	0	0	0.0	0.0
1889	6	0	0	0.0	0.0	0.0	0.0	0.0	0	0	0.0	0.0	0.0	0	0	0.0	0.0
1890	6	0	0	0.0	0.0	0.0	0.0	0.0	0	0	0.0	0.0	0.0	0	0	0.0	0.0
1891	6	0	0	0.0	0.0	0.0	0.0	0.0	0	0	0.0	0.0	0.0	0	0	0.0	0.0
1892	6	0	0	0.0	0.0	0.0	0.0	0.0	0	0	0.0	0.0	0.0	0	0	0.0	0.0

7.6 - ANNUAL AMOUNTS OF MAJOR POWER WAR

	ONSET--BY WAR								UNDERWAY					TERMINATION--BY WAR			
YEAR	NO. IN SYSTEM 1	NO. OF WARS BEGUN 2	NO. OF PARTIC-IPANTS 3	BATTLE DEATHS 000'S 4	NATION MONTHS 5	BATTLE DEATHS 000'S PER NATION MONTH 6	BATTLE DEATHS PER HUNDRED POPULA-TION 7	LOG OF BATTLE DEATHS PER MILLION POPULA-TION 8	NO. OF WARS UNDER-WAY 9	NO. OF NATIONS IN WAR 10	% OF NATIONS IN WAR 11	NATION MONTHS UNDER-WAY 12	% OF NATION MONTHS EX-HAUST-ED 13	NO. OF WARS ENDING 14	NO. OF PARTIC-IPANTS 15	NATION MONTHS 16	BATTLE DEATHS 000'S 17
1893	6	0	0	0.0	0.0	0.0	0.0	0.0	0	0	0.0	0.0	0.0	0	0	0.0	0.0
1894	6	1	1	6.0	9.7	0.62	0.0156	5.05	1	1	16.7	0.7	1.0	0	0	0.0	0.0
1895	7	1	1	9.0	10.5	0.86	0.0288	5.66	2	2	28.6	9.8	11.7	1	1	9.7	6.0
1896	7	0	0	0.0	0.0	0.0	0.0	0.0	1	1	14.3	9.7	11.5	1	1	10.5	9.0
1897	7	0	0	0.0	0.0	0.0	0.0	0.0	0	0	0.0	0.0	0.0	0	0	0.0	0.0
1898	7	0	0	0.0	0.0	0.0	0.0	0.0	0	0	0.0	0.0	0.0	0	0	0.0	0.0
1899	8	2	2	26.5	72.5	0.37	0.0226	5.42	2	2	25.0	13.6	14.2	0	0	0.0	0.0
1900	8	0	0	0.0	0.0	0.0	0.0	0.0	2	2	25.0	24.0	25.0	0	0	0.0	0.0
1901	8	0	0	0.0	0.0	0.0	0.0	0.0	2	2	25.0	24.0	25.0	0	0	0.0	0.0
1902	8	0	0	0.0	0.0	0.0	0.0	0.0	2	2	25.0	11.1	11.6	2	2	72.5	26.5
1903	8	0	0	0.0	0.0	0.0	0.0	0.0	0	0	0.0	0.0	0.0	0	0	0.0	0.0
1904	8	1	2	130.0	38.6	3.37	0.0692	6.54	1	2	25.0	21.6	22.5	0	0	0.0	0.0
1905	8	0	0	0.0	0.0	0.0	0.0	0.0	1	2	25.0	17.0	17.7	1	2	38.6	130.0
1906	8	0	0	0.0	0.0	0.0	0.0	0.0	0	0	0.0	0.0	0.0	0	0	0.0	0.0
1907	8	0	0	0.0	0.0	0.0	0.0	0.0	0	0	0.0	0.0	0.0	0	0	0.0	0.0
1908	8	0	0	0.0	0.0	0.0	0.0	0.0	0	0	0.0	0.0	0.0	0	0	0.0	0.0
1909	8	0	0	0.0	0.0	0.0	0.0	0.0	0	0	0.0	0.0	0.0	0	0	0.0	0.0
1910	8	0	0	0.0	0.0	0.0	0.0	0.0	0	0	0.0	0.0	0.0	0	0	0.0	0.0
1911	8	1	1	6.0	12.7	0.47	0.0172	5.15	1	1	12.5	3.1	3.2	0	0	0.0	0.0
1912	8	0	0	0.0	0.0	0.0	0.0	0.0	1	1	12.5	9.6	10.0	1	1	12.7	6.0
1913	8	0	0	0.0	0.0	0.0	0.0	0.0	0	0	0.0	0.0	0.0	0	0	0.0	0.0
1914	8	1	8	7734.3	356.6	21.69	1.3966	9.54	1	6	75.0	29.3	30.5	0	0	0.0	0.0
1915	8	0	0	0.0	0.0	0.0	0.0	0.0	1	7	87.5	79.3	82.6	0	0	0.0	0.0
1916	8	0	0	0.0	0.0	0.0	0.0	0.0	1	7	87.5	84.0	87.5	0	0	0.0	0.0
1917	8	0	0	0.0	0.0	0.0	0.0	0.0	1	8	100.0	91.6	96.4	0	0	0.0	0.0
1918	7	0	0	0.0	0.0	0.0	0.0	0.0	1	7	100.0	71.9	88.8	1	8	356.6	7734.3
1919	5	0	0	0.0	0.0	0.0	0.0	0.0	0	0	0.0	0.0	0.0	0	0	0.0	0.0
1920	5	0	0	0.0	0.0	0.0	0.0	0.0	0	0	0.0	0.0	0.0	0	0	0.0	0.0
1921	5	0	0	0.0	0.0	0.0	0.0	0.0	0	0	0.0	0.0	0.0	0	0	0.0	0.0
1922	6	0	0	0.0	0.0	0.0	0.0	0.0	0	0	0.0	0.0	0.0	0	0	0.0	0.0
1923	6	0	0	0.0	0.0	0.0	0.0	0.0	0	0	0.0	0.0	0.0	0	0	0.0	0.0
1924	6	0	0	0.0	0.0	0.0	0.0	0.0	0	0	0.0	0.0	0.0	0	0	0.0	0.0
1925	7	2	1	8.0	35.9	0.22	0.0098	4.59	2	1	14.3	14.2	16.9	0	0	0.0	0.0
1926	7	0	0	0.0	0.0	0.0	0.0	0.0	2	1	14.3	16.8	20.0	1	1	13.5	4.0
1927	7	0	0	0.0	0.0	0.0	0.0	0.0	1	1	14.3	5.0	6.0	1	1	22.4	4.0
1928	7	0	0	0.0	0.0	0.0	0.0	0.0	0	0	0.0	0.0	0.0	0	0	0.0	0.0
1929	7	0	0	0.0	0.0	0.0	0.0	0.0	0	0	0.0	0.0	0.0	0	0	0.0	0.0

	ONSET--BY WAR								UNDERWAY					TERMINATION--BY WAR			
YEAR	NO. IN SYSTEM 1	NO. OF WARS BEGUN 2	NO. OF PARTIC-IPANTS 3	BATTLE DEATHS 000'S 4	NATION MONTHS 5	BATTLE DEATHS 000'S PER NATION MONTH 6	BATTLE DEATHS PER HUNDRED POPULA-TION 7	LOG OF BATTLE DEATHS PER MILLION POPULA-TION 8	NO. OF WARS UNDER-WAY 9	NO. OF NATIONS IN WAR 10	% OF NATIONS IN WAR 11	NATION MONTHS UNDER-WAY 12	% OF NATION MONTHS EX-HAUST-ED 13	NO. OF WARS ENDING 14	NO. OF PARTIC-IPANTS 15	NATION MONTHS 16	BATTLE DEATHS 000'S 17
1930	7	0	0	0.0	0.0	0.0	0.0	0.0	0	0	0.0	0.0	0.0	0	0	0.0	0.0
1931	7	1	1	10.0	16.6	0.60	0.0154	5.04	1	1	14.3	0.4	0.5	0	0	0.0	0.0
1932	7	0	0	0.0	0.0	0.0	0.0	0.0	1	1	14.3	12.0	14.3	0	0	0.0	0.0
1933	7	0	0	0.0	0.0	0.0	0.0	0.0	1	1	14.3	4.1	4.9	1	1	16.6	10.0
1934	7	0	0	0.0	0.0	0.0	0.0	0.0	0	0	0.0	0.0	0.0	0	0	0.0	0.0
1935	7	1	1	4.0	7.2	0.56	0.0094	4.54	1	1	14.3	3.0	3.6	0	0	0.0	0.0
1936	7	0	0	0.0	0.0	0.0	0.0	0.0	1	1	14.3	4.3	5.1	1	1	7.2	4.0
1937	7	1	1	250.0	53.1	4.71	0.3602	8.19	1	1	14.3	5.8	6.9	0	0	0.0	0.0
1938	7	0	0	0.0	0.0	0.0	0.0	0.0	1	1	14.3	12.0	14.3	0	0	0.0	0.0
1939	7	3	7	13014.3	335.2	38.83	1.3097	9.48	4	5	71.4	33.3	39.6	1	2	8.4	16.0
1940	7	0	0	0.0	0.0	0.0	0.0	0.0	3	6	85.7	50.8	65.1	1	1	3.4	50.0
1941	6	0	0	0.0	0.0	0.0	0.0	0.0	2	6	100.0	55.1	76.5	1	1	53.1	250.0
1942	6	0	0	0.0	0.0	0.0	0.0	0.0	1	6	100.0	72.0	100.0	0	0	0.0	0.0
1943	6	0	0	0.0	0.0	0.0	0.0	0.0	1	6	100.0	68.0	98.6	0	0	0.0	0.0
1944	5	0	0	0.0	0.0	0.0	0.0	0.0	1	5	100.0	60.0	100.0	0	0	0.0	0.0
1945	6	2	2	96.0	113.2	0.85	0.1086	6.99	3	5	83.3	33.5	59.8	1	7	323.4	12948.3
1946	4	0	0	0.0	0.0	0.0	0.0	0.0	2	2	50.0	21.5	44.8	1	1	11.2	1.0
1947	4	1	1	1.5	20.2	0.07	0.0037	3.62	2	1	25.0	21.1	44.0	0	0	0.0	0.0
1948	4	0	0	0.0	0.0	0.0	0.0	0.0	2	1	25.0	23.0	47.9	1	1	20.2	1.5
1949	4	0	0	0.0	0.0	0.0	0.0	0.0	1	1	25.0	12.0	25.0	0	0	0.0	0.0
1950	5	1	4	955.0	135.8	7.03	0.1183	7.08	2	4	80.0	24.5	40.8	0	0	0.0	0.0
1951	5	0	0	0.0	0.0	0.0	0.0	0.0	2	4	80.0	60.0	100.0	0	0	0.0	0.0
1952	5	0	0	0.0	0.0	0.0	0.0	0.0	2	4	80.0	60.0	100.0	0	0	0.0	0.0
1953	5	0	0	0.0	0.0	0.0	0.0	0.0	2	4	80.0	39.2	65.3	1	4	135.8	955.0
1954	5	1	1	15.0	88.5	0.17	0.0349	5.85	2	1	20.0	7.0	11.7	1	1	102.0	95.0
1955	5	0	0	0.0	0.0	0.0	0.0	0.0	1	1	20.0	12.0	20.0	0	0	0.0	0.0
1956	5	3	4	47.0	37.9	1.24	0.0052	3.95	4	4	80.0	23.3	38.8	2	3	1.2	7.0
1957	5	0	0	0.0	0.0	0.0	0.0	0.0	2	2	40.0	24.0	40.0	0	0	0.0	0.0
1958	5	0	0	0.0	0.0	0.0	0.0	0.0	2	2	40.0	24.0	40.0	0	0	0.0	0.0
1959	5	0	0	0.0	0.0	0.0	0.0	0.0	2	2	40.0	14.7	24.5	1	1	36.7	40.0
1960	5	0	0	0.0	0.0	0.0	0.0	0.0	1	1	20.0	12.0	20.0	0	0	0.0	0.0
1961	5	0	0	0.0	0.0	0.0	0.0	0.0	1	1	20.0	12.0	20.0	0	0	0.0	0.0
1962	5	1	1	0.5	1.1	0.45	0.0001	-0.28	2	2	40.0	3.6	6.0	2	2	89.6	15.5
1963	5	0	0	0.0	0.0	0.0	0.0	0.0	0	0	0.0	0.0	0.0	0	0	0.0	0.0
1964	5	0	0	0.0	0.0	0.0	0.0	0.0	0	0	0.0	0.0	0.0	0	0	0.0	0.0
1965	5	0	0	0.0	0.0	0.0	0.0	0.0	0	0	0.0	0.0	0.0	0	0	0.0	0.0

7.7 - ANNUAL AMOUNTS OF MAJOR POWER INTERSTATE WAR

YEAR	NO. IN SYSTEM	NO. OF WARS BEGUN	NO. OF PARTIC-IPANTS	BATTLE DEATHS 000'S	NATION MONTHS	BATTLE DEATHS 000'S PER NATION MONTH	BATTLE DEATHS PER HUNDRED POPULA-TION	LOG OF BATTLE DEATHS PER MILLION POPULA-TION	NO. OF WARS UNDER-WAY	NO. OF NATIONS IN WAR	% OF NATIONS IN WAR	NATION MONTHS UNDER-WAY	% OF NATION MONTHS EX-HAUST-ED	NO. OF WARS ENDING	NO. OF PARTIC-IPANTS	NATION MONTHS	BATTLE DEATHS 000'S
	ONSET--BY WAR								UNDERWAY					TERMINATION--BY WAR			
	1	2	3	4	5	6	7	8	9	10	11	12	13	14	15	16	17
1816	5	0	0	0.0	0.0	0.0	0.0	0.0	0	0	0.0	0.0	0.0	0	0	0.0	0.0
1817	5	0	0	0.0	0.0	0.0	0.0	0.0	0	0	0.0	0.0	0.0	0	0	0.0	0.0
1818	5	0	0	0.0	0.0	0.0	0.0	0.0	0	0	0.0	0.0	0.0	0	0	0.0	0.0
1819	5	0	0	0.0	0.0	0.0	0.0	0.0	0	0	0.0	0.0	0.0	0	0	0.0	0.0
1820	5	0	0	0.0	0.0	0.0	0.0	0.0	0	0	0.0	0.0	0.0	0	0	0.0	0.0
1821	5	0	0	0.0	0.0	0.0	0.0	0.0	0	0	0.0	0.0	0.0	0	0	0.0	0.0
1822	5	0	0	0.0	0.0	0.0	0.0	0.0	0	0	0.0	0.0	0.0	0	0	0.0	0.0
1823	5	1	1	0.4	7.3	0.05	0.0013	2.54	1	1	20.0	7.3	12.2	1	1	7.3	0.4
1824	5	0	0	0.0	0.0	0.0	0.0	0.0	0	0	0.0	0.0	0.0	0	0	0.0	0.0
1825	5	0	0	0.0	0.0	0.0	0.0	0.0	0	0	0.0	0.0	0.0	0	0	0.0	0.0
1826	5	0	0	0.0	0.0	0.0	0.0	0.0	0	0	0.0	0.0	0.0	0	0	0.0	0.0
1827	5	1	3	0.2	0.3	0.60	0.0002	0.50	1	3	60.0	0.0	0.0	1	3	0.3	0.2
1828	5	1	1	50.0	16.7	2.99	0.0919	6.82	1	1	20.0	8.2	13.7	0	0	0.0	0.0
1829	5	0	0	0.0	0.0	0.0	0.0	0.0	1	1	20.0	8.4	14.0	1	1	16.7	50.0
1830	5	0	0	0.0	0.0	0.0	0.0	0.0	0	0	0.0	0.0	0.0	0	0	0.0	0.0
1831	5	0	0	0.0	0.0	0.0	0.0	0.0	0	0	0.0	0.0	0.0	0	0	0.0	0.0
1832	5	0	0	0.0	0.0	0.0	0.0	0.0	0	0	0.0	0.0	0.0	0	0	0.0	0.0
1833	5	0	0	0.0	0.0	0.0	0.0	0.0	0	0	0.0	0.0	0.0	0	0	0.0	0.0
1834	5	0	0	0.0	0.0	0.0	0.0	0.0	0	0	0.0	0.0	0.0	0	0	0.0	0.0
1835	5	0	0	0.0	0.0	0.0	0.0	0.0	0	0	0.0	0.0	0.0	0	0	0.0	0.0
1836	5	0	0	0.0	0.0	0.0	0.0	0.0	0	0	0.0	0.0	0.0	0	0	0.0	0.0
1837	5	0	0	0.0	0.0	0.0	0.0	0.0	0	0	0.0	0.0	0.0	0	0	0.0	0.0
1838	5	0	0	0.0	0.0	0.0	0.0	0.0	0	0	0.0	0.0	0.0	0	0	0.0	0.0
1839	5	0	0	0.0	0.0	0.0	0.0	0.0	0	0	0.0	0.0	0.0	0	0	0.0	0.0
1840	5	0	0	0.0	0.0	0.0	0.0	0.0	0	0	0.0	0.0	0.0	0	0	0.0	0.0
1841	5	0	0	0.0	0.0	0.0	0.0	0.0	0	0	0.0	0.0	0.0	0	0	0.0	0.0
1842	5	0	0	0.0	0.0	0.0	0.0	0.0	0	0	0.0	0.0	0.0	0	0	0.0	0.0
1843	5	0	0	0.0	0.0	0.0	0.0	0.0	0	0	0.0	0.0	0.0	0	0	0.0	0.0
1844	5	0	0	0.0	0.0	0.0	0.0	0.0	0	0	0.0	0.0	0.0	0	0	0.0	0.0
1845	5	0	0	0.0	0.0	0.0	0.0	0.0	0	0	0.0	0.0	0.0	0	0	0.0	0.0
1846	5	0	0	0.0	0.0	0.0	0.0	0.0	0	0	0.0	0.0	0.0	0	0	0.0	0.0
1847	5	0	0	0.0	0.0	0.0	0.0	0.0	0	0	0.0	0.0	0.0	0	0	0.0	0.0
1848	5	2	2	8.1	12.8	0.63	0.0161	5.08	2	2	40.0	9.2	15.3	0	0	0.0	0.0
1849	5	1	2	0.6	2.8	0.21	0.0009	2.15	3	3	60.0	6.4	10.7	3	3	15.6	8.7
1850	5	0	0	0.0	0.0	0.0	0.0	0.0	0	0	0.0	0.0	0.0	0	0	0.0	0.0
1851	5	0	0	0.0	0.0	0.0	0.0	0.0	0	0	0.0	0.0	0.0	0	0	0.0	0.0
1852	5	0	0	0.0	0.0	0.0	0.0	0.0	0	0	0.0	0.0	0.0	0	0	0.0	0.0

YEAR	NO. IN SYSTEM 1	NO. OF WARS BEGUN 2	NO. OF PARTIC-IPANTS 3	BATTLE DEATHS 000'S 4	NATION MONTHS 5	BATTLE DEATHS 000'S PER NATION MONTH 6	BATTLE DEATHS PER HUNDRED POPULA-TION 7	LOG OF BATTLE DEATHS PER MILLION POPULA-TION 8	NO. OF WARS UNDER-WAY 9	NO. OF NATIONS IN WAR 10	% OF NATIONS IN WAR 11	NATION MONTHS UNDER-WAY 12	% OF NATION MONTHS EX-HAUST-ED 13	NO. OF WARS ENDING 14	NO. OF PARTIC-IPANTS 15	NATION MONTHS 16	BATTLE DEATHS 000'S 17
	ONSET--BY WAR								UNDERWAY					TERMINATION--BY WAR			
1853	5	1	3	217.0	74.5	2.91	0.1597	7.38	1	1	20.0	2.3	3.8	0	0	0.0	0.0
1854	5	0	0	0.0	0.0	0.0	0.0	0.0	1	3	60.0	30.2	50.3	0	0	0.0	0.0
1855	5	0	0	0.0	0.0	0.0	0.0	0.0	1	3	60.0	36.0	60.0	0	C	0.0	0.0
1856	5	1	1	0.5	4.6	0.11	0.0017	2.84	2	3	60.0	8.2	13.7	1	3	74.5	217.0
1857	5	0	0	0.0	0.0	0.0	0.0	0.0	1	1	20.0	2.4	4.0	1	1	4.6	0.5
1858	5	0	0	0.0	0.0	0.0	0.0	0.0	0	0	0.0	0.0	0.0	0	0	0.0	0.0
1859	5	1	2	20.0	4.8	4.17	0.0279	5.63	1	2	40.0	4.8	8.0	1	2	4.8	20.0
1860	6	2	1	0.9	3.8	0.24	0.0021	3.02	2	1	16.7	3.2	4.4	1	1	0.6	0.3
1861	6	0	0	0.0	0.0	0.0	0.0	0.0	1	1	16.7	0.6	0.8	1	1	3.2	0.6
1862	6	1	1	8.0	57.7	0.14	0.0212	5.36	1	1	16.7	8.5	11.8	0	0	0.0	0.0
1863	6	0	0	0.0	0.0	0.0	0.0	0.0	1	1	16.7	12.0	16.7	0	0	0.0	0.0
1864	6	1	2	1.5	7.2	0.21	0.0027	3.31	2	3	50.0	19.4	26.9	1	2	7.2	1.5
1865	6	0	0	0.0	0.0	0.0	0.0	0.0	1	1	16.7	12.0	16.7	0	0	0.0	0.0
1866	6	1	3	34.0	4.2	8.10	0.0417	6.03	2	4	66.7	16.2	22.5	1	3	4.2	34.0
1867	6	0	0	0.0	0.0	0.0	0.0	0.0	1	1	16.7	1.2	1.7	1	1	57.7	8.0
1868	6	0	0	0.0	0.0	0.0	0.0	0.0	0	0	0.0	0.0	0.0	0	0	0.0	0.0
1869	6	0	0	0.0	0.0	0.0	0.0	0.0	0	0	0.0	0.0	0.0	0	0	0.0	0.0
1870	6	1	2	180.0	14.6	12.33	0.2329	7.75	1	2	33.3	11.0	15.3	0	0	0.0	0.0
1871	6	0	0	0.0	0.0	0.0	0.0	0.0	1	2	33.3	3.8	5.3	1	2	14.6	180.0
1872	6	0	0	0.0	0.0	0.0	0.0	0.0	0	0	0.0	0.0	0.0	0	0	0.0	0.0
1873	6	0	0	0.0	0.0	0.0	0.0	0.0	0	0	0.0	0.0	0.0	0	0	0.0	0.0
1874	6	0	0	0.0	0.0	0.0	0.0	0.0	0	0	0.0	0.0	0.0	0	0	0.0	0.0
1875	6	0	0	0.0	0.0	0.0	0.0	0.0	0	0	0.0	0.0	0.0	0	0	0.0	0.0
1876	6	0	0	0.0	0.0	0.0	0.0	0.0	0	0	0.0	0.0	0.0	0	0	0.0	0.0
1877	6	1	1	120.0	8.8	13.64	0.1279	7.15	1	1	16.7	8.7	12.1	0	0	0.0	0.0
1878	6	0	0	0.0	0.0	0.0	0.0	0.0	1	1	16.7	0.1	0.1	1	1	8.8	120.0
1879	6	0	0	0.0	0.0	0.0	0.0	0.0	0	0	0.0	0.0	0.0	0	0	0.0	0.0
1880	6	0	0	0.0	0.0	0.0	0.0	0.0	0	0	0.0	0.0	0.0	0	0	0.0	0.0
1881	6	0	0	0.0	0.0	0.0	0.0	0.0	0	0	0.0	0.0	0.0	0	0	0.0	0.0
1882	6	0	0	0.0	0.0	0.0	0.0	0.0	0	0	0.0	0.0	0.0	0	0	0.0	0.0
1883	6	0	0	0.0	0.0	0.0	0.0	0.0	0	0	0.0	0.0	0.0	0	0	0.0	0.0
1884	6	1	1	2.1	11.8	0.18	0.0055	4.01	1	1	16.7	6.6	9.2	0	0	0.0	0.0
1885	6	0	0	0.0	0.0	0.0	0.0	0.0	1	1	16.7	5.3	7.4	1	1	11.8	2.1
1886	6	0	0	0.0	0.0	0.0	0.0	0.0	0	0	0.0	0.0	0.0	0	0	0.0	0.0
1887	6	0	0	0.0	0.0	0.0	0.0	0.0	0	0	0.0	0.0	0.0	0	0	0.0	0.0
1888	6	0	0	0.0	0.0	0.0	0.0	0.0	0	0	0.0	0.0	0.0	0	0	0.0	0.0
1889	6	0	0	0.0	0.0	0.0	0.0	0.0	0	0	0.0	0.0	0.0	0	0	0.0	0.0
1890	6	0	0	0.0	0.0	0.0	0.0	0.0	0	0	0.0	0.0	0.0	0	0	0.0	0.0
1891	6	0	0	0.0	0.0	0.0	0.0	0.0	0	0	0.0	0.0	0.0	0	0	0.0	0.0
1892	6	0	0	0.0	0.0	0.0	0.0	0.0	0	0	0.0	0.0	0.0	0	0	0.0	0.0

7.7 - ANNUAL AMOUNTS OF MAJOR POWER INTERSTATE WAR

	ONSET--BY WAR								UNDERWAY					TERMINATION--BY WAR			
YEAR	NO. IN SYSTEM 1	NO. OF WARS BEGUN 2	NO. OF PARTIC-IPANTS 3	BATTLE DEATHS 000'S 4	NATION MONTHS 5	BATTLE DEATHS 000'S PER NATION MONTH 6	BATTLE DEATHS PER HUNDRED POPULA-TION 7	LOG OF BATTLE DEATHS PER MILLION POPULA-TION 8	NO. OF WARS UNDER-WAY 9	NO. OF NATIONS IN WAR 10	% OF NATIONS IN WAR 11	NATION MONTHS UNDER-WAY 12	% OF NATION MONTHS EX-HAUST-ED 13	NO. OF WARS ENDING 14	NO. OF PARTIC-IPANTS 15	NATION MONTHS 16	BATTLE DEATHS 000'S 17
1893	6	0	0	0.0	0.0	0.0	0.0	0.0	0	0	0.0	0.0	0.0	0	0	0.0	0.0
1894	6	0	0	0.0	0.0	0.0	0.0	0.0	0	0	0.0	0.0	0.0	0	0	0.0	0.0
1895	7	0	0	0.0	0.0	0.0	0.0	0.0	0	0	0.0	0.0	0.0	0	0	0.0	0.0
1896	7	0	0	0.0	0.0	0.0	0.0	0.0	0	0	0.0	0.0	0.0	0	0	0.0	0.0
1897	7	0	0	0.0	0.0	0.0	0.0	0.0	0	0	0.0	0.0	0.0	0	0	0.0	0.0
1898	7	0	0	0.0	0.0	0.0	0.0	0.0	0	0	0.0	0.0	0.0	0	0	0.0	0.0
1899	8	0	0	0.0	0.0	0.0	0.0	0.0	0	0	0.0	0.0	0.0	0	0	0.0	0.0
1900	8	0	0	0.0	0.0	0.0	0.0	0.0	0	0	0.0	0.0	0.0	0	0	0.0	0.0
1901	8	0	0	0.0	0.0	0.0	0.0	0.0	0	0	0.0	0.0	0.0	0	0	0.0	0.0
1902	8	0	0	0.0	0.0	0.0	0.0	0.0	0	0	0.0	0.0	0.0	0	0	0.0	0.0
1903	8	0	0	0.0	0.0	0.0	0.0	0.0	0	0	0.0	0.0	0.0	0	0	0.0	0.0
1904	8	1	2	130.0	38.6	3.37	0.0692	6.54	1	2	25.0	21.6	22.5	0	0	0.0	0.0
1905	8	0	0	0.0	0.0	0.0	0.0	0.0	1	2	25.0	17.0	17.7	1	2	38.6	130.0
1906	8	0	0	0.0	0.0	0.0	0.0	0.0	0	0	0.0	0.0	0.0	0	0	0.0	0.0
1907	8	0	0	0.0	0.0	0.0	0.0	0.0	0	0	0.0	0.0	0.0	0	0	0.0	0.0
1908	8	0	0	0.0	0.0	0.0	0.0	0.0	0	0	0.0	0.0	0.0	0	0	0.0	0.0
1909	8	0	0	0.0	0.0	0.0	0.0	0.0	0	0	0.0	0.0	0.0	0	0	0.0	0.0
1910	8	0	0	0.0	0.0	0.0	0.0	0.0	0	0	0.0	0.0	0.0	0	0	0.0	0.0
1911	8	1	1	6.0	12.7	0.47	0.0172	5.15	1	1	12.5	3.1	3.2	0	0	0.0	0.0
1912	8	0	0	0.0	0.0	0.0	0.0	0.0	1	1	12.5	9.6	10.0	1	1	12.7	6.0
1913	8	0	0	0.0	0.0	0.0	0.0	0.0	0	0	0.0	0.0	0.0	0	0	0.0	0.0
1914	8	1	8	7734.3	356.6	21.69	1.3966	9.54	1	6	75.0	29.3	30.5	0	0	0.0	0.0
1915	8	0	0	0.0	0.0	0.0	0.0	0.0	1	7	87.5	79.3	82.6	0	0	0.0	0.0
1916	8	0	0	0.0	0.0	0.0	0.0	0.0	1	7	87.5	84.0	87.5	0	0	0.0	0.0
1917	8	0	0	0.0	0.0	0.0	0.0	0.0	1	8	100.0	91.6	96.4	0	0	0.0	0.0
1918	7	0	0	0.0	0.0	0.0	0.0	0.0	1	7	100.0	71.9	88.8	1	8	356.6	7734.3
1919	5	0	0	0.0	0.0	0.0	0.0	0.0	0	0	0.0	0.0	0.0	0	0	0.0	0.0
1920	5	0	0	0.0	0.0	0.0	0.0	0.0	0	0	0.0	0.0	0.0	0	0	0.0	0.0
1921	5	0	0	0.0	0.0	0.0	0.0	0.0	0	0	0.0	0.0	0.0	0	0	0.0	0.0
1922	6	0	0	0.0	0.0	0.0	0.0	0.0	0	0	0.0	0.0	0.0	0	0	0.0	0.0
1923	6	0	0	0.0	0.0	0.0	0.0	0.0	0	0	0.0	0.0	0.0	0	0	0.0	0.0
1924	6	0	0	0.0	0.0	0.0	0.0	0.0	0	0	0.0	0.0	0.0	0	0	0.0	0.0
1925	7	0	0	0.0	0.0	0.0	0.0	0.0	0	0	0.0	0.0	0.0	0	0	0.0	0.0
1926	7	0	0	0.0	0.0	0.0	0.0	0.0	0	0	0.0	0.0	0.0	0	0	0.0	0.0
1927	7	0	0	0.0	0.0	0.0	0.0	0.0	0	0	0.0	0.0	0.0	0	0	0.0	0.0
1928	7	0	0	0.0	0.0	0.0	0.0	0.0	0	0	0.0	0.0	0.0	0	0	0.0	0.0
1929	7	0	0	0.0	0.0	0.0	0.0	0.0	0	0	0.0	0.0	0.0	0	0	0.0	0.0

YEAR	NO. IN SYSTEM 1	NO. OF WARS BEGUN 2	NO. OF PARTIC-IPANTS 3	BATTLE DEATHS 000'S 4	NATION MONTHS 5	BATTLE DEATHS 000'S PER NATION MONTH 6	BATTLE DEATHS PER HUNDRED POPULA-TION 7	LOG OF BATTLE DEATHS PER MILLION POPULA-TION 8	NO. OF WARS UNDER-WAY 9	NO. OF NATIONS IN WAR 10	% OF NATIONS IN WAR 11	NATION MONTHS UNDER-WAY 12	% OF NATION MONTHS EX-HAUST-ED 13	NO. OF WARS ENDING 14	NO. OF PARTIC-IPANTS 15	NATION MONTHS 16	BATTLE DEATHS 000'S 17
	ONSET--BY WAR								UNDERWAY					TERMINATION--BY WAR			
1930	7	0	0	0.0	0.0	0.0	0.0	0.0	0	0	0.0	0.0	0.0	0	0	0.0	0.0
1931	7	1	1	10.0	16.6	0.60	0.0154	5.04	1	1	14.3	0.4	0.5	0	0	0.0	0.0
1932	7	0	0	0.0	0.0	0.0	0.0	0.0	1	1	14.3	12.0	14.3	0	0	0.0	0.0
1933	7	0	0	0.0	0.0	0.0	0.0	0.0	1	1	14.3	4.1	4.9	1	1	16.6	10.0
1934	7	0	0	0.0	0.0	0.0	0.0	0.0	0	0	0.0	0.0	0.0	0	0	0.0	0.0
1935	7	1	1	4.0	7.2	0.56	0.0094	4.54	1	1	14.3	3.0	3.6	0	0	0.0	0.0
1936	7	0	0	0.0	0.0	0.0	0.0	0.0	1	1	14.3	4.3	5.1	1	1	7.2	4.0
1937	7	1	1	250.0	53.1	4.71	0.3602	8.19	1	1	14.3	5.8	6.9	0	0	0.0	0.0
1938	7	0	0	0.0	0.0	0.0	0.0	0.0	1	1	14.3	12.0	14.3	0	0	0.0	0.0
1939	7	3	7	13014.3	335.2	38.83	1.3097	9.48	4	5	71.4	33.3	39.6	1	2	8.4	16.0
1940	7	0	0	0.0	0.0	0.0	0.0	0.0	3	6	85.7	50.8	65.1	1	1	3.4	50.0
1941	6	0	0	0.0	0.0	0.0	0.0	0.0	2	6	100.0	55.1	76.5	1	1	53.1	250.0
1942	6	0	0	0.0	0.0	0.0	0.0	0.0	1	6	100.0	72.0	100.0	0	0	0.0	0.0
1943	6	0	0	0.0	0.0	0.0	0.0	0.0	1	6	100.0	68.0	98.6	0	0	0.0	0.0
1944	5	0	0	0.0	0.0	0.0	0.0	0.0	1	5	100.0	60.0	100.0	0	0	0.0	0.0
1945	6	0	0	0.0	0.0	0.0	0.0	0.0	1	5	83.3	30.8	55.0	1	7	323.4	12948.3
1946	4	0	0	0.0	0.0	0.0	0.0	0.0	0	0	0.0	0.0	0.0	0	0	0.0	0.0
1947	4	0	0	0.0	0.0	0.0	0.0	0.0	0	0	0.0	0.0	0.0	0	0	0.0	0.0
1948	4	0	0	0.0	0.0	0.0	0.0	0.0	0	0	0.0	0.0	0.0	0	0	0.0	0.0
1949	4	0	0	0.0	0.0	0.0	0.0	0.0	0	0	0.0	0.0	0.0	0	0	0.0	0.0
1950	5	1	4	955.0	135.8	7.03	0.1183	7.08	1	3	60.0	12.5	20.8	0	0	0.0	0.0
1951	5	0	0	0.0	0.0	0.0	0.0	0.0	1	4	80.0	48.0	80.0	0	0	0.0	0.0
1952	5	0	0	0.0	0.0	0.0	0.0	0.0	1	4	80.0	48.0	80.0	0	0	0.0	0.0
1953	5	0	0	0.0	0.0	0.0	0.0	0.0	1	4	80.0	27.2	45.3	1	4	135.8	955.0
1954	5	0	0	0.0	0.0	0.0	0.0	0.0	0	0	0.0	0.0	0.0	0	0	0.0	0.0
1955	5	0	0	0.0	0.0	0.0	0.0	0.0	0	0	0.0	0.0	0.0	0	0	0.0	0.0
1956	5	2	3	7.0	1.2	5.86	0.0024	3.17	2	3	60.0	1.2	2.0	2	3	1.2	7.0
1957	5	0	0	0.0	0.0	0.0	0.0	0.0	0	0	0.0	0.0	0.0	0	0	0.0	0.0
1958	5	0	0	0.0	0.0	0.0	0.0	0.0	0	0	0.0	0.0	0.0	0	0	0.0	0.0
1959	5	0	0	0.0	0.0	0.0	0.0	0.0	0	0	0.0	0.0	0.0	0	0	0.0	0.0
1960	5	0	0	0.0	0.0	0.0	0.0	0.0	0	0	0.0	0.0	0.0	0	0	0.0	0.0
1961	5	0	0	0.0	0.0	0.0	0.0	0.0	0	0	0.0	0.0	0.0	0	0	0.0	0.0
1962	5	1	1	0.5	1.1	0.45	0.0001	-0.28	1	1	20.0	1.1	1.8	1	1	1.1	0.5
1963	5	0	0	0.0	0.0	0.0	0.0	0.0	0	0	0.0	0.0	0.0	0	0	0.0	0.0
1964	5	0	0	0.0	0.0	0.0	0.0	0.0	0	0	0.0	0.0	0.0	0	0	0.0	0.0
1965	5	0	0	0.0	0.0	0.0	0.0	0.0	0	0	0.0	0.0	0.0	0	0	0.0	0.0

Extra-systemic War

In addition to the 50 wars in our century and a half that were fought within the interstate system, there are 43 additional ones in which a member of that system engaged in sufficiently sustained and bloody hostilities against either an independent nonmember of the system or an entity that was, in one way or another, less than independent. The annual amounts of war arising out of these imperial and colonial conflicts on the part of the interstate system members are shown in Table 7.8. Two points are worth emphasizing here. First, the data reflect *only the experience of the interstate system members* and include neither the war months nor the battle deaths experienced by the extra-systemic participants. Second, we have not presented separate tables for the imperial and colonial war participation of the two more restricted (that is, central and major power) sub-systems of the interstate system, since the extra-systemic wars were, for the most part, waged by these sub-system members. We can report, however, that for the 1816–1919 period, 74.7 percent of the nation months and 98.9 percent (from both interstate and extra-systemic wars) of the battle deaths were accounted for by *central* system members, and for the entire period, 37 percent of the nation months and 79.3 percent of the battle deaths were accounted for by the *major* powers alone. Thus, it is evident that additional tables for the extra-systemic war figures of these two sub-systems would not have differed appreciably from those presented here. And, once again, the user is quite free to return to the basic war list in Chapter Four and select the more restricted subpopulation.

RANKING THE YEARS

With the data now in on the annual amounts of war begun, underway, and terminated in each of our several systems and sub-systems, we can readily move on to additional analyses and summaries. But in order to look for chronological patterns such as secular trends, it is often necessary to convert these figures from a mere chronological ordering to a variety of rank orderings. Thus, we close this chapter with the presentation of several such listings, showing each year's rank position and its value, on several of the most useful and revealing measures.

The first of these (Table 7.9) shows the rank position of each of the 70 of our 150 years in which any international war *began;* they are ranked according to the number of battle deaths that resulted from all qualifying international wars which began in that year. In addition to the rank position score, we show the estimated number of these battle deaths, as well as the rank position (and value) for nation months of war which began in that year.

Next (Table 7.10) we rank all of the 126 years in which any international war was *underway,* according to two measures. First, there is the number of nation months of war which were underway during that year, along with the year's rank position on that measure; then, in order to permit comparisons over time, we normalize this figure by controlling for system size. This gives us the percentage of possible nation months ($12\times N$) which were indeed devoted to war, along with the year's position on this normalized figure. Worth noting here is that while there were only 70 years in which any war began, and 69 in which any ended (see below), 126 of a possible 150 years saw at least some international war underway large enough to satisfy our inclusion criteria.

Finally, we turn to measures of the amount of war that *ended* in any year. As in our onset measures, we show both the severity and the magnitude scores. The list is arranged according to the number of battle-connected deaths that resulted from all international wars which ended that year, but also includes the equivalent nation month figure and rank position (Table 7.11).

7.8 - ANNUAL AMOUNTS OF EXTRA-SYSTEMIC WAR

	ONSET--BY WAR								UNDERWAY					TERMINATION--BY WAR			
YEAR	NO. IN SYSTEM 1	NO. OF WARS BEGUN 2	NO. OF PARTIC-IPANTS 3	BATTLE DEATHS 000'S 4	NATION MONTHS 5	BATTLE DEATHS 000'S PER NATION MONTH 6	BATTLE DEATHS PER HUNDRED POPULA-TION 7	LOG OF BATTLE DEATHS PER MILLION POPULA-TION 8	NO. OF WARS UNDER-WAY 9	NO. OF NATIONS IN WAR 10	% OF NATIONS IN WAR 11	NATION MONTHS UNDER-WAY 12	% OF NATION MONTHS EX-HAUST-ED 13	NO. OF WARS ENDING 14	NO. OF PARTIC-IPANTS 15	NATION MONTHS 16	BATTLE DEATHS 000'S 17
1816	23	0	0	0.0	0.0	0.0	0.0	0.0	0	0	0.0	0.0	0.0	0	0	0.0	0.0
1817	23	1	1	2.0	6.9	0.29	0.0098	4.59	1	1	4.3	1.8	0.7	0	0	0.0	0.0
1818	23	0	0	0.0	0.0	0.0	0.0	0.0	1	1	4.3	5.1	1.8	1	1	6.9	2.0
1819	23	0	0	0.0	0.0	0.0	0.0	0.0	0	0	0.0	0.0	0.0	0	0	0.0	0.0
1820	23	0	0	0.0	0.0	0.0	0.0	0.0	0	0	0.0	0.0	0.0	0	0	0.0	0.0
1821	23	1	1	15.0	85.1	0.18	0.0607	6.41	1	1	4.3	9.3	3.4	0	0	0.0	0.0
1822	23	0	0	0.0	0.0	0.0	0.0	0.0	1	1	4.3	12.0	4.3	0	0	0.0	0.0
1823	23	1	1	15.0	29.1	0.52	0.0685	6.53	2	2	8.7	15.3	5.5	0	0	0.0	0.0
1824	23	0	0	0.0	0.0	0.0	0.0	0.0	2	2	8.7	24.0	8.7	0	0	0.0	0.0
1825	23	1	1	15.0	56.2	0.27	0.2542	7.84	3	3	13.0	29.3	10.6	0	0	0.0	0.0
1826	24	1	1	5.0	17.0	0.29	0.0095	4.55	4	4	16.7	28.9	10.0	1	1	29.1	15.0
1827	24	0	0	0.0	0.0	0.0	0.0	0.0	3	3	12.5	36.0	12.5	0	0	0.0	0.0
1828	25	0	0	0.0	0.0	0.0	0.0	0.0	3	3	12.0	17.7	5.9	2	2	102.1	20.0
1829	25	0	0	0.0	0.0	0.0	0.0	0.0	1	1	4.0	12.0	4.0	0	0	0.0	0.0
1830	26	0	0	0.0	0.0	0.0	0.0	0.0	1	1	3.8	2.9	0.9	1	1	56.2	15.0
1831	28	2	2	25.0	22.0	1.14	0.0314	5.75	2	2	7.1	10.3	3.1	1	1	8.3	15.0
1832	28	0	0	0.0	0.0	0.0	0.0	0.0	1	1	3.6	11.7	3.5	1	1	13.7	10.0
1833	28	0	0	0.0	0.0	0.0	0.0	0.0	0	0	0.0	0.0	0.0	0	0	0.0	0.0
1834	28	0	0	0.0	0.0	0.0	0.0	0.0	0	0	0.0	0.0	0.0	0	0	0.0	0.0
1835	28	1	1	1.0	6.7	0.15	0.0130	4.87	1	1	3.6	3.0	0.9	0	0	0.0	0.0
1836	28	0	0	0.0	0.0	0.0	0.0	0.0	1	1	3.6	3.7	1.1	1	1	6.7	1.0
1837	28	0	0	0.0	0.0	0.0	0.0	0.0	0	0	0.0	0.0	0.0	0	0	0.0	0.0
1838	30	1	1	20.0	48.4	0.41	0.0775	6.65	1	1	3.3	3.0	0.8	0	0	0.0	0.0
1839	31	1	2	10.0	5.7	1.76	0.0199	5.29	2	2	6.5	12.5	3.4	0	0	0.0	0.0
1840	31	0	0	0.0	0.0	0.0	0.0	0.0	2	2	6.5	17.2	4.6	1	2	5.7	10.0
1841	33	1	1	1.0	1.0	1.00	0.0769	6.65	2	2	6.1	13.0	3.3	1	1	1.0	1.0
1842	34	0	0	0.0	0.0	0.0	0.0	0.0	1	1	2.9	9.4	2.3	1	1	48.4	20.0
1843	35	0	0	0.0	0.0	0.0	0.0	0.0	0	0	0.0	0.0	0.0	0	0	0.0	0.0
1844	35	0	0	0.0	0.0	0.0	0.0	0.0	0	0	0.0	0.0	0.0	0	0	0.0	0.0
1845	35	1	1	1.5	2.9	0.52	0.0056	4.02	1	1	2.9	0.6	0.1	0	0	0.0	0.0
1846	35	0	0	0.0	0.0	0.0	0.0	0.0	1	1	2.9	2.2	0.5	1	1	2.9	1.5
1847	36	0	0	0.0	0.0	0.0	0.0	0.0	0	0	0.0	0.0	0.0	0	0	0.0	0.0
1848	37	2	3	61.0	17.2	3.55	0.0469	6.15	2	2	5.4	6.4	1.4	0	0	0.0	0.0
1849	38	0	0	0.0	0.0	0.0	0.0	0.0	2	3	7.9	10.7	2.3	2	3	17.2	61.0
1850	38	0	0	0.0	0.0	0.0	0.0	0.0	0	0	0.0	0.0	0.0	0	0	0.0	0.0
1851	39	0	0	0.0	0.0	0.0	0.0	0.0	0	0	0.0	0.0	0.0	0	0	0.0	0.0
1852	39	1	1	5.0	3.4	1.47	0.0198	5.29	1	1	2.6	1.0	0.2	0	0	0.0	0.0

7.8 - ANNUAL AMOUNTS OF EXTRA-SYSTEMIC WAR

	ONSET--BY WAR								UNDERWAY					TERMINATION--BY WAR			
YEAR	NO. IN SYSTEM 1	NO. OF WARS BEGUN 2	NO. OF PARTIC-IPANTS 3	BATTLE DEATHS 000'S 4	NATION MONTHS 5	BATTLE DEATHS 000'S PER NATION MONTH 6	BATTLE DEATHS PER HUNDRED POPULA-TION 7	LOG OF BATTLE DEATHS PER MILLION POPULA-TION 8	NO. OF WARS UNDER-WAY 9	NO. OF NATIONS IN WAR 10	% OF NATIONS IN WAR 11	NATION MONTHS UNDER-WAY 12	% OF NATION MONTHS EX-HAUST-ED 13	NO. OF WARS ENDING 14	NO. OF PARTIC-IPANTS 15	NATION MONTHS 16	BATTLE DEATHS 000'S 17
1853	39	0	0	0.0	0.0	0.0	0.0	0.0	1	1	2.6	2.4	0.5	1	1	3.4	5.0
1854	40	0	0	0.0	0.0	0.0	0.0	0.0	0	0	0.0	0.0	0.0	0	0	0.0	0.0
1855	41	0	0	0.0	0.0	0.0	0.0	0.0	0	0	0.0	0.0	0.0	0	0	0.0	0.0
1856	41	0	0	0.0	0.0	0.0	0.0	0.0	0	0	0.0	0.0	0.0	0	0	0.0	0.0
1857	41	1	1	3.5	22.9	0.15	0.0119	4.78	1	1	2.4	7.8	1.6	0	0	0.0	0.0
1858	41	1	1	3.0	12.9	0.23	0.0115	4.74	2	2	4.9	20.0	4.1	0	0	0.0	0.0
1859	42	0	0	0.0	0.0	0.0	0.0	0.0	2	2	4.8	8.2	1.6	2	2	35.8	6.5
1860	44	0	0	0.0	0.0	0.0	0.0	0.0	0	0	0.0	0.0	0.0	0	0	0.0	0.0
1861	40	0	0	0.0	0.0	0.0	0.0	0.0	0	0	0.0	0.0	0.0	0	0	0.0	0.0
1862	39	0	0	0.0	0.0	0.0	0.0	0.0	0	0	0.0	0.0	0.0	0	0	0.0	0.0
1863	39	1	1	5.0	14.9	0.34	0.0065	4.17	1	1	2.6	11.3	2.4	0	0	0.0	0.0
1864	39	1	2	110.0	123.5	0.89	0.8029	8.99	2	2	5.1	5.2	1.1	1	1	14.9	5.0
1865	39	0	0	0.0	0.0	0.0	0.0	0.0	1	2	5.1	21.9	4.7	0	0	0.0	0.0
1866	39	0	0	0.0	0.0	0.0	0.0	0.0	1	2	5.1	24.0	5.1	0	0	0.0	0.0
1867	37	0	0	0.0	0.0	0.0	0.0	0.0	1	2	5.4	24.0	5.4	0	0	0.0	0.0
1868	34	1	1	100.0	112.1	0.89	0.6024	8.70	2	3	8.8	26.7	6.5	0	0	0.0	0.0
1869	34	0	0	0.0	0.0	0.0	0.0	0.0	2	3	8.8	36.0	8.8	0	0	0.0	0.0
1870	34	0	0	0.0	0.0	0.0	0.0	0.0	2	3	8.8	16.0	3.9	1	2	123.5	110.0
1871	31	0	0	0.0	0.0	0.0	0.0	0.0	1	1	3.2	12.0	3.2	0	0	0.0	0.0
1872	31	0	0	0.0	0.0	0.0	0.0	0.0	1	1	3.2	12.0	3.2	0	0	0.0	0.0
1873	31	1	1	6.0	65.2	0.09	0.1622	7.39	2	2	6.5	21.2	5.7	0	0	0.0	0.0
1874	31	0	0	0.0	0.0	0.0	0.0	0.0	2	2	6.5	24.0	6.5	0	0	0.0	0.0
1875	32	1	1	10.0	21.4	0.47	0.0355	5.87	3	3	9.4	30.0	7.8	0	0	0.0	0.0
1876	32	0	0	0.0	0.0	0.0	0.0	0.0	3	3	9.4	36.0	9.4	0	0	0.0	0.0
1877	32	0	0	0.0	0.0	0.0	0.0	0.0	3	3	9.4	27.4	7.1	1	1	21.4	10.0
1878	34	2	2	7.5	20.3	0.37	0.0104	4.64	4	4	11.8	12.8	3.1	3	3	179.4	109.5
1879	34	1	1	3.5	5.7	0.61	0.0102	4.63	2	1	2.9	14.4	3.5	1	1	5.7	3.5
1880	34	0	0	0.0	0.0	0.0	0.0	0.0	1	1	2.9	8.1	2.0	1	1	18.2	4.0
1881	34	0	0	0.0	0.0	0.0	0.0	0.0	0	0	0.0	0.0	0.0	0	0	0.0	0.0
1882	35	2	2	24.5	65.3	0.38	0.0335	5.81	2	2	5.7	11.8	2.8	0	0	0.0	0.0
1883	35	0	0	0.0	0.0	0.0	0.0	0.0	2	2	5.7	24.0	5.7	0	0	0.0	0.0
1884	35	0	0	0.0	0.0	0.0	0.0	0.0	2	2	5.7	17.5	4.2	1	1	25.7	4.5
1885	35	1	1	2.0	1.2	1.67	0.1053	6.96	2	2	5.7	13.2	3.1	2	2	40.8	22.0
1886	35	0	0	0.0	0.0	0.0	0.0	0.0	0	0	0.0	0.0	0.0	0	0	0.0	0.0
1887	37	0	0	0.0	0.0	0.0	0.0	0.0	0	0	0.0	0.0	0.0	0	0	0.0	0.0
1888	38	0	0	0.0	0.0	0.0	0.0	0.0	0	0	0.0	0.0	0.0	0	0	0.0	0.0
1889	38	0	0	0.0	0.0	0.0	0.0	0.0	0	0	0.0	0.0	0.0	0	0	0.0	0.0

YEAR		ONSET--BY WAR							UNDERWAY					TERMINATION--BY WAR			
YEAR	NO. IN SYSTEM 1	NO. OF WARS BEGUN 2	NO. OF PARTIC-IPANTS 3	BATTLE DEATHS 000'S 4	NATION MONTHS 5	BATTLE DEATHS 000'S PER NATION MONTH 6	BATTLE DEATHS PER HUNDRED POPULA-TION 7	LOG OF BATTLE DEATHS PER MILLION POPULA-TION 8	NO. OF WARS UNDER-WAY 9	NO. OF NATIONS IN WAR 10	% OF NATIONS IN WAR 11	NATION MONTHS UNDER-WAY 12	% OF NATION MONTHS EX-HAUST-ED 13	NO. OF WARS ENDING 14	NO. OF PARTIC-IPANTS 15	NATION MONTHS 16	BATTLE DEATHS 000'S 17
1890	38	0	0	0.0	0.0	0.0	0.0	0.0	0	0	0.0	0.0	0.0	0	0	0.0	0.0
1891	38	0	0	0.0	0.0	0.0	0.0	0.0	0	0	0.0	0.0	0.0	0	0	0.0	0.0
1892	38	0	0	0.0	0.0	0.0	0.0	0.0	0	0	0.0	0.0	0.0	0	0	0.0	0.0
1893	38	0	0	0.0	0.0	0.0	0.0	0.0	0	0	0.0	0.0	0.0	0	0	0.0	0.0
1894	38	1	1	6.0	9.7	0.62	0.0156	5.05	1	1	2.6	0.7	0.2	0	0	0.0	0.0
1895	38	2	2	59.0	47.8	1.23	0.1194	7.09	3	3	7.9	20.0	4.4	1	1	9.7	6.0
1896	39	1	1	2.0	23.1	0.09	0.0110	4.70	3	2	5.1	28.8	6.2	1	1	10.5	9.0
1897	39	0	0	0.0	0.0	0.0	0.0	0.0	2	1	2.6	24.0	5.1	0	0	0.0	0.0
1898	40	0	0	0.0	0.0	0.0	0.0	0.0	2	1	2.5	7.0	1.5	2	1	60.4	52.0
1899	41	2	2	26.5	72.5	0.37	0.0226	5.42	2	2	4.9	13.6	2.8	0	0	0.0	0.0
1900	42	0	0	0.0	0.0	0.0	0.0	0.0	2	2	4.8	24.0	4.8	0	0	0.0	0.0
1901	42	0	0	0.0	0.0	0.0	0.0	0.0	2	2	4.8	24.0	4.8	0	0	0.0	0.0
1902	43	0	0	0.0	0.0	0.0	0.0	0.0	2	2	4.7	11.1	2.2	2	2	72.5	26.5
1903	43	0	0	0.0	0.0	0.0	0.0	0.0	0	0	0.0	0.0	0.0	0	0	0.0	0.0
1904	43	0	0	0.0	0.0	0.0	0.0	0.0	0	0	0.0	0.0	0.0	0	0	0.0	0.0
1905	44	0	0	0.0	0.0	0.0	0.0	0.0	0	0	0.0	0.0	0.0	0	0	0.0	0.0
1906	43	0	0	0.0	0.0	0.0	0.0	0.0	0	0	0.0	0.0	0.0	0	0	0.0	0.0
1907	43	0	0	0.0	0.0	0.0	0.0	0.0	0	0	0.0	0.0	0.0	0	0	0.0	0.0
1908	44	0	0	0.0	0.0	0.0	0.0	0.0	0	0	0.0	0.0	0.0	0	0	0.0	0.0
1909	44	0	0	0.0	0.0	0.0	0.0	0.0	0	0	0.0	0.0	0.0	0	0	0.0	0.0
1910	44	0	0	0.0	0.0	0.0	0.0	0.0	0	0	0.0	0.0	0.0	0	0	0.0	0.0
1911	44	0	0	0.0	0.0	0.0	0.0	0.0	0	0	0.0	0.0	0.0	0	0	0.0	0.0
1912	43	0	0	0.0	0.0	0.0	0.0	0.0	0	0	0.0	0.0	0.0	0	0	0.0	0.0
1913	43	0	0	0.0	0.0	0.0	0.0	0.0	0	0	0.0	0.0	0.0	0	0	0.0	0.0
1914	44	0	0	0.0	0.0	0.0	0.0	0.0	0	0	0.0	0.0	0.0	0	0	0.0	0.0
1915	44	0	0	0.0	0.0	0.0	0.0	0.0	0	0	0.0	0.0	0.0	0	0	0.0	0.0
1916	44	0	0	0.0	0.0	0.0	0.0	0.0	0	0	0.0	0.0	0.0	0	0	0.0	0.0
1917	44	1	1	50.0	39.3	1.27	0.0309	5.73	1	1	2.3	0.8	0.2	0	0	0.0	0.0
1918	48	0	0	0.0	0.0	0.0	0.0	0.0	1	1	2.1	12.0	2.1	0	0	0.0	0.0
1919	51	0	0	0.0	0.0	0.0	0.0	0.0	1	1	2.0	12.0	2.0	0	0	0.0	0.0
1920	61	0	0	0.0	0.0	0.0	0.0	0.0	1	1	1.6	12.0	1.6	0	0	0.0	0.0
1921	62	1	2	29.0	71.8	0.40	0.0463	6.14	2	2	3.2	8.0	1.1	1	1	39.3	50.0
1922	63	0	0	0.0	0.0	0.0	0.0	0.0	1	1	1.6	12.0	1.6	0	0	0.0	0.0
1923	63	0	0	0.0	0.0	0.0	0.0	0.0	1	1	1.6	12.0	1.6	0	0	0.0	0.0
1924	63	0	0	0.0	0.0	0.0	0.0	0.0	1	1	1.6	12.0	1.6	0	0	0.0	0.0
1925	63	1	1	4.0	22.4	0.18	0.0098	4.59	2	2	3.2	26.2	3.5	0	0	0.0	0.0
1926	64	0	0	0.0	0.0	0.0	0.0	0.0	2	2	3.1	21.6	2.8	1	2	71.8	29.0
1927	65	0	0	0.0	0.0	0.0	0.0	0.0	1	1	1.5	5.0	0.6	1	1	22.4	4.0
1928	65	0	0	0.0	0.0	0.0	0.0	0.0	0	0	0.0	0.0	0.0	0	0	0.0	0.0
1929	65	0	0	0.0	0.0	0.0	0.0	0.0	0	0	0.0	0.0	0.0	0	0	0.0	0.0

7.8 - ANNUAL AMOUNTS OF EXTRA-SYSTEMIC WAR

		CNSET--BY WAR							UNDERWAY					TERMINATION--BY WAR			
YEAR	NO. IN SYSTEM 1	NO. OF WARS BEGUN 2	NO. OF PARTIC-IPANTS 3	EATTLE DEATHS 000'S 4	NATION MONTHS 5	BATTLE DEATHS 000'S PER NATION MONTH 6	BATTLE DEATHS PER HUNDRED POPULA-TION 7	LOG OF BATTLE DEATHS PER MILLION POPULA-TION 8	NO. OF WARS UNDER-WAY 9	NO. OF NATIONS IN WAR 10	% OF NATIONS IN WAR 11	NATION MONTHS UNDER-WAY 12	% OF NATION MONTHS EX-HAUST-ED 13	NO. OF WARS ENDING 14	NO. OF PARTIC-IPANTS 15	NATION MONTHS 16	BATTLE DEATHS 000'S 17
1930	65	0	0	0.0	0.0	0.0	0.0	0.0	0	0	0.0	0.0	0.0	0	0	0.0	0.0
1931	65	0	0	0.0	0.0	0.0	0.0	0.0	0	0	0.0	0.0	0.0	0	0	0.0	0.0
1932	66	0	0	0.0	0.0	0.0	0.0	0.0	0	0	0.0	0.0	0.0	0	0	0.0	0.0
1933	66	0	0	0.0	0.0	0.0	0.0	0.0	0	0	0.0	0.0	0.0	0	0	0.0	0.0
1934	66	0	0	0.0	0.0	0.0	0.0	0.0	0	0	0.0	0.0	0.0	0	0	0.0	0.0
1935	66	0	0	0.0	0.0	0.0	0.0	0.0	0	0	0.0	0.0	0.0	0	0	0.0	0.0
1936	66	0	0	0.0	0.0	0.0	0.0	0.0	0	0	0.0	0.0	0.0	0	0	0.0	0.0
1937	66	0	0	0.0	0.0	0.0	0.0	0.0	0	0	0.0	0.0	0.0	0	0	0.0	0.0
1938	66	0	0	0.0	0.0	0.0	0.0	0.0	0	0	0.0	0.0	0.0	0	0	0.0	0.0
1939	65	0	0	0.0	0.0	0.0	0.0	0.0	0	0	0.0	0.0	0.0	0	0	0.0	0.0
1940	62	0	0	0.0	0.0	0.0	0.0	0.0	0	0	0.0	0.0	0.0	0	0	0.0	0.0
1941	55	0	0	0.0	0.0	0.0	0.0	0.0	0	0	0.0	0.0	0.0	0	0	0.0	0.0
1942	53	0	0	0.0	0.0	0.0	0.0	0.0	0	0	0.0	0.0	0.0	0	0	0.0	0.0
1943	52	0	0	0.0	0.0	0.0	0.0	0.0	0	0	0.0	0.0	0.0	0	0	0.0	0.0
1944	57	0	0	0.0	0.0	0.0	0.0	0.0	0	0	0.0	0.0	0.0	0	0	0.0	0.0
1945	64	2	3	96.4	124.4	0.77	0.0987	6.89	2	3	4.7	4.4	0.6	0	0	0.0	0.0
1946	66	0	0	0.0	0.0	0.0	0.0	0.0	2	3	4.5	31.0	3.9	1	2	22.4	1.4
1947	68	2	2	3.0	34.5	0.09	0.0007	1.94	3	2	2.9	23.3	2.9	0	0	0.0	0.0
1948	72	0	0	0.0	0.0	0.0	0.0	0.0	3	2	2.8	35.0	4.1	1	1	20.2	1.5
1949	75	0	0	0.0	0.0	0.0	0.0	0.0	2	2	2.7	12.0	1.3	1	1	14.3	1.5
1950	75	0	0	0.0	0.0	0.0	0.0	0.0	1	1	1.3	12.0	1.3	0	0	0.0	0.0
1951	75	0	0	0.0	0.0	0.0	0.0	0.0	1	1	1.3	12.0	1.3	0	0	0.0	0.0
1952	77	0	0	0.0	0.0	0.0	0.0	0.0	1	1	1.3	12.0	1.3	0	0	0.0	0.0
1953	78	0	0	0.0	0.0	0.0	0.0	0.0	1	1	1.3	12.0	1.3	0	0	0.0	0.0
1954	82	1	1	15.0	88.5	0.17	0.0349	5.85	2	1	1.2	7.0	0.7	1	1	102.0	95.0
1955	84	0	0	0.0	0.0	0.0	0.0	0.0	1	1	1.2	12.0	1.2	0	0	0.0	0.0
1956	87	1	1	40.0	36.7	1.09	0.0066	4.18	2	2	2.3	22.1	2.1	0	0	0.0	0.0
1957	89	0	0	0.0	0.0	0.0	0.0	0.0	2	2	2.2	24.0	2.2	0	0	0.0	0.0
1958	90	0	0	0.0	0.0	0.0	0.0	0.0	2	2	2.2	24.0	2.2	0	0	0.0	0.0
1959	89	0	0	0.0	0.0	0.0	0.0	0.0	2	2	2.2	14.7	1.4	1	1	36.7	40.0
1960	107	0	0	0.0	0.0	0.0	0.0	0.0	1	1	0.9	12.0	0.9	0	0	0.0	0.0
1961	111	0	0	0.0	0.0	0.0	0.0	0.0	1	1	0.9	12.0	0.9	0	0	0.0	0.0
1962	117	0	0	0.0	0.0	0.0	0.0	0.0	1	1	0.9	2.5	0.2	1	1	88.5	15.0
1963	119	0	0	0.0	0.0	0.0	0.0	0.0	0	0	0.0	0.0	0.0	0	0	0.0	0.0
1964	122	0	0	0.0	0.0	0.0	0.0	0.0	0	0	0.0	0.0	0.0	0	0	0.0	0.0
1965	124	0	0	0.0	0.0	0.0	0.0	0.0	0	0	0.0	0.0	0.0	0	0	0.0	0.0

7.9 - RANK ORDER OF YEARS BY AMOUNT OF WAR BEGUN

YEAR	BATTLE DEATHS FROM WARS BEGUN (000'S)	RANK	NATION MONTHS CF WAR BEGUN	RANK	YEAR	BATTLE DEATHS FROM WARS BEGUN (000'S)	RANK	NATION MONTHS OF WAR BEGUN	RANK
1939	15273.3	1.0	895.0	1.0	1821	15.0	37.0	85.1	13.0
1914	8555.8	2.0	607.8	2.0	1825	15.0	37.0	56.2	19.0
1950	1892.1	3.0	514.0	3.0	1954	15.0	37.0	88.5	12.0
1937	1000.0	4.0	106.2	10.0	1884	12.1	39.0	23.6	34.0
1877	285.0	5.0	17.6	44.0	1839	10.0	40.0	5.7	61.0
1853	264.2	6.0	116.5	7.0	1875	10.0	42.0	21.4	39.0
1870	187.5	7.0	27.0	31.0	1898	10.0	42.0	7.4	55.0
1828	130.0	9.0	33.4	29.0	1909	10.0	42.0	17.0	45.5
1904	130.0	9.0	38.6	27.0	1948	8.0	44.0	19.4	42.0
1932	130.0	9.0	71.8	15.5	1878	7.5	45.0	20.3	41.0
1864	114.5	11.0	134.3	5.0	1965	6.8	46.0	3.2	65.0
1868	100.0	12.0	112.1	9.0	1863	6.0	47.5	15.9	48.0
1945	96.4	13.0	124.4	6.0	1873	6.0	47.5	65.2	18.0
1912	82.0	14.0	20.4	40.0	1826	5.0	49.5	17.0	45.5
1848	76.0	15.0	42.8	23.0	1852	5.0	49.5	3.4	64.0
1956	75.2	16.0	39.3	25.5	1925	4.0	51.0	22.4	37.0
1919	61.0	17.0	93.4	11.0	1857	3.5	52.0	22.9	36.0
1913	60.5	18.0	4.2	63.0	1827	3.2	53.0	0.4	70.0
1931	60.0	19.0	33.2	30.0	1858	3.0	55.0	12.9	52.0
1895	59.0	20.0	47.8	21.0	1885	3.0	55.0	2.4	67.0
1917	50.0	21.0	39.3	25.5	1947	3.0	55.0	34.5	28.0
1866	36.1	22.0	14.5	49.0	1849	2.2	57.0	6.4	58.0
1859	32.5	23.0	17.7	43.0	1817	2.0	60.0	6.9	56.0
1921	29.0	24.0	71.8	15.5	1856	2.0	60.0	9.2	53.0
1899	26.5	25.0	72.5	14.0	1860	2.0	60.0	7.6	54.0
1831	25.0	26.0	22.0	38.0	1896	2.0	60.0	23.1	35.0
1882	24.5	27.0	65.3	17.0	1897	2.0	60.0	6.2	60.0
1894	21.0	28.0	25.7	32.0	1845	1.5	63.0	2.9	66.0
1838	20.0	30.5	48.4	20.0	1851	1.3	64.0	13.2	51.0
1862	20.0	30.5	115.4	8.0	1835	1.0	67.5	6.7	57.0
1911	20.0	30.5	25.4	33.0	1841	1.0	67.5	1.0	69.0
1935	20.0	30.5	14.4	50.0	1865	1.0	67.5	16.8	47.0
1879	17.5	33.0	176.0	4.0	1906	1.0	67.5	5.4	62.0
1846	17.0	34.0	42.2	24.0	1907	1.0	67.5	6.3	59.0
1823	16.0	35.0	43.7	22.0	1962	1.0	67.5	2.2	68.0

7.10 - RANK ORDER OF YEARS BY AMOUNT OF WAR UNDERWAY

YEAR	NATION MONTHS CF WAR UNDERWAY	RANK	% OF POSSIBLE NATION MONTHS EXHAUSTED	RANK	YEAR	NATION MONTHS CF WAR UNDERWAY	RANK	% OF POSSIBLE NATION MONTHS EXHAUSTED	RANK	YEAR	NATION MONTHS CF WAR UNDERWAY	RANK	% OF POSSIBLE NATION MONTHS EXHAUSTED	RANK
1952	204.0	1.0	22.1	8.0	1897	30.2	43.0	6.5	41.0	1841	13.0	85.5	3.3	75.0
1951	192.5	2.0	21.4	10.0	1875	30.0	44.0	7.8	37.0	1878	13.0	85.5	3.2	78.0
1944	184.3	3.0	26.9	5.0	1823	29.9	45.0	10.8	22.0	1857	12.6	87.0	2.6	88.0
1942	180.0	4.0	28.3	3.0	1825	29.3	46.0	10.6	25.0	1839	12.5	88.0	3.4	74.0
1943	178.5	5.0	28.6	2.0	1826	28.9	47.0	10.0	26.0	1949	12.4	89.0	1.4	104.0
1917	169.8	6.0	32.2	1.0	1829	28.8	48.5	9.6	28.0	1822	12.0	93.5	4.3	60.0
1916	146.3	7.0	27.7	4.0	1896	28.8	48.5	6.2	46.0	1860	12.0	93.5	2.3	93.0
1918	144.3	8.0	25.1	6.0	1848	27.6	50.0	6.2	44.0	1872	12.0	93.5	3.2	76.0
1941	144.0	9.0	21.8	9.0	1912	27.4	51.0	5.3	53.0	1923	12.0	93.5	1.6	100.5
1953	120.8	10.0	12.9	14.0	1868	26.7	52.0	6.5	40.0	1924	12.0	93.5	1.6	100.5
1940	118.2	11.0	15.9	12.0	1867	26.4	53.0	5.9	48.0	1955	12.0	93.5	1.2	107.0
1915	118.0	12.0	22.3	7.0	1925	26.2	54.0	3.5	72.0	1960	12.0	93.5	0.9	113.0
1945	97.3	13.0	12.7	15.0	1895	25.8	55.0	5.7	50.0	1961	12.0	93.5	0.9	115.0
1866	74.7	14.0	16.0	11.0	1885	25.0	56.0	6.0	47.0	1832	11.7	98.0	3.5	71.0
1939	66.8	15.0	8.6	35.0	1956	24.7	57.0	2.4	89.0	1909	11.6	99.5	2.2	96.0
1855	59.7	16.0	12.1	17.0	1849	24.3	58.0	5.3	52.0	1937	11.6	99.5	1.5	103.0
1883	56.2	17.0	13.4	13.0	1824	24.0	63.0	8.7	33.0	1902	11.1	101.0	2.2	97.0
1948	53.4	18.0	6.2	45.0	1847	24.0	63.0	5.6	51.0	1851	11.0	102.0	2.4	90.0
1865	50.3	19.0	10.7	24.0	1874	24.0	63.0	6.5	42.0	1894	10.7	103.0	2.3	91.0
1882	47.8	20.0	11.4	19.0	1900	24.0	63.0	4.8	56.5	1831	10.3	104.0	3.1	80.0
1877	44.8	21.0	11.7	18.0	1901	24.0	63.0	4.8	56.5	1842	9.4	105.0	2.3	92.0
1879	44.3	22.0	10.9	21.0	1934	24.0	63.0	3.0	81.5	1821	9.3	106.0	3.4	73.0
1950	44.2	23.0	4.9	55.0	1938	24.0	63.0	3.0	81.5	1936	8.6	107.0	1.1	110.0
1880	44.1	24.0	10.8	23.0	1957	24.0	63.0	2.2	94.0	1853	7.0	108.5	1.5	102.0
1854	42.2	25.0	8.8	32.0	1958	24.0	63.0	2.2	95.0	1954	7.0	108.5	0.7	118.0
1914	41.4	26.0	7.8	36.0	1947	23.3	68.0	2.9	85.0	1907	6.3	110.0	1.2	106.0
1864	40.3	27.0	8.6	34.0	1904	21.6	69.5	4.2	64.0	1911	6.2	111.0	1.2	108.0
1870	39.4	28.0	9.7	27.0	1926	21.6	69.5	2.8	86.0	1906	5.4	112.5	1.0	111.0
1919	38.6	29.0	6.3	43.0	1873	21.2	71.0	5.7	49.0	1910	5.4	112.5	1.0	112.0
1932	37.2	30.0	4.7	58.0	1859	20.1	72.0	4.0	68.0	1818	5.1	114.0	1.8	99.0
1863	36.3	31.0	7.8	38.0	1858	20.0	73.0	4.1	66.0	1927	5.0	115.0	0.6	121.0
1827	36.0	34.0	12.5	16.0	1846	17.6	74.0	4.2	63.0	1962	4.7	116.0	0.3	122.0
1869	36.0	34.0	8.8	30.5	1840	17.2	75.0	4.6	59.0	1836	3.7	117.0	1.1	109.0
1876	36.0	34.0	9.4	29.0	1862	17.0	76.5	3.6	70.0	1852	3.2	118.5	0.7	119.0
1881	36.0	34.0	8.8	30.5	1905	17.0	76.5	3.2	77.0	1965	3.2	118.5	0.2	124.0
1920	36.0	34.0	4.9	54.0	1935	16.8	78.0	2.1	98.0	1835	3.0	120.5	0.9	116.0
1828	34.1	37.0	11.4	20.0	1913	16.4	79.0	3.2	79.0	1838	3.0	120.5	0.8	117.0
1933	32.2	38.0	4.1	65.0	1871	15.8	80.0	4.2	62.0	1830	2.9	122.0	0.9	114.0
1921	32.0	39.0	4.3	61.0	1959	14.7	81.0	1.4	105.0	1817	1.8	123.0	0.7	120.0
1946	31.0	40.0	3.9	69.0	1856	14.4	82.5	2.9	84.0	1861	1.2	124.0	0.2	123.0
1884	30.7	41.0	7.3	39.0	1898	14.4	82.5	3.0	83.0	1931	0.8	125.0	0.1	126.0
1922	30.6	42.0	4.0	67.0	1899	13.6	84.0	2.8	87.0	1845	0.6	126.0	0.1	125.0

7.11 - RANK CRDER OF YEARS BY AMOUNT OF WAR TERMINATED

YEAR	BATTLE DEATHS FRCM WARS ENDING (000'S)	RANK	NATION MCNTHS OF WAR ENDING	RANK	YEAR	BATTLE DEATHS FROM WARS ENDING (000'S)	RANK	NATION MONTHS OF WAR ENDING	RANK
1945	15164.3	1.0	875.6	1.0	1826	15.0	37.0	29.1	31.0
1918	8555.8	2.0	607.8	2.0	1830	15.0	37.0	56.2	19.0
1953	1892.1	3.0	514.0	3.0	1831	15.0	37.0	8.3	53.0
1941	1000.0	4.0	106.2	9.0	1883	14.0	39.0	170.3	5.0
1878	394.5	5.0	197.0	4.0	1860	11.0	40.5	11.6	49.0
1856	264.2	6.0	116.5	7.0	1919	11.0	40.5	10.8	50.0
1871	187.5	7.0	27.0	32.0	1840	10.0	42.0	5.7	60.5
1913	142.5	8.0	24.6	37.0	1832	10.0	44.0	13.7	46.0
1829	130.0	10.0	33.4	28.0	1877	10.0	44.0	21.4	40.0
1905	130.0	10.0	38.6	25.0	1910	10.0	44.0	17.0	43.0
1935	130.0	10.0	71.8	15.5	1864	9.5	46.5	25.7	34.0
1870	110.0	12.0	123.5	6.0	1949	9.5	46.5	33.7	27.0
1954	95.0	13.0	102.0	11.0	1896	9.0	48.0	10.5	51.0
1940	90.0	14.0	6.8	55.0	1965	6.8	49.0	3.2	64.0
1849	78.2	15.0	49.2	20.0	1853	5.0	50.0	3.4	63.0
1898	62.0	16.0	67.8	17.0	1884	4.5	51.0	25.7	34.0
1933	60.0	17.0	33.2	29.0	1880	4.0	52.5	18.2	42.0
1921	50.0	18.5	39.3	24.0	1927	4.0	52.5	22.4	38.5
1922	50.0	18.5	82.6	13.0	1879	3.5	54.0	5.7	60.5
1959	40.0	20.0	36.7	26.0	1827	3.2	55.0	0.4	69.0
1866	37.1	21.0	31.3	30.0	1818	2.0	57.0	6.9	54.0
1956	35.2	22.0	2.6	66.0	1857	2.0	57.0	9.2	52.0
1885	35.1	23.0	65.6	18.0	1897	2.0	57.0	6.2	59.0
1859	29.0	24.5	43.1	22.0	1846	1.5	59.5	2.9	65.0
1926	29.0	24.5	71.8	15.5	1948	1.5	59.5	20.2	41.0
1902	26.5	26.0	72.5	14.0	1946	1.4	61.0	22.4	38.5
1895	21.0	27.0	25.7	34.0	1852	1.3	62.0	13.2	47.0
1828	20.0	30.0	102.1	10.0	1823	1.0	66.0	14.6	44.0
1842	20.0	30.0	48.4	21.0	1836	1.0	66.0	6.7	56.0
1867	20.0	30.0	115.4	8.0	1841	1.0	66.0	1.0	67.5
1912	20.0	30.0	25.4	36.0	1861	1.0	66.0	6.4	57.0
1936	20.0	30.0	14.4	45.0	1863	1.0	66.0	1.0	67.5
1939	19.0	33.0	12.6	48.0	1906	1.0	66.0	5.4	62.0
1848	17.0	34.0	42.2	23.0	1907	1.0	66.0	6.3	58.0
1962	16.0	35.0	90.7	12.0					

SUMMARY

For most theoretical purposes, the war data as presented in this chapter are the most important in the volume. First, they permit us to enter into empirical investigations on the basis of which we might generalize about the "causes" and the "consequences" of international war over the period since the Napoleonic Wars. Second, and of more immediate interest here, they provide us with the basis for a number of descriptive and analytic inquiries in the chapters which follow. Thus, we now turn to a consideration of trends (Chapter Eight) and cycles (Chapter Nine) in international war since 1816.

Chapter 8

Secular Trends in the Incidence of War

In the previous chapter we converted our data on the separate and particular wars into a form that permitted us to describe the amount of war in the system year by year. This shift of our unit of analysis from individual *wars* to the *system* as a whole produced 150 annual observations for a variety of measures on the incidence of war, and their fluctuations over time. Now we want to see whether these fluctuations reveal any sort of regular patterns over the century and a half that concerns us here.

Those patterns may be of two basic types: (a) steady upward or downward trends; and (b) recurrent cyclical fluctuations. In any historical process, we may find one, or both, or neither; furthermore, one may be sufficiently strong and the other sufficiently weak that only the stronger one is readily apparent. Hence, it is usually desirable (as economists, for example, have discovered) to try to disentangle them from one another, and this is what we undertake here. We begin with a search for secular trends in this chapter and then go on in the following one to look for any recurrent periodicities that may be concealed in the unanalyzed maze of annual figures.

PRIOR INVESTIGATIONS

One of the most frequently voiced notions in the international politics literature is that the system is not only undergoing constant change, but that as we move from decade to decade or generation to generation, things become so radically different that no legitimate comparisons may be made across time. This seems, for example, to be a major premise of those who hold that there can be no serious science of international politics. But how much evidence has been sought in an effort to test this proposition? With the exception of Sorokin's classic study (1937), which is only marginally concerned with this problem, and Russett's excellent little summary (*Trends in World Politics,* 1965) there are few relevant time series available.

When we shift from statements about "all" of international politics to those concerning the constancy of war alone, the problem becomes more manageable. Would we expect its incidence to rise or fall over the period since Waterloo? If so, why? Among the factors which might be expected to produce an *increase* in the frequency, severity, or magnitude of international war are increases in the lethality and range of offensive weapons, increases in the politicization of diplomacy, and the simple increase in the number of people and nations in the system. Among those which might produce a *diminishing* effect could be improvements in defensive weapon technology and military medicine, more sophisticated models of national behavior, the increasing efficacy of such intergovernmental organizations as the League and the United Nations, and an increasing reluctance to see the more modern and destructive weapons used. The mere listing of such factors makes evident the need to discriminate among the several measures of the incidence of war, since it is quite possible for wars to increase in frequency (for example) over time but not in severity, and so forth.

COMPARING SUCCESSIVE PERIODS FOR AMOUNT OF WAR IN THE SYSTEMS

In searching for an upward or downward secular trend, there are a good many computational approaches open to us, and each one can—depending on the number of categories and cutting points used—produce a somewhat different impression. At the simplest, we can divide our entire time span into two periods of 75 years each, indicate the total scores on our several measures and then ask whether the differences in the two periods' scores, if any, are likely to have occurred by sheer chance. This we do in Table 8.1, which is calculated as follows.

First, since the amounts of war underway and the amount begun (or terminated) in any period will be equal if the period is long enough and if the breaks do not come during any war, we need only use one set of measures; for our purposes, the onset data are as useful as any. Second, in order to cope with the strong upward trend in the system's size, we compute several of the measures in normalized as well as in absolute form. [Plotting a regression line for system size against time, we get a product moment correlation of 0.86 and a coefficient of determination (r^2) of 0.74; these values are significant at the .0001 level. Clearly, we must control for the number of states in the system.]

As to the *number of wars* in each period, we normalize by dividing that figure by $\overline{N}$ (which in this case is the average size of the system during each period). A more refined measure might have been achieved by dividing by $N(N-1)/2$, but that would only be appropriate if all or most of the wars in any class were bilateral; while this is largely true of the extra-systemic wars, it is only true of 60 percent of the interstate wars. Shifting from the frequency of war in a particular period to the total *magnitude* in nation months begun, we again normalized by the number of nations in the relevant system or sub-system during the "average" year of the period. As to *battle deaths,* if we knew the total combined population of all the nations in each of the systems examined, we could use that as a basis for normalization; but we do not yet have these figures. Furthermore, a case can be made for including some measures which are not normalized, since the latter procedure will certainly help to suppress any upward secular trend pattern.

What sort of visual pattern emerges from these computations? Or, to put it another way, how strong, if at all, is the deviation from the null model which predicts that the five individual measures for each of the three types of war should be approximately the same magnitude for each of the two periods? The picture is quite mixed. While the number of wars of all three types goes down for the second half of our 150 years, and declines even more sharply if we control for system size, the obverse holds true for magnitude and severity. That is, the number of nation months and battle deaths rises sharply for both the raw and the normalized figures. But this holds only for all international wars and for the interstate war subset; extra-systemic wars, conversely, decline not only in frequency, but in the total number of nation months and battle deaths arising from these wars.

In looking at these *extra-systemic* wars from the secular trend point of view, even though we compute normalized scores, they should not be taken very seriously, for as the size of the international system *increases,* the number of non-systemic entities *decreases.* That is, as more and more national units become qualified state members of the system, the opportunity for extra-systemic wars must inevitably diminish. In the next few decades, then, this class of war may become extinct.

Returning to the distributions of war in our successive time periods, we next ask whether the same general impressions emerge when we use a more discriminating set of time periods. In Table 8.2, we divide our 150 years into five periods of 30 years each, and it is apparent that the pattern is equally mixed. The number of wars fluctuates quite discernibly around the mean, and when we control for system size, the general frequency trend is downward. As for total nation months and battle deaths sustained during these five periods, there is again (despite the fluctuations) a general

TABLE 8.1 - COMPARING THE AMOUNT OF WAR BEGUN IN TWO SUCCESSIVE PERIODS

TYPE OF WAR	ONSET MEASURE	1816-1890	1891-1965	TOTALS	MEANS
	AVE. NO. OF NATIONS (N)	32.8	62.3		
	NUMBER OF WARS	52	41	93	46.5
	WARS/N	1.58	0.66	2.24	1.12
ALL INTERNATIONAL	NATION MONTHS	1452.0	3080.8	4532.8	2266.4
	NATION MONTHS/N	44.3	49.5	93.7	46.9
	BATTLE DEATHS	1484.1	27705.6	29189.7	14594.8
	NUMBER OF WARS	24	26	50	25.0
	WARS/N	0.73	0.42	1.15	0.57
INTERSTATE ONLY	NATION MONTHS	685.0	2510.1	3195.1	1597.5
	NATION MONTHS/N	20.9	40.3	61.2	30.6
	BATTLE DEATHS	1032.6	27374.7	28407.3	14203.6
	NUMBER OF WARS	28	15	43	21.5
	WARS/N	0.85	0.24	1.09	0.55
EXTRA-SYSTEMIC ONLY	NATION MONTHS	767.0	570.7	1337.7	668.8
	NATION MONTHS/N	23.4	9.2	32.5	16.3
	BATTLE DEATHS	451.5	330.9	782.4	391.2

upward trend in all wars and interstate wars, normalized or not. Once more, the extra-systemic war tendency is roughly a downward one.

Does a more consistent pattern emerge when we shift from 5 periods of 30 years each to 15 periods of 10 years each? Hardly. What we see, rather, is an accentuation of the fluctuating pattern which was present, but less evident, in the earlier breakdown. The muting effect of using ever smaller time periods that we saw in the shift from 2 to 5 periods is further emphasized when the number of observation periods is raised to 15; even the downward trend in the extra-systemic war indicators is less evident here.

To put it another way, the length of the time unit used can exercise an appreciable impact on the patterns that emerge. The Indian mathematician P. C. Mahalanobis reports a similar pattern when one correlates rainfall and temperature. With the month as the unit of analysis, there is a strong *positive* correlation; with the *day* as the unit, there is a strong *negative* correlation; and with the *week*, there is *no* correlation. The explanation, of course, is that rainfall occurs on the cool days of the hotter months. Even if we were to compute the deviations from the mean (that is, no trend) for each of the cells of our data, it is clear that no obvious trends, up or down, would emerge. All of this suggests, then, that our first impression may well have been misleading, and that an alternative mode of analysis is called for. Before doing so, however, one additional refinement might be worth considering.

TABLE 8.2 - CCMPARING THE AMOUNT OF WAR BEGUN IN FIVE SUCCESSIVE PERIODS

TYPE CF WAR	ONSET MEASURE	1816-1845	1846-1875	1876-1905	1906-1935	1936-1965	TOTALS	MEANS
AVE. NO. CF NATICNS (N)		27.1	37.4	37.7	55.0	80.4		
	NUMBER OF WARS	15	27	20	15	16	93	18.6
	WARS/N	0.55	0.72	0.53	0.27	0.20	2.28	0.46
ALL INTERNATIONAL	NATION MONTHS	329.4	817.4	526.5	1032.8	1826.7	4532.8	906.6
	NATION MONTHS/N	12.1	21.9	14.0	18.8	22.7	89.4	17.9
	BATTLE DEATHS	244.7	889.8	600.1	9084.3	18370.8	29189.7	5837.9
	NUMBER OF WARS	3	17	8	12	10	50	10.0
	WARS/N	0.11	0.45	0.21	0.22	0.12	1.12	0.22
INTERSTATE CNLY	NATION MONTHS	48.4	423.9	280.9	899.3	1542.6	3195.1	639.0
	NATION MONTHS/N	1.8	11.3	7.4	16.3	19.2	56.1	11.2
	BATTLE DEATHS	134.2	586.3	469.1	9001.3	18216.4	28407.3	5681.5
	NUMBER OF WARS	12	10	12	3	6	43	8.6
	WARS/N	0.44	0.27	0.32	0.05	0.07	1.16	0.23
EXTRA-SYSTEMIC ONLY	NATION MONTHS	281.0	393.5	245.6	133.5	284.1	1337.7	267.5
	NATION MONTHS/N	10.4	10.5	6.5	2.4	3.5	33.4	6.7
	BATTLE DEATHS	110.5	303.5	131.0	83.0	154.4	782.4	156.5

TABLE 8.3 - CCMPARING TEE AMOUNT OF WAR EEGUN IN FIFTEEN SUCCESSIVE PERIODS

TYPE OF WAR	ONSET MEASURE	1816-1825	1826-1835	1836-1845	1846-1855	1856-1865	1866-1875
AVE. NO. OF NATIONS (N)		23.0	26.4	32.0	38.2	40.5	33.4
	NUMBER CF WARS	5	6	4	9	13	5
	WARS/N	0.22	0.23	0.13	0.24	0.32	0.15
ALL INTERNATIONAL	NATION MONTHS	191.9	79.5	58.0	224.5	352.7	240.2
	NATION MONTHS/N	8.3	3.0	1.8	5.9	8.7	7.2
	EATTLE DEATHS	48.0	164.2	32.5	365.7	184.5	339.6
	NUMBER OF WARS	1	2	0	6	9	2
	WARS/N	0.04	0.08	0.0	0.16	0.22	0.06
INTERSTATE ONLY	NATION MONTHS	14.6	33.8	0.0	203.9	178.5	41.5
	NATION MONTHS/N	0.6	1.3	0.0	5.3	4.4	1.2
	EATTLE DEATHS	1.0	133.2	0.0	299.7	63.0	223.6
	NUMBER OF WARS	4	4	4	3	4	3
	WARS/N	0.17	0.15	0.13	0.08	0.10	0.09
EXTRA-SYSTEMIC CNLY	NATION MONTHS	177.3	45.7	58.0	20.6	174.2	198.7
	NATION MONTHS/N	7.7	1.7	1.8	0.5	4.3	5.9
	EATTLE DEATHS	47.0	31.0	32.5	66.0	121.5	116.0

TABLE 8.3 - COMPARING THE AMOUNT OF WAR BEGUN IN FIFTEEN SUCCESSIVE PERIODS

TYPE OF WAR	ONSET MEASURE	1876-1885	1886-1895	1896-1905	1906-1915	1916-1925	1926-1935
	AVE. NO. OF NATIONS (N)	34.0	37.6	41.6	43.6	56.2	65.3
	NUMBER OF WARS	10	4	6	7	5	3
	WARS/N	0.29	0.11	0.14	0.16	0.09	0.05
ALL INTERNATIONAL	NATION MONTHS	305.2	73.5	147.8	686.5	226.9	119.4
	NATION MONTHS/N	9.0	2.0	3.6	15.7	4.0	1.8
	BATTLE DEATHS	349.6	80.0	170.5	8730.3	144.0	210.0
	NUMBER OF WARS	4	1	3	7	2	3
	WARS/N	0.12	0.03	0.07	0.16	0.04	0.05
INTERSTATE ONLY	NATION MONTHS	212.7	16.0	52.2	686.5	93.4	119.4
	NATION MONTHS/N	6.3	0.4	1.3	15.7	1.7	1.8
	BATTLE DEATHS	312.1	15.0	142.0	8730.3	61.0	210.0
	NUMBER OF WARS	6	3	3	0	3	0
	WARS/N	0.18	0.08	0.07	0.0	0.05	0.0
EXTRA-SYSTEMIC ONLY	NATION MONTHS	92.5	57.5	95.6	0.0	133.5	0.0
	NATION MONTHS/N	2.7	1.5	2.3	0.0	2.4	0.0
	BATTLE DEATHS	37.5	65.0	28.5	0.0	83.0	0.0

TABLE 8.3 - COMPARING THE AMOUNT OF WAR BEGUN IN FIFTEEN SUCCESSIVE PERIODS

TYPE CF WAR	CNSET MEASURE	1936-1945	1946-1955	1956-1965	TOTALS	MEANS
	AVE. NO. CF NATIONS (N)	60.6	75.2	105.5		
	NUMBER OF WARS	6	5	5	93	6.2
	WARS/N	0.10	0.07	0.05	2.33	0.16
ALL INTERNATIONAL	NATION MONTHS	1125.6	656.4	44.7	4532.8	302.2
	NATION MONTHS/N	18.6	8.7	0.4	98.8	6.6
	BATTLE DEATHS	16369.7	1918.1	83.0	29189.7	1946.0
	NUMBER OF WARS	4	2	4	50	3.3
	WARS/N	0.07	0.03	0.04	1.15	0.08
INTERSTATE ONLY	NATION MONTHS	1001.2	533.4	8.0	3195.1	213.0
	NATION MONTHS/N	16.5	7.1	0.1	63.8	4.3
	BATTLE DEATHS	16273.3	1900.1	43.0	28407.3	1893.8
	NUMBER OF WARS	2	3	1	43	2.9
	WARS/N	0.03	0.04	0.01	1.18	0.08
EXTRA-SYSTEMIC CNLY	NATION MONTHS	124.4	123.0	36.7	1337.7	89.2
	NATION MONTHS/N	2.1	1.6	0.3	35.0	2.3
	BATTLE DEATHS	96.4	18.0	40.0	782.4	52.2

ISOLATING THE CENTRAL SYSTEM

That refinement concerns not so much the chronologically defined sub-systems, as the spatially defined ones. That is, any analysis which is based on the distribution of war in the total international system implies that the nations that comprise it are sufficiently interdependent to merit being treated as a single system. This would mean that there is some sort of empirical and causal link (direct or indirect) between wars and the decisions affecting them in such distant regions as South America, Europe, and Asia. At the moment we have no hard evidence as to how interdependent all the nations of the system were at different points in the time span under examination. But we do assume that the nations assigned to our central system (that is, most of Europe, plus the three or four most active non-European nations) from 1816 to 1920 *were* relatively interdependent. Thus, even if no upward or downward trend were visible in the total system, but one were indeed present when the peripheral nations of the first century (1816–1919) were left out of the analysis, we would be justified in speaking of that pattern as an historically meaningful trend. A glance at Table 8.4 indicates, however, that even within this more restricted population, there appears to be little in the way of a secular trend in the incidence of war. We omit any normalization here because the size of the system holds fairly constant, ranging from 13 in 1816 to 22 in 1919, when we no longer retain the sharp distinction between the central and peripheral system nations.

TABLE 8.4 - COMPARING THE AMOUNT OF WAR BEGUN IN CENTRAL SYSTEM IN TEN SUCCESSIVE PERIODS

TYPE OF WAR	ONSET MEASURE	1816-1825	1826-1835	1836-1845	1846-1855	1856-1865	1866-1875
	AVE. NO. OF NATIONS (N)	13.0	14.4	15.0	15.0	15.0	15.0
	NUMBER OF WARS	5	5	3	7	11	5
	WARS/N	0.38	0.35	0.20	0.47	0.73	0.33
ALL INTERNATIONAL	NATION MONTHS	191.9	72.8	57.0	165.5	146.6	217.5
	NATION MONTHS/N	14.8	5.1	3.8	11.0	9.8	14.5
	BATTLE DEATHS	48.0	163.2	31.5	345.8	52.2	330.0

TYPE OF WAR	ONSET MEASURE	1876-1885	1886-1895	1896-1905	1906-1915	TOTALS	MEANS
	AVE. NO. OF NATIONS (N)	16.6	17.2	19.8	22.0		
	NUMBER OF WARS	8	3	6	5	58	5.8
	WARS/N	0.48	0.17	0.30	0.23	3.65	0.37
ALL INTERNATIONAL	NATION MONTHS	121.9	57.5	144.1	666.3	1841.1	184.1
	NATION MONTHS/N	7.3	3.3	7.3	30.3	107.2	10.7
	BATTLE DEATHS	324.6	65.0	165.5	8720.3	10246.1	1024.6

REGRESSION LINES AS TREND INDICATORS

The second approach we use in examining the long-range trends in the incidence of war is that of linear regression. The idea here is to plot each set of measures along the vertical axis of a scattergram on which the longitudinal axis represents the successive years. By fitting a straight line which minimizes the square of the distance between that line and all of the data points on the scattergram, we can ascertain how much it departs from the horizontal (no trend) line over the 150 annual observations. Thus, if there *is* any clear upward or downward trend in a particular measure of war, it will become immediately apparent.

In Figure 8.5, we do this, with what is perhaps the best all-around indicator for these purposes: the amount of war underway, measured by normalized nation months. Visual inspection makes clear that the line which best fits the data shows only a very slight departure from the horizontal, suggesting the absence of any clear trend. The slope of this line may also be expressed statistically via the linear regression coefficients; for nation months underway (normalized for system size) the coefficient of determination (r^2) of the regression line, predicting from year of observation, is .014, which is so low as to have easily occurred by chance alone.

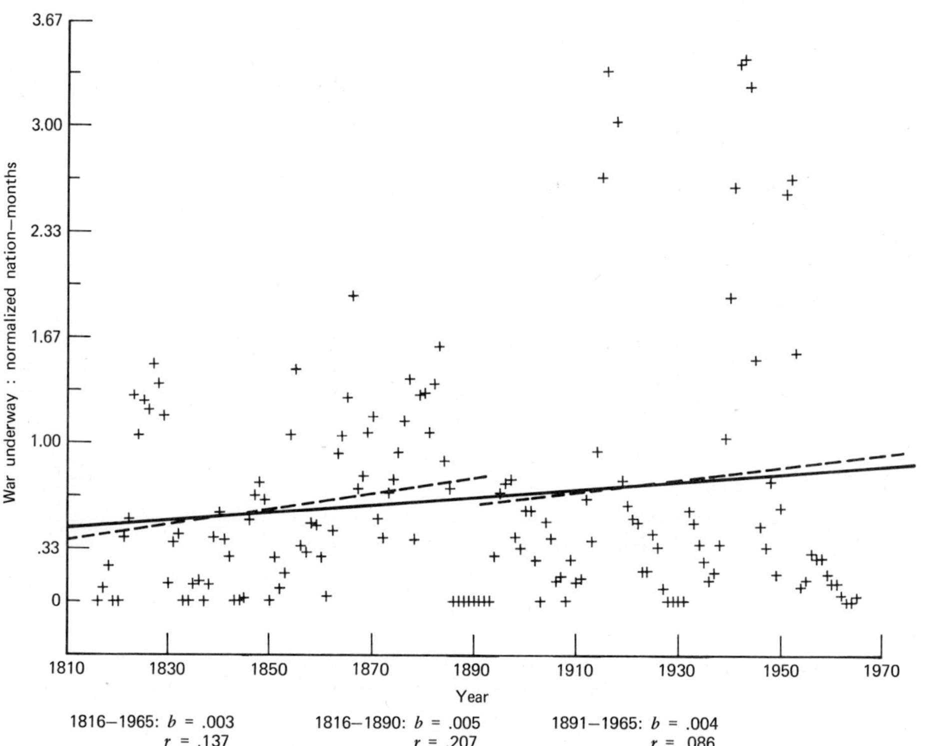

8.5 Regression line for normalized nation-months of war underway, annually, 1816–1965.

What happens when we do the same thing for a number of other measures of the incidence of war? In Table 8.6, we show the coefficients for a number of onset and underway measures. It is readily apparent that no clear trend, either upward or downward, is found for all wars or for the several types of interstate wars. Even the very modest upward (positive correlation) trends almost completely disappear when we normalize nation months of war for the number of nations in the system at hand. Sometimes, however, using a very short time unit can—because of the large number of fluctuations—obliterate a secular trend, and we have therefore reexamined some of these annual data after grouping them into periods of ten years each. The decade-by-decade analysis does produce a noticeable increase in the trend scores, as we found earlier in the visual presentations. For all international wars, the coefficient of determination rose to .146, and for central system wars only it rose to .283; but even this latter figure remains insignificant at the .05 level, using the *t* test. As in the prior analyses, then, we must conclude that war in its various forms (at least as we have measured its incidence) is neither on the wane nor on the rise.

8.6 LINEAR TREND STATISTICS FOR ANNUAL AMOUNTS OF WAR BEGUN AND UNDERWAY; 1816–1965 FOR INTERNATIONAL WAR ($N = 150$ ANNUAL OBSERVATIONS), 1816–1919 FOR CENTRAL SYSTEM WAR ($N = 104$ ANNUAL OBSERVATIONS)

Type of Measure	Variable	Correlation Coefficient with Time (r)	Coefficient of Determination (r^2)	Regression Coefficient (b)
	Nation months of international war	.12	.015	.279
	Nation months of international war/no. of nations in interstate system	.03	.001	.001
	Nation months of international war/no. of combatant nations	−.04	.002	−.019
	Nation months of central system war	.15	.022	.314
Onset	Nation months of central system war/no. of combatant nations	−.02	.000	−.011
	Battle deaths in international war	.12	.014	3861.52
	Battle deaths in international war/pre-war populations of combatant nations	.09	.007	.678
	Battle deaths in central system war	.16	.024	4347.78
	Battle deaths in central system war/pre-war populations of combatant nations	.16	.026	.845
	Nation months of international war	.32	.105	.315
Underway	Nation months of international war/no. of nations in interstate system	.14	.019	.003
	Nation months of international war/no. of combatant nations	.16	.026	.016

WAR RANK CORRELATIONS AS TREND INDICATORS

So far, we have, quite reasonably, used the year or other time span as our unit of analysis, and no discernible trends seem to be evident. But it occurs to us that one reason for the prevalent belief that war is on the increase is that the *wars* themselves may have become longer, larger, bloodier, or more intense. In other words, if we ignore the frequencies in war over time and the intervals between them, and just look at them in sequence as they unfold, we may discover a trend upward or downward in the magnitude, severity, or intensity of the wars themselves. The results of that approach, based on the data available in Chapter Six, are presented in Table 8.7, where we show the rank order correlation (Spearman rho) between the recency of the interstate wars and their rank position on battle deaths, battle deaths per capita, nation months, and nation months normalized by the system size at the onset of the war.

The results indicate that the unit of analysis (year or war) makes little difference. That is, if we look at the non-normalized measures, we find that the correlation between the recency of interstate war and the war's severity in battle deaths yields a coefficient of .31, indicating that wars are indeed becoming more severe; but the

8.7 RANK CORRELATIONS BETWEEN WAR DATE AND SEVERITY AND MAGNITUDE OF INTERSTATE WARS

Variable	Coefficient with War Onset Date (rho)	Attained Statistical Significance ($N = 50$)
Nation months	.04	n.s. at .05
Nation months/no. of combatant nations	−.02	n.s. at .05
Nation months/no. of nations in interstate system	−.10	n.s. at .05
Battle deaths	.31	$p < .05$
Battle deaths/pre-war populations of combatant nations	.13	n.s. at .05

trend is not very strong. The correlation between the recency of interstate war and magnitude in nation months indicates practically no upward trend at all, with a coefficient of .04. This is further reinforced when we examine the extent to which the normalized indicators correlate with war recency. The rank order coefficient of the wars' recency versus their battle death per capita scores is only .13 while that for nation months per system member at the time of the war's outbreak is only −.10. The negative correlation results, of course, from the fact that the system size increases at a very rapid rate (from 23 to 124 in 150 years).

TRENDS IN THE INTENSITY OF WAR

Although the evidence is fairly strong that we have only a slight upward trend in the incidence of war during the past century and a half (and that trend being in its severity), nevertheless it will be instructive to examine one other aspect of this phenomenon. That is, even if war is not becoming any more or less frequent, or increasing in magnitude, has it perhaps become more intense? Are there, for example, more battle deaths per nation month of war or per capita in the later decades of the period under study than in the earlier ones?

Rather than approach the question from the point of view of fixed time intervals, however, let us employ the analysis used in the previous section and examine this question in terms of the wars themselves. We do this because we have already ascertained that there is no significant increase in the frequency of war and because intensity is essentially a characteristic of individual wars rather than of years or decades. Furthermore, we again restrict our inquiry to interstate wars only, on the grounds that battle death figures for the non-member entities in extra-systemic wars are not available, thus reducing the usefulness of intensity ratios in these imperial and colonial wars.

For this analysis, we will use two different indicators. The first is that of battle deaths per nation month of interstate war, and the second is that of battle deaths per capita based on the pre-war size of the belligerents' total populations. And, as was indicated earlier, since there is a high correlation between this intensity figure and that based on armed forces size, we omit the latter. In order to make the visual presentation more manageable, we bring in the outlying high intensity cases (such as the Russo-Turkish War of 1877–1878, the Chaco War of 1932–1935, and the World Wars) by transforming the battle death per capita scores into $\log_e$ form. Since the data are found in Table 4.2, they need not be reproduced here; rather, we summarize them in graphic form via the scattergram in Figures 8.8 and 8.9.

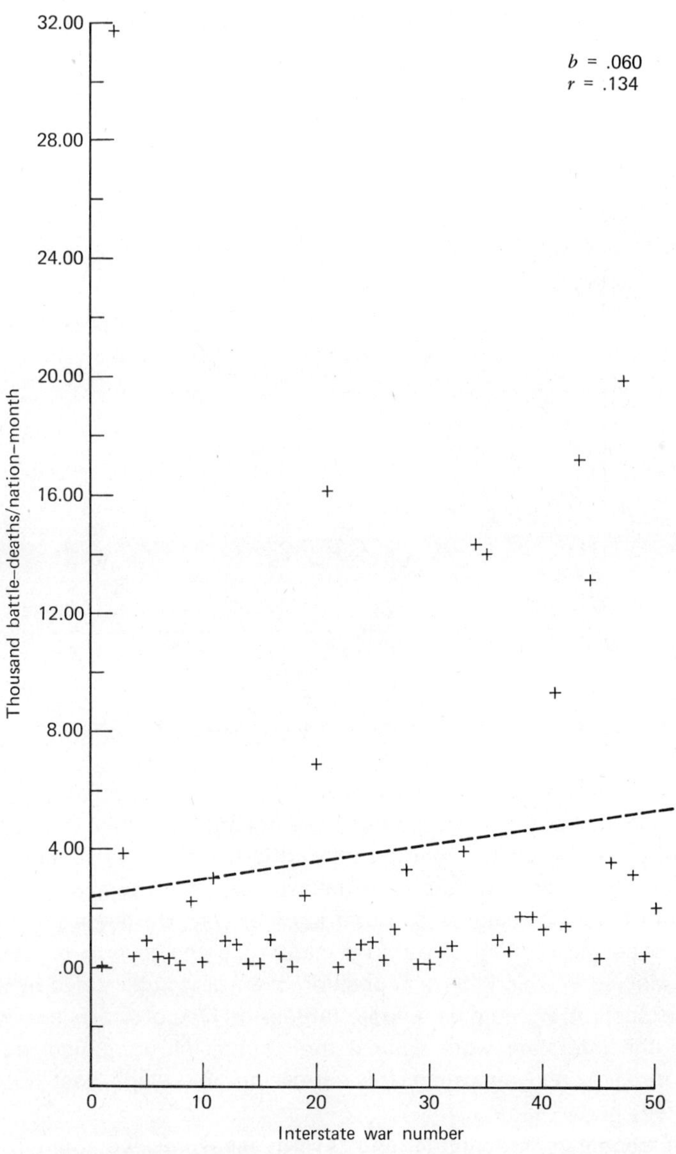

8.8 Scattergram of interstate war intensities: battle-deaths/nation-month.

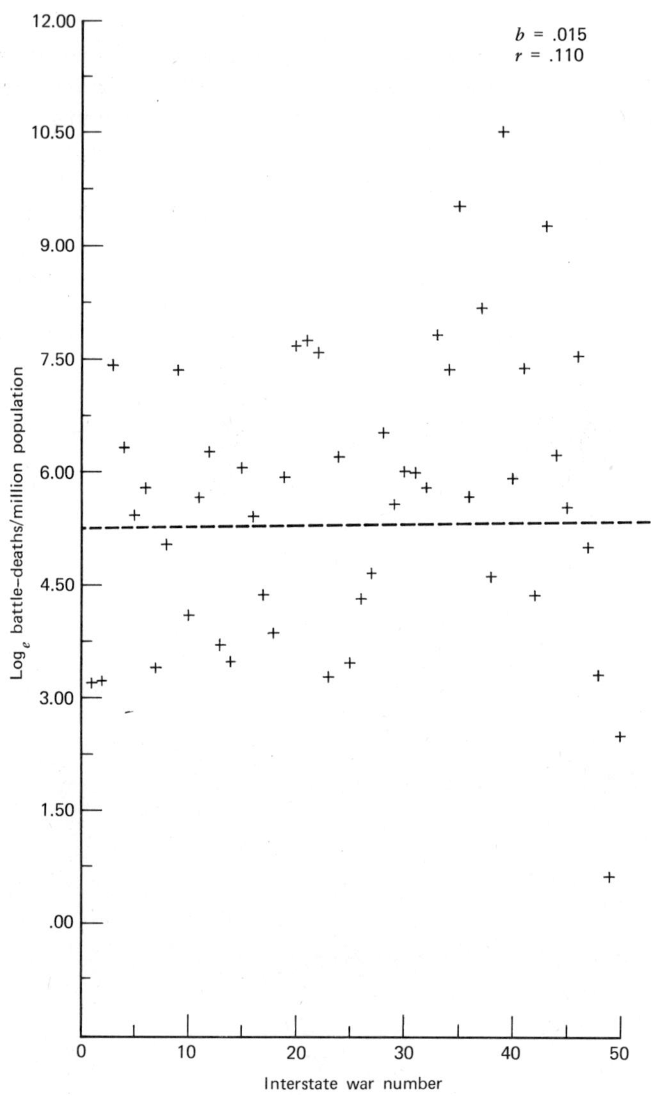

8.9 Scattergram of interstate war intensities: battle-deaths/population.

It should be pointed out that this method of searching for secular trends is different from the rank order correlation method utilized in the previous section. There, we compared the rank order of wars on four measures of severity and magnitude with the rank order of war on recency; to put it another way, we determined the extent to which the observed ranking of wars on magnitude and severity is the same as a hypothetical ranking in which the rank position of a war is determined by its recency in time. In this section, we employ a linear regression type of analysis as we plot the intensities of the interstate wars against their actual chronological occurrences (that is, not ranked), and determine the regression line which best describes the trend in intensity across time.

As with our frequency, magnitude, and severity measures, we again find a highly erratic and fluctuating pattern. And when we fit regression lines to the two different sets of plotted data, it is evident that, as before, any trend is more apparent than real. The regression coefficient for the battle deaths per nation month ratio is .06; a look at the points on the scattergram confirms the poor fit of the regression line, as indicated by a correlation of .13. What seemed to be a trend was largely the effect of six post-1900 wars: Second Balkan (1913), World War One (1914), Sino-Japanese (1937), World War Two (1939), Russo-Finnish (1939), and Russo-Hungarian (1956). On the other hand, the regression coefficient for the battle deaths per population ratio is only .02; its correlation (.11) is even lower than that for battle deaths per nation month. This correlation would be higher if we did not use the $\log_e$ values, as the transformation minimized the very high raw scores.

SUMMARY

Is war on the increase, as many scholars as well as laymen of our generation have been inclined to believe? The answer would seem to be a very unambiguous negative. Whether we look at the number of wars, their severity or their magnitude, there is no significant trend upward or down over the past 150 years. Even if we examine their intensities, we find that later wars are by and large no different than those of earlier periods. Likewise, even if we differentiate among different types of war, there seems to be no appreciable change in their frequency, when we control for their statistical probability as a function of the number of national units available to fight in these types of war. That is, the number of interstate wars per decade has risen no faster than the number of nations in the interstate system, and the number of extra-systemic wars has declined no faster than the number of extra-systemic nations in the world.

At first glance, our findings seem to run counter to other trend analyses such as that reported by Weiss (1963b). Using data from Wright, Richardson, and Sorokin, he discerned a clear upward trend in the *severity* (battle deaths) of war from 1820 to 1949. But he did not normalize for system size, did not differentiate between interstate and extra-systemic wars and, more importantly, when he looked at *frequency,* he found only a very modest upward trend. Moreover, in the analyses by Moyal (1949) and Richardson (1960a, pp. 137–142 and 157–167) no trend scores—either up or down—that could not have occurred by sheer chance, were uncovered.

What might account, then, for the widespread belief that war *is* on the rise? Four factors come to mind. First, modern communications make every war, in any part of the globe, known to us all in short order; we can no longer be oblivious to the violence and slaughter beyond our borders. Second, the two World Wars are a part of the memory of many of us, and their magnitudes and severities (as well as political consequences) remain all too salient. Third, the decades since World War Two have not only seen their normal share of war, but an allocation of resources and attention to the *preparation* for (some might say *prevention* of) war which certainly exceeds that of any earlier period. Finally, this study—for the reasons outlined earlier—is not addressed to that type of war which apparently *is* on the rise: civil war. Moreover, given the ideological, economic, and racial divisions that now mark the global system and its sub-systems, the indications are that intranational violence will be with us well into the future.

Whether these widely expected disasters will be concentrated within the next several years and then decline, or continue on indefinitely, is difficult to predict. If the historical record of interstate, imperial, and colonial wars is any guide, however, and if, furthermore, we fail to learn from that record, the optimistic may at least take hope from the fact that those wars have come and gone in a fairly cyclical fashion. The nature of that particular pattern constitutes our major concern in the next chapter.

Chapter 9

Cycles and Periodicity in the Incidence of War

As widely held as the belief that war is on the increase is the belief that war comes and goes in some clear and recurrent cyclical pattern. This latter belief, while more difficult to put to the test, is equally in keeping with the scientific mode which postulates a high degree of order and pattern in both the physical and the social worlds. Thus, in addition to the search for cyclical fluctuations in a wide range of *other* domains, there has been a consistent scholarly interest in the periodicity of war.

For those of us interested in ascertaining the causes of war, the periodicity problem is particularly critical. If, for example, there are no cyclical regularities in the incidence of war, we can safely assume that war is not caused by any single phenomenon with known periodicity. Conversely, if we do indeed find some sort of cyclical pattern, two interesting consequences follow. First, some might conclude that war is inherent in the great ebbs and flows of human activity, and is therefore not susceptible to rational intervention. But others, including ourselves, would be strengthened in the conviction that where there is regularity there is recurrent causation, and that once that causal pattern has been identified, our prospects for the control and elimination of war become considerably improved.

Perhaps the best known investigation of the question is that conducted by Sorokin as part of his ambitious study of social and cultural dynamics and reported in the third volume of *Fluctuations of Social Relationships, War and Revolution* (1937). Neither he nor Richardson (1960a, pp. 129–131), who worked with better data but a much shorter period, were able to find any strong evidence for such regularities. On the other hand, in secondary analyses of the Sorokin and Richardson data, as well as that of Wright, several researchers (Denton, 1966; and Denton and Phillips, 1968) concluded that there is indeed a discernible upswing in the incidence of war about every 30 years since 1680. Similarly, in a series of secondary analyses of Wheeler's estimates (1951), Dewey (1964) claims to find a number of discernible periodicities going back to 600 B.C. Another long-range study is Lee's (1931) analysis of Chinese internal wars from 221 B.C. to 1929; finding a recurrent cycle of about 800 years, with shorter cycles within, he fully anticipated the violence of the decades that followed. Given the broad range of the methods, as well as the diverse quality of the evidence used by our predecessors, we address ourselves to the point made in the most recent of the studies: "The possible effects of improved data are, of course, not known" (Denton and Phillips, 1968, p. 195).

In this search for regular fluctuations in the incidence of war, we will follow two separate approaches. In one, we will focus on the recurrent *outbreaks* of war in the various systems under investigation, and remain indifferent to other attributes of these wars such as their durations and the rate at which new participants enter and old participants leave them. These data on the frequency of war will be examined via two different statistical techniques: one will test for goodness of fit between the *observed* intervals of their onsets and the intervals that might be *expected* if they were quite random; the other will subject these intervals to a form of Fourier analysis known as spectral analysis. After analyzing these intervals between each successive war's beginning, we will shift to an approach which is more appropriate to phenomena which have not only a beginning, but which last long enough to show interesting fluctuations during their entire existence. There, we will apply the spectral analysis technique to the amount of war *underway*, year by year, for the entire century and a half.

FLUCTUATIONS IN THE ANNUAL AMOUNT OF WAR BEGUN

We begin here with an inquiry into the regularity of inter-war intervals in a variety of empirical settings. To what extent are the intervals between the beginnings of our 93 international wars equal in length? And if not equal, how nearly random is their distribution? If these intervals are indeed random, they should fit closely to the exponential Poisson density function $\phi(x) = \lambda e^{-\lambda x}$ (where $\lambda = 1/\bar{x}$, and $\bar{x}$ is the mean of the distribution of all intervals); thus the probability of any given interval falling between t_1 and t_2 is equal to $\lambda \int_{t_1}^{t_2} e^{-\lambda x}$. How close are the observed intervals to those predicted by the null model and found in such phenomena as the movement of vehicles past a given point (in moderate density traffic) or the emission of radioactive particles from a given source?

As Table 9.1 indicates, the intervals between the *onsets* of war come very close to the distribution predicted by the equation. That is, if we categorize our intervals on the basis of half-year units (with a half year or less as the shortest, 9 years as the longest interval between any two wars of *any* type, and 18.5 as the longest observed interval between the onset of any two *interstate* wars), we find that the observed distribution gives a very good fit to that which is predicted. Using the Chi-square test, we confirmed the randomness hypothesis in both cases at well above the critical .05 level of significance. Because an exponential Poisson distribution of intervals is always associated with a pure Poisson density distribution in the frequency of events

9.1 PREDICTED AND OBSERVED DISTRIBUTIONS OF INTER-WAR INTERVALS

Length of Interval in Six Month Units	All International Wars		Interstate Wars Only	
	Predicted	Observed	Predicted	Observed
1	.247	.231	.150	.208
2	.186	.275	.128	.104
3	.140	.131	.109	.104
4	.106	.099	.092	.125
5	.079	.088	.078	.146
6	.060	.044	.067	.063
7	.045	.044	.057	.021
8	.034	.029	.048	.000
9	.026	.033	.041	.021
10	.019	.000	.035	.042
11	.014	.000	.030	.021
12	.011	.011	.025	.042
13	.008	.000	.021	.021
14	.006	.000	.018	.021
15	.005	.000	.015	.021
16	.004	.000	.013	.000
17	.003	.000	.011	.021
18	.002	.011	—	—
37			.063	.021
	$x^2 = 13.55$; $p = >.05$		$x^2 = 11.95$; $p = >.05$	

per unit of time, these results fit nicely with Richardson's finding of a Poisson distribution in the number of wars occurring in each of the 110 years between 1820 and 1929.

We can also determine whether fluctuations in the amount of war occur in a cyclical fashion by correlating the amount of war beginning at each observation with the amount which began *k* observations earlier. Varying the lag factor, *k*, over a range of values from 1 to *m* would yield the autocorrelation or autocovariance function. These values would themselves be instructive as to the presence of periodicity in the series. However, any given autocorrelation coefficient will reflect the concurrent impact of several cycles in the series. If a given time series had known periodicities of 3, 4, and 6 years, we would find that the series exhibited a significant amount of autocorrelation at lag 12, although the apparent 12-year cycle was merely the concurrence of the shorter cycles. Each autocorrelation coefficient may reflect many cycles in the original series, and what is needed is a method of decomposing these coefficients in such a way as to reveal the underlying cycles that produce them.

Spectral analysis is such a method, and it may be used to decompose or "explain" either the autocorrelation function or autocovariance function, but in either case the substantive interpretation is the same. An analogy may be useful at this point to illustrate the utility of spectral analysis. If we sought to determine the color of a beam of light we would want to know the relative amounts of energy associated with different wavelengths of the electromagnetic spectrum. If we plotted the energy levels observed for an infinite number of wavelengths, the resulting continuous curve would be the spectral density function. The area under the curve would be equal to the total amount of energy emitted by the light source.

If the light were blue we would tend to find a sizeable proportion of the energy concentrated within a wavelength range of approximately 4500 to 5000 angstroms. This would be reflected as a peak in the spectral density function. In reality, however, we can only make a finite number of measurements for a relatively small number of wavelengths within a given band width (such as the visible portion of the spectrum) and estimate the function on the basis of these.

In the case of war we are trying to assess the impact of various cyclical factors of different frequencies on the variation in war. By taking measurements on a finite number of frequencies, we can estimate the spectral density function of war. The area under this curve will be proportional to the variance in the war series, and the general shape of the curve will reveal whether any range of frequencies dominates the variation in that series.

A flat spectral density function would indicate that all frequencies within the range investigated explain an equal amount of variation in the series. The existence of a peak, however, indicates that some frequencies account for a disproportionate amount of the variance.

The objective of spectral analysis is not to determine the strength of any particular cycle, but rather to estimate the general shape of the spectral density function underlying the autocovariance function. With these thoughts in mind, let us now turn to the consideration of the international war begun series.

To meet the assumption of stationarity implicit in spectral analysis, it is necessary to normalize the series given in Figure 9.2 by the size of the international system in each year and to detrend the series. When we subject this normalized series to spectral analysis with the longest cycle set at 40 years and the shortest at 2 years we produce the estimates and the approximating curve given in Figure 9.3.

The area under the curve in the figure is proportional to the variance in the series,

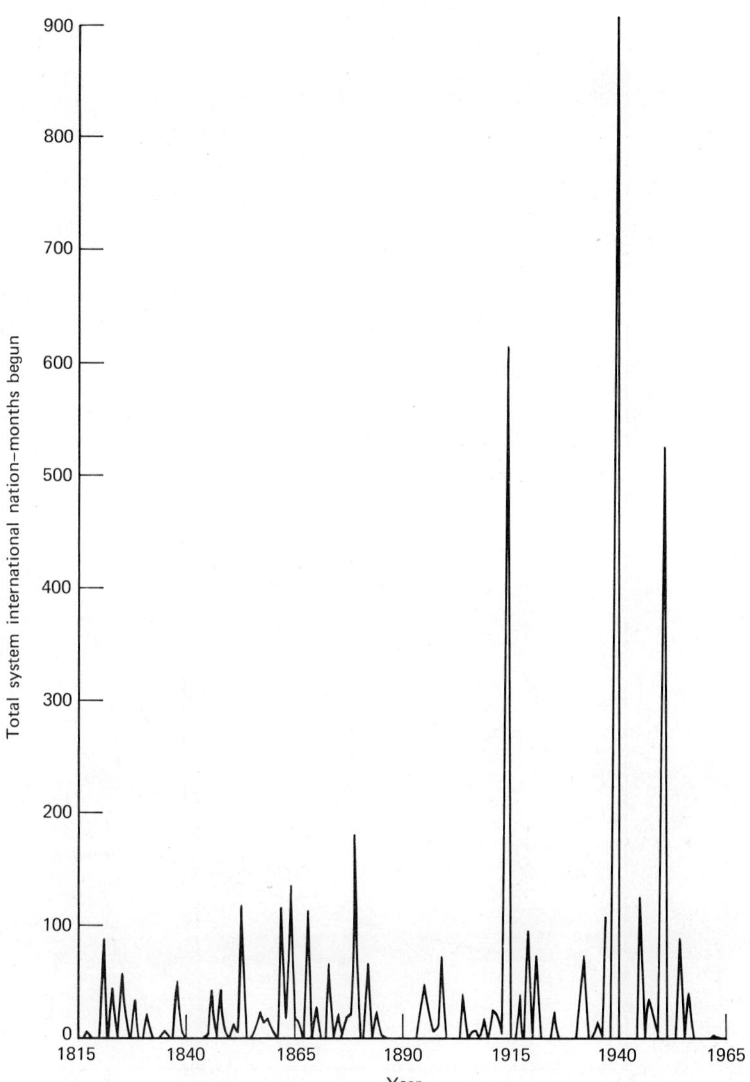

9.2 Annual amount of international war begun, 1816–1965.

and the flatness of the curve indicates that all cycles within the frequency band explain approximately the same amount of variance. The null hypothesis that the true spectrum is indeed flat was tested, and it could not be rejected at the .05 level of significance. Clearly there does not appear to be any periodicity of 40 years or less in international war begun.

Having found, via the exponential Poisson and spectral analysis methods, no evidence for the existence of periodicity in the incidence of war, can we safely conclude that such periodicity is merely a figment of the imagination of those who see pattern and regularity everywhere? Or have we overlooked some important point? As we indicated in introducing this section, one may look not only at data representing the annual amount of war *begun*, but also at the amount *underway*, and it is to those data which we must now turn before denying the existence of periodicity in the incidence of war.

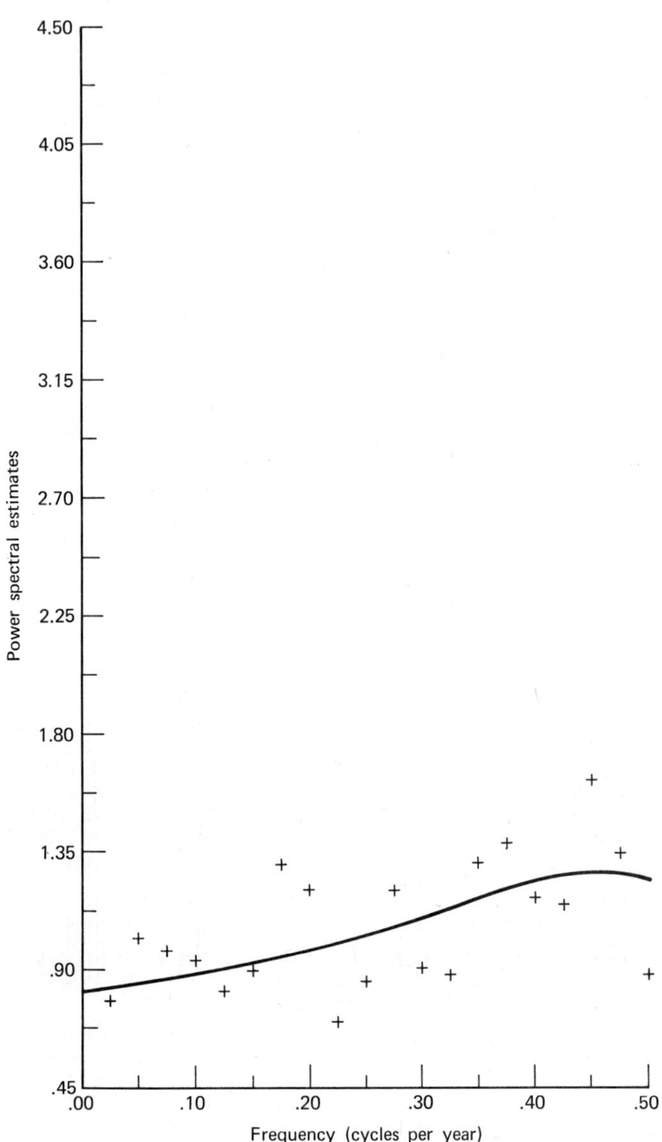

9.3 Graph of power spectral estimates of various frequencies for normalized nation-months of international war begun.

FLUCTUATIONS IN THE ANNUAL AMOUNT OF WAR UNDERWAY

Any search for periodicity in the incidence of war is likely to be informed by some theoretical framework which seeks to account for the hypothesized or observed periodicity. That framework is, in turn, quite likely to concern itself more with the amount of war that the system (or sub-system or nation) experienced *during each* of a series of years than with the amount that *began* at some fixed prior date. This, then, is one of the reasons for having computed and presented our war data in the underway as well as the onset and termination forms; it permits us to search for the existence of any

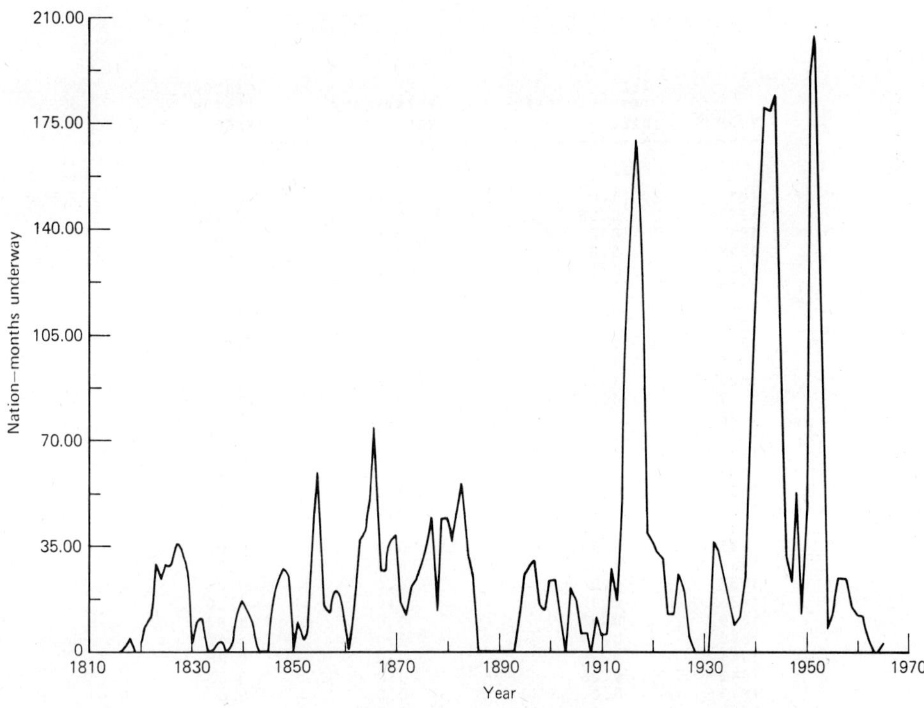

9.4 Annual amount of international war underway, 1816–1965.

fairly constant intervals from peak to peak and valley to valley in the longitudinal profile.

In this spectral analysis, we will again use the magnitude (nation month) rather than the severity (battle-connected death) figures; this is because they are readily and accurately normalized for system size, and because—as is evident from the earlier chapters—they correlate very strongly with the battle death figures.

We begin then with a graph very similar to that in Figure 9.2, but this time we show number of nation months of international war *underway* rather than *begun.* It is immediately apparent that we have a rather different longitudinal profile here. Instead of very sharp vertical rises and descents followed by long flat sections at the base line (for those years in which no war began), we have a profile of more continual fluctuations. This follows, of course, from the fact that while there were 80 years in which no wars *began,* there were only 24 years in which there was no war *underway.* In Table 9.5 we present, using data from Chapter Seven, the nation months of war underway (divided by system size for each year) for the amounts of international, interstate, and central system war.

When these underway data are subjected to the spectral analysis procedures outlined above, the results turn out to be appreciably different from those emerging from the onset data. As Figure 9.6 reveals, the spectral density curve is skewed toward the longer cycles (lower frequencies). The estimates for the 20- and 40-year cycles indicate that there is a peak in the true spectral density function in the vicinity of the frequencies .025 to .050. While we cannot say with certainty that war underway exhibits a 20- or 40-year cycle, we can say that this range of cycles is unusually powerful. A test of the hypothesis that the true spectrum is flat leads to its rejection at the .05 level of

9.5 - ANNUAL NATION MONTHS OF WAR UNDERWAY NORMALIZED BY SYSTEM SIZE

YEAR	ALL INTERNATIONAL WARS	INTERSTATE WARS	CENTRAL SYSTEM WARS
1816	0.0	0.0	0.0
1817	0.08	0.0	0.14
1818	0.22	0.0	0.39
1819	0.0	0.0	0.0
1820	0.0	0.0	0.0
1821	0.40	0.0	0.72
1822	0.52	0.0	0.92
1823	1.30	0.63	2.30
1824	1.04	0.0	1.85
1825	1.27	0.0	2.25
1826	1.20	0.0	2.22
1827	1.50	0.0	2.77
1828	1.36	0.66	2.44
1829	1.15	0.67	2.06
1830	0.11	0.0	0.19
1831	0.37	0.0	0.69
1832	0.42	0.0	0.78
1833	0.0	0.0	0.0
1834	0.0	0.0	0.0
1835	0.11	0.0	0.0
1836	0.13	0.0	0.0
1837	0.0	0.0	0.0
1838	0.10	0.0	0.20
1839	0.40	0.0	0.83
1840	0.55	0.0	1.15
1841	0.39	0.0	0.80
1842	0.28	0.0	0.63
1843	0.0	0.0	0.0
1844	0.0	0.0	0.0
1845	0.02	0.0	0.04
1846	0.50	0.44	0.15
1847	0.67	0.67	0.0
1848	0.75	0.57	1.65
1849	0.64	0.36	1.38
1850	0.0	0.0	0.0
1851	0.28	0.28	0.0
1852	0.08	0.06	0.07
1853	0.18	0.12	0.47
1854	1.05	1.05	2.81
1855	1.46	1.46	3.98
1856	0.35	0.35	0.81
1857	0.31	0.12	0.68
1858	0.49	0.0	1.33
1859	0.48	0.28	1.19
1860	0.27	0.27	0.40
1861	0.03	0.03	0.04
1862	0.44	0.44	0.57
1863	0.93	0.64	1.55
1864	1.03	0.90	1.78
1865	1.29	0.73	0.95
1866	1.92	1.30	1.36
1867	0.71	0.06	0.08
1868	0.79	0.0	0.18
1869	1.06	0.0	0.80
1870	1.16	0.69	1.53
1871	0.51	0.12	1.05
1872	0.39	0.0	0.80
1873	0.68	0.0	1.41
1874	0.77	0.0	1.60
1875	0.94	0.0	2.00
1876	1.12	0.0	2.40
1877	1.40	0.54	2.99
1878	0.38	0.01	0.76
1879	1.30	0.88	0.85
1880	1.30	1.06	0.48
1881	1.06	1.06	0.0
1882	1.37	1.03	0.69
1883	1.61	0.92	1.41
1884	0.88	0.38	1.42
1885	0.71	0.34	1.09
1886	0.0	0.0	0.0
1887	0.0	0.0	0.0
1888	0.0	0.0	0.0
1889	0.0	0.0	0.0
1890	0.0	0.0	0.0

9.5 - ANNUAL NATION MONTHS OF WAR UNDERWAY
NORMALIZED BY SYSTEM SIZE

YEAR	ALL INTERNATIONAL WARS	INTERSTATE WARS	CENTRAL SYSTEM WARS
1891	0.0	0.0	0.0
1892	0.0	0.0	0.0
1893	0.0	0.0	0.0
1894	0.28	0.26	0.04
1895	0.68	0.15	1.05
1896	0.74	0.0	1.52
1897	0.77	0.16	1.59
1898	0.36	0.18	0.56
1899	0.33	0.0	0.68
1900	0.57	0.0	1.20
1901	0.57	0.0	1.20
1902	0.26	0.0	0.55
1903	0.0	0.0	0.0
1904	0.50	0.50	1.08
1905	0.39	0.39	0.81
1906	0.13	0.13	0.0
1907	0.15	0.15	0.0
1908	0.0	0.0	0.0
1909	0.26	0.26	0.26
1910	0.12	0.12	0.12
1911	0.14	0.14	0.28
1912	0.64	0.64	1.25
1913	0.38	0.38	0.75
1914	0.94	0.94	1.80
1915	2.68	2.68	5.13
1916	3.32	3.32	6.36
1917	3.86	3.84	7.38
1918	3.01	2.76	5.34
1919	0.76	0.52	1.25
1920	0.59	0.39	
1921	0.52	0.39	
1922	0.49	0.30	
1923	0.19	0.0	
1924	0.19	0.0	
1925	0.42	0.0	
1926	0.34	0.0	
1927	0.08	0.0	
1928	0.0	0.0	
1929	0.0	0.0	
1930	0.0	0.0	
1931	0.01	0.01	
1932	0.56	0.56	
1933	0.49	0.49	
1934	0.36	0.36	
1935	0.25	0.25	
1936	0.13	0.13	
1937	0.18	0.18	
1938	0.36	0.36	
1939	1.03	1.03	
1940	1.91	1.91	
1941	2.62	2.62	
1942	3.40	3.40	
1943	3.43	3.43	
1944	3.23	3.23	
1945	1.52	1.45	
1946	0.47	0.0	
1947	0.34	0.0	
1948	0.74	0.26	
1949	0.17	0.01	
1950	0.59	0.43	
1951	2.57	2.41	
1952	2.65	2.49	
1953	1.55	1.39	
1954	0.09	0.0	
1955	0.14	0.0	
1956	0.28	0.03	
1957	0.27	0.0	
1958	0.27	0.0	
1959	0.17	0.0	
1960	0.11	0.0	
1961	0.11	0.0	
1962	0.04	0.02	
1963	0.0	0.0	
1964	0.0	0.0	
1965	0.03	0.03	

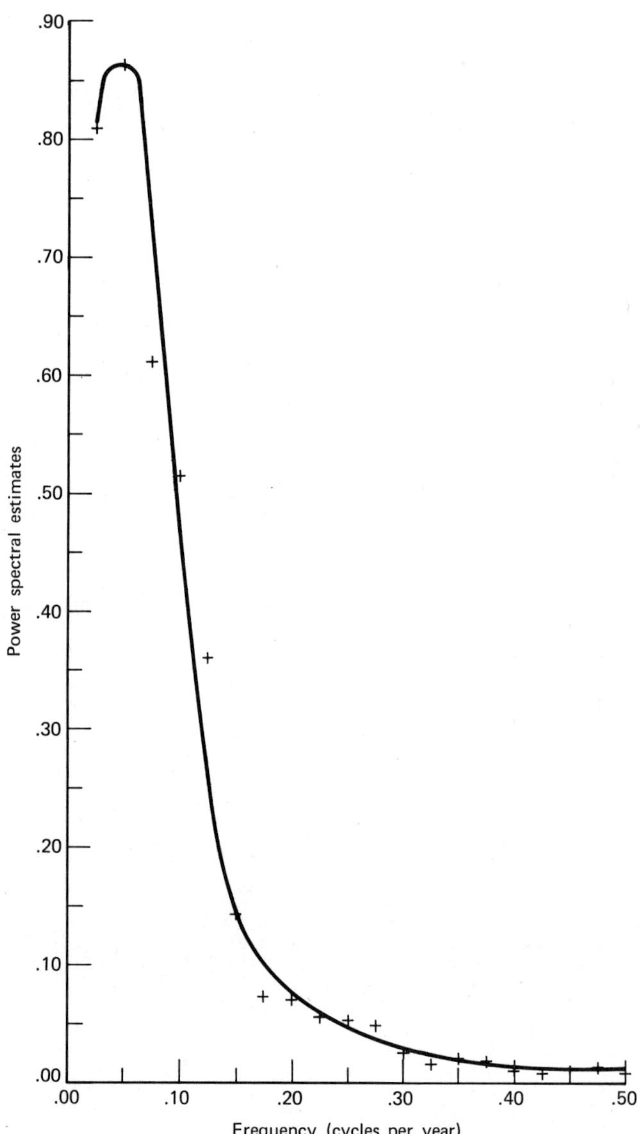

9.6 Graph of power spectral estimates of various frequencies for normalized nation-months of international war underway.

significance. This in turn leads us to conclude that there is some periodicity in international war underway.

Table 9.7 gives the results of similar analyses of interstate and central system wars as well as those for international war. The long cycle pattern seems to hold equally well for interstate wars only, and when we examine the more restricted domain of central system wars, it becomes even more pronounced.

In sum then, it seems clear that there does indeed exist one or more periodicities between 20 and 40 years in the fluctuations of the amount of war *underway* during the 150 years under study here.

9.7 POWER SPECTRAL ESTIMATES OF VARIOUS FREQUENCIES FOR NORMALIZED NATION MONTHS OF INTERNATIONAL, INTERSTATE, AND CENTRAL SYSTEM WAR UNDERWAY

Frequency (cycles per year)	Periodicity in Years (1.0/frequency)	International Wars (1816–1965)	Interstate Wars (1816–1965)	Central System Wars (1816–1919)
0.0		0.466	0.459	0.372
0.025	40.00	0.778	0.808	0.453
0.050	20.00	1.016	0.863	0.511
0.075	13.33	0.967	0.612	0.400
0.100	10.00	0.931	0.515	0.252
0.125	8.00	0.814	0.360	0.165
0.150	6.67	0.893	0.143	0.118
0.175	5.71	1.299	0.073	0.076
0.200	5.00	1.201	0.070	0.042
0.225	4.44	0.699	0.055	0.024
0.250	4.00	0.850	0.052	0.023
0.275	3.64	1.200	0.048	0.023
0.300	3.33	0.902	0.025	0.017
0.325	3.08	0.875	0.015	0.012
0.350	2.86	1.303	0.021	0.016
0.375	2.67	1.378	0.018	0.012
0.400	2.50	1.173	0.010	0.005
0.425	2.35	1.149	0.007	0.003
0.450	2.22	1.624	0.011	0.008
0.475	2.11	1.343	0.012	0.009
0.500	2.00	0.878	0.009	0.008

FLUCTUATIONS IN NATIONAL WAR EXPERIENCE INTERVALS

Up to this juncture, our concern has been with regularities in the flucutation of war for the international system as a whole. Such an approach, as we have readily acknowledged, may assume too much in the way of the interdependence of the nations comprising those systems. Even though we did find this fairly strong 20-year cycle in the amount of war underway in those empirical settings, it does not necessarily follow that the recurrences of war and the intervals between them are causally connected. We will, of course, be addressing ourselves to that question in the larger project, but in the interim it would make sense to shift our focus to the separate nations themselves. Thus, even though we will devote Chapter Eleven to purely national war experiences, we need to stop to examine the matter of periodicity at the national level of analysis here.

We are concerned only with *interstate* war experiences at this point; our later study will consider each nation's involvement in interstate, extra-systemic, and some level of *intra*-national conflict. We recognize here that participation in extra-systemic wars is *usually* at a much lower level, both of troop commitment and the resulting battle fatalities, and may, therefore, obscure any possible pattern of periodicity in interstate war involvement.

Our procedure is quite simple and straightforward. First, we turn to the master war list in Table 4.2, and for each nation we record the date on which it entered or left each interstate war. Then we compute the number of years (to the nearest half year) which intervene between each departure and the next entry in that nation's interstate war history. Finally, since the majority of nations participate in either no wars or only one (and therefore have no inter-war intervals) during their membership in the system, and since two wars would still give only one interval, we present these data only for the nations that fought in three or more interstate wars during the 1816–1965 period.

For those 19 nations, we list in Table 9.8 the number of interstate wars in which they did participate, and the number of years that elapsed between each of their war experiences. Recalling that these intervals run from the end of one war to the onset of the next (rather than onset to onset, as in the first of the systemic level analyses), we find our suspicions largely confirmed. A glance at the separate and average interval figures of the more war-prone nations indicates a very wide range of inter-war intervals. Even those nations with very frequent interstate war experience show little cyclical regularity. We might also note here that there was only one case of a nation's fighting two interstate wars simultaneously: Japan versus China, 1937–1941, and Japan versus Russia and Mongolia, 1939.

9.8 - INTER-WAR INTERVALS FOR NATIONS WHICH FOUGHT IN THREE OR MORE INTERSTATE WARS

CODE NO.	NATION	NO. OF WARS	INTER-WAR INTERVALS (IN YEARS)											MEAN
2	UNITED STATES	5	50.2	18.7	23.1	4.9								24.2
92	SALVADOR	3	21.1	0.6										10.8
200	ENGLAND	7	26.4	0.6	57.4	20.8	5.0	3.3						18.9
211	BELGIUM	3	21.5	10.6										16.1
220	FRANCE	12	3.9	21.5	4.7	3.2	2.8	3.4	13.3	29.1	20.8	5.4	3.3	10.1
230	SPAIN	5	35.9	5.6	31.9	10.9								21.1
255	GERMANY/PRUSSIA	6	14.6	1.9	4.0	43.4	20.8							16.9
300	AUSTRIA-HUNGARY	6	0.1	9.8	4.6	1.9	48.0							12.9
310	HUNGARY	3	21.9	11.8										16.8
325	ITALY/SARDINIA	10	5.8	3.2	1.2	0.0	5.4	45.2	2.6	16.9	4.1			9.4
345	YUGOSLAVIA/SERBIA	4	0.2	1.0	22.4									7.9
350	GREECE	7	15.4	0.2	3.9	0.5	18.0	9.7						8.0
355	BULGARIA	4	0.2	2.2	23.2									8.5
360	RUMANIA	4	3.1	1.3	21.9									8.8
365	RUSSIA	10	0.5	24.1	21.1	26.1	8.9	21.4	1.8	0.0	16.6			13.4
530	ETHIOPIA	3	4.7	9.8										7.3
640	TURKEY	11	0.5	24.1	21.1	19.1	14.4	0.0	0.2	1.2	0.5	28.0		10.9
710	CHINA	7	9.1	36.7	4.2	0.0	5.2	9.2						10.7
740	JAPAN	7	8.9	8.9	13.1	4.2	0.0	2.2						6.2

NOTE: 0.0 = A NATION LEFT ONE WAR AND ENTERED A NEW WAR ON THE SAME DAY (AS IN THE CASES OF CHINA AND JAPAN) OR LEFT ONE WAR AFTER STARTING A NEW WAR (AS IN THE CASE OF TURKEY).

There are, of course, two possible interpretations of the difference between systemic and national war periodicities. One is, as was suggested above, that there is indeed little interdependence among the system's members and that each nation (or small cluster of them) experiences its wars independently of the others. But the same data might equally support the inference that the system is sufficiently one (in terms of the interdependence of its component parts) that *it* reveals strong regularities irrespective of the interaction patterns of any specific nations. One criterion of system, as a matter of fact, is the extent to which the aggregation reveals pattern and regularity, despite randomness in the behavior of its components.

SUMMARY

The data and analyses presented in this chapter clearly show that we have only begun to scratch the surface of this fascinating and complex problem. As we indicated earlier, periodicity is one of the most important forms of regularity associated with the incidence of international violence, and one whose presence has important implications for its understanding and ultimate elimination. What have we found in this limited inquiry?

Looking at the larger international system first, the findings are far from consistent. On the one hand, there seems to be no uniformity in the intervals between the beginnings of successive wars during these 150 years; to the contrary, their distribution fits very closely to that predicted by the exponential Poisson model. But when we shift from the annual amount of war *beginning* to the amount *underway*, a rather strong periodicity emerges, with the dominant peaks about 20 years apart. This set of findings suggests not so much that discrete wars come and go with some regularity, but that, with *some* level of such violence almost always present, there are distinct and periodic fluctuations in the amount of that violence.

At least two possible sets of factors might account for this observed regularity. One, which would suggest that the finding might be spurious, is that the system size could have increased in sharp and clear steps, rather than quite incrementally. That is, if large numbers of new nations qualified for system membership at about the same time, and these bunchings occurred at intervals of 20 (or 40 or 60, etc.) years, that factor might possibly account for the pattern we discerned. As Table 2.2 makes clear, the accretion rate, while far from smooth, shows no such periodicity. A second, and more plausible element, might be the interaction effect resulting from systematic changes in: (a) the size of wartime partnerships; (b) the duration of the wars; and (c) the intervals between their onsets. Thus, even if none of these three factors shows any periodicity, it is nevertheless possible that their frequency distributions could well account for the periodicity in the amount of war underway. In a later paper, we hope to investigate this and similar relationships, but to do so now is beyond the task at hand.

Returning, then, to this observed periodicity, one possible inference we can draw is that we are no closer to getting at the causes or preconditions of war than before, but may only be closer to understanding the tempo of wars once they have begun. Our interpretation falls somewhere between these two views. That is, even though our periodicity pattern is largely a function of the fluctuations in the *amount* of war underway (in normalized nation months), this figure is also, by definition, partly dependent on fluctuations in the onset of war as well; wars must begin before they can produce high magnitude and severity levels. Furthermore, in the absence of evidence to the contrary, it seems prudent to assume that—despite certain obvious differences—the ecological and behavioral phenomena which produce the escalation and termination of war are essentially similar to those which produce war in the first place.

Shifting to more limited empirical domains, the pattern remains inconsistent. On the one hand, the 20-year periodicity is about as pronounced for interstate wars as for all international wars, and even more pronounced when we look only at central system wars. On the other hand, when we focus on the separate states themselves, no one of them reveals a particularly strong periodicity in its individual war experiences. Following the reasoning suggested in that context earlier, we take this—along with our other findings—as tentative evidence in support of the proposition that there is some underlying regularity in the incidence of war in the system, and that the identity of the specific states which experience that war is of minor consequence. But we must conclude this chapter on a highly tentative note, not only because the evidence is far from conclusive, but because of the inherently close connection between periodicity and a fuller understanding of the causes of these wars.

Chapter 10
Seasonal Concentrations in the Incidence of War

The importance of weather as a determinant of victory and defeat is well established in the folklore of military history. We are told that the Russian winter, for example, did as much to put Napoleon and Hitler to rout as the legions of the Czar and of Stalin. Similarly, once the northern Russian ports were frozen during the autumn of 1918, it was too late for the Americans to withdraw, with consequences for Soviet-American relations that continue to haunt us even now, a half century later.

Or consider the fact that many of Europe's statesmen were on vacation, avoiding the summer heat, when Archduke Franz Ferdinand was assassinated in June of 1914; to what extent could war have been averted had they been present in their capitals as the incident escalated into a crisis? Would the history of the twentieth century have been different had Gavrilo Princip fired the fatal shot in another month, instead of when British diplomats were at Ascot and the Kaiser was at Keil for the yacht races? And even if the chancelleries had been properly manned, the fact that July was a major harvesting month in Europe might well have played an inhibitory role.

Our concern here, then, is with the extent to which climate and season have determined not only the outcome of particular campaigns or wars, but how these variables may have influenced the timing, or even the occurrence, of wars. More specifically, we seek in this chapter to ascertain any regularities in the onset and termination of war that might be accounted for by season, climate, and the consequences of these considerations in national decision making. What might these considerations be?

First, before considering specific battlefield conditions, strategists pay attention to schedules for the planting and harvesting of crops. In the northern hemisphere, then, we can expect to find considerable reluctance to take men out of the fields and put them into combat if spring planting or fall harvesting (especially the latter) season is imminent. If the expectation is for a short war, decision makers may well delay the final confrontations until after a given seasonal activity is completed, hoping that most of the men will not only survive, but return home in time for the next upsurge in the need for manpower. Even if the hostilities are expected to continue for a year or more, the incentive to complete a final planting or harvesting can be quite powerful. These agricultural considerations will, of course, apply differentially across nations and across time, depending on the nature of the economy, demographic resources, the state of technology, and the potency of the military and political factors of the moment. Then, there are the myriad ways in which seasonal fluctuations may affect political and diplomatic activities. The willingness to move toward or away from war might well be affected by such seasonally determined factors as fiscal years, tax deadlines, elections, inaugurations, legislative recesses, and the like.

Second, there are the strategic and tactical considerations of war itself. Even in the twentieth century, such variables as temperature, precipitation, visibility, and atmospheric disturbance of communications can markedly affect the success of a campaign. Just as rainfall made the flintlock almost impossible to fire, the monsoon season in Vietnam today imposes serious (if asymmetric) constraints on the warring parties. We think, likewise, of the closing of northern ports during European winters, the importance of fog in many coastwise naval operations (even after radar's invention), the use of cloud cover for (or against) aerial activities, the crossing of ice-covered rivers and lakes, the bogging down of men, horses, and weaponry in mud, and the varying effect of darkness on guerrilla versus conventional forces.

In this volume, however, we cannot examine the testing of any specific hypotheses regarding the impact of seasonal phenomena on the incidence of war. They are too many, too complex, and too interrelated to examine in detail here. What we can do, however, is provide that body of data without which they could not be examined: the seasons and months which, over different time periods, have seen the most and least war begin and end.

As to coding procedures and format, a few preliminary comments are in order. First, in order to treat the northern and southern hemispheres together, we have converted all of the latter's months into their equivalents in the former; thus July in the southern hemisphere is treated as if it were January, August becomes February, and so on. Three wars were fought in and by southern hemisphere nations, and the dates were converted: Peruvian-Bolivian (1841), La Plata (1851–1852), and La Plata (1864–1870). However, four wars involve nations of both hemispheres: World War II, Korean, Ecuadorian-Colombian, and Spanish-Chilean. We decided to treat all four as northern hemisphere wars to minimize the number of date conversions. Since World War II and the Korean War were largely fought in and by northern hemisphere nations, our decision requires little explanation, but the other two were more complicated. Ecuador and Colombia straddle the equator, with parts of each in both hemispheres; we left the dates for Colombia (lying mostly in the northern hemisphere) unchanged, but converted the dates for Ecuador, which lies mostly south of the equator. The Spanish-Chilean war, which was fought *in* the southern hemisphere, involved both Peru and Chile from that region, against Spain from the northern hemisphere. Our decision to call the war a northern hemisphere war (therefore converting dates for Peru and Chile) was based on the fact that Spain initiated the war and was, from our viewpoint, a member of the more active and powerful sub-set of nations, the Central System.

In adopting this strategy we do not mean to suggest that winter in Brazil from June through September is exactly the same as winter in England from September to March. Nor do we insist that there is much difference between January and June in either equatorial or arctic climes. But since most of the war participants inhabit the northern and southern temperate zones, we feel there is enough similarity between respective winters and summers to justify the comparison.

Another point regarding seasons concerns the dates used to mark the breaks between them. We follow the conventional mode and define them as follows: winter, 22 December–21 March; spring, 22 March–21 June; summer, 22 June–21 September; and autumn, 22 September–21 December. When we collapse monthly figures into seasonal ones, therefore, we do not merely total up the three most appropriate months (such as October, November, and December for autumn) but actually go back to the accepted equinoctial dates as our cutting points.

Third, since a major assumption in this seasonal inquiry is that technological innovation in the fields of transport and weaponry particularly may gradually erode the importance of weather, geography, and distance, we define three different technological periods of approximately a half century each. Thus, many of our onset and termination figures are presented separately for these periods: 1816–1871, 1872–1919, and 1920–1965.

Fourth, the reader should be alerted to the special coding problem created by the wars that were interrupted by truces that occasionally extended across given months and seasons. Whereas we did not include periods of interrupted combat that lasted for more than a month, when computing each war's duration and magnitude; here we deviate partially from that rule. That is, we still treat each war as a single episode, but are indifferent to the length of any truce that may interrupt it when computing our seasonal distributions. Of course, a more detailed inquiry into the effects of seasonal phenomena might well want to take special note of the timing and duration of such interruptions of hostilities. Thus, the Austro-Sardinian and Schleswig-Holstein wars of 1848–1849 are both treated as single wars with only one onset and one termination date despite seven month truces; similarly, the Second Syrian war of 1839–1840 (an extra-systemic war) despite a 14-month truce, is treated as a single episode. Three other briefer interruptions should also be noted: Second Schleswig-Holestein, 1864 (2 months); Palestine, 1948–1949 (3 months); and Second British-Afghan, 1878–1880 (4 months).

Finally, it should be noted that this chapter is long on raw data and short on statistical analyses. That is, while we present a very large number of seasonal and monthly frequency distributions, we did not consider it useful to compute deviations from randomness. This is partly because these deviations are visually quite apparent when they do exist, and partly because—with the many cells and the somewhat arbitrary nature of the division between seasons and between months—it would convey more precision than is justified. On the other hand, every row of distributions is followed not only by a total figure for the variable, the historical period, and the class of war under examination, but by a mean for that row's entries. The *totals* are presented in order to maximize the frequency with which the user is provided with the important gross figures on the incidence of war, and also to give us ample opportunities for checking the accuracy of our multitudinous entries. The *means,* of course, provide a base line against which deviations above or below may be visually estimated, and also give a head start to those who may want to compute such deviations and compare them with random distributions.

With these preliminary points out of the way, we can now turn to the various compilations by which any seasonal concentration in the onset or termination of war might be uncovered.

CONCENTRATIONS IN THE ONSET OF WAR

As a first step in the search for any seasonal concentrations in the onset of war, we look at the most general and summary picture. Tables 10.1 to 10.3 show the number of international, interstate, and extra-systemic wars begun in each of the four seasons, plus the number of nation months and battle deaths (in thousands) which resulted from those wars. The simple frequency counts are given first, since, on balance, they offer the most valid and useful indicator here; that is, our main concern is the number of times that decisions regarding war, in which seasonal considerations might have played a part, were taken. Following the rows in which the figures for our entire 150-year span are given, we show how they differ in each of the three subperiods (1816–1871, 1872–1919, and 1920–1965). And because the high battle death figures from the World Wars might create a strong "outlier effect," we end up with the bottom row, showing these data for the entire time span, but with the two World War figures omitted.

Looking then at the seasonal distributions in the onset of the three classes of war in terms of frequency, magnitude, and severity, what sort of pattern emerges? In terms of the sheer frequency of war, and ignoring severity and magnitude, it is clear that the spring and autumn months are the ones which see the heaviest concentration of war beginnings, both within and without the interstate system. That pattern seems to hold most strongly for the earliest period (17 in autumn and 15 in spring, and only 4 each in winter and summer for all wars) but is less marked in the second period; the most modern of the periods, however, shows a strong trend toward autumn, with 10 of the 21 wars between 1920 and 1965 beginning in that season.

10.1 - SEASONAL DISTRIBUTIONS IN ONSET OF INTERNATIONAL WAR

	WINTER 22DEC-21MAR	SPRING 22MAR-21JUNE	SUMMER 22JUNE-21SEPT	AUTUMN 22SEPT-21DEC	MEAN	TOTAL
NUMBER OF INTERNATIONAL WARS BEGUN, 1816-1965	12	29	17	35	23.2	93
1816-1871	4	15	4	17	10.0	40
1872-1919	7	10	7	8	8.0	32
1920-1965	1	4	6	10	5.2	21
NATION MONTHS OF INTERNATICNAL WAR BEGUN, 1816-1965	389.2	897.1	2397.8	848.4	1133.1	4532.5
1816-1871	47.2	510.5	96.5	405.7	265.0	1059.9
1872-1919	305.3	262.6	708.1	156.3	358.1	1432.3
1920-1965	36.7	124.0	1593.2	286.4	510.1	2040.3
BATTLE DEATHS FROM INTERNATIONAL WARS BEGUN, 1816-1965	270.8	927.4	27034.0	957.5	7297.4	29189.7
1816-1871	25.8	386.3	263.0	443.4	279.6	1118.5
1872-1919	205.0	382.6	8674.8	195.0	2364.3	9457.4
1920-1965	40.0	158.5	18096.2	319.1	4653.5	18613.8
BATTLE DEATHS EXCLUDING WORLD WARS	270.8	927.4	3313.9	957.5	1367.4	5469.6

10.2 - SEASONAL DISTRIBUTIONS IN ONSET OF INTERSTATE WAR

	WINTER 22DEC-21MAR	SPRING 22MAR-21JUNE	SUMMER 22JUNE-21SEPT	AUTUMN 22SEPT-21DEC	MEAN	TOTAL
NUMBER OF INTERSTATE WARS BEGUN, 1816-1965	6	19	10	15	12.5	50
1816-1871	2	9	2	7	5.0	20
1872-1919	4	7	4	2	4.2	17
1920-1965	0	3	4	6	3.2	13
NATION MONTHS OF INTERSTATE WAR BEGUN, 1816-1965	245.4	511.8	2172.2	265.4	798.7	3194.8
1816-1871	24.0	259.4	28.2	160.4	118.0	472.0
1872-1919	221.4	148.6	645.0	45.8	265.2	1060.8
1920-1965	0.0	103.8	1499.0	59.2	415.5	1662.0
BATTLE DEATHS FRCM INTERSTATE WARS BEGUN, 1816-1965	152.8	770.9	26893.0	590.6	7101.8	28407.3
1816-1871	5.8	243.8	188.5	282.4	180.1	720.5
1872-1919	147.0	370.1	8641.3	102.0	2315.1	9260.4
1920-1965	0.0	157.0	18063.2	206.2	4606.6	18426.4
BATTLE DEATHS EXCLUDING WORLD WARS	152.8	770.9	3172.9	590.6	1171.8	4687.2

10.3 - SEASONAL DISTRIBUTIONS IN ONSET OF EXTRA-SYSTEMIC WAR

	WINTER 22DEC-21MAR	SPRING 22MAR-21JUNE	SUMMER 22JUNE-21SEPT	AUTUMN 22SEPT-21DEC	MEAN	TOTAL
NUMBER OF EXTRA-SYSTEMIC WARS BEGUN, 1816-1965	6	10	7	20	10.7	43
1816-1871	2	6	2	10	5.0	20
1872-1919	3	3	3	6	3.7	15
1920-1965	1	1	2	4	2.0	8
NATION MONTHS OF EXTRA-SYSTEMIC WAR BEGUN, 1816-1965	143.8	385.3	225.6	583.0	334.4	1337.7
1816-1871	23.2	251.1	68.3	245.3	147.0	587.9
1872-1919	83.9	114.0	63.1	110.5	92.9	371.5
1920-1965	36.7	20.2	94.2	227.2	94.6	378.3
BATTLE DEATHS FROM EXTRA-SYSTEMIC WARS BEGUN, 1816-1965	118.0	156.5	141.0	366.9	195.6	782.4
1816-1871	20.0	142.5	74.5	161.0	99.5	398.0
1872-1919	58.0	12.5	33.5	93.0	49.3	197.0
1920-1965	40.0	1.5	33.0	112.9	46.8	187.4

Does the spring and autumn concentration hold when we shift from the frequency of war to the number of *nation months* begun? Examining all international wars as well as the two sub-types, we find a much less clear picture. That is, more nation months of extra-systemic wars (at least in the first two periods) began in spring and autumn, but summer clearly leads as the season for beginning interstate wars of high magnitude. On the other hand, this deviation is largely accounted for by the more than 2000 nation months resulting from the World Wars and the Korean War.

As to the number of *battle deaths* incurred during the wars that began in each of the four seasons, we find that summer onset figures are not solely a function of the World Wars. That is, even without the more than 23 million battle deaths resulting from those conflicts, summer is the season in which most of the system's blood-letting has begun, with spring and autumn far behind. If, however, we return to the earliest of our three periods, we find that spring and autumn again show the heaviest concentration. A number of plausible explanations for these findings come to mind, but because these rough breakdowns may conceal some important differences, we defer that discussion until more detailed figures have been presented.

These more detailed presentations are nothing more than the original onset data which we combined in order to show the *seasonal* overview, now broken down into *monthly* frequencies. The format is the same as that used in the three seasonal tables, and once again shows all international wars first, followed by separate treatment of the 50 interstate and 43 extra-systemic wars (Tables 10.4–10.6). The operative question here is whether the longer time intervals (each season being three months) concealed any pattern that emerges with the use of the shorter observation intervals.

As to the frequency measure, we immediately see that April and October account for the concentration of war beginnings in spring and autumn. This holds fairly well for interstate wars in all three of the historical periods, but pretty well disappears for the imperial and colonial (extra-systemic) wars. Shifting to magnitude (measured in terms of nation months of war begun), April and October give way to June, July, and September. But the World Wars are again the key contributors, and if we look at the first period only (or all periods, but excluding the 1914 and 1939 holocausts), April

10.4 - MONTHLY DISTRIBUTIONS IN ONSET OF INTERNATIONAL WAR

PERIOD	JAN	FEB	MAR	APR	MAY	JUN	JUL	AUG	SEP	OCT	NOV	DEC	MEAN	TOTALS
NUMBER OF INTERNATIONAL WARS BEGUN														
ALL YEARS 1816-1965	2	8	6	10	8	6	10	2	7	18	9	7	7.7	93
1816-1871	1	2	2	6	3	2	3	0	4	11	4	2	3.3	40
1872-1919	1	6	2	4	3	2	4	1	2	2	2	3	2.7	32
1920-1965	0	0	2	0	2	2	3	1	1	5	3	2	1.7	21
NATION MONTHS OF INTERNATIONAL WAR BEGUN														
ALL YEARS 1816-1965	20.6	318.7	217.8	254.8	221.1	633.8	945.1	19.2	1000.0	418.2	282.2	201.0	377.7	4532.5
1816-1871	14.9	19.1	94.5	193.3	78.0	20.2	96.4	0.0	59.4	332.7	145.1	6.3	88.3	1059.9
1872-1919	5.7	299.6	66.4	61.5	111.1	27.8	648.3	16.0	65.0	52.0	19.4	59.5	119.4	1432.3
1920-1965	0.0	0.0	56.9	0.0	32.0	585.8	200.4	3.2	875.6	33.5	117.7	135.2	170.0	2040.3
BATTLE DEATHS FROM INTERNATIONAL WARS BEGUN														
ALL YEARS 1816-1965	8.5	221.0	72.5	492.2	103.5	2140.8	9816.1	21.8	15284.8	566.6	235.4	226.5	2432.5	29189.7
1816-1871	5.0	19.5	24.0	181.7	23.5	46.1	203.8	0.0	80.5	404.9	123.0	6.5	93.2	1118.5
1872-1919	3.5	201.5	7.0	310.5	53.0	72.6	8579.3	15.0	40.0	104.0	6.0	65.0	788.1	9457.4
1920-1965	0.0	0.0	41.5	0.0	27.0	2022.1	1033.0	6.8	15164.3	57.7	106.4	155.0	1551.2	18613.8

10.5 - MONTHLY DISTRIBUTIONS IN CNSET OF INTERSTATE WAR

PERIOD	JAN	FEB	MAR	APR	MAY	JUN	JUL	AUG	SEP	OCT	NOV	DEC	MEAN	TOTALS
NUMBER OF INTERSTATE WARS BEGUN														
ALL YEARS 1816-1871	1	5	2	9	5	5	4	2	3	11	2	1	4.2	50
1816-1871	1	1	1	6	1	1	1	0	1	6	1	0	1.7	20
1872-1919	0	4	1	3	2	2	2	1	1	1	0	0	1.4	17
1920-1965	0	0	0	0	2	2	1	1	1	4	1	1	1.1	13
NATION MONTHS OF INTERSTATE WAR BEGUN														
ALL YEARS 1816-1871	13.2	232.2	10.6	229.1	162.2	628.1	758.0	19.2	902.2	199.0	7.8	33.2	266.2	3194.8
1816-1871	13.2	10.8	9.4	193.3	42.2	14.5	27.0	0.0	1.2	159.4	1.0	0.0	39.3	472.0
1872-1919	0.0	221.4	1.2	35.8	88.0	27.8	624.8	16.0	25.4	20.4	0.0	0.0	88.4	1060.8
1920-1965	0.0	0.0	0.0	0.0	32.0	585.8	106.2	3.2	875.6	19.2	6.8	33.2	138.5	1662.0
BATTLE DEATHS FROM INTERSTATE WARS BEGUN														
ALL YEARS 1816-1871	1.3	151.5	10.0	487.7	95.0	2130.8	9753.3	21.8	15185.3	419.6	91.0	60.0	2367.3	28407.3
1816-1871	1.3	4.5	9.0	181.7	17.0	36.1	187.5	0.0	1.0	281.4	1.0	0.0	60.0	720.5
1872-1919	0.0	147.0	1.0	306.0	51.0	72.6	8565.8	15.0	20.0	82.0	0.0	0.0	771.7	9260.4
1920-1965	0.0	0.0	0.0	0.0	27.0	2022.1	1000.0	6.8	15164.3	56.2	90.0	60.0	1535.5	18426.4

10.6 - MONTHLY DISTRIBUTIONS IN ONSET OF EXTRA-SYSTEMIC WAR

PERIOD	JAN	FEB	MAR	APR	MAY	JUN	JUL	AUG	SEP	OCT	NOV	DEC	MEAN	TOTALS
NUMBER OF EXTRA-SYSTEMIC WARS BEGUN														
ALL YEARS 1816-1871	2	3	4	2	4	1	5	0	4	6	6	6	3.6	43
1816-1871	1	1	1	1	3	1	1	0	3	4	2	2	1.7	20
1872-1919	1	2	1	1	1	0	2	0	1	1	2	3	1.2	15
1920-1965	0	0	2	0	0	0	2	0	0	1	2	1	0.7	8
NATION MONTHS OF EXTRA-SYSTEMIC WAR BEGUN														
ALL YEARS 1816-1871	20.6	86.5	207.2	26.7	182.4	5.7	173.9	0.0	97.8	218.2	150.9	167.8	111.5	1337.7
1816-1871	14.9	8.3	85.1	1.0	159.3	5.7	56.2	0.0	58.2	172.3	20.6	6.3	49.0	587.9
1872-1919	5.7	78.2	65.2	25.7	23.1	0.0	23.5	0.0	39.6	31.6	19.4	59.5	31.0	371.5
1920-1965	0.0	0.0	56.9	0.0	0.0	0.0	94.2	0.0	0.0	14.3	110.9	102.0	31.5	378.3
BATTLE DEATHS FROM EXTRA-SYSTEMIC WARS BEGUN														
ALL YEARS 1816-1871	8.5	69.5	62.5	5.5	118.5	10.0	61.5	0.0	99.5	146.0	34.4	166.5	65.2	782.4
1816-1871	5.0	15.0	15.0	1.0	116.5	10.0	15.0	0.0	79.5	122.5	12.0	6.5	33.2	398.0
1872-1919	3.5	54.5	6.0	4.5	2.0	0.0	13.5	0.0	20.0	22.0	6.0	65.0	16.4	197.0
1920-1965	0.0	0.0	41.5	0.0	0.0	0.0	33.0	0.0	0.0	1.5	16.4	95.0	15.6	187.4

and October continue near the top as propitious months for the beginning of large and long interstate wars.

Looking at severity in battle deaths, the same general configuration seems to hold. For all international wars in all three periods, September ranks first, followed by July and June; among interstate wars this ordering is particularly strong, again in large measure as a result of the World Wars. But the extra-systemic wars seem to favor no particular month in frequency, magnitude, or severity.

So far, then, the general impression is that most wars begin in the spring month of April and the autumn month of October, but that the longer and bloodier ones begin in July and September. Is that impression borne out when we subdivide our 93 wars by their *duration* and then examine the frequency distributions? Looking at Table 10.7 and all international wars, it would seem only partially so. Combining the first three rows (durations of one year or less), April and October are again the leaders, but of the 42 wars that did last longer than one year, there is a much more even distribution, with 6 each in May and July, and 5 each in September and October. Leaving aside the extra-systemic wars (which show almost no discernible concentration) seems, moreover, to make little difference. The shorter interstate wars remain concentrated in April and October, while the longer ones show no significant tendency to begin in any particular month or season.

Rather than try to interpret these onset of war concentrations by themselves, it might be more useful to delay any further discussion until we have also examined the seasonal concentrations in the termination of international wars.

10.7 - MONTHLY DISTRIBUTIONS IN ONSET OF WARS OF VARYING DURATION

DURATION IN MONTHS	JAN	FEB	MAR	APR	MAY	JUN	JUL	AUG	SEP	OCT	NOV	DEC	MEAN	TOTALS
INTERNATIONAL														
.1 - 3	0	1	1	3	1	2	1	1	1	4	2	1	1.5	18
3.1 - 6	1	2	1	2	2	1	0	0	0	4	1	1	1.2	15
6.1 - 12	1	1	0	3	0	1	2	1	1	4	2	2	1.5	18
OVER 12	1	4	4	3	6	2	6	0	5	5	3	3	3.5	42
INTERSTATE														
.1 - 3	0	1	1	2	1	2	0	1	1	4	1	0	1.2	14
3.1 - 6	0	2	1	2	2	0	0	0	0	3	1	0	0.9	11
6.1 - 12	1	0	0	3	0	1	2	1	0	3	0	0	0.9	11
OVER 12	0	2	0	2	2	2	2	0	2	1	0	1	1.2	14
EXTRA-SYSTEMIC														
.1 - 3	0	0	0	1	0	0	1	0	0	0	1	1	0.3	4
3.1 - 6	1	0	0	0	0	1	0	0	0	1	0	1	0.3	4
6.1 - 12	0	1	0	0	0	0	0	0	1	1	2	2	0.6	7
OVER 12	1	2	4	1	4	0	4	0	3	4	3	2	2.3	28

CONCENTRATIONS IN THE TERMINATION OF WAR

If weather, terrain, crops, and the like have any impact on the time of year in which national elites "decide" to go to war, we might also expect similar considerations to be operative in decisions to terminate wars. In order to examine this side of the picture, then, we reproduce the same types of data as before, but for distributions in the *termination* of different types and lengths of war.

We begin, as before, with the general seasonal breakdown, and then proceed to a consideration of the month-by-month figures. In Tables 10.8 to 10.10, we show the

10.8 - SEASONAL DISTRIBUTIONS IN TERMINATION OF INTERNATIONAL WAR

	WINTER 22DEC-21MAR	SPRING 22MAR-21JUNE	SUMMER 22JUNE-21SEPT	AUTUMN 22SEPT-21DEC	MEAN	TOTAL
NUMBER OF INTERNATIONAL WARS ENDING, 1816-1965	19	30	21	23	23.2	93
1816-1871	11	11	9	8	9.7	39
1872-1919	3	12	9	7	7.7	31
1920-1965	5	7	3	8	5.7	23
NATION MONTHS OF INTERNATIONAL WAR ENDING, 1816-1965	711.8	825.3	1836.0	1159.4	1133.1	4532.5
1816-1871	374.2	243.2	237.4	93.0	236.9	947.8
1872-1919	169.3	229.8	196.4	827.0	355.6	1422.5
1920-1965	168.3	352.3	1402.2	239.4	540.5	2162.2
BATTLE DEATHS FROM INTERNATIONAL WARS ENDING, 1816-1965	1089.2	655.1	17678.0	9767.4	7297.4	29189.7
1816-1871	519.7	65.5	372.1	61.2	254.6	1018.5
1872-1919	405.0	211.6	230.5	8610.3	2364.3	9457.4
1920-1965	164.5	378.0	17075.4	1095.9	4678.5	18713.8
BATTLE DEATHS EXCLUDING WORLD WARS	874.7	353.1	2326.2	1133.2	1171.8	4687.2

10.9 - SEASONAL DISTRIBUTIONS IN TERMINATION OF INTERSTATE WAR

	WINTER 22DEC-21MAR	SPRING 22MAR-21JUNE	SUMMER 22JUNE-21SEPT	AUTUMN 22SEPT-21DEC	MEAN	TOTAL
NUMBER OF INTERSTATE WARS ENDING, 1816-1965	9	13	15	13	12.5	50
1816-1871	6	3	7	4	5.0	20
1872-1919	1	7	5	3	4.0	16
1920-1965	2	3	3	6	3.5	14
NATION MONTHS OF INTERSTATE WAR ENDING, 1816-1965	360.5	246.7	1570.4	1017.2	798.7	3194.8
1816-1871	316.7	36.6	101.8	16.9	118.0	472.0
1872-1919	17.6	90.7	66.4	803.5	244.5	978.2
1920-1965	26.2	119.4	1402.2	196.8	436.1	1744.6
BATTLE DEATHS FROM INTERSTATE WARS ENDING, 1816-1965	874.7	353.1	17490.5	9689.0	7101.8	28407.3
1816-1871	491.7	20.0	202.6	6.2	180.1	720.5
1872-1919	285.0	123.1	212.5	8589.8	2302.6	9210.4
1920-1965	98.0	210.0	17075.4	1093.0	4619.1	18476.4
BATTLE DEATHS EXCLUDING WORLD WARS	874.7	353.1	2326.2	1133.2	1171.8	4687.2

10.10 - SEASONAL DISTRIBUTIONS IN TERMINATION OF EXTRA-SYSTEMIC WAR

	WINTER 22DEC-21MAR	SPRING 22MAR-21JUNE	SUMMER 22JUNE-21SEPT	AUTUMN 22SEPT-21DEC	MEAN	TOTAL
NUMBER OF EXTRA-SYSTEMIC WARS ENDING, 1816-1965	10	17	6	10	10.7	43
1816-1871	5	8	2	4	4.7	19
1872-1919	2	5	4	4	3.7	15
1920-1965	3	4	0	2	2.2	9
NATION MONTHS OF EXTRA-SYSTEMIC WAR ENDING, 1816-1965	351.3	578.6	265.6	142.2	334.4	1337.7
1816-1871	57.5	206.6	135.6	76.1	118.9	475.8
1872-1919	151.7	139.1	130.0	23.5	111.1	444.3
1920-1965	142.1	232.9	0.0	42.6	104.4	417.6
BATTLE DEATHS FROM EXTRA-SYSTEMIC WARS ENDING, 1816-1965	214.5	302.0	187.5	78.4	195.6	782.4
1816-1871	28.0	45.5	169.5	55.0	74.5	298.0
1872-1919	120.0	88.5	18.0	20.5	61.8	247.0
1920-1965	66.5	168.0	0.0	2.9	59.3	237.4

amounts of war that ended in each season for all international wars, and then interstate and extra-systemic ones separately. In terms of all international wars, spring is the season in which most of them terminate, but with this pattern holding only for the second historical period. This effect is, however, mostly a consequence of the extra-systemic wars, with 17 of the 43 ending in the spring; the interstate wars, on the other hand, show very little in the way of a pronounced pattern, with winter the only season in which fewer than 12 wars ended.

In terms of the magnitude and severity indicators, spring again leads for the termination of colonial and imperial wars and gives way to summer (whether we include the World War figures or not), when interstate wars are our concern.

Shifting to the more discriminating month-by-month breakdowns, as shown in Tables 10.11 to 10.13, we find that the large number of wars ending in March (15) account for the high spring concentration. Looking at nation month and battle death figures, the earlier effect of the extra-systemic wars is diluted, since they generally lead to fewer casualties and, because they have fewer participants, fewer nation months as well. Thus, for all wars and for interstate ones, August, November, and July are the months that see the end of the largest amounts of war over the entire period. But it is well worth noting, once more, how much of this effect is the result of longer and bloodier wars of the more recent period.

As with the onset figures, let us briefly examine the effect of war durations on these distributions. It appears that the shortest wars (3 months or less) had the greatest tendency to end in July and November, but as we look at those lasting a year or more, we find that 7 months all saw 4 or more terminations. And when we discriminate between interstate and extra-systemic wars, the only noticeably high concentration is July for the ending of very short interstate hostilities, coupled with a more diffused pattern for the extra-systemic ones. This table also serves to remind us that even though wars of this latter type are of less magnitude and severity for the system members than are interstate ones, they have a strong tendency to last considerably longer.

10.11 - MONTHLY DISTRIBUTIONS IN TERMINATION OF INTERNATIONAL WAR

PERIOD	JAN	FEB	MAR	APR	MAY	JUN	JUL	AUG	SEP	OCT	NOV	DEC	MEAN	TOTALS
NUMBER OF INTERNATIONAL WARS ENDING														
ALL YEARS 1816-1965	4	7	15	9	7	7	10	4	7	9	7	7	7.7	93
1816-1871	1	6	9	4	1	2	5	1	2	3	3	2	3.2	39
1872-1919	1	1	2	5	3	2	4	2	3	4	1	3	2.6	31
1920-1965	2	0	4	0	3	3	1	1	2	2	3	2	1.9	23
NATION MONTHS OF INTERNATIONAL WAR ENDING														
ALL YEARS 1816-1965	57.7	356.0	540.9	216.2	197.1	265.3	625.4	905.9	172.4	209.5	633.9	352.2	377.7	4532.5
1816-1871	6.4	243.9	336.6	129.6	16.8	19.8	55.2	12.1	34.6	56.8	21.3	14.7	79.0	947.8
1872-1919	17.6	112.1	33.0	86.6	60.9	49.3	56.2	18.2	122.0	47.7	607.8	211.1	118.5	1422.5
1920-1965	33.7	0.0	171.3	0.0	119.4	196.2	514.0	875.6	15.8	105.0	4.8	126.4	180.2	2162.2
BATTLE DEATHS FROM INTERNATIONAL WARS ENDING														
ALL YEARS 1816-1965	295.5	345.8	638.2	168.5	136.0	250.6	2032.9	15244.8	296.8	128.1	8604.0	1048.5	2432.5	29189.7
1816-1871	1.0	245.8	418.2	24.5	1.0	5.0	71.3	59.5	131.0	38.2	12.0	11.0	84.9	1018.5
1872-1919	285.0	100.0	25.0	144.0	26.0	16.6	69.5	21.0	140.0	38.5	8555.8	36.0	788.1	9457.4
1920-1965	9.5	0.0	195.0	0.0	109.0	229.0	1892.1	15164.3	25.8	51.4	36.2	1001.5	1559.5	18713.8

10.12 - MONTHLY DISTRIBUTIONS IN TERMINATION OF INTERSTATE WAR

PERIOD	JAN	FEB	MAR	APR	MAY	JUN	JUL	AUG	SEP	OCT	NOV	DEC	MEAN	TOTALS
NUMBER OF INTERSTATE WARS ENDING														
ALL YEARS 1816-1871	3	3	7	3	4	2	8	4	5	3	5	3	4.2	50
1816-1871	1	3	4	0	1	0	5	1	2	1	1	1	1.7	20
1872-1919	1	0	2	3	1	1	2	2	1	1	1	1	1.3	16
1920-1965	1	0	1	0	2	1	1	1	2	1	3	1	1.2	14
NATION MONTHS OF INTERSTATE WAR ENDING														
ALL YEARS 1816-1871	43.4	184.6	185.3	27.9	70.6	95.4	578.8	907.0	89.0	108.1	627.2	277.5	266.2	3194.8
1816-1871	6.4	184.6	145.5	0.0	16.8	0.0	55.2	13.2	34.6	0.1	14.6	1.0	39.3	472.0
1872-1919	17.6	0.0	33.0	27.9	6.2	23.6	9.6	18.2	38.6	25.4	607.8	170.3	81.5	978.2
1920-1965	19.4	0.0	6.8	0.0	47.6	71.8	514.0	875.6	15.8	82.6	4.8	106.2	145.4	1744.6
BATTLE DEATHS FROM INTERSTATE WARS ENDING														
ALL YEARS 1816-1871	294.0	224.5	400.2	84.0	83.0	142.1	2024.9	15186.6	286.8	73.2	8593.0	1015.0	2367.3	28407.3
1816-1871	1.0	224.5	285.2	0.0	1.0	0.0	71.3	1.3	131.0	3.2	1.0	1.0	60.0	720.5
1872-1919	285.0	0.0	25.0	84.0	2.0	12.1	61.5	21.0	130.0	20.0	8555.8	14.0	767.5	9210.4
1920-1965	8.0	0.0	90.0	0.0	80.0	130.0	1892.1	15164.3	25.8	50.0	36.2	1000.0	1539.7	18476.4

10.13 - MONTHLY DISTRIBUTIONS IN TERMINATION OF EXTRA-SYSTEMIC WAR

PERIOD	JAN	FEB	MAR	APR	MAY	JUN	JUL	AUG	SEP	OCT	NOV	DEC	MEAN	TOTALS
NUMBER OF EXTRA-SYSTEMIC WARS ENDING														
ALL YEARS 1816-1871	1	3	7	6	4	5	2	1	3	6	1	4	3.6	43
1816-1871	0	2	4	4	1	2	0	1	1	2	1	1	1.6	19
1872-1919	0	1	0	2	2	1	2	0	2	3	0	2	1.2	15
1920-1965	1	0	3	0	1	2	0	0	0	1	0	1	0.8	9
NATION MONTHS OF EXTRA-SYSTEMIC WAR ENDING														
ALL YEARS 1816-1871	14.3	158.2	232.1	188.3	127.5	169.9	46.6	12.1	206.9	101.4	5.7	74.7	111.5	1337.7
1816-1871	0.0	46.1	67.6	129.6	1.0	19.8	0.0	12.1	123.5	56.7	5.7	13.7	39.6	475.8
1872-1919	0.0	112.1	0.0	58.7	54.7	25.7	46.6	0.0	83.4	22.3	0.0	40.8	37.0	444.3
1920-1965	14.3	0.0	164.5	0.0	71.8	124.4	0.0	0.0	0.0	22.4	0.0	20.2	34.8	417.6
BATTLE DEATHS FROM EXTRA-SYSTEMIC WARS ENDING														
ALL YEARS 1816-1871	1.5	120.0	128.0	84.5	54.0	108.5	8.0	59.5	120.0	54.9	10.0	33.5	65.2	782.4
1816-1871	0.0	20.0	23.0	24.5	1.0	5.0	0.0	59.5	110.0	35.0	10.0	10.0	24.8	298.0
1872-1919	0.0	100.0	0.0	60.0	24.0	4.5	8.0	0.0	10.0	18.5	0.0	22.0	20.6	247.0
1920-1965	1.5	0.0	105.0	0.0	29.0	99.0	0.0	0.0	0.0	1.4	0.0	1.5	19.8	237.4

10.14 - MONTHLY DISTRIBUTIONS IN TERMINATION OF WARS OF VARYING DURATION

DURATION IN MONTHS	JAN	FEB	MAR	APR	MAY	JUN	JUL	AUG	SEP	OCT	NOV	DEC	MEAN	TOTALS
INTERNATIONAL														
.1 - 3	0	0	1	2	1	0	5	0	2	2	3	2	1.5	18
3.1 - 6	2	0	6	0	1	0	2	2	1	0	1	0	1.2	15
6.1 - 12	1	1	2	2	2	2	1	2	0	4	1	0	1.5	18
OVER 12	1	5	5	5	4	5	2	1	5	3	1	5	3.5	42
INTERSTATE														
.1 - 3	0	0	0	2	0	0	5	0	2	1	3	1	1.2	14
3.1 - 6	2	0	4	0	1	0	1	2	1	0	0	0	0.9	11
6.1 - 12	1	1	2	1	2	1	1	1	0	0	1	0	0.9	11
OVER 12	0	2	1	0	1	1	1	1	2	2	1	2	1.2	14
EXTRA-SYSTEMIC														
.1 - 3	0	0	1	0	1	0	0	0	0	1	0	1	0.3	4
3.1 - 6	0	0	2	0	0	0	1	0	0	0	1	0	0.3	4
6.1 - 12	0	0	0	1	0	1	0	1	0	4	0	0	0.6	7
OVER 12	1	3	4	5	3	4	1	0	3	1	0	3	2.3	28

SEASONAL CONCENTRATIONS FOR THE INDIVIDUAL NATIONS

Having examined a variety of indicators reflecting seasonal and monthly concentrations in the amount of war begun and ended in the international system and its several sub-systems, let us now shift to the seasonal experiences of the separate nations. While the various totals and subtotals will reveal the same general pattern as those found in the earlier sections, these more detailed breakdowns will permit certain analyses which are not possible at the systemic level of inquiry. One might, for example, want to ascertain whether seasonal incentives and constraints operate differentially, depending on each nation's level of industrialization, access to technology, size of the domestic agricultural sector, age or literacy profile, dependence on foreign sources or markets, political cycles, and so forth. Alternatively, for those whose research treats war as an independent variable, such a compilation permits the systematic investigation of the way in which the timing of a nation's entry into or departure from war might affect cyclical patterns in economic activity, births and deaths, marriage and divorce, homicide and suicide, elections, political unrest, etc.

Thus, in Tables 10.15 and 10.16, we show our best estimate of the day of each month in which each nation in the system entered into (10.15) or departed from (10.16) each of the international wars in which it participated during its membership in the system. The format of both tables is identical. The first column identifies the season and the second shows the specific month of each entry or departure; here we also indicate in which of the three historical periods the specific entries and departures occurred. After identifying the specific nations in columns 3 and 4, we give our estimate of the precise day, month, and year, followed by each war's code number (column 6). Finally, in columns 7 and 8 are shown that nation's battle deaths (in thousands) for the separate wars that it entered or left that month, and the length of its participation. An asterisk (*) signifies any nation which fought in three or more wars, as only they will be used in our two summary tables, later in this chapter. Finally, the rows that appear after each month's listing are used to summarize the number of nations that enter or leave all wars and interstate wars (in parentheses) during that month for each of the three historical periods, accompanied by the respective national battle deaths and war months. We split March, June, September, and December, marking the end of a given season (at the end of the table are totals showing the national summaries for each entire season). And although we present these four months so that the seasonal break is obvious, we must emphasize that the totals are *monthly* totals which ignore the seasonal break at the 21st.

With the data provided in Tables 10.15 and 10.16, we can go a step further in summarizing the seasonal concentrations in national war decisions. Working on the assumption that a single decision to enter or leave a war on the part of any one nation

10.15 - MONTHLY AND SEASONAL ENTRIES INTO WAR BY NATIONS

SEASON 1	MONTH AND PERIOD 2	CODE NO. 3	NATION NAME 4	DATE OF ENTRY 5	WAR NO. 6	BATTLE DEATHS (000'S) 7	WAR MONTHS 8
WINTER	JANUARY						
	1ST	140	*BRAZIL	7-19-1851	8	0.5	6.6
		160	ARGENTINA	7-19-1851	8	0.8	6.6
		325	*ITALY/SARDINIA	1-10-1855	9	2.2	13.7
		365	*RUSSIA	1-22-1863	68	5.0	14.9
	2ND	200	*ENGLAND	1-11-1879	75	3.5	5.7
	3RD	530	*ETHIOPIA	1-24-1941	43	5.0	5.3
		140	*BRAZIL	7-06-1944	43	1.0	10.1
		210	*HOLLAND	1-20-1951	46	0.1	30.2
		211	*BELGIUM	1-20-1951	46	0.1	30.2
		220	*FRANCE	1-01-1951	46	0.3	30.8
		350	*GREECE	1-20-1951	46	0.2	30.2
		800	THAILAND	1-20-1951	46	0.1	30.2
	1ST		1816-1871: 4 (3)			8.5 (3.5)	41.8 (26.9)
	2ND		1872-1919: 1 (0)			3.5 (0.0)	5.7 (0.0)
	3RD		1920-1965 7 (7)			6.8 (6.8)	167.0 (167.0)
	JANUARY		12 (10)			18.8 (10.3)	214.5 (193.9)
WINTER	FEBRUARY						
	1ST	365	*RUSSIA	2-07-1831	56	15.0	8.3
		255	*GERMANY/PRUSSIA	2-01-1864	17	1.0	3.6
		300	*AUSTRIA-HUNGARY	2-01-1864	17	0.5	3.6
		390	DENMARK	2-01-1864	17	3.0	3.6
	2ND	230	*SPAIN	2-24-1895	80	50.0	37.3
		640	*TURKEY	2-15-1897	26	1.4	3.1
		350	*GREECE	2-15-1897	26	0.6	3.1
		2	*UNITED STATES	2-04-1899	83	4.5	40.9
		740	*JAPAN	2-08-1904	28	85.0	19.3
		365	*RUSSIA	2-08-1904	28	45.0	19.3
		93	NICARAGUA	2-19-1907	30	0.4	2.1
		91	HONDURAS	2-19-1907	30	0.3	2.1
		92	*SALVADOR	2-19-1907	30	0.3	2.1
	1ST		1816-1871: 4 (3)			19.5 (4.5)	19.1 (10.8)
	2ND		1872-1919: 9 (7)			187.5 (133.0)	129.3 (51.1)
	FEBRUARY		13 (10)			207.0 (137.5)	148.4 (61.9)

NOTES: * = NATION IN 3 OR MORE WARS
( ) = TOTALS FOR INTERSTATE WARS ONLY

10.15 - MONTHLY AND SEASONAL ENTRIES INTO WAR BY NATIONS

SEASON 1	MONTH AND PERIOD 2	CODE NO. 3	NATION NAME 4	DATE OF ENTRY 5	WAR NO. 6	BATTLE DEATHS (000'S) 7	WAR MONTHS 8
WINTER	MARCH						
	2ND	235	PORTUGAL	3-01-1916	35	7.0	32.4
	3RD	560	SOUTH AFRICA	9-06-1939	43	8.7	71.3
		900	AUSTRALIA	9-03-1939	43	29.4	71.4
		920	NEW ZEALAND	9-03-1939	43	17.3	71.4
		710	*CHINA	3-01-1956	93	40.0	36.7
***** END OF WINTER *****							
SPRING	MARCH						
	1ST	640	*TURKEY	3-25-1821	52	15.0	85.1
		300	*AUSTRIA-HUNGARY	3-24-1848	5	5.6	4.7
		325	*ITALY/SARDINIA	3-24-1848	5	3.4	4.7
		200	*ENGLAND	3-31-1854	9	22.0	23.1
		220	*FRANCE	3-31-1854	9	95.0	23.1
	2ND	210	*HOLLAND	3-26-1873	71	6.0	65.2
		92	*SALVADOR	3-28-1885	24	0.2	0.6
		90	GUATEMALA	3-28-1885	24	0.8	0.6
	3RD	220	*FRANCE	3-29-1947	90	1.5	20.2
	1ST		1816-1871: 5 (4)			141.0 (126.0)	140.7 (55.6)
	2ND		1872-1919: 4 (3)			14.0 (8.0)	98.8 (33.6)
	3RD		1920-1965 5 (3)			96.9 (55.4)	271.0 (214.1)
	MARCH		14 (10)			251.9 (189.4)	510.5 (303.3)
SPRING	APRIL						
	1ST	220	*FRANCE	4-07-1823	1	0.4	7.3
		230	*SPAIN	4-07-1823	1	0.6	7.3
		365	*RUSSIA	4-26-1828	3	50.0	16.7
		640	*TURKEY	4-26-1828	3	80.0	16.7
		135	*PERU	10-19-1841	61	1.0	1.0
		255	*GERMANY/PRUSSIA	4-10-1848	6	2.5	8.1
		390	DENMARK	4-10-1848	6	3.5	8.1
		220	*FRANCE	4-30-1849	7	0.5	1.0
		327	PAPAL STATES	4-30-1849	7	1.5	1.8
		325	*ITALY/SARDINIA	4-29-1859	11	2.5	2.5
		300	*AUSTRIA-HUNGARY	4-29-1859	11	12.5	2.5
		70	*MEXICO	4-16-1862	15	12.0	57.7
		220	*FRANCE	4-16-1862	15	8.0	57.7
		155	CHILE	10-25-1865	18	0.1	6.5

NOTES: * = NATION IN 3 OR MORE WARS
( ) = TOTALS FOR INTERSTATE WARS ONLY

SEASON 1	MONTH AND PERIOD 2	CODE NO. 3	NATION NAME 4	DATE OF ENTRY 5	WAR NO. 6	BATTLE DEATHS (000'S) 7		WAR MONTHS 8	
	2ND	365	*RUSSIA	4-12-1877	21	120.0		8.8	
		640	*TURKEY	4-12-1877	21	165.0		8.8	
		220	*FRANCE	4-25-1882	76	4.5		25.7	
		2	*UNITED STATES	4-21-1898	27	5.0		3.7	
		230	*SPAIN	4-21-1898	27	5.0		3.7	
		2	*UNITED STATES	4-17-1917	35	126.0		18.9	
		315	CZECHOSLOVAKIA	4-16-1919	36	2.0		3.6	
		360	*RUMANIA	4-16-1919	36	3.0		3.6	
		310	*HUNGARY	4-16-1919	36	6.0		3.6	
	3RD	220	*FRANCE	4-12-1925	86	4.0		13.5	
		385	NORWAY	4-09-1940	43	2.0		2.0	
		345	*YUGOSLAVIA/SERBIA	4-06-1941	43	5.0		0.4	
	1ST		1816-1871: 14 (13)			175.1	(174.1)	194.9	(193.9)
	2ND		1872-1919: 9 (8)			436.5	(432.0)	80.4	(54.7)
	3RD		1920-1965 3 (2)			11.0	(7.0)	15.9	(2.4)
	APRIL		26 (23)			622.6	(613.1)	291.2	(251.0)
SPRING	MAY								
	1ST	2	*UNITED STATES	5-12-1846	4	11.0		21.1	
		70	*MEXICO	5-12-1846	4	6.0		21.1	
		300	*AUSTRIA-HUNGARY	5-08-1849	7	0.1		1.8	
		329	TWO SICILIES	5-08-1849	7	0.1		1.8	
		200	*ENGLAND	5-10-1857	66	3.5		22.9	
		640	*TURKEY	5-04-1858	67	3.0		12.9	
		220	*FRANCE	5-03-1859	11	7.5		2.3	
		130	ECUADOR	11-22-1863	16	0.7		0.5	
		140	*BRAZIL	11-12-1864	69	100.0		63.6	
	2ND	230	*SPAIN	5-30-1896	82	2.0		23.1	
		90	GUATEMALA	5-27-1906	29	0.4		1.8	
		91	HONDURAS	5-27-1906	29	0.3		1.8	
		92	*SALVADOR	5-27-1906	29	0.3		1.8	
		325	*ITALY/SARDINIA	5-23-1915	35	650.0		41.7	
		640	*TURKEY	5-05-1919	37	20.0		41.3	
		350	*GREECE	5-05-1919	37	30.0		41.3	
	3RD	365	*RUSSIA	5-11-1939	42	1.0		4.2	
		712	MONGOLIA	5-11-1939	42	3.0		4.2	
		740	*JAPAN	5-11-1939	42	15.0		4.2	
		210	*HOLLAND	5-10-1940	43	6.2		0.2	
		211	*BELGIUM	5-10-1940	43	9.6		0.6	
		666	ISRAEL	5-15-1948	45	3.0		4.7	
		645	IRAQ	5-15-1948	45	0.5		2.5	

NOTES: * = NATION IN 3 OR MORE WARS
( ) = TOTALS FOR INTERSTATE WARS ONLY

10.15 - MONTHLY AND SEASONAL ENTRIES INTO WAR BY NATIONS

SEASON 1	MONTH AND PERIOD 2	CODE NO. 3	NATION NAME 4	DATE OF ENTRY 5	WAR NO. 6	BATTLE DEATHS (000'S) 7		WAR MONTHS 8	
		651	U.A.R.	5-15-1948	45	2.0		4.7	
		652	SYRIA	5-15-1948	45	1.0		2.5	
		660	LEBANON	5-15-1948	45	0.5		2.5	
		663	JORDAN	5-15-1948	45	1.0		2.5	
		530	*ETHIOPIA	5-01-1951	46	0.1		26.9	
	1ST		1816-1871: 9 (6)			131.9	(25.4)	148.0	(48.6)
	2ND		1872-1919: 7 (6)			703.0	(701.0)	152.8	(129.7)
	3RD		1920-1965 12 (12)			42.9	(42.9)	59.7	(59.7)
	MAY		28 (24)			877.8	(769.3)	360.5	(238.0)
SPRING	JUNE								
	1ST	640	*TURKEY	6-10-1839	60	10.0		3.1	
		255	*GERMANY/PRUSSIA	6-15-1866	19	10.0		1.4	
		325	*ITALY/SARDINIA	6-15-1866	19	4.0		1.4	
		240	HANOVER	6-15-1866	19	0.5		0.5	
		245	BAVARIA	6-15-1866	19	0.5		1.4	
		267	BADEN	6-15-1866	19	0.1		1.4	
		269	SAXONY	6-15-1866	19	0.6		1.4	
		271	WUERTTEMBERG	6-15-1866	19	0.1		1.4	
		273	HESSE ELECTORAL	6-15-1866	19	0.1		1.4	
		275	HESSE GRAND DUCAL	6-15-1866	19	0.1		1.4	
		280	MECKLENBURG-SCHWERIN	6-15-1866	19	0.1		1.4	
		300	*AUSTRIA-HUNGARY	6-15-1866	19	20.0		1.4	
	2ND	220	*FRANCE	6-15-1884	23	2.1		11.8	
		710	*CHINA	6-15-1884	23	10.0		11.8	
	3RD	325	*ITALY/SARDINIA	6-10-1940	43	60.0		38.8	
		900	AUSTRALIA	12-10-1950	46	0.3		31.6	
		100	COLOMBIA	6-06-1951	46	0.1		25.7	
***** END OF SPRING *****									
SUMMER	JUNE								
	2ND	345	*YUGOSLAVIA/SERBIA	6-30-1913	34	18.5		1.0	
		350	*GREECE	6-30-1913	34	2.5		1.0	
		355	*BULGARIA	6-30-1913	34	18.0		1.0	
		350	*GREECE	6-29-1917	35	5.0		16.5	
	3RD	365	*RUSSIA	6-22-1941	43	7500.0		46.7	
		310	*HUNGARY	6-27-1941	43	40.0		42.8	
		360	*RUMANIA	6-22-1941	43	290.0		38.1	
		375	FINLAND	6-25-1941	43	42.0		38.9	
		2	*UNITED STATES	6-27-1950	46	54.0		37.0	

NOTES: * = NATION IN 3 OR MORE WARS
( ) = TOTALS FOR INTERSTATE WARS ONLY

SEASON 1	MONTH AND PERIOD 2	CODE NO. 3	NATION NAME 4	DATE OF ENTRY 5	WAR NO. 6	BATTLE DEATHS (000'S) 7	WAR MONTHS 8
		732	KOREA SOUTH	6-24-1950	46	415.0	37.1
		731	KOREA NORTH	6-24-1950	46	520.0	37.1
	1ST		1816-1871: 12 (11)			46.1 (36.1)	17.6 (14.5)
	2ND		1872-1919: 6 (6)			56.1 (56.1)	43.1 (43.1)
	3RD		1920-1965 10 (10)			8921.4 (8921.4)	373.8 (373.8)
	JUNE		28 (27)			9023.6 (9013.6)	434.5 (431.4)
SUMMER	JULY						
	1ST	210	*HOLLAND	7-23-1825	54	15.0	56.2
		365	*RUSSIA	7-16-1849	63	14.5	1.0
		135	*PERU	1-14-1866	18	0.6	3.8
		245	BAVARIA	7-19-1870	20	5.5	3.9
		255	*GERMANY/PRUSSIA	7-19-1870	20	40.0	7.3
		267	BADEN	7-19-1870	20	1.0	4.2
		271	WUERTTEMBERG	7-19-1870	20	1.0	4.3
		220	*FRANCE	7-19-1870	20	140.0	7.3
	2ND	640	*TURKEY	7-03-1875	72	10.0	21.4
		300	*AUSTRIA-HUNGARY	7-29-1878	73	3.5	2.1
		230	*SPAIN	7-07-1909	31	2.0	8.5
		600	MOROCCO	7-07-1909	31	8.0	8.5
		360	*RUMANIA	7-11-1913	34	1.5	0.7
		640	*TURKEY	7-15-1913	34	20.0	0.5
		345	*YUGOSLAVIA/SERBIA	7-29-1914	35	48.0	51.5
		300	*AUSTRIA-HUNGARY	7-29-1914	35	1200.0	51.2
	3RD	230	*SPAIN	7-18-1921	86	25.0	58.3
		220	*FRANCE	7-18-1925	87	4.0	22.4
		740	*JAPAN	7-07-1937	41	250.0	53.1
		710	*CHINA	7-07-1937	41	750.0	53.1
	1ST		1816-1871: 8 (6)			217.6 (188.1)	88.0 (30.8)
	2ND		1872-1919: 8 (6)			1293.0 (1279.5)	144.4 (120.9)
	3RD		1920-1965 4 (2)			1029.0 (1000.0)	186.9 (106.2)
	JULY		20 (14)			2539.6 (2467.6)	419.3 (257.9)
SUMMER	AUGUST						
	2ND	155	CHILE	2-14-1879	22	3.0	57.9
		145	BOLIVIA	2-14-1879	22	1.0	57.9
		740	*JAPAN	8-01-1894	25	5.0	8.0
		710	*CHINA	8-01-1894	25	10.0	8.0

NOTES: * = NATION IN 3 OR MORE WARS
( ) = TOTALS FOR INTERSTATE WARS ONLY

10.15 - MONTHLY AND SEASONAL ENTRIES INTO WAR BY NATIONS

SEASON 1	MONTH AND PERIOD 2	CODE NO. 3	NATION NAME 4	DATE OF ENTRY 5	WAR NO. 6	BATTLE DEATHS (000'S) 7	WAR MONTHS 8
		200	*ENGLAND	8-05-1914	35	908.0	51.2
		211	*BELGIUM	8-04-1914	35	87.5	51.3
		220	*FRANCE	8-03-1914	35	1350.0	51.3
		365	*RUSSIA	8-01-1914	35	1700.0	40.2
		740	*JAPAN	8-23-1914	35	0.3	50.7
		255	*GERMANY/PRUSSIA	8-01-1914	35	1800.0	51.4
		360	*RUMANIA	8-27-1916	35	335.0	15.4
	3RD	712	MONGOLIA	8-10-1945	43	3.0	0.2
		200	*ENGLAND	8-29-1950	46	0.7	35.0
		770	PAKISTAN	8-05-1965	50	3.8	1.6
		750	*INDIA	8-05-1965	50	3.0	1.6
	2ND	1872-1919:	11 (11)			6199.8 (6199.8)	443.3 (443.3)
	3RD	1920-1965	4 (4)			10.5 (10.5)	38.4 (38.4)
	AUGUST		15 (15)			6210.3 (6210.3)	481.7 (481.7)
SUMMER	SEPTEMBER						
	1ST	200	*ENGLAND	9-09-1840	60	0.0	2.6
		300	*AUSTRIA-HUNGARY	9-09-1848	63	45.0	11.1
		325	*ITALY/SARDINIA	9-11-1860	13	0.3	0.6
		327	PAPAL STATES	9-11-1860	13	0.7	0.6
		160	ARGENTINA	3-05-1865	69	10.0	59.9
	2ND	200	*ENGLAND	9-13-1882	77	20.0	39.6
	3RD	20	CANADA	9-10-1939	43	39.3	71.2
		200	*ENGLAND	9-03-1939	43	270.0	71.4
		220	*FRANCE	9-03-1939	43	210.0	19.4
		290	POLAND	9-01-1939	43	320.0	0.9
		255	*GERMANY/PRUSSIA	9-01-1939	43	3500.0	68.2
		355	*BULGARIA	9-09-1944	43	1.0	7.9
		360	*RUMANIA	9-09-1944	43	10.0	7.9
		840	PHILIPPINES	9-16-1950	46	0.1	34.4
***** END OF SUMMER *****							
AUTUMN	SEPTEMBER						
	1ST	200	*ENGLAND	9-24-1823	53	15.0	29.1
		365	*RUSSIA	9-28-1826	55	5.0	17.0
	2ND	325	*ITALY/SARDINIA	9-29-1911	32	6.0	12.7
		640	*TURKEY	9-29-1911	32	14.0	12.7

NOTES: * = NATION IN 3 OR MORE WARS
( ) = TOTALS FOR INTERSTATE WARS ONLY

SEASON 1	MONTH AND PERIOD 2	CODE NO. 3	NATION NAME 4	DATE OF ENTRY 5	WAR NO. 6	BATTLE DEATHS (000'S) 7		WAR MONTHS 8	
	1ST		1816-1871: 7 (2)			76.0	(1.0)	120.9	(1.2)
	2ND		1872-1919: 3 (2)			40.0	(20.0)	65.0	(25.4)
	3RD		1920-1965 8 (8)			4350.4	(4350.4)	281.3	(281.3)
	SEPTEMBER		18 (12)			4466.4	(4371.4)	467.2	(307.9)
AUTUMN	OCTOBER								
	1ST	200	*ENGLAND	10-20-1827	2	0.1		0.1	
		220	*FRANCE	10-20-1827	2	0.0		0.1	
		365	*RUSSIA	10-20-1827	2	0.1		0.1	
		640	*TURKEY	10-20-1827	2	3.0		0.1	
		70	*MEXICO	10-01-1835	58	1.0		6.7	
		200	*ENGLAND	10-01-1838	59	20.0		48.4	
		200	*ENGLAND	10-10-1848	64	1.5		5.1	
		640	*TURKEY	10-23-1853	9	45.0		28.3	
		365	*RUSSIA	10-23-1853	9	100.0		28.3	
		200	*ENGLAND	10-25-1856	10	0.5		4.6	
		630	IRAN	10-25-1856	10	1.5		4.6	
		230	*SPAIN	10-22-1859	12	4.0		5.2	
		600	MOROCCO	10-22-1859	12	6.0		5.2	
		325	*ITALY/SARDINIA	10-15-1860	14	0.6		3.2	
		329	TWO SICILIES	10-15-1860	14	0.4		3.2	
		230	*SPAIN	10-25-1865	18	0.3		6.5	
		230	*SPAIN	10-10-1868	70	100.0		112.1	
	2ND	135	*PERU	4-05-1879	22	10.0		54.5	
		200	*ENGLAND	10-11-1899	84	22.0		31.6	
		345	*YUGOSLAVIA/SERBIA	10-17-1912	33	15.0		4.1	
		350	*GREECE	10-17-1912	33	5.0		6.1	
		355	*BULGARIA	10-17-1912	33	32.0		4.1	
		640	*TURKEY	10-17-1912	33	30.0		6.1	
		640	*TURKEY	10-28-1914	35	325.0		48.5	
		355	*BULGARIA	10-12-1915	35	14.0		35.6	
	3RD	325	*ITALY/SARDINIA	10-03-1935	40	4.0		7.2	
		530	*ETHIOPIA	10-03-1935	40	16.0		7.2	
		350	*GREECE	10-25-1940	43	10.0		5.9	
		325	*ITALY/SARDINIA	10-18-1943	43	17.5		18.7	
		750	*INDIA	10-26-1947	91	1.5		14.3	
		640	*TURKEY	10-18-1950	46	0.7		33.3	
		710	*CHINA	10-27-1950	46	900.0		33.0	
		365	*RUSSIA	10-23-1956	47	7.0		0.8	
		310	*HUNGARY	10-23-1956	47	25.0		0.8	
		666	ISRAEL	10-31-1956	48	0.2		0.3	
		651	U.A.R.	10-31-1956	48	3.0		0.3	
		710	*CHINA	10-20-1962	49	0.5		1.1	
		750	*INDIA	10-20-1962	49	0.5		1.1	

NOTES: * = NATION IN 3 OR MORE WARS
( ) = TOTALS FOR INTERSTATE WARS ONLY

10.15 - MONTHLY AND SEASONAL ENTRIES INTO WAR BY NATIONS

SEASON 1	MONTH AND PERIOD 2	CODE NO. 3	NATION NAME 4		DATE OF ENTRY 5	WAR NO. 6	BATTLE DEATHS (000'S) 7		WAR MONTHS 8	
	1ST		1816-1871:	17 (13)			284.0	(161.5)	261.8	(89.5)
	2ND		1872-1919:	8 (7)			453.0	(431.0)	190.6	(159.0)
	3RD		1920-1965	13 (12)			985.9	(984.4)	124.0	(109.7)
	OCTOBER			38 (32)			1722.9	(1576.9)	576.4	(358.2)
AUTUMN	NOVEMBER									
	1ST	200	*ENGLAND		11-06-1817	51	2.0		6.9	
		640	*TURKEY		11-01-1831	57	10.0		13.7	
		100	COLOMBIA		11-22-1863	16	0.3		0.5	
	2ND	200	*ENGLAND		11-20-1878	74	4.0		18.2	
		345	*YUGOSLAVIA/SERBIA		11-02-1885	78	2.0		1.2	
	3RD	365	*RUSSIA		11-30-1939	44	50.0		3.4	
		375	FINLAND		11-30-1939	44	40.0		3.4	
		200	*ENGLAND		11-10-1945	88	1.0		11.2	
		210	*HOLLAND		11-10-1945	88	0.4		11.2	
		220	*FRANCE		11-01-1954	92	15.0		88.5	
		200	*ENGLAND		11-02-1956	48	0.0		0.2	
		220	*FRANCE		11-02-1956	48	0.0		0.2	
	1ST		1816-1871:	3 (1)			12.3	(0.3)	21.1	(0.5)
	2ND		1872-1919:	2 (0)			6.0	(0.0)	19.4	(0.0)
	3RD		1920-1965	7 (4)			106.4	(90.0)	118.1	(7.2)
	NOVEMBER			12 (5)			124.7	(90.3)	158.6	(7.7)
AUTUMN	DECEMBER									
	1ST	200	*ENGLAND		12-13-1845	62	1.5		2.9	
		640	*TURKEY		12-02-1852	65	5.0		3.4	
	2ND	220	*FRANCE		12-12-1894	79	6.0		9.7	
		325	*ITALY/SARDINIA		12-07-1895	81	9.0		10.5	
		365	*RUSSIA		12-09-1917	85	50.0		39.3	
	3RD	740	*JAPAN		12-19-1931	38	10.0		16.6	
		710	*CHINA		12-19-1931	38	50.0		16.6	
		150	PARAGUAY		6-15-1932	39	50.0		35.9	
		145	BOLIVIA		6-15-1932	39	80.0		35.9	
		2	*UNITED STATES		12-07-1941	43	408.3		44.3	
		710	*CHINA		12-07-1941	43	1350.0		44.3	
		355	*BULGARIA		12-08-1941	43	9.0		33.0	
		740	*JAPAN		12-07-1941	43	1000.0		44.3	
		220	*FRANCE		12-01-1945	89	95.0		102.0	

NOTES: * = NATION IN 3 OR MORE WARS
( ) = TOTALS FOR INTERSTATE WARS ONLY

SEASON 1	MONTH AND PERIOD 2	CODE NO. 3	NATION NAME 4	DATE OF ENTRY 5	WAR NO. 6	BATTLE DEATHS (000'S) 7	WAR MONTHS 8
		20	CANADA	12-19-1950	46	0.3	31.3
	1ST		1816-1871: 2 (0)			6.5 (0.0)	6.3 (0.0)
	2ND		1872-1919: 3 (0)			65.0 (0.0)	59.5 (0.0)
	3RD		1920-1965 10 (9)			3052.6 (2957.6)	404.2 (302.2)
	DECEMBER		15 (9)			3124.1 (2957.6)	470.0 (302.2)

*** SEASONAL TOTALS ***

PERIOD	NO. OF NATIONS ENTERING WAR		BATTLE DEATHS (000'S)	WAR MONTHS
	WINTER: DECEMBER 22 - MARCH 21			
1ST	1816-1871:	8 (6)	28.0 (8.0)	60.9 (37.7)
2ND	1872-1919:	11 (8)	198.0 (140.0)	167.4 (83.5)
3RD	1920-1965	11 (10)	102.2 (62.2)	417.8 (381.1)
WINTER		30 (24)	328.2 (210.2)	646.1 (502.3)
	SPRING: MARCH 22 - JUNE 21			
1ST	1816-1871:	40 (34)	494.1 (361.6)	501.2 (312.6)
2ND	1872-1919:	21 (18)	1158.6 (1146.1)	323.2 (209.2)
3RD	1920-1965	19 (17)	115.8 (110.3)	191.9 (158.2)
SPRING		80 (69)	1768.5 (1618.0)	1016.3 (680.0)
	SUMMER: JUNE 22 - SEPTEMBER 21			
1ST	1816-1871:	13 (8)	273.6 (189.1)	162.8 (32.0)
2ND	1872-1919:	24 (21)	7556.8 (7523.3)	646.8 (583.7)
3RD	1920-1965	23 (21)	14250.9 (14221.9)	784.3 (703.6)
SUMMER		60 (50)	22081.3 (21934.2)	1593.9 (1319.3)
	SEPTEMBER 22 - DECEMBER 21			
1ST	1816-1871:	24 (14)	322.8 (161.8)	335.3 (90.0)
2ND	1872-1919:	15 (9)	544.0 (451.0)	294.9 (184.4)
3RD	1920-1965	30 (25)	4145.0 (4032.1)	646.3 (419.1)
AUTUMN		69 (48)	5011.7 (4644.8)	1276.5 (693.5)

NOTE: ( ) = TOTALS FOR INTERSTATE WARS ONLY

10.16 - MONTHLY AND SEASONAL DEPARTURES FROM WAR BY NATIONS

SEASON 1	MONTH AND PERIOD 2	CODE NO. 3	NATION NAME 4	DATE OF DEPARTURE 5	WAR NO. 6	BATTLE DEATHS (000'S) 7		WAR MONTHS 8	
WINTER	JANUARY								
	1ST	325	*ITALY/SARDINIA	1-19-1861	14	0.6		3.2	
		329	TWO SICILIES	1-19-1861	14	0.4		3.2	
	2ND	365	*RUSSIA	1-03-1878	21	120.0		8.8	
		640	*TURKEY	1-03-1878	21	165.0		8.8	
	3RD	310	*HUNGARY	1-20-1945	43	40.0		42.8	
		666	ISRAEL	1-07-1949	45	3.0		4.7	
		651	U.A.R.	1-07-1949	45	2.0		4.7	
		750	*INDIA	1-01-1949	91	1.5		14.3	
		900	AUSTRALIA	7-27-1953	46	0.3		31.6	
	1ST		1816-1871: 2 (2)			1.0	(1.0)	6.4	(6.4)
	2ND		1872-1919: 2 (2)			285.0	(285.0)	17.6	(17.6)
	3RD		1920-1965 5 (4)			46.8	(45.3)	98.1	(83.8)
	JANUARY		9 (8)			332.8	(331.3)	122.1	(107.8)
WINTER	FEBRUARY								
	1ST	200	*ENGLAND	2-24-1826	53	15.0		29.1	
		365	*RUSSIA	2-28-1828	55	5.0		17.0	
		2	*UNITED STATES	2-12-1848	4	11.0		21.1	
		70	*MEXICO	2-12-1848	4	6.0		21.1	
		70	*MEXICO	2-05-1867	15	12.0		57.7	
		220	*FRANCE	2-05-1867	15	8.0		57.7	
		255	*GERMANY/PRUSSIA	2-26-1871	20	40.0		7.3	
		220	*FRANCE	2-26-1871	20	140.0		7.3	
	2ND	230	*SPAIN	2-10-1878	70	100.0		112.1	
	3RD	560	SOUTH AFRICA	8-14-1945	43	8.7		71.3	
		900	AUSTRALIA	8-14-1945	43	29.4		71.4	
		920	NEW ZEALAND	8-14-1945	43	17.3		71.4	
	1ST		1816-1871: 8 (6)			237.0	(217.0)	218.3	(172.2)
	2ND		1872-1919: 1 (0)			100.0	(0.0)	112.1	(0.0)
	3RD		1920-1965 3 (3)			55.4	(55.4)	214.1	(214.1)
	FEBRUARY		12 (9)			392.4	(272.4)	544.5	(386.3)

NOTES: * = NATION IN 3 OR MORE WARS
( ) = TOTALS FOR INTERSTATE WARS ONLY

SEASON 1	MONTH AND PERIOD 2	CODE NO. 3	NATION NAME 4	DATE OF DEPARTURE 5	WAR NO. 6	BATTLE DEATHS (000'S) 7	WAR MONTHS 8
WINTER	MARCH						
	1ST	200	*ENGLAND	3-09-1846	62	1.5	2.9
		200	*ENGLAND	3-12-1849	64	1.5	5.1
		640	*TURKEY	3-13-1853	65	5.0	3.4
		200	*ENGLAND	3-01-1856	9	22.0	23.1
		220	*FRANCE	3-01-1856	9	95.0	23.1
		325	*ITALY/SARDINIA	3-01-1856	9	2.2	13.7
		640	*TURKEY	3-01-1856	9	45.0	28.3
		365	*RUSSIA	3-01-1856	9	100.0	28.3
		200	*ENGLAND	3-14-1857	10	0.5	4.6
		630	IRAN	3-14-1857	10	1.5	4.6
	3RD	365	*RUSSIA	3-18-1921	85	50.0	39.3
		365	*RUSSIA	3-12-1940	44	50.0	3.4
		375	FINLAND	3-12-1940	44	40.0	3.4
		220	*FRANCE	3-17-1962	92	15.0	88.5
***** END OF WINTER *****							
SPRING	MARCH						
	1ST	210	*HOLLAND	3-28-1830	54	15.0	56.2
		300	*AUSTRIA-HUNGARY	3-23-1849	5	5.6	4.7
		325	*ITALY/SARDINIA	3-23-1849	5	3.4	4.7
		230	*SPAIN	3-26-1860	12	4.0	5.2
		600	MOROCCO	3-26-1860	12	6.0	5.2
	2ND	740	*JAPAN	3-30-1895	25	5.0	8.0
		710	*CHINA	3-30-1895	25	10.0	8.0
		230	*SPAIN	3-23-1910	31	2.0	8.5
		600	MOROCCO	3-23-1910	31	8.0	8.5
	3RD	710	*CHINA	3-22-1959	93	40.0	36.7
	1ST		1816-1871: 15 (11)			308.2 (285.2)	213.1 (145.5)
	2ND		1872-1919: 4 (4)			25.0 (25.0)	33.0 (33.0)
	3RD		1920-1965 5 (2)			195.0 (90.0)	171.3 (6.8)
	MARCH		24 (17)			528.2 (400.2)	417.4 (185.3)
SPRING	APRIL						
	1ST	640	*TURKEY	4-25-1828	52	15.0	85.1
		70	*MEXICO	4-22-1836	58	1.0	6.7
		200	*ENGLAND	4-07-1859	66	3.5	22.9
		365	*RUSSIA	4-19-1864	68	5.0	14.9

NOTES: * = NATION IN 3 OR MORE WARS
( ) = TOTALS FOR INTERSTATE WARS ONLY

10.16 - MONTHLY AND SEASONAL DEPARTURES FROM WAR BY NATIONS

SEASON 1	MONTH AND PERIOD 2	CODE NO. 3	NATION NAME 4	DATE OF DEPARTURE 5	WAR NO. 6	BATTLE DEATHS (000'S) 7	WAR MONTHS 8
	2ND	640	*TURKEY	4-12-1877	72	10.0	21.4
		135	*PERU	10-20-1883	22	10.0	54.5
		92	*SALVADOR	4-15-1885	24	0.2	0.6
		90	GUATEMALA	4-15-1885	24	0.8	0.6
		230	*SPAIN	4-02-1898	80	50.0	37.3
		93	NICARAGUA	4-23-1907	30	0.4	2.1
		91	HONDURAS	4-23-1907	30	0.3	2.1
		92	*SALVADOR	4-23-1907	30	0.3	2.1
		345	*YUGOSLAVIA/SERBIA	4-19-1913	33	15.0	4.1
		350	*GREECE	4-19-1913	33	5.0	6.1
		355	*BULGARIA	4-19-1913	33	32.0	4.1
		640	*TURKEY	4-19-1913	33	30.0	6.1
	3RD	345	*YUGOSLAVIA/SERBIA	4-17-1941	43	5.0	0.4
		350	*GREECE	4-23-1941	43	10.0	5.9
	1ST		1816-1871: 4 (0)			24.5 (0.0)	129.6 (0.0)
	2ND		1872-1919: 12 (10)			154.0 (94.0)	141.1 (82.4)
	3RD		1920-1965 2 (2)			15.0 (15.0)	6.3 (6.3)
	APRIL		18 (12)			193.5 (109.0)	277.0 (88.7)
SPRING	MAY						
	1ST	135	*PERU	11-18-1841	61	1.0	1.0
		230	*SPAIN	5-09-1866	18	0.3	6.5
	2ND	640	*TURKEY	5-19-1897	26	1.4	3.1
		350	*GREECE	5-19-1897	26	0.6	3.1
		230	*SPAIN	5-01-1898	82	2.0	23.1
		200	*ENGLAND	5-31-1902	84	22.0	31.6
	3RD	220	*FRANCE	5-27-1926	86	4.0	13.5
		230	*SPAIN	5-27-1926	86	25.0	58.3
		740	*JAPAN	5-06-1933	38	10.0	16.6
		710	*CHINA	5-06-1933	38	50.0	16.6
		325	*ITALY/SARDINIA	5-09-1936	40	4.0	7.2
		530	*ETHIOPIA	5-09-1936	40	16.0	7.2
		210	*HOLLAND	5-14-1940	43	6.2	0.2
		211	*BELGIUM	5-28-1940	43	9.6	0.6
		325	*ITALY/SARDINIA	5-07-1945	43	17.5	18.7
		355	*BULGARIA	5-07-1945	43	1.0	7.9
		360	*RUMANIA	5-07-1945	43	10.0	7.9
		255	*GERMANY/PRUSSIA	5-07-1945	43	3500.0	68.2

NOTES: * = NATION IN 3 OR MORE WARS
( ) = TOTALS FOR INTERSTATE WARS ONLY

SEASON 1	MCNTH AND PERIOD 2	CODE NO. 3	NATION NAME 4	DATE OF DEPARTURE 5	WAR NO. 6	BATTLE DEATHS (000'S) 7	WAR MONTHS 8
	1ST		1816-1871: 2 (1)			1.3 (0.3)	7.5 (6.5)
	2ND		1872-1919: 4 (2)			26.0 (2.0)	60.9 (6.2)
	3RD		1920-1965 12 (10)			3653.3 (3624.3)	222.9 (151.1)
	MAY		18 (13)			3680.6 (3[illegible].6)	291.3 (163.8)
SPRING	JUNE						
	1ST	200	*ENGIAND	6-03-1818	51	2.0	6.9
		640	*TURKEY	6-00-1859	67	3.0	12.9
		130	ECUADOR	12-06-1863	16	0.7	0.5
	2ND	155	CHIIE	12-11-1883	22	3.0	57.9
		145	BOIIVIA	12-11-1883	22	1.0	57.9
		220	*FRANCE	6-14-1884	76	4.5	25.7
		220	*FRANCE	6-09-1885	23	2.1	11.8
		710	*CHINA	6-09-1885	23	10.0	11.8
	3RD	220	*FRANCE	6-00-1927	87	4.0	22.4
		385	NORWAY	6-09-1940	43	2.0	2.0
		220	*FRANCE	6-01-1954	89	95.0	102.0
***** END OF SPRING *****							
SUMMER	JUNE						
	1ST	240	HANCVER	6-29-1866	19	0.5	0.5
	1ST		1816-1871: 4 (2)			6.2 (1.2)	20.8 (1.0)
	2ND		1872-1919: 5 (4)			20.6 (16.1)	165.1 (139.4)
	3RD		1920-1965 3 (1)			101.0 (2.0)	126.4 (2.0)
	JUNE		12 (7)			127.8 (19.3)	312.3 (142.4)
SUMMER	JULY						
	1ST	255	*GERMANY/PRUSSIA	7-10-1849	6	2.5	8.1
		390	DENMARK	7-10-1849	6	3.5	8.1
		220	*FRANCE	7-01-1849	7	0.5	1.0
		300	*AUSTRIA-HUNGARY	7-01-1849	7	0.1	1.8
		329	TWO SICILIES	7-01-1849	7	0.1	1.8
		327	PAPAL STATES	7-01-1849	7	1.5	1.8
		220	*FRANCE	7-12-1859	11	7.5	2.3
		325	*ITALY/SARDINIA	7-12-1859	11	2.5	2.5
		300	*AUSTRIA-HUNGARY	7-12-1859	11	12.5	2.5
		255	*GERMANY/PRUSSIA	7-20-1864	17	1.0	3.6
		300	*AUSTRIA-HUNGARY	7-20-1864	17	0.5	3.6
		390	DENMARK	7-20-1864	17	3.0	3.6

NOTES: * = NATION IN 3 OR MORE WARS
( ) = TOTALS FOR INTERSTATE WARS ONLY

10.16 - MONTHLY AND SEASONAL DEPARTURES FROM WAR BY NATIONS

SEASON 1	MONTH AND PERIOD 2	CODE NO. 3	NATION NAME 4	DATE OF DEPARTURE 5	WAR NO. 6	BATTLE DEATHS (000'S) 7	WAR MONTHS 8
		255	*GERMANY/PRUSSIA	7-26-1866	19	10.0	1.4
		325	*ITALY/SARDINIA	7-26-1866	19	4.0	1.4
		245	BAVARIA	7-26-1866	19	0.5	1.4
		267	BADEN	7-26-1866	19	0.1	1.4
		269	SAXONY	7-26-1866	19	0.6	1.4
		271	WUERTTEMBERG	7-26-1866	19	0.1	1.4
		273	HESSE ELECTORAL	7-26-1866	19	0.1	1.4
		275	HESSE GRAND DUCAL	7-26-1866	19	0.1	1.4
		280	MECKLENBURG-SCHWERIN	7-26-1866	19	0.1	1.4
		300	*AUSTRIA-HUNGARY	7-26-1866	19	20.0	1.4
	2ND	200	*ENGLAND	7-04-1879	75	3.5	5.7
		2	*UNITED STATES	7-04-1902	83	4.5	40.9
		90	GUATEMALA	7-20-1906	29	0.4	1.8
		91	HONDURAS	7-20-1906	29	0.3	1.8
		92	*SALVADOR	7-20-1906	29	0.3	1.8
		345	*YUGOSLAVIA/SERBIA	7-30-1913	34	18.5	1.0
		350	*GREECE	7-30-1913	34	2.5	1.0
		360	*RUMANIA	7-30-1913	34	1.5	0.7
		640	*TURKEY	7-30-1913	34	20.0	0.5
		355	*BULGARIA	7-30-1913	34	18.0	1.0
	3RD	530	*ETHIOPIA	7-03-1941	43	5.0	5.3
		2	*UNITED STATES	7-27-1953	46	54.0	37.0
		20	CANADA	7-27-1953	46	0.3	31.3
		100	COLOMBIA	7-27-1953	46	0.1	25.7
		200	*ENGLAND	7-27-1953	46	0.7	35.0
		210	*HOLLAND	7-27-1953	46	0.1	30.2
		211	*BELGIUM	7-27-1953	46	0.1	30.2
		220	*FRANCE	7-27-1953	46	0.3	30.8
		350	*GREECE	7-27-1953	46	0.2	30.2
		530	*ETHIOPIA	7-27-1953	46	0.1	26.9
		640	*TURKEY	7-27-1953	46	0.7	33.3
		732	KOREA SOUTH	7-27-1953	46	415.0	37.1
		800	THAILAND	7-27-1953	46	0.1	30.2
		840	PHILIPPINES	7-27-1953	46	0.1	34.4
		710	*CHINA	7-27-1953	46	900.0	33.0
		731	KOREA NORTH	7-27-1953	46	520.0	37.1
	1ST		1816-1871: 22 (22)			70.8 (70.8)	54.7 (54.7)
	2ND		1872-1919: 10 (8)			69.5 (61.5)	56.2 (9.6)
	3RD		1920-1965 16 (16)			1896.8 (1896.8)	487.7 (487.7)
	JULY		48 (46)			2037.1 (2029.1)	598.6 (552.0)

NOTES: * = NATION IN 3 OR MORE WARS
( ) = TOTALS FOR INTERSTATE WARS ONLY

SEASON 1	MONTH AND PERIOD 2	CODE NO. 3	NATION NAME 4	DATE OF DEPARTURE 5	WAR NO. 6	BATTLE DEATHS (000'S) 7	WAR MONTHS 8
SUMMER	AUGUST						
	1ST	300	*AUSTRIA-HUNGARY	8-13-1849	63	45.0	11.1
		365	*RUSSIA	8-13-1849	63	14.5	1.0
		140	*BRAZIL	2-03-1852	8	0.5	6.6
		160	ARGENTINA	2-03-1852	8	0.8	6.6
	2ND	2	*UNITED STATES	8-12-1898	27	5.0	3.7
		230	*SPAIN	8-12-1898	27	5.0	3.7
		315	CZECHOSLOVAKIA	8-04-1919	36	2.0	3.6
		360	*RUMANIA	8-04-1919	36	3.0	3.6
		310	*HUNGARY	8-04-1919	36	6.0	3.6
	3RD	360	*RUMANIA	8-23-1944	43	290.0	38.1
		2	*UNITED STATES	8-14-1945	43	408.3	44.3
		20	CANADA	8-14-1945	43	39.3	71.2
		200	*ENGLAND	8-14-1945	43	270.0	71.4
		220	*FRANCE	8-14-1945	43	210.0	19.4
		365	*RUSSIA	8-14-1945	43	7500.0	46.7
		710	*CHINA	8-14-1945	43	1350.0	44.3
		712	MONGOLIA	8-14-1945	43	3.0	0.2
		740	*JAPAN	8-14-1945	43	1000.0	44.3
	1ST		1816-1871: 4 (2)			60.8 (1.3)	25.3 (13.2)
	2ND		1872-1919: 5 (5)			21.0 (21.0)	18.2 (18.2)
	3RD		1920-1965 9 (9)			11070.6 (11070.6)	379.9 (379.9)
	AUGUST		18 (16)			11152.4 (11092.9)	423.4 (411.3)
SUMMER	SEPTEMBER						
	1ST	365	*RUSSIA	9-14-1829	3	50.0	16.7
		640	*TURKEY	9-14-1829	3	80.0	16.7
		140	*BRAZIL	3-01-1870	69	100.0	63.6
		160	ARGENTINA	3-01-1870	69	10.0	59.9
	2ND	210	*HOLLAND	9-00-1878	71	6.0	65.2
		200	*ENGLAND	9-02-1880	74	4.0	18.2
		740	*JAPAN	9-15-1905	28	85.0	19.3
		365	*RUSSIA	9-15-1905	28	45.0	19.3
	3RD	365	*RUSSIA	9-16-1939	42	1.0	4.2
		712	MONGOLIA	9-16-1939	42	3.0	4.2
		740	*JAPAN	9-16-1939	42	15.0	4.2
		325	*ITALY/SARDINIA	9-02-1943	43	60.0	38.8
		355	*BULGARIA	9-08-1944	43	9.0	33.0

NOTES: * = NATION IN 3 OR MORE WARS
( ) = TOTALS FOR INTERSTATE WARS ONLY

10.16 - MONTHLY AND SEASONAL DEPARTURES FROM WAR BY NATIONS

SEASON 1	MONTH AND PERIOD 2	CODE NO. 3	NATION NAME 4	DATE OF DEPARTURE 5	WAR NO. 6	BATTLE DEATHS (000'S) 7	WAR MONTHS 8
		375	FINLAND	9-19-1944	43	42.0	38.9
***** END OF SUMMER *****							
AUTUMN	SEPTEMBER						
	1ST	325	*ITALY/SARDINIA	9-29-1860	13	0.3	0.6
		327	PAPAL STATES	9-29-1860	13	0.7	0.6
	2ND	355	*BULGARIA	9-29-1918	35	14.0	35.6
	3RD	290	POLAND	9-27-1939	43	320.0	0.9
		770	PAKISTAN	9-23-1965	50	3.8	1.6
		750	*INDIA	9-23-1965	50	3.0	1.6
	1ST		1816-1871: 6 (4)			241.0 (131.0)	158.1 (34.6)
	2ND		1872-1919: 5 (3)			154.0 (144.0)	157.6 (74.2)
	3RD		1920-1965 9 (9)			456.8 (456.8)	127.4 (127.4)
	SEPTEMBR		20 (16)			851.8 (731.8)	443.1 (236.2)
AUTUMN	OCTOBER						
	1ST	200	*ENGLAND	10-20-1827	2	0.1	0.1
		220	*FRANCE	10-20-1827	2	0.0	0.1
		365	*RUSSIA	10-20-1827	2	0.1	0.1
		640	*TURKEY	10-20-1827	2	3.0	0.1
		365	*RUSSIA	10-18-1831	56	15.0	8.3
		200	*ENGLAND	10-12-1842	59	20.0	48.4
	2ND	300	*AUSTRIA-HUNGARY	10-00-1878	73	3.5	2.1
		220	*FRANCE	10-01-1895	79	6.0	9.7
		325	*ITALY/SARDINIA	10-21-1896	81	9.0	10.5
		325	*ITALY/SARDINIA	10-18-1912	32	6.0	12.7
		640	*TURKEY	10-18-1912	32	14.0	12.7
	3RD	640	*TURKEY	10-11-1922	37	20.0	41.3
		350	*GREECE	10-11-1922	37	30.0	41.3
		200	*ENGLAND	10-15-1946	88	1.0	11.2
		210	*HOLLAND	10-15-1946	88	0.4	11.2
		645	IRAQ	10-31-1948	45	0.5	2.5
		652	SYRIA	10-31-1948	45	1.0	2.5
		660	LEBANON	10-31-1948	45	0.5	2.5
		663	JORDAN	10-31-1948	45	1.0	2.5

NOTES: * = NATION IN 3 OR MORE WARS
( ) = TOTALS FOR INTERSTATE WARS ONLY

SEASON 1	MONTH AND PERIOD 2	CODE NO. 3	NATION NAME 4	DATE OF DEPARTURE 5	WAR NO. 6	BATTLE DEATHS (000'S) 7	WAR MONTHS 8
	1ST		1816-1871: 6 (4)			38.2 (3.2)	57.1 (0.4)
	2ND		1872-1919: 5 (2)			38.5 (20.0)	47.7 (25.4)
	3RD		1920-1965 8 (6)			54.4 (53.0)	115.0 (92.6)
	OCTOBER		19 (12)			131.1 (76.2)	219.8 (118.4)
AUTUMN	NOVEMBER						
	1ST	220	*FRANCE	11-13-1823	1	0.4	7.3
		230	*SPAIN	11-13-1823	1	0.6	7.3
		200	*ENGLAND	11-27-1840	60	0.0	2.6
		640	*TURKEY	11-27-1840	60	10.0	3.1
		135	*PERU	5-09-1866	18	0.6	3.8
		155	CHILE	5-09-1866	18	0.1	6.5
		245	BAVARIA	11-15-1870	20	5.5	3.9
		267	BADEN	11-22-1870	20	1.0	4.2
		271	WUERTTEMBERG	11-25-1870	20	1.0	4.3
	2ND	2	*UNITED STATES	11-11-1918	35	126.0	18.9
		200	*ENGLAND	11-11-1918	35	908.0	51.2
		211	*BELGIUM	11-11-1918	35	87.5	51.3
		220	*FRANCE	11-11-1918	35	1350.0	51.3
		235	PORTUGAL	11-11-1918	35	7.0	32.4
		325	*ITALY/SARDINIA	11-11-1918	35	650.0	41.7
		345	*YUGOSLAVIA/SERBIA	11-11-1918	35	48.0	51.5
		350	*GREECE	11-11-1918	35	5.0	16.5
		740	*JAPAN	11-11-1918	35	0.3	50.7
		255	*GERMANY/PRUSSIA	11-11-1918	35	1800.0	51.4
		300	*AUSTRIA-HUNGARY	11-03-1918	35	1200.0	51.2
		640	*TURKEY	11-11-1918	35	325.0	48.5
	3RD	140	*BRAZIL	5-07-1945	43	1.0	10.1
		365	*RUSSIA	11-14-1956	47	7.0	0.8
		310	*HUNGARY	11-14-1956	47	25.0	0.8
		200	*ENGLAND	11-07-1956	48	0.0	0.2
		220	*FRANCE	11-07-1956	48	0.0	0.2
		666	ISRAEL	11-07-1956	48	0.2	0.3
		651	U.A.R.	11-07-1956	48	3.0	0.3
		710	*CHINA	11-22-1962	49	0.5	1.1
		750	*INDIA	11-22-1962	49	0.5	1.1
	1ST		1816-1871: 9 (7)			19.2 (9.2)	43.0 (37.3)
	2ND		1872-1919: 12 (12)			6506.8 (6506.8)	516.6 (516.6)
	3RD		1920-1965 9 (9)			37.2 (37.2)	14.9 (14.9)
	NOVEMBER		30 (28)			6563.2 (6553.2)	574.5 (568.8)

NOTES: * = NATION IN 3 OR MORE WARS
( ) = TOTALS FOR INTERSTATE WARS ONLY

10.16 - MONTHLY AND SEASONAL DEPARTURES FROM WAR BY NATIONS

SEASON 1	MONTH AND PERIOD 2	CODE NO. 3	NATION NAME 4	DATE OF DEPARTURE 5	WAR NO. 6	BATTLE DEATHS (000'S) 7		WAR MONTHS 8	
AUTUMN	DECEMBER								
	1ST	640	*TURKEY	12-21-1832	57	10.0		13.7	
		100	COLOMBIA	12-06-1863	16	0.3		0.5	
	2ND	345	*YUGOSLAVIA/SERBIA	12-07-1885	78	2.0		1.2	
		360	*RUMANIA	12-09-1917	35	335.0		15.4	
		365	*RUSSIA	12-05-1917	35	1700.0		40.2	
	3RD	150	PARAGUAY	6-12-1935	39	50.0		35.9	
		145	BOLIVIA	6-12-1935	39	80.0		35.9	
		740	*JAPAN	12-07-1941	41	250.0		53.1	
		710	*CHINA	12-07-1941	41	750.0		53.1	
		220	*FRANCE	12-01-1948	90	1.5		20.2	
***** END OF AUTUMN *****									
WINTER	DECEMBER								
	2ND	200	*ENGLAND	12-30-1885	77	20.0		39.6	
	1ST		1816-1871: 2 (1)			10.3	(0.3)	14.2	(0.5)
	2ND		1872-1919: 4 (2)			2057.0	(2035.0)	96.4	(55.6)
	3RD		1920-1965 5 (4)			1131.5	(1130.0)	198.2	(178.0)
	DECEMBER		11 (7)			3198.8	(3165.3)	308.8	(234.1)

10.16 - MONTHLY AND SEASONAL DEPARTURES FROM WAR BY NATIONS

*** SEASONAL TOTALS ***

PERIOD	NO. OF NATIONS LEAVING WAR		BATTLE DEATHS (000'S)		WAR MONTHS	
	WINTER: DECEMBER 22 - MARCH 21					
1ST	1816-1871:	20 (15)	512.2	(484.2)	361.8	(304.3)
2ND	1872-1919:	4 (2)	405.0	(285.0)	169.3	(17.6)
3RD	1920-1965	12 (9)	257.2	(190.7)	446.8	(304.7)
WINTER		36 (26)	1174.4	(959.9)	977.9	(626.6)
	SPRING: MARCH 22 - JUNE 21					
1ST	1816-1871:	14 (6)	65.5	(20.0)	233.4	(26.8)
2ND	1872-1919:	25 (20)	225.6	(137.1)	400.1	(261.0)
3RD	1920-1965	18 (13)	3809.3	(3641.3)	392.3	(159.4)
SPRING		57 (39)	4100.4	(3798.4)	1025.8	(447.2)
	SUMMER: JUNE 22 - SEPTEMBER 21					
1ST	1816-1871:	31 (27)	372.1	(202.6)	237.4	(101.8)
2ND	1872-1919:	19 (15)	230.5	(212.5)	196.4	(66.4)
3RD	1920-1965	31 (31)	13097.4	(13097.4)	990.9	(990.9)
SUMMER		81 (73)	13700.0	(13512.5)	1424.7	(1159.1)
	SEPTEMBER 22 - DECEMBER 21					
1ST	1816-1871:	19 (14)	68.7	(13.7)	115.5	(39.4)
2ND	1872-1919:	21 (17)	8596.3	(8575.8)	656.7	(633.2)
3RD	1920-1965	25 (22)	1549.9	(1547.0)	332.2	(289.6)
AUTUMN		65 (53)	10214.9	(10136.5)	1104.4	(962.2)

NOTE: ( ) = TOTALS FOR INTERSTATE WARS ONLY

10.17 - TOTAL MONTHLY ENTRIES INTO WAR BY WAR-PRONE NATIONS

CODE	NATION NAME	JAN	FEB	MAR	APR	MAY	JUN	JUL	AUG	SEP	OCT	NOV	DEC	TOTAL
2	UNITED STATES	0	1	0	2	1	1	0	0	0	0	0	1	6
70	MEXICO	0	0	0	1	1	0	0	0	0	1	0	0	3
92	SALVADOR	0	1	1	0	1	0	0	0	0	0	0	0	3
135	PERU	0	0	0	1	0	0	1	0	0	1	0	0	3
140	BRAZIL	2	0	0	0	1	0	0	0	0	0	0	0	3
200	ENGLAND	1	0	1	0	1	0	0	2	4	5	4	1	19
210	HOLLAND	1	0	1	0	1	0	1	0	0	0	1	0	5
211	BELGIUM	1	0	0	0	1	0	0	1	0	0	0	0	3
220	FRANCE	1	0	2	5	1	1	2	1	1	1	2	2	19
230	SPAIN	0	1	0	2	1	0	2	0	0	3	0	0	9
255	GERMANY/PRUSSIA	0	1	0	1	0	1	1	1	1	0	0	0	6
300	AUSTRIA-HUNGARY	0	1	1	1	1	1	2	0	1	0	0	0	8
310	HUNGARY	0	0	0	1	0	1	0	0	0	1	0	0	3
325	ITALY/SARDINIA	1	0	1	1	1	2	0	0	2	3	0	1	12
345	YUGOSLAVIA/SERBIA	0	0	0	1	0	1	1	0	0	1	1	0	5
350	GREECE	1	1	0	0	1	2	0	0	0	2	0	0	7
355	BULGARIA	0	0	0	0	0	1	0	0	1	2	0	1	5
360	RUMANIA	0	0	0	1	0	1	1	1	1	0	0	0	5
365	RUSSIA	1	2	0	2	1	1	1	1	1	3	1	1	15
530	ETHIOPIA	1	0	0	0	1	0	0	0	0	1	0	0	3
640	TURKEY	0	1	1	2	2	1	2	0	1	5	1	1	17
710	CHINA	0	0	1	0	0	1	1	1	0	2	0	2	8
740	JAPAN	0	1	0	0	1	0	1	2	0	0	0	2	7
750	INDIA	0	0	0	0	0	0	0	1	0	2	0	0	3
	** TOTALS	10	10	9	21	17	15	16	11	13	33	10	12	177

10.18 - TOTAL MONTHLY DEPARTURES FROM WAR BY WAR-PRONE NATIONS

CODE	NATION NAME	JAN	FEB	MAR	APR	MAY	JUN	JUL	AUG	SEP	OCT	NOV	DEC	TOTAL
2	UNITED STATES	0	1	0	0	0	0	2	2	0	0	1	0	6
70	MEXICO	0	2	0	1	0	0	0	0	0	0	0	0	3
92	SALVADOR	0	0	0	2	0	0	1	0	0	0	0	0	3
135	PERU	0	0	0	1	1	0	0	0	0	0	1	0	3
140	BRAZIL	0	0	0	0	0	0	0	1	1	0	1	0	3
200	ENGLAND	0	1	4	1	1	1	2	1	1	3	3	1	19
210	HOLLAND	0	0	1	0	1	0	1	0	1	1	0	0	5
211	BELGIUM	0	0	0	0	1	0	1	0	0	0	1	0	3
220	FRANCE	0	2	2	0	1	4	3	1	0	2	3	1	19
230	SPAIN	0	1	2	1	3	0	0	1	0	0	1	0	9
255	GERMANY/PRUSSIA	0	1	0	0	1	0	3	0	0	0	1	0	6
300	AUSTRIA-HUNGARY	0	0	1	0	0	0	4	1	0	1	1	0	8
310	HUNGARY	1	0	0	0	0	0	0	1	0	0	1	0	3
325	ITALY/SARDINIA	1	0	2	0	2	0	2	0	2	2	1	0	12
345	YUGOSLAVIA/SERBIA	0	0	0	2	0	0	1	0	0	0	1	1	5
350	GREECE	0	0	0	2	1	0	2	0	0	1	1	0	7
355	BULGARIA	0	0	0	1	1	0	1	0	2	0	0	0	5
360	RUMANIA	0	0	0	0	1	0	1	2	0	0	0	1	5
365	RUSSIA	1	1	3	1	0	0	0	2	3	2	1	1	15
530	ETHIOPIA	0	0	0	0	1	0	2	0	0	0	0	0	3
640	TURKEY	1	0	2	3	1	1	2	0	1	3	2	1	17
710	CHINA	0	0	2	0	1	1	1	1	0	0	1	1	8
740	JAPAN	0	0	1	0	1	0	0	1	2	0	1	1	7
750	INDIA	1	0	0	0	0	0	0	0	1	0	1	0	3
	** TOTALS	5	9	20	15	18	7	29	14	14	15	23	8	177

may very well be a matter of pure chance, we focus next on those nations that made at least 6 such decisions, via participation in at least 3 wars. Since the cumulative effect of the less war-prone nations' behavior has already made itself apparent in all the prior tables, we can disregard those events and move on to an examination of the patterns of the more war-prone of the system members (Table 10.17 and 10.18).

The results here tend, in general, to echo those emerging in Tables 10.4 to 10.6 and 10.11 to 10.13; most of the war entries and departures (as we will see in Chapter Eleven) are accounted for by the small fraction of the system's members that contributed inordinately to the incidence of war in the 150 years under study, and that groups is represented in the tables below. Thus, we again find that October and April are the preferred entry months for those nations having the most war experience. England, Russia, and Turkey show a marked "preference" for October, and if these decisions *are* at all autonomous, it is clear that French and Spanish (and to a lesser extent, American) decision makers lean toward April as a propitious month for entry into war. On the other hand, we should note that the really high war-prone nations are well represented in almost all months (and certainly all seasons) of the year.

As to the ending of wars or departure from those which continue on, July is the most "popular" month, followed by November and March. But the most war-prone system members show much less of a concentration here than in their entry into wars; France, England, Russia, and Turkey all reveal a fairly flat distribution in their "choice" of war departure dates.

SUMMARY

We find in Wright's *Study of War* that 98 percent of the battles of the Middle Ages, 87 percent of those in the seventeenth and eighteenth centuries, and 78 percent in the last two centuries occurred during spring and summer. Do our data reflect the same sort of seasonal concentrations? If specific battles were as important in more recent periods as they were in determining the outcome of earlier wars, we might be able to compare our findings with those of Wright; but even without such data, some useful generalizations are possible.

Two patterns seem to stand out, and would therefore merit further investigation. First, in sheer number of joint decisions to go to war over the past century and a half, April and October are clearly the preferred months. Second, the passage of time and associated developments in the technology of war, communications, and agriculture seem to have exercised little impact on seasonal concentrations; modest concentrations which appear in the 1816–1871 period, for example, disappear in the middle period, and then show up again in the post-1920 decades. None of the other patterns noted in the chapter is sufficiently strong and clear to merit recapitulation here. As a matter of fact, a quick analysis of the days of the week on which wars began also shows an essentially random distribution.

On the other hand, this absence of many strong patterns hardly justifies a turning away from the subject. Rather, what seems to be required next is a more detailed analysis of both the aggregate data presented here and the specific cases on which the figures are originally based. As we ourselves move into those specific cases—as well as the other cases of conflict that did *not* eventuate in war—it is likely that seasonal factors will have been far from negligible in decisions to enter, leave, or avoid war.

Part D
The Nations

Chapter 11

The War-Proneness of Nations

Up to this point, our major concern has been with war as a *systemic* phenomenon; we have examined the incidence of various types of war in the international system and its several sub-systems, and presented our best estimates of its fluctuations and distributions. For many researchers, that may be the most useful orientation, but we hope to make this volume equally valuable to scholars who concentrate not on the larger systemic setting, but on a particular geographic region, a given pair of nations, or even a single such entity. In this chapter, therefore, we shift our level of analysis and offer a wide range of war data showing the war experienced by each individual *nation* during its membership in the system.

The literature of international politics fairly brims over with hunches, hypotheses, propositions, and allegations about which particular nations—or classes of nations—are most war-prone. Sometimes the argument is based on the geographical locus or resources of the nations, sometimes on the type of political system or style of leadership, and not infrequently on some putative innate characteristic of the people. While much of this literature is often stronger on rhetoric than on evidence, the general question—why some nations are more war-prone than others—merits investigation. We insist, however, on a considerable broadening of the inquiry and urge not only that a wide range of attributes be examined, but that as much attention be paid to those characteristics which change and fluctuate as to those of a relatively enduring nature.

Thus, any search for correlations between the attributes of the nations and their war-proneness during all or part of their tenure in the system might well look at both the more stable and the more erratic aspects of their physical, structural, and cultural attributes. Among the *physical* attributes to which we will be turning as possible predictors of national war-proneness are: population, birth and death rates, ethnic composition and homogeneity, basic geography, natural resources, industrial production, military capability, and so forth. Some of the *structural* attributes worth investigating might be governmental structure, party number and strength, economic patterns and wealth distribution, educational facilities, religious institutions, mass media circulation, and of course, rates of change therein. As to the *cultural* dimensions possibly meriting investigations, there might be not only national character, military and diplomatic traditions, religiosity, and family orientations, but the direction and rates of change in such elite and mass phenomena as xenophobia, future-orientedness, propensity for risk-taking, and the like.

Regardless of the national attribute or attributes selected for a possible correlational analysis, however, no satisfactory results are possible unless we know precisely which nations, during which periods, experienced what amounts of war. In this chapter, we present data on the nations individually; in subsequent chapters, we will give similar data for all possible pairs of nations during their post-Napoleonic histories, and also for each of the major regions of the globe. The first two tables arrange the nations geographically and show a variety of indicators of national war experience, the third and fourth bring the nations together for rank order comparisons, and the fifth table shows the correlations among the various indicators used.

SPECIFIC WAR EXPERIENCE OF THE NATIONS

In Table 11.1 each nation is listed by its region in order of its nation code number. We control for such important factors as duration of membership in the international system, and the magnitude and severity of the wars a nation fought, in Table 11.2, but our first concern is to present the national war experience data in its most raw and least converted or interpreted form.

The first set of columns (1 to 3) shows the frequency with which each nation has been involved in all international wars and in interstate and extra-systemic ones, respectively; each such war is identified only by its code number, since the name, dates, and participants have already been specified in Tables 4.2 and 4.4 . Next (columns 4 and 5), the number of war months and battle deaths is shown, first in total and below that in terms of each specific war experience. As we noted in Chapter Three, the battle death figures must not be interpreted too literally. While the estimates for some nations in some wars are probably accurate to a man (such as the 40 French deaths in Navarino Bay) and therefore given in that form, others are clearly approximations (such as China's 1,350,000 in World War II) and are therefore rounded off as was indicated earlier. Thus, each nation's total figure is somewhat less precise than the numbers might convey. These figures are followed in turn by the two most useful of our three intensity measures: battle deaths per nation month for each war (column 6) as well as its battle deaths per capita, based on its population prior to each of its wars (column 7). Finally, for those with a geopolitical bent (and in anticipation of the next chapter), we indicate (column 8) the continental region or regions in which that nation fought in each war.

At the end of each region's list is a series of figures summing up the war experiences of all of the nations in that region; these figures will be repeated and expanded in the next chapter, but are included here to offer a base line against which individual national experiences can be compared. In the first three columns, the total number of all international war experiences as well as interstate and extra-systemic experiences of all nations in the region are shown; in the next two, respectively, are the total number of war months experienced and the total number of battle-connected deaths suffered. Since many, if not most, of the interstate wars involve only nations from the same region, the effect is to count many of the war and war month experiences more than once. Although these aggregate figures may be of real value for certain theoretical purposes, they are not an accurate indication of the war experiences of the region *qua* region. The battle death sum, on the other hand, is not likely to be misinterpreted since—unlike wars and war months—fatalities cannot be shared. They are strictly (but in the statistical sense only) a single nation's loss and therefore may be summed up quite unambiguously.

TOTAL AND AVERAGE WAR EXPERIENCE OF THE NATIONS

In this section, we shift our focus from the specific wars in which the nations fought, and the magnitude, severity, and intensity of each of those war experiences, to each nation's total war experiences during the period in which it was a qualified member of the interstate system. Besides presenting a nation's total war record, we will compute its average war experience, and control for the duration of its tenure in the system—its life span, if we may anthropomorphize for a moment. For instance, we feel that there is an important qualitative difference between a nation whose wars are on the average brief with light losses, and one which fought fewer wars which are of greater duration and severity, and that there is a difference between a nation which engaged in five wars in 150 years and one which engaged in five during the brief span of perhaps 25 years.

11.1 - NATIONAL WAR EXPERIENCES SUMMARIZED AND SPECIFIED

CODE NUMBER AND NATION NAME	WAR FREQUENCIES AND CODE NUMBERS ALL 1	INTER-STATE 2	EXTRA SYS-TEMIC 3	NATION MONTHS 4	BATTLE DEATHS 5	BATTLE DEATHS PER NATION MONTH 6	BATTLE DEATHS PER MILLION POP. 7	REGION WHERE WAR WAS FOUGHT 8
WESTERN HEMISPHERE								
2 UNITED STATES	6	5	1	165.9	608800			
		4		21.1	11000	521.3	476.2	WH
		27		3.7	5000	1351.4	65.8	WH
		35		18.9	126000	6666.7	1312.5	EU
		43		44.3	408300	9216.7	3140.8	EU AF ME AS
		46		37.0	54000	1459.5	347.7	AS
			83	40.9	4500	110.0	59.2	AS
20 CANADA	2	2	0	102.5	39610			
		43		71.2	39300	552.0	3447.4	EU
		46		31.3	310	9.9	22.6	AS
70 MEXICO	3	2	1	85.5	19000			
		4		21.1	6000	284.4	800.0	WH
		15		57.7	12000	208.0	1428.6	WH
			58	6.7	1000	149.3	129.9	WH
90 GUATEMALA	2	2	0	2.4	1200			
		24		0.6	800	1333.3	615.4	WH
		29		1.8	400	222.2	210.5	WH
91 HONDURAS	2	2	0	3.9	600			
		29		1.8	300	166.7	428.6	WH
		30		2.1	300	142.9	428.6	WH
92 SALVADOR	3	3	0	4.5	800			
		24		0.6	200	333.3	285.7	WH
		29		1.8	300	166.7	272.7	WH
		30		2.1	300	142.9	272.7	WH

CODE NUMBER AND NATION NAME	WAR FREQUENCIES AND CODE NUMBERS ALL 1	INTER-STATE 2	EXTRA SYS-TEMIC 3	NATION MONTHS 4	BATTLE DEATHS 5	BATTLE DEATHS PER NATION MONTH 6	BATTLE DEATHS PER MILLION POP. 7	REGION WHERE WAR WAS FOUGHT 8
93 NICARAGUA	1	1	0	2.1	400			
		30		2.1	400	190.5	666.7	WH
100 COLOMBIA	2	2	0	26.2	440			
		16		0.5	300	600.0	100.0	WH
		46		25.7	140	5.4	10.3	AS
130 ECUADOR	1	1	0	0.5	700			
		16		0.5	700	1400.0	500.0	WH
135 PERU	3	2	1	59.3	11600			
		18		3.8	600	157.9	187.5	WH
		22		54.5	10000	183.5	3703.7	WH
			61	1.0	1000	1000.0	769.2	WH
140 BRAZIL	3	2	1	80.3	101500			
		8		6.6	500	75.8	68.5	WH
		43		10.1	1000	99.0	25.3	EU
			69	63.6	100000	1572.3	8474.6	WH
145 BOLIVIA	2	2	0	93.8	81000			
		22		57.9	1000	17.3	434.8	WH
		39		35.9	80000	2228.4	32000.0	WH
150 PARAGUAY	1	1	0	35.9	50000			
		39		35.9	50000	1392.8	55555.6	WH
155 CHILE	2	2	0	64.4	3100			
		18		6.5	100	15.4	55.6	WH
		22		57.9	3000	51.8	1500.0	WH

11.1 - NATIONAL WAR EXPERIENCES SUMMARIZED AND SPECIFIED

CODE NUMBER AND NATION NAME	WAR FREQUENCIES AND CODE NUMBERS ALL 1	INTER-STATE 2	EXTRA SYS-TEMIC 3	NATION MONTHS 4	BATTLE DEATHS 5	BATTLE DEATHS PER NATION MONTH 6	BATTLE DEATHS PER MILLION POP. 7	REGION WHERE WAR WAS FOUGHT 8
160 ARGENTINA	2	1	1	66.5	10800			
		8		6.6	800	121.2	727.3	WH
			69	59.9	10000	166.9	5263.2	WH
WESTERN HEMISPHERE TOTALS	35	30	5	793.7	929550			

11.1 - NATIONAL WAR EXPERIENCES SUMMARIZED AND SPECIFIED

CODE NUMBER AND NATION NAME	WAR FREQUENCIES AND CODE NUMBERS ALL 1	INTER-STATE 2	EXTRA SYS-TEMIC 3	NATION MONTHS 4	BATTLE DEATHS 5	BATTLE DEATHS PER NATION MONTH 6	BATTLE DEATHS PER MILLION POP. 7	REGION WHERE WAR WAS FOUGHT 8
EUROPE								
200 ENGLAND	19	7	12	409.8	1295280			
		2		0.1	80	800.0	3.5	EU
		9		23.1	22000	952.4	766.6	EU
		10		4.6	500	108.7	17.1	ME
		35		51.2	908000	17734.4	19653.7	EU AF ME AS
		43		71.4	270000	3781.5	5684.2	EU AF ME AS
		46		35.0	670	19.1	13.4	AS
		48		0.2	20	100.0	0.4	ME
			51	6.9	2000	289.9	98.0	AS
			53	29.1	15000	515.5	684.9	AS
			59	48.4	20000	413.2	775.2	AS
			60	2.6	10	3.8	0.4	ME
			62	2.9	1500	517.2	55.6	AS
			64	5.1	1500	294.1	54.9	AS
			66	22.9	3500	152.8	119.0	AS
			74	18.2	4000	219.8	118.0	AS
			75	5.7	3500	614.0	102.3	AF
			77	39.6	20000	505.1	568.2	ME
			84	31.6	22000	696.2	531.4	AF
			88	11.2	1000	89.3	20.2	AS
210 HOLLAND	5	2	3	163.0	27710			
		43		0.2	6200	31000.0	712.6	EU
		46		30.2	110	3.6	10.8	AS
			54	56.2	15000	266.9	2542.4	AS
			71	65.2	6000	92.0	1621.6	AS
			88	11.2	400	35.7	43.0	AS
211 BEIGIUM	3	3	0	82.1	97200			
		35		51.3	87500	1705.7	11513.2	EU
		43		0.6	9600	16000.0	1142.9	EU
		46		30.2	100	3.3	11.5	AS

11.1 - NATIONAL WAR EXPERIENCES SUMMARIZED AND SPECIFIED

CODE NUMBER AND NATICN NAME	WAR FREQUENCIES AND CODE NUMBERS ALL 1	INTER-STATE 2	EXTRA SYS-TEMIC 3	NATION MONTHS 4	BATTLE DEATHS 5	BATTLE DEATHS PER NATION MONTH 6	BATTLE DEATHS PER MILLION POP. 7	REGION WHERE WAR WAS FOUGHT 8
220 FRANCE	19	12	7	494.3	1943840			
		1		7.3	400	54.8	12.7	EU
		2		0.1	40	400.0	1.2	EU
		7		1.0	500	500.0	14.0	EU
		9		23.1	95000	4112.6	2638.9	EU
		11		2.3	7500	3260.9	201.6	EU
		15		57.7	8000	138.6	212.2	WH
		20		7.3	140000	19178.1	3589.7	EU
		23		11.8	2100	178.0	55.1	AS
		35		51.3	1350000	26315.8	32926.8	EU AF ME
		43		19.4	210000	10824.7	5109.5	EU
		46		30.8	290	9.4	6.9	AS
		48		0.2	10	50.0	0.2	ME
			76	25.7	4500	175.1	118.7	AS
			79	9.7	6000	618.6	156.3	AF
			86	13.5	4000	296.3	98.3	ME
			87	22.4	4000	178.6	98.3	ME
			89	102.0	95000	931.4	2435.9	AS
			90	20.2	1500	74.3	37.5	AF
			92	88.5	15000	169.5	348.8	ME
230 SPAIN	9	5	4	262.0	188900			
		1		7.3	600	82.2	53.1	EU
		12		5.2	4000	769.2	248.4	ME
		18		6.5	300	46.2	18.3	WH
		27		3.7	5000	1351.4	271.7	WH
		31		8.5	2000	235.3	102.6	ME
			70	112.1	100000	892.1	6024.1	WH
			80	37.3	50000	1340.5	2762.4	WH
			82	23.1	2000	86.6	109.9	AS
			86	58.3	25000	428.8	1136.4	ME
235 PORTUGAL	1	1	0	32.4	7000			
		35		32.4	7000	216.0	1129.0	EU
240 HANOVER	1	1	0	0.5	500			
		19		0.5	500	1000.0	5000.0	EU

CODE NUMBER AND NATION NAME	ALL 1	INTER-STATE 2	EXTRA SYS-TEMIC 3	NATION MONTHS 4	BATTLE DEATHS 5	BATTLE DEATHS PER NATION MONTH 6	BATTLE DEATHS PER MILLION POP. 7	REGION WHERE WAR WAS FOUGHT 8
	WAR FREQUENCIES AND CODE NUMBERS							
245 BAVARIA	2	2	0	5.3	6000			
		19		1.4	500	357.1	104.2	EU
		20		3.9	5500	1410.3	1122.4	EU
255 GERMANY/PRUSSIA	6	6	0	140.0	5353500			
		6		8.1	2500	308.6	156.2	EU
		17		3.6	1000	277.8	51.8	EU
		19		1.4	10000	7142.9	423.7	EU
		20		7.3	40000	5479.4	1044.4	EU
		35		51.4	1800000	35019.5	26865.7	EU AF ME AS
		43		68.2	3500000	51319.6	44416.2	EU AF ME
267 BADEN	2	2	0	5.6	1100			
		19		1.4	100	71.4	71.4	EU
		20		4.2	1000	238.1	666.7	EU
269 SAXONY	1	1	0	1.4	600			
		19		1.4	600	428.6	250.0	EU
271 WUERTTEMBERG	2	2	0	5.7	1100			
		19		1.4	100	71.4	55.6	EU
		20		4.3	1000	232.6	555.6	EU
273 HESSE ELECTORAL	1	1	0	1.4	100			
		19		1.4	100	71.4	142.9	EU
275 HESSE GRAND DUCAL	1	1	0	1.4	100			
		19		1.4	100	71.4	125.0	EU
280 MECKLENBURG-SCHWERIN	1	1	0	1.4	100			
		19		1.4	100	71.4	166.7	EU

11.1 - NATIONAL WAR EXPERIENCES SUMMARIZED AND SPECIFIED

CODE NUMBER AND NATION NAME	WAR FREQUENCIES AND CODE NUMBERS ALL 1	INTER-STATE 2	EXTRA SYS-TEMIC 3	NATION MONTHS 4	BATTLE DEATHS 5	BATTLE DEATHS PER NATION MONTH 6	BATTLE DEATHS PER MILLION POP. 7	REGION WHERE WAR WAS FOUGHT 8
290 POLAND	1	1	0	0.9	320000			
		43		0.9	320000	355555.6	9169.1	EU
300 AUSTRIA-HUNGARY	8	6	2	78.4	1287200			
		5		4.7	5600	1191.5	163.3	EU
		7		1.8	100	55.6	2.9	EU
		11		2.5	12500	5000.0	361.3	EU
		17		3.6	500	138.9	14.2	EU
		19		1.4	20000	14285.7	561.8	EU
		35		51.2	1200000	23437.5	22641.5	EU
			63	11.1	45000	4054.1	1312.0	EU
			73	2.1	3500	1666.7	90.9	EU
310 HUNGARY	3	3	0	47.2	71000			
		36		3.6	6000	1666.7	750.0	EU
		43		42.8	40000	934.6	4347.8	EU
		47		0.8	25000	31250.0	2551.0	EU
315 CZECHCSLOVAKIA	1	1	0	3.6	2000			
		36		3.6	2000	555.6	153.8	EU
325 ITALY/SARDINIA	12	11	1	155.7	759500			
		5		4.7	3400	723.4	693.9	EU
		9		13.7	2200	160.6	423.1	EU
		11		2.5	2500	1000.0	480.8	EU
		13		0.6	300	500.0	13.7	EU
		14		3.2	600	187.5	27.4	EU
		19		1.4	4000	2857.1	179.4	EU
		32		12.7	6000	472.4	171.9	ME
		35		41.7	650000	15587.5	18465.9	EU
		40		7.2	4000	555.6	93.9	AF
		43		18.7	17500	935.8	401.4	EU AF ME
		43		38.8	60000	1546.4	1376.1	EU
			81	10.5	9000	857.1	287.5	AF

CODE NUMBER AND NATION NAME	WAR FREQUENCIES AND CODE NUMBERS ALL 1	INTER-STATE 2	EXTRA SYS-TEMIC 3	NATION MONTHS 4	BATTLE DEATHS 5	BATTLE DEATHS PER NATION MONTH 6	BATTLE DEATHS PER MILLION POP. 7	REGION WHERE WAR WAS FOUGHT 8
327 PAPAL STATES	2	2	0	2.4	2200			
		7		1.8	1500	833.3	517.2	EU
		13		0.6	700	1166.7	225.8	EU
329 TWO SICILIES	2	2	0	5.0	500			
		7		1.8	100	55.6	32.3	EU
		14		3.2	400	125.0	41.2	EU
345 YUGOSLAVIA/SERBIA	5	4	1	58.2	88500			
		33		4.1	15000	3658.5	5172.4	EU ME
		34		1.0	18500	18500.0	4111.1	EU
		35		51.5	48000	932.0	10666.7	EU
		43		0.4	5000	12500.0	324.7	EU
			78	1.2	2000	1666.7	1052.6	EU
350 GREECE	7	7	0	104.1	53270			
		26		3.1	600	193.5	250.0	EU
		33		6.1	5000	819.7	1851.9	EU ME
		34		1.0	2500	2500.0	925.9	EU
		35		16.5	5000	303.0	1851.9	EU
		37		41.3	30000	726.4	11111.1	EU ME
		43		5.9	10000	1694.9	1408.5	EU
		46		30.2	170	5.6	22.4	AS
355 BULGARIA	5	5	0	81.6	74000			
		33		4.1	32000	7804.9	7441.9	EU
		34		1.0	18000	18000.0	3750.0	EU
		35		35.6	14000	393.3	2916.7	EU
		43		7.9	1000	126.6	158.7	EU
		43		33.0	9000	272.7	1428.6	EU

11.1 - NATIONAL WAR EXPERIENCES SUMMARIZED AND SPECIFIED

CODE NUMBER AND NATION NAME	WAR FREQUENCIES AND CODE NUMBERS ALL 1	INTER-STATE 2	EXTRA SYS-TEMIC 3	NATION MONTHS 4	BATTLE DEATHS 5	BATTLE DEATHS PER NATION MONTH 6	BATTLE DEATHS PER MILLION POP. 7	REGION WHERE WAR WAS FOUGHT 8
360 RUMANIA	5	5	0	65.7	639500			
		34		0.7	1500	2142.9	211.3	EU
		35		15.4	335000	21753.2	47183.1	EU
		36		3.6	3000	833.3	187.5	EU
		43		7.9	10000	1265.8	500.0	EU
		43		38.1	290000	7611.5	14500.0	EU
365 RUSSIA	15	10	5	249.0	9662560			
		2		0.1	60	600.0	1.1	EU
		3		16.7	50000	2994.0	919.1	EU ME
		9		28.3	100000	3533.6	1404.5	EU
		21		8.8	120000	13636.4	1279.3	EU ME
		28		19.3	45000	2331.6	319.6	AS
		35		40.2	1700000	42288.6	10493.8	EU ME
		42		4.2	1000	238.1	5.9	AS
		43		46.7	7500000	160599.6	43988.3	EU AS
		44		3.4	50000	14705.9	293.3	EU
		47		0.8	7000	8750.0	35.0	EU
			55	17.0	5000	294.1	94.7	ME
			56	8.3	15000	1807.2	265.0	EU
			63	1.0	14500	14500.0	212.0	EU
			68	14.9	5000	335.6	64.9	EU
			85	39.3	50000	1272.3	308.6	EU
375 FINLAND	2	2	0	42.3	82000			
		43		38.9	42000	1079.7	10769.2	EU
		44		3.4	40000	11764.7	10256.4	EU
385 NORWAY	1	1	0	2.0	2000			
		43		2.0	2000	1000.0	689.7	EU
390 DENMARK	2	2	0	11.7	6500			
		6		8.1	3500	432.1	1521.7	EU
		17		3.6	3000	833.3	1578.9	EU
EUROPE TOTALS	144	109	35	2514.1	21973760			

11.1 - NATIONAL WAR EXPERIENCES SUMMARIZED AND SPECIFIED

CODE NUMBER AND NATION NAME		WAR FREQUENCIES AND CODE NUMBERS ALL 1	INTER-STATE 2	EXTRA SYS-TEMIC 3	NATION MONTHS 4	BATTLE DEATHS 5	BATTLE DEATHS PER NATION MONTH 6	BATTLE DEATHS PER MILLION POP. 7	REGION WHERE WAR WAS FOUGHT 8
AFRICA									
530 ETHIOPIA		3	3	0	39.4	21120			
			40		7.2	16000	2222.2	1600.0	AF
			43		5.3	5000	943.4	500.0	AF
			46		26.9	120	4.5	7.6	AS
560 SOUTH AFRICA		1	1	0	71.3	8700			
			43		71.3	8700	122.0	870.0	AF
AFRICA	TOTALS	4	4	0	110.7	29820			

11.1 - NATIONAL WAR EXPERIENCES SUMMARIZED AND SPECIFIED

CODE NUMBER AND NATION NAME	WAR FREQUENCIES AND CODE NUMBERS: ALL 1	INTER-STATE 2	EXTRA SYS-TEMIC 3	NATION MONTHS 4	BATTLE DEATHS 5	BATTLE DEATHS PER NATION MONTH 6	BATTLE DEATHS PER MILLION POP. 7	REGION WHERE WAR WAS FOUGHT 8
MIDDLE EAST								
600 MOROCCO	2	2	0	13.7	14000			
		12		5.2	6000	1153.8	2307.7	ME
		31		8.5	8000	941.2	1600.0	ME
630 IRAN	1	1	0	4.6	1500			
		10		4.6	1500	326.1	340.9	ME
640 TURKEY	17	11	6	339.0	757120			
		2		0.1	3000	30000.0	126.1	EU
		3		16.7	80000	4790.4	3347.3	EU ME
		9		28.3	45000	1590.1	1764.7	EU
		21		8.8	165000	18750.0	5851.1	EU ME
		26		3.1	1400	451.6	57.6	EU
		32		12.7	14000	1102.4	564.5	ME
		33		6.1	30000	4918.0	1363.6	EU ME
		34		0.5	20000	40000.0	1081.1	EU
		35		48.5	325000	6701.0	17567.6	ME
		37		41.3	20000	484.3	1818.2	EU ME
		46		33.3	720	21.6	34.3	AS
			52	85.1	15000	176.3	607.3	EU
			57	13.7	10000	729.9	432.9	ME
			60	3.1	10000	3225.8	416.7	ME
			65	3.4	5000	1470.6	198.4	EU
			67	12.9	3000	232.6	114.9	EU
			72	21.4	10000	467.3	354.6	EU
645 IRAQ	1	1	0	2.5	500			
		45		2.5	500	200.0	108.7	ME
651 U.A.R.	2	2	0	5.0	5000			
		45		4.7	2000	425.5	104.2	ME
		48		0.3	3000	10000.0	128.8	ME

CODE NUMBER AND NATION NAME	WAR FREQUENCIES AND CODE NUMBERS ALL 1	INTER-STATE 2	EXTRA SYS-TEMIC 3	NATION MONTHS 4	BATTLE DEATHS 5	BATTLE DEATHS PER NATION MONTH 6	BATTLE DEATHS PER MILLION POP. 7	REGION WHERE WAR WAS FOUGHT 8
652 SYRIA	1	1	0	2.5	1000			
		45		2.5	1000	400.0	322.6	ME
660 LEBANON	1	1	0	2.5	500			
		45		2.5	500	200.0	416.7	ME
663 JORDAN	1	1	0	2.5	1000			
		45		2.5	1000	400.0	769.2	ME
666 ISRAEL	2	2	0	5.0	3200			
		45		4.7	3000	638.3	2142.9	ME
		48		0.3	200	666.7	105.3	ME
MIDDLE EAST TOTALS	28	22	6	377.3	783820			

11.1 - NATIONAL WAR EXPERIENCES SUMMARIZED AND SPECIFIED

CODE NUMBER AND NATION NAME	WAR FREQUENCIES AND CODE NUMBERS ALL 1	INTER-STATE 2	EXTRA SYS-TEMIC 3	NATION MONTHS 4	BATTLE DEATHS 5	BATTLE DEATHS PER NATION MONTH 6	BATTLE DEATHS PER MILLION POP. 7	REGION WHERE WAR WAS FOUGHT 8
ASIA								
710 CHINA	8	7	1	204.6	3110500			
		23		11.8	10000	847.5	23.3	AS
		25		8.0	10000	1250.0	22.7	AS
		38		16.6	50000	3012.0	95.0	AS
		41		53.1	750000	14124.3	1395.6	AS
		43		44.3	1350000	30474.0	·2495.4	AS
		46		33.0	900000	27272.7	1607.1	AS
		49		1.1	500	454.5	0.8	AS
			93	36.7	40000	1089.9	65.6	AS
712 MONGOLIA	2	2	0	4.4	6000			
		42		4.2	3000	714.3	5000.0	AS
		43		0.2	3000	15000.0	5000.0	AS
731 KOREA NORTH	1	1	0	37.1	520000			
		46		37.1	520000	14016.2	53608.2	AS
732 KOREA SOUTH	1	1	0	37.1	415000			
		46		37.1	415000	11186.0	19951.9	AS
740 JAPAN	7	7	0	196.2	1365300			
		25		8.0	5000	625.0	125.0	AS
		28		19.3	85000	4404.1	1804.7	AS
		35		50.7	300	5.9	5.6	AS
		38		16.6	10000	602.4	154.3	AS
		41		53.1	250000	4708.1	3602.3	AS
		42		4.2	15000	3571.4	212.5	AS
		43		44.3	1000000	22573.4	14164.3	AS

CODE NUMBER AND NATION NAME	WAR FREQUENCIES AND CODE NUMBERS ALL 1	INTER-STATE 2	EXTRA SYS-TEMIC 3	NATION MONTHS 4	BATTLE DEATHS 5	BATTLE DEATHS PER NATION MONTH 6	BATTLE DEATHS PER MILLION POP. 7	REGION WHERE WAR WAS FOUGHT 8
750 INDIA	3	2	1	17.0	5000			
		49		1.1	500	454.5	1.1	AS
		50		1.6	3000	1875.0	6.2	AS
			91	14.3	1500	104.9	3.9	AS
770 PAKISTAN	1	1	0	1.6	3800			
		50		1.6	3800	2375.0	33.4	AS
800 THAILAND	1	1	0	30.2	110			
		46		30.2	110	3.6	5.4	AS
840 PHILIPPINES	1	1	0	34.4	90			
		46		34.4	90	2.6	4.4	AS
900 AUSTRALIA	2	2	0	103.0	29670			
		43		71.4	29400	411.8	4323.5	AF ME AS
		46		31.6	270	8.5	32.9	AS
920 NEW ZEALAND	1	1	0	71.4	17300			
		43		71.4	17300	242.3	10812.5	AF ME AS
ASIA TOTALS	28	26	2	737.0	5472770			

The nations are listed in Table 11.2 within their regions, and, as in the previous table, in order of the nations' three-digit code numbers. The first column shows the duration of the nation's system membership in the total system, thus providing the basis for normalizing the later columns. The next two (columns 2 and 3) show the total number of wars—interstate and extra-systemic—in which the nation fought, and the total number of battle deaths resulting from those wars. Next (column 4) we give the nation's total war months. The following three columns, in which we control for length of system membership, show: the nation's battle deaths per year of membership in the total system (column 5); the number of wars per year of tenure (column 6); and its war months per year of membership in the system (column 7). In the final set of columns are three figures which are the result of controlling for the number of wars experienced. We compute the following *war averages:* average length of the nation's participation in war, or its nation months per war (column 8); average number of battle-connected deaths per war (column 9); and finally, the average number of such deaths for each war month (column 10).

Once these three sets of figures are presented for each nation in a given continental region, we compute Regional Sums and Regional Means, which permit a modest comparison among the nations of the separate regions. For each region, we first show, under the Totals columns, the total number of years in which that region's nations have been system members, and then (column 2) the number of national war experiences for the region. It should be noted that, as in some of the Table 11.1 figures, the latter is strictly an arithmetical sum of nation-wars and takes no account of the fact that many of these will have been the same wars. Thus, it is *not* the number of discrete wars fought by the nations of that region, but a larger number: it reflects nation-wars rather than region-wars. Likewise, the war-month figure (column 4) shows the summation of the war-months experienced by each nation of that region, despite the fact that many of these will have been "shared" war-months. The column 3 total (if we may skip around here for emphasis) is also a sum—total battle-connected deaths of all nations in the region—but in this case, there is no danger of misinterpretation. As emphasized earlier, a given war can be "shared," as can a war-month, but a battle fatality may be assigned only to a single nation. Therefore, that figure would be the same whether we merely summed all nations' battle-connected deaths or computed the battle deaths of all of the wars in which these nations fought, regardless of how many of them participated.

Shifting from the columns devoted to sums (1 to 4) to those covering averages (5 to 7 and 8 to 10), we have computed only the Regional Means, but there is still some chance of misinterpreting these figures. Under Averages we add up the separate national average figures and divide them by the number of nations comprising the region. That is, we present only an arithmetic mean here, whereas in the next chapter, we present the annual war average for the regions *qua* regions. Thus, for battle deaths, wars, and war-months per year we compute the mean of all the region members' annual war experience averages; all of the averages are added together and divided by the number of nations in the region. In the final set of columns (8 to 10), the regional means of national war averages are exactly that: the months per war, and battle deaths per war and per war-month are designed only to show the mean figure for all the nations in the region, and not to show the war experiences of the region as a single unit.

11.2 - NATIONAL WAR EXPERIENCE TOTALED, AVERAGED, AND NORMALIZED

CODE NO.	NATION NAME	TOTAL YEARS IN SYSTEM 1	NO. OF WARS 2	TOTAL BATTLE DEATHS (000'S) 3	TOTAL WAR MONTHS 4	BATTLE DEATHS (000'S) PER YEAR 5	WARS PER YEAR 6	WAR MONTHS PER YEAR 7	MONTHS PER WAR 8	BATTLE DEATHS (000'S) PER WAR 9	BATTLE DEATHS (000'S) PER MONTH 10
	WESTERN HEMISPHERE										
2	UNITED STATES	150	6	608.80	165.9	4.059	0.040	1.11	27.65	101.47	3.670
20	CANADA	46	2	39.61	102.5	0.861	0.043	2.23	51.25	19.80	0.386
40	CUBA	64	0	0.0	0.0	0.0	0.0	0.0	0.0	0.0	0.0
41	HAITI	107	0	0.0	0.0	0.0	0.0	0.0	0.0	0.0	0.0
42	DOMINICAN REPUBLIC	79	0	0.0	0.0	0.0	0.0	0.0	0.0	0.0	0.0
51	JAMAICA	4	0	0.0	0.0	0.0	0.0	0.0	0.0	0.0	0.0
52	TRINIDAD-TOBAGO	4	0	0.0	0.0	0.0	0.0	0.0	0.0	0.0	0.0
70	MEXICO	135	3	19.00	85.5	0.141	0.022	0.63	28.50	6.33	0.222
90	GUATEMALA	117	2	1.20	2.4	0.010	0.017	0.02	1.20	0.60	0.500
91	HONDURAS	67	2	0.60	3.9	0.009	0.030	0.06	1.95	0.30	0.154
92	SALVADOR	91	3	0.80	4.5	0.009	0.033	0.05	1.50	0.27	0.178
93	NICARAGUA	66	1	0.40	2.1	0.006	0.015	0.03	2.10	0.40	0.190
94	COSTA RICA	46	0	0.0	0.0	0.0	0.0	0.0	0.0	0.0	0.0
95	PANAMA	46	0	0.0	0.0	0.0	0.0	0.0	0.0	0.0	0.0
100	COLOMBIA	135	2	0.44	26.2	0.003	0.015	0.19	13.10	0.22	0.017
101	VENEZUELA	125	0	0.0	0.0	0.0	0.0	0.0	0.0	0.0	0.0
130	ECUADOR	112	1	0.70	0.5	0.006	0.009	0.00	0.50	0.70	1.400
135	PERU	128	3	11.60	59.3	0.091	0.023	0.46	19.77	3.87	0.196
140	BRAZIL	140	3	101.50	80.3	0.725	0.021	0.57	26.77	33.83	1.264
145	BOLIVIA	118	2	81.00	93.8	0.686	0.017	0.79	46.90	40.50	0.864
150	PARAGUAY	70	1	50.00	35.9	0.714	0.014	0.51	35.90	50.00	1.393
155	CHILE	127	2	3.10	64.4	0.024	0.016	0.51	32.20	1.55	0.048
160	ARGENTINA	125	2	10.80	66.5	0.086	0.016	0.53	33.25	5.40	0.162
165	URUGUAY	84	0	0.0	0.0	0.0	0.0	0.0	0.0	0.0	0.0
REGIONAL SUMMARY		REGIONAL SUM OF NATIONAL TOTALS				REGIONAL MEANS OF NATIONAL ANNUAL AVERAGES			REGIONAL MEANS OF NATIONAL WAR AVERAGES		
	24 NATIONS	2186	35	929.55	793.7	0.310	0.014	0.32	13.44	11.05	0.443

11.2 - NATIONAL WAR EXPERIENCE TOTALED, AVERAGED, AND NORMALIZED

CODE NO.	NATION NAME	TOTAL YEARS IN SYSTEM 1	NO. OF WARS 2	TOTAL BATTLE DEATHS (000'S) 3	TOTAL WAR MONTHS 4	BATTLE DEATHS (000'S) PER YEAR 5	WARS PER YEAR 6	WAR MONTHS PER YEAR 7	MONTHS PER WAR 8	BATTLE DEATHS (000'S) PER WAR 9	BATTLE DEATHS (000'S) PER MONTH 10
	EUROPE										
200	ENGLAND	150	19	1295.28	409.8	8.635	0.127	2.73	21.57	68.17	3.161
205	IRELAND	44	0	0.0	0.0	0.0	0.0	0.0	0.0	0.0	0.0
210	HOLLAND	145	5	27.71	163.0	0.191	0.034	1.12	32.60	5.54	0.170
211	BELGIUM	131	3	97.20	82.1	0.742	0.023	0.63	27.37	32.40	1.184
212	LUXEMBURG	42	0	0.0	0.0	0.0	0.0	0.0	0.0	0.0	0.0
220	FRANCE	148	19	1943.84	494.3	13.134	0.128	3.34	26.02	102.31	3.933
225	SWITZERLAND	150	0	0.0	0.0	0.0	0.0	0.0	0.0	0.0	0.0
230	SPAIN	150	9	188.90	262.0	1.259	0.060	1.75	29.11	20.99	0.721
235	PORTUGAL	150	1	7.00	32.4	0.047	0.007	0.22	32.40	7.00	0.216
240	HANOVER	29	1	0.50	0.5	0.017	0.034	0.02	0.50	0.50	1.000
245	BAVARIA	55	2	6.00	5.3	0.109	0.036	0.10	2.65	3.00	1.132
255	GERMANY/PRUSSIA	130	6	5353.50	140.0	41.181	0.046	1.08	23.33	892.25	38.239
260	GERMANY WEST	11	0	0.0	0.0	0.0	0.0	0.0	0.0	0.0	0.0
265	GERMANY EAST	12	0	0.0	0.0	0.0	0.0	0.0	0.0	0.0	0.0
267	BADEN	55	2	1.10	5.6	0.020	0.036	0.10	2.80	0.55	0.196
269	SAXONY	52	1	0.60	1.4	0.012	0.019	0.03	1.40	0.60	0.429
271	WUERTTEMBERG	55	2	1.10	5.7	0.020	0.036	0.10	2.85	0.55	0.193
273	HESSE ELECTORAL	51	1	0.10	1.4	0.002	0.020	0.03	1.40	0.10	0.071
275	HESSE GRAND DUCAL	52	1	0.10	1.4	0.002	0.019	0.03	1.40	0.10	0.071
280	MECKLENBURG-SCHWERIN	25	1	0.10	1.4	0.004	0.040	0.06	1.40	0.10	0.071
290	POLAND	41	1	320.00	0.9	7.805	0.024	0.02	0.90	320.00	355.555
300	AUSTRIA-HUNGARY	103	8	1287.20	78.4	12.497	0.078	0.76	9.80	160.90	16.418
305	AUSTRIA	30	0	0.0	0.0	0.0	0.0	0.0	0.0	0.0	0.0
310	HUNGARY	47	3	71.00	47.2	1.511	0.064	1.00	15.73	23.67	1.504
315	CZECHOSLOVAKIA	42	1	2.00	3.6	0.048	0.024	0.09	3.60	2.00	0.556
325	ITALY/SARDINIA	150	12	759.50	155.7	5.063	0.080	1.04	12.97	63.29	4.878
327	PAPAL STATES	45	2	2.20	2.4	0.049	0.044	0.05	1.20	1.10	0.917
329	TWO SICILIES	46	2	0.50	5.0	0.011	0.043	0.11	2.50	0.25	0.100
332	MODENA	19	0	0.0	0.0	0.0	0.0	0.0	0.0	0.0	0.0
335	PARMA	10	0	0.0	0.0	0.0	0.0	0.0	0.0	0.0	0.0
337	TUSCANY	45	0	0.0	0.0	0.0	0.0	0.0	0.0	0.0	0.0
338	MALTA	2	0	0.0	0.0	0.0	0.0	0.0	0.0	0.0	0.0
339	ALBANIA	47	0	0.0	0.0	0.0	0.0	0.0	0.0	0.0	0.0
345	YUGOSLAVIA/SERBIA	85	5	88.50	58.2	1.041	0.059	0.68	11.64	17.70	1.521
350	GREECE	134	7	53.27	104.1	0.398	0.052	0.78	14.87	7.61	0.512
352	CYPRUS	6	0	0.0	0.0	0.0	0.0	0.0	0.0	0.0	0.0
355	BULGARIA	58	5	74.00	81.6	1.276	0.086	1.41	16.32	14.80	0.907
360	RUMANIA	88	5	639.50	65.7	7.267	0.057	0.75	13.14	127.90	9.734

CODE NO.	NATION NAME	TOTAL YEARS IN SYSTEM 1	NO. OF WARS 2	TOTAL BATTLE DEATHS (000'S) 3	TOTAL WAR MONTHS 4	BATTLE DEATHS (000'S) PER YEAR 5	WARS PER YEAR 6	WAR MONTHS PER YEAR 7	MONTHS PER WAR 8	BATTLE DEATHS (000'S) PER WAR 9	BATTLE DEATHS (000'S) PER MONTH 10
365	RUSSIA	150	15	9662.56	249.0	64.417	0.100	1.66	16.60	644.17	38.805
366	ESTONIA	23	0	0.0	0.0	0.0	0.0	0.0	0.0	0.0	0.0
367	LATVIA	23	0	0.0	0.0	0.0	0.0	0.0	0.0	0.0	0.0
368	LITHUANIA	23	0	0.0	0.0	0.0	0.0	0.0	0.0	0.0	0.0
375	FINLAND	47	2	82.00	42.3	1.745	0.043	0.90	21.15	41.00	1.939
380	SWEDEN	150	0	0.0	0.0	0.0	0.0	0.0	0.0	0.0	0.0
385	NORWAY	56	1	2.00	2.0	0.036	0.018	0.04	2.00	2.00	1.000
390	DENMARK	145	2	6.50	11.7	0.045	0.014	0.08	5.85	3.25	0.556
395	ICELAND	22	0	0.0	0.0	0.0	0.0	0.0	0.0	0.0	0.0
REGIONAL SUMMARY		REGIONAI SUM OF NATIONAL TOTALS				REGIONAL MEANS OF NATIONAL ANNUAL AVERAGES			REGIONAL MEANS OF NATIONAL WAR AVERAGES		
	47 NATIONS	3274	144	21973.74	2514.1	3.587	0.031	0.44	7.55	54.55	10.334

11.2 - NATIONAL WAR EXPERIENCE TOTALED, AVERAGED, AND NORMALIZED

CODE NO.	NATION NAME	TOTAL YEARS IN SYSTEM 1	NO. OF WARS 2	TOTAL BATTLE DEATHS (000'S) 3	TOTAL WAR MONTHS 4	BATTLE DEATHS (000'S) PER YEAR 5	WARS PER YEAR 6	WAR MONTHS PER YEAR 7	MONTHS PER WAR 8	BATTLE DEATHS (000'S) PER WAR 9	BATTLE DEATHS (000'S) PER MONTH 10
	AFRICA										
420	GAMEIA	1	0	0.0	0.0	0.0	0.0	0.0	0.0	0.0	0.0
432	MALI	6	0	0.0	0.0	0.0	0.0	0.0	0.0	0.0	0.0
433	SENEGAL	6	0	0.0	0.0	0.0	0.0	0.0	0.0	0.0	0.0
434	DAHOMEY	6	0	0.0	0.0	0.0	0.0	0.0	0.0	0.0	0.0
435	MAURITANIA	6	0	0.0	0.0	0.0	0.0	0.0	0.0	0.0	0.0
436	NIGER	6	0	0.0	0.0	0.0	0.0	0.0	0.0	0.0	0.0
437	IVORY COAST	6	0	0.0	0.0	0.0	0.0	0.0	0.0	0.0	0.0
438	GUINEA	8	0	0.0	0.0	0.0	0.0	0.0	0.0	0.0	0.0
439	UPFER VOLTA	6	0	0.0	0.0	0.0	0.0	0.0	0.0	0.0	0.0
450	LIBEFIA	46	0	0.0	0.0	0.0	0.0	0.0	0.0	0.0	0.0
451	SIERRA LEONE	5	0	0.0	0.0	0.0	0.0	0.0	0.0	0.0	0.0
452	GHANA	9	0	0.0	0.0	0.0	0.0	0.0	0.0	0.0	0.0
461	TOGO	6	0	0.0	0.0	0.0	0.0	0.0	0.0	0.0	0.0
471	CAMERCUN	6	0	0.0	0.0	0.0	0.0	0.0	0.0	0.0	0.0
475	NIGERIA	6	0	0.0	0.0	0.0	0.0	0.0	0.0	0.0	0.0
481	GABON	6	0	0.0	0.0	0.0	0.0	0.0	0.0	0.0	0.0
482	CENTRAL AFRICAN REPB	6	0	0.0	0.0	0.0	0.0	0.0	0.0	0.0	0.0
483	CHAD	6	0	0.0	0.0	0.0	0.0	0.0	0.0	0.0	0.0
484	CONGO (ERAZZAVILLE)	6	0	0.0	0.0	0.0	0.0	0.0	0.0	0.0	0.0
490	CONGO (KINSHASA)	6	0	0.0	0.0	0.0	0.0	0.0	0.0	0.0	0.0
500	UGANDA	4	0	0.0	0.0	0.0	0.0	0.0	0.0	0.0	0.0
501	KENYA	3	0	0.0	0.0	0.0	0.0	0.0	0.0	0.0	0.0
510	TANZANIA	5	0	0.0	0.0	0.0	0.0	0.0	0.0	0.0	0.0
511	ZANZIEAR	2	0	0.0	0.0	0.0	0.0	0.0	0.0	0.0	0.0
516	BURUNDI	4	0	0.0	0.0	0.0	0.0	0.0	0.0	0.0	0.0
517	RWANDA	4	0	0.0	0.0	0.0	0.0	0.0	0.0	0.0	0.0
520	SOMALIA	6	0	0.0	0.0	0.0	0.0	0.0	0.0	0.0	0.0
530	ETHIOFIA	63	3	21.12	39.4	0.335	0.048	0.63	13.13	7.04	0.536
551	ZAMEIA (N. RHODESIA)	2	0	0.0	0.0	0.0	0.0	0.0	0.0	0.0	0.0
553	MAIAWI	2	0	0.0	0.0	0.0	0.0	0.0	0.0	0.0	0.0
560	SOUTH AFRICA	46	1	8.70	71.3	0.189	0.022	1.55	71.30	8.70	0.122
580	MALAGASY	6	0	0.0	0.0	0.0	0.0	0.0	0.0	0.0	0.0
REGIONAL SUMMARY		REGIONAL SUM OF NATIONAL TOTALS				REGIONAL MEANS OF NATIONAL ANNUAL AVERAGES			REGIONAL MEANS OF NATIONAL WAR AVERAGES		
	32 NATIONS	306	4	29.82	110.7	0.016	0.002	0.07	2.64	0.49	0.021

CODE NO.	NATION NAME	TOTAL YEARS IN SYSTEM 1	NO. OF WARS 2	TOTAL BATTLE DEATHS (000'S) 3	TOTAL WAR MONTHS 4	BATTLE DEATHS (000'S) PER YEAR 5	WARS PER YEAR 6	WAR MONTHS PER YEAR 7	MONTHS PER WAR 8	BATTLE DEATHS (000'S) PER WAR 9	BATTLE DEATHS (000'S) PER MONTH 10
	MIDDLE EAST										
600	MOROCCO	74	2	14.00	13.7	0.189	0.027	0.19	6.85	7.00	1.022
615	ALGERIA	4	0	0.0	0.0	0.0	0.0	0.0	0.0	0.0	0.0
616	TUNISIA	10	0	0.0	0.0	0.0	0.0	0.0	0.0	0.0	0.0
620	LIBYA	14	0	0.0	0.0	0.0	0.0	0.0	0.0	0.0	0.0
625	SUDAN	10	0	0.0	0.0	0.0	0.0	0.0	0.0	0.0	0.0
630	IRAN	111	1	1.50	4.6	0.014	0.009	0.04	4.60	1.50	0.326
640	TURKEY	150	17	757.12	339.0	5.047	0.113	2.26	19.94	44.54	2.233
645	IRAQ	34	1	0.50	2.5	0.015	0.029	0.07	2.50	0.50	0.200
651	U.A.R.	29	2	5.00	5.0	0.172	0.069	0.17	2.50	2.50	1.000
652	SYRIA	17	1	1.00	2.5	0.059	0.059	0.15	2.50	1.00	0.400
660	LEBANCN	20	1	0.50	2.5	0.025	0.050	0.13	2.50	0.50	0.200
663	JORDAN	20	1	1.00	2.5	0.050	0.050	0.13	2.50	1.00	0.400
666	ISRAEL	18	2	3.20	5.0	0.178	0.111	0.28	2.50	1.60	0.640
670	SAUDI ARABIA	39	0	0.0	0.0	0.0	0.0	0.0	0.0	0.0	0.0
678	YEMEN	40	0	0.0	0.0	0.0	0.0	0.0	0.0	0.0	0.0
690	KUWAIT	5	0	0.0	0.0	0.0	0.0	0.0	0.0	0.0	0.0
REGIONAL SUMMARY		REGIONAI SUM OF NATIONAL TCTALS				REGIONAL MEANS OF NATIONAL ANNUAL AVERAGES			REGIONAL MEANS OF NATIONAL WAR AVERAGES		
	16 NATIONS	595	28	783.82	377.3	0.359	0.032	0.21	2.90	3.76	0.401

11.2 - NATIONAL WAR EXPERIENCE TOTALED, AVERAGED, AND NORMALIZED

CODE NO.	NATION NAME	TOTAL YEARS IN SYSTEM 1	NO. OF WARS 2	TOTAL BATTLE DEATHS (000'S) 3	TOTAL WAR MONTHS 4	BATTLE DEATHS (000'S) PER YEAR 5	WARS PER YEAR 6	WAR MONTHS PER YEAR 7	MONTHS PER WAR 8	BATTLE DEATHS (000'S) PER WAR 9	BATTLE DEATHS (000'S) PER MONTH 10
	ASIA										
700	AFGHANISTAN	46	0	0.0	0.0	0.0	0.0	0.0	0.0	0.0	0.0
710	CHINA	106	8	3110.50	204.6	29.344	0.075	1.93	25.57	388.81	15.203
712	MONGOLIA	45	2	6.00	4.4	0.133	0.044	0.10	2.20	3.00	1.364
713	TAIWAN	17	0	0.0	0.0	0.0	0.0	0.0	0.0	0.0	0.0
730	KOREA	18	0	0.0	0.0	0.0	0.0	0.0	0.0	0.0	0.0
731	KOREA NCRTH	18	1	520.00	37.1	28.889	0.056	2.06	37.10	520.00	14.016
732	KOREA SOUTH	17	1	415.00	37.1	24.412	0.059	2.18	37.10	415.00	11.186
740	JAPAN	99	7	1365.30	196.2	13.791	0.071	1.98	28.03	195.04	6.959
750	INDIA	19	3	5.00	17.0	0.263	0.158	0.89	5.67	1.67	0.294
770	PAKISTAN	19	1	3.80	1.6	0.200	0.053	0.08	1.60	3.80	2.375
775	BURMA	18	0	0.0	0.0	0.0	0.0	0.0	0.0	0.0	0.0
780	CEYLON	18	0	0.0	0.0	0.0	0.0	0.0	0.0	0.0	0.0
781	MALDIVE ISLANDS	1	0	0.0	0.0	0.0	0.0	0.0	0.0	0.0	0.0
790	NEPAL	46	0	0.0	0.0	0.0	0.0	0.0	0.0	0.0	0.0
800	THAILAND	79	1	0.11	30.2	0.001	0.013	0.38	30.20	0.11	0.004
811	CAMBODIA	13	0	0.0	0.0	0.0	0.0	0.0	0.0	0.0	0.0
812	LAOS	12	0	0.0	0.0	0.0	0.0	0.0	0.0	0.0	0.0
816	VIETNAM NORTH	12	0	0.0	0.0	0.0	0.0	0.0	0.0	0.0	0.0
817	VIETNAM SOUTH	12	0	0.0	0.0	0.0	0.0	0.0	0.0	0.0	0.0
820	MALAYSIA (MALAYA)	9	0	0.0	0.0	0.0	0.0	0.0	0.0	0.0	0.0
830	SINGAPORE	1	0	0.0	0.0	0.0	0.0	0.0	0.0	0.0	0.0
840	PHILIPPINES	20	1	0.09	34.4	0.004	0.050	1.72	34.40	0.09	0.003
850	INDONESIA	17	0	0.0	0.0	0.0	0.0	0.0	0.0	0.0	0.0
900	AUSTRALIA	46	2	29.67	103.0	0.645	0.043	2.24	51.50	14.83	0.288
920	NEW ZEALAND	46	1	17.30	71.4	0.376	0.022	1.55	71.40	17.30	0.242
REGIONAL SUMMARY		REGIONAL SUM OF NATIONAL TOTALS				REGIONAL MEANS OF NATIONAL ANNUAL AVERAGES			REGIONAL MEANS OF NATIONAL WAR AVERAGES		
	25 NATIONS	754	28	5472.76	737.0	3.922	0.026	0.61	12.99	62.39	2.077

RANKING THE NATIONS BY WAR EXPERIENCE

In the first two sections, we have provided the basic data by which the major empirical question of this chapter may be answered: which nations have been most war-prone during the period under investigation? The next step is to rearrange these data so as to offer precise evidence for that answer. Quite clearly, the war-proneness of a nation, and therefore its rank order among other nations, may be measured in a variety of ways; our intention is to use several such criteria and thus provide a variety of rank order hierarchies.

In Table 11.3, the six measures that we consider most useful are offered, and for each measure of war-proneness, each nation's rank position and raw score are shown. Of the possible measures permitted by our data, we believe that the "best" all-around index of a nation's war-proneness since the Congress of Vienna is the number of battle-connected deaths resulting from all of its international (that is, extra-systemic as well as interstate) wars. Thus, we present this set of figures first (columns 1 and 2) and list the 67 nations with any war experience at all according to their rank on this measure. In contrast to Tables 11.1 and 11.2, we dispense with the regional breakdowns and deal with the population of the system as a whole.

Since the total number of battle deaths might not be a particularly valid index of a nation's war-proneness because it disregards the time span covered, we next control for length of tenure in the system and list the rank order and battle deaths per year figures for all members of the system in columns 3 and 4. Some might argue that, for the reasons we adduced in Chapter Three, war months experienced provides a better index of war-proneness; thus, each nation's rank and raw score on that measure is shown next (columns 5 and 6), followed by a normalized index in which we again (as for battle deaths) control for length of membership (columns 7 and 8).

Whereas the first eight columns reflect *severity* and *magnitude* of national war experience, the remaining four reflect national equivalents of its *intensity.* For each nation, we next show the average of battle deaths per war (columns 9 and 10), followed by an index based on battle deaths per war month in columns 11 and 12. Each of these indices is nothing more than a statistical mean of the intensity scores of each nation's experience in each of its wars. With these alternative measures of war-proneness, many different theoretical viewpoints may be accommodated, but only within certain limits, as the final section of this chapter, focusing on the intercorrelations among these six indicators, will make clear.

Because of the unique nature of the two World Wars, as we have noted above (Chapter Six), we see fit to present our data excluding those extraordinary conflicts. Thus we offer in Table 11.4 the ranks of the nations according to their battle deaths in *all* wars, and then according to battle deaths in all wars except for World War One and World War Two. The first two columns give the battle deaths totals and the rank position, by which the nations are listed. The next set gives each nation's battle deaths excluding those from the World Wars and the rank position on this measure. So that the effect of excluding the World War fatalities can be seen more clearly, we also give a listing of the nations according to their ranks on the battle deaths without the World Wars. The rank position only is given in the final column, and the figures are not repeated, since they are easily found in the middle column.

CORRELATIONS AMONG WAR EXPERIENCE INDICATORS

Having presented nine alternative indicators of national war experience, along with the rank orders based on six of them, it might now be useful to ascertain the extent to

11.3 - RANK ORDER OF NATIONS BY WAR EXPERIENCE INDICATORS

CODE NO.	NATION NAME	SEVERITY RANK 1	SEVERITY BATTLE DEATHS 2	SEVERITY RANK 3	SEVERITY BATTLE DEATHS PER YEAR 4	MAGNITUDE RANK 5	MAGNITUDE WAR MONTHS 6	MAGNITUDE RANK 7	MAGNITUDE WAR MONTHS PER WAR 8	INTENSITY RANK 9	INTENSITY BATTLE DEATHS PER WAR 10	INTENSITY RANK 11	INTENSITY BATTLE DEATHS PER WAR MONTH 12
365	RUSSIA	1.0	9662560	1.0	64417	5.0	249.0	12.0	1.66	2.0	644171	2.0	33805
255	GERMANY/PRUSSIA	2.0	5353500	2.0	41181	11.0	140.0	18.0	1.08	1.0	892250	3.0	33239
710	CHINA	3.0	3110500	3.0	29344	6.0	204.6	9.0	1.93	5.0	388813	5.0	15203
220	FRANCE	4.0	1943840	7.0	13134	1.0	494.3	1.0	3.34	10.0	102307	11.0	3933
740	JAPAN	5.0	1365300	6.0	13791	7.0	196.2	8.0	1.98	7.0	195043	9.0	6959
200	ENGLAND	6.0	1295280	9.0	8635	2.0	409.8	2.0	2.73	12.0	68173	13.0	3161
300	AUSTRIA-HUNGARY	7.0	1287200	8.0	12497	20.0	78.4	25.0	0.76	8.0	160900	4.0	16418
325	ITALY/SARDINIA	8.0	759500	12.0	5063	10.0	155.7	19.0	1.04	13.0	63292	10.0	4878
640	TURKEY	9.0	757120	13.0	5047	3.0	339.0	3.0	2.26	15.0	44536	15.0	2233
360	RUMANIA	10.0	639500	11.0	7267	24.0	65.7	26.0	0.75	9.0	127900	8.0	9734
2	UNITED STATES	11.0	608800	14.0	4059	8.0	165.9	17.0	1.11	11.0	101467	12.0	3670
731	KOREA NORTH	12.0	520000	4.0	28889	31.5	37.1	7.0	2.06	3.0	520000	6.0	14016
732	KOREA SOUTH	13.0	415000	5.0	24412	31.5	37.1	6.0	2.18	4.0	415000	7.0	11186
290	POLAND	14.0	320000	10.0	7805	65.0	0.9	64.0	0.02	6.0	320000	1.0	355556
230	SPAIN	15.0	188900	18.0	1259	4.0	262.0	10.0	1.75	21.0	20989	32.0	721
140	BRAZIL	16.0	101500	22.0	725	19.0	80.3	31.0	0.57	18.0	33833	22.0	1264
211	BELGIUM	17.0	97200	21.0	742	17.0	82.1	29.0	0.63	19.0	32400	23.0	1184
345	YUGOSLAVIA/SERBIA	18.0	88500	19.0	1041	27.0	58.2	27.0	0.68	23.0	17700	17.0	1521
375	FINLAND	19.0	82000	15.0	1745	29.0	42.3	21.0	0.90	16.0	41000	16.0	1939
145	BOLIVIA	20.0	81000	24.0	686	15.0	93.8	23.0	0.79	17.0	40500	31.0	864
355	BULGARIA	21.0	74000	17.0	1276	18.0	81.6	15.0	1.41	26.0	14800	30.0	907
310	HUNGARY	22.0	71000	16.0	1511	28.0	47.2	20.0	1.00	20.0	23667	18.0	1504
350	GREECE	23.0	53270	26.0	398	12.0	104.1	24.0	0.78	28.0	7610	37.0	512
150	PARAGUAY	24.0	50000	23.0	714	33.0	35.9	33.0	0.51	14.0	50000	20.0	1393
20	CANADA	25.0	39610	20.0	861	14.0	102.5	5.0	2.23	22.0	19805	42.0	386
900	AUSTRALIA	26.0	29670	25.0	645	13.0	103.0	4.0	2.24	25.0	14835	45.0	288
210	HOLLAND	27.0	27710	31.0	191	9.0	163.0	16.0	1.12	33.0	5542	56.0	170
530	ETHIOPIA	28.0	21120	28.0	335	30.0	39.4	30.0	0.63	29.0	7040	36.0	536
70	MEXICO	29.0	19000	36.0	141	16.0	85.5	28.0	0.63	32.0	6333	47.0	222
920	NEW ZEALAND	30.0	17300	27.0	376	21.0	71.4	13.0	1.55	24.0	17300	46.0	242
600	MOROCCO	31.0	14000	32.0	189	39.0	13.7	40.0	0.19	30.5	7000	25.0	1022
135	PERU	32.0	11600	39.0	91	26.0	59.3	35.0	0.46	35.0	3867	52.0	196
160	ARGENTINA	33.0	10800	40.0	86	23.0	66.5	32.0	0.53	34.0	5400	57.0	162
560	SOUTH AFRICA	34.0	8700	33.0	189	22.0	71.3	14.0	1.55	27.0	8700	59.0	122
235	PORTUGAL	35.0	7000	45.0	47	35.0	32.4	38.0	0.22	30.5	7000	48.0	216
390	DENMARK	36.0	6500	46.0	45	40.0	11.7	52.0	0.08	37.0	3250	34.5	556
245	BAVARIA	37.5	6000	38.0	109	43.0	5.3	49.0	0.10	38.5	3000	24.0	1132
712	MONGOLIA	37.5	6000	37.0	133	49.0	4.4	48.0	0.10	38.5	3000	21.0	1364
651	U.A.R.	39.5	5000	35.0	172	45.0	5.0	41.0	0.17	40.0	2500	27.0	1000

CODE NO.	NATION NAME	SEVERITY RANK 1	BATTLE DEATHS 2	RANK 3	BATTLE DEATHS PER YEAR 4	MAGNITUDE RANK 5	WAR MONTHS 6	RANK 7	WAR MONTHS PER WAR 8	INTENSITY RANK 9	BATTLE DEATHS PER WAR 10	RANK 11	BATTLE DEATHS PER WAR MONTH 12
750	INDIA	39.5	5000	29.0	263	38.0	17.0	22.0	0.89	43.0	1667	44.0	294
770	PAKISTAN	41.0	3800	30.0	200	60.0	1.6	51.0	0.08	36.0	3800	14.0	2375
666	ISRAEL	42.0	3200	34.0	178	45.0	5.0	37.0	0.28	44.0	1600	33.0	640
155	CHILE	43.0	3100	49.0	24	25.0	64.4	34.0	0.51	45.0	1550	64.0	48
327	PAPAL STATES	44.0	2200	43.0	49	56.5	2.4	56.0	0.05	47.0	1100	29.0	917
315	CZECHOSLOVAKIA	45.5	2000	44.0	48	51.0	3.6	50.0	0.09	41.5	2000	34.5	556
385	NORWAY	45.5	2000	47.0	36	59.0	2.0	59.0	0.04	41.5	2000	27.0	1000
630	IRAN	47.0	1500	54.0	14	47.0	4.6	58.0	0.04	46.0	1500	43.0	326
90	GUATEMALA	48.0	1200	57.0	10	56.5	2.4	65.0	0.02	51.5	600	38.0	500
267	BADEN	49.5	1100	50.5	20	42.0	5.6	47.0	0.10	53.5	550	51.0	196
271	WUERTTEMBERG	49.5	1100	50.5	20	41.0	5.7	46.0	0.10	53.5	550	53.0	193
652	SYRIA	51.5	1000	41.0	59	53.5	2.5	42.0	0.15	48.5	1000	40.5	400
663	JORDAN	51.5	1000	42.0	50	53.5	2.5	43.5	0.13	48.5	1000	40.5	400
92	SALVADOR	53.0	800	59.0	9	48.0	4.5	57.0	0.05	60.0	267	55.0	178
130	ECUADOR	54.0	700	60.0	6	66.5	0.5	67.0	0.00	50.0	700	19.0	1400
91	HONDURAS	55.5	600	58.0	9	50.0	3.9	54.0	0.06	59.0	300	58.0	154
269	SAXONY	55.5	600	55.0	12	62.5	1.4	62.5	0.03	51.5	600	39.0	429
240	HANOVER	58.5	500	52.0	17	66.5	0.5	66.0	0.02	56.0	500	27.0	1000
329	TWO SICILIES	58.5	500	56.0	11	45.0	5.0	45.0	0.11	61.0	250	60.0	100
645	IRAQ	58.5	500	53.0	15	53.5	2.5	53.0	0.07	56.0	500	49.5	200
660	LEBANON	58.5	500	48.0	25	53.5	2.5	43.5	0.13	56.0	500	49.5	200
100	COLOMBIA	61.0	440	64.0	3	37.0	26.2	39.0	0.19	62.0	220	65.0	17
93	NICARAGUA	62.0	400	61.0	6	58.0	2.1	60.0	0.03	58.0	400	54.0	190
800	THAILAND	63.0	110	67.0	1	36.0	30.2	36.0	0.38	63.0	110	66.0	4
273	HESSE ELECTORAL	65.0	100	65.0	2	62.5	1.4	61.0	0.03	65.0	100	62.0	71
275	HESSE GRAND DUCAL	65.0	100	66.0	2	62.5	1.4	62.5	0.03	65.0	100	62.0	71
280	MECKLENBURG-SCHWERIN	65.0	100	63.0	4	62.5	1.4	55.0	0.06	65.0	100	62.0	71
840	PHILIPPINES	67.0	90	62.0	5	34.0	34.4	11.0	1.72	67.0	90	67.0	3

11.4 - RANK ORDER OF NATIONS BY TOTAL BATTLE DEATHS AND BY BATTLE DEATHS EXCLUDING THOSE SUSTAINED IN WORLD WARS

	BATTLE DEATHS ALL WARS (000'S)	RANK	BATTLE DEATHS EXCL. WORLD WARS I AND II (000'S)	RANK	RANK POSITION ACCORDING TO BATTLE DEATHS EXCLUDING WORLD WAR I AND II	
RUSSIA	9662.56	1.0	462.56	3.0	CHINA	1.0
GERMANY/PRUSSIA	5353.50	2.0	53.50	14.0	KOREA NORTH	2.0
CHINA	3110.50	3.0	1760.50	1.0	RUSSIA	3.0
FRANCE	1943.84	4.0	383.84	6.0	TURKEY	4.0
JAPAN	1365.30	5.0	365.00	7.0	KOREA SOUTH	5.0
ENGLAND	1295.28	6.0	117.28	9.0	FRANCE	6.0
AUSTRIA-HUNGARY	1287.20	7.0	87.20	11.0	JAPAN	7.0
ITALY/SARDINIA	759.50	8.0	32.00	20.0	SPAIN	8.0
TURKEY	757.12	9.0	432.12	4.0	ENGLAND	9.0
RUMANIA	639.50	10.0	4.50	32.0	BRAZIL	10.0
UNITED STATES	608.80	11.0	74.50	13.0	AUSTRIA-HUNGARY	11.0
KOREA NORTH	520.00	12.0	520.00	2.0	BOLIVIA	12.0
KOREA SOUTH	415.00	13.0	415.00	5.0	UNITED STATES	13.0
POLAND	320.00	14.0	0.0	65.0	GERMANY/PRUSSIA	14.0
SPAIN	188.90	15.0	188.90	8.0	PARAGUAY	15.5
BRAZIL	101.50	16.0	100.50	10.0	BULGARIA	15.5
BELGIUM	97.20	17.0	0.10	58.0	FINLAND	17.0
YUGOSLAVIA/SERBIA	88.50	18.0	35.50	19.0	GREECE	18.0
FINLAND	82.00	19.0	40.00	17.0	YUGOSLAVIA/SERBIA	19.0
BOLIVIA	81.00	20.0	81.00	12.0	ITALY/SARDINIA	20.0
BULGARIA	74.00	21.0	50.00	15.5	HUNGARY	21.0
HUNGARY	71.00	22.0	31.00	21.0	HOLLAND	22.0
GREECE	53.27	23.0	38.27	18.0	MEXICO	23.0
PARAGUAY	50.00	24.0	50.00	15.5	ETHIOPIA	24.0
CANADA	39.61	25.0	0.31	55.0	MOROCCO	25.0
AUSTRALIA	29.67	26.0	0.27	56.0	PERU	26.0
HOLLAND	27.71	27.0	21.51	22.0	ARGENTINA	27.0
ETHIOPIA	21.12	28.0	16.12	24.0	DENMARK	28.0
MEXICO	19.00	29.0	19.00	23.0	BAVARIA	29.0
NEW ZEALAND	17.30	30.0	0.0	65.0	U.A.R.	30.5
MOROCCO	14.00	31.0	14.00	25.0	INDIA	30.5
PERU	11.60	32.0	11.60	26.0	RUMANIA	32.0
ARGENTINA	10.80	33.0	10.80	27.0	PAKISTAN	33.0
SOUTH AFRICA	8.70	34.0	0.0	65.0	ISRAEL	34.0
PORTUGAL	7.00	35.0	0.0	65.0	CHILE	35.0
DENMARK	6.50	36.0	6.50	28.0	MONGOLIA	36.0
BAVARIA	6.00	37.5	6.00	29.0	PAPAL STATES	37.0
MONGOLIA	6.00	37.5	3.00	36.0	CZECHOSLOVAKIA	38.0
U.A.R.	5.00	39.5	5.00	30.5	IRAN	39.0
INDIA	5.00	39.5	5.00	30.5	GUATEMALA	40.0
PAKISTAN	3.80	41.0	3.80	33.0	BADEN	41.5
ISRAEL	3.20	42.0	3.20	34.0	WUERTTEMBERG	41.5
CHILE	3.10	43.0	3.10	35.0	SYRIA	43.5

	BATTLE DEATHS ALL WARS (000'S)	RANK	BATTLE DEATHS EXCL. WORLD WARS I AND II (000'S)	RANK	RANK POSITION ACCORDING TO BATTLE DEATHS EXCLUDING WORLD WAR I AND II	
PAPAL STATES	2.20	44.0	2.20	37.0	JCRDAN	43.5
CZECHOSLOVAKIA	2.00	45.5	2.00	38.0	SALVADOR	45.0
NORWAY	2.00	45.5	0.0	65.0	ECUADOR	46.0
IRAN	1.50	47.0	1.50	39.0	HCNDURAS	47.5
GUATEMALA	1.20	48.0	1.20	40.0	SAXONY	47.5
BADEN	1.10	49.5	1.10	41.5	HANOVER	50.5
WUERTTEMBERG	1.10	49.5	1.10	41.5	TWO SICILIES	50.5
SYRIA	1.00	51.5	1.00	43.5	IRAQ	50.5
JORDAN	1.00	51.5	1.00	43.5	LEBANON	50.5
SALVADOR	0.80	53.0	0.80	45.0	COLOMBIA	53.0
ECUADOR	0.70	54.0	0.70	46.0	NICARAGUA	54.0
HONDURAS	0.60	55.5	0.60	47.5	CANADA	55.0
SAXONY	0.60	55.5	0.60	47.5	AUSTRALIA	56.0
HANOVER	0.50	58.5	0.50	50.5	THAILAND	57.0
TWO SICILIES	C.50	58.5	0.50	50.5	BELGIUM	58.0
IRAQ	0.50	58.5	0.50	50.5	HESSE ELECTORAL	60.0
LEBANON	0.50	58.5	0.50	50.5	HESSE GRAND DUCAL	60.0
COLOMBIA	0.44	61.0	0.44	53.0	MECKLENBURG-SCHWERIN	60.0
NICARAGUA	0.40	62.0	0.40	54.0	PHILIPPINES	62.0
THAILAND	0.11	63.0	0.11	57.0	PORTUGAL	65.0
HESSE ELECTCRAL	0.10	65.0	0.10	60.0	POLAND	65.0
HESSE GRAND DUCAL	0.10	65.0	0.10	60.0	NORWAY	65.0
MECKLENBURG-SCHWERIN	0.10	65.0	0.10	60.0	SOUTH AFRICA	65.0
PHILIPPINES	0.09	67.0	0.09	62.0	NEW ZEALAND	65.0

which these various measures tap the same basic phenomenon. In Table 11.5 are shown the Kendall's *tau* rank order coefficients among the six indicators by which we ranked the nations in Table 11.3. A brief glance at the results shows that the only three fairly high correlations are among the indicators based on battle deaths: battle deaths versus battle deaths per year, battle deaths versus battle deaths per war, and battle deaths per year versus battle deaths per war. The only other coefficient above .70 is that between war months and war months per year. Using the *Z*-test (tau ÷ s.d. of rank orders), we did find, however, that all the coefficients are significant at the .01 level or better.

11.5 RANK ORDER CORRELATIONS AMONG NATIONAL WAR EXPERIENCE INDICATORS

	Battle deaths	Battle deaths per year	War months	War months per year	Battle deaths per war	Battle deaths per war month
Battle deaths	1.00					
Battle deaths per year	.84	1.00				
War months	.62	.54	1.00			
War months per year	.56	.59	.75	1.00		
Battle deaths per war	.87	.83	.54	.53	1.00	
Battle deaths per war month	.63	.67	.26	.26	.66	1.00

SUMMARY

Having computed the amounts of war experienced by each nation during the years in which it was a system member, and rearranged these figures into rank orderings, we can now summarize our findings. In doing so, we might again emphasize that war-proneness need not be thought of primarily as a function of a nation's attributes or behavior, but should also be examined in the light of the geographical, temporal, and political setting in which it found itself. Here, then, we report only on the dependent variable, and suggest the need for further inquiry along the lines set out at the beginning of the chapter.

In sheer number of wars, the two dominant powers of the nineteenth century—France and England—lead the field with 19 wars each, followed by Turkey (17), Russia (15), and Italy, including its predecessor, Sardinia (12). Each of these was also a charter member of our interstate system. In their 150 years in the system, Spain participated in 9 international wars, followed by the United States with 6. For those with a shorter tenure, Austria-Hungary and China were in 8 wars, Greece and Japan were in 7, and Germany (including the predecessor, Prussia) was in 6. Another way of putting this, on the basis of column 6 in Table 11.2, is that five nations were involved in an average of more than one war per decade: France, England, Turkey, Russia, and Israel, which is an exceptional case, having been in the system for only 18 of the years under study, but having fought in two wars; were the study to extend beyond 1965, that nation's wars per year figure would be even higher.

Do the same nations stand out on the more refined measures of war experience? As Table 11.3 makes evident, essentially the same nations sustained the most battle deaths; Russia, Germany, China, France, Japan, England, Austria-Hungary, Italy, and Turkey, in that order, all had more than 750,000 battle deaths, and all but the last two had over a million such losses. On total war months experienced (but not controlling for duration of system membership), we find the following at the top of the list: France, England, Turkey, Spain, Russia, China, Japan, and the United States.

This same pattern is evident when we note that 1754.1 of the 4532.7 nation months of international war, or 39 percent, were accounted for by only five of the system's members: France (494.3), England (409.8), Turkey (339), Spain (262.0), and Russia (249). Likewise, if we look at extra-systemic wars, we find that 39 of the 43 were accounted for by the following 7 nations: England (12), France (7), Turkey (6), Russia (5), Spain (4), Holland (3), and Austria-Hungary (2).

We can summarize these results by saying that most of the war in the system has been accounted for by a small fraction of the nations, most of which would be found near the top of any hierarchy based on diplomatic status, military-industrial capability, or related indicators.[1] It is not surprising that every one of the nations cited so far was a member of what we defined as the central system. Further, of the highly war-prone nations, only Turkey, Holland, Spain, and Greece were not, at one time or another, major powers. Thus, even though we urge a distinction between war-proneness and military aggressiveness, one may nevertheless conclude that the top-ranked nations were compelled to fight often and at length either to maintain their position, or to achieve it. In subsequent reports, we will examine this pattern in greater detail, looking at the frequency with which these nations were the initiators or defenders, and the extent to which either role was accounted for by top positions in the hierarchy or movement toward or away from the top. To put it differently, we will want to ask how often, and under what conditions, upward and downward mobility—as well as perpetual high status—are associated with war-proneness.

[1] Using the rank order of nations on geographic centrality, as given by Gleditsch (1967), and fitting into his list our "extinct" system members, we correlated all 6 war-proneness indicators (from Table 11.3) with centrality. This measure was computed by summing each nation's capital-to-capital distance to each other nation, and produces a list from Italy as the most central to Australia and New Zealand as the least central. The correlations were all quite low (from −.08 to .14), which could be expected when such war-prone nations as China, Japan, United States, and even Russia appear far down in the list, below most of the nonwarring nations of Africa.

Chapter 12

The War-Proneness of Regions

In the preceding chapter, we suggested a number of variables which might account for ranges in the magnitude and type of war that the individual nations have experienced, and went on to provide the data by which the dependent variable—national war experience—might be measured over time. If, as some scholars have argued, the national or multinational state is little more than a combination of legal fiction and historical accident, and therefore not a fit object of analysis for scientific research, the continental region offers an even more dubious object of analysis. The region, as Russett (1968) and others have argued, may safely be identified in geographical terms, but to treat it as an integrated or homogeneous unit is risky indeed. We are not, however, make any such assumptions or treating it as a single and coherent behavioral entity; to the contrary, regions are used here primarily as the milieu or environment within which specific nations happen to be located. And even though territoriality and its associated variables may be of declining importance in world politics, it would nevertheless seem to be of considerable consequence for the historical period under investigation.

Several uses of regionally arranged war data come to mind. First, despite the above reservations, regions often reflect a concentration of nations of a given cultural or ethnic type, or of a given level of technology, and therefore permit some rough and preliminary generalizations regarding which types of nations are most war-prone. Second, since they are often characterized by a moderately uniform climate, topography, and distribution of natural resources, such a computation permits certain forms of geopolitical analysis. Third, since a great many intergovernmental organizations are built on a regional basis, and one of the motives behind their establishment is the direct or indirect reduction of war in the region, such data permit one particular measure of the efficacy of these organizations.

Our purpose in this chapter, then, is to examine the war-proneness of the standard geographical regions. It should be emphasized, however, that our major focus here is not so much the regions *in which* these wars have been fought, as the regions *from which* the combatant nations come, and while they often add up to the same thing, they frequently do not. This distinction is, for example, most clearly dramatized when we shift our attention from interstate wars, most of which tend to be fought on or near home territory, to extra-systemic wars, which were often waged by the European powers in distant overseas theaters.

Although we have already discussed in the previous chapter a few measures which reflect the differing war experience of the five major geographical regions of the world (Tables 11.1 and 11.2), it is clear that these measures were largely by-products of *national* war experience data. They permitted us to generalize to some extent about the nations on a region-by-region basis, but not to treat the separate regions as distinct empirical domains. In this chapter, we hope to rectify that inadequacy and to present data which permit us to deal with the regions in such a manner that they may be compared and ranked according to their war-proneness. First, we reproduce in Table 12.1 the aggregated sums and means of national war experience from Tables 11.1 and 11.2 in the previous chapter; next (Table 12.2) are the comparable figures but with the regions treated as distinct analytical entities rather than as aggregates of their separate nations. Finally, we show (Table 12.3) the amounts of war that actually *occurred within* the region rather than the amounts experienced both in or out of the region by the nations that constitute the region. These distinctions will become more evident as each table is presented. One point worth emphasizing, as the five main regions are examined, is that certain comparisons must be made and interpreted with considerable caution, given the disparity in the number of nations that comprise those regions, and the length of the nations' membership in the interstate system during the total 150 years. We do, of course, control for that factor by computing the total number of nation years for each region, and then using that figure as the denominator in several of the indicators.

REGIONAL AGGREGATIONS OF NATIONAL WAR EXPERIENCES

Looking first at the regional groupings of the nations, and aggregating the war experiences of the nations in these regions, Table 12.1 shows first the total number of nation years accounted for by that region's system members (column 1), followed by the total number of all international nation wars (column 2), and the interstate and extra-systemic nation wars separately (columns 3 and 4). The next set of columns (5 to 7) gives the total number of nation months in all wars, interstate wars, and extra-systemic wars. Similarly, in columns 8 to 10, we present the battle deaths from all international wars, interstate wars, and extra-systemic wars. Then, using the number of nation years contributed to the interstate system by the nations of each region as a baseline for normalizing, we compute the last three columns: number of nation wars per nation year (column 11), number of nation months of war per nation year (column 12), and number of battle deaths per nation year (column 13).

Not unexpectedly, the European nations lead by a wide margin in the frequency of involvement in both interstate and extra-systemic wars, and in nation months and battle deaths resulting from such wars. Of course, most of the extra-systemic wars (33 of the 43) were fought outside of Europe and against non-European political entities, and if the latters' war involvement measures were included, the disparity would probably be less dramatic. Does the greater war-proneness of the European nations still appear when we control for the number of nations in each region and the length of their tenure in the interstate system? Generally speaking, the answer is yes, but with the gap markedly reduced. That is, in national war experiences per nation year of system membership, the Middle East edges ahead of Europe, and on normalized nation months and battle deaths, Asian nations show a slightly higher score than the Europeans or any of the others. To some extent, however, assigning Turkey to the Middle East accounts for much of this pattern; the "sick man of Europe" fought in 17 wars for a total of 339 war months and 757,120 battle-connected fatalities. Had these sums been assigned to Europe, the latter's figures would have remained highest even after normalizing for nation years.

TOTAL AND AVERAGE WAR EXPERIENCE OF REGIONAL GROUPINGS

Let us shift now from the rough aggregate scores in which a good many nation wars (and their accompanying magnitude measures) are counted more than once, to a more restricted and perhaps more valid set of indicators. Here, instead of totaling *all* of the war experiences of each of the nations in a given region (that is, nation wars), we count only the number of wars in which at least one nation from that region participated; whether the war involved one or a dozen of them, it is counted only once for frequency. Its nation months and battle deaths are, likewise, only counted once in arriving at regional sums. It should also be reiterated that the following figures (Table 12.2) are based not on *where* the wars were *fought* but the region in which the participating *nations* were *located.*

12.1 - REGIONAL AGGREGATIONS OF NATIONAL WAR EXPERIENCES

		NO. OF NATION-WARS			NATION MONTHS OF WAR			BATTLE DEATHS (000'S)			ANNUAL AVERAGES		
REGIONAL GROUP	NATION YEARS IN TOTAL SYSTEM	ALL WARS	INTER-STATE WARS	EXTRA-SYS-TEMIC WARS	ALL WARS	INTER-STATE WARS	EXTRA-SYS-TEMIC WARS	ALL WARS	INTER-STATE WARS	EXTRA-SYS-TEMIC WARS	NATION-WARS PER NATION-YEAR	NATION MONTHS PER NATION-YEAR	BATTLE DEATHS (000'S) PER NATION-YEAR
	1	2	3	4	5	6	7	8	9	10	11	12	13
WESTERN HEMISPHERE	2186	35	30	5	793.7	621.6	172.1	929.5	813.0	116.5	0.016	0.363	0.425
EUROPE	3274	144	109	35	2514.1	1539.1	975.0	21973.7	21402.3	571.4	0.044	0.768	6.712
AFRICA	306	4	4	0	110.7	110.7	0.0	29.8	29.8	0.0	0.013	0.362	0.097
MIDDLE EAST	595	28	22	6	377.3	237.7	139.6	783.8	730.8	53.0	0.047	0.634	1.317
ASIA	754	28	26	2	737.0	686.0	51.0	5472.8	5431.3	41.5	0.037	0.977	7.258

Here, after giving the number of years in which at least one nation from a particular region was a qualified system member (column 1), we show the number of international, interstate, and extra-systemic wars that involved one or more nations from that region (columns 2 to 4). This is followed by the number of war months devoted to each class of war by one or more nations from that region (columns 5 to 7); the latter figure is a *regional* war month, and not a sum of *national* war months. After listing the total number of battle-connected deaths (column 8) sustained by all of the nations coming from each region, we present three different annual averages for the region. First is the number of wars that involved one or more nations from the region, divided by the number of years during which the region had at least one qualified nation member in the interstate system (column 9). Next are the war months per year (column 10); again, these are not nation months but regional war months. Last in this series are battle-connected deaths per year (column 11). In the final four columns (12 to 15) we shift from *annual* averages to *war* averages in order to permit some inter-regional comparisons of wars fought by the nations of each region; average duration in months per war (column 12); average magnitude in nation months per war (column 13) computed from the total nation months of wars in which one or more nations from that region fought, and *not* from the total nation months of nations from that region; average severity in battle deaths per war (column 14); and average intensity in battle deaths per regional war month (column 15).

Does this more restricted set of regional war data reveal a pattern any different from the earlier compilation? In terms of frequency of war experiences, the European nations again lead by an appreciable, if slightly smaller, margin; the same holds for war months and battle deaths. Examining annual averages (which are not quite com-

12.2 - TCTAL ANC AVERAGE WAR EXPERIENCE OF REGIONAL GROUPINGS

REGIONAL GRCUPING	NO. OF YEARS REGION HAC AT LEAST CNE SYSTEM MEMEER	NO. OF WARS INVOLVING AT LEAST ONE NATION FROM SPECIFIED REGION: ALL WARS	INTER-STATE WARS	EXTRA-SYSTEMIC WARS	REGIONAL WAR-MONTHS: ALL WARS	INTER-STATE WARS	EXTRA-SYS-TEMIC WARS	BATTLE DEATHS (000'S) FROM ALL WARS
	1	2	3	4	5	6	7	8
WESTERN HEMISPHERE	150	18	14	4	466.7	354.5	112.2	929.5
EUROPE	150	68	36	32	1405.3	455.5	949.8	21973.7
AFRICA	64	3	3	0	115.8	115.8	0.0	29.8
MIDDLE EAST	150	22	16	6	369.6	230.0	139.6	783.8
ASIA	106	13	11	2	326.8	275.8	51.0	5472.8

REGIONAL GROUPING	ANNUAL AVERAGES: WARS PER YEAR	WAR-MONTHS PER YEAR	BATTLE DEATHS (000'S) PER YEAR	WAR AVERAGES: AVERAGE DURATION OF WARS IN MONTHS	AVERAGE MAGNITUDE OF WARS IN NATION MONTHS	AVERAGE SEVERITY OF WARS IN BATTLE DEATHS (000'S)	AVERAGE INTENSITY: BATTLE DEATHS (000'S) PER WAR-MONTH
	9	10	11	12	13	14	15
WESTERN HEMISPHERE	0.12	3.1	6.2	25.9	145.6	1440.3	55.6
EUROPE	0.45	9.4	146.5	20.7	54.1	407.8	19.7
AFRICA	0.05	1.8	0.5	38.6	468.0	5692.1	147.5
MIDDLE EAST	0.15	2.5	5.2	16.8	74.0	519.6	30.9
ASIA	0.12	3.1	51.6	25.1	175.7	2069.0	82.3

parable, since the earlier data are based on nation year memberships in the system and those here are based on the mere number of years that the region had at least one system member), the lead of the European nations is even more pronounced, as is clear when we compare columns 9 to 11 here with columns 11 to 13 in Table 12.1. The other difference is that the Western Hemisphere nations drop from second to third place in war frequencies, but remain in second place in nation months and battle deaths (given the fact that these can only be counted once). Finally, this second table, by examining wars rather than nation war experiences, permits us to compare the regions in terms of their war averages. On these dimensions (columns 12 to 15) we find that the African nations' wars are, while markedly fewer than the others', of greater average duration, magnitude, severity, and intensity. This is wholly a consequence of the fact that South Africa and Ethiopia participated—albeit modestly—in World War II, and the latter participated in the Korean War, plus one other relatively short war (Italo-Ethiopian, 1935–1936), whereas the other regions' members saw more war of varying magnitude and severity. But even with the greater frequency and variation in the war experiences of the other regions, we find that on these war average figures, the European nations score lowest on magnitude, severity, and intensity. Let us shift now to a third possible way of comparing regional war experiences over the past 150 years.

TOTAL AND AVERAGE WAR EXPERIENCE IN EACH REGION

Turning from a focus on the regions as locales from which the warring nations *come,* to locales *in* which the wars are fought, we are dealing, of necessity, with somewhat more ambiguous material. This is the result of two sorts of cases. First, there were the wars that were fought largely within a given geographical region, but that nevertheless also saw *some* limited combat in other regions; illustrative would be the Spanish-American naval encounter in Manila Bay in 1898, quite distinct from the main Caribbean theater. In such cases, we treat the war experience as if it had all taken place in the major combat zone. Second, there were the wars that saw major campaigns in more than one continental region. It would be nearly impossible to ascertain how many battle deaths were sustained in each of the regions and to assign specific war months to each. Thus, for the five wars (asterisked in Table 12.4) that did produce sustained military action in more than one region, we assigned the war experiences of each participant that fought in more than one region to *each* such region; that is, a given set of figures may have been counted *more than once.* For example, the total battle deaths and war months of England and the United States in World War II appear in their entirety four times (Asia, Europe, Africa, and Middle East). This procedure inflates the totals of these regions, but it portrays a more accurate picture than one in which we either assign fractions of war months and battle deaths to each participating region or merely include only the region that saw most of the fighting.

Bearing in mind this unavoidable artificiality, we present in Table 12.3 the number of wars fought partially or wholly within the bounds of each region (columns 1 to 3), the months of war fought in each region (columns 4 to 6) and the total battle deaths sustained by all system members that fought in each region (columns 7 to 9). We then move on to the annual averages of wars within the regions: wars per year (column 10), war months per year (column 11), and battle deaths per year (column 12). We conclude with war averages for wars fought within the regions: months per war (column 13), battle deaths per war (column 14), and battle deaths per war month (column 15).

12.3 - TOTAL AND AVERAGE WAR EXPERIENCE IN EACH REGION

REGION WHERE WARS WERE FOUGHT	NO. OF WARS FOUGHT IN SPECIFIED REGION			MONTHS OF WAR FOUGHT IN SPECIFIED REGION			BATTLE DEATHS (000'S) FROM WARS FOUGHT IN SPECIFIED REGION		
	ALL WARS 1	INTER-STATE WARS 2	EXTRA-SYS-TEMIC WARS 3	ALL WARS 4	INTER-STATE WARS 5	EXTRA-SYS-TEMIC WARS 6	ALL WARS 7	INTER-STATE WARS 8	EXTRA-SYS-TEMIC WARS 9
WESTERN HEMISPHERE	16	11	5	415.1	194.4	220.7	459.3	197.3	262.0
EUROPE	33	23	10	476.3	276.6	199.7	22430.1	22262.1	168.0
AFRICA	8	3	5	207.7	130.0	77.7	8376.2	8334.2	42.0
MIDDLE EAST	19	12	7	474.3	231.7	242.6	10986.7	10893.7	93.0
ASIA	27	11	16	784.4	275.6	508.8	16639.7	16422.3	217.4

REGION WHERE WARS WERE FOUGHT	ANNUAL AVERAGES			WAR AVERAGES		
	WARS PER YEAR 10	MONTHS OF WAR PER YEAR 11	BATTLE DEATHS (000'S) PER YEAR 12	MONTHS PER WAR 13	BATTLE DEATHS (000'S) PER WAR 14	BATTLE DEATHS (000'S) PER MONTH OF WAR 15
WESTERN HEMISPHERE	0.11	2.8	3.1	25.9	28.7	1.1
EUROPE	0.22	3.2	149.5	14.4	679.7	47.1
AFRICA	0.05	1.4	55.8	26.0	1047.0	40.3
MIDDLE EAST	0.13	3.2	73.2	25.0	578.2	23.2
ASIA	0.18	5.2	110.9	29.1	616.3	21.2

When we use region as the locale of war, what generalizations emerge from the data? Europe, of course, sees more interstate wars than the other regions (column 2), but is second to Asia in extra-systemic ones (column 3). Asia also leads in the months of war (columns 4 to 6), largely because of the 509 months of extra-systemic war fought—by outsiders—on its territory, but Europe again outstrips the other regions in terms of the total number of combatants killed on its soil (columns 7 to 9).

Shifting over to annual averages (columns 10 to 12), Europe leads in wars per year and battle deaths per year, but falls to second position behind Asia in war months divided by 150, the entire span of our study. And as to averages based on wars fought in the separate regions, Europe again saw most battle deaths per month of war (column 15), but ranked second behind Africa in battle deaths per war (column 14), and with her more numerous short wars, ranked last on average duration (column 13).

Finally in Table 12.4, we have listed all 93 of the international wars and their code numbers under the region or regions in which sustained hostilities occurred. Those assigned to more than one region are marked by an asterisk, and the interstate wars (numbered 1 to 50) are separated in each column from the extra-systemic ones (numbered 51 to 93) by a double space.

SUMMARY

As the above findings are summarized, it is worth noting that even though Europe has experienced, according to most of our indicators, more war than any other region, this may well be a consequence of our selection criteria. First, our definition of system membership is a very Europe-centered one and, second, we are only looking at wars which involved our system members. Moreover, when the extra-systemic wars are examined and quantified, only the war experience of the system members is counted, omitting the many battle deaths and war months of the peoples of these other regions.

Finally, the fact that we are not looking at civil wars can lead to some bias in the cross-regional comparisons; Europe, for example, has probably seen fewer civil wars in the past 150 years than the Western Hemisphere, even though in severity there may be little difference. In passing, however, we might note that one reason for the relatively low incidence of international war in the Western Hemisphere was the combination of British policy, their naval power, and in the twentieth century, the Monroe Doctrine. While this might not have affected the incidence of intra-regional wars in Latin America, it could have significantly reduced the opportunities for war between these states and those of Europe.

In sum, then, we are suggesting that these compilations of war experience in, and by, the several continental regions may be quite useful, but that comparisons among them must be used with caution. There are enough dissimilarities from region to region to make overly explicit comparisons quite misleading.

12.4 REGIONAL BATTLEGROUNDS OF INTERNATIONAL WARS

WESTERN HEMISPHERE	EUROPE	MIDDLE EAST	AFRICA	ASIA
4. Mexican-American	1. Franco-Spanish	*3. Russo-Turkish	*35. World War One	23. Sino-French
8. La Plata	2. Navarino Bay	10. Anglo-Persian	40. Italo-Ethiopian	25. Sino-Japanese
15. Franco-Mexican	*3. Russo-Turkish	12. Spanish-Moroccan	*43. World War Two	28. Russo-Japanese
16. Ecuadorian-Colombian	5. Austro-Sardinian	*21. Russo-Turkish		*35. World War One
18. Spanish-Chilean	6. 1st Schles.-Holstein	31. Spanish-Moroccan	75. British-Zulu	38. Manchurian
22. Pacific	7. Roman Republic	32. Italo-Turkish	79. Franco-Madagascan	41. Sino-Japanese
24. Central American	9. Crimean	*33. First Balkan	81. Italo-Ethiopian	42. Russo-Japanese
27. Spanish-American	11. Italian Unification	*35. World War One	84. Boer	*43. World War Two
29. Central American	13. Italo-Roman	*37. Greco-Turkish	90. Madagascan	46. Korean
30. Central American	14. Italo-Sicilian	*43. World War Two		49. Sino-Indian
39. Chaco	17. 2nd Schles.-Holstein	45. Palestine		50. Second Kashmir
	19. Seven Weeks	48. Sinai		
58. Texan	20. Franco-Prussian			51. British-Maharattan
61. Peruvian-Bolivian	*21. Russo-Turkish	55. Russo-Persian		53. 1st Anglo-Burmese
69. La Plata	26. Greco-Turkish	57. First Syrian		54. Javanese
70. Ten Years	*33. First Balkan	60. Second Syrian		59. 1st British-Afghan
80. Cuban	34. Second Balkan	77. Mahdist		62. 1st British-Sikh
	*35. World War One	86. Riffian		64. 2nd British-Sikh
	36. Hungarian-Allies	87. Druze		66. Sepoy
	*37. Greco-Turkish	92. Algerian		71. Dutch-Achinese
	*43. World War Two			74. 2nd British-Afghan
	44. Russo-Finnish			76. Franco-Indochinese
	47. Russo-Hungarian			82. 1st Philippine
				83. 2nd Philippine
	52. Greek			88. Indonesian
	56. First Polish			89. Indochinese
	63. Hungarian			91. First Kashmir
	65. 1st Turco-Montenegran			93. Tibetan
	67. 2nd Turco-Montenegran			
	68. Second Polish			
	72. Balkan			
	73. Bosnian			
	78. Serbo-Bulgarian			
	85. Russian Nationalities			

* before war indicates war fought in more than one region.

Chapter 13

Pair-Wise War Frequencies: Traditional Enmity and Enduring Friendship

By definition, every war involves at least two parties, and it is often more profitable to examine the specific combinations of nations that have the most or the least war experience, than to examine them singly and in isolation. Is it more likely for two nations to fight one another if they are highly similar or quite different? Do they tend to be similar on cultural dimensions and different in their structural or physical attributes? Are they close together geographically? Do they sit astride one another's trade routes or are they separated by a given number and type of neighboring nation? How interdependent have they been, and how strong or weak were the links and bonds between them before each of their wars? In many of the social sciences it is becoming increasingly clear that much more is to be learned from the *relationships* between and among our objects of analysis than from an exhaustive investigation of their *discrete properties*, and we therefore provide here the sort of data which will permit and encourage this same approach to the understanding of international military conflict. (A vigorous defense of this viewpoint, with some supporting evidence, is found in Rummel, 1965.) As in prior chapters, we will not present data on any of the independent or intervening variables, but only the data that seem to measure best the dependent variable, and that might provide the basis for testing pair-wise factors such as those suggested above.

One caveat is, however, very much in order here. Just as in the physical sciences, where there was little progress in *N*-body problems until certain two-body problems had begun to reveal their secrets, most of us in the social sciences have tended to focus on dyadic relationships and interactions at the outset. In doing so, however, it should be stressed that this is often an artificial mode of analysis, dictated more by our methodological inadequacies and the state of the discipline than by any theoretical conviction. In subsequent analyses, we hope to return to the *N*-body problem, but for now we must restrict ourselves to the straightforward pair-wise analysis. Here, then, we present a range of indicators that reflect the extent to which all pairs of nations have fought against, or alongside of, one another, and that may permit us to identify the pairs of nations that deserve to be classified as "traditional enmities" and "enduring friendships."

PAIR-WISE WAR EXPERIENCES AS PARTNERS AND AS OPPONENTS

Although there are persuasive reasons for treating pair-wise experience in which the two nations fight *alongside* one another separately from those data reflecting their roles as *adversaries,* we begin by combining the two sets of data. Theoretically, this has the virtue of treating each dyad in a more complete and summary fashion. And mechanically, it eliminates the need to repeat a very lengthy list. One alternative would have been a large matrix of all the nations ever in the system ($N=144$), but two major considerations mitigated against adoption of such a format. First, each cell intersection of two nations which had experienced war as partners and/or opponents would have had to include the separate war month and battle death figures (several of which run to 6 digits) for partnerships and enmities; such a layout would be very confusing and difficult to read. Second, such a matrix could not possibly be printed on a single page, therefore necessitating a fold-out sheet of considerable size; we think that such a fold-out would either *not* be used very often or would soon be torn to shreds!

Thus, in Table 13.1, we list each nation once in alphabetical order at the left margin and then list (again alphabetically) in the next column every other nation with whom, or against whom, it has ever fought a war. (Since imperial and colonial wars are, by definition, those in which one side does not include a system member, our data for extra-systemic war show *partnerships* only: those wars in which two system members fought together against a non-system member.) When all those who have been partners or opponents of the left-hand nation have been listed, we skip a line, identify the next nation in alphabetical order and continue as before. In this way, of course, every pair will be shown twice; early in the list you will find, for example, England-Russia and further down in the list you will find Russia-England. Even though this produces a rather lengthy list, it makes it more useful to scholars interested in certain particular nations. We have not, however, listed any pair which had *no* war experience vis-à-vis one another. Finally, the reader is reminded that there are the three succession states of Prussia/Germany, Sardinia/Italy, and Serbia/Yugoslavia. These nations are listed in the left-hand column as Germany/Prussia, Italy/Sardinia, and Yugoslavia/Serbia.

In both of a pair's locations, the following figures are shown. As partners, there is the total number of wars fought alongside one another (column 1), plus the total duration in months (column 2) of that pair's partnerships. It should be emphasized that one or both parties may not only *not* have participated in the full duration of these wars but need not have fought side-by-side in the same combat zone; the only requirement is that they were on the same side during *some* shared amount of time. For example, we do not count Belgium (which left World War Two in 1940) and Mongolia (which entered that war in 1945) as partners in World War Two; however, we do count France and Poland as partners in that conflict. That is, even though French troops did not fight in Poland, both nations were at war at the same time against a common enemy. Next there is column 3 showing the number of battle-connected deaths, in thousands, sustained by the first named co-belligerent during all the wars in which the second named nation was its partner, either for all or part of the conflict's duration. Next (column 4) are the battle deaths in thousands sustained by the second named nation. Finally, in column 5 we present the decile in which the *combined* battle deaths of both partners are ranked. More will be said about the decile ranking in the next section.

Shifting over to the "As Opponents" columns, we find the same sets of figures. First, there is the number of wars in which the two nations were on opposite sides (column 6) and then the total duration in months of their opposition (column 7). Similarly, columns 8 and 9 show the number of battle-connected deaths, in thousands, sustained by the first named and second named nations during all those wars in which they fought on opposite sides. And again (column 10) we present the decile rank of the combined battle deaths as opponents.

RANKING NATION-PAIRS BY SHARED EXPERIENCE AS WARTIME PARTNERS

Despite what we hope to be a useful presentation, the data shown in Table 13.1 are too raw and too numerous to permit any rapid and convenient interpretation. What is required for such purposes is a transformation of the raw data into a set of rank order presentations such that the researcher can not only ascertain quickly which dyads were most war-prone and which most frequently allied in war, but where each

13.1 - NATIONAL WAR EXPERIENCE AS PARTNERS AND OPPONENTS

		AS PARTNERS					AS OPPONENTS				
				-BATTLE DEATHS- (000'S)					-BATTLE DEATHS- (000'S)		
		NO. OF WARS 1	WAR MONTHS 2	FIRST NAMED 3	SECOND NAMED 4	DECILE BATTLE DEATHS 5	NO. OF WARS 6	WAR MONTHS 7	FIRST NAMED 8	SECOND NAMED 9	DECILE BATTLE DEATHS 10
ARGENTINA	AND: BRAZIL	1	59.9	10.00	100.00	6	1	6.6	0.80	0.50	10
AUSTRALIA	AND: BELGIUM	2	30.8	29.67	9.70	7					
	BRAZIL	1	10.1	29.40	1.00	8					
	BULGARIA	1	7.9	29.40	1.00	8	1	33.0	29.40	9.00	9
	CANADA	2	102.5	29.67	39.61	6					
	CHINA	1	44.3	29.40	1350.00	2	1	31.6	0.27	900.00	4
	COLOMBIA	1	25.7	0.27	0.14	10					
	ENGLAND	2	103.0	29.67	270.67	5					
	ETHIOPIA	2	32.2	29.67	5.12	8					
	FINLAND						1	38.9	29.40	42.00	8
	FRANCE	2	50.2	29.67	210.29	5					
	GERMANY/PRUSSIA						1	68.1	29.40	3500.00	2
	GREECE	2	36.1	29.67	10.17	7					
	HOLLAND	2	30.4	29.67	6.31	7					
	HUNGARY						1	42.8	29.40	40.00	8
	ITALY/SARDINIA	1	18.7	29.40	17.50	7	1	38.8	29.40	60.00	7
	JAPAN						1	44.3	29.40	1000.00	4
	KOREA NORTH						1	31.6	0.27	520.00	5
	KOREA SOUTH	1	31.6	0.27	415.00	4					
	MONGOLIA	1	0.2	29.40	3.00	8					
	NEW ZEALAND	1	71.4	29.40	17.30	7					
	NORWAY	1	2.0	29.40	2.00	8					
	PHILIPPINES	1	31.6	0.27	0.09	10					
	POLAND	1	0.8	29.40	320.00	4					
	RUMANIA	1	7.9	29.40	10.00	7	1	38.1	29.40	290.00	6
	RUSSIA	1	46.7	29.40	7500.00	1					
	SOUTH AFRICA	1	71.3	29.40	8.70	7					
	THAILAND	1	30.2	0.27	0.11	10					
	TURKEY	1	31.6	0.27	0.72	9					
	UNITED STATES	2	75.9	29.67	462.30	3					
	YUGOSLAVIA/SERBIA	1	0.4	29.40	5.00	8					
AUSTRIA-HUNGARY	AND: BADEN	1	1.4	20.00	0.10	8					
	BAVARIA	1	1.4	20.00	0.50	8					
	BELGIUM						1	51.0	1200.00	87.50	3
	BULGARIA	1	35.6	1200.00	14.00	3					
	DENMARK						1	3.6	0.50	3.00	10
	ENGLAND						1	51.0	1200.00	908.00	2
	FRANCE	1	1.0	0.10	0.50	10	2	53.4	1212.50	1357.50	2
	GERMANY/PRUSSIA	2	54.7	1200.50	1801.00	1	1	1.4	20.00	10.00	9
	GREECE						1	16.2	1200.00	5.00	3
	HANOVER	1	0.5	20.00	0.50	8					
	HESSE ELECTORAL	1	1.4	20.00	0.10	8					
	HESSE GRAND DUCAL	1	1.4	20.00	0.10	8					
	ITALY/SARDINIA						4	50.0	1238.10	659.90	2

			AS PARTNERS					AS OPPONENTS				
					-BATTLE DEATHS- (000'S)					-BATTLE DEATHS- (000'S)		
			NO. OF WARS 1	WAR MONTHS 2	FIRST NAMED 3	SECOND NAMED 4	DECILE BATTLE DEATHS 5	NO. OF WARS 6	WAR MONTHS 7	FIRST NAMED 8	SECOND NAMED 9	DECILE BATTLE DEATHS 10
		JAPAN						1	50.4	1200.00	0.30	3
		MECKLENBURG-SCHWERIN	1	1.4	20.00	0.10	8					
		PAPAL STATES						1	1.8	0.10	1.50	10
		PORTUGAL						1	32.1	1200.00	7.00	3
		RUMANIA						1	15.4	1200.00	335.00	2
		RUSSIA	1	1.0	45.00	14.50	6	1	40.2	1200.00	1700.00	2
		SAXONY	1	1.4	20.00	0.60	8					
		TURKEY	1	48.2	1200.00	325.00	2					
		TWO SICILIES	1	1.8	0.10	0.10	10					
		UNITED STATES						1	18.6	1200.00	126.00	3
		WUERTTEMBERG	1	1.4	20.00	0.10	8					
		YUGOSLAVIA/SERBIA						1	51.2	1200.00	48.00	3
BADEN	AND:	AUSTRIA-HUNGARY	1	1.4	0.10	20.00	8					
		BAVARIA	2	5.3	1.10	6.00	9					
		FRANCE						1	4.2	1.00	140.00	7
		GERMANY/PRUSSIA	1	4.2	1.00	40.00	7	1	1.4	0.10	10.00	9
		HANOVER	1	0.5	0.10	0.50	10					
		HESSE ELECTORAL	1	1.4	0.10	0.10	10					
		HESSE GRAND DUCAL	1	1.4	0.10	0.10	10					
		ITALY/SARDINIA						1	1.4	0.10	4.00	10
		MECKLENBURG-SCHWERIN	1	1.4	0.10	0.10	10					
		SAXONY	1	1.4	0.10	0.60	10					
		WUERTTEMBERG	2	5.6	1.10	1.10	9					
BAVARIA	AND:	AUSTRIA-HUNGARY	1	1.4	0.50	20.00	8					
		BADEN	2	5.3	6.00	1.10	9					
		FRANCE						1	3.9	5.50	140.00	7
		GERMANY/PRUSSIA	1	3.9	5.50	40.00	7	1	1.4	0.50	10.00	9
		HANOVER	1	0.5	0.50	0.50	9					
		HESSE ELECTORAL	1	1.4	0.50	0.10	10					
		HESSE GRAND DUCAL	1	1.4	0.50	0.10	10					
		ITALY/SARDINIA						1	1.4	0.50	4.00	10
		MECKLENBURG-SCHWERIN	1	1.4	0.50	0.10	10					
		SAXONY	1	1.4	0.50	0.60	9					
		WUERTTEMBERG	2	5.3	6.00	1.10	9					
BELGIUM	AND:	AUSTRALIA	2	30.8	9.70	29.67	7					
		AUSTRIA-HUNGARY						1	51.0	87.50	1200.00	3
		BULGARIA						1	35.6	87.50	14.00	7
		CANADA	2	30.8	9.70	39.61	6					
		CHINA						1	30.2	0.10	900.00	5
		COLOMBIA	1	25.7	0.10	0.14	10					
		ENGLAND	3	82.0	97.20	1178.67	3					
		ETHIOPIA	1	26.9	0.10	0.12	10					
		FRANCE	3	82.1	97.20	1560.29	2					
		GERMANY/PRUSSIA						2	51.9	97.10	5300.00	1

13.1 - NATIONAL WAR EXPERIENCE AS PARTNERS AND OPPONENTS

			AS PARTNERS					AS OPPONENTS				
			NO. OF WARS 1	WAR MONTHS 2	-BATTLE DEATHS- (000'S) FIRST NAMED 3	SECOND NAMED 4	DECILE BATTLE DEATHS 5	NO. OF WARS 6	WAR MONTHS 7	-BATTLE DEATHS- (000'S) FIRST NAMED 8	SECOND NAMED 9	DECILE BATTLE DEATHS 10
		GREECE	2	46.7	87.60	5.17	6					
		HOLLAND	2	30.4	9.70	6.31	8					
		ITALY/SARDINIA	1	41.7	87.50	650.00	3					
		JAPAN	1	50.7	87.50	0.30	6					
		KOREA NORTH						1	30.2	0.10	520.00	6
		KOREA SOUTH	1	30.2	0.10	415.00	4					
		NEW ZEALAND	1	0.6	9.60	17.30	8					
		NORWAY	1	0.6	9.60	2.00	9					
		PHILIPPINES	1	30.2	0.10	0.09	10					
		PORTUGAL	1	32.4	87.50	7.00	6					
		RUMANIA	1	15.4	87.50	335.00	4					
		RUSSIA	1	40.1	87.50	1700.00	2					
		SOUTH AFRICA	1	0.6	9.60	8.70	8					
		THAILAND	1	30.2	0.10	0.11	10					
		TURKEY	1	30.2	0.10	0.72	10	1	48.5	87.50	325.00	6
		UNITED STATES	2	49.1	87.60	180.00	5					
		YUGOSLAVIA/SERBIA	1	51.3	87.50	48.00	5					
BOLIVIA	AND:	CHILE						1	57.9	1.00	3.00	10
		PARAGUAY						1	35.9	80.00	50.00	7
		PERU	1	54.5	1.00	10.00	9					
BRAZIL	AND:	ARGENTINA	1	59.9	100.00	10.00	6	1	6.6	0.50	0.80	10
		AUSTRALIA	1	10.1	1.00	29.40	8					
		BULGARIA	1	7.9	1.00	1.00	9	1	2.1	1.00	9.00	9
		CANADA	1	10.1	1.00	39.30	7					
		CHINA	1	10.1	1.00	1350.00	3					
		ENGLAND	1	10.1	1.00	270.00	5					
		FINLAND						1	2.5	1.00	42.00	9
		FRANCE	1	6.5	1.00	210.00	5					
		GERMANY/PRUSSIA						1	10.1	1.00	3500.00	2
		HUNGARY						1	6.5	1.00	40.00	9
		ITALY/SARDINIA	1	10.1	1.00	17.50	8					
		JAPAN						1	10.1	1.00	1000.00	4
		NEW ZEALAND	1	10.1	1.00	17.30	8					
		RUMANIA	1	7.9	1.00	10.00	9	1	1.6	1.00	290.00	7
		RUSSIA	1	10.1	1.00	7500.00	1					
		SOUTH AFRICA	1	10.1	1.00	8.70	9					
		UNITED STATES	1	10.1	1.00	408.30	4					
BULGARIA	AND:	AUSTRALIA	1	7.9	1.00	29.40	8	1	33.0	9.00	29.40	9
		AUSTRIA-HUNGARY	1	35.6	14.00	1200.00	3					
		BELGIUM						1	35.6	14.00	87.50	7
		BRAZIL	1	7.9	1.00	1.00	9	1	2.1	9.00	1.00	9
		CANADA	1	7.9	1.00	39.30	7	1	33.0	9.00	39.30	9
		CHINA	1	7.9	1.00	1350.00	3	1	33.0	9.00	1350.00	3
		ENGLAND	1	7.9	1.00	270.00	5	2	68.6	23.00	1178.00	3

		AS PARTNERS					AS OPPONENTS				
		NO. OF WARS	WAR MONTHS	-BATTLE DEATHS- (000'S) FIRST NAMED	SECOND NAMED	DECILE BATTLE DEATHS	NO. OF WARS	WAR MONTHS	-BATTLE DEATHS- (000'S) FIRST NAMED	SECOND NAMED	DECILE BATTLE DEATHS
		1	2	3	4	5	6	7	8	9	10
	FINLAND	1	33.0	9.00	42.00	6	1	0.4	1.00	42.00	9
	FRANCE	1	6.5	1.00	210.00	5	1	35.6	14.00	1350.00	3
	GERMANY/PRUSSIA	2	68.6	23.00	5300.00	1	1	7.9	1.00	3500.00	2
	GREECE	1	4.1	32.00	5.00	7	2	16.0	32.00	7.50	9
	HUNGARY	1	33.0	9.00	40.00	7	1	4.4	1.00	40.00	9
	ITALY/SARDINIA	2	28.7	10.00	77.50	6	2	46.3	23.00	667.50	5
	JAPAN	1	33.0	9.00	1000.00	3	2	43.5	15.00	1000.30	4
	NEW ZEALAND	1	7.9	1.00	17.30	8	1	33.0	9.00	17.30	9
	PORTUGAL						1	31.0	14.00	7.00	9
	RUMANIA	2	40.4	10.00	300.00	5	2	16.1	32.00	336.50	6
	RUSSIA	1	7.9	1.00	7500.00	1	2	58.8	23.00	9200.00	1
	SOUTH AFRICA	1	7.9	1.00	8.70	9	1	33.0	9.00	8.70	9
	TURKEY	1	35.6	14.00	325.00	4	2	4.6	50.00	50.00	7
	UNITED STATES	1	7.9	1.00	408.30	4	2	50.4	23.00	534.30	5
	YUGOSLAVIA/SERBIA	1	4.1	32.00	15.00	7	2	36.6	32.00	66.50	7
CANADA	AND: AUSTRALIA	2	102.5	39.61	29.67	6					
	BELGIUM	2	30.8	39.61	9.70	6					
	BRAZIL	1	10.1	39.30	1.00	7					
	BULGARIA	1	7.9	39.30	1.00	7	1	33.0	39.30	9.00	9
	CHINA	1	44.3	39.30	1350.00	2	1	31.3	0.31	900.00	4
	COLOMBIA	1	25.7	0.31	0.14	10					
	ENGLAND	2	102.5	39.61	270.67	5					
	ETHIOPIA	2	32.2	39.61	5.12	7					
	FINLAND						1	38.9	39.30	42.00	8
	FRANCE	2	50.0	39.61	210.29	5					
	GERMANY/PRUSSIA						1	67.9	39.30	3500.00	1
	GREECE	2	36.1	39.61	10.17	6					
	HOLLAND	2	30.4	39.61	6.31	7					
	HUNGARY						1	42.8	39.30	40.00	8
	ITALY/SARDINIA	1	18.7	39.30	17.50	6	1	38.8	39.30	60.00	7
	JAPAN						1	44.3	39.30	1000.00	4
	KOREA NORTH						1	31.3	0.31	520.00	5
	KOREA SOUTH	1	31.3	0.31	415.00	4					
	MONGOLIA	1	0.2	39.30	3.00	7					
	NEW ZEALAND	1	71.2	39.30	17.30	6					
	NORWAY	1	2.0	39.30	2.00	7					
	PHILIPPINES	1	31.3	0.31	0.09	10					
	POLAND	1	0.6	39.30	320.00	4					
	RUMANIA	1	7.9	39.30	10.00	7	1	38.1	39.30	290.00	6
	RUSSIA	1	46.7	39.30	7500.00	1					
	SOUTH AFRICA	1	71.2	39.30	8.70	7					
	THAILAND	1	30.2	0.31	0.11	10					
	TURKEY	1	31.3	0.31	0.72	9					
	UNITED STATES	2	75.6	39.61	462.30	3					
	YUGOSLAVIA/SERBIA	1	0.4	39.30	5.00	7					

13.1 - NATIONAL WAR EXPERIENCE AS PARTNERS AND OPPONENTS

		AS PARTNERS					AS OPPONENTS				
		NO. OF WARS	WAR MONTHS	-BATTLE DEATHS- (000'S) FIRST NAMED	SECOND NAMED	DECILE BATTLE DEATHS	NO. OF WARS	WAR MONTHS	-BATTLE DEATHS- (000'S) FIRST NAMED	SECOND NAMED	DECILE BATTLE DEATHS
		1	2	3	4	5	6	7	8	9	10
CHILE	AND: BOLIVIA						1	57.9	3.00	1.00	10
	PERU	1	3.8	0.10	0.60	10	1	54.5	3.00	10.00	9
	SPAIN						1	6.5	0.10	0.30	10
CHINA	AND: AUSTRALIA	1	44.3	1350.00	29.40	2	1	31.6	900.00	0.27	4
	BELGIUM						1	30.2	900.00	0.10	5
	BRAZIL	1	10.1	1350.00	1.00	3					
	BULGARIA	1	7.9	1350.00	1.00	3	1	33.0	1350.00	9.00	3
	CANADA	1	44.3	1350.00	39.30	2	1	31.3	900.00	0.31	4
	COLOMBIA						1	25.7	900.00	0.14	5
	ENGLAND	1	44.3	1350.00	270.00	2	1	33.0	900.00	0.67	4
	ETHIOPIA						1	26.9	900.00	0.12	5
	FINLAND						1	33.4	1350.00	42.00	3
	FRANCE	1	9.7	1350.00	210.00	2	2	42.6	910.00	2.39	4
	GERMANY/PRUSSIA						1	41.0	1350.00	3500.00	1
	GREECE						1	30.2	900.00	0.17	4
	HOLLAND						1	30.2	900.00	0.11	5
	HUNGARY						1	37.5	1350.00	40.00	3
	INDIA						1	1.1	0.50	0.50	10
	ITALY/SARDINIA	1	18.7	1350.00	17.50	2	1	20.9	1350.00	60.00	3
	JAPAN						4	122.0	2160.00	1265.00	2
	KOREA NORTH	1	33.0	900.00	520.00	2					
	KOREA SOUTH						1	33.0	900.00	415.00	3
	MONGOLIA	1	0.2	1350.00	3.00	3					
	NEW ZEALAND	1	44.3	1350.00	17.30	2					
	PHILIPPINES						1	33.0	900.00	0.09	5
	RUMANIA	1	7.9	1350.00	10.00	2	1	32.6	1350.00	290.00	2
	RUSSIA	1	41.2	1350.00	7500.00	1					
	SOUTH AFRICA	1	44.3	1350.00	8.70	2					
	THAILAND						1	30.2	900.00	0.11	5
	TURKEY						1	33.0	900.00	0.72	4
	UNITED STATES	1	44.3	1350.00	408.30	2	1	33.0	900.00	54.00	4
COLOMBIA	AND: AUSTRALIA	1	25.7	0.14	0.27	10					
	BELGIUM	1	25.7	0.14	0.10	10					
	CANADA	1	25.7	0.14	0.31	10					
	CHINA						1	25.7	0.14	900.00	5
	ECUADOR						1	0.5	0.30	0.70	10
	ENGLAND	1	25.7	0.14	0.67	10					
	ETHIOPIA	1	25.7	0.14	0.12	10					
	FRANCE	1	25.7	0.14	0.29	10					
	GREECE	1	25.7	0.14	0.17	10					
	HOLLAND	1	25.7	0.14	0.11	10					
	KOREA NORTH						1	25.7	0.14	520.00	5
	KOREA SOUTH	1	25.7	0.14	415.00	4					
	PHILIPPINES	1	25.7	0.14	0.09	10					

			AS PARTNERS					AS OPPONENTS				
			NO. OF WARS	WAR MONTHS	-BATTLE DEATHS- (000'S) FIRST NAMED	SECOND NAMED	DECILE BATTLE DEATHS	NO. OF WARS	WAR MONTHS	-BATTLE DEATHS- (000'S) FIRST NAMED	SECOND NAMED	DECILE BATTLE DEATHS
			1	2	3	4	5	6	7	8	9	10
		THAILAND	1	25.7	0.14	0.11	10					
		TURKEY	1	25.7	0.14	0.72	9					
		UNITED STATES	1	25.7	0.14	54.00	6					
CZECHOSLOVAKIA	AND:	HUNGARY						1	3.6	2.00	6.00	10
		RUMANIA	1	3.6	2.00	3.00	9					
DENMARK	AND:	AUSTRIA-HUNGARY						1	3.6	3.00	0.50	10
		GERMANY/PRUSSIA						2	11.7	6.50	3.50	9
ECUADOR	AND:	COLOMBIA						1	0.5	0.70	0.30	10
ENGLAND	AND:	AUSTRALIA	2	103.0	270.67	29.67	5					
		AUSTRIA-HUNGARY						1	51.0	908.00	1200.00	2
		BELGIUM	3	82.0	1178.67	97.20	3					
		BRAZIL	1	10.1	270.00	1.00	5					
		BULGARIA	1	7.9	270.00	1.00	5	2	68.6	1178.00	23.00	3
		CANADA	2	102.5	270.67	39.61	5					
		CHINA	1	44.3	270.00	1350.00	2	1	33.0	0.67	900.00	4
		COLOMBIA	1	25.7	0.67	0.14	10					
		ETHIOPIA	2	32.2	270.67	5.12	5					
		FINLAND						1	38.9	270.00	42.00	6
		FRANCE	6	124.8	1200.77	1655.34	1					
		GERMANY/PRUSSIA						2	119.3	1178.00	5300.00	1
		GREECE	3	52.6	1178.67	15.17	3					
		HOLLAND	3	41.6	271.67	6.71	5					
		HUNGARY						1	42.8	270.00	40.00	7
		IRAN						1	4.6	0.50	1.50	10
		ISRAEL	1	0.2	0.02	0.20	10					
		ITALY/SARDINIA	3	74.1	1200.00	669.70	2	1	38.8	270.00	60.00	6
		JAPAN	1	50.7	908.00	0.30	3	1	44.3	270.00	1000.00	3
		KOREA NORTH						1	35.0	0.67	520.00	5
		KOREA SOUTH	1	35.0	0.67	415.00	4					
		MONGOLIA	1	0.2	270.00	3.00	5					
		NEW ZEALAND	1	71.4	270.00	17.30	5					
		NORWAY	1	2.0	270.00	2.00	5					
		PHILIPPINES	1	34.4	0.67	0.09	10					
		POLAND	1	0.8	270.00	320.00	3					
		PORTUGAL	1	32.4	908.00	7.00	3					
		RUMANIA	2	23.3	1178.00	345.00	2	1	38.1	270.00	290.00	5
		RUSSIA	3	86.8	1178.08	9200.06	1	1	23.1	22.00	100.00	7
		SOUTH AFRICA	1	71.3	270.00	8.70	5					
		THAILAND	1	30.2	0.67	0.11	10					
		TURKEY	3	59.0	22.68	55.72	6	2	48.6	908.08	328.00	3
		U.A.R.						1	0.2	0.02	3.00	10
		UNITED STATES	3	98.2	1178.67	588.30	2					
		YUGOSLAVIA/SERBIA	2	51.6	1178.00	53.00	3					

13.1 - NATIONAL WAR EXPERIENCE AS PARTNERS AND OPPONENTS

		AS PARTNERS					AS OPPONENTS				
				-BATTLE DEATHS- (000'S)					-BATTLE DEATHS- (000'S)		
		NO. OF WARS	WAR MONTHS	FIRST NAMED	SECOND NAMED	DECILE BATTLE DEATHS	NO. OF WARS	WAR MONTHS	FIRST NAMED	SECOND NAMED	DECILE BATTLE DEATHS
		1	2	3	4	5	6	7	8	9	10
ETHIOPIA	AND: AUSTRALIA	2	32.2	5.12	29.67	8					
	BELGIUM	1	26.9	0.12	0.10	10					
	CANADA	2	32.2	5.12	39.61	7					
	CHINA						1	26.9	0.12	900.00	5
	COLOMBIA	1	25.7	0.12	0.14	10					
	ENGLAND	2	32.2	5.12	270.67	5					
	FINLAND						1	0.3	5.00	42.00	9
	FRANCE	1	26.9	0.12	0.29	10					
	GERMANY/PRUSSIA						1	5.3	5.00	3500.00	2
	GREECE	2	29.9	5.12	10.17	8					
	HOLLAND	1	26.9	0.12	0.11	10					
	HUNGARY						1	0.2	5.00	40.00	9
	ITALY/SARDINIA						2	12.5	21.00	64.00	8
	KOREA NORTH						1	26.9	0.12	520.00	6
	KOREA SOUTH	1	26.9	0.12	415.00	4					
	NEW ZEALAND	1	5.3	5.00	17.30	8					
	PHILIPPINES	1	26.9	0.12	0.09	10					
	RUMANIA						1	0.4	5.00	290.00	7
	RUSSIA	1	0.4	5.00	7500.00	1					
	SOUTH AFRICA	1	5.3	5.00	8.70	9					
	THAILAND	1	26.9	0.12	0.11	10					
	TURKEY	1	26.9	0.12	0.72	10					
	UNITED STATES	1	26.9	0.12	54.00	6					
	YUGOSLAVIA/SERBIA	1	0.4	5.00	5.00	9					
FINLAND	AND: AUSTRALIA						1	38.9	42.00	29.40	8
	BRAZIL						1	2.5	42.00	1.00	9
	BULGARIA	1	33.0	42.00	9.00	6	1	0.4	42.00	1.00	9
	CANADA						1	38.9	42.00	39.30	8
	CHINA						1	33.4	42.00	1350.00	3
	ENGLAND						1	38.9	42.00	270.00	6
	ETHIOPIA						1	0.3	42.00	5.00	9
	GERMANY/PRUSSIA	1	38.9	42.00	3500.00	1					
	HUNGARY	1	38.8	42.00	40.00	6					
	ITALY/SARDINIA	1	26.3	42.00	60.00	6	1	11.1	42.00	17.50	8
	JAPAN	1	33.4	42.00	1000.00	3					
	NEW ZEALAND						1	38.9	42.00	17.30	8
	RUMANIA	1	38.0	42.00	290.00	4	1	0.4	42.00	10.00	8
	RUSSIA						2	42.3	82.00	7550.00	1
	SOUTH AFRICA						1	38.9	42.00	8.70	8
	UNITED STATES						1	33.4	42.00	408.30	6
FRANCE	AND: AUSTRALIA	2	50.2	210.29	29.67	5					
	AUSTRIA-HUNGARY	1	1.0	0.50	0.10	10	2	53.4	1357.50	1212.50	2
	BADEN						1	4.2	140.00	1.00	7
	BAVARIA						1	3.9	140.00	5.50	7

		AS PARTNERS					AS OPPONENTS				
		NO. OF WARS	WAR MONTHS	-BATTLE DEATHS- (000'S) FIRST NAMED	SECOND NAMED	DECILE BATTLE DEATHS	NO. OF WARS	WAR MONTHS	-BATTLE DEATHS- (000'S) FIRST NAMED	SECOND NAMED	DECILE BATTLE DEATHS
		1	2	3	4	5	6	7	8	9	10
	BELGIUM	3	82.1	1560.29	97.20	2					
	BRAZIL	1	6.5	210.00	1.00	5					
	BULGARIA	1	6.5	210.00	1.00	5	1	35.6	1350.00	14.00	3
	CANADA	2	50.0	210.29	39.61	5					
	CHINA	1	9.7	210.00	1350.00	2	2	42.6	2.39	910.00	4
	COLOMBIA	1	25.7	0.29	0.14	10					
	ENGLAND	6	124.8	1655.34	1200.77	1					
	ETHIOPIA	1	26.9	0.29	0.12	10					
	GERMANY/PRUSSIA						3	74.7	1700.00	5340.00	1
	GREECE	2	46.7	1350.29	5.17	3					
	HOLLAND	2	30.4	210.29	6.31	5					
	HUNGARY						1	3.0	210.00	40.00	7
	ISRAEL	1	0.2	0.01	0.20	10					
	ITALY/SARDINIA	4	64.2	1662.50	672.20	1	1	0.4	210.00	60.00	7
	JAPAN	1	50.7	1350.00	0.30	3	1	9.7	210.00	1000.00	3
	KOREA NORTH						1	30.8	0.29	520.00	5
	KOREA SOUTH	1	30.8	0.29	415.00	4					
	MEXICO						1	57.7	8.00	12.00	9
	MONGOLIA	1	0.2	210.00	3.00	5					
	NEW ZEALAND	1	19.4	210.00	17.30	5					
	NORWAY	1	2.0	210.00	2.00	5					
	PAPAL STATES						1	1.0	0.50	1.50	10
	PHILIPPINES	1	30.8	0.29	0.09	10					
	POLAND	1	0.8	210.00	320.00	3					
	PORTUGAL	1	32.4	1350.00	7.00	3					
	RUMANIA	2	21.9	1560.00	345.00	1					
	RUSSIA	3	46.9	1560.04	9200.06	1	1	23.1	95.00	100.00	7
	SOUTH AFRICA	1	19.3	210.00	8.70	5					
	SPAIN	1	13.5	4.00	25.00	8	1	7.3	0.40	0.60	10
	THAILAND	1	30.2	0.29	0.11	10					
	TURKEY	2	53.9	95.29	45.72	5	2	48.6	1350.04	328.00	2
	TWO SICILIES	1	1.0	0.50	0.10	10					
	U.A.R.						1	0.2	0.01	3.00	10
	UNITED STATES	3	59.4	1560.29	588.30	1					
	WUERTTEMBERG						1	4.3	140.00	1.00	7
	YUGOSLAVIA/SERBIA	1	51.3	1350.00	48.00	2					
GERMANY/PRUSSIA	AND: AUSTRALIA						1	68.1	3500.00	29.40	2
	AUSTRIA-HUNGARY	2	54.7	1801.00	1200.50	1	1	1.4	10.00	20.00	9
	BADEN	1	4.2	40.00	1.00	7	1	1.4	10.00	0.10	9
	BAVARIA	1	3.9	40.00	5.50	7	1	1.4	10.00	0.50	9
	BELGIUM						2	51.9	5300.00	97.10	1
	BRAZIL						1	10.1	3500.00	1.00	2
	BULGARIA	2	68.6	5300.00	23.00	1	1	7.9	3500.00	1.00	2
	CANADA						1	67.9	3500.00	39.30	1
	CHINA						1	41.0	3500.00	1350.00	1
	DENMARK						2	11.7	3.50	6.50	9

13.1 - NATIONAL WAR EXPERIENCE AS PARTNERS AND OPPONENTS

		AS PARTNERS					AS OPPONENTS				
		NO. OF WARS	WAR MONTHS	-BATTLE DEATHS- (000'S) FIRST NAMED	SECOND NAMED	DECILE BATTLE DEATHS	NO. OF WARS	WAR MONTHS	-BATTLE DEATHS- (000'S) FIRST NAMED	SECOND NAMED	DECILE BATTLE DEATHS
		1	2	3	4	5	6	7	8	9	10
	ENGLAND						2	119.3	5300.00	1178.00	1
	ETHIOPIA						1	5.3	3500.00	5.00	2
	FINLAND	1	38.9	3500.00	42.00	1					
	FRANCE						3	74.7	5340.00	1700.00	1
	GREECE						2	22.4	5300.00	15.00	1
	HANOVER						1	0.5	10.00	0.50	9
	HESSE ELECTORAL						1	1.4	10.00	0.10	9
	HESSE GRAND DUCAL						1	1.4	10.00	0.10	9
	HOLLAND						1	0.2	3500.00	6.20	2
	HUNGARY	1	42.8	3500.00	40.00	1					
	ITALY/SARDINIA	2	40.2	3510.00	64.00	1	2	60.4	5300.00	667.50	1
	JAPAN	1	41.0	3500.00	1000.00	1	1	50.7	1800.00	0.30	2
	MECKLENBURG-SCHWERIN						1	1.4	10.00	0.10	9
	NEW ZEALAND						1	68.1	3500.00	17.30	2
	NORWAY						1	2.0	3500.00	2.00	2
	POLAND						1	0.9	3500.00	320.00	1
	PORTUGAL						1	32.4	1800.00	7.00	2
	RUMANIA	1	38.1	3500.00	290.00	1	2	23.3	5300.00	345.00	1
	RUSSIA						2	86.7	5300.00	9200.00	1
	SAXONY						1	1.4	10.00	0.60	9
	SOUTH AFRICA						1	68.0	3500.00	8.70	2
	TURKEY	1	48.5	1800.00	325.00	1					
	UNITED STATES						2	59.9	5300.00	534.30	1
	WUERTTEMBERG	1	4.3	40.00	1.00	7	1	1.4	10.00	0.10	9
	YUGOSLAVIA/SERBIA						2	51.8	5300.00	53.00	1
GREECE	AND: AUSTRALIA	2	36.1	10.17	29.67	7					
	AUSTRIA-HUNGARY						1	16.2	5.00	1200.00	3
	BELGIUM	2	46.7	5.17	87.60	6					
	BULGARIA	1	4.1	5.00	32.00	7	2	16.0	7.50	32.00	9
	CANADA	2	36.1	10.17	39.61	6					
	CHINA						1	30.2	0.17	900.00	4
	COLOMBIA	1	25.7	0.17	0.14	10					
	ENGLAND	3	52.6	15.17	1178.67	3					
	ETHIOPIA	2	29.9	10.17	5.12	8					
	FRANCE	2	46.7	5.17	1350.29	3					
	GERMANY/PRUSSIA						2	22.4	15.00	5300.00	1
	HOLLAND	1	30.2	0.17	0.11	10					
	ITALY/SARDINIA	1	16.5	5.00	650.00	3	1	5.9	10.00	60.00	8
	JAPAN	1	16.5	5.00	0.30	9					
	KOREA NORTH						1	30.2	0.17	520.00	5
	KOREA SOUTH	1	30.2	0.17	415.00	4					
	NEW ZEALAND	1	5.9	10.00	17.30	8					
	PHILIPPINES	1	30.2	0.17	0.09	10					
	PORTUGAL	1	16.5	5.00	7.00	9					
	RUMANIA	2	6.1	7.50	336.50	4					
	RUSSIA	1	5.3	5.00	1700.00	2					

			AS PARTNERS					AS OPPONENTS				
					-BATTLE DEATHS- (000'S)					-BATTLE DEATHS- (000'S)		
			NO. OF WARS 1	WAR MONTHS 2	FIRST NAMED 3	SECOND NAMED 4	DECILE BATTLE DEATHS 5	NO. OF WARS 6	WAR MONTHS 7	FIRST NAMED 8	SECOND NAMED 9	DECILE BATTLE DEATHS 10
		SOUTH AFRICA	1	5.9	10.00	8.70	8					
		THAILAND	1	30.2	0.17	0.11	10					
		TURKEY	2	30.7	2.67	20.72	8	4	67.0	40.60	376.40	6
		UNITED STATES	2	46.7	5.17	180.00	5					
		YUGOSLAVIA/SERBIA	4	22.0	22.50	86.50	6					
GUATEMALA	AND:	HONDURAS						1	1.8	0.40	0.30	10
		SALVADOR						2	2.4	1.20	0.50	10
HANOVER	AND:	AUSTRIA-HUNGARY	1	0.5	0.50	20.00	8					
		BADEN	1	0.5	0.50	0.10	10					
		BAVARIA	1	0.5	0.50	0.50	9					
		GERMANY/PRUSSIA						1	0.5	0.50	10.00	9
		HESSE ELECTORAL	1	0.5	0.50	0.10	10					
		HESSE GRAND DUCAL	1	0.5	0.50	0.10	10					
		ITALY/SARDINIA						1	0.5	0.50	4.00	10
		MECKLENBURG-SCHWERIN	1	0.5	0.50	0.10	10					
		SAXONY	1	0.5	0.50	0.60	9					
		WUERTTEMBERG	1	0.5	0.50	0.10	10					
HESSE ELECTORAL	AND:	AUSTRIA-HUNGARY	1	1.4	0.10	20.00	8					
		BADEN	1	1.4	0.10	0.10	10					
		BAVARIA	1	1.4	0.10	0.50	10					
		GERMANY/PRUSSIA						1	1.4	0.10	10.00	9
		HANOVER	1	0.5	0.10	0.50	10					
		HESSE GRAND DUCAL	1	1.4	0.10	0.10	10					
		ITALY/SARDINIA						1	1.4	0.10	4.00	10
		MECKLENBURG-SCHWERIN	1	1.4	0.10	0.10	10					
		SAXONY	1	1.4	0.10	0.60	10					
		WUERTTEMBERG	1	1.4	0.10	0.10	10					
HESSE GRAND DUCAL	AND:	AUSTRIA-HUNGARY	1	1.4	0.10	20.00	8					
		BADEN	1	1.4	0.10	0.10	10					
		BAVARIA	1	1.4	0.10	0.50	10					
		GERMANY/PRUSSIA						1	1.4	0.10	10.00	9
		HANOVER	1	0.5	0.10	0.50	10					
		HESSE ELECTORAL	1	1.4	0.10	0.10	10					
		ITALY/SARDINIA						1	1.4	0.10	4.00	10
		MECKLENBURG-SCHWERIN	1	1.4	0.10	0.10	10					
		SAXONY	1	1.4	0.10	0.60	10					
		WUERTTEMBERG	1	1.4	0.10	0.10	10					
HOLLAND	AND:	AUSTRALIA	2	30.4	6.31	29.67	7					
		BELGIUM	2	30.4	6.31	9.70	8					
		CANADA	2	30.4	6.31	39.61	7					
		CHINA						1	30.2	0.11	900.00	5
		COLOMBIA	1	25.7	0.11	0.14	10					

13.1 - NATIONAL WAR EXPERIENCE AS PARTNERS AND OPPONENTS

			AS PARTNERS					AS OPPONENTS				
			NO. OF WARS	WAR MONTHS	-BATTLE DEATHS- (000'S) FIRST NAMED	SECOND NAMED	DECILE BATTLE DEATHS	NO. OF WARS	WAR MONTHS	-BATTLE DEATHS- (000'S) FIRST NAMED	SECOND NAMED	DECILE BATTLE DEATHS
			1	2	3	4	5	6	7	8	9	10
		ENGLAND	3	41.6	6.71	271.67	5					
		ETHIOPIA	1	26.9	0.11	0.12	10					
		FRANCE	2	30.4	6.31	210.29	5					
		GERMANY/PRUSSIA						1	0.2	6.20	3500.00	2
		GREECE	1	30.2	0.11	0.17	10					
		KOREA NORTH						1	30.2	0.11	520.00	6
		KOREA SOUTH	1	30.2	0.11	415.00	4					
		NEW ZEALAND	1	0.2	6.20	17.30	8					
		NORWAY	1	0.2	6.20	2.00	9					
		PHILIPPINES	1	30.2	0.11	0.09	10					
		SOUTH AFRICA	1	0.2	6.20	8.70	8					
		THAILAND	1	30.2	0.11	0.11	10					
		TURKEY	1	30.2	0.11	0.72	10					
		UNITED STATES	1	30.2	0.11	54.00	6					
HONDURAS	AND:	GUATEMALA						1	1.8	0.30	0.40	10
		NICARAGUA						1	2.1	0.30	0.40	10
		SALVADOR	2	3.9	0.60	0.60	9					
HUNGARY	AND:	AUSTRALIA						1	42.8	40.00	29.40	8
		BRAZIL						1	6.5	40.00	1.00	9
		BULGARIA	1	33.0	40.00	9.00	7	1	4.4	40.00	1.00	9
		CANADA						1	42.8	40.00	39.30	8
		CHINA						1	37.5	40.00	1350.00	3
		CZECHOSLOVAKIA						1	3.6	6.00	2.00	10
		ENGLAND						1	42.8	40.00	270.00	7
		ETHIOPIA						1	0.2	40.00	5.00	9
		FINLAND	1	38.8	40.00	42.00	6					
		FRANCE						1	3.0	40.00	210.00	7
		GERMANY/PRUSSIA	1	42.8	40.00	3500.00	1					
		ITALY/SARDINIA	1	26.2	40.00	60.00	6	1	15.1	40.00	17.50	8
		JAPAN	1	37.5	40.00	1000.00	3					
		NEW ZEALAND						1	42.8	40.00	17.30	8
		RUMANIA	1	37.9	40.00	290.00	5	2	8.0	46.00	13.00	8
		RUSSIA						2	43.6	65.00	7507.00	1
		SOUTH AFRICA						1	42.8	40.00	8.70	8
		UNITED STATES						1	37.5	40.00	408.30	6
INDIA	AND:	CHINA						1	1.1	0.50	0.50	10
		PAKISTAN						1	1.6	3.00	3.80	10
IRAN	AND:	ENGLAND						1	4.6	1.50	0.50	10
IRAQ	AND:	ISRAEL						1	2.5	0.50	3.00	10
		JORDAN	1	2.5	0.50	1.00	9					
		LEBANON	1	2.5	0.50	0.50	9					
		SYRIA	1	2.5	0.50	1.00	9					

			AS PARTNERS					AS OPPONENTS				
		NO. OF WARS	WAR MONTHS	-BATTLE DEATHS- (000'S) FIRST NAMED	SECOND NAMED	DECILE BATTLE DEATHS	NO. OF WARS	WAR MONTHS	-BATTLE DEATHS- (000'S) FIRST NAMED	SECOND NAMED	DECILE BATTLE DEATHS
		1	2	3	4	5	6	7	8	9	10
	U.A.R.	1	2.5	0.50	2.00	9					
ISRAEL	AND: ENGLAND	1	0.2	0.20	0.02	10					
	FRANCE	1	0.2	0.20	0.01	10					
	IRAQ						1	2.5	3.00	0.50	10
	JORDAN						1	2.5	3.00	1.00	10
	LEBANON						1	2.5	3.00	0.50	10
	SYRIA						1	2.5	3.00	1.00	10
	U.A.R.						2	5.0	3.20	5.00	10
ITALY/SARDINIA	AND: AUSTRALIA	1	18.7	17.50	29.40	7	1	38.8	60.00	29.40	7
	AUSTRIA-HUNGARY						4	50.0	659.90	1238.10	2
	BADEN						1	1.4	4.00	0.10	10
	BAVARIA						1	1.4	4.00	0.50	10
	BELGIUM	1	41.7	650.00	87.50	3					
	BRAZIL	1	10.1	17.50	1.00	8					
	BULGARIA	2	28.7	77.50	10.00	6	2	46.3	667.50	23.00	5
	CANADA	1	18.7	17.50	39.30	6	1	38.8	60.00	39.30	7
	CHINA	1	18.7	17.50	1350.00	2	1	20.9	60.00	1350.00	3
	ENGLAND	3	74.1	669.70	1200.00	2	1	38.8	60.00	270.00	6
	ETHIOPIA						2	12.5	64.00	21.00	8
	FINLAND	1	26.3	60.00	42.00	6	1	11.1	17.50	42.00	8
	FRANCE	4	64.2	672.20	1662.50	1	1	0.4	60.00	210.00	7
	GERMANY/PRUSSIA	2	40.2	64.00	3510.00	1	2	60.4	667.50	5300.00	1
	GREECE	1	16.5	650.00	5.00	3	1	5.9	60.00	10.00	8
	HANOVER						1	0.5	4.00	0.50	10
	HESSE ELECTORAL						1	1.4	4.00	0.10	10
	HESSE GRAND DUCAL						1	1.4	4.00	0.10	10
	HUNGARY	1	26.2	60.00	40.00	6	1	15.1	17.50	40.00	8
	JAPAN	2	62.6	710.00	1000.30	2	1	18.7	17.50	1000.00	4
	MECKLENBURG-SCHWERIN						1	1.4	4.00	0.10	10
	NEW ZEALAND	1	18.7	17.50	17.30	7	1	38.8	60.00	17.30	8
	PAPAL STATES						1	0.6	0.30	0.70	10
	PORTUGAL	1	32.4	650.00	7.00	3					
	RUMANIA	3	49.7	727.50	635.00	2	1	10.2	17.50	290.00	7
	RUSSIA	2	49.2	667.50	9200.00	1	2	40.1	62.20	7600.00	1
	SAXONY						1	1.4	4.00	0.60	10
	SOUTH AFRICA	1	18.7	17.50	8.70	8	1	38.8	60.00	8.70	8
	TURKEY	1	13.7	2.20	45.00	7	2	54.4	656.00	339.00	4
	TWO SICILIES						1	3.2	0.60	0.40	10
	UNITED STATES	2	37.6	667.50	534.30	3	1	20.9	60.00	408.30	6
	WUERTTEMBERG						1	1.4	4.00	0.10	10
	YUGOSLAVIA/SERBIA	1	41.7	650.00	48.00	3	1	0.4	60.00	5.00	8
JAPAN	AND: AUSTRALIA						1	44.3	1000.00	29.40	4
	AUSTRIA-HUNGARY						1	50.4	0.30	1200.00	3
	BELGIUM	1	50.7	0.30	87.50	6					

13.1 - NATIONAL WAR EXPERIENCE AS PARTNERS AND OPPONENTS

			AS PARTNERS					AS OPPONENTS				
					-BATTLE DEATHS- (000'S)					-BATTLE DEATHS- (000'S)		
			NO. OF WARS	WAR MONTHS	FIRST NAMED	SECOND NAMED	DECILE BATTLE DEATHS	NO. OF WARS	WAR MONTHS	FIRST NAMED	SECOND NAMED	DECILE BATTLE DEATHS
			1	2	3	4	5	6	7	8	9	10
		BRAZIL						1	10.1	1000.00	1.00	4
		BULGARIA	1	33.0	1000.00	9.00	3	2	43.5	1000.30	15.00	4
		CANADA						1	44.3	1000.00	39.30	4
		CHINA						4	122.0	1265.00	2160.00	2
		ENGLAND	1	50.7	0.30	908.00	3	1	44.3	1000.00	270.00	3
		FINLAND	1	33.4	1000.00	42.00	3					
		FRANCE	1	50.7	0.30	1350.00	3	1	9.7	1000.00	210.00	3
		GERMANY/PRUSSIA	1	41.0	1000.00	3500.00	1	1	50.7	0.30	1800.00	2
		GREECE	1	16.5	0.30	5.00	9					
		HUNGARY	1	37.5	1000.00	40.00	3					
		ITALY/SARDINIA	2	62.6	1000.30	710.00	2	1	18.7	1000.00	17.50	4
		MONGOLIA						2	4.4	1015.00	6.00	4
		NEW ZEALAND						1	44.3	1000.00	17.30	4
		PORTUGAL	1	32.4	0.30	7.00	9					
		RUMANIA	2	48.0	1000.30	625.00	2	1	7.9	1000.00	10.00	4
		RUSSIA	1	39.5	0.30	1700.00	2	3	64.7	1100.00	7546.00	1
		SOUTH AFRICA						1	44.3	1000.00	8.70	4
		TURKEY						1	48.5	0.30	325.00	6
		UNITED STATES	1	18.9	0.30	126.00	6	1	44.3	1000.00	408.30	3
		YUGOSLAVIA/SERBIA	1	50.7	0.30	48.00	7					
JORDAN	AND:	IRAQ	1	2.5	1.00	0.50	9					
		ISRAEL						1	2.5	1.00	3.00	10
		LEBANON	1	2.5	1.00	0.50	9					
		SYRIA	1	2.5	1.00	1.00	9					
		U.A.R.	1	2.5	1.00	2.00	9					
KOREA NORTH	AND:	AUSTRALIA						1	31.6	520.00	0.27	5
		BELGIUM						1	30.2	520.00	0.10	6
		CANADA						1	31.3	520.00	0.31	5
		CHINA	1	33.0	520.00	900.00	2					
		COLOMBIA						1	25.7	520.00	0.14	5
		ENGLAND						1	35.0	520.00	0.67	5
		ETHIOPIA						1	26.9	520.00	0.12	6
		FRANCE						1	30.8	520.00	0.29	5
		GREECE						1	30.2	520.00	0.17	5
		HOLLAND						1	30.2	520.00	0.11	6
		KOREA SOUTH						1	37.1	520.00	415.00	4
		PHILIPPINES						1	34.4	520.00	0.09	6
		THAILAND						1	30.2	520.00	0.11	6
		TURKEY						1	33.3	520.00	0.72	5
		UNITED STATES						1	37.0	520.00	54.00	5
KOREA SOUTH	AND:	AUSTRALIA	1	31.6	415.00	0.27	4					
		BELGIUM	1	30.2	415.00	0.10	4					
		CANADA	1	31.3	415.00	0.31	4					
		CHINA						1	33.0	415.00	900.00	3

			AS PARTNERS					AS OPPONENTS				
					-BATTLE DEATHS- (000'S)					-BATTLE DEATHS- (000'S)		
			NO. OF WARS 1	WAR MONTHS 2	FIRST NAMED 3	SECOND NAMED 4	DECILE BATTLE DEATHS 5	NO. OF WARS 6	WAR MONTHS 7	FIRST NAMED 8	SECOND NAMED 9	DECILE BATTLE DEATHS 10
		COLOMBIA	1	25.7	415.00	0.14	4					
		ENGLAND	1	35.0	415.00	0.67	4					
		ETHIOPIA	1	26.9	415.00	0.12	4					
		FRANCE	1	30.8	415.00	0.29	4					
		GREECE	1	30.2	415.00	0.17	4					
		HOLLAND	1	30.2	415.00	0.11	4					
		KOREA NORTH						1	37.1	415.00	520.00	4
		PHILIPPINES	1	34.4	415.00	0.09	4					
		THAILAND	1	30.2	415.00	0.11	4					
		TURKEY	1	33.3	415.00	0.72	4					
		UNITED STATES	1	37.0	415.00	54.00	3					
LEBANON	AND:	IRAQ	1	2.5	0.50	0.50	9					
		ISRAEL						1	2.5	0.50	3.00	10
		JORDAN	1	2.5	0.50	1.00	9					
		SYRIA	1	2.5	0.50	1.00	9					
		U.A.R.	1	2.5	0.50	2.00	9					
MECKLENBURG-SCHWERIN	AND:	AUSTRIA-HUNGARY	1	1.4	0.10	20.00	8					
		BADEN	1	1.4	0.10	0.10	10					
		BAVARIA	1	1.4	0.10	0.50	10					
		GERMANY/PRUSSIA						1	1.4	0.10	10.00	9
		HANOVER	1	0.5	0.10	0.50	10					
		HESSE ELECTORAL	1	1.4	0.10	0.10	10					
		HESSE GRAND DUCAL	1	1.4	0.10	0.10	10					
		ITALY/SARDINIA						1	1.4	0.10	4.00	10
		SAXONY	1	1.4	0.10	0.60	10					
		WUERTTEMBERG	1	1.4	0.10	0.10	10					
MEXICO	AND:	FRANCE						1	57.7	12.00	8.00	9
		UNITED STATES						1	21.1	6.00	11.00	9
MONGOLIA	AND:	AUSTRALIA	1	0.2	3.00	29.40	8					
		CANADA	1	0.2	3.00	39.30	7					
		CHINA	1	0.2	3.00	1350.00	3					
		ENGLAND	1	0.2	3.00	270.00	5					
		FRANCE	1	0.2	3.00	210.00	5					
		JAPAN						2	4.4	6.00	1015.00	4
		NEW ZEALAND	1	0.2	3.00	17.30	8					
		RUSSIA	2	4.4	6.00	7501.00	1					
		SOUTH AFRICA	1	0.2	3.00	8.70	9					
		UNITED STATES	1	0.2	3.00	408.30	4					
MOROCCO	AND:	SPAIN						2	13.7	14.00	6.00	9
NEW ZEALAND	AND:	AUSTRALIA	1	71.4	17.30	29.40	7					
		BELGIUM	1	0.6	17.30	9.60	8					

13.1 - NATIONAL WAR EXPERIENCE AS PARTNERS AND OPPONENTS

		AS PARTNERS					AS OPPONENTS				
		NO. OF WARS 1	WAR MONTHS 2	-BATTLE DEATHS- (000'S) FIRST NAMED 3	SECOND NAMED 4	DECILE BATTLE DEATHS 5	NO. OF WARS 6	WAR MONTHS 7	-BATTLE DEATHS- (000'S) FIRST NAMED 8	SECOND NAMED 9	DECILE BATTLE DEATHS 10
	BRAZIL	1	10.1	17.30	1.00	8					
	BULGARIA	1	7.9	17.30	1.00	8	1	33.0	17.30	9.00	9
	CANADA	1	71.2	17.30	39.30	6					
	CHINA	1	44.3	17.30	1350.00	2					
	ENGLAND	1	71.4	17.30	270.00	5					
	ETHIOPIA	1	5.3	17.30	5.00	8					
	FINLAND						1	38.9	17.30	42.00	8
	FRANCE	1	19.4	17.30	210.00	5					
	GERMANY/PRUSSIA						1	68.1	17.30	3500.00	2
	GREECE	1	5.9	17.30	10.00	8					
	HOLLAND	1	0.2	17.30	6.20	8					
	HUNGARY						1	42.8	17.30	40.00	8
	ITALY/SARDINIA	1	18.7	17.30	17.50	7	1	38.8	17.30	60.00	8
	JAPAN						1	44.3	17.30	1000.00	4
	MONGOLIA	1	0.2	17.30	3.00	8					
	NORWAY	1	2.0	17.30	2.00	8					
	POLAND	1	0.8	17.30	320.00	4					
	RUMANIA	1	7.9	17.30	10.00	8	1	38.1	17.30	290.00	7
	RUSSIA	1	46.7	17.30	7500.00	1					
	SOUTH AFRICA	1	71.3	17.30	8.70	8					
	UNITED STATES	1	44.3	17.30	408.30	4					
	YUGOSLAVIA/SERBIA	1	0.4	17.30	5.00	8					
NICARAGUA	AND: HONDURAS						1	2.1	0.40	0.30	10
	SALVADOR						1	2.1	0.40	0.30	10
NORWAY	AND: AUSTRALIA	1	2.0	2.00	29.40	8					
	BELGIUM	1	0.6	2.00	9.60	9					
	CANADA	1	2.0	2.00	39.30	7					
	ENGLAND	1	2.0	2.00	270.00	5					
	FRANCE	1	2.0	2.00	210.00	5					
	GERMANY/PRUSSIA						1	2.0	2.00	3500.00	2
	HOLLAND	1	0.2	2.00	6.20	9					
	NEW ZEALAND	1	2.0	2.00	17.30	8					
	SOUTH AFRICA	1	2.0	2.00	8.70	9					
PAKISTAN	AND: INDIA						1	1.6	3.80	3.00	10
PAPAL STATES	AND: AUSTRIA-HUNGARY						1	1.8	1.50	0.10	10
	FRANCE						1	1.0	1.50	0.50	10
	ITALY/SARDINIA						1	0.6	0.70	0.30	10
	TWO SICILIES						1	1.8	1.50	0.10	10
PARAGUAY	AND: BOLIVIA						1	35.9	50.00	80.00	7
PERU	AND: BOLIVIA	1	54.5	10.00	1.00	9					
	CHILE	1	3.8	0.60	0.10	10	1	54.5	10.00	3.00	9

		AS PARTNERS					AS OPPONENTS				
		NO. OF WARS	WAR MONTHS	-BATTLE DEATHS- (000'S) FIRST NAMED	SECOND NAMED	DECILE BATTLE DEATHS	NO. OF WARS	WAR MONTHS	-BATTLE DEATHS- (000'S) FIRST NAMED	SECOND NAMED	DECILE BATTLE DEATHS
		1	2	3	4	5	6	7	8	9	10
	SPAIN						1	3.8	0.60	0.30	10
PHILIPPINES	AND: AUSTRALIA	1	31.6	0.09	0.27	10					
	BELGIUM	1	30.2	0.09	0.10	10					
	CANADA	1	31.3	0.09	0.31	10					
	CHINA						1	33.0	0.09	900.00	5
	COLOMBIA	1	25.7	0.09	0.14	10					
	ENGLAND	1	34.4	0.09	0.67	10					
	ETHIOPIA	1	26.9	0.09	0.12	10					
	FRANCE	1	30.8	0.09	0.29	10					
	GREECE	1	30.2	0.09	0.17	10					
	HOLLAND	1	30.2	0.09	0.11	10					
	KOREA NORTH						1	34.4	0.09	520.00	6
	KOREA SOUTH	1	34.4	0.09	415.00	4					
	THAILAND	1	30.2	0.09	0.11	10					
	TURKEY	1	33.3	0.09	0.72	10					
	UNITED STATES	1	34.4	0.09	54.00	6					
POLAND	AND: AUSTRALIA	1	0.8	320.00	29.40	4					
	CANADA	1	0.6	320.00	39.30	4					
	ENGLAND	1	0.8	320.00	270.00	3					
	FRANCE	1	0.8	320.00	210.00	3					
	GERMANY/PRUSSIA						1	0.9	320.00	3500.00	1
	NEW ZEALAND	1	0.8	320.00	17.30	4					
	SOUTH AFRICA	1	0.7	320.00	8.70	5					
PORTUGAL	AND: AUSTRIA-HUNGARY						1	32.1	7.00	1200.00	3
	BELGIUM	1	32.4	7.00	87.50	6					
	BULGARIA						1	31.0	7.00	14.00	9
	ENGLAND	1	32.4	7.00	908.00	3					
	FRANCE	1	32.4	7.00	1350.00	3					
	GERMANY/PRUSSIA						1	32.4	7.00	1800.00	2
	GREECE	1	16.5	7.00	5.00	9					
	ITALY/SARDINIA	1	32.4	7.00	650.00	3					
	JAPAN	1	32.4	7.00	0.30	9					
	RUMANIA	1	15.4	7.00	335.00	4					
	RUSSIA	1	21.2	7.00	1700.00	2					
	TURKEY						1	32.4	7.00	325.00	6
	UNITED STATES	1	18.9	7.00	126.00	6					
	YUGOSLAVIA/SERBIA	1	32.4	7.00	48.00	6					
RUMANIA	AND: AUSTRALIA	1	7.9	10.00	29.40	7	1	38.1	290.00	29.40	6
	AUSTRIA-HUNGARY						1	15.4	335.00	1200.00	2
	BELGIUM	1	15.4	335.00	87.50	4					
	BRAZIL	1	7.9	10.00	1.00	9	1	1.6	290.00	1.00	7
	BULGARIA	2	40.4	300.00	10.00	5	2	16.1	336.50	32.00	6
	CANADA	1	7.9	10.00	39.30	7	1	38.1	290.00	39.30	6

13.1 - NATIONAL WAR EXPERIENCE AS PARTNERS AND OPPONENTS

			AS PARTNERS					AS OPPONENTS				
			NO. OF WARS	WAR MONTHS	-BATTLE DEATHS- (000'S) FIRST NAMED	SECOND NAMED	DECILE BATTLE DEATHS	NO. OF WARS	WAR MONTHS	-BATTLE DEATHS- (000'S) FIRST NAMED	SECOND NAMED	DECILE BATTLE DEATHS
			1	2	3	4	5	6	7	8	9	10
		CHINA	1	7.9	10.00	1350.00	2	1	32.6	290.00	1350.00	2
		CZECHOSLOVAKIA	1	3.6	3.00	2.00	9					
		ENGLAND	2	23.3	345.00	1178.00	2	1	38.1	290.00	270.00	5
		ETHIOPIA						1	0.4	290.00	5.00	7
		FINLAND	1	38.0	290.00	42.00	4	1	0.4	10.00	42.00	8
		FRANCE	2	21.9	345.00	1560.00	1					
		GERMANY/PRUSSIA	1	38.1	290.00	3500.00	1	2	23.3	345.00	5300.00	1
		GREECE	2	6.1	336.50	7.50	4					
		HUNGARY	1	37.9	290.00	40.00	5	2	8.0	13.00	46.00	8
		ITALY/SARDINIA	3	49.7	635.00	727.50	2	1	10.2	290.00	17.50	7
		JAPAN	2	48.0	625.00	1000.30	2	1	7.9	10.00	1000.00	4
		NEW ZEALAND	1	7.9	10.00	17.30	8	1	38.1	290.00	17.30	7
		PORTUGAL	1	15.4	335.00	7.00	4					
		RUSSIA	2	23.2	345.00	9200.00	1	1	38.1	290.00	7500.00	1
		SOUTH AFRICA	1	7.9	10.00	8.70	8	1	38.1	290.00	8.70	7
		TURKEY	1	0.5	1.50	20.00	8	1	15.4	335.00	325.00	5
		UNITED STATES	2	15.7	345.00	534.30	3	1	32.6	290.00	408.30	5
		YUGOSLAVIA/SERBIA	2	16.1	336.50	66.50	4					
RUSSIA	AND:	AUSTRALIA	1	46.7	7500.00	29.40	1					
		AUSTRIA-HUNGARY	1	1.0	14.50	45.00	6	1	40.2	1700.00	1200.00	2
		BELGIUM	1	40.1	1700.00	87.50	2					
		BRAZIL	1	10.1	7500.00	1.00	1					
		BULGARIA	1	7.9	7500.00	1.00	1	2	58.8	9200.00	23.00	1
		CANADA	1	46.7	7500.00	39.30	1					
		CHINA	1	41.2	7500.00	1350.00	1					
		ENGLAND	3	86.8	9200.06	1178.08	1	1	23.1	100.00	22.00	7
		ETHIOPIA	1	0.4	7500.00	5.00	1					
		FINLAND						2	42.3	7550.00	82.00	1
		FRANCE	3	46.9	9200.06	1560.04	1	1	23.1	100.00	95.00	7
		GERMANY/PRUSSIA						2	86.7	9200.00	5300.00	1
		GREECE	1	5.3	1700.00	5.00	2					
		HUNGARY						2	43.6	7507.00	65.00	1
		ITALY/SARDINIA	2	49.2	9200.00	667.50	1	2	40.1	7600.00	62.20	1
		JAPAN	1	39.5	1700.00	0.30	2	3	64.7	7546.00	1100.00	1
		MONGOLIA	2	4.4	7501.00	6.00	1					
		NEW ZEALAND	1	46.7	7500.00	17.30	1					
		PORTUGAL	1	21.2	1700.00	7.00	2					
		RUMANIA	2	23.2	9200.00	345.00	1	1	38.1	7500.00	290.00	1
		SOUTH AFRICA	1	46.7	7500.00	8.70	1					
		TURKEY						5	91.2	1970.06	618.00	2
		UNITED STATES	2	48.9	9200.00	534.30	1					
		YUGOSLAVIA/SERBIA	1	40.2	1700.00	48.00	2					
SALVADOR	AND:	GUATEMALA						2	2.4	0.50	1.20	10
		HONDURAS	2	3.9	0.60	0.60	9					
		NICARAGUA						1	2.1	0.30	0.40	10

		AS PARTNERS					AS OPPONENTS				
		NO. OF WARS	WAR MONTHS	-BATTLE DEATHS- (000'S) FIRST NAMED	SECOND NAMED	DECILE BATTLE DEATHS	NO. OF WARS	WAR MONTHS	-BATTLE DEATHS- (000'S) FIRST NAMED	SECOND NAMED	DECILE BATTLE DEATHS
		1	2	3	4	5	6	7	8	9	10
SAXONY	AND: AUSTRIA-HUNGARY	1	1.4	0.60	20.00	8					
	BADEN	1	1.4	0.60	0.10	10					
	BAVARIA	1	1.4	0.60	0.50	9					
	GERMANY/PRUSSIA						1	1.4	0.60	10.00	9
	HANOVER	1	0.5	0.60	0.50	9					
	HESSE ELECTORAL	1	1.4	0.60	0.10	10					
	HESSE GRAND DUCAL	1	1.4	0.60	0.10	10					
	ITALY/SARDINIA						1	1.4	0.60	4.00	10
	MECKLENBURG-SCHWERIN	1	1.4	0.60	0.10	10					
	WUERTTEMBERG	1	1.4	0.60	0.10	10					
SOUTH AFRICA	AND: AUSTRALIA	1	71.3	8.70	29.40	7					
	BELGIUM	1	0.6	8.70	9.60	8					
	BRAZIL	1	10.1	8.70	1.00	9					
	BULGARIA	1	7.9	8.70	1.00	9	1	33.0	8.70	9.00	9
	CANADA	1	71.2	8.70	39.30	7					
	CHINA	1	44.3	8.70	1350.00	2					
	ENGLAND	1	71.3	8.70	270.00	5					
	ETHIOPIA	1	5.3	8.70	5.00	9					
	FINLAND						1	38.9	8.70	42.00	8
	FRANCE	1	19.3	8.70	210.00	5					
	GERMANY/PRUSSIA						1	68.0	8.70	3500.00	2
	GREECE	1	5.9	8.70	10.00	8					
	HOLLAND	1	0.2	8.70	6.20	8					
	HUNGARY						1	42.8	8.70	40.00	8
	ITALY/SARDINIA	1	18.7	8.70	17.50	8	1	38.8	8.70	60.00	8
	JAPAN						1	44.3	8.70	1000.00	4
	MONGOLIA	1	0.2	8.70	3.00	9					
	NEW ZEALAND	1	71.3	8.70	17.30	8					
	NORWAY	1	2.0	8.70	2.00	9					
	POLAND	1	0.7	8.70	320.00	5					
	RUMANIA	1	7.9	8.70	10.00	8	1	38.1	8.70	290.00	7
	RUSSIA	1	46.7	8.70	7500.00	1					
	UNITED STATES	1	44.3	8.70	408.30	4					
	YUGOSLAVIA/SERBIA	1	0.4	8.70	5.00	9					
SPAIN	AND: CHILE						1	6.5	0.30	0.10	10
	FRANCE	1	13.5	25.00	4.00	8	1	7.3	0.60	0.40	10
	MOROCCO						2	13.7	6.00	14.00	9
	PERU						1	3.8	0.30	0.60	10
	UNITED STATES						1	3.7	5.00	5.00	9
SYRIA	AND: IRAQ	1	2.5	1.00	0.50	9					
	ISRAEL						1	2.5	1.00	3.00	10
	JORDAN	1	2.5	1.00	1.00	9					
	LEBANON	1	2.5	1.00	0.50	9					

13.1 - NATIONAL WAR EXPERIENCE AS PARTNERS AND OPPONENTS

		AS PARTNERS					AS OPPONENTS				
		NO. OF WARS	WAR MONTHS	-BATTLE DEATHS- (000'S) FIRST NAMED	SECOND NAMED	DECILE BATTLE DEATHS	NO. OF WARS	WAR MONTHS	-BATTLE DEATHS- (000'S) FIRST NAMED	SECOND NAMED	DECILE BATTLE DEATHS
		1	2	3	4	5	6	7	8	9	10
	U.A.R.	1	2.5	1.00	2.00	9					
THAILAND	AND: AUSTRALIA	1	30.2	0.11	0.27	10					
	BELGIUM	1	30.2	0.11	0.10	10					
	CANADA	1	30.2	0.11	0.31	10					
	CHINA						1	30.2	0.11	900.00	5
	COLOMBIA	1	25.7	0.11	0.14	10					
	ENGLAND	1	30.2	0.11	0.67	10					
	ETHIOPIA	1	26.9	0.11	0.12	10					
	FRANCE	1	30.2	0.11	0.29	10					
	GREECE	1	30.2	0.11	0.17	10					
	HOLLAND	1	30.2	0.11	0.11	10					
	KOREA NORTH						1	30.2	0.11	520.00	6
	KOREA SOUTH	1	30.2	0.11	415.00	4					
	PHILIPPINES	1	30.2	0.11	0.09	10					
	TURKEY	1	30.2	0.11	0.72	10					
	UNITED STATES	1	30.2	0.11	54.00	6					
TURKEY	AND: AUSTRALIA	1	31.6	0.72	0.27	9					
	AUSTRIA-HUNGARY	1	48.2	325.00	1200.00	2					
	BELGIUM	1	30.2	0.72	0.10	10	1	48.5	325.00	87.50	6
	BULGARIA	1	35.6	325.00	14.00	4	2	4.6	50.00	50.00	7
	CANADA	1	31.3	0.72	0.31	9					
	CHINA						1	33.0	0.72	900.00	4
	COLOMBIA	1	25.7	0.72	0.14	9					
	ENGLAND	3	59.0	55.72	22.68	6	2	48.6	328.00	908.08	3
	ETHIOPIA	1	26.9	0.72	0.12	10					
	FRANCE	2	53.9	45.72	95.29	5	2	48.6	328.00	1350.04	2
	GERMANY/PRUSSIA	1	48.5	325.00	1800.00	1					
	GREECE	2	30.7	20.72	2.67	8	4	67.0	376.40	40.60	6
	HOLLAND	1	30.2	0.72	0.11	10					
	ITALY/SARDINIA	1	13.7	45.00	2.20	7	2	54.4	339.00	656.00	4
	JAPAN						1	48.5	325.00	0.30	6
	KOREA NORTH						1	33.3	0.72	520.00	5
	KOREA SOUTH	1	33.3	0.72	415.00	4					
	PHILIPPINES	1	33.3	0.72	0.09	10					
	PORTUGAL						1	32.4	325.00	7.00	6
	RUMANIA	1	0.5	20.00	1.50	8	1	15.4	325.00	335.00	5
	RUSSIA						5	91.2	618.00	1970.06	2
	THAILAND	1	30.2	0.72	0.11	10					
	UNITED STATES	1	33.3	0.72	54.00	6	1	18.9	325.00	126.00	6
	YUGOSLAVIA/SERBIA	1	0.5	20.00	18.50	7	2	52.6	355.00	63.00	6
TWO SICILIES	AND: AUSTRIA-HUNGARY	1	1.8	0.10	0.10	10					
	FRANCE	1	1.0	0.10	0.50	10					
	ITALY/SARDINIA						1	3.2	0.40	0.60	10
	PAPAL STATES						1	1.8	0.10	1.50	10

		AS PARTNERS					AS OPPONENTS				
		NO. OF WARS	WAR MONTHS	-BATTLE DEATHS- (000'S) FIRST NAMED	SECOND NAMED	DECILE BATTLE DEATHS	NO. OF WARS	WAR MONTHS	-BATTLE DEATHS- (000'S) FIRST NAMED	SECOND NAMED	DECILE BATTLE DEATHS
		1	2	3	4	5	6	7	8	9	10
U.A.R.	AND: ENGLAND						1	0.2	3.00	0.02	10
	FRANCE						1	0.2	3.00	0.01	10
	IRAQ	1	2.5	2.00	0.50	9					
	ISRAEL						2	5.0	5.00	3.20	10
	JORDAN	1	2.5	2.00	1.00	9					
	LEBANON	1	2.5	2.00	0.50	9					
	SYRIA	1	2.5	2.00	1.00	9					
UNITED STATES	AND: AUSTRALIA	2	75.9	462.30	29.67	3					
	AUSTRIA-HUNGARY						1	18.6	126.00	1200.00	3
	BELGIUM	2	49.1	180.00	87.60	5					
	BRAZIL	1	10.1	408.30	1.00	4					
	BULGARIA	1	7.9	408.30	1.00	4	2	50.4	534.30	23.00	5
	CANADA	2	75.6	462.30	39.61	3					
	CHINA	1	44.3	408.30	1350.00	2	1	33.0	54.00	900.00	4
	COLOMBIA	1	25.7	54.00	0.14	6					
	ENGLAND	3	98.2	588.30	1178.67	2					
	ETHIOPIA	1	26.9	54.00	0.12	6					
	FINLAND						1	33.4	408.30	42.00	6
	FRANCE	3	59.4	588.30	1560.29	1					
	GERMANY/PRUSSIA						2	59.9	534.30	5300.00	1
	GREECE	2	46.7	180.00	5.17	5					
	HOLLAND	1	30.2	54.00	0.11	6					
	HUNGARY						1	37.5	408.30	40.00	6
	ITALY/SARDINIA	2	37.6	534.30	667.50	3	1	20.9	408.30	60.00	6
	JAPAN	1	18.9	126.00	0.30	6	1	44.3	408.30	1000.00	3
	KOREA NORTH						1	37.0	54.00	520.00	5
	KOREA SOUTH	1	37.0	54.00	415.00	3					
	MEXICO						1	21.1	11.00	6.00	9
	MONGOLIA	1	0.2	408.30	3.00	4					
	NEW ZEALAND	1	44.3	408.30	17.30	4					
	PHILIPPINES	1	34.4	54.00	0.09	6					
	PORTUGAL	1	18.9	126.00	7.00	6					
	RUMANIA	2	15.7	534.30	345.00	3	1	32.6	408.30	290.00	5
	RUSSIA	2	48.9	534.30	9200.00	1					
	SOUTH AFRICA	1	44.3	408.30	8.70	4					
	SPAIN						1	3.7	5.00	5.00	9
	THAILAND	1	30.2	54.00	0.11	6					
	TURKEY	1	33.3	54.00	0.72	6	1	18.9	126.00	325.00	6
	YUGOSLAVIA/SERBIA	1	18.9	126.00	48.00	5					
WUERTTEMBERG	AND: AUSTRIA-HUNGARY	1	1.4	0.10	20.00	8					
	BADEN	2	5.6	1.10	1.10	9					
	BAVARIA	2	5.3	1.10	6.00	9					
	FRANCE						1	4.3	1.00	140.00	7
	GERMANY/PRUSSIA	1	4.3	1.00	40.00	7	1	1.4	0.10	10.00	9

13.1 - NATIONAL WAR EXPERIENCE AS PARTNERS AND OPPONENTS

		AS PARTNERS					AS OPPONENTS				
		NO. OF WARS	WAR MONTHS	-BATTLE DEATHS- (000'S) FIRST NAMED	SECOND NAMED	DECILE BATTLE DEATHS	NO. OF WARS	WAR MONTHS	-BATTLE DEATHS- (000'S) FIRST NAMED	SECOND NAMED	DECILE BATTLE DEATHS
		1	2	3	4	5	6	7	8	9	10
	HANOVER	1	0.5	0.10	0.50	10					
	HESSE ELECTORAL	1	1.4	0.10	0.10	10					
	HESSE GRAND DUCAL	1	1.4	0.10	0.10	10					
	ITALY/SARDINIA						1	1.4	0.10	4.00	10
	MECKLENBURG-SCHWERIN	1	1.4	0.10	0.10	10					
	SAXONY	1	1.4	0.10	0.60	10					
YUGOSLAVIA/SERBIA AND:	AUSTRALIA	1	0.4	5.00	29.40	8					
	AUSTRIA-HUNGARY						1	51.2	48.00	1200.00	3
	BELGIUM	1	51.3	48.00	87.50	5					
	BULGARIA	1	4.1	15.00	32.00	7	2	36.6	66.50	32.00	7
	CANADA	1	0.4	5.00	39.30	7					
	ENGLAND	2	51.6	53.00	1178.00	3					
	ETHIOPIA	1	0.4	5.00	5.00	9					
	FRANCE	1	51.3	48.00	1350.00	2					
	GERMANY/PRUSSIA						2	51.8	53.00	5300.00	1
	GREECE	4	22.0	86.50	22.50	6					
	ITALY/SARDINIA	1	41.7	48.00	650.00	3	1	0.4	5.00	60.00	8
	JAPAN	1	50.7	48.00	0.30	7					
	NEW ZEALAND	1	0.4	5.00	17.30	8					
	PORTUGAL	1	32.4	48.00	7.00	6					
	RUMANIA	2	16.1	66.50	336.50	4					
	RUSSIA	1	40.2	48.00	1700.00	2					
	SOUTH AFRICA	1	0.4	5.00	8.70	9					
	TURKEY	1	0.5	18.50	20.00	7	2	52.6	63.00	355.00	6
	UNITED STATES	1	18.9	48.00	126.00	5					

pair stands vis-à-vis all other pairs. It does not help, for example, to assert that "France and Russia have been traditional friends" unless we can say how much more, or less, war they have experienced as partners than a number of other pairs; the same holds true for the allegedly enduring enmities of traditional opposition. Thus, in Table 13.2 we show the rank ordering of all possible pairs based on the number of battle-connected deaths that they sustained during the wars in which they fought together, as well as the number of war months during which they were on the same side.

Several caveats are necessary in regard to our rankings. First, we decided against using the exact rank order numbers for the pair-wise combined battle deaths measure. As we have emphasized before, our battle death figures are only estimates and therefore an exact rank order number would be too refined; in other words, to say that the Italian-Japanese partnership with 1,710,300 combined battle deaths ranks higher than that of Portugal-Russia with 1,707,000 combined battle deaths is to take the estimates too literally. Moreover, we have no measure of the battle deaths sustained on a monthly basis, so that even if two nations were not partners or opponents for the whole duration of a war, we must nevertheless give their battle deaths for the entire conflict. Therefore, we have used decile groupings, and the above pairs are represented only as being in the second decile.

Second, we had three options in interpreting the meaning of decile, in dividing the range of pairwise war experience into distinct groups. We could have taken the range of *scores* and divided it into ten sectors of magnitude. But this method was rejected because the combined battle death scores were as low as 190 and as high as 14.5 million. Each sector would have been more than one million battle deaths in range, and nearly all pairs would have fallen into the lowest sector. Or we could have defined decile in its literal fashion, and assigned one tenth of the pairs to each such group. But there were many ties and the decile divisions often fell within a group of ties. A third method, and the one finally used, takes into account the number of *different* scores. For example, in dividing the combined battle death scores for partners into groups, we counted first the number of pairs who were ever partners ($N=317$) and then the number of pairs that had different battle death totals ($N=246$), leaving 71 pairs which were tied with one or another of the 246. Each decile therefore embraces 24 or 25 different *scores,* but varies in size (number of pairs) depending on the number of pairs with tied scores. In the same manner, the 117 different scores for shared war months were divided into approximate deciles, with 11 or 12 different scores in each. On this measure, 200 of the 317 pairs had ties.

Table 13.2 lists all pairs of nations (but only once, since a pair can only have one rank position) according to the total number of battle-connected deaths sustained by them, in combination, while participating in wars on the same side during some period of partial or complete overlap. Pairs are arranged alphabetically; that is, the first-named nation is higher in the alphabet. Each pair's identity is followed by the number of their "shared" fatalities in thousands. Next are the total number of months they experienced as wartime partners, followed by the decile grouping into which that number of months would put them. We do not rank nations according to number of wars because there would be a great many tied scores.

These data require little in the way of verbal summary. Naturally, the major power participants in the World Wars and their partners dominate the top groupings; even a one-time partnership such as Canada-Russia shows up in the top group because of Russia's extremely severe losses in World War Two. It is noteworthy that there seems to be little relationship between the combined battle death rank decile and that based

13.2 - NATION PAIRS RANKED BY COMBINED DEATHS AS WARTIME <u>PARTNERS</u>

		BATTLE DEATHS (000'S)	SHARED WAR MONTHS	WAR MONTH DECILE			BATTLE DEATHS (000'S)	SHARED WAR MONTHS	WAR MONTH DECILE
				*** DECILE 1 ***					
FRANCE	-RUSSIA	10760.10	46.9	4	BULGARIA	-RUSSIA	7501.00	7.9	8
ENGLAND	-RUSSIA	10378.14	86.8	1	BULGARIA	-GERMANY/PRUSSIA	5323.00	68.6	2
ITALY/SARDINIA	-RUSSIA	9867.50	49.2	3	GERMANY/PRUSSIA	-JAPAN	4500.00	41.0	4
RUSSIA	-UNITED STATES	9734.30	48.9	3	GERMANY/PRUSSIA	-RUMANIA	3790.00	38.1	5
RUMANIA	-RUSSIA	9545.00	23.2	7	GERMANY/PRUSSIA	-ITALY/SARDINIA	3574.00	40.2	4
CHINA	-RUSSIA	8850.00	41.2	4	FINLAND	-GERMANY/PRUSSIA	3542.00	38.9	5
CANADA	-RUSSIA	7539.30	46.7	4	GERMANY/PRUSSIA	-HUNGARY	3540.00	42.8	4
AUSTRALIA	-RUSSIA	7529.40	46.7	4	AUSTRIA-HUNGARY	-GERMANY/PRUSSIA	3001.50	54.7	2
NEW ZEALAND	-RUSSIA	7517.30	46.7	4	ENGLAND	-FRANCE	2856.11	124.8	1
RUSSIA	-SOUTH AFRICA	7508.70	46.7	4	FRANCE	-ITALY/SARDINIA	2334.70	64.2	2
MONGOLIA	-RUSSIA	7507.00	4.4	9	FRANCE	-UNITED STATES	2148.59	59.4	2
ETHIOPIA	-RUSSIA	7505.00	0.4	10	GERMANY/PRUSSIA	-TURKEY	2125.00	48.5	3
BRAZIL	-RUSSIA	7501.00	10.1	8	FRANCE	-RUMANIA	1905.00	21.9	7
				*** DECILE 2 ***					
ENGLAND	-ITALY/SARDINIA	1869.70	74.1	1	CHINA	-FRANCE	1560.00	9.7	8
BELGIUM	-RUSSIA	1787.50	40.1	4	AUSTRIA-HUNGARY	-TURKEY	1525.00	48.2	3
ENGLAND	-UNITED STATES	1766.97	98.2	1	ENGLAND	-RUMANIA	1523.00	23.3	7
CHINA	-UNITED STATES	1758.30	44.3	4	CHINA	-KOREA NORTH	1420.00	33.0	6
RUSSIA	-YUGOSLAVIA/SERBIA	1748.00	40.2	4	FRANCE	-YUGOSLAVIA/SERBIA	1398.00	51.3	3
ITALY/SARDINIA	-JAPAN	1710.30	62.6	2	CANADA	-CHINA	1389.30	44.3	4
PORTUGAL	-RUSSIA	1707.00	21.2	7	AUSTRALIA	-CHINA	1379.40	44.3	4
GREECE	-RUSSIA	1705.00	5.3	9	CHINA	-ITALY/SARDINIA	1367.50	18.7	8
JAPAN	-RUSSIA	1700.30	39.5	4	CHINA	-NEW ZEALAND	1367.30	44.3	4
BELGIUM	-FRANCE	1657.49	82.1	1	ITALY/SARDINIA	-RUMANIA	1362.50	49.7	3
JAPAN	-RUMANIA	1625.30	48.0	3	CHINA	-RUMANIA	1360.00	7.9	8
CHINA	-ENGLAND	1620.00	44.3	4	CHINA	-SOUTH AFRICA	1358.70	44.3	4
				*** DECILE 3 ***					
FRANCE	-PORTUGAL	1357.00	32.4	6	BULGARIA	-JAPAN	1009.00	33.0	6
FRANCE	-GREECE	1355.46	46.7	4	ENGLAND	-PORTUGAL	915.00	32.4	6
CHINA	-MONGOLIA	1353.00	0.2	10	ENGLAND	-JAPAN	908.30	50.7	3
BRAZIL	-CHINA	1351.00	10.1	8	RUMANIA	-UNITED STATES	879.30	15.7	8
BULGARIA	-CHINA	1351.00	7.9	8	BELGIUM	-ITALY/SARDINIA	737.50	41.7	4
FRANCE	-JAPAN	1350.30	50.7	3	ITALY/SARDINIA	-YUGOSLAVIA/SERBIA	698.00	41.7	4
BELGIUM	-ENGLAND	1275.87	82.0	1	ITALY/SARDINIA	-PORTUGAL	657.00	32.4	6
ENGLAND	-YUGOSLAVIA/SERBIA	1231.00	51.6	3	GREECE	-ITALY/SARDINIA	655.00	16.5	8
AUSTRIA-HUNGARY	-BULGARIA	1214.00	35.6	5	ENGLAND	-POLAND	590.00	0.8	10
ITALY/SARDINIA	-UNITED STATES	1201.80	37.6	5	FRANCE	-POLAND	530.00	0.8	10
ENGLAND	-GREECE	1193.84	52.6	2	CANADA	-UNITED STATES	501.91	75.6	1
FINLAND	-JAPAN	1042.00	33.4	6	AUSTRALIA	-UNITED STATES	491.97	75.9	1
HUNGARY	-JAPAN	1040.00	37.5	5	KOREA SOUTH	-UNITED STATES	469.00	37.0	5

		BATTLE DEATHS (000'S)	SHARED WAR MONTHS	WAR MONTH DECILE			BATTLE DEATHS (000'S)	SHARED WAR MONTHS	WAR MONTH DECILE
				*** DECILE 4 ***					
NEW ZEALAND	-UNITED STATES	425.60	44.3	4	BELGIUM	-KOREA SOUTH	415.10	30.2	6
BELGIUM	-RUMANIA	422.50	15.4	8	KOREA SOUTH	-PHILIPPINES	415.09	34.4	5
SOUTH AFRICA	-UNITED STATES	417.00	44.3	4	MONGOLIA	-UNITED STATES	411.30	0.2	10
KOREA SOUTH	-TURKEY	415.72	33.3	6	BRAZIL	-UNITED STATES	409.30	10.1	8
ENGLAND	-KOREA SOUTH	415.67	35.0	5	BULGARIA	-UNITED STATES	409.30	7.9	8
CANADA	-KOREA SOUTH	415.31	31.3	6	RUMANIA	-YUGOSLAVIA/SERBIA	403.00	16.1	8
FRANCE	-KOREA SOUTH	415.29	30.8	6	CANADA	-POLAND	359.30	0.6	10
AUSTRALIA	-KOREA SOUTH	415.27	31.6	6	AUSTRALIA	-POLAND	349.40	0.8	10
GREECE	-KOREA SOUTH	415.17	30.2	6	GREECE	-RUMANIA	344.00	6.1	9
COLOMBIA	-KOREA SOUTH	415.14	25.7	7	PORTUGAL	-RUMANIA	342.00	15.4	8
ETHIOPIA	-KOREA SOUTH	415.12	26.9	7	BULGARIA	-TURKEY	339.00	35.6	5
HOLLAND	-KOREA SOUTH	415.11	30.2	6	NEW ZEALAND	-POLAND	337.30	0.8	10
KOREA SOUTH	-THAILAND	415.11	30.2	6	FINLAND	-RUMANIA	332.00	38.0	5
				*** DECILE 5 ***					
HUNGARY	-RUMANIA	330.00	37.9	5	CANADA	-FRANCE	249.90	50.0	3
POLAND	-SOUTH AFRICA	328.70	0.7	10	AUSTRALIA	-FRANCE	239.96	50.2	3
CANADA	-ENGLAND	310.28	102.5	1	FRANCE	-NEW ZEALAND	227.30	19.4	7
BULGARIA	-RUMANIA	310.00	40.4	4	FRANCE	-SOUTH AFRICA	218.70	19.3	8
AUSTRALIA	-ENGLAND	300.34	103.0	1	FRANCE	-HCLLAND	216.60	30.4	6
ENGLAND	-NEW ZEALAND	287.30	71.4	1	FRANCE	-MONGOLIA	213.00	0.2	10
ENGLAND	-SOUTH AFRICA	278.70	71.3	1	FRANCE	-NORWAY	212.00	2.0	10
ENGLAND	-HOLLAND	278.38	41.6	4	BRAZIL	-FRANCE	211.00	6.5	9
ENGLAND	-ETHIOPIA	275.79	32.2	6	BULGARIA	-FRANCE	211.00	6.5	9
ENGLAND	-MONGOLIA	273.00	0.2	10	GREECE	-UNITED STATES	185.17	46.7	4
ENGLAND	-NORWAY	272.00	2.0	10	UNITED STATES	-YUGOSLAVIA/SERBIA	174.00	18.9	8
BRAZIL	-ENGLAND	271.00	10.1	8	FRANCE	-TURKEY	141.01	53.9	2
BULGARIA	-ENGLAND	271.00	7.9	8	BELGIUM	-YUGOSLAVIA/SERBIA	135.50	51.3	3
BELGIUM	-UNITED STATES	267.60	49.1	3					
				*** DECILE 6 ***					
PORTUGAL	-UNITED STATES	133.00	18.9	8	AUSTRIA-HUNGARY	-RUSSIA	59.50	1.0	10
JAPAN	-UNITED STATES	126.30	18.9	8	CANADA	-ITALY/SARDINIA	56.80	18.7	8
ARGENTINA	-BRAZIL	110.00	59.9	2	CANADA	-NEW ZEALAND	56.60	71.2	2
GREECE	-YUGOSLAVIA/SERBIA	109.00	22.0	7	PORTUGAL	-YUGOSLAVIA/SERBIA	55.00	32.4	6
FINLAND	-ITALY/SARDINIA	102.00	26.3	7	TURKEY	-UNITED STATES	54.72	33.3	6
HUNGARY	-ITALY/SARDINIA	100.00	26.2	7	COLOMBIA	-UNITED STATES	54.14	25.7	7
BELGIUM	-PORTUGAL	94.50	32.4	6	ETHIOPIA	-UNITED STATES	54.12	26.9	7
BELGIUM	-GREECE	92.77	46.7	4	HOLLAND	-UNITED STATES	54.11	30.2	6
BELGIUM	-JAPAN	87.80	50.7	3	THAILAND	-UNITED STATES	54.11	30.2	6
BULGARIA	-ITALY/SARDINIA	87.50	28.7	7	PHILIPPINES	-UNITED STATES	54.09	34.4	5
FINLAND	-HUNGARY	82.00	38.8	5	BULGARIA	-FINLAND	51.00	33.0	6
ENGLAND	-TURKEY	78.40	59.0	2	CANADA	-GREECE	49.78	36.1	5
AUSTRALIA	-CANADA	69.28	102.5	1	BELGIUM	-CANADA	49.31	30.8	6

13.2 - NATION PAIRS RANKED BY COMBINED DEATHS AS WARTIME <u>PARTNERS</u>

		BATTLE DEATHS (000'S)	SHARED WAR MONTHS	WAR MONTH DECILE			BATTLE DEATHS (000'S)	SHARED WAR MONTHS	WAR MONTH DECILE
				*** DECILE 7 ***					
CANADA	-RUMANIA	49.30	7.9	8	CANADA	-NORWAY	41.30	2.0	10
BULGARIA	-HUNGARY	49.00	33.0	6	BADEN	-GERMANY/PRUSSIA	41.00	4.2	9
JAPAN	-YUGOSLAVIA/SERBIA	48.30	50.7	3	GERMANY/PRUSSIA	-WUERTTEMBERG	41.00	4.3	9
CANADA	-SOUTH AFRICA	48.00	71.2	2	BRAZIL	-CANADA	40.30	10.1	8
ITALY/SARDINIA	-TURKEY	47.20	13.7	8	BULGARIA	-CANADA	40.30	7.9	8
BULGARIA	-YUGOSLAVIA/SERBIA	47.00	4.1	9	AUSTRALIA	-GREECE	39.84	36.1	5
AUSTRALIA	-ITALY/SARDINIA	46.90	18.7	8	AUSTRALIA	-RUMANIA	39.40	7.9	8
AUSTRALIA	-NEW ZEALAND	46.70	71.4	1	AUSTRALIA	-BELGIUM	39.37	30.8	6
CANADA	-HOLLAND	45.92	30.4	6	TURKEY	-YUGOSLAVIA/SERBIA	38.50	0.5	10
BAVARIA	-GERMANY/PRUSSIA	45.50	3.9	9	AUSTRALIA	-SOUTH AFRICA	38.10	71.3	1
CANADA	-ETHIOPIA	44.73	32.2	6	BULGARIA	-GREECE	37.00	4.1	9
CANADA	-YUGOSLAVIA/SERBIA	44.30	0.4	10	AUSTRALIA	-HOLLAND	35.98	30.4	6
CANADA	-MONGOLIA	42.30	0.2	10	ITALY/SARDINIA	-NEW ZEALAND	34.80	18.7	8
				*** DECILE 8 ***					
AUSTRALIA	-ETHIOPIA	34.79	32.2	6	AUSTRIA-HUNGARY	-BAVARIA	20.50	1.4	10
AUSTRALIA	-YUGOSLAVIA/SERBIA	34.40	0.4	10	AUSTRIA-HUNGARY	-HANOVER	20.50	0.5	10
AUSTRALIA	-MONGOLIA	32.40	0.2	10	MONGOLIA	-NEW ZEALAND	20.30	0.2	10
AUSTRALIA	-NORWAY	31.40	2.0	10	AUSTRIA-HUNGARY	-BADEN	20.10	1.4	10
AUSTRALIA	-BRAZIL	30.40	10.1	8	AUSTRIA-HUNGARY	-HESSE ELECTORAL	20.10	1.4	10
AUSTRALIA	-BULGARIA	30.40	7.9	8	AUSTRIA-HUNGARY	-HESSE GRAND DUCAL	20.10	1.4	10
FRANCE	-SPAIN	29.00	13.5	8	AUSTRIA-HUNGARY	-MECKLENBURG-SCHWERIN	20.10	1.4	10
GREECE	-NEW ZEALAND	27.30	5.9	9	AUSTRIA-HUNGARY	-WUERTTEMBERG	20.10	1.4	10
NEW ZEALAND	-RUMANIA	27.30	7.9	8	NEW ZEALAND	-NORWAY	19.30	2.0	10
BELGIUM	-NEW ZEALAND	26.90	0.6	10	GREECE	-SOUTH AFRICA	18.70	5.9	9
ITALY/SARDINIA	-SOUTH AFRICA	26.20	18.7	8	RUMANIA	-SOUTH AFRICA	18.70	7.9	8
NEW ZEALAND	-SOUTH AFRICA	26.00	71.3	1	BRAZIL	-ITALY/SARDINIA	18.50	10.1	8
HOLLAND	-NEW ZEALAND	23.50	0.2	10	BELGIUM	-SOUTH AFRICA	18.30	0.6	10
GREECE	-TURKEY	23.39	30.7	6	BRAZIL	-NEW ZEALAND	18.30	10.1	8
ETHIOPIA	-NEW ZEALAND	22.30	5.3	9	BULGARIA	-NEW ZEALAND	18.30	7.9	8
NEW ZEALAND	-YUGOSLAVIA/SERBIA	22.30	0.4	10	BELGIUM	-HOLLAND	16.01	30.4	6
RUMANIA	-TURKEY	21.50	0.5	10	ETHIOPIA	-GREECE	15.29	29.9	7
AUSTRIA-HUNGARY	-SAXONY	20.60	1.4	10	HOLLAND	-SOUTH AFRICA	14.90	0.2	10

		BATTLE DEATHS (000'S)	SHARED WAR MONTHS	WAR MONTH DECILE			BATTLE DEATHS (000'S)	SHARED WAR MONTHS	WAR MONTH DECILE
				*** DECILE 9 ***					
ETHIOPIA	-SOUTH AFRICA	13.70	5.3	9	SYRIA	-U.A.R.	3.00	2.5	10
SOUTH AFRICA	-YUGOSLAVIA/SERBIA	13.70	0.4	10	IRAQ	-U.A.R.	2.50	2.5	10
GREECE	-PORTUGAL	12.00	16.5	8	LEBANON	-U.A.R.	2.50	2.5	10
MONGOLIA	-SOUTH AFRICA	11.70	0.2	10	BADEN	-WUERTTEMBERG	2.20	5.6	9
BELGIUM	-NORWAY	11.60	0.6	10	BRAZIL	-BULGARIA	2.00	7.9	8
BOLIVIA	-PERU	11.00	54.5	2	JORDAN	-SYRIA	2.00	2.5	10
BRAZIL	-RUMANIA	11.00	7.9	8	IRAQ	-JORDAN	1.50	2.5	10
NORWAY	-SOUTH AFRICA	10.70	2.0	10	IRAQ	-SYRIA	1.50	2.5	10
ETHIOPIA	-YUGOSLAVIA/SERBIA	10.00	0.4	10	JORDAN	-LEBANON	1.50	2.5	10
BRAZIL	-SOUTH AFRICA	9.70	10.1	8	LEBANON	-SYRIA	1.50	2.5	10
BULGARIA	-SOUTH AFRICA	9.70	7.9	8	HONDURAS	-SALVADOR	1.20	3.9	9
HOLLAND	-NORWAY	8.20	0.2	10	BAVARIA	-SAXONY	1.10	1.4	10
JAPAN	-PORTUGAL	7.30	32.4	6	HANOVER	-SAXONY	1.10	0.5	10
BADEN	-BAVARIA	7.10	5.3	9	CANADA	-TURKEY	1.03	31.3	6
BAVARIA	-WUERTTEMBERG	7.10	5.3	9	BAVARIA	-HANOVER	1.00	0.5	10
GREECE	-JAPAN	5.30	16.5	8	IRAQ	-LEBANON	1.00	2.5	10
CZECHOSLOVAKIA	-RUMANIA	5.00	3.6	10	AUSTRALIA	-TURKEY	0.99	31.6	6
JORDAN	-U.A.R.	3.00	2.5	10	COLOMBIA	-TURKEY	0.86	25.7	7

13.2 - NATION PAIRS RANKED BY COMBINED DEATHS AS WARTIME PARTNERS

		BATTLE DEATHS (000'S)	SHARED WAR MONTHS	WAR MONTH DECILE			BATTLE DEATHS (000'S)	SHARED WAR MONTHS	WAR MONTH DECILE
*** DECILE 10 ***									
ETHIOPIA	-TURKEY	0.84	26.9	7	FRANCE	-PHILIPPINES	0.38	30.8	6
HOLLAND	-TURKEY	0.83	30.2	6	AUSTRALIA	-PHILIPPINES	0.36	31.6	6
THAILAND	-TURKEY	0.83	30.2	6	COLOMBIA	-GREECE	0.31	25.7	7
BELGIUM	-TURKEY	0.82	30.2	6	GREECE	-HOLLAND	0.28	30.2	6
COLOMBIA	-ENGLAND	0.81	25.7	7	GREECE	-THAILAND	0.28	30.2	6
PHILIPPINES	-TURKEY	0.81	33.3	6	COLOMBIA	-ETHIOPIA	0.26	25.7	7
ENGLAND	-THAILAND	0.78	30.2	6	GREECE	-PHILIPPINES	0.26	30.2	6
ENGLAND	-PHILIPPINES	0.76	34.4	5	COLOMBIA	-HOLLAND	0.25	25.7	7
BADEN	-SAXONY	0.70	1.4	10	COLOMBIA	-THAILAND	0.25	25.7	7
CHILE	-PERU	0.70	3.8	9	BELGIUM	-COLOMBIA	0.24	25.7	7
HESSE ELECTORAL	-SAXONY	0.70	1.4	10	COLOMBIA	-PHILIPPINES	0.23	25.7	7
HESSE GRAND DUCAL	-SAXONY	0.70	1.4	10	ETHIOPIA	-HOLLAND	0.23	26.9	7
MECKLENBURG-SCHWERIN	-SAXONY	0.70	1.4	10	ETHIOPIA	-THAILAND	0.23	26.9	7
SAXONY	-WUERTTEMBERG	0.70	1.4	10	BELGIUM	-ETHIOPIA	0.22	26.9	7
AUSTRIA-HUNGARY	-FRANCE	0.60	1.0	10	ENGLAND	-ISRAEL	0.22	0.2	10
BADEN	-HANOVER	0.60	0.5	10	HOLLAND	-THAILAND	0.22	30.2	6
BAVARIA	-HESSE ELECTORAL	0.60	1.4	10	BELGIUM	-THAILAND	0.21	30.2	6
BAVARIA	-HESSE GRAND DUCAL	0.60	1.4	10	ETHIOPIA	-PHILIPPINES	0.21	26.9	7
BAVARIA	-MECKLENBURG-SCHWERIN	0.60	1.4	10	FRANCE	-ISRAEL	0.21	0.2	10
FRANCE	-TWO SICILIES	0.60	1.0	10	AUSTRIA-HUNGARY	-TWO SICILIES	0.20	1.8	10
HANOVER	-HESSE ELECTORAL	0.60	0.5	10	BADEN	-HESSE ELECTORAL	0.20	1.4	10
HANOVER	-HESSE GRAND DUCAL	0.60	0.5	10	BADEN	-HESSE GRAND DUCAL	0.20	1.4	10
HANOVER	-MECKLENBURG-SCHWERIN	0.60	0.5	10	BADEN	-MECKLENBURG-SCHWERIN	0.20	1.4	10
HANOVER	-WUERTTEMBERG	0.60	0.5	10	HESSE ELECTORAL	-HESSE GRAND DUCAL	0.20	1.4	10
CANADA	-COLOMBIA	0.45	25.7	7	HESSE ELECTORAL	-MECKLENBURG-SCHWERIN	0.20	1.4	10
COLOMBIA	-FRANCE	0.43	25.7	7	HESSE ELECTORAL	-WUERTTEMBERG	0.20	1.4	10
CANADA	-THAILAND	0.42	30.2	6	HESSE GRAND DUCAL	-MECKLENBURG-SCHWERIN	0.20	1.4	10
AUSTRALIA	-COLOMBIA	0.41	25.7	7	HESSE GRAND DUCAL	-WUERTTEMBERG	0.20	1.4	10
ETHIOPIA	-FRANCE	0.41	26.9	7	HOLLAND	-PHILIPPINES	0.20	30.2	6
CANADA	-PHILIPPINES	0.40	31.3	6	MECKLENBURG-SCHWERIN	-WUERTTEMBERG	0.20	1.4	10
FRANCE	-THAILAND	0.40	30.2	6	PHILIPPINES	-THAILAND	0.20	30.2	6
AUSTRALIA	-THAILAND	0.38	30.2	6	BELGIUM	-PHILIPPINES	0.19	30.2	6

on shared war months; partners that are in the first group on shared war months are spread fairly evenly over the first eight deciles on the combined battle death ranking. On the other hand, there are no pairs which scored in the top ranks on shared war months and in the bottom ranks of shared battle fatalities, and this is quite understandable. It would be nearly impossible for any pair to build up a record of a very long partnership in shared war months without scoring above the lowest ranks on the combined battle death indicator. In any event, the extent to which the war month rankings do differ from those based on combined battle deaths is more fully revealed in Table 13.3.

RANKING NATION PAIRS BY SHARED EXPERIENCE AS WARTIME OPPONENTS

Having examined the pair-wise patterns as wartime partners, let us look now at the other side of the coin. In Table 13.4 we follow the same format as in Table 13.2, beginning with the total number of *battle deaths* sustained by both nations during all the wars in which they fought on opposing sides. This is again followed by the number of months during which they fought on opposite sides and the resulting decile position on this variable. The 209 pairs which opposed each other have 178 different scores, making the decile about 18 scores in range.

Comparing these rankings with those based on wartime partnerships, we begin to find some tentative evidence for the notion of traditional friendships and enmities. That is, we find very different pairs of nations in the first and second deciles of these two sets of tables. With the exception of the three nations that shifted sides during World War Two (Italy, Rumania, and Bulgaria), the top two deciles in the listing of opponents contain none of the same pairs as those found in Table 13.2. As we noted in our discussion of the former table, the results are largely determined by the fatalities of the participants in the World Wars.

Again we offer a simple rank list of the shared war month scores for opposing pairs. One look at both Tables 13.4 and 13.5 shows that there is a much higher correspondence between an *opposing* pair's rank on the combined battle death measure and the shared war month indicator than we found for the *partnerships.* This suggests that, while partners with very high combined battle fatality scores had not necessarily fought for many months together, the pairs of nations that opposed each other did so more often and at greater cost in lives. This and other patterns can now be more fully examined as we turn in the next section to an examination of "traditional" alliances and enmities.

PURE FORMS OF MILITARY ENMITY, FRIENDSHIP, AND INDIFFERENCE

In the previous sections, we have looked only at the pairs of nations that have had some mutual wartime experience, either on opposing or allied sides. To list the nations that have never had any type of military relations would be a fruitless task, since we would need to list some 12,000-odd pairs. Moreover, to discover that Ecuador and Switzerland or Gabon and Haiti have not shared mutual war experience is not particularly helpful. However, there is much more we can do with the data already presented as we move into fascinating questions involving legendary historical bonds between nations.

13.3 - NATION PAIRS RANKED BY SHARED WAR MONTHS AS PARTNERS

*** DECILE 1 ***

Nation	Partner	Months	Nation	Partner	Months
ENGLAND	- FRANCE	124.8	AUSTRALIA	- UNITED STATES	75.9
AUSTRALIA	- ENGLAND	103.0	CANADA	- UNITED STATES	75.6
AUSTRALIA	- CANADA	102.5	ENGLAND	- ITALY/SARDINIA	74.1
CANADA	- ENGLAND	102.5	AUSTRALIA	- NEW ZEALAND	71.4
ENGLAND	- UNITED STATES	98.2	ENGLAND	- NEW ZEALAND	71.4
ENGLAND	- RUSSIA	86.8	AUSTRALIA	- SOUTH AFRICA	71.3
BELGIUM	- FRANCE	82.1	ENGLAND	- SOUTH AFRICA	71.3
BELGIUM	- ENGLAND	82.0	NEW ZEALAND	- SOUTH AFRICA	71.3

*** DECILE 2 ***

Nation	Partner	Months	Nation	Partner	Months
CANADA	- NEW ZEALAND	71.2	FRANCE	- UNITED STATES	59.4
CANADA	- SOUTH AFRICA	71.2	ENGLAND	- TURKEY	59.0
BULGARIA	- GERMANY/PRUSSIA	68.6	AUSTRIA-HUNGARY	- GERMANY/PRUSSIA	54.7
FRANCE	- ITALY/SARDINIA	64.2	BOLIVIA	- PERU	54.5
ITALY/SARDINIA	- JAPAN	62.6	FRANCE	- TURKEY	53.9
ARGENTINA	- BRAZIL	59.9	ENGLAND	- GREECE	52.6

*** DECILE 3 ***

Nation	Partner	Months	Nation	Partner	Months
ENGLAND	- YUGOSLAVIA/SERBIA	51.6	CANADA	- FRANCE	50.0
BELGIUM	- YUGOSLAVIA/SERBIA	51.3	ITALY/SARDINIA	- RUMANIA	49.7
FRANCE	- YUGOSLAVIA/SERBIA	51.3	ITALY/SARDINIA	- RUSSIA	49.2
BELGIUM	- JAPAN	50.7	BELGIUM	- UNITED STATES	49.1
ENGLAND	- JAPAN	50.7	RUSSIA	- UNITED STATES	48.9
FRANCE	- JAPAN	50.7	GERMANY/PRUSSIA	- TURKEY	48.5
JAPAN	- YUGOSLAVIA/SERBIA	50.7	AUSTRIA-HUNGARY	- TURKEY	48.2
AUSTRALIA	- FRANCE	50.2	JAPAN	- RUMANIA	48.0

*** DECILE 4 ***

Nation	Partner	Months	Nation	Partner	Months
FRANCE	- RUSSIA	46.9	NEW ZEALAND	- UNITED STATES	44.3
AUSTRALIA	- RUSSIA	46.7	SOUTH AFRICA	- UNITED STATES	44.3
BELGIUM	- GREECE	46.7	GERMANY/PRUSSIA	- HUNGARY	42.8
CANADA	- RUSSIA	46.7	BELGIUM	- ITALY/SARDINIA	41.7
FRANCE	- GREECE	46.7	ITALY/SARDINIA	- YUGOSLAVIA/SERBIA	41.7
GREECE	- UNITED STATES	46.7	ENGLAND	- HOLLAND	41.6
NEW ZEALAND	- RUSSIA	46.7	CHINA	- RUSSIA	41.2
RUSSIA	- SOUTH AFRICA	46.7	GERMANY/PRUSSIA	- JAPAN	41.0
AUSTRALIA	- CHINA	44.3	BULGARIA	- RUMANIA	40.4
CANADA	- CHINA	44.3	GERMANY/PRUSSIA	- ITALY/SARDINIA	40.2
CHINA	- ENGLAND	44.3	RUSSIA	- YUGOSLAVIA/SERBIA	40.2
CHINA	- NEW ZEALAND	44.3	BELGIUM	- RUSSIA	40.1
CHINA	- SOUTH AFRICA	44.3	JAPAN	- RUSSIA	39.5
CHINA	- UNITED STATES	44.3			

*** DECILE 5 ***

FINLAND	- GERMANY/PRUSSIA	38.9	AUSTRALIA	- GREECE	36.1
FINLAND	- HUNGARY	38.8	CANADA	- GREECE	36.1
GERMANY/PRUSSIA	- RUMANIA	38.1	AUSTRIA-HUNGARY	- BULGARIA	35.6
FINLAND	- RUMANIA	38.0	BULGARIA	- TURKEY	35.6
HUNGARY	- RUMANIA	37.9	ENGLAND	- KOREA SOUTH	35.0
ITALY/SARDINIA	- UNITED STATES	37.6	ENGLAND	- PHILIPPINES	34.4
HUNGARY	- JAPAN	37.5	KOREA SOUTH	- PHILIPPINES	34.4
KOREA SOUTH	- UNITED STATES	37.0	PHILIPPINES	- UNITED STATES	34.4

*** DECILE 6 ***

FINLAND	- JAPAN	33.4	GREECE	- TURKEY	30.7
KOREA SOUTH	- TURKEY	33.3	AUSTRALIA	- HOLLAND	30.4
PHILIPPINES	- TURKEY	33.3	BELGIUM	- HOLLAND	30.4
TURKEY	- UNITED STATES	33.3	CANADA	- HOLLAND	30.4
BULGARIA	- FINLAND	33.0	FRANCE	- HOLLAND	30.4
BULGARIA	- HUNGARY	33.0	AUSTRALIA	- THAILAND	30.2
BULGARIA	- JAPAN	33.0	BELGIUM	- KOREA SOUTH	30.2
CHINA	- KOREA NORTH	33.0	BELGIUM	- PHILIPPINES	30.2
BELGIUM	- PORTUGAL	32.4	BELGIUM	- THAILAND	30.2
ENGLAND	- PORTUGAL	32.4	BELGIUM	- TURKEY	30.2
FRANCE	- PORTUGAL	32.4	CANADA	- THAILAND	30.2
ITALY/SARDINIA	- PORTUGAL	32.4	ENGLAND	- THAILAND	30.2
JAPAN	- PORTUGAL	32.4	FRANCE	- THAILAND	30.2
PORTUGAL	- YUGOSLAVIA/SERBIA	32.4	GREECE	- HOLLAND	30.2
AUSTRALIA	- ETHIOPIA	32.2	GREECE	- KOREA SOUTH	30.2
CANADA	- ETHIOPIA	32.2	GREECE	- PHILIPPINES	30.2
ENGLAND	- ETHIOPIA	32.2	GREECE	- THAILAND	30.2
AUSTRALIA	- KOREA SOUTH	31.6	HOLLAND	- KOREA SOUTH	30.2
AUSTRALIA	- PHILIPPINES	31.6	HOLLAND	- PHILIPPINES	30.2
AUSTRALIA	- TURKEY	31.6	HOLLAND	- THAILAND	30.2
CANADA	- KOREA SOUTH	31.3	HOLLAND	- TURKEY	30.2
CANADA	- PHILIPPINES	31.3	HOLLAND	- UNITED STATES	30.2
CANADA	- TURKEY	31.3	KOREA SOUTH	- THAILAND	30.2
AUSTRALIA	- BELGIUM	30.8	PHILIPPINES	- THAILAND	30.2
BELGIUM	- CANADA	30.8	THAILAND	- TURKEY	30.2
FRANCE	- KOREA SOUTH	30.8	THAILAND	- UNITED STATES	30.2
FRANCE	- PHILIPPINES	30.8			

13.3 - NATION PAIRS RANKED BY SHARED WAR MONTHS AS PARTNERS

*** DECILE 7 ***

Nation		Partner	Months
ETHIOPIA	-	GREECE	29.9
BULGARIA	-	ITALY/SARDINIA	28.7
BELGIUM	-	ETHIOPIA	26.9
ETHIOPIA	-	FRANCE	26.9
ETHIOPIA	-	HOLLAND	26.9
ETHIOPIA	-	KOREA SOUTH	26.9
ETHIOPIA	-	PHILIPPINES	26.9
ETHIOPIA	-	THAILAND	26.9
ETHIOPIA	-	TURKEY	26.9
ETHIOPIA	-	UNITED STATES	26.9
FINLAND	-	ITALY/SARDINIA	26.3
HUNGARY	-	ITALY/SARDINIA	26.2
AUSTRALIA	-	COLOMBIA	25.7
BELGIUM	-	COLOMBIA	25.7
CANADA	-	COLOMBIA	25.7
COLOMBIA	-	ENGLAND	25.7
COLOMBIA	-	ETHIOPIA	25.7
COLOMBIA	-	FRANCE	25.7
COLOMBIA	-	GREECE	25.7
COLOMBIA	-	HOLLAND	25.7
COLOMBIA	-	KOREA SOUTH	25.7
COLOMBIA	-	PHILIPPINES	25.7
COLOMBIA	-	THAILAND	25.7
COLOMBIA	-	TURKEY	25.7
COLOMBIA	-	UNITED STATES	25.7
ENGLAND	-	RUMANIA	23.3
RUMANIA	-	RUSSIA	23.2
GREECE	-	YUGOSLAVIA/SERBIA	22.0
FRANCE	-	RUMANIA	21.9
PORTUGAL	-	RUSSIA	21.2
FRANCE	-	NEW ZEALAND	19.4

*** DECILE 8 ***

Nation		Partner	Months
FRANCE	-	SOUTH AFRICA	19.3
JAPAN	-	UNITED STATES	18.9
PORTUGAL	-	UNITED STATES	18.9
UNITED STATES	-	YUGOSLAVIA/SERBIA	18.9
AUSTRALIA	-	ITALY/SARDINIA	18.7
CANADA	-	ITALY/SARDINIA	18.7
CHINA	-	ITALY/SARDINIA	18.7
ITALY/SARDINIA	-	NEW ZEALAND	18.7
ITALY/SARDINIA	-	SOUTH AFRICA	18.7
GREECE	-	ITALY/SARDINIA	16.5
GREECE	-	JAPAN	16.5
GREECE	-	PORTUGAL	16.5
RUMANIA	-	YUGOSLAVIA/SERBIA	16.1
RUMANIA	-	UNITED STATES	15.7
BELGIUM	-	RUMANIA	15.4
PORTUGAL	-	RUMANIA	15.4
ITALY/SARDINIA	-	TURKEY	13.7
FRANCE	-	SPAIN	13.5
AUSTRALIA	-	BRAZIL	10.1
BRAZIL	-	CANADA	10.1
BRAZIL	-	CHINA	10.1
BRAZIL	-	ENGLAND	10.1
BRAZIL	-	ITALY/SARDINIA	10.1
BRAZIL	-	NEW ZEALAND	10.1
BRAZIL	-	RUSSIA	10.1
BRAZIL	-	SOUTH AFRICA	10.1
BRAZIL	-	UNITED STATES	10.1
CHINA	-	FRANCE	9.7
AUSTRALIA	-	BULGARIA	7.9
AUSTRALIA	-	RUMANIA	7.9
BRAZIL	-	BULGARIA	7.9
BRAZIL	-	RUMANIA	7.9
BULGARIA	-	CANADA	7.9
BULGARIA	-	CHINA	7.9
BULGARIA	-	ENGLAND	7.9
BULGARIA	-	NEW ZEALAND	7.9
BULGARIA	-	RUSSIA	7.9
BULGARIA	-	SOUTH AFRICA	7.9
BULGARIA	-	UNITED STATES	7.9
CANADA	-	RUMANIA	7.9
CHINA	-	RUMANIA	7.9
NEW ZEALAND	-	RUMANIA	7.9
RUMANIA	-	SOUTH AFRICA	7.9

*** DECILE 9 ***

BRAZIL	- FRANCE	6.5	GREECE	- RUSSIA	5.3
BULGARIA	- FRANCE	6.5	MONGOLIA	- RUSSIA	4.4
GREECE	- RUMANIA	6.1	GERMANY/PRUSSIA	- WUERTTEMBERG	4.3
GREECE	- NEW ZEALAND	5.9	BADEN	- GERMANY/PRUSSIA	4.2
GREECE	- SOUTH AFRICA	5.9	BULGARIA	- GREECE	4.1
BADEN	- WUERTTEMBERG	5.6	BULGARIA	- YUGOSLAVIA/SERBIA	4.1
BADEN	- BAVARIA	5.3	BAVARIA	- GERMANY/PRUSSIA	3.9
BAVARIA	- WUERTTEMBERG	5.3	HONDURAS	- SALVADOR	3.9
ETHIOPIA	- NEW ZEALAND	5.3	CHILE	- PERU	3.8
ETHIOPIA	- SOUTH AFRICA	5.3			

13.3 - NATION PAIRS RANKED BY SHARED WAR MONTHS AS PARTNERS

*** DECILE 10 ***

CZECHOSLOVAKIA	- RUMANIA	3.6	SAXONY	- WUERTTEMBERG	1.4
IRAQ	- JORDAN	2.5	AUSTRIA-HUNGARY	- FRANCE	1.0
IRAQ	- LEBANON	2.5	AUSTRIA-HUNGARY	- RUSSIA	1.0
IRAQ	- SYRIA	2.5	FRANCE	- TWO SICILIES	1.0
IRAQ	- U.A.R.	2.5	AUSTRALIA	- POLAND	0.8
JORDAN	- LEBANON	2.5	ENGLAND	- POLAND	0.8
JORDAN	- SYRIA	2.5	FRANCE	- POLAND	0.8
JORDAN	- U.A.R.	2.5	NEW ZEALAND	- POLAND	0.8
LEBANON	- SYRIA	2.5	POLAND	- SOUTH AFRICA	0.7
LEBANON	- U.A.R.	2.5	BELGIUM	- NEW ZEALAND	0.6
SYRIA	- U.A.R.	2.5	BELGIUM	- NORWAY	0.6
AUSTRALIA	- NORWAY	2.0	BELGIUM	- SOUTH AFRICA	0.6
CANADA	- NORWAY	2.0	CANADA	- POLAND	0.6
ENGLAND	- NORWAY	2.0	AUSTRIA-HUNGARY	- HANOVER	0.5
FRANCE	- NORWAY	2.0	BADEN	- HANOVER	0.5
NEW ZEALAND	- NORWAY	2.0	BAVARIA	- HANOVER	0.5
NORWAY	- SOUTH AFRICA	2.0	HANOVER	- HESSE ELECTORAL	0.5
AUSTRIA-HUNGARY	- TWO SICILIES	1.8	HANOVER	- HESSE GRAND DUCAL	0.5
AUSTRIA-HUNGARY	- BADEN	1.4	HANOVER	- MECKLENBURG-SCHWERIN	0.5
AUSTRIA-HUNGARY	- BAVARIA	1.4	HANOVER	- SAXONY	0.5
AUSTRIA-HUNGARY	- HESSE ELECTORAL	1.4	HANOVER	- WUERTTEMBERG	0.5
AUSTRIA-HUNGARY	- HESSE GRAND DUCAL	1.4	RUMANIA	- TURKEY	0.5
AUSTRIA-HUNGARY	- MECKLENBURG-SCHWERIN	1.4	TURKEY	- YUGOSLAVIA/SERBIA	0.5
AUSTRIA-HUNGARY	- SAXONY	1.4	AUSTRALIA	- YUGOSLAVIA/SERBIA	0.4
AUSTRIA-HUNGARY	- WUERTTEMBERG	1.4	CANADA	- YUGOSLAVIA/SERBIA	0.4
BADEN	- HESSE ELECTORAL	1.4	ETHIOPIA	- RUSSIA	0.4
BADEN	- HESSE GRAND DUCAL	1.4	ETHIOPIA	- YUGOSLAVIA/SERBIA	0.4
BADEN	- MECKLENBURG-SCHWERIN	1.4	NEW ZEALAND	- YUGOSLAVIA/SERBIA	0.4
BADEN	- SAXONY	1.4	SOUTH AFRICA	- YUGOSLAVIA/SERBIA	0.4
BAVARIA	- HESSE ELECTORAL	1.4	AUSTRALIA	- MONGOLIA	0.2
BAVARIA	- HESSE GRAND DUCAL	1.4	CANADA	- MONGOLIA	0.2
BAVARIA	- MECKLENBURG-SCHWERIN	1.4	CHINA	- MONGOLIA	0.2
BAVARIA	- SAXONY	1.4	ENGLAND	- ISRAEL	0.2
HESSE ELECTORAL	- HESSE GRAND DUCAL	1.4	ENGLAND	- MONGOLIA	0.2
HESSE ELECTORAL	- MECKLENBURG-SCHWERIN	1.4	FRANCE	- ISRAEL	0.2
HESSE ELECTORAL	- SAXONY	1.4	FRANCE	- MONGOLIA	0.2
HESSE ELECTORAL	- WUERTTEMBERG	1.4	HOLLAND	- NEW ZEALAND	0.2
HESSE GRAND DUCAL	- MECKLENBURG-SCHWERIN	1.4	HOLLAND	- NORWAY	0.2
HESSE GRAND DUCAL	- SAXONY	1.4	HOLLAND	- SOUTH AFRICA	0.2
HESSE GRAND DUCAL	- WUERTTEMBERG	1.4	MONGOLIA	- NEW ZEALAND	0.2
MECKLENBURG-SCHWERIN	- SAXONY	1.4	MONGOLIA	- SOUTH AFRICA	0.2
MECKLENBURG-SCHWERIN	- WUERTTEMBERG	1.4	MONGOLIA	- UNITED STATES	0.2

13.4 - NATION PAIRS RANKED BY COMBINED DEATHS AS WARTIME OPPONENTS

		BATTLE DEATHS (000'S)	SHARED WAR MONTHS	WAR MONTH DECILE			BATTLE DEATHS (000'S)	SHARED WAR MONTHS	WAR MONTH DECILE
				*** DECILE 1 ***					
GERMANY/PRUSSIA	-RUSSIA	14500.00	86.7	1	GERMANY/PRUSSIA	-ITALY/SARDINIA	5967.50	60.4	2
BULGARIA	-RUSSIA	9223.00	58.8	2	GERMANY/PRUSSIA	-UNITED STATES	5834.30	59.9	2
JAPAN	-RUSSIA	8646.00	64.7	1	GERMANY/PRUSSIA	-RUMANIA	5645.00	23.3	6
RUMANIA	-RUSSIA	7790.00	38.1	4	BELGIUM	-GERMANY/PRUSSIA	5397.10	51.9	2
ITALY/SARDINIA	-RUSSIA	7662.20	40.1	4	GERMANY/PRUSSIA	-YUGOSLAVIA/SERBIA	5353.00	51.8	2
FINLAND	-RUSSIA	7632.00	42.3	4	GERMANY/PRUSSIA	-GREECE	5315.00	22.4	6
HUNGARY	-RUSSIA	7572.00	43.6	3	CHINA	-GERMANY/PRUSSIA	4850.00	41.0	4
FRANCE	-GERMANY/PRUSSIA	7040.00	74.7	1	GERMANY/PRUSSIA	-POLAND	3820.00	0.9	10
ENGLAND	-GERMANY/PRUSSIA	6478.00	119.3	1	CANADA	-GERMANY/PRUSSIA	3539.30	67.9	1
				*** DECILE 2 ***					
AUSTRALIA	-GERMANY/PRUSSIA	3529.40	68.1	1	RUSSIA	-TURKEY	2588.06	91.2	1
GERMANY/PRUSSIA	-NEW ZEALAND	3517.30	68.1	1	AUSTRIA-HUNGARY	-FRANCE	2570.00	53.4	2
GERMANY/PRUSSIA	-SOUTH AFRICA	3508.70	68.0	1	AUSTRIA-HUNGARY	-ENGLAND	2108.00	51.0	3
GERMANY/PRUSSIA	-HOLLAND	3506.20	0.2	10	AUSTRIA-HUNGARY	-ITALY/SARDINIA	1898.00	50.0	3
ETHIOPIA	-GERMANY/PRUSSIA	3505.00	5.3	8	GERMANY/PRUSSIA	-PORTUGAL	1807.00	32.4	5
GERMANY/PRUSSIA	-NORWAY	3502.00	2.0	10	GERMANY/PRUSSIA	-JAPAN	1800.30	50.7	3
BRAZIL	-GERMANY/PRUSSIA	3501.00	10.1	8	FRANCE	-TURKEY	1678.04	48.6	3
BULGARIA	-GERMANY/PRUSSIA	3501.00	7.9	8	CHINA	-RUMANIA	1640.00	32.6	5
CHINA	-JAPAN	3425.00	122.0	1	AUSTRIA-HUNGARY	-RUMANIA	1535.00	15.4	7
AUSTRIA-HUNGARY	-RUSSIA	2900.00	40.2	4					
				*** DECILE 3 ***					
CHINA	-ITALY/SARDINIA	1410.00	20.9	6	ENGLAND	-JAPAN	1270.00	44.3	3
JAPAN	-UNITED STATES	1408.30	44.3	3	AUSTRIA-HUNGARY	-YUGOSLAVIA/SERBIA	1248.00	51.2	2
CHINA	-FINLAND	1392.00	33.4	5	ENGLAND	-TURKEY	1236.08	48.6	3
CHINA	-HUNGARY	1390.00	37.5	4	FRANCE	-JAPAN	1210.00	9.7	8
BULGARIA	-FRANCE	1364.00	35.6	5	AUSTRIA-HUNGARY	-PORTUGAL	1207.00	32.1	5
BULGARIA	-CHINA	1359.00	33.0	5	AUSTRIA-HUNGARY	-GREECE	1205.00	16.2	7
AUSTRIA-HUNGARY	-UNITED STATES	1326.00	18.6	7	BULGARIA	-ENGLAND	1201.00	68.6	1
CHINA	-KOREA SOUTH	1315.00	33.0	5	AUSTRIA-HUNGARY	-JAPAN	1200.30	50.4	3
AUSTRIA-HUNGARY	-BELGIUM	1287.50	51.0	3					

13.4 - NATION PAIRS RANKED BY COMBINED DEATHS AS WARTIME OPPONENTS

		BATTLE DEATHS (000'S)	SHARED WAR MONTHS	WAR MONTH DECILE			BATTLE DEATHS (000'S)	SHARED WAR MONTHS	WAR MONTH DECILE
				*** DECILE 4 ***					
CANADA	-JAPAN	1039.30	44.3	3	ITALY/SARDINIA	-TURKEY	995.00	54.4	2
AUSTRALIA	-JAPAN	1029.40	44.3	3	CHINA	-UNITED STATES	954.00	33.0	5
JAPAN	-MONGOLIA	1021.00	4.4	9	KOREA NORTH	-KOREA SOUTH	935.00	37.1	4
ITALY/SARDINIA	-JAPAN	1017.50	18.7	7	CHINA	-FRANCE	912.39	42.6	4
JAPAN	-NEW ZEALAND	1017.30	44.3	3	CHINA	-TURKEY	900.72	33.0	5
BULGARIA	-JAPAN	1015.30	43.5	3	CHINA	-ENGLAND	900.67	33.0	5
JAPAN	-RUMANIA	1010.00	7.9	8	CANADA	-CHINA	900.31	31.3	6
JAPAN	-SOUTH AFRICA	1008.70	44.3	3	AUSTRALIA	-CHINA	900.27	31.6	5
BRAZIL	-JAPAN	1001.00	10.1	8	CHINA	-GREECE	900.17	30.2	6
				*** DECILE 5 ***					
CHINA	-COLOMBIA	900.14	25.7	6	ENGLAND	-RUMANIA	560.00	38.1	4
CHINA	-ETHIOPIA	900.12	26.9	6	BULGARIA	-UNITED STATES	557.30	50.4	3
CHINA	-HOLLAND	900.11	30.2	6	KOREA NORTH	-TURKEY	520.72	33.3	5
CHINA	-THAILAND	900.11	30.2	6	ENGLAND	-KOREA NORTH	520.67	35.0	5
BELGIUM	-CHINA	900.10	30.2	6	CANADA	-KOREA NORTH	520.31	31.3	6
CHINA	-PHILIPPINES	900.09	33.0	5	FRANCE	-KOREA NORTH	520.29	30.8	6
RUMANIA	-UNITED STATES	698.30	32.6	5	AUSTRALIA	-KOREA NORTH	520.27	31.6	5
BULGARIA	-ITALY/SARDINIA	690.50	46.3	3	GREECE	-KOREA NORTH	520.17	30.2	6
RUMANIA	-TURKEY	660.00	15.4	7	COLOMBIA	-KOREA NORTH	520.14	25.7	6
KOREA NORTH	-UNITED STATES	574.00	37.0	4					
				*** DECILE 6 ***					
ETHIOPIA	-KOREA NORTH	520.12	26.9	6	GREECE	-TURKEY	417.00	67.0	1
HOLLAND	-KOREA NORTH	520.11	30.2	6	BELGIUM	-TURKEY	412.50	48.5	3
KOREA NORTH	-THAILAND	520.11	30.2	6	BULGARIA	-RUMANIA	368.50	16.1	7
BELGIUM	-KOREA NORTH	520.10	30.2	6	PORTUGAL	-TURKEY	332.00	32.4	5
KOREA NORTH	-PHILIPPINES	520.09	34.4	5	ENGLAND	-ITALY/SARDINIA	330.00	38.8	4
ITALY/SARDINIA	-UNITED STATES	468.30	20.9	6	CANADA	-RUMANIA	329.30	38.1	4
TURKEY	-UNITED STATES	451.00	18.9	6	JAPAN	-TURKEY	325.30	48.5	3
FINLAND	-UNITED STATES	450.30	33.4	5	AUSTRALIA	-RUMANIA	319.40	38.1	4
HUNGARY	-UNITED STATES	448.30	37.5	4	ENGLAND	-FINLAND	312.00	38.9	4
TURKEY	-YUGOSLAVIA/SERBIA	418.00	52.6	2					

		BATTLE DEATHS (000'S)	SHARED WAR MONTHS	WAR MONTH DECILE			BATTLE DEATHS (000'S)	SHARED WAR MONTHS	WAR MONTH DECILE
				*** DECILE 7 ***					
ENGLAND	-HUNGARY	310.00	42.8	3	BADEN	-FRANCE	141.00	4.2	9
ITALY/SARDINIA	-RUMANIA	307.50	10.2	8	FRANCE	-WUERTTEMBERG	141.00	4.3	9
NEW ZEALAND	-RUMANIA	307.30	38.1	4	BOLIVIA	-PARAGUAY	130.00	35.9	5
RUMANIA	-SOUTH AFRICA	298.70	38.1	4	ENGLAND	-RUSSIA	122.00	23.1	6
ETHIOPIA	-RUMANIA	295.00	0.4	10	BELGIUM	-BULGARIA	101.50	35.6	5
BRAZIL	-RUMANIA	291.00	1.6	10	BULGARIA	-TURKEY	100.00	4.6	8
FRANCE	-ITALY/SARDINIA	270.00	0.4	10	CANADA	-ITALY/SARDINIA	99.30	38.8	4
FRANCE	-HUNGARY	250.00	3.0	9	BULGARIA	-YUGOSLAVIA/SERBIA	98.50	36.6	4
FRANCE	-RUSSIA	195.00	23.1	6	AUSTRALIA	-ITALY/SARDINIA	89.40	38.8	4
BAVARIA	-FRANCE	145.50	3.9	9					
				*** DECILE 8 ***					
ETHIOPIA	-ITALY/SARDINIA	85.00	12.5	7	FINLAND	-ITALY/SARDINIA	59.50	11.1	7
CANADA	-FINLAND	81.30	38.9	4	FINLAND	-NEW ZEALAND	59.30	38.9	4
CANADA	-HUNGARY	79.30	42.8	3	HUNGARY	-RUMANIA	59.00	8.0	8
ITALY/SARDINIA	-NEW ZEALAND	77.30	38.8	4	HUNGARY	-ITALY/SARDINIA	57.50	15.1	7
AUSTRALIA	-FINLAND	71.40	38.9	4	HUNGARY	-NEW ZEALAND	57.30	42.8	3
GREECE	-ITALY/SARDINIA	70.00	5.9	8	FINLAND	-RUMANIA	52.00	0.4	10
AUSTRALIA	-HUNGARY	69.40	42.8	3	FINLAND	-SOUTH AFRICA	50.70	38.9	4
ITALY/SARDINIA	-SOUTH AFRICA	68.70	38.8	4	HUNGARY	-SOUTH AFRICA	48.70	42.8	3
ITALY/SARDINIA	-YUGOSLAVIA/SERBIA	65.00	0.4	10					
				*** DECILE 9 ***					
BULGARIA	-CANADA	48.30	33.0	5	BULGARIA	-SOUTH AFRICA	17.70	33.0	5
ETHIOPIA	-FINLAND	47.00	0.3	10	MEXICO	-UNITED STATES	17.00	21.1	6
ETHIOPIA	-HUNGARY	45.00	0.2	10	CHILE	-PERU	13.00	54.5	2
BRAZIL	-FINLAND	43.00	2.5	9	GERMANY/PRUSSIA	-SAXONY	10.60	1.4	10
BULGARIA	-FINLAND	43.00	0.4	10	BAVARIA	-GERMANY/PRUSSIA	10.50	1.4	10
BRAZIL	-HUNGARY	41.00	6.5	8	GERMANY/PRUSSIA	-HANOVER	10.50	0.5	10
BULGARIA	-HUNGARY	41.00	4.4	9	BADEN	-GERMANY/PRUSSIA	10.10	1.4	10
BULGARIA	-GREECE	39.50	16.0	7	GERMANY/PRUSSIA	-HESSE ELECTORAL	10.10	1.4	10
AUSTRALIA	-BULGARIA	38.40	33.0	5	GERMANY/PRUSSIA	-HESSE GRAND DUCAL	10.10	1.4	10
AUSTRIA-HUNGARY	-GERMANY/PRUSSIA	30.00	1.4	10	GERMANY/PRUSSIA	-MECKLENBURG-SCHWERIN	10.10	1.4	10
BULGARIA	-NEW ZEALAND	26.30	33.0	5	GERMANY/PRUSSIA	-WUERTTEMBERG	10.10	1.4	10
BULGARIA	-PORTUGAL	21.00	31.0	6	BRAZIL	-BULGARIA	10.00	2.1	9
FRANCE	-MEXICO	20.00	57.7	2	DENMARK	-GERMANY/PRUSSIA	10.00	11.7	7
MOROCCO	-SPAIN	20.00	13.7	7	SPAIN	-UNITED STATES	10.00	3.7	9

13.4 - NATION PAIRS RANKED BY COMBINED DEATHS AS WARTIME OPPONENTS

*** DECILE 10 ***

		BATTLE DEATHS (000'S)	SHARED WAR MONTHS	WAR MONTH DECILE			BATTLE DEATHS (000'S)	SHARED WAR MONTHS	WAR MONTH DECILE
ISRAEL	-U.A.R.	8.20	5.0	8	FRANCE	-U.A.R.	3.01	0.2	10
CZECHOSLOVAKIA	-HUNGARY	8.00	3.6	9	ENGLAND	-IRAN	2.00	4.6	8
INDIA	-PAKISTAN	6.80	1.6	10	FRANCE	-PAPAL STATES	2.00	1.0	10
ITALY/SARDINIA	-SAXONY	4.60	1.4	10	GUATEMALA	-SALVADOR	1.70	2.4	9
BAVARIA	-ITALY/SARDINIA	4.50	1.4	10	AUSTRIA-HUNGARY	-PAPAL STATES	1.60	1.8	10
HANOVER	-ITALY/SARDINIA	4.50	0.5	10	PAPAL STATES	-TWO SICILIES	1.60	1.8	10
BADEN	-ITALY/SARDINIA	4.10	1.4	10	ARGENTINA	-BRAZIL	1.30	6.6	8
HESSE ELECTORAL	-ITALY/SARDINIA	4.10	1.4	10	CHINA	-INDIA	1.00	1.1	10
HESSE GRAND DUCAL	-ITALY/SARDINIA	4.10	1.4	10	COLOMBIA	-ECUADOR	1.00	0.5	10
ITALY/SARDINIA	-MECKLENBURG-SCHWERIN	4.10	1.4	10	FRANCE	-SPAIN	1.00	7.3	8
ITALY/SARDINIA	-WUERTTEMBERG	4.10	1.4	10	ITALY/SARDINIA	-PAPAL STATES	1.00	0.6	10
BOLIVIA	-CHILE	4.00	57.9	2	ITALY/SARDINIA	-TWO SICILIES	1.00	3.2	9
ISRAEL	-JORDAN	4.00	2.5	9	PERU	-SPAIN	0.90	3.8	9
ISRAEL	-SYRIA	4.00	2.5	9	GUATEMALA	-HONDURAS	0.70	1.8	10
AUSTRIA-HUNGARY	-DENMARK	3.50	3.6	9	HONDURAS	-NICARAGUA	0.70	2.1	9
IRAQ	-ISRAEL	3.50	2.5	9	NICARAGUA	-SALVADOR	0.70	2.1	9
ISRAEL	-LEBANON	3.50	2.5	9	CHILE	-SPAIN	0.40	6.5	8
ENGLAND	-U.A.R.	3.02	0.2	10					

13.5 - NATION PAIRS RANKED BY SHARED WAR MONTHS AS <u>OPPONENTS</u>

*** DECILE 1 ***

CHINA	-JAPAN	122.0	AUSTRALIA	-GERMANY/PRUSSIA	68.1
ENGLAND	-GERMANY/PRUSSIA	119.3	GERMANY/PRUSSIA	-NEW ZEALAND	68.1
RUSSIA	-TURKEY	91.2	GERMANY/PRUSSIA	-SOUTH AFRICA	68.0
GERMANY/PRUSSIA	-RUSSIA	86.7	CANADA	-GERMANY/PRUSSIA	67.9
FRANCE	-GERMANY/PRUSSIA	74.7	GREECE	-TURKEY	67.0
BULGARIA	-ENGLAND	68.6	JAPAN	-RUSSIA	64.7

*** DECILE 2 ***

GERMANY/PRUSSIA	-ITALY/SARDINIA	60.4	ITALY/SARDINIA	-TURKEY	54.4
GERMANY/PRUSSIA	-UNITED STATES	59.9	AUSTRIA-HUNGARY	-FRANCE	53.4
BULGARIA	-RUSSIA	58.8	TURKEY	-YUGOSLAVIA/SERBIA	52.6
BOLIVIA	-CHILE	57.9	BELGIUM	-GERMANY/PRUSSIA	51.9
FRANCE	-MEXICO	57.7	GERMANY/PRUSSIA	-YUGOSLAVIA/SERBIA	51.8
CHILE	-PERU	54.5	AUSTRIA-HUNGARY	-YUGOSLAVIA/SERBIA	51.2

*** DECILE 3 ***

AUSTRIA-HUNGARY	-BELGIUM	51.0	CANADA	-JAPAN	44.3
AUSTRIA-HUNGARY	-ENGLAND	51.0	ENGLAND	-JAPAN	44.3
GERMANY/PRUSSIA	-JAPAN	50.7	JAPAN	-NEW ZEALAND	44.3
AUSTRIA-HUNGARY	-JAPAN	50.4	JAPAN	-SOUTH AFRICA	44.3
BULGARIA	-UNITED STATES	50.4	JAPAN	-UNITED STATES	44.3
AUSTRIA-HUNGARY	-ITALY/SARDINIA	50.0	HUNGARY	-RUSSIA	43.6
ENGLAND	-TURKEY	48.6	BULGARIA	-JAPAN	43.5
FRANCE	-TURKEY	48.6	AUSTRALIA	-HUNGARY	42.8
BELGIUM	-TURKEY	48.5	CANADA	-HUNGARY	42.8
JAPAN	-TURKEY	48.5	ENGLAND	-HUNGARY	42.8
BULGARIA	-ITALY/SARDINIA	46.3	HUNGARY	-NEW ZEALAND	42.8
AUSTRALIA	-JAPAN	44.3	HUNGARY	-SOUTH AFRICA	42.8

*** DECILE 4 ***

CHINA	-FRANCE	42.6	ITALY/SARDINIA	-NEW ZEALAND	38.8
FINLAND	-RUSSIA	42.3	ITALY/SARDINIA	-SOUTH AFRICA	38.8
CHINA	-GERMANY/PRUSSIA	41.0	AUSTRALIA	-RUMANIA	38.1
AUSTRIA-HUNGARY	-RUSSIA	40.2	CANADA	-RUMANIA	38.1
ITALY/SARDINIA	-RUSSIA	40.1	ENGLAND	-RUMANIA	38.1
AUSTRALIA	-FINLAND	38.9	NEW ZEALAND	-RUMANIA	38.1
CANADA	-FINLAND	38.9	RUMANIA	-RUSSIA	38.1
ENGLAND	-FINLAND	38.9	RUMANIA	-SOUTH AFRICA	38.1
FINLAND	-NEW ZEALAND	38.9	CHINA	-HUNGARY	37.5
FINLAND	-SOUTH AFRICA	38.9	HUNGARY	-UNITED STATES	37.5
AUSTRALIA	-ITALY/SARDINIA	38.8	KOREA NORTH	-KOREA SOUTH	37.1
CANADA	-ITALY/SARDINIA	38.8	KOREA NORTH	-UNITED STATES	37.0
ENGLAND	-ITALY/SARDINIA	38.8	BULGARIA	-YUGOSLAVIA/SERBIA	36.6

13.5 - NATION PAIRS RANKED BY SHARED WAR MONTHS AS OPPONENTS

*** DECILE 5 ***

Nation	Nation	Months	Nation	Nation	Months
BOLIVIA	-PARAGUAY	35.9	CHINA	-ENGLAND	33.0
BELGIUM	-BULGARIA	35.6	CHINA	-KOREA SOUTH	33.0
BULGARIA	-FRANCE	35.6	CHINA	-PHILIPPINES	33.0
ENGLAND	-KOREA NORTH	35.0	CHINA	-TURKEY	33.0
KOREA NORTH	-PHILIPPINES	34.4	CHINA	-UNITED STATES	33.0
CHINA	-FINLAND	33.4	CHINA	-RUMANIA	32.6
FINLAND	-UNITED STATES	33.4	RUMANIA	-UNITED STATES	32.6
KOREA NORTH	-TURKEY	33.3	GERMANY/PRUSSIA	-PORTUGAL	32.4
AUSTRALIA	-BULGARIA	33.0	PORTUGAL	-TURKEY	32.4
BULGARIA	-CANADA	33.0	AUSTRIA-HUNGARY	-PORTUGAL	32.1
BULGARIA	-CHINA	33.0	AUSTRALIA	-CHINA	31.6
BULGARIA	-NEW ZEALAND	33.0	AUSTRALIA	-KOREA NORTH	31.6
BULGARIA	-SOUTH AFRICA	33.0			

*** DECILE 6 ***

Nation	Nation	Months	Nation	Nation	Months
CANADA	-CHINA	31.3	CHINA	-ETHIOPIA	26.9
CANADA	-KOREA NORTH	31.3	ETHIOPIA	-KOREA NORTH	26.9
BULGARIA	-PORTUGAL	31.0	CHINA	-COLOMBIA	25.7
FRANCE	-KOREA NORTH	30.8	COLOMBIA	-KOREA NORTH	25.7
BELGIUM	-CHINA	30.2	GERMANY/PRUSSIA	-RUMANIA	23.3
BELGIUM	-KOREA NORTH	30.2	ENGLAND	-RUSSIA	23.1
CHINA	-GREECE	30.2	FRANCE	-RUSSIA	23.1
CHINA	-HOLLAND	30.2	GERMANY/PRUSSIA	-GREECE	22.4
CHINA	-THAILAND	30.2	MEXICO	-UNITED STATES	21.1
GREECE	-KOREA NORTH	30.2	CHINA	-ITALY/SARDINIA	20.9
HOLLAND	-KOREA NORTH	30.2	ITALY/SARDINIA	-UNITED STATES	20.9
KOREA NORTH	-THAILAND	30.2	TURKEY	-UNITED STATES	18.9

*** DECILE 7 ***

Nation	Nation	Months	Nation	Nation	Months
ITALY/SARDINIA	-JAPAN	18.7	RUMANIA	-TURKEY	15.4
AUSTRIA-HUNGARY	-UNITED STATES	18.6	HUNGARY	-ITALY/SARDINIA	15.1
AUSTRIA-HUNGARY	-GREECE	16.2	MOROCCO	-SPAIN	13.7
BULGARIA	-RUMANIA	16.1	ETHIOPIA	-ITALY/SARDINIA	12.5
BULGARIA	-GREECE	16.0	DENMARK	-GERMANY/PRUSSIA	11.7
AUSTRIA-HUNGARY	-RUMANIA	15.4	FINLAND	-ITALY/SARDINIA	11.1

		*** DECILE 8 ***			
ITALY/SARDINIA	-RUMANIA	10.2	ARGENTINA	-BRAZIL	6.6
BRAZIL	-GERMANY/PRUSSIA	10.1	BRAZIL	-HUNGARY	6.5
BRAZIL	-JAPAN	10.1	CHILE	-SPAIN	6.5
FRANCE	-JAPAN	9.7	GREECE	-ITALY/SARDINIA	5.9
HUNGARY	-RUMANIA	8.0	ETHIOPIA	-GERMANY/PRUSSIA	5.3
BULGARIA	-GERMANY/PRUSSIA	7.9	ISRAEL	-U.A.R.	5.0
JAPAN	-RUMANIA	7.9	BULGARIA	-TURKEY	4.6
FRANCE	-SPAIN	7.3	ENGLAND	-IRAN	4.6
		*** DECILE 9 ***			
BULGARIA	-HUNGARY	4.4	FRANCE	-HUNGARY	3.0
JAPAN	-MONGOLIA	4.4	BRAZIL	-FINLAND	2.5
FRANCE	-WUERTTEMBERG	4.3	IRAQ	-ISRAEL	2.5
BADEN	-FRANCE	4.2	ISRAEL	-JORDAN	2.5
BAVARIA	-FRANCE	3.9	ISRAEL	-LEBANON	2.5
PERU	-SPAIN	3.8	ISRAEL	-SYRIA	2.5
SPAIN	-UNITED STATES	3.7	GUATEMALA	-SALVADOR	2.4
AUSTRIA-HUNGARY	-DENMARK	3.6	BRAZIL	-BULGARIA	2.1
CZECHOSLOVAKIA	-HUNGARY	3.6	HONDURAS	-NICARAGUA	2.1
ITALY/SARDINIA	-TWO SICILIES	3.2	NICARAGUA	-SALVADOR	2.1
		*** DECILE 10 ***			
GERMANY/PRUSSIA	-NORWAY	2.0	ITALY/SARDINIA	-SAXONY	1.4
AUSTRIA-HUNGARY	-PAPAL STATES	1.8	ITALY/SARDINIA	-WUERTTEMBERG	1.4
GUATEMALA	-HONDURAS	1.8	CHINA	-INDIA	1.1
PAPAL STATES	-TWO SICILIES	1.8	FRANCE	-PAPAL STATES	1.0
BRAZIL	-RUMANIA	1.6	GERMANY/PRUSSIA	-POLAND	0.9
INDIA	-PAKISTAN	1.6	ITALY/SARDINIA	-PAPAL STATES	0.6
AUSTRIA-HUNGARY	-GERMANY/PRUSSIA	1.4	COLOMBIA	-ECUADOR	0.5
BADEN	-GERMANY/PRUSSIA	1.4	GERMANY/PRUSSIA	-HANOVER	0.5
BADEN	-ITALY/SARDINIA	1.4	HANOVER	-ITALY/SARDINIA	0.5
BAVARIA	-GERMANY/PRUSSIA	1.4	BULGARIA	-FINLAND	0.4
BAVARIA	-ITALY/SARDINIA	1.4	ETHIOPIA	-RUMANIA	0.4
GERMANY/PRUSSIA	-HESSE ELECTORAL	1.4	FINLAND	-RUMANIA	0.4
GERMANY/PRUSSIA	-HESSE GRAND DUCAL	1.4	FRANCE	-ITALY/SARDINIA	0.4
GERMANY/PRUSSIA	-MECKLENBURG-SCHWERIN	1.4	ITALY/SARDINIA	-YUGOSLAVIA/SERBIA	0.4
GERMANY/PRUSSIA	-SAXONY	1.4	ETHIOPIA	-FINLAND	0.3
GERMANY/PRUSSIA	-WUERTTEMBERG	1.4	ENGLAND	-U.A.R.	0.2
HESSE ELECTORAL	-ITALY/SARDINIA	1.4	ETHIOPIA	-HUNGARY	0.2
HESSE GRAND DUCAL	-ITALY/SARDINIA	1.4	FRANCE	-U.A.R.	0.2
ITALY/SARDINIA	-MECKLENBURG-SCHWERIN	1.4	GERMANY/PRUSSIA	-HOLLAND	0.2

Thus, in order to find out more about traditional allies and enemies, we list in Table 13.6 the nations that have fought *alongside* one another at least twice, but have never fought *against* one another, and in Table 13.7, those which have fought on *opposite* sides at least twice, while never fighting on the *same* side. We chose this threshold of pair-wise war experience because we felt that a lower threshold—such as single partnership with no opposition—might yield a rather lengthy list with misleading results. To speak with greater confidence of traditional enmity and enduring friendship (as measured here), we need to go beyond a simple listing of single cases which may be nothing more than a chance occurrence. Alternatively, one might set some minimal threshold of war months or battle deaths, rather than mere frequency, and use that as the differentiating characteristic, but this hardly seems necessary in light of the figures presented in the earlier tables.

Of course, wars restricted to the magnitude or severity thresholds used here are only one of the many forms which inter-nation interaction may take, and fairly strong rivalries and friendships may well have been acted out in a variety of non-military (or low-level military) activities over the years. Certain pairs may never have fought against one another and yet may well turn out to have had relatively sustained relationships of antipathy during the period; some possible examples might be Russia and Sweden or the United States and Argentina. Likewise, certain pairs may never have fought alongside one another, while nevertheless enjoying a long and essentially cooperative relationship; such might be France and Switzerland, or Sweden and Finland. Finally, for nations that have never fought in the same war, with or against one another, we should not automatically assume that their paths have never crossed or that they have experienced little or no interdependence.

When we sort out our pairs according to these criteria, is the earlier impression of traditional friendships and hostilities further strengthened? In both Tables 13.6 and 13.7, we see most of the pairs that were top ranking on shared war months. It should be pointed out that each pair is listed twice (since the lists are short) and that, unless notated with a number following the pair in each of the tables, the number of times each pair was a partner or opponent is two. Of the 41 pairs who were partners at least twice and never opponents, only 8 were partners more than twice, and of the 18 pairs who were opponents at least two times without fighting on the same side, only 4 opposed each other more than twice. We also see that almost all of the relationships can be accounted for by the two World Wars. That is, if we were interested in nations that had no experience as enemies and some (at least two) experience as allies, and we eliminated the two World Wars, only 5 dyads of the 41 would remain: Baden-Bavaria, Baden-Wuerttemberg, Bavaria-Wuerttemberg, Salvador-Honduras, and England-France. As for pairs with no experience as allies and at least two experiences as enemies, eliminating the World Wars narrows that list down to seven pairs: Austria-Hungary–Italy (Sardinia), China–Japan, Denmark–Germany (Prussia), Guatemala–Salvador, Israel–U.A.R., Morocco–Spain, and Russia–Turkey.

13.6 - PAIRS OF NATIONS WITH TWO OR MORE WARTIME PARTNERSHIPS AND NO ENMITIES (N=41)

Nation	Partner	Count
AUSTRALIA	- BELGIUM	
	- CANADA	
	- ENGLAND	
	- ETHIOPIA	
	- FRANCE	
	- GREECE	
	- HOLLAND	
	- UNITED STATES	
BADEN	- BAVARIA	
	- WUERTTEMBERG	
BAVARIA	- BADEN	
	- WUERTTEMBERG	
BELGIUM	- AUSTRALIA	
	- CANADA	
	- ENGLAND	3
	- FRANCE	3
	- GREECE	
	- HOLLAND	
	- UNITED STATES	
CANADA	- AUSTRALIA	
	- BELGIUM	
	- ENGLAND	
	- ETHIOPIA	
	- FRANCE	
	- GREECE	
	- HOLLAND	
	- UNITED STATES	
ENGLAND	- AUSTRALIA	
	- BELGIUM	3
	- CANADA	
	- ETHIOPIA	
	- FRANCE	6
	- GREECE	3
	- HOLLAND	3
	- UNITED STATES	3
	- YUGOSLAVIA/SERBIA	
ETHIOPIA	- AUSTRALIA	
	- CANADA	
	- ENGLAND	
	- GREECE	
FRANCE	- AUSTRALIA	
	- BELGIUM	3
	- CANADA	
	- ENGLAND	6
	- GREECE	
	- HOLLAND	
	- RUMANIA	
	- UNITED STATES	3
GREECE	- AUSTRALIA	
	- BELGIUM	
	- CANADA	
	- ENGLAND	3
	- ETHIOPIA	
	- FRANCE	
	- RUMANIA	
	- UNITED STATES	
	- YUGOSLAVIA/SERBIA	4
HOLLAND	- AUSTRALIA	
	- BELGIUM	
	- CANADA	
	- ENGLAND	3
	- FRANCE	
HONDURAS	- SALVADOR	
MONGOLIA	- RUSSIA	
RUMANIA	- FRANCE	
	- GREECE	
	- YUGOSLAVIA/SERBIA	
RUSSIA	- MONGOLIA	
	- UNITED STATES	
SALVADOR	- HONDURAS	
UNITED STATES	- AUSTRALIA	
	- BELGIUM	
	- CANADA	
	- ENGLAND	3
	- FRANCE	3
	- GREECE	
	- RUSSIA	
WUERTTEMBERG	- BADEN	
	- BAVARIA	
YUGOSLAVIA/SERBIA	- ENGLAND	
	- GREECE	4
	- RUMANIA	

13.7 - PAIRS OF NATIONS WITH TWO OR MORE WARTIME ENMITIES AND NO PARTNERSHIPS (N=18)

AUSTRIA-HUNGARY	- ITALY/SARDINIA	4
BELGIUM	- GERMANY/PRUSSIA	
CHINA	- JAPAN	4
DENMARK	- GERMANY/PRUSSIA	
ENGLAND	- GERMANY/PRUSSIA	
ETHIOPIA	- ITALY/SARDINIA	
FINLAND	- RUSSIA	
FRANCE	- GERMANY/PRUSSIA	3
GERMANY/PRUSSIA	- BELGIUM	
	- DENMARK	
	- ENGLAND	
	- FRANCE	3
	- GREECE	
	- RUSSIA	
	- UNITED STATES	
	- YUGOSLAVIA/SERBIA	
GREECE	- GERMANY/PRUSSIA	
GUATEMALA	- SALVADOR	
HUNGARY	- RUSSIA	
ISRAEL	- U.A.R.	
ITALY/SARDINIA	- AUSTRIA-HUNGARY	4
	- ETHIOPIA	
JAPAN	- CHINA	4
	- MONGOLIA	
MONGOLIA	- JAPAN	
MOROCCO	- SPAIN	
RUSSIA	- FINLAND	
	- GERMANY/PRUSSIA	
	- HUNGARY	
	- TURKEY	5
SALVADOR	- GUATEMALA	
SPAIN	- MOROCCO	
TURKEY	- RUSSIA	5
U.A.R.	- ISRAEL	
UNITED STATES	- GERMANY/PRUSSIA	
YUGOSLAVIA/SERBIA	- GERMANY/PRUSSIA	

SUMMARY

In the *Statistics of Deadly Quarrels* (1960, pp. 196-99), Richardson reports that of the 186 total pairs of opposed belligerents in the wars from 1820 to 1929 which he examined, 89 (or 48 percent) had already fought against one another in the past, and that only 54 (or 29 percent) had been wartime allies at least once prior to warring against one another. While not dramatic, these figures certainly strengthen the impression of historical friends and enemies in the international system. Our results, using a somewhat more restricted set of wars, a longer time period, and a differing set of indicators, seem to point in a different direction. That is, of the 209 pairs who ever fought in opposition, 39 (or 19 percent) had fought against one another at least once before; but 44 (or 21 percent) had been *partners* on at least one occasion in the past. In order to look at a more restricted set of cases, let us exclude from the 449 pairs of nations which had *some* wartime experience as partners or enemies, the 313 one-time cases (of which 199 were single partnerships and 114 were single oppositions). Of the remaining 136 pairs, how consistent were their interaction patterns?

There were 95 pairs, for example, with some experience as opponents, but 77 of them also fought at least once on the *same* side. Moreover, 44 of these wartime alliances followed at least one occasion on which the partners had fought *against* one another. And of the 60 pairs whose first interaction was as enemies, 42 subsequently fought as allies; in 6 cases, they had fought twice against one another before joining forces as allies in combat. As for consistent friendships, the picture remains equally mixed. While 41 of the 136 pairs with some wartime partnership experience never fought against each other, the remaining 95 did; moreover, 8 of them ended up on opposing sides after two experiences as allies. And if we look at that even more restricted set of pairs—those 46 pairs with three or more joint wartime experiences—the pattern is equally irregular. Only 8 were always partners and 4 were always enemies, with the other pairs showing typically irregular alignments.

In sum, there seems to be only modest evidence in support of the notion that nations have highly consistent sets of fundamental relationships with one another. Whether that belief flows from some alleged continuity in national interests, the inexorable pressures of geography, or deep-seated cultural loves and hates, it hardly stands up. Most nations, despite occupying essentially the same piece of real estate and embracing essentially the same ethnic stock, show a remarkable flexibility in "selecting" their partners and adversaries. And it is probably this general *inconsistency* that makes the few remaining pairs of traditional allies and traditional enemies all the more outstanding and visible.

Be that as it may, the fact that the past century and a half reveals so small a number of traditional enmities offers some hope for the future. If most nations find it possible to cooperate with almost any other ones in wartime, such cooperation in the avoidance of war may not be as impossible to achieve as the pessimists might have us believe. And if almost none of them find it necessary to war against one another over and over, that, too, may offer some grounds for optimism.

Chapter 14
Victory, Defeat and Battle Deaths

Depending on one's point of view and theoretical interpretation of the evidence, those who guide the destinies of nations are seen as entering into war for a multitude of reasons and with a degree of choice ranging from great to infinitesimal. But regardless of the model preferred, almost all points of view recognize that the decision makers are partially influenced by their estimate of the consequences of going into, or when possible, postponing or avoiding the commitment to war. Whether the anticipated consequences of combat weigh more or less heavily than those associated with a nonwar option is, of course, an empirical question, and despite many case studies and a few multicase analyses, the evidence is far from complete. In principle, at least, these decisions (if and when they can be called that) could be more rational if some of the consequences of the prowar strategy were more readily estimated. That is, if those who decide for their nations were in a better position to not only predict who the "winner" will be, but to predict the losses which *all* must expect, there might be a reduced propensity toward war all around. Despite the discontinuities between past and future, owing to sweeping changes in everything from weapons technology to command and control procedures, it may well be that history has something to teach us.

In addition to providing statistical regularities in battle deaths and nation months over the interstate wars of the past century and a half, these data may also have some practical relevance for those cases in which war was not successfully avoided. As we pointed out in Chapter One, one of the major motives behind the Klingberg study (1966) for the United States War Department in World War Two was the possibility that casualty figures of the past might give some clue as to the point at which Japan might sue for peace. Klingberg's failure to find strong regularities and patterns *might* have been the result of his often incomplete and uncomparable casualty estimates. Given the better quality of the data and the greater similarity of the types of war presented here, the inquiry might profitably be conducted anew. Thus, the computations that follow might enable us to deal with three general questions.

First, when gross battle deaths reach a given level, does the losing side tend to sue for peace? Conversely, is there a battle death threshold at which the winning side tends to reduce its "war objectives" and entertain peace negotiations short of total victory or some other inflated set of aspirations? Second, are these thresholds to be found, not in absolute fatality figures, but in such normalized (or intensity) figures as battle deaths per month or per capita? Third, and perhaps most interestingly, does the critical figure lie in some ratio between combat fatalities of the victor and those of the vanquished?

Concerning the distinction between victor and vanquished, two possible weaknesses should be noted. First, we treat every nation that qualified as an active participant on the victorious side as a "victor," regardless of its contribution to that victory or the costs it sustained; the same holds for all those which fought on the vanquished side in these interstate wars. On occasion, some of the nations that we labeled victors suffered far more than the vanquished. Pyrrhic victors like Poland and Belgium in World War Two were defeated on the field of battle and returned only at war's end as political victors. Despite their total absorption by the vanquished, we consider them to have been part of the winning coalition which shared in the spoils in 1945.

Second, we offer no operational indicators of our own by which the victorious and defeated sides may be differentiated. We merely follow the consensus among the acknowledged specialists in deciding which side "won" each war. In other words, even if it turns out that there are systematic differences in the fatalities between victor and vanquished, it is not these which provide the basis for discerning winners and losers; as a matter of fact, that classification was made before the present body of data had been assembled and analyzed. While we had some difficulties in discerning a true victor in several of the 50 interstate wars, only one was judged to be a draw: the Korean War of 1950–1953. Although the United States and its allies repelled the initial invasion, the nature of the war and the criteria of victory changed dramatically when it was decided in the winter of 1950 to try to reunify all of Korea by force. Because the North Koreans and their Chinese allies repelled this advance into *their* territory and because the war terminated with a situation close to the status quo ante bellum, we classified the entire conflict as a draw. For those who disagree with our coding decision, and prefer to treat one side or the other as a victor, the condensed figures for the Korean conflict (number 46) are as follows:

	Battle Deaths (000's)	BD per NM	BD per 100,000 Pop.	Battle Death Ratios		
					BD ÷ BD	BD/Pop ÷ BD/Pop
S. Korea, UN	472.1	1063.5	115.9	S.Kor/N.Kor	.33	.46
N. Korea, China	1420.0	20256.8	249.3	N.Kor/S.Kor	3.01	2.15

In the following sections we present the raw figures, relative scores, and ratios that permit us both to compare the fatalities of the victorious and vanquished (as well as the initiating and responding) nations over time, and to ascertain whether there are any consistent casualty thresholds at which wars have had a high probability of terminating.

BATTLE DEATHS FOR OPPOSING SIDES IN INTERSTATE WARS

In attempting to generalize about the relative battle fatalities of the nations that "won" and those which "lost" in the interstate wars (extra-systemic wars are discussed later in this chapter) of the past century and a half, the first step is to list each of these wars and then show the most relevant severity and intensity figures for those which participated on the winning and losing sides. This we do in Table 14.1, with the code number of the war in the left-hand column and the names of the participating nations on the victorious and vanquished sides listed under the appropriate headings. Then, for each of these nations, we show its battle deaths in thousands, battle deaths per nation month, and battle deaths per 100,000 of the pre-war population. (We do not reproduce the ratio between armed force size and battle deaths, since as we noted in earlier chapters, this figure reflects the size of the army in existence at the beginning of the year in which the war started. In many of the wars under consideration, the battle death figures easily surpass the armed force size figures and thus lead to a misleading ratio.) At the end of each war's participant list, we present the totals for these three variables for the nations on the winning and losing sides, respectively.

With these severity and intensity figures, we can then compute, for each war, the two most revealing ratios between vanquished and victorious nations: first, the ratio of the defeated nations' battle deaths to those of the victors and, second, the ratio between their battle death per capita scores. Given the fact that in most wars the nation months are the same for all participants, there is little use in computing a ratio between the battle deaths per nation month scores; this would always be identical to, or close to, the straight battle death ratio. With these eight figures for each war, a basis for comparison becomes readily available.

As one reads down the columns of battle losses for each side in these 49 wars, and the ratios between them, it is apparent that the range is wide indeed; even without computing the standard deviation, it is evident that any measure of central tendency would be of little value. Neither the winning nor the losing side seems to show any consistent figure, in either raw battle death terms or in terms of the two ratios, and even among those nations on the same side (victor or vanquished) in a multilateral war, the differences are quite pronounced.

COMPARING BATTLE DEATHS OF VANQUISHED AND VICTORIOUS NATIONS

Given the above results, it might seem pointless to examine further the ratios between the losses of the opposing sides in interstate wars. But it is just possible that certain regularities are indeed concealed in the data, and could be uncovered in a separate listing of these ratios: that which compares: (a) the battle deaths sustained by the defeated side with those of the winning side; and (b) the losses when we control for population size. Thus, in Table 14.2, we present both of these ratios, ranked by the amount by which the defeated nations' fatalities exceeded those of the victors'.

The impression one again draws is that the ratios range widely indeed. In sheer battle fatalities, the defeated side lost from almost 17 times as many military personnel as the victor to less than half of the latter's. When we control for total population, the range increases even further. Second, there are quite a few interstate wars (14 of the 49) in which the victorious side actually sustains greater combat losses than the defeated side, as indicated by those ratios which are less than 1.00. Third, whether or not we control for population, there are a good many wars in which the losses of both sides are approximately equal.

Before assuming, however, that there really are no sharp and clear patterns in the ratio of vanquished-victorious battle losses, we should note how disparate this population of wars may be. Not only do the wars differ among themselves in terms of epoch, locale, duration, severity, intensity, and number of participants, but the latter also differ appreciably in terms of size, capability, organization, tactics, and technology. Therefore, if we were to subdivide the entire set of wars into subsets on the basis of such distinguishing characteristics, we might well find that the original range in the two victor-vanquished ratios becomes much smaller within each of these separate subsets. This, then, is what we have done in Table 14.3; for all interstate wars (excluding the Korean), we have computed and shown, for both battle death and battle death per capita ratios, the mean, median, range of ratios, standard deviation, and coefficient of variability. This last measure permits more valid comparision of the dispersion in data sets with quite different means and standard deviations. We then did the same for five specific subsets, looking only at battle death ratios. These subsets are as follows: (a) those which involved at least one major power and those which did not; (b) those which occurred in the nineteenth century and in the twentieth century; (c) those with 20,000 battle deaths or more, and those with less; (d) those which lasted 6 months or more, and those which were shorter; and (e) those which involved only one qualified participant on each side and those

14.1 - SEVERITY AND INTENSITY INDICATORS FOR VICTOR AND VANQUISHED IN EACH INTERSTATE WAR

WAR NO.	NATION NAME (VICTOR)	BATTLE DEATHS (000'S)	BATTLE DEATHS PER NATION MONTH	BATTLE DEATHS PER 100,000 POPULATION	NATION NAME (VANQUISHED)	BATTLE DEATHS (000'S)	BATTLE DEATHS PER NATION MONTH	BATTLE DEATHS PER 100,000 POPULATION	RATIOS: BATTLE DEATHS VANQ./ BATTLE DEATHS VICTOR	RATIOS: BATTLE DEATHS/POP VANQ.// BATTLE DEATHS/POP VICTOR
1	FRANCE	0.4	54.8	1.3	SPAIN	0.6	82.2	5.3	1.50	4.19
	(TOTAL)	0.4	54.8	1.3	(TOTAL)	0.6	82.2	5.3		
2	ENGLAND	0.1	800.0	0.3	TURKEY	3.0	30000.0	12.6	16.67	76.19
	FRANCE	0.0	400.0	0.1						
	RUSSIA	0.1	600.0	0.1						
	(TOTAL)	0.2	600.0	0.2	(TOTAL)	3.0	30000.0	12.6		
3	RUSSIA	50.0	2994.0	91.9	TURKEY	80.0	4790.4	334.7	1.60	3.64
	(TOTAL)	50.0	2994.0	91.9	(TOTAL)	80.0	4790.4	334.7		
4	UNITED STATES	11.0	521.3	47.6	MEXICO	6.0	284.4	80.0	0.55	1.68
	(TOTAL)	11.0	521.3	47.6	(TOTAL)	6.0	284.4	80.0		
5	AUSTRIA-HUNGARY	5.6	1191.5	16.3	ITALY/SARDINIA	3.4	723.4	69.4	0.61	4.25
	(TOTAL)	5.6	1191.5	16.3	(TOTAL)	3.4	723.4	69.4		
6	GERMANY/PRUSSIA	2.5	308.6	15.6	DENMARK	3.5	432.1	152.2	1.40	9.74
	(TOTAL)	2.5	308.6	15.6	(TOTAL)	3.5	432.1	152.2		
7	FRANCE	0.5	500.0	1.4	PAPAL STATES	1.5	833.3	51.7	2.14	54.01
	AUSTRIA-HUNGARY	0.1	55.6	0.3						
	TWO SICILIES	0.1	55.6	3.2						
	(TOTAL)	0.7	152.2	1.0	(TOTAL)	1.5	833.3	51.7		
8	BRAZIL	0.5	75.8	6.8	ARGENTINA	0.8	121.2	72.7	1.60	10.62
	(TOTAL)	0.5	75.8	6.8	(TOTAL)	0.8	121.2	72.7		
9	ENGLAND	22.0	952.4	76.7	RUSSIA	100.0	3533.6	140.4	0.61	0.82
	FRANCE	95.0	4112.6	263.9						
	ITALY/SARDINIA	2.2	160.6	42.3						
	TURKEY	45.0	1590.1	176.5						
	(TOTAL)	164.2	1861.7	172.1	(TOTAL)	100.0	3533.6	140.4		

14.1 - SEVERITY AND INTENSITY INDICATORS FOR VICTOR AND VANQUISHED IN EACH INTERSTATE WAR

WAR NO.	VICTOR: NATION NAME	VICTOR: BATTLE DEATHS (000'S)	VICTOR: BATTLE DEATHS PER NATION MONTH	VICTOR: BATTLE DEATHS PER 100,000 POPULATION	VANQUISHED: NATION NAME	VANQUISHED: BATTLE DEATHS (000'S)	VANQUISHED: BATTLE DEATHS PER NATION MONTH	VANQUISHED: BATTLE DEATHS PER 100,000 POPULATION	RATIOS: BATTLE DEATHS VANQ./ BATTLE DEATHS VICTOR	RATIOS: BATTLE DEATHS/POP VANQ.// BATTLE DEATHS/POP VICTOR
10	ENGLAND	0.5	108.7	1.7	IRAN	1.5	326.1	34.1	3.00	19.91
	(TOTAL)	0.5	108.7	1.7	(TOTAL)	1.5	326.1	34.1		
11	FRANCE	7.5	3260.9	20.2	AUSTRIA-HUNGARY	12.5	5000.0	36.1	1.25	1.53
	ITALY/SARDINIA	2.5	1000.0	48.1						
	(TOTAL)	10.0	2083.3	23.6	(TOTAL)	12.5	5000.0	36.1		
12	SPAIN	4.0	769.2	24.8	MOROCCO	6.0	1153.8	230.8	1.50	9.29
	(TOTAL)	4.0	769.2	24.8	(TOTAL)	6.0	1153.8	230.8		
13	ITALY/SARDINIA	0.3	500.0	1.4	PAPAL STATES	0.7	1166.7	22.6	2.33	16.48
	(TOTAL)	0.3	500.0	1.4	(TOTAL)	0.7	1166.7	22.6		
14	ITALY/SARDINIA	0.6	187.5	2.7	TWO SICILIES	0.4	125.0	4.1	0.67	1.51
	(TOTAL)	0.6	187.5	2.7	(TOTAL)	0.4	125.0	4.1		
15	MEXICO	12.0	208.0	142.9	FRANCE	8.0	138.6	21.2	0.67	0.15
	(TOTAL)	12.0	208.0	142.9	(TOTAL)	8.0	138.6	21.2		
16	COLOMBIA	0.3	600.0	10.0	ECUADOR	0.7	1400.0	50.0	2.33	5.00
	(TOTAL)	0.3	600.0	10.0	(TOTAL)	0.7	1400.0	50.0		
17	GERMANY/PRUSSIA	1.0	277.8	5.2	DENMARK	3.0	833.3	157.9	2.00	57.47
	AUSTRIA-HUNGARY	0.5	138.9	1.4						
	(TOTAL)	1.5	208.3	2.7	(TOTAL)	3.0	833.3	157.9		
18	PERU	0.6	157.9	18.8	SPAIN	0.3	46.2	1.8	0.43	0.13
	CHILE	0.1	15.4	5.6						
	(TOTAL)	0.7	68.0	14.0	(TOTAL)	0.3	46.2	1.8		

WAR NO.	VICTOR: NATION NAME	VICTOR: BATTLE DEATHS (000'S)	VICTOR: BATTLE DEATHS PER NATION MONTH	VICTOR: BATTLE DEATHS PER 100,000 POPULATION	VANQUISHED: NATION NAME	VANQUISHED: BATTLE DEATHS (000'S)	VANQUISHED: BATTLE DEATHS PER NATION MONTH	VANQUISHED: BATTLE DEATHS PER 100,000 POPULATION	RATIOS: BATTLE DEATHS VANQ./ BATTLE DEATHS VICTOR	RATIOS: BATTLE DEATHS/POP VANQ.// BATTLE DEATHS/POP VICTOR
19	GERMANY/PRUSSIA	10.0	7142.9	42.4	HANOVER	0.5	1000.0	500.0	1.58	1.50
	ITALY/SARDINIA	4.0	2857.1	17.9	BAVARIA	0.5	357.1	10.4		
					BADEN	0.1	71.4	7.1		
					SAXONY	0.6	428.6	25.0		
					WUERTTEMBERG	0.1	71.4	5.6		
					HESSE ELECTORAL	0.1	71.4	14.3		
					HESSE GRAND DUCAL	0.1	71.4	12.5		
					MECKLENBURG-SCHWERIN	0.1	71.4	16.7		
					AUSTRIA-HUNGARY	20.0	14285.7	56.2		
	(TOTAL)	14.0	5000.0	30.5	(TOTAL)	22.1	1888.9	45.9		
20	BAVARIA	5.5	1410.3	112.2	FRANCE	140.0	19178.1	359.0	2.95	3.51
	GERMANY/PRUSSIA	40.0	5479.4	104.4						
	BADEN	1.0	238.1	66.7						
	WUERTTEMBERG	1.0	232.6	55.6						
	(TOTAL)	47.5	2411.2	102.2	(TOTAL)	140.0	19178.1	359.0		
21	RUSSIA	120.0	13636.4	127.9	TURKEY	165.0	18750.0	585.1	1.37	4.57
	(TOTAL)	120.0	13636.4	127.9	(TOTAL)	165.0	18750.0	585.1		
22	CHILE	3.0	51.8	150.0	PERU	10.0	183.5	370.4	3.67	1.47
					BOLIVIA	1.0	17.3	43.5		
	(TOTAL)	3.0	51.8	150.0	(TOTAL)	11.0	97.9	220.0		
23	FRANCE	2.1	178.0	5.5	CHINA	10.0	847.5	2.3	4.76	0.42
	(TOTAL)	2.1	178.0	5.5	(TOTAL)	10.0	847.5	2.3		
24	SALVADOR	0.2	333.3	28.6	GUATEMALA	0.8	1333.3	61.5	4.00	2.15
	(TOTAL)	0.2	333.3	28.6	(TOTAL)	0.8	1333.3	61.5		
25	JAPAN	5.0	625.0	12.5	CHINA	10.0	1250.0	2.3	2.00	0.18
	(TOTAL)	5.0	625.0	12.5	(TOTAL)	10.0	1250.0	2.3		

14.1 - SEVERITY AND INTENSITY INDICATORS FOR VICTOR AND VANQUISHED IN EACH INTERSTATE WAR

WAR NO.	NATION NAME (VICTOR)	BATTLE DEATHS (000'S)	BATTLE DEATHS PER NATION MONTH	BATTLE DEATHS PER 100,000 POPULATION	NATION NAME (VANQUISHED)	BATTLE DEATHS (000'S)	BATTLE DEATHS PER NATION MONTH	BATTLE DEATHS PER 100,000 POPULATION	RATIOS: BATTLE DEATHS VANQ./ BATTLE DEATHS VICTOR	RATIOS: BATTLE DEATHS/POP VANQ.// BATTLE DEATHS/POP VICTOR
26	TURKEY	1.4	451.6	5.8	GREECE	0.6	193.5	25.0	0.43	4.34
	(TOTAL)	1.4	451.6	5.8	(TOTAL)	0.6	193.5	25.0		
27	UNITED STATES	5.0	1351.4	6.6	SPAIN	5.0	1351.4	27.2	1.00	4.13
	(TOTAL)	5.0	1351.4	6.6	(TOTAL)	5.0	1351.4	27.2		
28	JAPAN	85.0	4404.1	180.5	RUSSIA	45.0	2331.6	32.0	0.53	0.18
	(TOTAL)	85.0	4404.1	180.5	(TOTAL)	45.0	2331.6	32.0		
29	GUATEMALA	0.4	222.2	21.1	HONDURAS	0.3	166.7	42.9	1.50	1.58
					SALVADOR	0.3	166.7	27.3		
	(TOTAL)	0.4	222.2	21.1	(TOTAL)	0.6	166.7	33.3		
30	NICARAGUA	0.4	190.5	66.7	HONDURAS	0.3	142.9	42.9	1.50	0.50
					SALVADOR	0.3	142.9	27.3		
	(TOTAL)	0.4	190.5	66.7	(TOTAL)	0.6	142.9	33.3		
31	SPAIN	2.0	235.3	10.3	MOROCCO	8.0	941.2	160.0	4.00	15.60
	(TOTAL)	2.0	235.3	10.3	(TOTAL)	8.0	941.2	160.0		
32	ITALY/SARDINIA	6.0	472.4	17.2	TURKEY	14.0	1102.4	56.5	2.33	3.28
	(TOTAL)	6.0	472.4	17.2	(TOTAL)	14.0	1102.4	56.5		
33	YUGOSLAVIA/SERBIA	15.0	3658.5	517.2	TURKEY	30.0	4918.0	136.4	0.58	0.26
	GREECE	5.0	819.7	185.2						
	BULGARIA	32.0	7804.9	744.2						
	(TOTAL)	52.0	3636.4	525.3	(TOTAL)	30.0	4918.0	136.4		
34	YUGOSLAVIA/SERBIA	18.5	18500.0	411.1	BULGARIA	18.0	18000.0	375.0	0.42	2.89
	GREECE	2.5	2500.0	92.6						
	RUMANIA	1.5	2142.9	21.1						
	TURKEY	20.0	40000.0	108.1						
	(TOTAL)	42.5	13281.2	129.6	(TOTAL)	18.0	18000.0	375.0		

WAR NO.	VICTOR: NATION NAME	BATTLE DEATHS (000'S)	BATTLE DEATHS PER NATION MONTH	BATTLE DEATHS PER 100,000 POPULATION	VANQUISHED: NATION NAME	BATTLE DEATHS (000'S)	BATTLE DEATHS PER NATION MONTH	BATTLE DEATHS PER 100,000 POPULATION	RATIOS: BATTLE DEATHS VANQ./ BATTLE DEATHS VICTOR	RATIOS: BATTLE DEATHS/POP VANQ.// BATTLE DEATHS/POP VICTOR
35	UNITED STATES	126.0	6666.7	131.2	GERMANY/PRUSSIA	1800.0	35019.5	2686.6	0.64	2.06
	ENGLAND	908.0	17734.4	1965.4	AUSTRIA-HUNGARY	1200.0	23437.5	2264.2		
	BELGIUM	87.5	1705.7	1151.3	BULGARIA	14.0	393.3	291.7		
	FRANCE	1350.0	26315.8	3292.7	TURKEY	325.0	6701.0	1756.8		
	PORTUGAL	7.0	216.0	112.9						
	ITALY/SARDINIA	650.0	15587.5	1846.6						
	YUGOSLAVIA/SERBIA	48.0	932.0	1066.7						
	GREECE	5.0	303.0	185.2						
	RUMANIA	335.0	21753.2	4718.3						
	RUSSIA	1700.0	42288.6	1049.4						
	JAPAN	0.3	5.9	0.6						
	(TOTAL)	5216.8	12388.5	1129.4	(TOTAL)	3339.0	17884.3	2330.1		
36	CZECHOSLOVAKIA	2.0	555.6	15.4	HUNGARY	6.0	1666.7	75.0	1.20	4.35
	RUMANIA	3.0	833.3	18.8						
	(TOTAL)	5.0	694.4	17.2	(TOTAL)	6.0	1666.7	75.0		
37	TURKEY	20.0	484.3	181.8	GREECE	30.0	726.4	1111.1	1.50	6.11
	(TOTAL)	20.0	484.3	181.8	(TOTAL)	30.0	726.4	1111.1		
38	JAPAN	10.0	602.4	15.4	CHINA	50.0	3012.0	9.5	5.00	0.62
	(TOTAL)	10.0	602.4	15.4	(TOTAL)	50.0	3012.0	9.5		
39	PARAGUAY	50.0	1392.8	5555.6	BOLIVIA	80.0	2228.4	3200.0	1.60	0.58
	(TOTAL)	50.0	1392.8	5555.6	(TOTAL)	80.0	2228.4	3200.0		
40	ITALY/SARDINIA	4.0	555.6	9.4	ETHIOPIA	16.0	2222.2	160.0	4.00	17.04
	(TOTAL)	4.0	555.6	9.4	(TOTAL)	16.0	2222.2	160.0		
41	JAPAN	250.0	4708.1	360.2	CHINA	750.0	14124.3	139.6	3.00	0.39
	(TOTAL)	250.0	4708.1	360.2	(TOTAL)	750.0	14124.3	139.6		

14.1 - SEVERITY AND INTENSITY INDICATORS FOR VICTOR AND VANQUISHED IN EACH INTERSTATE WAR

WAR NO.	VICTOR: NATION NAME	VICTOR: BATTLE DEATHS (000'S)	VICTOR: BATTLE DEATHS PER NATION MONTH	VICTOR: BATTLE DEATHS PER 100,000 POPULATION	VANQUISHED: NATION NAME	VANQUISHED: BATTLE DEATHS (000'S)	VANQUISHED: BATTLE DEATHS PER NATION MONTH	VANQUISHED: BATTLE DEATHS PER 100,000 POPULATION	RATIOS: BATTLE DEATHS VANQ./ BATTLE DEATHS VICTOR	RATIOS: BATTLE DEATHS/POP VANQ.// BATTLE DEATHS/POP VICTOR
42	RUSSIA	1.0	238.1	0.6	JAPAN	15.0	3571.4	21.2	3.75	9.09
	MONGOLIA	3.0	714.3	500.0						
	(TOTAL)	4.0	476.2	2.3	(TOTAL)	15.0	3571.4	21.2		
43	UNITED STATES	408.3	9216.7	314.1	GERMANY/PRUSSIA	3500.0	51319.6	4441.6	0.48	2.41
	CANADA	39.3	552.0	344.7	HUNGARY	40.0	934.6	434.8		
	BRAZIL	1.0	99.0	2.5	ITALY/SARDINIA	60.0	1546.4	137.6		
	ENGLAND	270.0	3781.5	568.4	BULGARIA	9.0	272.7	142.9		
	HOLLAND	6.2	31000.0	71.3	RUMANIA	290.0	7611.5	1450.0		
	BELGIUM	9.6	16000.0	114.3	FINLAND	42.0	1079.7	1076.9		
	FRANCE	210.0	10824.7	510.9	JAPAN	1000.0	22573.4	1416.4		
	POLAND	320.0	355555.6	916.9						
	ITALY/SARDINIA	17.5	935.8	40.1						
	YUGOSLAVIA/SERBIA	5.0	12500.0	32.5						
	GREECE	10.0	1694.9	140.8						
	BULGARIA	1.0	126.6	15.9						
	RUMANIA	10.0	1265.8	50.0						
	RUSSIA	7500.0	160599.6	4398.8						
	NORWAY	2.0	1000.0	69.0						
	ETHIOPIA	5.0	943.4	50.0						
	SOUTH AFRICA	8.7	122.0	87.0						
	CHINA	1350.0	30474.0	249.5						
	MONGOLIA	3.0	15000.0	500.0						
	AUSTRALIA	29.4	411.8	432.4						
	NEW ZEALAND	17.3	242.3	1081.2						
	(TOTAL)	10223.3	17888.6	883.4	(TOTAL)	4941.0	16248.0	2126.1		
44	RUSSIA	50.0	14705.9	29.3	FINLAND	40.0	11764.7	1025.6	0.80	34.97
	(TOTAL)	50.0	14705.9	29.3	(TOTAL)	40.0	11764.7	1025.6		
45	ISRAEL	3.0	638.3	214.3	IRAQ	0.5	200.0	10.9	1.67	0.08
					U.A.R.	2.0	425.5	10.4		
					SYRIA	1.0	400.0	32.3		
					LEBANON	0.5	200.0	41.7		
					JORDAN	1.0	400.0	76.9		
	(TOTAL)	3.0	638.3	214.3	(TOTAL)	5.0	340.1	17.0		

WAR NO.	NATION NAME	VICTOR: BATTLE DEATHS (000'S)	VICTOR: BATTLE DEATHS PER NATION MONTH	VICTOR: BATTLE DEATHS PER 100,000 POPULATION	NATION NAME	VANQUISHED: BATTLE DEATHS (000'S)	VANQUISHED: BATTLE DEATHS PER NATION MONTH	VANQUISHED: BATTLE DEATHS PER 100,000 POPULATION	RATIOS: BATTLE DEATHS VANQ./ BATTLE DEATHS VICTOR	RATIOS: BATTLE DEATHS/POP VANQ.// BATTLE DEATHS/POP VICTOR
47	RUSSIA	7.0	8750.0	3.5	HUNGARY	25.0	31250.0	255.1	3.57	72.81
	(TOTAL)	7.0	8750.0	3.5	(TOTAL)	25.0	31250.0	255.1		
48	ENGLAND	0.0	100.0	0.0	U.A.R.	3.0	10000.0	12.9	13.04	54.47
	FRANCE	0.0	50.0	0.0						
	ISRAEL	0.2	666.7	10.5						
	(TOTAL)	0.2	328.6	0.2	(TOTAL)	3.0	10000.0	12.9		
49	CHINA	0.5	454.5	0.1	INDIA	0.5	454.5	0.1	1.00	1.46
	(TOTAL)	0.5	454.5	0.1	(TOTAL)	0.5	454.5	0.1		
50	PAKISTAN	3.8	2375.0	3.3	INDIA	3.0	1875.0	0.6	0.79	0.18
	(TOTAL)	3.8	2375.0	3.3	(TOTAL)	3.0	1875.0	0.6		

14.2 - INTERSTATE WARS RANKED BY VANQUISHED/VICTOR BATTLE DEATH RATIOS

BATTLE DEATHS			BATTLE DEATHS/POPULATION		
RANK	RATIO	WAR NAME AND NUMBER	RANK	RATIO	WAR NAME AND NUMBER
1.0	16.67	2 NAVARINO BAY	1.0	76.19	2 NAVARINO BAY
2.0	13.04	48 SINAI	2.0	72.81	47 RUSSO-HUNGARIAN
3.0	5.00	38 MANCHURIAN	3.0	57.47	17 SECOND SCHLESWIG-HOLSTEIN
4.0	4.76	23 SINO-FRENCH	4.0	54.47	48 SINAI
6.0	4.00	24 CENTRAL AMERICAN	5.0	54.01	7 ROMAN REPUBLIC
6.0	4.00	31 SPANISH-MOROCCAN	6.0	34.97	44 RUSSO-FINNISH
6.0	4.00	40 ITALO-ETHIOPIAN	7.0	19.91	10 ANGLO-PERSIAN
8.0	3.75	42 RUSSO-JAPANESE	8.0	17.04	40 ITALO-ETHIOPIAN
9.0	3.67	22 PACIFIC	9.0	16.48	13 ITALO-ROMAN
10.0	3.57	47 RUSSO-HUNGARIAN	10.0	15.60	31 SPANISH-MOROCCAN
11.5	3.00	10 ANGLO-PERSIAN	11.0	10.62	8 LA PLATA
11.5	3.00	41 SINO-JAPANESE	12.0	9.74	6 FIRST SCHLESWIG-HOLSTEIN
13.0	2.95	20 FRANCO-PRUSSIAN	13.0	9.29	12 SPANISH-MOROCCAN
15.0	2.33	13 ITALO-ROMAN	14.0	9.09	42 RUSSO-JAPANESE
15.0	2.33	16 ECUADORIAN-COLOMBIAN	15.0	6.11	37 GRECO-TURKISH
15.0	2.33	32 ITALO-TURKISH	16.0	5.00	16 ECUADORIAN-COLOMBIAN
17.0	2.14	7 ROMAN REPUBLIC	17.0	4.57	21 RUSSO-TURKISH
18.5	2.00	17 SECOND SCHLESWIG-HOLSTEIN	18.0	4.35	36 HUNGARIAN-ALLIES
18.5	2.00	25 SINO-JAPANESE	19.0	4.34	26 GRECO-TURKISH
20.0	1.67	45 PALESTINE	20.0	4.25	5 AUSTRO-SARDINIAN
22.0	1.60	3 RUSSO-TURKISH	21.0	4.19	1 FRANCO-SPANISH
22.0	1.60	8 LA PLATA	22.0	4.13	27 SPANISH-AMERICAN
22.0	1.60	39 CHACO	23.0	3.64	3 RUSSO-TURKISH
24.0	1.58	19 SEVEN WEEKS	24.0	3.51	20 FRANCO-PRUSSIAN
27.0	1.50	1 FRANCO-SPANISH	25.0	3.28	32 ITALO-TURKISH
27.0	1.50	12 SPANISH-MOROCCAN	26.0	2.89	34 SECOND BALKAN
27.0	1.50	29 CENTRAL AMERICAN	27.0	2.41	43 WORLD WAR II
27.0	1.50	30 CENTRAL AMERICAN	28.0	2.15	24 CENTRAL AMERICAN
27.0	1.50	37 GRECO-TURKISH	29.0	2.06	35 WORLD WAR I
30.0	1.40	6 FIRST SCHLESWIG-HOLSTEIN	30.0	1.68	4 MEXICAN-AMERICAN
31.0	1.37	21 RUSSO-TURKISH	31.0	1.58	29 CENTRAL AMERICAN
32.0	1.25	11 ITALIAN UNIFICATION	32.0	1.53	11 ITALIAN UNIFICATION
33.0	1.20	36 HUNGARIAN-ALLIES	33.0	1.51	14 ITALO-SICILIAN
34.5	1.00	27 SPANISH-AMERICAN	34.0	1.50	19 SEVEN WEEKS
34.5	1.00	49 SINO-INDIAN	35.0	1.47	22 PACIFIC
36.0	0.80	44 RUSSO-FINNISH	36.0	1.46	49 SINO-INDIAN
37.0	0.79	50 SECOND KASHMIR	37.0	0.82	9 CRIMEAN
38.5	0.67	14 ITALO-SICILIAN	38.0	0.62	38 MANCHURIAN
38.5	0.67	15 FRANCO-MEXICAN	39.0	0.58	39 CHACO
40.0	0.64	35 WORLD WAR I	40.0	0.50	30 CENTRAL AMERICAN
41.0	0.61	9 CRIMEAN	41.0	0.42	23 SINO-FRENCH
42.0	0.61	5 AUSTRO-SARDINIAN	42.0	0.39	41 SINO-JAPANESE
43.0	0.58	33 FIRST BALKAN	43.0	0.26	33 FIRST BALKAN
44.0	0.55	4 MEXICAN-AMERICAN	44.0	0.18	50 SECOND KASHMIR
45.0	0.53	28 RUSSO-JAPANESE	45.0	0.18	25 SINO-JAPANESE
46.0	0.48	43 WORLD WAR II	46.0	0.18	28 RUSSO-JAPANESE
47.5	0.43	18 SPANISH-CHILEAN	47.0	0.15	15 FRANCO-MEXICAN
47.5	0.43	26 GRECO-TURKISH	48.0	0.13	18 SPANISH-CHILEAN
49.0	0.42	34 SECOND BALKAN	49.0	0.08	45 PALESTINE

which were multilateral. Other bases of subdividing our population are, of course, possible, depending on one's theoretical concerns, but this range should suffice for many needs.

In examining these figures, we must again note that the standard deviation in many of them is sufficiently large to make one question the validity of the ratios. If, however, we concentrate on a few particular subsets, a more consistent pattern emerges. The wars with more than 20,000 battle dead, those lasting 6 or more months, and those that were purely bilateral all show very small standard deviations (1.33, 1.44, and 1.35), while those which were less severe, shorter, and multilateral all show larger spreads. Moreover, those with the small dispersion around the mean also show a very consistent mean ratio of vanquished to victor battle deaths: 1.72, 1.95, and 1.98. If we construct a combined subset by looking at the 19 wars that were bilateral and satisfied either of the other two criteria (6 or more months; 20,000 or more deaths), the standard deviation is 1.43 and the mean battle death ratio is 2.20. However, the subset of the 11 wars that were bilateral, less than 6 months long, and had fewer than 20,000

14.3 CENTRAL TENDENCY AND DISPERSION IN THE DISTRIBUTION OF VANQUISHED/VICTOR BATTLE DEATH RATIOS

	N	Mean	Median	Range	Standard Deviation	Coefficient of Variability (*V*): s.d./mean
Interstate wars	49	2.36	1.50	.42–16.67	2.91	1.23
Interstate wars, battle death per capita ratios	49	11.59	3.50	.08–88.33	20.25	1.75
Major power wars	29	2.87	1.60	.48–16.67	3.60	1.25
Non-major power wars	20	1.61	1.50	.42–4.00	1.12	.70
19th century wars	27	2.32	1.58	.43–16.67	3.08	1.33
20th century wars	22	2.41	1.50	.42–13.04	2.75	1.14
Wars with 20,000 or more battle deaths	20	1.72	1.44	.42–5.00	1.33	.77
Wars with fewer than 20,000 battle deaths	29	2.79	1.60	.43–16.67	3.58	1.28
Wars of 6 months duration or longer	24	1.95	1.55	.43–5.00	1.44	.73
Wars of less than 6 months duration	25	2.75	1.50	.42–16.67	3.82	1.39
Bilateral wars	30	1.98	1.55	.43–5.00	1.35	.68
Multilateral wars	19	2.95	1.50	.42–16.67	4.36	1.48

battle deaths were even more concentrated, with a standard deviation of 1.16 around a mean of 1.61. The 10 wars that were bilateral, longer than 6 months, *and* resulted in at least 20,000 deaths also showed a small dispersion, with a standard deviation of 1.44 around the mean of 2.16. Interestingly, 8 of these 10 wars were major power wars.

The much higher means and standard deviations of subsets such as the multilateral, less severe, and shorter wars suggest not only a greater range in battle death ratios but also that the victors were able to keep their losses relatively lower vis-à-vis those of the vanquished side. However, an examination of the actual ratios as ranked in Table 14.2 indicates that the very extreme ratios of 2 wars account for much of the dispersion reported in those rows of Table 14.3: war number 2 (Navarino Bay) and war number 48 (Sinai), were both very short, multilateral, and resulted in a very few battle deaths for the victors, but a proportionally much higher number for the vanquished. Without these 2 wars' ratios, the mean for the other 47 interstate wars' battle death ratios would be only 1.83, with a quite low standard deviation of 1.25.

Another way of interpreting these ratios is to divide the wars into those which had a given range of battle death and battle death per capita ratios. A brief summary reveals even more clearly that few generalizations can be made about the relationship between casualty levels and war outcome.

There were 12 wars in which the vanquished lost 3 or more times as many military personnel as the victor(s), that is, the battle death ratios were equal to or greater than 3.00; these 12 were distributed nearly equally between the dichotomies presented in Table 14.3: longer or shorter than 6 months, bilateral or multilateral, etc. However, 9 of these 12 were major power wars. A closer examination of a slightly larger subset of wars—those with ratios at or above the mean of 2.36—shows that 12 of the 16 wars in this range are major power wars, and of these 12, 10 involved major powers who were victorious over a non-major power, while the other 2 saw a major power with allies defeat an unallied major power. Similarly, with the 12 wars having a battle death per capita vanquished/victor ratio at or above the mean of 11.59, the highest 10 were major power victors versus non-major powers, while the 11th ranking ratio represents a central system member (Spain) victorious over a peripheral system member (Morocco).

There were 21 interstate wars with vanquished/victor battle death ratios ranging from 1.01 to 2.99, and 16 wars in which the victors lost as many or more in battle than the vanquished (ratios of 1.00 or less); these subsets are very evenly distributed between the dichotomies, including that of major versus non-major power. The only other distribution of note involves again the per capita ratios, which are so widely spread as to suggest only very cautious generalizations: of the 13 wars in which the victors lost as many or more military personnel per capita of total population (ratios of 1.00 or less), 10 wars were of 6 months or more in duration, suggesting perhaps that there is a greater chance for a war to be costly to the victors in terms of per capita losses if the war is quite long. This generalization gains some support from the fact that, of the 14 interstate wars lasting a year or more, 7 have vanquished/victor battle death per capita ratios of less than 1.00, and 6 fall within the range of 1.01 to 4.16—all well below the mean ratio of 11.59.

We will return to this type of generalization in our concluding remarks, in the context of our search for the relationship between battle fatalities and the termination of war.

SUCCESS, FAILURE, AND BATTLE DEATHS IN EXTRA-SYSTEMIC WARS

So far in this chapter we have looked only at interstate wars, and have ignored the problem of wars that involved a system member on one side, versus an independent political entity which is not a qualified system member, or versus a non-independent entity. Turning to these wars, it will be recalled that battle death figures were not gathered for the non-system members, making it impossible to calculate victor-vanquished comparisons in the sense used above. On the other hand, an equally important question is whether or not the absolute and relative fatality scores of the system members reveal any significant differences between those cases in which they were able to more or less impose their will on their non-member adversaries (that is, "win") and those in which that military effort was largely unsuccessful. By again following the consensus among scholarly specialists, we can arrive at an intuitively satisfactory classification of the imperial and colonial war cases, in order to see whether there is any discernible relationship between a system member's success or failure in these types of wars and the absolute, per war month, and per capita battle deaths it sustained. While in most of these extra-systemic conflicts there was indeed consensus among historians regarding the victory or defeat of the system member involved, we feel a special note should be made about the ambiguous Russian Nationalities war of 1917–1921 (war number 85). We classified Russia as the loser in this war, although Russia won on many of the widespread battle fronts. A more detailed description of this conflict is given in Appendix B, where we list the sources from which we gathered our data.

In Table 14.4, then, we first list those 28 extra-systemic wars in which the system

14.4 - BATTLE DEATHS OF VICTORIOUS AND VANQUISHED SYSTEM MEMBERS IN EXTRA-SYSTEMIC WARS

WAR NO. AND NAME OF SYSTEM MEMBER(S)	BATTLE DEATHS (000'S)	BATTLE DEATHS PER WAR MONTH	BATTLE DEATHS PER MILLION POPULATION
VICTORS (N=28)			
51 ENGLAND	2.00	289.9	98.0
53 ENGLAND	15.00	515.5	684.9
54 HOLLAND	15.00	266.9	2542.4
55 RUSSIA	5.00	294.1	94.7
56 RUSSIA	15.00	1807.2	265.0
59 ENGLAND	20.00	413.2	775.2
60 ENGLAND	0.01	3.8	0.4
TURKEY	10.00	3225.8	416.7
(COMBINED)	10.01	1756.1	199.0
62 ENGLAND	1.50	517.2	55.6
63 AUSTRIA-HUNGARY	45.00	4054.1	1312.0
RUSSIA	14.50	14500.0	212.0
(COMBINED)	59.50	4917.4	579.4
64 ENGLAND	1.50	294.1	54.9
66 ENGLAND	3.50	152.8	119.0
68 RUSSIA	5.00	335.6	64.9
69 BRAZIL	100.00	1572.3	8474.6
ARGENTINA	10.00	166.9	5263.2
(COMBINED)	110.00	890.7	8029.2
70 SPAIN	100.00	892.1	6024.1
71 HOLLAND	6.00	92.0	1621.6
73 AUSTRIA-HUNGARY	3.50	1666.7	90.9

14.4 - BATTLE DEATHS OF VICTORIOUS AND VANQUISHED SYSTEM MEMBERS IN EXTRA-SYSTEMIC WARS

WAR NO. AND NAME OF SYSTEM MEMBER(S)	BATTLE DEATHS (000'S)	BATTLE DEATHS PER WAR MONTH	BATTLE DEATHS PER MILLION POPULATION
74 ENGLAND	4.00	219.8	118.0
75 ENGLAND	3.50	614.0	102.3
76 FRANCE	4.50	175.1	118.7
79 FRANCE	6.00	618.6	156.2
82 SPAIN	2.00	86.6	109.9
83 UNITED STATES	4.50	110.0	59.2
84 ENGLAND	22.00	696.2	531.4
86 FRANCE	4.00	296.3	98.3
SPAIN	25.00	428.8	1136.4
(COMBINED)	29.00	403.9	462.5
87 FRANCE	4.00	178.6	98.3
90 FRANCE	1.50	74.3	37.5
91 INDIA	1.50	104.9	3.9
93 CHINA	40.00	1089.9	65.6

14.4 - BATTLE DEATHS OF VICTORIOUS AND VANQUISHED SYSTEM MEMBERS IN EXTRA-SYSTEMIC WARS

WAR NO. AND NAME OF SYSTEM MEMBER(S)	BATTLE DEATHS (000'S)	BATTLE DEATHS PER WAR MONTH	BATTLE DEATHS PER MILLION POPULATION
VANQUISHED (N=15)			
52 TURKEY	15.00	176.3	607.3
57 TURKEY	10.00	729.9	432.9
58 MEXICO	1.00	149.3	129.9
61 PERU	1.00	1000.0	769.2
65 TURKEY	5.00	1470.6	198.4
67 TURKEY	3.00	232.6	114.9
72 TURKEY	10.00	467.3	354.6
77 ENGLAND	20.00	505.1	568.2
78 YUGOSLAVIA/SERBIA	2.00	1666.7	1052.6
80 SPAIN	50.00	1340.5	2762.4
81 ITALY/SARDINIA	9.00	857.1	287.5
85 RUSSIA	50.00	1272.3	308.6
88 ENGLAND	1.00	89.3	20.2
HOLLAND	0.40	35.7	43.0
(COMBINED)	1.40	62.5	23.9
89 FRANCE	95.00	931.4	2435.9
92 FRANCE	15.00	169.5	348.8

member (or members) was, according to the historians' consensus, successful in more or less imposing its will on the entity against whose forces it was fighting, and then follow with those 15 cases in which the non-member was able to resist or defeat the system member's forces. For each of these 43 wars, we show the war's code number and the name of the system member(s) involved, followed by its battle deaths in that war, its battle deaths per war month, and its battle deaths per million of its own population.

This listing reveals that the colonial powers were fairly successful in the nineteenth century (winning 23 of 34 wars) but somewhat less so in the twentieth century (winning 5 of 9). We see that the *major* powers rarely lost to colonial entities until the twentieth century and that a handful of nations, led by England and Russia, participated in a disproportionate number of extra-systemic wars. Interestingly, although the victors often seem to have paid a greater cost to win their wars than some of the vanquished paid in a losing cause, the mean number of system members' losses (in thousands of battle deaths) is only slightly lower for the victorious enterprises (17.7) than for those wars in which they were defeated (19.2). We also find that the battle death range is quite large. The lack of any consistent pattern in battle loss figures is well reflected in Table 14.5; here we find, as with the interstate wars, a fairly large dispersion around the mean, particularly in the data for the victorious system members.

NATIONAL VICTORY AND DEFEAT TABULATIONS

In Chapter Eleven we presented a variety of indicators by which we could rank the nations of the interstate system on the war-proneness dimension. Here, as a by-product of our major concern, we have the information that permits a rough ranking on the success-failure dimension. If a sports metaphor may be allowed, the earlier chapter indicated how many games each team played, and how rough the several games were. Here, we can ascertain how well they did in terms of overall wins and losses, even though we have no intention here of going into the sort of diagnostic detail found in Cook's *Percentage Baseball* (1964). As should be evident by now, these performance records are based only on wars that met our various inclusion criteria, and only for the period during which each nation was a qualified system member. For example, even though Bulgaria won the extra-systemic Serbo-Bulgarian War of 1885 (war number 78), this victory is not included since Bulgaria did not qualify for system membership until 1908. In Table 14.6, we list every nation that engaged in at least one international war while it was a member of the system and then show its victories and defeats in all of its international wars, followed by its performance in interstate wars only. The one war which resulted in a stalemate—the Korean War—is, of course, not considered in this tabulation; therefore, those nations such as Thailand and the Philippines, whose only war experience was the Korean War, are not among the nations listed. Furthermore, Italy, Rumania, and Bulgaria, who fought on both sides during World War II, are considered to have participated in two wars during the 1940–1945 period, one of which they lost and one of which they won.

The nations are listed, not by a percentage index, but by the difference between defeats and victories, inasmuch as the number of wars varied considerably from nation to nation. For those who prefer an alternate ranking criterion, the necessary data are ready at hand in Table 14.6, but the scheme used here places the United States, which won five and lost no wars, in fifth place behind those four nations which lost some wars but whose won-lost difference is greater than five. Among

14.5 CENTRAL TENDENCY AND DISPERSION IN THE DISTRIBUTION OF EXTRA-SYSTEMIC WAR DEATHS, BATTLE DEATHS PER WAR MONTH, AND BATTLE DEATHS PER POPULATION

	N	Mean	Median	Range	Standard Deviation	Coefficient of Variability (*V*): s.d./mean
Battle Deaths (in thousands)						
All extra-systemic wars	43	18.2	6.0	1.0–110.0	26.83	1.47
Wars in which system member was victor	28	17.7	5.0	1.5–110.0	27.54	1.56
Wars in which system member was defeated	15	19.2	10.0	1.0–95.0	25.42	1.32
Battle Deaths per War Month						
All extra-systemic wars	43	709.4	505.1	62.5–4917.4	825.2	1.16
Wars in which system member was victor	28	695.5	408.6	74.3–4917.4	950.1	1.37
Wars in which system member was defeated	15	735.4	729.9	62.5–1666.7	515.9	.70
Battle Deaths per Million Population						
All extra-systemic wars	43	780.4	199.0	3.9–8029.2	1547.4	1.98
Wars in which system member was victor	28	827.2	118.4	3.9–8029.2	1820.0	2.20
Wars in which system member was defeated	15	693.0	354.6	23.9–2762.4	793.1	1.14

the several nations whose won-lost differences are the same—say, one or two—no specific *rank* is implied in our ordering, nor were these "tied" nations listed in any other specific order, for example, by nation number or alphabetically.

Thanks to their choice of allies and enemies, as well as military skills and capability,

14.6 - NATIONAL PERFORMANCE IN INTERNATIONAL WAR

NATION NAME	ALL WARS	INTERSTATE WARS	NATION NAME	ALL WARS	INTERSTATE WARS
ENGLAND	16 - 2	6 - 0	BAVARIA	1 - 1	1 - 1
FRANCE	14 - 4	9 - 2	BADEN	1 - 1	1 - 1
RUSSIA	12 - 3	8 - 2	WUERTTEMBERG	1 - 1	1 - 1
ITALY/SARDINIA	9 - 3	9 - 2	GUATEMALA	1 - 1	1 - 1
UNITED STATES	5 - 0	4 - 0	ETHIOPIA	1 - 1	1 - 1
JAPAN	5 - 2	5 - 2	CHINA	3 - 4	2 - 4
YUGOSLAVIA/SERBIA	4 - 1	4 - 0	BULGARIA	2 - 3	2 - 3
RUMANIA	4 - 1	4 - 1	MEXICO	1 - 2	1 - 1
BRAZIL	3 - 0	2 - 0	PERU	1 - 2	1 - 1
AUSTRIA-HUNGARY	5 - 3	3 - 3	SALVADOR	1 - 2	1 - 2
GERMANY/PRUSSIA	4 - 2	4 - 2	INDIA	1 - 2	0 - 2
GREECE	4 - 2	4 - 2	IRAN	0 - 1	0 - 1
HOLLAND	3 - 1	1 - 0	ECUADOR	0 - 1	0 - 1
CHILE	2 - 0	2 - 0	HANOVER	0 - 1	0 - 1
BELGIUM	2 - 0	2 - 0	SAXONY	0 - 1	0 - 1
MONGOLIA	2 - 0	2 - 0	HESSE ELECTORAL	0 - 1	0 - 1
ISRAEL	2 - 0	2 - 0	HESSE GRAND DUCAL	0 - 1	0 - 1
SPAIN	5 - 4	2 - 3	MECKLENBURG-SCHWERIN	0 - 1	0 - 1
COLOMBIA	1 - 0	1 - 0	IRAQ	0 - 1	0 - 1
NICARAGUA	1 - 0	1 - 0	SYRIA	0 - 1	0 - 1
PORTUGAL	1 - 0	1 - 0	LEBANON	0 - 1	0 - 1
CZECHOSLOVAKIA	1 - 0	1 - 0	JORDAN	0 - 1	0 - 1
PARAGUAY	1 - 0	1 - 0	DENMARK	0 - 2	0 - 2
CANADA	1 - 0	1 - 0	PAPAL STATES	0 - 2	0 - 2
POLAND	1 - 0	1 - 0	MOROCCO	0 - 2	0 - 2
NORWAY	1 - 0	1 - 0	BOLIVIA	0 - 2	0 - 2
SOUTH AFRICA	1 - 0	1 - 0	HONDURAS	0 - 2	0 - 2
AUSTRALIA	1 - 0	1 - 0	FINLAND	0 - 2	0 - 2
NEW ZEALAND	1 - 0	1 - 0	U.A.R.	0 - 2	0 - 2
PAKISTAN	1 - 0	1 - 0	HUNGARY	0 - 3	0 - 3
TWO SICILIES	1 - 1	1 - 1	TURKEY	5 - 11	4 - 6
ARGENTINA	1 - 1	0 - 1			

most of the major powers have fared quite successfully in the international war league, occupying the first six positions in the overall standings. If we look at the nine nations that were, at one time or another, in the major power category, we find that they hold 8 of the first 11, and that China is the only one of them which lost more wars than it won. And even this nation, after achieving major power status in 1950, succeeded in winning 2 of its 3 wars, and holding the United States to a stalemate in the Korean conflict. Also of interest is the fact that while Turkey compiled a record as dismal as its reputation for martial prowess, one of the nations most maligned by military historians—Italy—ended up on the winning side in 9 out of its 12 wars. Perhaps diplomatic skill and related virtues are, in the last resort, more determining than manpower and hardware in the outcome of these confrontations.

This matter of competence leads, in turn, to one of the points raised in the introduction: whether the capacity to predict the consequences of a given war might affect the decision to choose war in the first place. To put it another way, how well do the initiators of war do, compared to their opponents? Let us attempt here, however tentatively, to answer these two questions: (a) to what extent did the initiators of the 50 interstate wars studied here succeed in gaining that "victory" which must have been an important motivation in many, but not all, of the cases; and (b) whether victorious or not, are their battle deaths systematically lower than those whose entry into the war was less voluntary?

In Table 14.7, we list 48 of the interstate wars by war number, identify the side whose forces were the initiators, identify the opponent(s), indicate whether the initiator was victorious or not, and then compute the extent to which the responding side's battle deaths exceeded those of the initiator, if indeed they did. As our language should make very clear, we are not labeling any government the "aggressor" in these wars, or trying to reach a firm, data-based conclusion as to which participant "caused" the war, whether by action, threat, or other provocation. Our classification (like that of victory and defeat) is as crude as it is tentative, resting as it does solely on the historians' consensus as to whose battalions made the first attack in strength on their opponents' armies or territories; indeed, one of the major objectives in our subsequent investigations will be to uncover precisely the sequence of events that converted mere conflict into bloody battle.

Before presenting our classification and results, a number of the particularly ambiguous cases and our tentative coding decisions merit special comment, as follows:

(a) Navarino Bay, 1827: This war has been left out of our computation because of its unique nature. The allied fleets of England, France, and Russia blockaded the Turkish fleet, which then tried to run the blockade; in a formal sense, then, the latter initiated this one-day naval engagement.

(b) Mexican-American, 1846–1848: Although General Taylor reported that "American blood was shed on American soil," the evidence seems to be that his army first moved into an area claimed by Mexico.

(c) Crimean, 1853–1856: The Russians may have made certain movements which led the Turkish army to attack (with allied approval), but Turkey must be labeled the military initiator.

(d) Italian Independence, 1859: While the Sardinians gave political support to the Italians within Austrian-held territories, and may even have lent some military assistance, our evidence is that Austria-Hungary was the initiator of serious hostilities.

(e) Second Balkan, 1913: A contingent of Bulgarians under General Savov violated official policy by crossing a border into enemy territory, thus giving the Serbians and their allies the casus belli for which they were looking.

(f) Korean, 1950–1953: The North Korean army *could* probably be identified as the initiator, but because neither side was victorious, we have not included this conflict.

(g) Sino-Indian, 1962: Although China is considered the initiator, Indian forces made the first major provocative, but *bloodless,* move into the disputed territory. Several weeks later they were attacked by the Chinese. India *could* be considered the aggressor, because she had the weakest legal and historical claims to the area and, moreover, spurned Chinese offers to negotiate their differences.

(h) Second Kashmir, 1965: We have coded India as the initiator, but it should be noted that their forces moved to meet pro-Pakistani *irregulars* who had infiltrated the Indian sphere in Kashmir.

While recognizing that the factors that lead a government to initiate military hostilities are myriad indeed, and certainly go beyond some primitive expectation of victory, it is also likely that the relative prospects for—and relative costs of—victory or defeat will play a key role in such a decision. Granting that premise for the moment, how well have the initiators done over the past 150 years? First, the initiating forces emerged victorious in 34 (or 71 percent) of the 48 cases, suffering 14 defeats. This pattern varies little if we subdivide our 150 years into briefer periods. In the period 1816–1871, the initiators won 14 out of 19, or 74 percent; from 1872 to 1919, they won 12 out of 17, or 71 percent; and in the 1920–1965 period, initiators were victorious 8 out of 12 times, or in 67 percent of the wars. Even if we restrict our focus to wars largely in the European theater (16 of the 25 initiators were victorious, or 64 percent), or to those in which a major power was the initiator (19 of 25 were victorious, or 76 percent), the picture remains essentially the same. However, certain subsets of these major power wars indicate a different pattern. There were 18 wars initiated by major powers against minor powers, and the majors were successful in all but one (the French war against Mexico, 1862–1867), or 94 percent of the cases. But when a major power initiated war against another major power, the initiator was victorious in only 3 of 8 such wars, or 37.5 percent. (This subset includes the Crimean War in which minor power Turkey initiated against major power Russia and was later joined by major power allies England and France.) The 21 wars that were waged exclusively by minor powers again result in a lower percent of victories for initiators: they were successful in 14 such wars, or 67 percent.

Did the initiators do better or worse than their adversaries in regard to relative battle fatalities? Apparently better, or more accurately, less badly. In 36 (or 75 percent) of the 48 cases, the initiators lost the same number or fewer men in battle than did their opponents; and they were victorious in 6 of those 12 wars in which their losses were greater than their opponents'. Shifting from simple battle death ratios to those in which we normalize for national population, we find that the initiators do not do quite as well. Using this measure, we see that their losses are fewer than their adversaries' in only 29 (or 60 percent) of the 48 wars. Finally, the mean battle death

14.7 INITIATION, VICTORY, AND BATTLE DEATH RATIOS IN INTERSTATE WARS

War Number	Initiator	Opponent(s)	Initiator Victor?		Battle Death Ratios Opponent/Initiator	
			Yes	No	BD	BD/Pop
1	France	Spain	X		1.50	4.09
3	Russia	Turkey	X		1.60	4.16
4	United States	Mexico	X		.55	1.68
5	Sardinia	Austria-Hungary		X	1.65	.26
6	Prussia	Denmark	X		1.40	16.00
7	France	Papal States	X		2.14	50.32
8	Brazil	Argentina	X		1.60	10.62
9	Turkey	Russia	X		.61	.80
10	England	Persia	X		3.00	19.09
11	Austria-Hungary	France, Italy		X	.80	.62
12	Spain	Morocco	X		1.50	8.65
13	Italy	Papal States	X		2.33	16.56
14	Italy	Two Sicilies	X		.67	1.51
15	France	Mexico		X	1.50	6.62
16	Colombia	Ecuador	X		2.33	5.00
17	Prussia	Denmark	X		2.00	62.50
18	Spain	Peru, Chile		X	2.33	7.37
19	Prussia	A.-H., German Allies	X		1.58	1.49
20	France	Prussia, etc.		X	.34	.26
21	Russia	Turkey	X		1.37	5.21
22	Chile	Peru, Bolivia	X		3.67	1.47
23	France	China	X		4.76	.42
24	Guatemala	Salvador		X	.25	.47
25	Japan	China	X		2.00	.18

14.7 INITIATION, VICTORY, AND BATTLE DEATH RATIOS IN INTERSTATE WARS

War Number	Initiator	Opponent(s)	Initiator Victor? Yes	Initiator Victor? No	Battle Death Ratios Opponent/Initiator BD	Battle Death Ratios Opponent/Initiator BD/Pop
26	Greece	Turkey		X	2.33	.20
27	United States	Spain	X		1.00	4.00
28	Japan	Russia	X		.53	.18
29	Guatemala	Honduras, Salvador	X		1.50	1.58
30	Nicaragua	Honduras, Salvador	X		1.50	.50
31	Spain	Morocco	X		4.00	15.20
32	Italy	Turkey	X		2.33	3.50
33	Serbia	Turkey	X		.58	.24
34	Bulgaria	Serbia, Greece, etc.		X	2.36	.30
35	Austria-Hungary	England, Allies		X	1.56	.48
36	Rumania	Hungary	X		1.20	4.35
37	Greece	Turkey		X	.67	.09
38	Japan	China	X		5.00	.61
39	Paraguay	Bolivia	X		1.60	.56
40	Italy	Ethiopia	X		4.00	30.55
41	Japan	China	X		3.00	.39
42	Japan	Russia, Mongolia		X	.27	.11
43	Germany	England, Allies		X	2.07	.41
44	Russia	Finland	X		.80	36.11
45	Egypt et al	Israel		X	.60	12.61
47	Russia	Hungary	X		3.57	71.43
48	Israel	Egypt	X		13.04	54.15
49	China	India	X		1.00	1.50
50	India	Pakistan		X	1.27	6.33

ratio for the defenders versus the initiators was 2.02, and the mean battle death per population ratio was 9.81, when all cases are considered.

If we compare the relative costs in human life to the initiating nations vis-à-vis their opponents, with that of the victorious nations and *their* opponents, we find fairly similar patterns. That is, the vanquished nations lost an average of 2.36 men for each lost by the victors. And they lost more men than the victors in 34 of the cases; controlling for population size, that figure rises to 35, or 73 percent of the time. The tactical, demographic, and technological factors that may account for these results lie beyond our immediate concern, but for some historical battle figures, and a discussion of the advantages and costs to attacker and defender, see Fuller (1961, p. 105) and O'Neill (1966, p. 154).

In sum, we can say that the initiation of military hostilities has not been a particularly safe activity in the past. The nations whose forces appear to have made the first overt military move in strength not only lost the war in nearly one third of the cases, but with about the same frequency, also suffered more battle fatalities than did their putative victims.

SUMMARY

In opening this chapter, we suggested several possible questions of a general nature to which these data might offer partial answers. Three of them have been of concern here: (a) how much more costly is war to the defeated side than to the victor in terms of battle fatalities; (b) how well does the initiator of hostilities do, vis-à-vis the adversary; and (c) is there any constant set of absolute or relative battle death levels at which wars are likely to terminate?

As to the first, we can summarize here by saying that, when all of the nearly 100 international wars are examined, there is no discernible pattern. The mean of the vanquished-victor battle death ratios is 2.36, and that for wars which are multilateral, short, and not severe hovers around 2.85; but the dispersion of these ratios is quite high. On the other hand, if we look at interstate wars which are purely bilateral, last more than 6 months or lead to at least 20,000 battle deaths, there is a more constant ratio, and this is about 1.85.

Regarding the second, we find that the initiator-responder ratios are about the same as those for the victor vis-à-vis the vanquished. Those who strike the first blow, despite some of the military folklore, suffer on the average half of the fatalities suffered by their victims. On the other hand, regardless of the time period we focus on, the initiating side—if our coding decisions are correct—loses from one quarter to one third of the interstate wars in which it becomes involved. These figures do not lend themselves, at the moment, to any confident interpretations. We not only have some reservations about our win-lose and initiate-respond classifications, but would need to examine several other variables in order to make any judgment regarding the processes leading up to these wars. Is the relatively poor win-lose score of the initiators a function of incompetence in the game of realpolitik? If so, was the trouble largely in faulty estimates of relative capability, erroneous predictions of the adversary's behavior, misperceptions of *N*th power moves, etc.? Or, did the initiators find themselves all too often in escalatory processes which had gotten beyond their control earlier than expected? To what extent did their domestic politics create the sort of constraints and pressures which shut off the most promising avenues of escape from war? Or, as has happened in more than one case, did other nations put them in such a position that they were, in the last analysis, driven into war?

One might, of course, look at the won-lost figures and interpret them as indicative of a fairly high level of success for the initiators. To win 71 percent of the time is not, one might argue, a poor record. From that viewpoint, it could be urged that foreign policy decision makers are indeed quite competent in evaluating capabilities, discerning tendencies, and predicting behavior, not to mention in picking their enemies. Furthermore, treating 34 victories in 48 contests as a strong record, one might go on to conclude that the pre-war process is indeed a highly rational one (in the limited, problem-solving sense) rather than one in which the environmental conditions determine the outcome, or in which the nations are largely the pawns of random events. Either interpretation is, in our judgment, premature. Neither the limited material presented here, nor the many case studies that now exist, provide a sufficient basis for evaluating the processes by which nations move from peace to war. This will, of course, be a major preoccupation in the later stages of this project.

Turning to the third of our general questions, it seems quite clear that there is not any absolute or relative battle death threshold at which nations withdraw, or at which wars come to an end. When we look at the raw or the normalized battle losses for either the winning or losing side, the range is wide indeed. We uncover, at least for the more important interstate and extra-systemic wars, no particular threshold at which either the ultimate victors or the ultimate losers appear to modify their expectations and their bargaining positions sufficiently to bring hostilities to a close.

Others have, however, reached somewhat different conclusions. In a pioneering analysis of the Richardson data, Weiss (1963a) proposed a model that might account for the probability of a war ending at a given point in time, depending on "the cumulative number of casualties and the time in which they have been incurred" (p. 102). On the basis of severity and duration to date (using our labels), he found a Markov model that generated a frequency distribution very close to that found in Richardson's data. This model (itself an extension of an earlier one in which cumulative casualties alone predicted to termination) was later modified by Horvath (1968), who found that the distribution of war durations could be accounted for by the theory of extreme values, ignoring battle death data. Urging that "a theory based on the number of war dead will never be adequately confirmed" (because of the data quality), his model only "assumes that the duration of a conflict is a probabilistic process independent of the number of people involved, and that the observed distribution of durations is a property of the underlying statistical fluctuations" (p. 18). His model—based on the duration of U. S. labor disputes, as well as Richardson's duration figures—gave a predicted frequency distribution fit very close to that reported in *Statistics of Deadly Quarrels*. A third effort (Voevodsky, 1969), built around the five major wars in U.S. history—Civil, World Wars One and Two, Korean, and Vietnamese I (1961–1964)—returns to battle deaths as a predictor of termination, along with non-fatal casualties, combat troop strength, and time; it further requires that those data be observed for a fairly large number of regular periods *within* the war, rather than just the total figures for each war. Using incremental changes in (as well as ratios between) fatalities, casualties, and strength, Voevodsky found that all three growth rates show a distinct leveling-off prior to the end of each war. But he also found that this leveling-off can be the precursor of radical escalation; hence, his distinction between Vietnam Wars I and II, with 1965 marking the beginning of the second phase.

In sum, the relationship between battle deaths and war termination remains blurred. It seems reasonable to expect that these variables are associated, but it also seems clear that additional variables must be considered; perhaps those suggested in the above papers, or those in Calahan (1944), Coffey (1965), or Kecskemeti (1958). A strong model, then, might also need to include such phenomena as sudden changes in battle death ratios, the defeat of a crack military unit, the loss of a key geographical area, accelerating attrition of materiel, a faltering economy, elimination of an ally, high civilian casualties, crumbling popular support at home, and so forth.

Another reason for the poor predictive power of combat losses is that, even though they were severe in individual and humanitarian terms, they tended to be negligible from a demographic point of view. In only 7 of the 50 interstate wars did the battle death figure exceed 100,000; and in terms of fatalities per capita, the most severe losses were for all participants in the Chaco War (1932–1935), and for the defeated nations in the World Wars, with average figures of a little more than 4 and 2 percent, respectively. Even the Russian military personnel losses in World War Two and those of Paraguay in the Chaco War were as low as 4.5 and 6.3 percent of the pre-war populations, respectively. We seriously doubt whether the inclusion of civilian deaths would have made the costs of war sufficiently greater and the correlation between such losses and the end of war any higher. Finally, if as Clausewitz has argued, war is a means to political objectives, and thus purely instrumental, the cumulative body count would be of infrequent importance in conventional interstate wars, even though—as is apparent in the Vietnam War now underway—it would be a fairly important factor in the political maneuvering associated with guerrilla combat. In brief, it would seem to take more than the systematic extinction of human lives to bring national governments to the conference table.

Chapter 15

Summary and Projection

Summing up a volume like this seems to be an impossible task. As distinct from most social science books, there is no dominant theoretical strand, no culminating argument, no recurrent cadenza. We have tested few hypotheses, confirmed no causal models, fortified no theories, and completed no critical experiment. All we have done is to generate a particular set of data and then refined and systematized it into a multitude of potentially useful forms. An enterprise such as this offers little opportunity for creative expression; in current jargon, it was a nit-picking operation all the way. Tedious, frustrating, expensive, and time-consuming, but hopefully valuable in the end.

By itself, this enterprise is of no greater scientific usefulness than any other competent piece of systematic description. It is, as advertised, merely a statistical handbook that measures and describes some of the "wages of war" over the past century and a half. Its value is more instrumental than intrinsic, but even that value may turn out to be negligible unless we and others fully exploit the data that it brings together. That exploitation will only occur, however, in the context of a particular type of research strategy, and the sort of strategy we have in mind is being embraced, in our view, by too few, too slowly. Before specifying the general nature of that strategy, though, let us devote a few paragraphs to the more immediate payoffs that arise out of a work such as this. More specifically, what do we and our readers know now that we did not know before?

A CAPSULE RECAPITULATION

As we indicated at the very outset, this is by no means the first serious effort to describe the incidence of war within any extended spatial-temporal domain in a systematic fashion. But we have enjoyed certain advantages denied to Wright, Richardson, and the others, and can therefore regard our data with greater confidence. What information do these data convey?

First, they operationally define the fluctuating composition of the interstate system, and all of the international wars of any appreciable magnitude and severity in which the members of that system became involved. Second, they give us a variety of indicators by which these wars may be measured and compared: duration, location, participants, pre-war population and armed force size, battle-connected fatalities, and identity of the initiators and victors in each. More specifically, the data permit us to speak with some precision regarding the severity, magnitude, and intensity of each of the interstate and extra-systemic wars. With each of the wars of the several types so scaled, compared, and ranked on these dimensions, we can aggregate the individual war indicators and measure the incidence of war's occurrence in the system and its sub-systems. Thus, Part C begins with a number of measures of the amount of war that began, ended, and was underway each year in each of the relevant empirical settings.

There we find that, according to our particular measures, there were 50 interstate wars and 43 imperial and colonial wars, leading directly to the death of over 29 million military personnel, exclusive of civilians. There was some sort of international war underway in all but 24 of the 150 years covered, consuming over 4500 nation months of active combat; with 144 nations having been in the system at one time or another, and its size ranging from 23 to 124, this is 5.2 percent of the total nation months available. On the average, an interstate war began every three years and an extra-systemic one began every three and a half years. In terms of possible nation months, 1917 and 1943 were the most warlike years in the century and a half, with 169.8 and 178.5 nation months of war underway, respectively, or 32.2 and 28.6 percent of the maximum possible. And while we could not compute the number of battle deaths sustained on an annual basis, 1939 and 1914 were the bloodiest in terms of military personnel killed during the wars that began in those years, with over 15 million and over 8 million, respectively; with civilian casualties included, these figures would be appreciably greater.

Looking at the entire period, there is no solid evidence that war has been on the increase. The number of wars, the battle deaths, and the nation months have fluctuated considerably over time, with the "average" decade seeing 6.2 wars, over 300 nation months of war, and almost 2 million battle deaths. Nor have later wars generally been any more intense, in terms of deaths per capita or per nation month. On the other hand, there is some tentative evidence for the general belief in war cycles. Wars do not seem to *begin* according to any cyclical pattern, but there is some suggestion of a 20-year periodicity between peaks in the amount of war underway at any given time. Shifting from annual to seasonal observations, we discovered that more wars begin in spring and autumn than in winter and summer, with April and October the preferred months. On the other hand, advances in the technology of war, agriculture, and industry seem to have had only a modest impact on these seasonal propensities.

Looking next at the nations and their regions, we find to no one's surprise that the Europeans were far and away the most war-prone. The top position goes to France and England with 19 wars each, followed by Turkey with 17, Russia with 15, Italy with 12, and Spain with 9. Essentially the same nations led in battle deaths sustained, with the following all sustaining more than a million battle deaths during their tenure in the system: Russia, Germany, China, France, Japan, England, and Austria-Hungary, in that order. Similarly, of the more than 4500 nation months of war that the system experienced, almost 40 percent of them were accounted for by France, England, Turkey, Spain, and Russia.

Do these, or the less war-prone nations, show any consistent preferences in their "choice" of enemies and allies? Apparently not. Outside of such well-identified historical enmities as the Russo-Turkish, Sino-Japanese, and the Franco-German, and in the twentieth century, the recurring partnerships of France, England, and the United States, the lines of hostility and alliance have been remarkably fluid. Most of the nations seem to have found it quite feasible to fight alongside of, as well as against, a goodly number of their neighbors at one time or another.

Finally, our data permit us to say some interesting things about the immediate results of these wars, in terms of victory, defeat, and battle-connected fatalities. Despite the search for some battle death threshold (absolute or relative) at which wars might be expected to end, none was found. Not only do the defeated nations not respond to a given number of losses, but there seems to be almost no constant advantage to the victorious side in terms of battle death ratios. The victors actually lose as many or more men than their enemies in nearly a third of the interstate wars. If the victors often do this badly in the immediate costs of the war, how well do those who actually initiated these hostilities do? For one thing, the initiators "win" in 70 percent of the interstate wars, and they sustain fewer battle deaths than their "victims" in nearly 80 percent of the cases.

A final comment in regard to our findings concerns their similarity with the patterns uncovered by Richardson, Sorokin, Wright, and others. As we noted in Chapter Five, our data base differs in several ways from theirs, and the question is whether that difference affects, in any appreciable way, the statistical regularities that turn up. We can, of course, make only the most tentative sort of response to that question now, given the fact that the present volume is limited in its coverage to the dependent variable only, whereas our three major predecessors report relationships between and among a much larger set of variables. But on this limited basis, there is indeed a surprising degree of consistency, as our several chapter summaries make clear. Whether these consistencies are merely a function of the "law of large numbers," reflecting statistical regularities that are found in a wide variety of social systems, or more significant than that, we cannot yet say. Nor can we answer, at this juncture, the more fundamental question as to whether the differing data bases will produce markedly different patterns as we move on to inquire into the correlates, predictors, and causes of international war.

A PROJECTED STRATEGY

Given these statistical patterns, and the data base from which they are sampled, how do we go about accounting for them and explaining them? Where do we go from here in trying to identify—and hopefully, mitigate—the causes of modern international war? The range of alternative research strategies is large indeed, and we do not presume to evaluate them in any dogmatic fashion. The theoretical and empirical basis for such an evaluation is painfully inadequate, and the stakes are much too high. On the other hand, since we cannot follow several distinct paths simultaneously, each researcher must decide on his own priorities and research strategies. The general outlines of our particular strategy were laid down about five years ago, as the project went through that incremental metamorphosis from casual speculation to serious commitment. While certain elements have been refined along the way, we have found no reason—either in the findings to date or in the comments of our colleagues—to make any fundamental changes in our basic research design. Let us, therefore, summarize it briefly here, in order to put the present volume into proper context and to suggest one possible approach to those who may pick up the challenge which these war data pose.

Beginning with the key epistemological arguments, it is obvious that we believe strongly in the need for an inductive, empirical approach. Our fairly systematic examination of both the limited data-based work and the extensive speculative work persuades us of two things in this regard. First, there are many plausible hunches and models regarding the causes of war, many of which are logically incompatible with one another. Second, outside of the more trivial ones, few of these models or hunches —whether concerned with all international wars, a particular subset of them, or even those few which are bounded by a given time-space frame—have yet been successfully confirmed or disconfirmed. This is not to say that we find all of the contending notions equally plausible, but only to emphasize the importance of distinguishing between a priori plausibility and post-investigative comparison of the models with the evidence. From this, it follows that we must indeed be tentative enough to begin with a search for the *correlates* of war; hence the name of the project. In other words, we are engaged in a systematic "fishing expedition" during this phase of the enterprise.

Such an approach need not, however, be either mindless or atheoretical. We, like others of this persuasion, have some clear ideas as to which potentially "causal" variables ought to be examined first, and rather definite views as to the methods by which their explanatory power may eventually be appraised. Regarding the latter, our investment will continue to be heaviest in the multivariate statistical analysis approach. Our immediate objective is to discover which particular clusters of variables, singly and in combination, show the consistently strongest association with fluctuations in the incidence of war over the 150 years under study. To put it simply, we want first to discover what sorts of conditions and events are most regularly associated with periods and places characterized by the highest and lowest incidence of such violence. Once those patterns have been satisfactorily ascertained, we can move on to the more fundamental question: what events and conditions most sharply differentiate between those international conflicts of the past 150 years which terminated in war and those which found another and less violent resolution?

Of course, the social sciences are already well-equipped to begin such an inquiry. We can, and will, utilize such simple techniques as the scatter diagram, rank order and product-moment correlations, and the multiple regression type of data analysis. But we also have available an increasing number of more complex and powerful techniques, including a variety of causal inference types of longitudinal analysis. The generic name for such techniques already indicates that the line between the search for correlation and for causality is far from sharp and clear. Thus, as the statistical regularities become increasingly apparent, the mode of inquiry becomes increasingly theoretical, and the search for causal patterns and sequences becomes more intense.

Moreover, as the more causal models are systematically tested against our data, and those which give the best fit are more clearly identified, the use of a further analytical tool becomes quite appropriate. Reference is to computerized dynamic modeling, permitting us not only to discover which historical configurations best account for the incidence of war, but also to deal with a range of "what if . . ." questions. One of the more frequent criticisms of the longitudinal, ex post facto, experimental type of study underway here is that it can only handle events and conditions which *did* appear in the referent world, and must therefore be forever inadequate in dealing with what *might* have occurred. This criticism loses much of its salience when one can move back and forth between ideas and evidence, gradually improving one's models. As these explanatory schemes, based on configurations which *could* have obtained, as well as those which we have indeed observed, become more refined and subtle, the relevance of this strategy becomes increasingly apparent. That is, we are no longer restricted to accounting for wars that erupted in the past, but are in an increasingly strong position to search for configurations that could well erupt into war in the future.

So much for the tools and techniques we employ. What types of evidence are to be evaluated? There are four basic sets of data in which we expect to find our independent and intervening (or less rigidly put, our predictor) variables. First, there are the physical, structural, and cultural attributes of the international system itself. Using operational observations taken on an annual or other regular basis, we can describe not only the state of the system (or any of its sub-systems) at a given point in time, but can also measure and record the directions and rates of change therein over time. These particular data will permit us both to identify the systemic patterns that are most strongly associated with fluctuations in the incidence of war under varying time-lag conditions, and to control for the ecological constraints and opportunities that are at work as the specific international conflicts unfold.

Second, there are the attributes of the nations themselves. Using a variety of indicators by which their physical, structural, and cultural characteristics may be operationally measured, we can go on to ascertain which particular types of nations, at which particular stages in their history, have been most and least war prone. In

Chapter Eleven of this volume, we merely identify which specific nations have been most war prone during their entire tenure in the system, but with the above indicators we will be able to generalize about *classes* of nations and *stages* in their social, economic, and political history. When we use our systemic and national attribute data together, our analyses should tell us something about which types of nation in which particular ecological contexts have been—and might be—most likely to get into war, either by initiative or response, or more likely, some combination of the two.

A third set of predictor variables are those which describe the fluctuating relationships between and among specific pairs and clusters of nations over time. Reflecting the strength and types of interdependence that characterize all dyads and groups of system members, these measures get at the diplomatic, military, political, economic, and cultural links between and among them. They also provide the observational basis on which we can build many of the structural indicators of the larger system itself.

The fourth and final set of variables is, at once, the most intriguing and the most elusive of those which we expect to help us identify the causes of war. Reference is to the behavioral and interactional sequences that characterize each inter-nation conflict process. In the complex stages by which pairs and groups of nations move from modest competition through sustained rivalry into conflict and crisis, there may well be certain modes of behavior which regularly lead to war and others which lead to a less violent outcome. When we use a feedback type of scheme, these data should permit us to identify the national decisions and moves that are most often self-aggravating in their effects, and those which tend to be self-correcting. Controlling for the state of the larger system, the types of nations engaged in the conflict, and their pre-conflict relationships, we should be able to discover which strategies and resulting interaction patterns have been—and may continue to be—most likely to lead to large-scale international violence (see Singer, 1972).

CONCLUSION

The above comments, then, serve to summarize the data presented in this volume and to indicate the directions we are following in trying to account for those data. They cannot, of course, do justice either to the richness of these distributions on the incidence of war, or to the complexities of the research strategy to which we adhere. But our hope is that both the availability of the material presented in the preceding chapters, and the sort of investigative design outlined in this chapter will stimulate a renewed attack on the causes of war problem. Much more in the way of energy, resources, creativity, and rigor will be necessary before we have either diagnosed this deadly disease or put the tools of prevention in the hands of those who have the need for—and will to use—them. Thus, we reiterate the theme of our dedication page, and hope that an applied science of war prevention will be created in time to make unnecessary any further editions of a volume such as this.

Appendix

Appendix A
Summary of Definitions

SYSTEM AND SUB-SYSTEM MEMBERS

International System:

All national or quasi-national entities that have ever been independent, a colony, a mandate or trust, or even militarily occupied, as long as population is 10,000 or more.

Interstate System, 1816–1919:

National entities, with independent control over own foreign policy, population of at least 500,000, and diplomatic recognition from Great Britain and France.

Interstate System, 1920–1965:

National entities, with independent control over own foreign policy, and either (a) membership in League of Nations or United Nations, *or* (b) population of at least 500,000 and diplomatic recognition from any two major powers.

Central Sub-System, 1816–1919:

The most powerful, industrialized, and diplomatically active members of the interstate system, generally coinciding with the "European state system."

Major Power Sub-System:

Great Britain, 1816–1965
Italy, 1860–1943
Japan, 1895–1945
United States, 1899–1965
China, 1950–1965
France, 1816–1940, 1945–1965
Russia, 1816–1917, 1922–1965
Austria-Hungary, 1816–1918
Germany/Prussia, 1816–1918, 1925–1945

TYPES OF INTERNATIONAL WAR

Interstate War:

Conflict involving at least one member of interstate system on each side of the war, resulting in a total of 1000 or more battle deaths. Thresholds for individual nations' participation are at least 100 battle deaths or at least 1,000 troops in active combat.

Central System War:

International war, in which at least one participant was, at the onset of that war, a member of the Central Sub-System.

Major Power War:

International war, in which at least one participant was, at the onset of that war, a major power.

Extra-Systemic War:

International war in which there was a member of the interstate system on only one side of the war, resulting in an average of 1000 battle deaths per year for system member participants.

Imperial War: System member versus independent *non-member* of the interstate system.

Colonial War: System member versus ethnically different, *non-independent non-member* of the interstate system.

DEFINITION OF MEASURES

Magnitude:

The sum total of the months of war experienced by all participants in each war, expressed in "nation months" and calculated to the nearest tenth of a month (= 30.44 days).

War Month: In various contexts, referring to a month of a war's duration, a month of a nation's participation, or a month of war fought by any number of nations in a given season or geographical region.

Severity:

Battle-connected deaths of all military personnel of participating members of the interstate system sustained in active combat, or resulting from wounds, disease, or exposure in the combat zone.

Intensity:

The ratios of battle deaths to (a) nation months, (b) pre-war population of each participant, and (c) pre-war armed forces size of each participant.

Appendix B:
Wars That Are Included: Explanatory Notes and References

In the list that follows, we break down all of the 93 international wars that are included in this study into two main classes: interstate ($N=50$) and extra-systemic ($N=43$). For each of these, we list the sources from which we gathered our basic information on that war, including participants, dates, and fatality estimates. For the wars whose inclusion might not be obvious (given our criteria for inclusion-exclusion) or whose duration, magnitude, or severity may be ambiguous, we also provide a brief explanatory note.

It should be stressed that these references are by no means exhaustive; we began in almost every case with the more obvious monographs and then worked our way through additional ones until we were satisfied that the information we needed was accurate and complete. Moreover, we have not listed all of the sources that we consulted, particularly those whose estimates or interpretations we ultimately rejected. Thus, for the British-Zulu War of 1879, we were able to get all the information we required from a single source (Morris, 1965), and for World War One we consulted the eight studies shown but did not find it necessary to utilize such an otherwise valuable study as Liddle-Hart (1930). In addition to the specialized studies that are listed for each war, we found much valuable information in the following more general sources:

> *The Annual Register, Encyclopedia Americana, Encyclopaedia Britannica,* Helen Keller's *Dictionary of Dates* (1934), William Langer's *Encyclopedia of World History* (1948), *World Almanac, Almanach de Gotha, New York Times, Keesing's Contemporary Archives,* and René Albrecht-Carrié's *A Diplomatic History of Europe Since the Congress of Vienna* (1958).

INTERSTATE WARS

1. *Franco-Spanish,* 1823:

   Although the French fought on the side of, and at the "request" of, the deposed Spanish Bourbons against the Liberal Government, this war was not considered an internationalized civil war because the Spanish Liberals had controlled the country for three years.

   Hume (1900); Clarke (1906); Phillips (1914); Bodart (1916); Geoffrey de Grandmaison (1928); Artz (1934); Richardson (1960a).

2. *Navarino Bay,* 1827:

   The British, French, and Russian governments ordered their navies to bottle up the Turkish-Egyptian fleet in the bay in order to aid the Greeks in their war for independence. Although the ensuing battle was "accidental," the Allies were prepared to use force, and Ibrahim, the Ottoman commander, was prepared to resist the blockade.

Anderson (1952).

3. *Russo-Turkish,* 1828–1829:

In the Russian van, naturally, were Greeks and other Balkan peoples who made minor contributions to the war effort.

Russell (1877); von Sternegg (1891–1895); von Sax (1913); Crawley (1930); Woodhouse (1952); Florinsky (1953); Allen and Muratoff (1953).

4. *Mexican-American,* 1846–1848:

Wilcox (1892); Smith (1919)' Bemis (1936); Morris (1953); Peterson (1957); Singletary (1960).

5. *Austro-Sardinian,* 1848–1849:

Fighting alongside the Sardinian Army were irregulars from several Austrian provinces and duchies in Italy.

Friedjung (1912); Bodart (1916); Sorokin (1937); Urlanis (1960).

6. *First Schleswig-Holstein,* 1848–1849:

von Sternegg (1892–1898); Bodart (1916); Sorokin (1937); Urlanis (1960).

7. *Roman Republic,* 1849:

The Roman Republic was established in 1848, and the Pope was divested of his temporal powers. The subsequent war to overthrow the secular Republic was fought by Austrian, French, and Sicilian troops for the Pope, who had no forces of his own. This war differed from similar uprisings in Venice and Milan in that it involved independent nations on each side (the Allies on one and the Republic, the successor to the Papal States, on the other), and resulted in the requisite number of battle deaths. The Milanese and Venetian rebellions do not even qualify as colonial wars in this latter respect.

King (1899); Johnston (1901); Harbottle (1904); Bodart (1916); Berkeley (1932); Sorokin (1937).

8. *La Plata,* 1851–1852:

The wars of La Plata began in the late 1830s. Since French and British intervention resulted in few battle deaths, European participation was excluded. During the next decade, fighting continued among and between Uruguayans and Argentinians, but Argentina, the only system member of the two (Uruguay had not crossed the population threshold), did not suffer the requisite number of battle deaths. Brazil's entry into the fray in 1851 finally qualified the conflict as an interstate war.

Dawson (1935); Levene (1937); Cady (1950); Best, vol. 2 (1960); Calogeras (1963).

9. *Crimean,* 1853–1856:

Russell (1877); Bodart (1916); Dumas and Vedel-Peterson (1923); Sorokin (1937); Allen and Muratoff (1953); Urlanis (1960).

10. *Anglo-Persian,* 1856–1857:

Fortescue, vol. 13 (1930).

11. *Italian Unification,* 1859:

The Sardinians were aided by Italian nationals from Austrian territories.

King (1899); Bodart (1916); Dumas and Vedel-Peterson (1923); Sorokin (1937); Richardson (1960a); Urlanis (1960).

12. *Spanish-Moroccan,* 1859–1860:

Harbottle (1904); Dumas and Vedel-Peterson (1923); Usborne (1936); Sorokin (1937); Spain, Servicio Historico Militar (1947); Richardson (1960a); Urlanis (1960); Miege (1961).

13. *Italo-Roman,* 1860:

This war and the following war (Italo-Sicilian) were part of the struggle for Italian unification. Although Rome and Sicily were in philosophical and political agreement, they resisted the emerging Italian state separately in time and place.

Nolan (1865); King (1899); Harbottle (1904); Thayer (1911).

14. *Italo-Sicilian,* 1860–1861:

Garibaldi's landing in the Kingdom of the Two Sicilies and his celebrated conquest of Naples were not included as part of this interstate war between Victor Emmanuel's armies and the Sicilians.

Same sources as 13.

15. *Franco-Mexican,* 1862–1867:

Some Mexicans fought on the French side. Although Maximillian was Austrian, the Austro-Hungarian government sent no troops. The British and Spanish forces which originally landed with the French in 1861 withdrew before hostilities began.

Niox (1874); Harbottle (1904); Bodart (1916); Dumas and Vedel-Peterson (1923); Dawson (1935); Urlanis (1960); Bock (1966).

16. *Ecuadorian-Colombian,* 1863:

Berthe (1903); Harbottle (1904); Le Gouhir y Rodas (1925); Pattee (1941); Richardson (1960a).

17. *Second Schleswig-Holstein,* 1864:

Bodart (1916); Dumas and Vedel-Peterson (1923); Steefel (1932); Clark (1934); Friedjung (1935); Urlanis (1960).

18. *Spanish-Chilean,* 1865–1866:

Although Bolivia and Ecuador opposed Spain, they did not engage Spanish forces and were not treated as participants in our study.

Markham (1892); Galvez (1919); Galdames (1941); Dellepiane (1943); Davis (1950); Encina (1950); Richardson (1960a).

19. *Seven Weeks,* 1866:

Bodart (1916); Dumas and Vedel-Peterson (1923); Clark (1934); Friedjung (1935); Urlanis (1960).

20. *Franco-Prussian,* 1870–1871:

Baden, Bavaria, and Württemberg, who began the war as independent states, became part of the emerging German Empire by late 1870 and, consequently, were not included as belligerents after that date. The bloody fighting in and around the Paris Commune was excluded because of its civil nature.

France, Ministry of Foreign Affairs (1915); Bodart (1916); Dumas and Vedel-Peterson (1923); Sorokin (1937); Urlanis (1960).

21. *Russo-Turkish,* 1877–1878:

Russia was again aided by Balkan peoples, but Turkey had defeated most of their forces in engagements from 1875 to 1877.

von Sternegg (1866–1889); Hozier (1878); von Sax (1913); Sumner (1937); Seton-Watson (1952); Allen and Muratoff (1953); Richardson (1960a).

22. *Pacific,* 1879–1883:

Markham (1892); Dumas and Vedel-Peterson (1923); Galdames (1941); Dellepiane (1943); Richardson (1960a).

23. *Sino-French,* 1884–1885:

From 1882 to 1884, the French waged an imperial war against the Annamese and the Chinese-supported Black Flag guerrillas of Tonkin [see 76]. In the treaty of Hué of 1883, the French protectorate over what is now South Vietnam and part of North Vietnam was established, but fighting continued with guerrillas, at which time irregular Chinese forces engaged the French. A temporary agreement between France and China in 1884 led to misunderstanding and full-scale war (now an interstate war because of China's open participation).

Cordier (1902); Bodart (1916); Kiernan (1929); Khôi (1955); Taboulet (1955); Li (1956); Buttinger (1958); Lancaster (1961); Roberts (1963); Eastman (1967); McAleavy (1968).

24. *Central American,* 1885:

Burgess (1926); Meza (1935); Richardson (1960a); Karnes (1961).

25. *Sino-Japanese,* 1894–1895:

Cordier (1902); Li (1914); Morse (1918); Ono (1922); Richardson (1960a).

26. *Greco-Turkish,* 1897:

    Harbottle (1904); Dumas and Vedel-Peterson (1923); Sorokin (1937); Richardson (1960a).

27. *Spanish-American,* 1898:

    More than 4000 of the American battle deaths were attributed to disease.

    White (1909); Sorokin (1937); Morris (1953).

28. *Russo-Japanese,* 1904–1905:

    Dumas and Vedel-Peterson (1923); Ogawa (1923); Akagi (1936); Seton-Watson (1952); Richardson (1960a); Urlanis (1960); Martin (1967).

29. *Central American,* 1906:

    This conflict naturally was closely related to the one that followed.

    Castellanos (1925); Karnes (1961).

30. *Central American,* 1907:

    Castellanos (1925).

31. *Spanish-Moroccan,* 1909–1910:

    Usborne (1936); Sorokin (1937).

32. *Italo-Turkish,* 1911–1912:

    The Italians continued fighting in Tripoli against Senussi tribesmen until the 1920s, but after the war with Turkey, the number of Italian battle deaths drops below the inclusion threshold.

    Beehler (1913); McClure (1913); Sorokin (1937); Askew (1942); Urlanis (1960).

33. *First Balkan,* 1912–1913:

    Fried (1914); Report of International Commission (1914); Young (1915); Dumas and Vedel-Peterson (1923); Helmreich (1938); Urlanis (1960).

34. *Second Balkan,* 1913:

    Report of the International Commission (1914); Young (1915); Helmreich (1938); Richardson (1960a).

35. *World War One,* 1914–1918:

    Battle death figures are most likely conservative, since casualty statistics are unreliable for Eastern Europe and Russia.

    Dumas and Vedel-Peterson (1923); Fay (1928); Schmitt (1930); Sorokin (1937); Albertini (1932–1957); Falls (1959); Urlanis (1960); Esposito (1964a).

36. *Hungarian-Allies,* 1919:

    Kiritzesco (1934).

37. *Greco-Turkish,* 1919–1922:

Allied participation was limited both in terms of troops actively engaged and battle deaths.

Urlanis (1960).

38. *Manchurian,* 1931–1933:

Lei (1932); "Chinese-Japan Truce" (1933); Snow (1933); Richardson (1960a).

39. *Chaco,* 1932–1935:

Ireland (1938); La Foy (1946); Richardson (1960a); Zook (1960); Garner (1966).

40. *Italo-Ethiopian,* 1935–1936:

Badoglio (1937); Sandford (1946); Richardson (1960a).

41. *Sino-Japanese,* 1937–1941:

This undeclared war which started with the Marco Polo Bridge incident was treated as part of World War II after December 7, 1941.

Chambers, Harris, and Bayley (1950); Esposito (1964b).

42. *Russo-Japanese,* 1939:

Keesing's 3 (1940); Phillips (1942); Friters (1949); Jones (1954); Rupen (1964);

43. *World War Two,* 1939–1945:

As in World War I, battle death figures are on the conservative side because of unreliable reports from Eastern Europe.

When Germany established de facto control of the governments in such countries as France, Belgium, and Poland, these nations were dropped as participants in the war, even though the Free French, Free Belgian, and other similar military contingents fought with the Allies until the war's end. In the case of Holland, although a sizable Dutch force resisted the Japanese in Indonesia in early 1942, the contingent was, for all intents and purposes, an arm of the Anglo-American command in the Far East, supplied and, indeed, directed by the Allies. Consequently, Dutch participation is said to have ceased when she capitulated to Germany in 1940.

Partisan and underground fighting in France, Yugoslavia, and Greece is not included. Thailand and Mexico, who sent less than 1000 troops into active combat, suffered few battle deaths and were therefore excluded. The Russian invasion of Poland in September 1939 was not included because it was relatively unopposed and resulted in few battle deaths for both sides.

Chambers, Harris, and Bayley (1950); Burt (1956); Aron (1958); *Geschichte des Zweiten Weltkrieges 1939–1945* (1960); Cline (1963); Esposito (1964b).

44. *Russo-Finish,* 1939–1940:

Brody (1940); Coates (1941).

45. *Palestine,* 1948–1949:

During the last months of British occupation (Fall 1947 through May 1948), the British army lost several hundred troops in clashes with both Arab and Jewish forces. Arab-Israeli incidents between 1949 and 1956 and 1957 and 1967 do not reach our battle death threshold.

O'Ballance (1956); Glubb (1957); Israel Office of Information (1960); Kimche (1960); Lorch (1961); Abdel-Kader (1962).

46. *Korean,* 1950–1953:

Given the size of the contingent and the structure of the command, the Chinese "volunteers" have been considered official representatives of the Chinese government in this war.

Keesing's 8 (1952); United Nations Command (1953); Barclay (1954); Leckie (1962); Rees (1964).

47. *Russo-Hungarian,* 1956:

Following the war, Indian Prime Minister Nehru delivered a speech in which he presented fatality estimates, which came to serve as the basis for most other estimates of battle deaths. The military history of the Hungarian revolt remains to be written. Completely accurate figures for the size of the "freedom fighter" army, let alone their casualties, probably never will be ascertained. We do not consider this war a civil war, even though the official Hungarian government requested Soviet intervention; very few natives aided the Soviets.

Meray (1959); Vali (1961); Zinner (1962).

48. *Sinai,* 1956:

Bromberger and Bromberger (1957); Henriques (1957); Marshall (1958); Thomas (1967).

49. *Sino-Indian,* 1962:

Early in this war, some Indian sources suggested that their forces had suffered 2500 battle deaths. At war's end, however, this figure, according to Prime Minister Nehru, was around 200, excluding "missing." Unofficial estimates range from the 200 figure to 5000 for India and a like number for China.

New York Times (10/30/62; 11/04/62; 11/22/62); *United Asia* (1962); *Communist China, 1962* (1963); *Facts on File* (17–23 Jan. 1963). *Britannica Book of the Year* (1963); Rouland (1967); Kaul (1967), Maxwell (1970).

50. *Second Kashmir,* 1965:

Facts on File (1965); Lamb (1967).

EXTRA-SYSTEMIC WARS

51. *British-Maharattan,* 1817–1818:

This war was treated as an imperial war because the Maharattan tribes had never been part of the British Raj.

Frazer (1897); Fortescue, vol. 11 (1923).

52. *Greek,* 1821–1828:

Phillips (1897); Crawley (1930); Woodhouse (1952).

53. *First Anglo-Burmese,* 1823–1826:

The other two major Anglo-Burmese wars do not meet our battle death criterion.

Fortescue, vol. 11 (1923); Harvey (1929); Cady (1958).

54. *Javanese,* 1825–1830:

Klerck (1938); Vlekke (1960).

55. *Russo-Persian,* 1826–1828:

von Schlechta-Wssehrd (1866); Schiemann (1913); Sykes (1951).

56. *First Polish,* 1831:

Exaggerated patriotic first-hand accounts such as the first three cited reported that handfuls of courageous Polish freedom fighters slaughtered 100,000 Russian troops. While many Russians did not return from the front, most of the deaths, including that of the Commander-in-Chief, can be attributed to disease. During much of the nineteenth century, disease was the major killer in wars in Eastern Europe and the Middle East.

Hordynski (1832); Brzozowski (1833); Gnorowski (1839); Puzyrewsky (1893); Schiemann (1913); Grunwald (1955); Leslie (1956); Reddaway (1961); Curtis (1965).

57. *First Syrian,* 1831–1832:

Mehemet Ali of Egypt asked his Ottoman suzerain for all of Syria as reward for Egypt's aid to Turkey in Greece. When the Porte refused, Ali took Syria and advanced almost to Constantinople. Fearing the Egyptians would take the Straits, Russia landed troops on the Asiatic side of the Bosporus and, in effect, stopped the war without firing a shot.

Sabry (1930); Dodwell (1931); Polites (1931); Cattaui and Cattaui (1950).

58. *Texan,* 1835–1836:

Some fighting continued after 1836 until the abortive New Mexican campaign of 1842, but these skirmishes involved only a handful of men.

Bancroft (1885); Stephenson (1921); Callcott (1936); Alessio Robles (1945–1946).

59. *First British-Afghan,* 1838–1842:

Thompson and Garrett (1934); Sykes (1940); Majumdar (1948); Fletcher (1965); Macrory (1966); Norris (1967).

60. *Second Syrian,* 1839–1840:

British and Austrian participation was limited to naval bombardment of the Syrian coast and relatively bloodless occupation of Mehemet Ali's strongholds.

Jochmus (1883); Jordan (1923); Sabry (1930); Dodwell (1931); Polites (1931); Moltke (1935); Cattaui and Cattaui (1950); Anderson (1952); Temperly (1964).

61. *Peruvian-Bolivian,* 1841:

Arguedas (1923); Basadre (1940); Dellepiane (1943); Vásquez-Machicado and Gisbert (1963).

62. *First British-Sikh,* 1845–1846:

This war was treated as an imperial war because the Sikhs had never been a part of the British Raj.

Gough and Innes (1897); Fortescue, vol. 12 (1927); Majumdar (1948); Burt (1956); Singh (1966); Bond (1967).

63. *Hungarian,* 1848–1849:

Headley (1852); Bodart (1916); Curtis (1965).

64. *Second British-Sikh,* 1848–1849:

Same sources as for 62.

65. *First Turco-Montenegran,* 1852–1853:

Frilley and Wlahovitj (1876); Gopcevic (1877).

66. *Sepoy,* 1857–1859:

Originally an army mutiny, this conflict reached such proportion as to qualify as an Indian war for liberation from the British.

Collier (1963); Edwardes (1963).

67. *Second Turco-Montenegran,* 1858–1859.

Same sources as for 65.

68. *Second Polish,* 1863–1864:

Edwards (1865); Reddaway (1961); Leslie (1963).

69. *La Plata,* 1864–1870:

Because Paraguay had a population of about 450,000 in 1864 (and, therefore, did not meet the requirements for system membership), this long and bloody conflict qualified as an imperial, rather than as an interstate, war.

Almanach de Gotha (1865); Box (1927); Levene (1937); Warren (1949); Laine (1956); Best, vol. 2 (1960); Calogeras (1963); Kolinski (1965).

70. *Ten Years' War,* 1868–1878:

While fighting continued on into the 1880s, the last major rebel force signed a peace with the Spanish in 1878.

Barrios y Carrion (1888–1890); Clarke (1906); Beals (1933); Guerra y Sanchez (1950); Ponte Dominguez (1958); Payne (1967).

71. *Dutch-Achinese,* 1873–1878:

The Dutch did not completely subdue the Achinese until 1908, but the first and major phase of the conflict ended in 1878. Although Dutch forces suffered 10,000 battle deaths from 1878 to 1908, in incessant border warfare and raiding, the requirement of an average of 1000 deaths a year was not met.

Kielstra (1883); Rose (1915); Vlekke (1960).

72. *Balkan,* 1875–1877:

Hozier (1878); Langer (1931); Summer (1937); Stavrianos (1963); Mackenzie (1967).

73. *Bosnian,* 1878:

Dumas and Vedel-Peterson (1923); Haumant (1930).

74. *Second British-Afghan,* 1878–1880:

Hanna (1910).

75. *British-Zulu,* 1879:

Morris (1965).

76. *Franco-Indochinese,* 1882–1884.

Bodart (1916); Cordier (1920); Kiernan (1939); Khôi (1955); Li (1956); Buttinger (1958); Lancaster (1961); Roberts (1963).

77. *Mahdist,* 1882–1885:

After Tel-El-Kebir in 1882, England seized control of Egyptian affairs. Consequently, losses suffered by Egyptian forces under British command in the Sudan were considered British battle deaths. After the debacle of Gordon's death at Khartoum, the British withdrew from the Sudan and temporarily gave up hopes of reconquest. They resumed the campaign from 1896–1899, but the combined Anglo-Egyptian armies suffered surprisingly light casualties.

Churchill (1900); Alford and Sword (1932); Theobald (1951); Shibeika (1952); Holt (1958); Magnus (1958).

78. *Serbo-Bulgarian,* 1885:

Mallat (1902); Mijatovich (1917); Dumas and Vedel-Peterson (1923); MacDermott (1962).

79. *Franco-Madagascan,* 1894–1895:

Resistance continued in the interior for several years.

Bodart (1916); Deschamps (1960).

80. *Cuban,* 1895–1896:

Clarke (1906); Beals (1933); Portell Vilá (1949); Smith (1965).

81. *Italo-Ethiopian,* 1895–1896:

The several skirmishes that took place before the official declaration of war were not included because they were neither severe nor sustained. Italian forces also engaged Mahdist bands, but these contests resulted in relatively few battle deaths.

Berkeley (1935); Italy, Comitato per la Documentazione Dell'Opera Dell'Italia in Africa (1952); Battaglia (1958).

82. *First Philippine,* 1896–1898:

Although Aguinaldo agreed to a truce in the winter of 1897 and left the islands, several rebel chieftains did not surrender.

Kalaw (1925); Zaide (1954); Agoncilla (1956).

83. *Second Philippine,* 1899–1902:

Heitman (1903); Storey and Lichauco (1926); Grunder and Livezey (1951).

84. *Boer,* 1899–1902:

Dumas and Vedel-Peterson (1923); Pemberton (1964).

85. *Russian Nationalities,* 1917–1921:

Finns, Ukrainians, Latvians, Estonians, Lithuanians, Poles, and others, versus the Bolsheviks. The Russian Revolutionary government had a mixed record in these wars. They crushed the independence movement in the Ukraine, Georgia, and other areas of Asian Russia, but they lost to the Poles, Finns, Latvians, Estonians, and Lithuanians. Of course, during this period, the Soviets were also successfully waging a war against White and foreign troops on several fronts from Siberia to the Black Sea.

Doroshenko (1939); Graves (1941); Hrushevsky (1941); Carr (1950–1953); Bilmanis (1951); Reshetar (1952); Ironside (1953); Unterberger (1956); Rauch (1957); Smith (1958); Senn (1959); Page (1959); Reddaway, vol. 2 (1961); Sullivant (1962); Jutikkala (1962); Wuorinen (1965).

86. *Riffian,* 1921–1926:

The Spanish were harassed by rebels in Morocco from 1910 through 1921, but they did not suffer sufficient battle deaths until 1921, when the Rifs began an organized rebellion. After the capture of Abd-El-Krim in 1926, desultory fighting continued on into the 1930s.

L'Afrique Française (1926); Jacques (1927); Harris (1927); Usborne (1936); Fontaine (1950); Gabrielle (1953); Landau (1956); Payne (1967); Woolman (1968).

87. *Druze,* 1925–1927:

MacCallum (1928); Longrigg (1958).

88. *Indonesian,* 1945–1946:

Only during the brief period of British occupation did the battle deaths of British and Dutch troops reach the appropriate threshold. This first uprising was marked by the bloody battle of Surabaya. During the second phase of the revolt (1946–1949), only the Dutch participated and their battle deaths were insufficient to merit inclusion.

Wehl (1948); Wolf (1948); Gebrandy (1950); Kahin (1952); Woodman (1955).

89. *Indochinese,* 1945–1954:

Keesing's 9 (1954); Fall (1963); O'Ballance (1964).

90. *Madagascan,* 1947–1948:

Deschamps (1960); Thompson and Adloff (1965).

91. *First Kashmir,* 1947–1949:

The official forces of Indian and Kashmir opposed Pathan tribes, Kashmir rebels, and Pakistani irregulars. The army of Pakistan did participate in a minor way, supplying the Kashmiris and defending strategic points behind the battle lines. Generally the Indians were circumspect in engaging Pakistani troops. Given these considerations, the conflict in the disputed territories was tenuously classified as an imperial war between the Indian government and the people of Kashmir.

India, Ministry of Information (1949); Mellor (1951); Birwood (1954); Korbel (1959); Poplai (1959); Williams (1962); Lamb (1967).

92. *Algerian,* 1954–1962:

Deadline Data (1957, 1961, 1962).

93. *Tibetan,* 1956–1959:

Thomas (1959); Patterson (1960); Richardson (1962).

Appendix C
Wars That Are Excluded: Explanatory Notes and References

Throughout this enterprise we have frequently been surprised by the relatively low fatalities arising out of wars which have been not only famous, but allegedly quite bloody. In addition, colleagues have occasionally asked why one of their "favorite" wars was not to be found in our compilation. The purpose of this appendix is to indicate the sources from which we gathered the information which justifies our exclusion of a good many wars, including some which the traditional literature would have us believe "should" be included. These are the monographs on which we have based our decisions to exclude many of the wars listed by Richardson, Wright, Sorokin, and others, and in Table 5.2 the reason for such exclusion is shown.

Here, we again break the wars down into our two main classes (interstate and extra-systemic) and then add a third: civil wars that became internationalized via the intervention of an external power. In all three classes the major sources are shown, and for the imperial and colonial wars we also include a battle death estimate (in brackets immediately following the dates) when available. When no source is indicated, as is the case with most of the post-1945 conflicts, we used the *New York Times, Keesing's, Britannica Book of the Year,* and *Facts on File.*

Finally, we list wars that were excluded because they continued beyond our cut-off date of 31 December 1965. In Appendix D, we offer some data estimates for wars that have been terminated since that date.

Two of the excluded wars merit an additional comment. Regarding the Boxer Rebellion of 1900, eight foreign powers (Austria, France, Germany, Italy, England, Russia, Japan, and the United States) mounted an allied expedition to relieve the Boxers' siege of the legations in Peking. But the struggle was against troops whom the Chinese authorities largely disowned, and did not result in sufficient fatalities to merit inclusion in our list; in the several clashes at Tientsin and Peking, only a few hundred of the foreign forces were killed. Even though the events were of profound political importance, they did not constitute an international war by our criteria. Likewise, in the Russian-Khivan War of 1839–1842, an imperial war in which the Russians lost most of their 5000-man force, the battle death threshold was not satisfied. Dispatched to the wilds of Central Asia, many of these troops died of disease and starvation, even before experiencing the little combat that did occur.

INTERSTATE WARS EXCLUDED

1. Belgian Independence (England and France versus Holland), 1830–1832: Blok (1912).
2. Boxer Rebellion, 1900: Anthouard (1902), *Deutschland in China* (1902), Fleming (1959), Purcell (1963).

3. Third Afghan (England versus Afghanistan), 1919: Fletcher (1965).
4. Russo-Japanese (Changkufeng Incident), 1938: Dallin (1948).
5. British-Iraqi, 1941: Great Britain Central Office of Information (1948), Khadduri (1960).
6. Occupation of Iran (England and Russia versus Iran), 1941: Lenczowski (1949).
7. Russo-Iranian, 1946–1948: Lenczowski (1949).
8. Burmese-Nationalist Chinese, 1950–1953.
9. Formosa Straits (China versus Taiwan), 1950, 1954–1956.
10. Nicaraguan-Costa Rican, 1955.
11. Yemeni-Adenese (Yemen versus England), 1956–1960.
12. Honduran-Nicaraguan, 1957.
13. Dutch-Indochinese (West Irian), 1960–1962.
14. Portuguese-Indian (Goa), 1961.
15. Egyptian-Somalian, 1963–1964.
16. Algerian-Moroccan, 1963–1964.
17. Malaysian-Indonesian (Malaysia and England versus Indonesia), 1964–1966.

EXTRA-SYSTEMIC WARS EXCLUDED

(I) = Imperial, (C) = Colonial

1. British-Ashanti (I), 1824–1826 [1500 dead]: Fortescue 11 (1923).
2. British-Bhartapur (I), 1825 [500 dead]: Fortescue 11 (1923).
3. Russian-Khivan (I), 1839–1842 [5000 dead]: Allworth (1967).
4. Opium (England versus China) (I), 1842 [500 dead]: Fortescue 12 (1927), Costin (1937).
5. Anglo-Sindian (I), 1843 [500 dead]: Thompson and Garrett (1934), Huttenback (1962).
6. British-Ashanti (I), 1873: Ward (1959).
7. Russian-Turkmen (Geok Tepe) (I), 1879–1881 [800 dead]: Pierce (1960), Allworth (1967).
8. British-Boer (I), 1881: Mansford (1967).
9. Anglo-Egyptian (I), 1882: Maurice and Arthur (1924).
10. Anglo-Burmese (I), 1885: Scott (1924), Woodman (1955), Cady (1958).
11. Belgian-Arab (C), 1892–1894: Wack (1905), Martelli (1962).
12. Germany-Southwest Africans (Germany versus Herreros and Hottentots) (C), 1904–1907 [1600]: Germany, Armee Grosser Generalstab (1906–1907), Johnston (1913), Maclean (1918), Hintrager (1955), First (1963).
13. Germany-Tanganyika (Maji-Maji) (C), 1905: Buell (1908), Johnston (1913), Listowel (1965).
14. Anglo-Iraqi (C), 1920 [400 dead]: Foster (1935), Hasluck (1938), Longrigg (1953).
15. Arabian-Yemeni (I), 1934: Wenner (1967).
16. Nationalist Chinese-Formosan (C), 1947 [100 dead]: Kerr (1965).

17. Indian-Hyderabad (I), 1948.
18. British-Malayan (C), 1948–1960: Pye (1956), Short (1958), O'Ballance (1966b).
19. Sino-Tibetan (C), 1950.
20. British-Kenyan (Mau Mau) (C), 1952–1955 [591 dead]: Great Britain, Colonial Office (1960), Listowel (1965), Rosberg (1966).
21. French-Cameroons (C), 1956–1958: Levine (1964).
22. British-Cypriote (C), 1955–1959.
23. Rwanda- Watusi (C), 1963–1964.

INTERNATIONALIZED CIVIL WARS

(showing regions, dates, and name of intervening nations)

1. Naples, 1820: Austria-Hungary. Harbottle (1904), Romani (1950).
2. Sardinia, 1821: Austria-Hungary. King (1899), Artz (1934).
3. Portugal, 1828–1834: Spain, England, France. Fortescue 11 (1923), Seton-Watson (1938).
4. Spain, 1833–1840: England. Fortescue 11 (1923), Seton-Watson (1938).
5. La Plata, 1838–1850: France, England, Argentina. Cady (1950).
6. Revolutions in German nations, 1848–1849: Prussia, Baden, Bavaria, et al. Droz (1957).
7. Dominican Republic, 1904: United States. Perkins (1941), Callcott (1942), Bemis (1943), Munro (1964).
8. Cuba, 1906: United States, Fitzgibbon (1935).
9. Nicaragua, 1911–1912: United States. Perkins (1941), Callcott (1942), Bemis (1943), Munro (1964).
10. Mexico, 1914, 1916–1917: United States. Bemis (1943), Cline (1963).
11. Haiti, 1915–1920: United States. Perkins (1941), Callcott (1942), Bemis (1943), Munro (1964).
12. Dominican Republic, 1916: United States. Perkins (1941), Callcott (1942), Bemis (1943), Munro (1964).
13. Cuba, 1917: United States, Fitzgibbon (1935).
14. Russia, 1918: England, France, Japan, United States, Germany. Brinkley (1966).
15. Nicaragua, 1927–1933: United States. Perkins (1941), Bemis (1943), Macauley (1967).
16. Spain, 1936–1939: Germany, Italy, Russia, Portugal. Payne (1967).
17. Greece, 1944–1946: England, Albania, Yugoslavia, Bulgaria. O'Ballance (1966a).
18. China, 1945–1949: United States.
19. Greece, 1947: United States, Albania, Yugoslavia, Bulgaria. O'Ballance (1966a).
20. Iran (Azerbaijan), 1946: U.S.S.R.
21. Laos, 1953–1963: United States, North Vietnam.
22. Guatemala, 1954: United States.
23. Muscat and Oman, 1957: Great Britain.
24. Jordan, 1958: Great Britain.

25. Lebanon, 1958: United States.
26. Congo, 1960: United Nations.
27. Cuba (Bay of Pigs), 1961: United States.
28. Yemen, 1961: United Arab Republic, Saudi Arabia.
29. Cyprus, 1963–1965: Greece, Turkey, United Nations.
30. Tanganyika, 1964: Great Britain.
31. Uganda, 1964: Great Britain.
32. Kenya, 1964: Great Britain.
33. Gabon, 1964: France.
34. Dominican Republic, 1965: United States, O.A.S.

WARS CONTINUING AFTER 31 DECEMBER 1965

1. Royal Government of Yemen and Saudi Arabia and Jordan versus Republic of Yemen and United Arab Republic.
2. North Vietnam and Viet Cong versus South Vietnam, United States, Philippines, South Korea, Australia, Thailand, and Cambodia.
3. United States and Laos versus Pathet Lao and North Vietnam.
4. Portugal versus Angola.
5. England versus Adenese.

Appendix D
Epilogue

One of the most frequent queries we encounter in describing the Correlates of War project (of which this is the first book-length report) is whether such research will be relevant to the contemporary historical period and the near future. Although this specific study only covers the period 1816 through 1965, we continue to gather data on the international system since then, and plan to update our analyses as such data become available. Thus, we add these few *very tentative* pages to put the world's more recent wars into context and to make our report somewhat more timely.

First, several *interstate* wars began and ended between 1966 and 1971, and two of them met our criteria for inclusion (see Table D.1). The first of these was the Six Day War in the Middle East which resulted in about 21,000 battle-connected deaths. Since its termination on 10 June 1967, there have been intermittent border raids, artillery barrages, and aircraft attacks between Israel and its Arab neighbors. While these hostilities—and those which preceded the war—have probably led to an additional 3000 battle fatalities, they have not been sufficiently sustained to merit inclusion as interstate wars. The second post-1965 interstate war is the so-called Football War of 14–18 July 1969, between the forces of Honduras and Salvador; this brief war would add approximately 1900 battle deaths to our listing. Here, again, we would not include the series of border incidents which occurred during the ten days prior to the outbreak of full-scale hostilities.

A third interstate war, the celebrated Sino-Soviet border conflicts of March and August 1969, would not be included in any revised compilation, despite the political importance which some have attached to those confrontations. Information is sketchy in the West, but it appears that the combined military losses of both sides did not approach the 1000 battle death level.

One internationalized civil war, however, merits inclusion in an up-to-date catalogue of wars which have ended since 1965. The United Arab Republic (and perhaps Saudi Arabia and Jordan as well) participated in sufficient numbers in the civil war in Yemen from 1962 to 1970 to convert that conflict into an international war of one type or another. There is no doubt about the extent of Egyptian involvement, but it might well be that the other two—on the side of the royalists—supplied more material

D.1 TENTATIVE ESTIMATES FOR INTERSTATE WARS, 1966–1971

Name of War and Participants	Dates	Battle Deaths
Six Days' War	6/5/67–6/10/67	20,800
Israel		700
United Arab Republic		11,500
Syria		2,500
Jordan		6,100
Football War	7/14/69–7/18/69	1,900
Honduras		1,200
Salvador		700

and political support than military manpower. In September 1962, pro-Egyptian Yemenis staged a revolution against the Royal government and established effective control of the capital and the surrounding regions. On September 27, Royal Yemeni troops, backed by Saudi Arabia and Jordan, staged a counter-offensive and the long and bloody civil war was launched. Almost immediately, Egyptian ground and air forces poured into Yemen, and in a few short months the more than 40,000 troops sent by Cairo were doing the bulk of the fighting for the new regime. The Egyptian forces pulled out in December 1967 and thus terminated the internationalized phase of the Yemeni conflict; the civil war itself was brought to a conclusion in April 1970. Although information on Egyptian battle deaths is not yet available, it is likely that they ran into the thousands; thus, by our criteria, this war was clearly internationalized. If Saudi Arabia and Jordan (especially the former) suffered the requisite battle deaths, or if one considers the Royal government of Yemen as the legitimate regime against which the U.A.R. troops were engaged, then this war could be considered an interstate war from the end of 1962 to the end of 1967.

The most troublesome recent case—in both the classificatory and human meanings of the word—is the continuing warfare in Indochina. As this volume goes to press, the death toll for combatants has probably surpassed the million mark and that for civilians is considerably higher. In addition, despite the fact that no war has ever been so thoroughly reported, we find that neither recency nor journalistic energy provides assurance of complete and accurate data. We are, for example, much more confident of our magnitude and severity estimates for the first war on our list—that between France and Spain in 1823—than we are of the Indochinese, or the Sino-Indian and Kashmir wars, for that matter.

Despite these constraints, let us attempt a very tentative delineation of these destructive confrontations (see Table D.2). Between December 1945 and June 1954, we found a *colonial* war (number 89 in our listing) in which the French sought to reimpose their pre-World War II authority over the colonies in Indochina. With the fall of Dien Bien Phu on 7 May 1954 and the conclusion of the Geneva conference, that war—which cost about 95,000 French battle deaths—came to an end. But South Vietnam (separated from the North by the 17th Parallel) and Laos were plunged into civil war before the decade was over. Taking the South Vietnamese case first, the Bao Dai monarchy was deposed in the referendum of October 1955 and replaced by a republic under Ngo Dinh Diem, who enjoyed strong political support from the United States. During the late 1950s, opposition to that regime increased, and by 1960 the guerrillas were sufficiently organized and aggressive to commence—with some assistance from the North Vietnamese government of Ho Chi Minh—a bona fide *civil war.* The conversion of this conflict into an *internationalized civil war* and then into an *interstate* war was a complex and elusive process which we nevertheless try to summarize here.

Despite the United States claim that it was never really a civil war because of the massive North Vietnamese "aggression" against the legitimate government in Saigon, the evidence publicly available points in the opposite direction. Thus, even though the National Liberation Front (Viet Cong) received aid, training, and some weapons from the North, those who fought under its colors were predominantly Southerners seeking to erect their own independent regime in the South.

During the Eisenhower presidency, U.S. military advisers slowly increased in activity and numbers alongside troops of the Diem government. There were about 800 of them in South Vietnam by January 1961 when Kennedy took office, and their role appears to have been restricted to training in the use and maintenance of the U.S.-

D.2 INDOCHINESE WARS, 1960–1970

Name of War and Participants	Civil War	Int'lized Civil War	Interstate War
		Dates	
Vietnam War	3/--/60–	1/1/61–	2/7/65–
South Vietnam-government	3/--/60–	1/1/61–	2/7/65–
United States		1/1/61–	2/7/65–
Australia			7/1/65–
South Korea			5/1/66–
Philippines			10/1/66–
Thailand			10/1/67–
Cambodia			3/--/70–
South Vietnam-Viet Cong (NLF)	3/--/60–	1/1/61–	2/7/65–
North Vietnam			2/7/65–
First Lao War	10/--/60– 7/--/62		
Royal Lao group			
Neutralists			
Pathet Lao			
Second Lao War	2/--/63–	5/--/64–	
Souvanna Phouma's government	2/--/63–	5/--/64–	
United States		5/--/64–	
Pathet Lao	2/--/63–	5/--/64–	
Dissident Neutralists	2/--/63–	5/--/64–	

supplied weaponry, plus guidance in counter-insurgency tactics. The fact that there were probably no American advisers killed until early 1961, and that the U.S. Department of Defense begins its battle death tabulation as of 1 January 1961, suggests that this conflict was an internationalized civil war *before* it became an interstate war.

It will be recalled that a civil war is internationalized under our coding criteria when a sovereign system member intervenes with a combat force of at least 1000 regular troops *alongside* the regime. It becomes an interstate war only when a member of the system fights on the *insurgent* side. Thus, even though the Hanoi government was also providing supplies and advisers—but to the forces of the National Liberation Front—during the late 1950s and early 1960s, they apparently did not contribute sufficient numbers of soldiers for the conflict to qualify as an interstate war.

As to the escalation into an interstate war, that date is equally difficult to ascertain. From 1961 to the mid-1960s, several thousand North Vietnamese probably joined those Southerners and emigres fighting under the banner of the National Liberation Front, but they apparently did not fight in identifiable North Vietnamese battle contingents. As late as the spring of 1965, the U.S. government could only confirm (publicly at least) the presence in the South of one North Vietnamese battalion numbering around 500 men. By that time, many more were indeed operating in some form in the South, but most of them were indistinguishable from local Southern rebels. The problem is further complicated by the temporary division in 1954 of Vietnam at the 17th Parallel, raising some question as to the legality and permanence of the North-South boundary.

As for American and South Vietnamese military action directed against the North, South Vietnamese naval contingents, supported by American air and naval power, raided areas of the North Vietnam coast in early August 1964. This activity was followed almost immediately by the controversial Tonkin Gulf incident, which was followed in turn by U.S. air attacks against mainland North Vietnam on 4 August 1964. These attacks, described as limited punitive raids against the bases harboring the patrol boats that allegedly torpedoed the American fleet in the Gulf of Tonkin, involved one (and perhaps the first) day's combat between the United States and North Vietnamese forces. Six months later, on 6 February 1965, the U.S. air base at Pleiku was shelled, and the United States began to bomb the North in a more or less sustained fashion on the next day. That bombing, which continued until October 1968, was followed by a steady increase of infiltration of men and supplies from the North.

We may never know at what precise point in time North Vietnamese began fighting Americans and South Vietnamese with a force of over 1000 men engaged in sustained combat (or vice versa). Our best estimate is to date arbitrarily the interstate phase of the Vietnamese conflict from 7 February 1965, even though (as noted above) several months later Americans could only find a single battalion of North Vietnamese regulars in the South.

Four other state members of the international system joined the United States and South Vietnam with combat troops numbering 1000 or more. Australian forces began fighting at that level about 1 July 1965, South Korea about 1 May 1966, the Philippines about 1 October 1966, and Thailand about 1 October 1967. New Zealand also contributed a number of troops but the contingent never approached the 1000 men threshold.

The situation is even more ambiguous in Cambodia and Laos. In the early months of 1970, North Vietnamese, Viet Cong, and Khmer Rouge Cambodian troops began to challenge the Cambodian government troops of Lon Nol. The Cambodian *civil* war began in earnest about the end of March, and was probably internationalized from the onset. Cambodia became a participant in the Indochinese *interstate* war on 30 April 1970, when American and South Vietnamese troops crossed its border to attack the North Vietnamese and Viet Cong sanctuaries there. Although the American incursion was limited in its penetration into Cambodia, the South Vietnamese moved all the way to the capital at Phnom Penh where they helped to train the new Cambodian army and protect the regime of Lon Nol. As we go to press, the war in Cambodia still smolders, with American air power and South Vietnamese ground troops playing a major role.

Laos is still another story. In the Fall of 1960, sustained hostilities broke out between the Royal Lao government headed by Phoumi Nosavan, and the neutralist forces of Souvanna Phouma and Kong Le. The communist-oriented Pathet Lao soon joined with the neutralists to fight the American-backed government in Vientiane. This war was essentially a *civil* war despite American military aid to the Royal government, Thailand's blockading of Vientiane to support that same government, and the Soviet Union's airlift of economic aid to the other side; it was terminated by the Geneva agreements in July 1962. In February 1963, a new conflict arose between the neutralist forces that supported Prime Minister Souvanna Phouma's pro-American policy and dissident neutralists who were soon joined by the Pathet Lao contingents.

In May 1964, the United States assumed an active combat role in Laos when they began to bomb Pathet Lao positions. In that month, the Second Laotian Civil war clearly became *internationalized.* Prior to this period, the United States government financed secret mercenary armies as well as Laotian government troops, and perhaps even engaged in limited and covert military missions; all this time, the Pathet Lao, similarly, received support from North Vietnam. After the American bombing began, North Vietnamese support troops joined the Pathet Lao in greater numbers. Some were in the northeast part of Laos (in the Plaines des Jarres region), but were not necessarily coordinating their activities with those regular troops who had used and continued to use sanctuaries along the Laos-Vietnam frontier. The latter contingents were clearly engaged in the *interstate* war in Vietnam, but information on the direct combat role of their compatriots in the northeast is scanty. Our interpretation is that the Laotian civil war—while clearly internationalized—never became an interstate war, since Laotian and United States elements never directly confronted the North Vietnamese in any sustained fashion in the northeastern theater of combat.

In a legalistic sense, the situation did not change very much when South Vietnamese units and fleets of American helicopter gun ships crossed into Laos on 8 February 1971. This incursion was quite limited in space and time, and when the South Vietnamese engaged the North Vietnamese, they did not really fight in the name of the Laotian government; nor did they engage Pathet Lao troops. Thus, we would have to conclude that while the recent Laos incursion may have "widened" the major war, Laos itself does not qualify as a participant in the *interstate* Indochinese war. Artificial though the distinction might be, we tentatively conclude that the war in Laos should be treated separately from the wars in Vietnam and Cambodia which merged in the Spring of 1970.

As difficult as it may be to disentangle the chronology of military events in Indochina, the battle death estimates pose an even more difficult question. The "body counts" reported by all of the military commands must be regarded with the same skepticism that we acquired in examining the 93 wars included in the 1816–1965 period. Not only are there the standard temptations to exaggerate the adversaries' casualties and underreport one's own, but in a savage war of this type, it is unlikely that we will ever know how many of the victims were combatants.

Complicating matters further is Hanoi's reluctance to issue any battle death figures, a reluctance related to their insistence that North Vietnamese troops have not participated in the conflict in the South. The National Liberation Front and the Pathet Lao have also refrained from entering the body count game. Even the American figures must be looked at suspiciously. There have been suggestions that in order to make the war appear less costly, the Pentagon has not included deaths from wounds and disease suffered in the combat zone in their official tallies for American battle deaths. Given these difficult problems of analysis and interpretation and the fact that the figure is still moving upward as we go to press, we will not offer battle death estimates for the Indochinese Wars for the time being.

As the Correlates of War project continues, and our analyses are extended into the more recent period, we will go into these post-1965 wars in greater detail. In subsequent reports, then, more solid measures and classifications may be expected.

Besides the regular press coverage of these conflicts discussed above, the following books and articles were consulted:

Six Days War: Safran (1969).

Indochinese Wars: Vietnam: Pike (1966); Buttinger (1967); Fall (1967); Kahin and Lewis (1969); United States Senate (1969); Gettleman (1970); Cooper (1970); Grant (1970); *New York Times* (1971).

Laos: Chomsky (1970); Langer and Zasloff (1970); McCoy (1970); Shaplen (1970).

References

These references include, in alphabetical order by author, all of the books, reports, and articles that are mentioned in the book or that we used to ascertain or confirm our estimates of each war's magnitude, severity, or intensity. The historical specialist may, however, note the omission of certain standard sources, and such omissions are quite intentional. That is, since we are interested here in the sort of detailed breakdowns which show (for example) the number of fatalities sustained by all participants in a given single battle, or the ratio between officer and enlisted losses, we have not cited—or made much use of—these highly detailed studies. A classic example might be **Albert G. Love's** *Medical and Casualty Statistics* (vol. 15 of U.S. Army Medical Department history of World War I, 1925).

We might also indicate that the citation format represents our small contribution to the war on unselective redundancy. In order to make the References as legible and useful as possible, we have eliminated much of what appears in the classic citation. No one needs, for example, to be told that a London publishing house is in England, or that Lippincott is a publishing company, or that the University of California Press is the publisher of a book identified as "Berkeley: Univ. of California, etc." Nor need we clutter up our lists with "Vol. 59, No. 3" or "pp. 90–105" when "59/3" (before the month and year of the journal's publication) and "90–105" (following it) will do just as well. Thus, we have only used the full traditional citations when there was a danger of misinterpretation, especially by those of our readers that are not in the American social science subculture.

Abdel-Kader, A. Razak. *Le Conflit Judéo-Arabe.* Paris: François Maspero, 1962.

L'Afrique Française. 36/6 (June 1926), 327–37.

Agoncilla, Teodoro A. *The Revolt of the Masses.* Quezon City: Univ. of Philippines, 1956.

Akagi, Roy. *Japan's Foreign Relations: A Short History 1542–1936.* Tokyo: Hokuseido, 1936.

Albertini, Luigi. *The Origins of the War of 1914.* 3 vols. (Trans. Isabella Massey.) London: Oxford Univ., 1952–1957.

Albrecht-Carrié, René. *A Diplomatic History of Europe Since the Congress of Vienna.* New York: Harper, 1958.

Alessio Robles, Vito. *Coahuila y Texas.* 2 vols. Mexico City: Antigua Libreroa Robredo, 1945–1946.

Alford, Henry and W. Denniston Sword. *The Egyptian Sudan: Its Loss and Recovery.* London: Macmillan, 1932.

Allen, W. E. D. and Paul Muratoff. *Caucasian Battlefields.* Cambridge: Cambridge Univ., 1953.

Allworth, Edward (ed). *Central Asia.* New York: Columbia Univ., 1967.

Almanach de Gotha. Gotha: Justus Perthes, 1764–1940.

Anderson, R. C. *Naval Wars in the Levant.* Princeton: Princeton Univ., 1952.

Annual Register of World Events. London: Longmans, 1758–.

Anthouard, Albert F. *Les Boxeurs.* Paris: Plon-Nourrit, 1902.

Arguedas, Alcides. *Histoire Générale de la Bolivie.* Paris: Alcan, 1923.

Aron, Robert. *The Vichy Regime 1940–1944.* London: Putnam, 1958.

"The Art of War," *Military Review,* 40/3 (June 1960), 72.

"The Art of War," *U.S. Naval Institute Proceedings,* 86/11 (November 1960), 151.

Artz, Frederick B. *Reaction and Revolution 1814–1832.* New York: Harpers, 1934.

Askew, William C. *Europe and Italy's Acquisition of Libya 1911–1912.* Durham, N.C.: Duke Univ., 1942.

Badoglio, Pietro. *The War in Abyssinia.* London: Methuen, 1937.

Bancroft, Hubert Howe. *History of Mexico,* San Francisco: A. L. Bancroft, 1885.

Barclay, C. N. *The First Commonwealth Division.* Aldershot, U.K.: Gale and Polden, 1954.

Barrios y Carrion, Leopoldo. *Sobre la Historia de la Guerra de Cuba.* Barcelona: Revista Cientifico-Militar y Biblioteca Militar, 1888–1890.

Basadre, Jorge. *Historia de la Republica del Peru.* Lima: Editorial Cultura Anartica S. A., 1940, Vol. 1.

Battaglia, Roberto. *La Prima Guerra D'Africa.* Rome: Einaudi, 1958.

Beals, Carleton. *The Crime of Cuba.* Philadelphia: Lippincott, 1933.

Beebe, Gilbert and Michael de Bakey. *Battle Casualties: Incidence, Mortality and Logistic Considerations.* Springfield, Ill.: C. C. Thomas, 1952.

Beehler, William H. *The History of the Italian-Turkish War.* Annapolis, Md.: Advertiser-Republican, 1913.

Bemis, Samuel Flagg. *A Diplomatic History of the United States.* New York: Holt, 1936.

———. *The Latin American Policy of the United States.* New York: Harcourt, 1943.

Benoit, Emile and Harold Lubell. "World Defense Expenditures." *Journal of Peace Research,* 3 (1966), 97–113.

Berkeley, George F. H. *The Campaign of Adowa and the Rise of Menelik.* London: Constable, 1935.

———. *Italy in the Making 1815–1846.* Vol. I. Cambridge: Cambridge Univ., 1932.

Berndt, Otto. *Die Zahl im Kriege.* Vienna: Freytag u. Berndt, 1897.

Berthe, Augustine. *Garcia Moreno.* Vol. I. Paris: Librairie de la "Sainte Famille," 1903.

Best, Felix. *Historia de las Guerras Argentinas.* 2 vols. Buenos Aires: Peuser, 1960.

Bilmanis, Alfred. *A History of Latvia.* Princeton: Princeton Univ., 1951.

Birwood, Christopher. *India and Pakistan.* New York: Praeger, 1954.

Bloch, Ivan. *The Future of War.* New York: Doubleday & McClure, 1899.

Blok, Petrus J. *A History of the People of the Netherlands.* New York: Putnams, 1912.

Blumenfeld, Ralph D. "A Hundred Years War of Today," *Harper's Monthly,* 103 (August, 1901), 367–74.

Bock, Carl H. *Prelude to Tragedy.* Philadelphia: Univ. of Pennsylvania, 1966.

Bodart, Gaston. *Militär-historisches Kriegs-Lexikon (1618–1905).* Vienna: C. W. Stern, 1908.

______. *Losses of Life in Modern Wars.* London: Oxford Univ., 1916.

Bond, Brian (ed.). *Victorian Military Campaigns.* New York: Praeger, 1967.

Box, Pelham Horton. *Origins of the Paraguayan War.* Urbana: Univ. of Illinois, 1927.

Brinkley, George A. *The Volunteer Army and Allied Intervention in Southern Russia, 1917–1921.* South Bend, Ind.: Univ. of Notre Dame, 1966.

Britannica Book of the Year 1962. Chicago: Encyclopaedia Britannica, 1963.

Brody, Alter, et al. (eds.). *War and Peace in Finland.* New York: Soviet Russia Today, 1940.

Bromberger, Merry and Serge. *Secrets of Suez.* London: Pan, 1957.

Brzozowski, Marie. *La Guerre de Pologne en 1831.* Leipzig: Brockhaus, 1833.

Buell, Raymond Leslie. *The Native Problem in Africa.* Vol. 1. New York: Macmillan, 1908.

Burgess, Paul. *Justo Ruffino Barrios.* Philadelphia: Dorrance, 1926.

Burr, Robert N. "The Balance of Power in Nineteenth Century South America: An Exploratory Essay." *The Hispanic American Historical Review,* 25 (February 1955), 37–60.

Burt, Alfred L. *The Evolution of the British Empire and Commonwealth.* Boston: Heath, 1956.

Buttinger, Joseph. *The Smaller Dragon.* New York: Praeger, 1958.

______. *Vietnam, A Dragon Embattled.* Vol. 2. New York: Praeger, 1967.

Cady, John F. *Foreign Intervention in the Rio Del Plata 1838–1850.* Philadelphia: Univ. of Pennsylvania, 1950.

______. *A History of Modern Burma.* Ithaca: Cornell Univ., 1958.

Calahan, H. A. *What Makes a War End?* New York: Vanguard, 1944.

Callcott, Wilfred H. *Santa Anna.* Norman: Univ. of Oklahoma, 1936.

______. *The Caribbean Policy of the United States.* Baltimore: Johns Hopkins, 1942.

Calogeras, Joao P. *A History of Brazil.* (Trans. and Ed. Percy A. Martin.) New York: Russell and Russell, 1963.

Carr, Edward H. *The Bolshevik Revolution 1917–1923.* 3 vols. London: Macmillan, 1950–1953.

Carroll, Berenice A. "Germany Disarmed and Rearming, 1925–1935," *Journal of Peace Research,* 3 (1966) 114–124.

Castellanos, Pedro Zamora. *Vida Militar de Centro America.* Guatemala City: 1925.

Cattaui, Réné and Georges. *Mohamed Aly et l'Europe.* Paris: Libraire Orientaliste, 1950.

Chadwick, H. Munro. *The Nationalities of Europe and the Growth of National Ideologies.* Cambridge: Cambridge Univ., 1945.

Chambers, Frank, Christina Harris, and Charles Bayley. *This Age of Conflict.* New York: Harcourt, 1950.

"The Chinese-Japanese Truce of Tangku." *Literary Digest.* 115/23 (June 10, 1933), 11.

Chomsky, Naom. "Destroying Laos." *New York Review of Books,* 15/2 (23 July 1970), 21–33.

Churchill, Winston S. *The River War.* 2 vols. London: Longmans, 1900.

Clark, Chester Wells. *Franz Joseph and Bismarck: The Diplomacy of Austria Before the War of 1866.* Cambridge: Harvard Univ., 1934.

Clarke, Henry Butler. *Modern Spain 1815–1898.* Cambridge: Cambridge Univ., 1906.

Cline, Howard. *The United States and Mexico.* New York: Atheneum, 1963.

Coates, William P. and Zelda. *The Soviet Finnish Campaign.* London: Eldon, 1941.

Coffey, Rosemary K. "The Heart of Deterrence," *Bulletin of the Atomic Scientists,* 21/4 (April 1965), 27–29.

Collier, Richard. *The Sound of Fury.* London: Collins, 1963.

Communist China, 1962. Hong Kong: Union Research, 1963.

Cook, Earnshaw. *Percentage Baseball.* Cambridge: Massachusetts Inst. of Technology, 1964.

Cooper, Chester. *The Lost Crusade.* New York: Dodd, Mead, 1970.

Cordier, Henri. *Histoire des Relations de la Chine avec les Puissances Occidentales.* Vol. 3. Paris: F. Alcan, 1902.

———. *Histoire Générale de la Chine et de ses Relations avec les pays étrangers depuis les temps les plus anciens jusqu'à la chute de la dynastie Mandchou.* Vol. 4. Paris: Geuthner, 1920.

Costin, W. C. *Great Britain and China, 1833–1860.* London: Oxford Univ., 1937.

Cousins, Norman. "Electronic Brain on War and Peace: A Report of an Imaginary Experiment," *St. Louis Post-Dispatch,* December 13, 1953.

———. "The Electronic Case for Peace," *Saturday Review,* 37/23 (June 5, 1954), 22–23.

Crawley, Charles William. *The Question of Greek Independence.* Cambridge: Cambridge Univ., 1930.

Curtis, John Shelton. *The Russian Army Under Nicholas I.* Durham: Duke Univ., 1965.

Dallin, David J. *Soviet Russia and the Far East.* New Haven: Yale Univ., 1948.

Davis, William Columbus. *The Last Conquistadores.* Athens: Univ. of Georgia, 1950. Georgia, 1950.

Dawson, Daniel. *The Mexican Adventure.* London: G. Bell and Sons, 1935.

Deadline Data on World Affairs. New York: Deadline Data (weekly since 1955).

Dellepiane, Carlos. *Historia Militar del Peru.* Vol. 1. Lima: Imprenta del Ministero de Guerra, 1943.

Denton, Frank H. "Some Regularities in International Conflict, 1820–1949," *Background,* 9/4 (February 1966), 283–296.

——— **and Warren Phillips.** "Some Patterns in the History of Violence," *Journal of Conflict Resolution,* 12/2 (June 1968), 182–195.

Deschamps, Hubert. *Histoire de Madagascar.* Paris: Berger-Levrault, 1960.

Deutschland in China, 1900–1901. Dusseldorf: A. Bagel, 1902.

Dewey, Edward R. *The 177-Year Cycle in War, 600 B.C.–A.D. 1957.* Pittsburgh: Foundation for the Study of Cycles, 1964.

Dodwell, Henry. *The Founder of Modern Egypt: A Study of Muhammad 'Ali.* Cambridge: Cambridge Univ., 1931.

Droz, Jacques. *Les Revolutions Allemandes de 1848.* Paris: Presses Universitaires de France, 1957.

Doroshenko, Dmitro. *History of the Ukraine.* (Trans. and abr. Hanna Chikalenko-Keller.) Edmonton, Alberta: Institute Press, 1939.

Dumas, Samuel and Knud Otto Vedel-Peterson. *Losses of Life Caused by War.* London: Oxford Univ., 1923.

Eastman, Lloyd E. *Throne and Mandarins.* Cambridge: Harvard Univ., 1967.

Eckstein, Harry (ed). *Internal War.* New York: Free Press, 1964.

Edwardes, Michael. *Battles of the India Mutiny.* London: Batsford, 1963.

Edwards, H. Sutherland. *The Private History of a Polish Insurrection.* London: Saunders, 1865.

Eggenberger, David. *A Dictionary of Battles.* New York: Crowell, 1967.

Ellis, C. H. *The British "Intervention" in Transcaspia, 1918–1919.* Berkeley: Univ. of California, 1963.

Encina, Francisco Antonio. *Historia de Chile.* Vol. 14. Santiago: Editorial Nascimento, 1950.

Encyclopaedia Britannica. Chicago: Encyclopaedia Britannica, 1967 ed.

Encyclopedia Americana. New York: Americana Corp., 1967 ed.

Esposito, Vincent J. (ed). *A Concise History of World War I.* New York: Praeger, 1964a.

______. *A Concise History of World War II.* New York: Praeger, 1964b.

Facts on File. New York: Facts on File (weekly since 1940).

Fall, Bernard. *Street Without Joy.* Harrisburg: Stackpole, 1963.

______. *The Two Viet-Nams.* New York: Praeger, 1967.

Falls, Cyril. *The Great War.* New York: Putnams, 1959.

Fay, Sidney B. *The Origins of the World War.* 2 vols. New York: Macmillan, 1928.

Field, G. Lowell. *Comparative Political Development: The Precedent of the West.* Ithaca: Cornell Univ., 1967.

First, Ruth. *South West Africa.* London: Penguin, 1963.

Fitzgibbon, Russell H. *Cuba and the United States.* Menasha, Wis.: George Banta, 1935.

Fleming, Peter. *The Siege at Peking.* London: Hart-Davis, 1959.

Fletcher, Arnold. *Afghanistan: Highway of Conquest.* Ithaca: Cornell Univ., 1965.

Florinsky, Michael T. *Russia: A History and an Interpretation.* Vol. II. New York: Macmillan, 1953.

Fontaine, Pierre. *Abd-El-Krim.* Paris: Le Sept Couleurs, 1950.

Fortescue, Sir John W. *History of the British Army.* Vols. 11, 12, and 13. London: Macmillan, 1923, 1927, 1930.

Foster, Henry. *The Making of Modern Iraq.* Norman: Univ. of Oklahoma, 1935.

France, Ministry of Foreign Affairs. *Les Oirgines Diplomatiques de la Guerre de 1870–1871.* Paris: G. Ficker, 1915.

Frazer, R. W. *British India.* New York: Putnams, 1897.

Fried, Alfred H. "A Few Lessons Taught by the Balkan War," *International Conciliation,* 74 (January 1914).

Friedjung, Heinrich. *Osterreich von 1848 bis 1860.* Stuttgart: J. G. Cotta, 1912.

______. *The Struggle for Supremacy in Germany 1859–1866.* (Trans. A. J. P. Taylor and W. L. McIvee.) London: Macmillan, 1935.

Frilley, G. and Jovan Wlahovitj. *Le Monténégro Contemporain.* Paris: E. Plon, 1876.

Friters, Gerard M. *Outer Mongolia and Its International Position.* Baltimore: Johns Hopkins Univ., 1949.

Fuller, J. F. C. *The Conduct of War, 1789–1961.* London: Eyre and Spottiswoode, 1961.

Gabrielle, Léon. *Abd-El-Krim et les Événements du Rif.* Casablanca: Editions Atlantides, 1953.

Galdames, Luis. *A History of Chile.* Chapel Hill: Univ. of North Carolina, 1941.

Galvez, Juan Ignacio. *El Peru Contra Colombia, Ecuador y Chile.* Santiago: Sociedad Imprentalitografia Universo, 1919.

Garner, William R. *The Chaco Dispute.* Washington: Public Affairs Press, 1966.

Gebrandy, P. S. *Indonesia.* London: Hutchinson, 1950.

Geoffroy de Grandmaison, Charles Alexander. *L'Expedition Française D'Espagne en 1823.* Paris: Plon, 1928.

Germany. Armee Grosser General Stab. Kriegsgeschicht Abteilung. *Die Kampfe der deutschen Truppen in Sudwest Africa.* 2 vols. Berlin: 1906–1907.

Geschichte des Zweiten Weltkrieges 1939–1945. Wurzburg: A. G. Ploetz, 1960.

Gettleman, Marvin (ed). *Vietnam.* New York: Fawcett, 1970.

Gleditsch, Nils P. "The International Airline Network: A Test of the Zipf and Stouffer Hypotheses," *Peace Research Society Papers* 11 (1969), 123–53.

Glubb, John Bagot. *A Soldier with the Arabs.* London: Hoddon and Stoughton, 1957.

Gnorowski, S. B. *Insurrection of Poland.* London: James Ridgeway, 1839.

Gopcevic, Spiridion. *Le Monténégro et les Monténégrins.* Paris: Plon, 1877.

Gough, Charles and Arthur Innes. *The Sikhs and the Sikh Wars.* London: A. D. Innes, 1897.

Grant, Jonathan, Jonathan Unger, and Laurance A. G. Moss (eds). *Cambodia: The Widening War in Indochina.* New York: Simon and Schuster, 1970.

Graves, W. S. *America's Siberian Adventure, 1918–1920.* New York: P. Smith, 1941.

Great Britain. Central Office of Information. *Paiforce.* London: H.M.S.O., 1948.

Great Britain. Colonial Office. *Historical Survey of the Origins and Growth of Mau Mau.* London: H.M.S.O., 1960.

Greaves, Fielding L. "Peace in Our Time—Fact or Fable," *Military Review,* 42/12 (December 1962), 55–58.

______. "Peace in Our Time," *New York Times Magazine* (April 14, 1963), 16 and 124.

Grunder, Garel and William Livezey. *The Philippines and the United States.* Norman: Univ. of Oklahoma, 1951.

Grunwald, Constantin de. *Tsar Nicholas I.* (Trans. Brigit Patmore.) New York: Macmillan, 1955.

Guerra y Sanchez, Ramiro. *Guerra de los Diez Años.* 2 vols. Havana: Cultural, 1950.

Hanna, Henry B. *The Second Afghan War.* Vol. 3. London: Constable, 1910.

Harbottle, Thomas Benfield. *Dictionary of Battles from the Earliest Date to the Present Time.* London: S. Sonneschein, 1904.

Harris, Walter. *France, Spain, and the Rif.* London: Arnold, 1927.

Harvey, George E. *The Cambridge History of India.* Cambridge: Cambridge Univ., 1929.

Hasluck, E. L. *Foreign Affairs, 1919–1937.* New York: Macmillan, 1938.

Haumant, Emile. *La Formation de la Yugoslavie.* Paris: Bossard, 1930.

Haydon, Brownlee. *The Great Statistics of Wars Hoax.* Santa Monica, Calif.: Rand Corp., November 1962.

Headley, P. C. *The Life of Louis Kossuth.* Auburn, N.Y.: Derby and Miller, 1852.

Heitman, Francis B. *Historical Registry and Directory of the United States Army.* Vol. 2. Washington, D.C.: G.P.O., 1903.

Helmreich, Ernst Christian. *The Diplomacy of the Balkan Wars, 1912–1913.* Cambridge: Harvard Univ., 1938.

Henriques, Robert. *100 Hours to Suez.* New York: Viking, 1957.

Hintrager, Oskar. *Sudwest Afrika in der deutschen Zeit.* Munich: R. Oldenbourg, 1955.

Holt, Peter M. *The Madhist State in the Sudan, 1881–1898.* London: Oxford, 1958.

Hordynski, Joseph. *History of the Late Polish Revolution.* Boston: Carter and Hendle, 1832.

Horvath, William. "A Statistical Model for the Duration of Wars and Strikes," *Behavioral Science,* 13/1 (January 1968), 18–28.

_____ **and Caxton C. Foster.** "Stochastic Models of War Alliances," *Journal of Conflict Resolution,* 7/2 (June 1963), 110–116.

Hozier, Henry Montague. *The Russo-Turkish War.* 2 vols. London: W. Mackenzie, 1878.

Hrushevsky, Michael. *A History of the Ukraine.* New Haven: Yale Univ., 1941.

Hume, Martin A. S. *Modern Spain.* London: Putnams, 1900.

Huttenback, Robert A. *British Relations with Sind, 1799–1843.* Berkeley: Univ. of California, 1962.

Hyamson, Albert M. *Palestine Under the Mandate.* London: Methuen, 1950.

India. Ministry of Information and Broadcasting. *Defending Kashmir.* Delhi: 1949.

Institut Français de Polémologie. "Periodicité et Intensité des Actions de Guerre de 1200 à 1945." *Guerre et Paix,* 2 (1968), 20–32.

Ireland, Gordon. *Boundaries, Possessions and Conflicts in South America.* Cambridge: Harvard Univ., 1938.

Ironside, Edmund. *Archangel, 1918–1919.* London: Constable, 1953.

Israel Office of Information. *Israel's Struggle for Peace.* New York: Israel Office of Information, 1960.

Italy. Comitato per la Documentazione Dell'Opera Dell'Italia in Africa. *Italia in Africa.* Rome: Istituto Poligrafico Dello Stato, 1952, vol. I, pt. 2.

Jacques, Hubert. *L'Aventure Riffaine et ses Dessous Politiques.* Paris: Bossard, 1927.

Jenkins, Gwilym M. and J. G. Watts. *Spectral Analysis and its Applications.* San Francisco: Holden Day, 1968.

Jochmus, Augustus. *The Syrian War and the Decline of the Ottoman Empire.* 2 vols. Berlin: Albert Cohn, 1883.

Johnston, Harry H. *A History of the Colonization of Africa by Alien Races.* Cambridge: Cambridge Univ., 1913.

Johnston, Robert. *The Roman Theocracy and the Republic.* London: Macmillan, 1901.

Jones, F. C. *Japan's New Order in East Asia.* London: Oxford Univ. Press, 1954.

Jones, Ronald D. "Construct Mapping." Kansas City: Univ. of Missouri, June 1966, mimeo.

Jordan, Karl G. *Der Aegyptisch-Turkische Krieg, 1839.* Zurich: Borsig, 1923.

Jutikkala, Eino. *A History of Finland.* New York: Praeger, 1962.

Kaas, Albert and Fedor De Lazarovics. *Bolshevism in Hungary.* London: Grant Richards, 1931.

Kahin, George. *Nationalism and Revolution in Indonesia.* Ithaca: Cornell Univ., 1952.

_____ **and John Lewis.** *The United States in Vietnam.* New York: Dial, 1969.

Kalaw, Teodoro M. *The Philippine Revolution.* Manila: Manila Book Co., 1925.

Karnes, Thomas L. *The Failure of Union: Central America 1824–1960.* Chapel Hill: Univ. of North Carolina, 1961.

Kaul, B. M. *The Untold Story.* Bombay: Allied Publishers, 1967.

Kecskemeti, Paul. *Strategic Surrender.* Stanford: Stanford Univ., 1958.

Keesing's Contemporary Archives. London: Keesing's, since 1931.

Keller, Helen Rex. *A Dictionary of Dates.* 2 vols. New York: Macmillan, 1934.

Kennan, George F. *The Decision to Intervene.* Princeton: Princeton Univ., 1958.

———. *Russia and the West under Lenin and Stalin.* Boston: Little, Brown, 1960.

Kerr, George H. *Formosa Betrayed.* Boston: Houghton-Mifflin, 1965.

Khadduri, Majid. *Independent Iraq, 1932–1958.* London: Oxford Univ., 1960.

Khôi, Lê Thành. *Le Viet-Nam.* Paris: Editions de Minuit, 1955.

Kielstra, E. B. *Beschrijving van den Atjeh-Oorlog.* 3 vols. 's Gravenhage: Van Cleef, 1883.

Kiernan, E. V. *British Diplomacy in China, 1880–1885.* Cambridge: Cambridge Univ., 1939.

Kimche, Jon and David. *A Clash of Destinies.* New York: Praeger, 1960.

King, Bolton. *A History of Italian Unity.* 2 vols. London: J. Nisbet, 1899.

Kiritzesco, Constantin. *La Roumanie dans la Guerre Mondiale, 1916–1919.* Paris: Payot, 1934.

de Klerck, E. S. *History of the Netherlands East Indies.* Vol. 2. Rotterdam: Brusse, 1938.

Klingberg, Frank L. *Historical Study of War Casualties.* Washington, D.C.: United States, Secretary of War Office, 1945.

———. "Predicting the Termination of War: Battle Casualties and Population Losses," *Journal of Conflict Resolution,* 10/2 (June 1966), 129–71.

Kolinski, Charles J. *Independence or Death.* Gainesville: Univ. of Florida, 1965.

Korbel, Josef. *Danger in Kashmir.* Princeton: Princeton Univ., 1959.

La Foy, Margaret. *The Chaco Dispute and the League of Nations.* Bryn Mawr, Pa.: Bryn Mawr Press, 1946.

Laine, Philip. *Paraguay.* New Brunswick, N.J.: Scarecrow, 1956.

Lamb, Alastair. *The Kashmir Problem.* New York: Praeger, 1967.

Lancaster, Donald. *The Emancipation of French Indochina.* London: Oxford Univ., 1961.

Landau, Rom. *Moroccan Drama.* San Francisco: American Academy of Asian Studies, 1956.

Langer, Paul F. and Joseph J. Zasloff. *North Vietnam and Laos.* Cambridge, Mass.: Harvard, 1970.

Langer, William L. *European Alliances and Alignments.* New York: Knopf, 1931.

——— (ed). *An Encyclopedia of World History.* Boston: Houghton-Mifflin, 1948.

Leckie, Robert. *Conflict.* New York: Putnams, 1962.

Lee, J. S. "The Periodic Recurrence of Internecine Wars in China," *The China Journal,* 14/3 (March 1931), 111–115, 159–162.

Le Gouhir y Rodas, José. *Historia de la Republic del Ecuador.* Quito: Prensa Católica, 1925.

Lei, K. N. (ed). *Information and Opinion Concerning the Japanese Invasion of Manchuria and Shanghai from Sources Other than Chinese.* Shanghai: Shanghai Bar Association, 1932.

Lenczowski, George. *Russia and the West in Iran.* Ithaca: Cornell Univ., 1949.

Leslie, R. F. *Polish Politics and the Revolution of November, 1930.* London: London Univ., 1956.

———. *Reform and Insurrection in Russian Poland.* London: London Univ., 1963.

Lettrich, Joseph. *History of Modern Slovakia.* New York: Praeger, 1955.

Levene, Ricardo. *A History of Argentina.* Chapel Hill: Univ. of North Carolina, 1937.

Levine, Victor T. *The Cameroons.* Berkeley: Univ. of California, 1964.

Li, Chien-Nung. *The Political History of China, 1840–1928.* Princeton: Van Nostrand, 1956.

Li, Ung Bing. *Outlines of Chinese History.* Shanghai: Commercial Press, 1914.

Liddell-Hart, B. H. *The Real War, 1914–1918.* Boston: Little, Brown, 1930.

Listowel, Judith. *The Making of Tanganyika.* London: Chatto and Windus, 1965.
Lobanov-Rostovsky, Andrei. *Russia And Asia.* Ann Arbor: Wahr, 1951.
Longrigg, Stephen Hemsley. *Iraq, 1900 to 1950.* London: Oxford Univ. Press, 1953.
______. *Syria and Lebanon Under French Mandate.* London: Oxford Univ., 1958.
Lorch, Netanel. *The Edge of the Sword.* New York: Putnams, 1961.
Lyons, Eugene. *Assignment in Utopia.* New York: Harcourt, Brace, 1937.
Macauley, Neill. *The Sandino Affair.* Chicago: Quadrangle, 1967.
MacCallum, Elizabeth. *The Nationalist Crusade in Syria.* New York: Foreign Policy Assn., 1928.
MacDermott, Marcia. *A History of Bulgaria.* London: Allen and Unwin, 1962.
Mackenzie, David. *The Serbs and Russian Pan-Slavism, 1875–1878.* Ithaca: Cornell Univ., 1967.
MacLean, Frank. *Germany's Colonial Failure.* Boston: Houghton-Mifflin, 1918.
Macrory, Patrick. *Signal Catastrophe.* London: Hodder and Staughton, 1966.
Magnus, Philip. *Kitchener.* London: John Murray, 1958.
Majumdar, R. C., H. C. Raychaudhuri, and Kalikinkar Datta. *An Advanced History of India.* London: Macmillan, 1948.
Mallat, Joseph. *La Serbie Contemporaine.* Vol. 1. Paris: Librarie Orientale et Américaine, 1902.
Mansford, Oliver. *The Battle of Majuba Hill.* New York: Crowell, 1967.
Markham, Clement R. *A History of Peru.* Chicago: C. H. Sergel, 1892.
Marshall, S. L. A. *Sinai Victory.* New York: William Morrow, 1958.
Martelli, George. *Leopold to Lumumba.* London: Chapman and Hall, 1962.
Martin, Christopher. *The Russo-Japanese War.* New York: Abelard Schulman, 1967.
Maurice, John Frederick. *Hostilities without Declaration of War.* London: H.M.S.O., 1883.
Maurice, F. and George Arthur. *The Life of Lord Wolseley.* Garden City, N.Y.: Doubleday, 1924.
Maxwell, Neville. *India's China War.* London: Jonathan Cape, 1970.
McAleavy, Henry. *Black Flags in Vietnam.* New York: Macmillan, 1968.
McClure, William K. *Italy in North Africa.* London: Constable, 1913.
McCoy, Al and Nina Adams (eds). *Laos: War and Revolution.* New York: Harper and Row, 1970.
Mellor, Andrew. *India Since Partition.* New York: Praeger, 1951.
Mentre, François. *Les Générations Sociales.* Paris: Bossard, 1920.
Meray, Tibor. *Thirteen Days that Shook the Kremlin.* New York: Praeger, 1959.
Meza, Rafael. *Centro America: Campana National de 1885.* Guatemala City: Tipográfia Nácional, 1935.
Miege, Jean-Louis. *Le Maroc et L'Europe.* Vol. II. Paris: Presses Universaires de France, 1961.
Mijatovich, Chedomille. *The Memoirs of a Balkan Diplomat.* London: Cassell, 1917.
Mikus, Joseph. *Slovakia.* Milwaukee: Marquette Univ., 1963.
Miller, William. *The Ottoman Empire and its Successors.* 2 vols. Cambridge: Cambridge Univ., 1936.
von Moltke, Helmuth. *Darstellung des Turkisch-Aegyptischen Feldzugs in Sommer 1839.* Berlin: Junker und Dunnhaupt, 1935.
Moore, Harriet L. *Soviet Far Eastern Policy, 1931–1945.* Princeton: Princeton Univ., 1945.
Moore, Joel R. et al. *The History of the American Expedition Fighting the Bolsheviki.* Detroit: Polar Bear, 1921.
Morris, Donald. *Washing of the Spears.* New York: Simon and Schuster, 1965.

Morris, Richard (ed). *Encyclopedia of American History.* Vol. I. New York: Harper, 1953.

Morse, Hosea Ballou. *The International Relations of the Chinese Empire.* Vol. III. London: Longmans, 1918.

Moyal, J. E. "The Distribution of Wars in Time," *Journal of the Royal Statistical Society* (Series A), 112/4 (1949), 446–49.

Munro, Dana G. *Intervention and Dollar Diplomacy in the Caribbean.* Princeton, N.J.: Princeton Univ., 1964.

New York Times. Oct. 30, 1962; November 4, 1962; November 22, 1962.

______. *The Pentagon Papers.* New York, Bantam, 1971.

Niox, Gustave. *Expedition du Mexique 1861–1867.* Paris: J. Dumaine, 1874.

Nolan, Edward H. *The Liberators of Italy.* London: J. S. Virtue, 1865.

Norris, J. A. *The First Afghan War 1838–1842.* Cambridge: Cambridge Univ., 1967.

O'Ballance, Edgar. *The Arab-Israeli War.* London: Faber and Faber, 1956.

______. *The Indo-China War 1945–1954.* London: Faber and Faber, 1964.

______. *The Greek Civil War, 1944–1949.* New York: Praeger, 1966a.

______. *Malaya: The Communist Insurgent War, 1948–1960.* Hamden, Connecticut: Archon, 1966b.

Ogawa, Gotaro. *Expenditures of the Russo-Japanese War.* New York: Oxford Univ., 1923.

O'Neill, Robert. "Doctrine and Training in the German Army," in Michael Howard (ed). *The Theory and Practice of War.* New York: Praeger, 1966.

Ono, Giichi. *Expenditures of the Sino-Japanese War.* New York: Oxford Univ., 1922.

Page, Stanley. *The Formation of the Baltic States.* Cambridge: Harvard Univ., 1959.

Pattee, Richard. *Gabriel Garcia Moreno y el Ecuador de su Tiempo.* Quito: Editorial Ecuatoriana, 1941.

Patterson, George. *Tibet in Revolt.* London: Faber and Faber, 1960.

Payne, Stanley. *Politics and the Military in Modern Spain.* Stanford, Calif.: Stanford Univ., 1967.

Pemberton, W. Baring. *Battles of the Boer War.* London: Batsford, 1964.

Perce, Elbert. *The Battle Roll.* New York: Mason Bros., 1858.

Perkins, Dexter. *Hands Off.* Boston: Little, Brown, 1941.

______. *The American Approach to Foreign Policy.* Cambridge: Harvard Univ., 1952.

Peterson, Clarence Stewart. *Known Military Dead During Mexican War, 1846–1848.* Baltimore: by author, 1957.

Phillips, G. D. R. *Russia, Japan and Mongolia.* London: Frederick Muller, 1942.

Phillips, Walter Alison. *The War of Greek Independence.* London: Smith, Elder, 1897.

______. *The Confederation of Europe: A Study of the European Alliance, 1813–1823.* London: Longmans, 1914.

Phillipson, Coleman. *Termination of War and Treaties of Peace.* London: T. Fisher Unwin, 1916.

Pierce, Richard. *Russian Central Asia.* Berkeley: Univ. of California, 1960.

Pike, Douglas. *Viet Kong.* Cambridge: M.I.T., 1966.

Pohler, Johann. *Bibliotheca Historico-Militaris. Systematische Übersicht d. Erscheinungen Aller Sprachen auf dem Gebiete d. Geschichte d. Kriege und Kriegswissenschaft seit Erfindung d. Buchdruckerkunst b. z. Schluss des Jahres 1880.* 4 vols. 1880. Vol. 2. New York: Burt Franklin, 1961.

Polites, Athanase G. *Le Conflit Turko-Egyptien.* Cairo: Institut Française D'Archéologie Orientale du Caire, 1931.

Ponte Dominguéz. Francisco J. *Historia de la Guerra de los Diez Años.* 2 vols. Havana: A. Muñiz, 1958.

Poplai, S. L. *India, 1947–1950.* Vol. 2. London: Oxford Univ., 1959.

Portell Vilá, Herminio. *Historia de la Guerra de Cuba y los Etados Unidos contra España.* Havana: 1949.

Prinzing, Friedrich. *Epidemics Resulting from Wars.* Oxford: Clarendon, 1916.

Purcell, Victor. *The Boxer Uprising.* Cambridge: Cambridge Univ., 1963.

Puzyrewsky, Alexander. *Der Polnisch-Russische Krieg, 1831.* 3 vols. Vienna: Kreisel and Gröger, 1893.

Pye, Lucien. *Guerilla Communism in Malaya.* Princeton: Princeton Univ., 1956.

Rapoport, Anatol. "Lewis F. Richardson's Mathematical Theory of War," *Journal of Conflict Resolution,* 1/3 (September 1957), 249–307.

von Rauch, George. *A History of Soviet Russia.* New York: Praeger, 1957.

Reddaway, W. F., et al. *Cambridge History of Poland.* 2 vols., Cambridge: Cambridge Univ., 1961.

Rees, David. *Korea: The Limited War.* New York: St. Martin's, 1964.

Report of the International Commission to Inquire into the Causes and Conduct of the Balkan Wars. Geneva: Carnegie Endowment for International Peace, 1914.

Reshetar, John S. *The Ukrainian Revolution, 1917–1920.* Princeton: Princeton Univ., 1952.

Richardson, H. E. *Tibet and its History.* London: Oxford Univ., 1962.

Richardson, Lewis F. "Generalized Foreign Politics," *British Journal of Psychology,* Suppl. Monograph 23 (June 1939), 1–91.

______. "Frequency of Occurrence of Wars and Other Fatal Quarrels," *Nature,* 148/3759 (15 November 1941), p. 598.

______. "The Distribution of Wars in Time," *Journal of the Royal Statistical Society,* 107, (1945), 242–250.

______. "Variation of the Frequency of Fatal Quarrels with Magnitude," *Journal of the American Statistical Society,* 43 (1948), 523–46.

______. *Statistics of Deadly Quarrels.* Pittsburgh: Boxwood, 1960a.

______. *Arms and Insecurity.* Pittsburgh: Boxwood, 1960b.

Roberts, Stephen H. *The History of French Colonial Policy.* Hamden, Conn.: Archon, 1963.

Robertson, Priscilla. *Revolutions of 1848: A Social History.* Princeton: Princeton Univ., 1952.

Romani, George T. *The Neopolitan Revolution of 1820–1821.* Evanston: Northwestern Univ., 1950.

Rosberg, Carl G., Jr. and John Nottingham. *The Myth of "Mau Mau": Nationalism in Kenya.* New York: Praeger, 1966.

Rose, J. Holland. *The Development of European Nations 1870–1919.* Cambridge: Cambridge Univ., 1915.

Rosenau, James N. (ed.). *International Aspects of Civil Strife.* Princeton: Princeton Univ., 1964.

Ross, Frank E. "The American Naval Attack on Shimonoseki in 1863," *Chinese Social and Political Science Review,* 18/1 (April 1934), 146–155.

Rouland, John. *A History of Sino-Indian Relations.* Princeton: Van Nostrand, 1967.

Rummel, R. J. "A Field Theory of Social Action with Application to Conflict Within Nations," *Yearbook of the Society for General Systems,* X, 1965, 183–211.

Rupen, Robert A. *Mongols of the Twentieth Century.* Vol. I. Bloomington: Indiana Univ., 1964.

Russell, Frank S. *Russian Wars with Turkey.* London: Henry S. King, 1877.

Russett, Bruce M., *Trends in World Politics.* New York: Macmillan, 1965.

______. *International Regions and the International System: A Study in Political Ecology.* Chicago: Rand McNally, 1967.

______. "Delineating International Regions," in J. David Singer (ed). *Quantitative International Politics: Insights and Evidence.* New York: Free Press, 1968.

______, **J. David Singer and Melvin Small.** "National Political Units in the Twentieth Century: A Standardized List." *American Political Science Review,* 62/3 (September 1968), 932–51.

Sabry, M. *L'Empire Égyptien sous Mohamed-Ali et la Question d'Orient.* Paris: Librairie Orientaliste, 1930.

Safran, Nadev. *From War to War.* New York: Pegasus, 1969.

Sandford, Christine. *Ethiopia under Haile Selassie.* London: J. M. Dent, 1946.

von Sax, Carl Ritter. *Geschichte des Machtverfalls der Türkei.* Vienna: Manziche k. u. k. Hof Verlags und Universitäts Buchhandlung, 1913.

Schiemann, Theodor. *Geschichte Russlands unter Kaiser Nikolaus I.* Vol. 3. Berlin: George Reimer, 1913.

von Schlechta-Wssehdr, Ottokar. "Der Letzte Persiche-Russische Krieg" in *Zeitschrift der Deutschen Morgen Landischen Gesellschaft.* 20, (1866), 288–305.

Schmitt, Bernadotte. *Coming of the War 1914.* New York: Scribners, 1930.

Scott, J. G. *Burma.* New York: Knopf, 1924.

Senn, Alfred E. *The Emergence of Modern Lithuania.* New York: Columbia, 1959.

Seton-Watson, Hugh. *The Decline of Imperial Russia, 1855–1914.* London: Methuen, 1952.

Seton-Watson, Robert William. *Britain in Europe 1789–1914.* Cambridge: Cambridge Univ., 1938.

Shaplen, Robert. "Our Involvement in Laos," *Foreign Affairs,* 48/3 (April 1970), 478–93.

Shibeika, Mekki. *British Policy in the Sudan 1882–1902.* London: Oxford, 1952.

Short, Anthony. "Communism and the Emergency," in Gung wu Wang (ed.). *Malaysia.* London: Pall Mall, 1958.

Singer, J. David. "The Correlates of War Project: Interim Report," *World Politics* 24/2 (1972), 243–70.

______ **and Melvin Small.** "The Composition and Status Ordering of the International System, 1815–1940," *World Politics,* 18/2 (January 1966), 236–282.

______. "Formal Alliances, 1815–1939: A Quantitative Description," *Journal of Peace Research,* 1966/1 (January), 1–32.

______. "National Alliance Commitments and War Involvement, 1815–1945," *Peace Research Society Papers,* 4 (1967), 109–140.

______. "Alliance Aggregation and the Onset of War, 1815–1945," in J. David Singer, (ed.). *Quantitative International Politics: Insights and Evidence.* New York: Free Press, 1968, 247–286.

______ **and Michael Wallace.** "Inter-Governmental Organization in the Global System, 1816–1964: A Quantitative Description, *International Organization* 24/2, 239–87.

______ et al. "The Military-Industrial Capability of Nations, 1816–1965: A Quantitative Assessment." Ann Arbor, Mich.: MHRI Preprint [forthcoming].

Singh, Khushwant. *A History of the Sikhs.* Vol. 2. Princeton: Princeton Univ., 1966.

Singletary, Otis A. *The Mexican War.* Chicago: Univ. of Chicago, 1960.

Small, Melvin and J. David Singer. "Formal Alliances, 1816–1965: An Extension of the Basic Data," *Journal of Peace Research 6 (1969), 257–282.*

———. "Patterns in International Warfare, 1816–1965," *Annals* 391 (Sept. 1970), 145–155.

Smith, C. Jay, Jr. *Finland and the Russian Revolution.* Athens: Univ. of Georgia, 1958.

Smith, Justin H. *The War with Mexico.* 2 vols. New York: Macmillan, 1919.

Smith, Rhea Marsh. *Spain.* Ann Arbor: Univ. of Michigan, 1965.

Snow, Edgar. *Far Eastern Front.* New York: H. Smith and R. Haas, 1933.

Sorokin, Pitirim A. *Social and Cultural Dynamics.* Vol. 3 (*Fluctuation of Social Relationships, War and Revolution*) New York: American Book, 1937.

Spain. Servicio Historico Militar. *Historia de las Campanas de Marrueces.* Vol. I. Madrid: Impr. del Servicio Geografico del Ejercito, 1947.

Stavrianos, Leften S. *The Balkans Since 1453.* New York: Holt, Rinehart and Winston, 1963.

Steefel, Lawrence C. *The Schleswig-Holstein Question.* Cambridge: Harvard Univ., 1932.

Stephenson, Nathaniel W. *Texas and the Mexican War.* New Haven: Yale Univ., 1921.

von Sternegg, J. K. *Schlacten-Atlas des XIX. Jahrhunderts: der deutsche-dänische Krieg, 1848–1850.* Leipzig: P. Bauerle, 1892(?)–1898(?).

———. *Schlacten-Atlas des XIX. Jahrhunderts: der russisch-turkische Krieg, 1828–1829.* Leipzig: P. Bauerle, 1891(?)–1895(?).

———. *Schlacten-Atlas des XIX. Jahrhunderts: der russisch-turkische Krieg, 1877–1878.* Leipzig: P. Bauerle, 1886(?)–1899(?).

Stewart, George. *The White Armies of Russia.* New York: Macmillan, 1933.

Storey, Moorfield and Marcial P. Lichauco. *The Conquest of the Philippines by the United States.* New York: Putnam, 1926.

Sullivant, Robert S. *Soviet Politics and the Ukraine 1917–1957.* New York: Columbia Univ., 1962.

Sumner, Benedict H. *Russia and the Balkans 1870–1880.* Oxford: Oxford Univ., 1937.

Sykes, Percy Molesworth. *A History of Afghanistan,* London: Macmillan, 1940.

———. *A History of Persia.* 2 vols. London: Macmillan, 1951.

Taboulet, Georges (ed). *La Geste Française en Indochine.* Paris: Adrien-Maisonneuve, 1955.

Tang, Peter S. H. *Russia and Soviet Policy in Manchuria and Outer Mongolia.* Durham: Duke Univ., 1959.

Taylor, A. J. P. *The Struggle for Mastery in Europe, 1848–1918.* Oxford: Clarendon, 1954.

Temperly, Harold. *England and the Near East.* Hamden, Conn.: Archon, 1964.

Thayer, William Roscoe. *The Life and Times of Cavour.* Vol. 2. Boston: Houghton-Mifflin, 1911.

Theobald, A. B. *The Mahdiya.* London: Longmans, 1951.

Thomas, Hugh. *The Spanish Civil War.* New York: Harper, 1961.

———. *Suez.* New York: Harper & Row, 1967.

Thomas, Lowell. *The Silent War in Tibet.* Garden City, N.Y.: Doubleday, 1959.

Thompson, Edward John and G. T. Garrett. *The Rise and Fulfillment of British Rule in India.* London: Macmillan, 1934.

Thompson, Virginia and B. Richard Adloff. *The Malagasy Republic.* Stanford: Stanford Univ., 1965.

Time, September 24, 1965, pp. 30–31.

Ullman, Richard. *Intervention and the War.* Princeton: Princeton Univ. 1961.

United Asia, 14/12 (December 1962), 691–708.

United Nations Command. Report to United Nations Secretary General. October 23, 1953.

United States Department of the Army. Historical Section. *Order of Battle of the United States Army Forces in the World War.* Washington, D.C.: G.P.O., 1937.

United States Senate. Committee on Foreign Relations. *Hearings Before a Subcommittee on U.S. Security Agreements Abroad.* 91st Congress, First Session, Part Two. 20, 21, 22, 28 October 1969.

Unterberger, Betty. *America's Siberian Expedition 1918–1920.* Durham, N.C.: Duke Univ., 1956.

Urlanis, B. T. *Voeni i Narodo-Nacelenie Evropi (Wars and the Population of Europe).* Moscow: Government Publishing House, 1960.

Usborne, C. V. *The Conquest of Morocco.* London: Stanley Paul, 1936.

Vali, Ferenc A. *Rift and Revolt in Hungary.* Cambridge: Harvard Univ., 1961.

Vásquez-Machicado, Humberto and José de Mesa y Teresa Gisbert. *Manual de Historia de Bolivia.* La Paz: Libreroas Editores, 1963.

Vial, Jean. *Le Maroc Héroique.* Paris: Hachette, 1938.

Vlekke, Bernard. *Nusantara.* Chicago: Quadrangle, 1960.

Voevodsky, John. "Quantitative Behavior of Warring Nations." *Journal of Psychology,* 72 (July 1969), 269–292.

Wack, Henry Wellington. *The Story of the Congo Free State.* New York: Putnams, 1905.

Ward, W. E. F. *A History of Ghana.* London: Allen and Unwin, 1959.

Warren, Harris Gaylord. *Paraguay.* Norman: Univ. of Oklahoma, 1949.

Wehl, David. *The Birth of Indonesia.* London: Allen and Unwin, 1948.

Weiss, Herbert K. "Stochastic Models for the Duration and Magnitude of a 'Deadly Quarrel'," *Operations Research,* 11/1 (1963), 101–121.

———. "Trends in World Involvement in War." Los Angeles: Aerospace Corporation, mimeo, 1963.

Wenner, Manfred W. *Modern Yemen, 1918–1966.* Baltimore: Johns Hopkins Univ., 1967.

Werth, Alexander. *Russia at War.* New York: E. P. Dutton, 1964.

Wheeler, Geoffrey. *Modern History of Soviet Central Asia.* London: Weidenfeld and Nicholson, 1964.

Wheeler, Raymond H. *War, 599 B.C.–1950 A.D.: Indexes of International and Civil War Battles of the World.* Pittsburgh: Foundation for the Study of Cycles, 1951.

White, George F. *A History of Spain and Portugal.* London: Methuen, 1909.

White, John A. *The Siberian Intervention.* Princeton: Princeton Univ., 1950.

Wilcox, Cadmus M. *History of the Mexican War.* Washington, D.C.: Church News, 1892.

Williams, C. F. Rushbrook. *The State of Pakistan.* London: Faber & Faber, 1962.

Wolf, Charles, Jr. *The Indonesian Story.* New York: John Day, 1948.

Woodhouse, C. M. *Greek War of Independence.* London: Hutchinson House, 1952.

Woodman, Dorothy. *The Republic of Indonesia.* New York: Philosophical Library, 1955.

———. *The Making of Burma.* London: Cresset, 1962.

Woods, Frederick Adams and Alexander Baltzly. *Is War Diminishing?* Boston: Houghton Mifflin, 1915.

Woolman, David. *Rebels in the Rif.* Stanford: Stanford Univ., 1968.

The World Almanac. New York: *World Telegram and Sun,* 1886–1965.

Wright, Quincy. "When Does War Exist?" *American Journal of International Law,* 26/2 (April 1932), 362–368.

______. *A Study of War.* 2 vols. Chicago: Univ. of Chicago, 1942 (revised edition, 1965, vol. 1.)

Wuorinen, John H. *A History of Finland.* New York: Columbia Univ., 1965.

Young, George. *Nationalism and War in the Near East.* Oxford: Clarendon, 1915.

Zaide, Gregorio F. *The Philippine Revolution.* Manila: Modern Book Co., 1954.

Zinner, Paul E. *Revolution in Hungary.* New York: Columbia Univ., 1962.

Zook, David. H. *The Conduct of the Chaco War.* New York: Bookman, 1960.

AMOUNT OF INTERNATIONAL
WAR UNDERWAY, 1816-1965
NATION MONTHS UNDERWAY
0
25
50
75
100
125
150
175
200
1815
1825
1835
1845
1855
1865
1875